⑤ 2161488

Contemporary Authors®

ISSN 0010-7468

Contemporary Authors®

A Bio-Bibliographical Guide to
Current Writers in Fiction, General Nonfiction,
Poetry, Journalism, Drama, Motion Pictures,
Television, and Other Fields

volume 226

THOMSON

GALE

Detroit • New York • San Francisco • San Diego • New Haven, Conn. • Waterville, Maine • London • Munich

Contemporary Authors, Vol. 226

Project Editor
Julie Keppen

Editorial
Katy Balcer, Sara Constantakis, Michelle Kazensky, Joshua Kondek, Lisa Kumar, Mary Ruby, Lemma Shomali, Susan Strickland, Maikue Vang, Tracey Watson

Permissions
Jacqueline Key, William Sampson

Imaging and Multimedia
Lezlie Light, Kelly A. Quin

Composition and Electronic Capture
Carolyn Roney

Manufacturing
Lori Kessler

LIBRARY OF CONGRESS CATALOG CARD NUMBER 62-52046

ISBN 0-7876-6706-4
ISSN 0010-7468

Printed in the United States of America
10 9 8 7 6 5 4 3 2 1

Contents

> **Indexing note:** All *Contemporary Authors* entries are indexed in the *Contemporary Authors* cumulative index, which is published separately and distributed twice a year.
>
> **As always, the most recent Contemporary Authors cumulative index continues to be the user's guide to the location of an individual author's listing.**

Preface

Contemporary Authors (*CA*) provides information on approximately 115,000 writers in a wide range of media, including:

- Current writers of fiction, nonfiction, poetry, and drama whose works have been issued by commercial publishers, risk publishers, or university presses (authors whose books have been published only by known vanity or author-subsidized firms are ordinarily not included)

- Prominent print and broadcast journalists, editors, photojournalists, syndicated cartoonists, graphic novelists, screenwriters, television scriptwriters, and other media people

- Notable international authors

- Literary greats of the early twentieth century whose works are popular in today's high school and college curriculums and continue to elicit critical attention

A *CA* listing entails no charge or obligation. Authors are included on the basis of the above criteria and their interest to *CA* users. Sources of potential listees include trade periodicals, publishers' catalogs, librarians, and other users of the series.

How to Get the Most out of *CA*: Use the Index

The key to locating an author's most recent entry is the *CA* cumulative index, which is published separately and distributed twice a year. It provides access to *all* entries in *CA* and *Contemporary Authors New Revision Series* (*CANR*). Always consult the latest index to find an author's most recent entry.

For the convenience of users, the *CA* cumulative index also includes references to all entries in these Thomson Gale literary series: *Authors and Artists for Young Adults, Authors in the News, Bestsellers, Black Literature Criticism, Black Literature Criticism Supplement, Black Writers, Children's Literature Review, Concise Dictionary of American Literary Biography, Concise Dictionary of British Literary Biography, Contemporary Authors Autobiography Series, Contemporary Authors Bibliographical Series, Contemporary Dramatists, Contemporary Literary Criticism, Contemporary Novelists, Contemporary Poets, Contemporary Popular Writers, Contemporary Southern Writers, Contemporary Women Poets, Dictionary of Literary Biography, Dictionary of Literary Biography Documentary Series, Dictionary of Literary Biography Yearbook, DISCovering Authors, DISCovering Authors: British, DISCovering Authors: Canadian, DISCovering Authors: Modules* (including modules for Dramatists, Most-Studied Authors, Multicultural Authors, Novelists, Poets, and Popular/Genre Authors), *DISCovering Authors 3.0, Drama Criticism, Drama for Students, Feminist Writers, Hispanic Literature Criticism, Hispanic Writers, Junior DISCovering Authors, Major Authors and Illustrators for Children and Young Adults, Major 20th-Century Writers, Native North American Literature, Novels for Students, Poetry Criticism, Poetry for Students, Short Stories for Students, Short Story Criticism, Something about the Author, Something about the Author Autobiography Series, St. James Guide to Children's Writers, St. James Guide to Crime & Mystery Writers, St. James Guide to Fantasy Writers, St. James Guide to Horror, Ghost & Gothic Writers, St. James Guide to Science Fiction Writers, St. James Guide to Young Adult Writers, Twentieth-Century Literary Criticism, 20th Century Romance and Historical Writers, World Literature Criticism,* and *Yesterday's Authors of Books for Children.*

A Sample Index Entry:

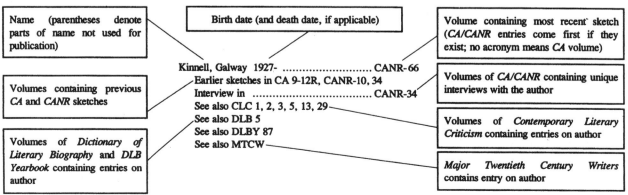

How Are Entries Compiled?

The editors make every effort to secure new information directly from the authors; listees' responses to our questionnaires and query letters provide most of the information featured in *CA*. For deceased writers, or those who fail to reply to requests for data, we consult other reliable biographical sources, such as those indexed in Thomson Gale's *Biography and Genealogy Master Index,* and bibliographical sources, including *National Union Catalog, LC MARC,* and *British National Bibliography.* Further details come from published interviews, feature stories, and book reviews, as well as information supplied by the authors' publishers and agents.

An asterisk (*) at the end of a sketch indicates that the listing has been compiled from secondary sources believed to be reliable but has not been personally verified for this edition by the author sketched.

What Kinds of Information Does An Entry Provide?

Sketches in *CA* contain the following biographical and bibliographical information:

- **Entry heading:** the most complete form of author's name, plus any pseudonyms or name variations used for writing

- **Personal information:** author's date and place of birth, family data, ethnicity, educational background, political and religious affiliations, and hobbies and leisure interests

- **Addresses:** author's home, office, or agent's addresses, plus e-mail and fax numbers, as available

- **Career summary:** name of employer, position, and dates held for each career post; resume of other vocational achievements; military service

- **Membership information:** professional, civic, and other association memberships and any official posts held

- **Awards and honors:** military and civic citations, major prizes and nominations, fellowships, grants, and honorary degrees

- **Writings:** a comprehensive, chronological list of titles, publishers, dates of original publication and revised editions, and production information for plays, television scripts, and screenplays

- **Adaptations:** a list of films, plays, and other media which have been adapted from the author's work

- **Work in progress:** current or planned projects, with dates of completion and/or publication, and expected publisher, when known

- **Sidelights:** a biographical portrait of the author's development; information about the critical reception of the author's works; revealing comments, often by the author, on personal interests, aspirations, motivations, and thoughts on writing

- **Interview:** a one-on-one discussion with authors conducted especially for *CA*, offering insight into authors' thoughts about their craft

- **Autobiographical essay:** an original essay written by noted authors for *CA*, a forum in which writers may present themselves, on their own terms, to their audience

- **Photographs:** portraits and personal photographs of notable authors

- **Biographical and critical sources:** a list of books and periodicals in which additional information on an author's life and/or writings appears

- **Obituary Notices** in *CA* provide date and place of birth as well as death information about authors whose full-length sketches appeared in the series before their deaths. The entries also summarize the authors' careers and writings and list other sources of biographical and death information.

Related Titles in the *CA* Series

Contemporary Authors Autobiography Series complements *CA* original and revised volumes with specially commissioned autobiographical essays by important current authors, illustrated with personal photographs they provide. Common topics include their motivations for writing, the people and experiences that shaped their careers, the rewards they derive from their work, and their impressions of the current literary scene.

Contemporary Authors Bibliographical Series surveys writings by and about important American authors since World War II. Each volume concentrates on a specific genre and features approximately ten writers; entries list works written by and about the author and contain a bibliographical essay discussing the merits and deficiencies of major critical and scholarly studies in detail.

Available in Electronic Formats

GaleNet. *CA* is available on a subscription basis through GaleNet, an online information resource that features an easy-to-use end-user interface, powerful search capabilities, and ease of access through the World-Wide Web. For more information, call 1-800-877-GALE.

Licensing. *CA* is available for licensing. The complete database is provided in a fielded format and is deliverable on such media as disk, CD-ROM, or tape. For more information, contact Thomson Gale's Business Development Group at 1-800-877-GALE, or visit us on our website at www.galegroup.com/bizdev.

Suggestions Are Welcome

The editors welcome comments and suggestions from users on any aspect of the *CA* series. If readers would like to recommend authors for inclusion in future volumes of the series, they are cordially invited to write the Editors at *Contemporary Authors*, Thomson Gale, 27500 Drake Rd., Farmington Hills, MI 48331-3535; or call at 1-248-699-4253; or fax at 1-248-699-8054.

Contemporary Authors Product Advisory Board

The editors of *Contemporary Authors* are dedicated to maintaining a high standard of excellence by publishing comprehensive, accurate, and highly readable entries on a wide array of writers. In addition to the quality of the content, the editors take pride in the graphic design of the series, which is intended to be orderly yet inviting, allowing readers to utilize the pages of *CA* easily and with efficiency. Despite the longevity of the *CA* print series, and the success of its format, we are mindful that the vitality of a literary reference product is dependent on its ability to serve its users over time. As literature, and attitudes about literature, constantly evolve, so do the reference needs of students, teachers, scholars, journalists, researchers, and book club members. To be certain that we continue to keep pace with the expectations of our customers, the editors of *CA* listen carefully to their comments regarding the value, utility, and quality of the series. Librarians, who have firsthand knowledge of the needs of library users, are a valuable resource for us. The *Contemporary Authors* Product Advisory Board, made up of school, public, and academic librarians, is a forum to promote focused feedback about *CA* on a regular basis. The six-member advisory board includes the following individuals, whom the editors wish to thank for sharing their expertise:

- **Anne M. Christensen,** Librarian II, Phoenix Public Library, Phoenix, Arizona.

- **Barbara C. Chumard,** Reference/Adult Services Librarian, Middletown Thrall Library, Middletown, New York.

- **Eva M. Davis,** Youth Department Manager, Ann Arbor District Library, Ann Arbor, Michigan.

- **Adam Janowski, Jr.,** Library Media Specialist, Naples High School Library Media Center, Naples, Florida.

- **Robert Reginald,** Head of Technical Services and Collection Development, California State University, San Bernadino, California.

- **Stephen Weiner,** Director, Maynard Public Library, Maynard, Massachusetts.

International Advisory Board

Well-represented among the 115,000 author entries published in *Contemporary Authors* are sketches on notable writers from many non-English-speaking countries. The primary criteria for inclusion of such authors has traditionally been the publication of at least one title in English, either as an original work or as a translation. However, the editors of *Contemporary Authors* came to observe that many important international writers were being overlooked due to a strict adherence to our inclusion criteria. In addition, writers who were publishing in languages other than English were not being covered in the traditional sources we used for identifying new listees. Intent on increasing our coverage of international authors, including those who write only in their native language and have not been translated into English, the editors enlisted the aid of a board of advisors, each of whom is an expert on the literature of a particular country or region. Among the countries we focused attention on are Mexico, Puerto Rico, Germany, Luxembourg, Belgium, the Netherlands, Norway, Sweden, Denmark, Finland, Taiwan, Singapore, Spain, Italy, South Africa, Israel, and Japan, as well as England, Scotland, Wales, Ireland, Australia, and New Zealand. The sixteen-member advisory board includes the following individuals, whom the editors wish to thank for sharing their expertise:

- **Lowell A. Bangerter,** Professor of German, University of Wyoming, Laramie, Wyoming.

- **Nancy E. Berg,** Associate Professor of Hebrew and Comparative Literature, Washington University, St. Louis, Missouri.

- **Frances Devlin-Glass,** Associate Professor, School of Literary and Communication Studies, Deakin University, Burwood, Victoria, Australia.

- **David William Foster,** Regent's Professor of Spanish, Interdisciplinary Humanities, and Women's Studies, Arizona State University, Tempe, Arizona.

- **Hosea Hirata,** Director of the Japanese Program, Associate Professor of Japanese, Tufts University, Medford, Massachusetts.

- **Jack Kolbert,** Professor Emeritus of French Literature, Susquehanna University, Selinsgrove, Pennsylvania.

- **Mark Libin,** Professor, University of Manitoba, Winnipeg, Manitoba, Canada.

- **C. S. Lim,** Professor, University of Malaya, Kuala Lumpur, Malaysia.

- **Eloy E. Merino,** Assistant Professor of Spanish, Northern Illinois University, DeKalb, Illinois.

- **Linda M. Rodríguez Guglielmoni,** Associate Professor, University of Puerto Rico—Mayagüez, Puerto Rico.

- **Sven Hakon Rossel,** Professor and Chair of Scandinavian Studies, University of Vienna, Vienna, Austria.

- **Steven R. Serafin,** Director, Writing Center, Hunter College of the City University of New York, New York City.

- **David Smyth,** Lecturer in Thai, School of Oriental and African Studies, University of London, England.

- **Ismail S. Talib,** Senior Lecturer, Department of English Language and Literature, National University of Singapore, Singapore.

- **Dionisio Viscarri,** Assistant Professor, Ohio State University, Columbus, Ohio.

- **Mark Williams,** Associate Professor, English Department, University of Canterbury, Christchurch, New Zealand.

CA Numbering System and Volume Update Chart

Occasionally questions arise about the *CA* numbering system and which volumes, if any, can be discarded. Despite numbers like "29-32R," "97-100" and "225," the entire *CA* print series consists of only 277 physical volumes with the publication of *CA* Volume 226. The following charts note changes in the numbering system and cover design, and indicate which volumes are essential for the most complete, up-to-date coverage.

CA **First Revision**	• 1-4R through 41-44R (11 books) *Cover:* Brown with black and gold trim. There will be no further First Revision volumes because revised entries are now being handled exclusively through the more efficient *New Revision Series* mentioned below.
CA **Original Volumes**	• 45-48 through 97-100 (14 books) *Cover:* Brown with black and gold trim. 101 through 226 (126 books) *Cover:* Blue and black with orange bands. The same as previous *CA* original volumes but with a new, simplified numbering system and new cover design.
CA **Permanent Series**	• *CAP*-1 and *CAP*-2 (2 books) *Cover:* Brown with red and gold trim. There will be no further Permanent Series volumes because revised entries are now being handled exclusively through the more efficient *New Revision Series* mentioned below.
CA **New Revision Series**	• CANR-1 through CANR-132 (132 books) *Cover:* Blue and black with green bands. Includes only sketches requiring significant changes; **sketches are taken from any previously published CA, CAP, or CANR volume.**

If You Have:	You May Discard:
CA First Revision Volumes 1-4R through 41-44R and *CA Permanent Series* Volumes 1 and 2	*CA* Original Volumes 1, 2, 3, 4 Volumes 5-6 through 41-44
CA Original Volumes 45-48 through 97-100 and 101 through 226	**NONE:** These volumes will not be superseded by corresponding revised volumes. Individual entries from these and all other volumes appearing in the left column of this chart may be revised and included in the various volumes of the *New Revision Series*.
CA New Revision Series Volumes *CANR*-1 through *CANR*-132	**NONE:** The *New Revision Series* does not replace any single volume of *CA*. Instead, volumes of *CANR* include entries from many previous *CA* series volumes. All *New Revision Series* volumes must be retained for full coverage.

A Sampling of Authors and Media People
Featured in This Volume

Eleanor Jack Gibson
A trained psychologist, Gibson received much attention for her research in the field of perceptual development in children. Overcoming prejudices against women scientists in the mid-twentieth century to earn her own place as a respected professor, Gibson formulated the well-known experiment gauging young children's depth perception by enticing them to crawl off a table and onto a plate-glass surface. As most children refused, Gibson was able to demonstrate the presence of depth perception in infants, an ability to help them avoid falls. Many of her works focused on the concept of perception, particularly tracing the development of a child's interaction with others, interest in objects, and development of motor skills.

Linda Hogan
Hogan is an award-winning poet and novelist of American-Indian decent who has earned wide-spread acclaim for her examination of the Native experience in contemporary culture. Many of her works follow characters as they explore their Native ancestors, learning a different perspective about nature, family, and the spirit. A university professor, Hogan also has a great interest in the natural world, researching and writing about the migration of gray whales and editing collections about the relationships between women and nature. An autobiographical essay by Hogan is included in this volume of *CA*.

Gregory Maguire
An acclaimed author of fiction for children and young adults, Maguire is known for his work which traces the journey of a character to a greater understanding of him or herself. In works ranging from folklore to fantasy, Maguire frequently writes books that deal with the loss of a close family member, feature well-detailed plots, and contain richly-drawn characters. Turning his hand to adult fiction, the author received high acclaim for his story *Wicked: The Life and Times of the Wicked Witch of the West,* an imaginative examination of the true nature of the much-maligned creature from Oz. An autobiographical essay by Maguire is included in this volume of *CA*.

Gregory E. Pence
Noted medical ethicist Pence writes about emerging and sometimes controversial issues in modern science, such as human cloning and bioengineered food. Pence is author of *Classic Cases in Medical Ethics: Accounts of Cases That Have Shaped Medical Ethics, with Philosophical, Legal, and Historical Backgrounds,* a text considered valuable for its examination of medical issues, including in vitro fertilization, euthanasia, and fetal tissue research. Particularly interested in how scientific developments are incorporated into human life, Pence explores the fields of cloning in *Who's Afraid of Human Cloning* and the landscape of genetically modified plants in *Designer Food: Mutant Harvest or Breadbasket,* works commended for their well-informed deliberation of highly charged scientific issues.

Alex Sanchez
A former youth and family counselor, Mexican-born, American-raised Sanchez examines the sexual maturation process of gay teens in his award-winning works for young adults. Considered a promising young writer in the newly emerging field of books that chronicle the coming-of-age of gay, lesbian, bisexual, transgender, and questioning youths, Sanchez offers readers works that examine the nature of relationships between individuals, regardless of sexual orientation. In the highly commended *Rainbow Boys,* the author follows the high-school events of three young men as they deal with issues of self-worth, discrimination, and acceptance in their community and families.

Beth Saulnier
Former journalist Saulnier is the author of the "Alex Bernier" mystery series that feature the detective skills of a young reporter from New York state. Alex investigates crimes, suicides, and other unusual events, unearthing evidence that causes authorities to look at these mysteries in a new light. Applauded for her intelligent, humorous, and charming protagonist, Saulnier has been awarded much praise for her well-developed plots and ability to create vivid settings, interesting characters, and entertaining stories.

Greg Tate
Researching the world of famous African Americans, Tate shares with readers the influence of prominent black writers, musicians, and celebrities on mainstream American culture. In *Midnight Lightning: Jimi Hendrix and the Black Experience,* Tate expresses how Hendrix transcended the lines of race in America and was warmly embraced by both black and white listeners. Tate has also compiled a collection of essays, *Everything but the Burden: What White People Are Taking from Black Cul-*

ture, which explores the idea that marginalized black culture contributes greatly to the wider American culture and is often the source for emerging trends in music, literature, and pop culture.

Ludmila Ulitskaya

Born in Siberia, Ulitskaya is a Russian author of fiction. Educated as a biologist at Moscow State University, Ulitskaya encountered trouble from the Soviet authorities with her translation of *Exodus,* Leon Uris's novel about the birth of the State of Israel, a book banned in the Union of Soviet Socialist Republics. Ulitskaya, however, began writing her own works, including well-received screenplays, short stories, and novels. Noted for her books in the style of nineteenth century authors, Ulitskaya has received awards from around the world for her books, earning the author comparisons to the esteemed Russian man of letters, Leo Tolstoy.

Acknowledgments

Grateful acknowledgment is made to those publishers, photographers, and artists whose work appear with these authors's essays. Following is a list of the copyright holders who have granted us permission to reproduce material in this volume of *CA*. Every effort has been made to trace copyright, but if omissions have been made, please let us know.

Photographs/Art

Hogan, Linda: All photographs reproduced by permission of Linda Hogan.

Keshavjee, Rafique: Photograph. Reproduced by permission of Gregory Maguire.

Maguire, Gregory: All photographs reproduced by permission of Gregory Maguire.

A

Indicates that a listing has been compiled from secondary sources believed to be reliable, but has not been personally verified for this edition by the author sketched.

ABBOTT, Edith 1876-1957

PERSONAL: Born September 26, 1876, in Grand Island, NE; died, July 28, 1957, in Grand Island, NE; daughter of Othman Ali (an attorney and former lieutenant governor of Nebraska), and Elizabeth Maletta (Griffin) Abbott. *Education:* University of Nebraska, B.A., 1901; University of Chicago, Ph.D. (with honors), 1905; postdoctoral study at the London School of Economics.

CAREER: Taught high school in Grand Island and Lincoln, NE, beginning 1893; Women's Trade Union League, Boston, MA, secretary, 1905-06; Wellesley College, instructor in political economics, 1907-08; Chicago School of Civics and Philanthropy (became University of Chicago School of Social Service Administration, 1920), Chicago, IL, codirector and professor of social economy, 1908-42, dean, 1924-42. President, National Conference of Social Work, 1937; member of advisory committee on emigration, International Labor Organization.

MEMBER: National Association of Social Workers (former president).

AWARDS, HONORS: Carnegie fellowship, 1903.

WRITINGS:

The Wages of Unskilled Labor in the United States, 1850-1900, University of Chicago Press (Chicago, IL), 1905.
Women in Industry: A Study in American Economic History, Appleton (New York, NY), 1910.

(With Sophonisba P. Breckinridge) *The Delinquent Child and the Home,* (Chicago, IL), 1912, reprinted, Arno Press (New York, NY), 1970.
The Real Jail Problem, Hale-Crossley (Chicago, IL), 1915.
(With Sophonisba P. Breckinridge) *Truancy and Non-Attendance in the Chicago Schools: A Study of the Social Aspects of the Compulsory Education and Child Labor Legislation of Illinois,* University of Chicago Press (Chicago, IL), 1917.
(With Sophonisba P. Breckinridge) *The Administration of the Aid-to-Mothers Law in Illinois,* United States Children's Bureau (Washington, DC), 1921, published in *The Family and Social Services in the 1920s,* Arno Press (New York, NY), 1972.
(Editor) *Immigration: Select Documents and Case Records,* University of Chicago Press (Chicago, IL), 1924.
(Editor) *Historical Aspects of the Immigration Problem: Select Documents,* University of Chicago Press (Chicago, IL), 1926.
Report on Crime and the Foreign Born, University of Chicago Press (Chicago, IL), 1931.
Social Welfare and Professional Education, University of Chicago Press (Chicago, IL), 1931, revised and enlarged edition, 1942.
(With Sophonisba P. Breckinridge, and others) *The Tenements of Chicago, 1908-1935,* University of Chicago Press (Chicago, IL), 1936.
(Editor) *Some American Pioneers in Social Welfare: Selected Documents,* University of Chicago Press (Chicago, IL), 1937.
Public Assistance, University of Chicago Press (Chicago, IL), 1940.

(Editor) Grace Abbott, *From Relief to Social Security: The Development of the New Public Welfare Services,* 1941.

Also author of *The One Hundred and One County Jails of Illinois and Why They Ought to Be Abolished,* 1916, *Twenty-one Years of University Education for Social Service,* 1942, and, with Sophonisba P. Breckinridge, *The Wage-Earning Woman and the State,* Boston Equal Suffrage Association for Good Government (Boston, MA). Cofounder and editor of *Social Service Review,* 1927-53, and of University of Chicago Social Service monograph series. Contributor to *New Republic, Social Service Review,* and *Nation.* Abbott's manuscript collections are maintained at the Joseph Regenstein Library, University of Chicago; Archives of Social Welfare History at the University of Minnesota; and the Nebraska State Historical Association.

SIDELIGHTS: Edith Abbott was a social reformer who helped open new opportunities for women to become social workers. Much of her dedication stemmed from the influence of her mother, Elizabeth Griffin Abbott, who had taught both Edith and her sister Grace the values of independence, pacifism, and woman's suffrage. Although they had their differences, both sisters dedicated themselves to improving the situation of working women and labored throughout their lifetimes to further this cause.

Following her studies at the University of Chicago, Abbott left for Boston to become the secretary of the Women's Trade Union League and to do a research assignment on wages and employment of women for the Carnegie Institution. In the process of this research, her interest in women's work as it related to economic history heightened, eventually becoming the impetus for her book *Women in Industry: A Study in American Economic History.* Within a year of research, Abbott had accumulated enough data to begin the book—a lengthy, detailed historical volume—that was published in 1910. *Women in Industry* depicts the lives and conditions of women in industries, records the first women's labor movements, and polled 1909 public opinion. Beginning in 1906, portions of the book regularly appeared in the *Journal of Political Economy.*

After traveling to England, where she studied at the London School of Economics under noted Fabian economists Beatrice and Sidney Webb, Abbott returned to Chicago, where she joined the staff at Hull House, the famous the settlement house founded by Jane Addams. Here she worked with her sister Grace and Sophonisba P. Breckinridge, who had been her mentor when she was a university student. At the settlement residence, Abbott became familiar with the problems of immigrants. It was there that her social work training would begin, as she tried to improve the lot of immigrant women. The rights of women workers were of special concern to her, and she sought legislation for a ten-hour working day, worked toward bringing women into labor unions, and attempted to help immigrants find better living quarters and secure them their rights. In 1920, Abbott and Breckinridge incorporated the School of Civics and Philanthropy into the University of Chicago, where it became the School of Social Service Administration. Four years later, when Breckinridge resigned from the school, Abbott became dean.

Over her long career, Abbott wrote over one hundred articles and books covering many topics. As a scholar, she relied on factual evidence to lay the foundation for concrete solutions to the problems of women and children working long hours and living in poor conditions—a situation that became a particular concern during the Great Depression. With friend and collaborator Breckinridge, Abbott established the *Social Service Review* in 1927 and began a well-respected monograph series for the University of Chicago that included such documents as *Immigration: Select Documents and Case Records* and *Historical Aspects of the Immigration Problem: Select Documents.*

Over the years, the once-shy Abbott blossomed into a woman of action, but, following her sister's death in 1939, she became more withdrawn and increasingly more demanding of her students. Resolute in her belief that women were intellectually equal to their male counterparts and therefore equally deserving of an education, Abbott served as a major influence both in the formation of guidelines for the research and study of social work and in creating unique opportunities for women to contribute to each other's success in the field.

BIOGRAPHICAL AND CRITICAL SOURCES:

BOOKS

Costin, Lela B., *Two Sisters for Social Justice: A Biography of Grace and Edith Abbott,* University of Illinois Press (Urbana, IL), 1983.*

ABRAMS, J. J.
    See ABRAMS, Jeffrey

*   *   *

ABRAMS, Jeffrey 1966-
    (J. J. Abrams)

PERSONAL: Born 1966, in New York, NY; son of Gerald W. Adams (a producer); married Joya Tillem, November 24, 2000; children: Max, Madelaine.

ADDRESSES: Agent—Endeavor, 9701 Wilshire Blvd., 10th Floor, Beverly Hills, CA 90212.

CAREER: Producer, director, actor, and screenwriter. Producer of films, including (with others) *Regarding Henry,* Paramount, 1991; (executive producer) *Forever Young,* Warner Bros., 1992; *The Pallbearer,* Miramax, 1996; (under the name J. J. Abrams) *The Suburbans,* Ignite Entertainment/Motion Picture Corporation of America, 1999; and (under the name J. J. Abrams) *Joy Ride* (also known as *Road Kill*), Twentieth Century-Fox, 2001. Actor in films, including (as delivery boy) *Regarding Henry,* Paramount, 1991; (as Doug) *Six Degrees of Separation,* Metro-Goldwyn-Mayer, 1993; (as second video photographer) *Diabolique,* Warner Bros., 1996; (under the name J. J. Abrams; as rock journalist) *The Suburbans,* Ignite Entertainment/Motion Picture Corporation of America, 1999.

Worked on television series under the name J. J. Abrams, including (as creator, executive producer, director of some episodes, and theme song performer and composer) *Felicity,* Warner Bros., Inc. (WB), 1998-2002; and (as creator, executive producer, title designer, director of some episodes, and composer of main theme and other music) *Alias,* American Broadcasting Companies, Inc. (ABC), 2001—. Composer of music and creator of sound effects for the film *Nightbeast,* 1983.

WRITINGS:

SCREENPLAYS

Regarding Henry, Paramount, 1991.
Forever Young, Warner Bros., 1992.
(With Jill Mazursky) *Gone Fishin',* Buena Vista, 1997.

(As J. J. Abrams; with others) *Armageddon,* Buena Vista, 1998.
(As J. J. Abrams; with Clay Tarver) *Joy Ride* (also known as *Road Kill*), Twentieth Century-Fox, 2001.

Also author of, with Jill Mazursky, *Taking Care of Business* (also known as *Filofax*), 1991.

TELEVISION SERIES; AS J. J. ABRAMS; WITH OTHERS

Felicity, WB, 1998-2002.
Alias, ABC, 2001—.

OTHER

With Breen Frazier, wrote the *Alias* video game, 2003.

WORK IN PROGRESS: A screenplay for a new *Superman* movie.

SIDELIGHTS: Although he has been a screenwriter on several successful films, including *Forever Young* and *Armageddon,* Jeffrey Abrams is probably best known for creating two hit television series, *Felicity* and *Alias.* Although both shows feature young-adult women struggling to figure out who they are, the similarities end there. *Felicity* stars former Mouseketeer Keri Russell as Felicity Porter, a curly-haired, insecure young lady who follows her high school crush, Ben, to New York when he goes to college there. Alas, despite writing a seemingly loving note in Felicity's yearbook, Ben actually has no romantic interest in her. Now Felicity is far from home, forced to define herself and decide what she wants to do with her life. *Variety* reviewer Ray Richmond noted the similarities between *Felicity* and other series about confused young women, including *Ally McBeal* and *My So-Called Life,* but continued, "shows that are this shamelessly imitative aren't supposed to be this good." *Felicity* "astutely transmits the conflicting blend of giddy anticipation and neurotic dread that defines the early college experience," Richmond concluded. Writing in *Entertainment Weekly,* Ken Tucker attributed much of the show's success to its "vivid, quick-witted ensemble" cast, but noted that "cocreators J. J. Abrams and Matt Reeves have known just what to fine-tune about the show" to keep it successful after the first season.

Abrams described his next series, *Alias,* as "very much a comic book come to life" to an *Entertainment Weekly* weekly interviewer. The show stars *Felicity* alumna Jennifer Garner as Sidney Bristow, a graduate student who is also an agent for the Central Intelligence Agency (CIA). Or at least she thinks she is a CIA agent; after her fiancé is murdered in the series premiere, Bristow discovers that she has actually been working for a rogue intelligence agency and CIA rival, SD-6. She therefore goes to the real CIA and becomes a double agent. Her always-distant father is also a CIA/SD-6 double agent, she soon discovers. "On a human level," the growing relationship between Bristow and her father "is the most interesting thing" in the show, thought *Variety* reviewer Phil Gallo. There are also other plot lines of human interest in the show, including Bristow's discovery of what really happened to her mother and her budding romance with fellow agent Vaughn. Although the show is driven by its high-action stories, "having strong, balanced characters is important to me," Abrams told *Daily Variety*'s Josef Adalian. "Identifying with a character and feeling there's a struggle worth telling is important."

Besides being a screenwriter, director, and producer, Abrams is also a composer who writes much of the music for his shows, mostly notably the techno-beats used in *Alias.* "Anyone who knows me says that I create TV shows so that I can create themes to them," Abrams joked in his *Entertainment Weekly* interview. "It's very rare to have someone who's good at virtually every element of the business, but that's what J. J. is," ABC Entertainment Television Group chairman Lloyd Braun told Adalian. "He's the whole package in every respect."

BIOGRAPHICAL AND CRITICAL SOURCES:

PERIODICALS

Cosmopolitan, February, 1993, Guy Flatley, review of *Forever Young,* p. 14.

Daily Herald (Arlington Heights, IL), May 3, 1996, Dann Gire, review of *The Pallbearer,* p. 22; June 4, 1997, Dann Gire, review of *Gone Fishin',* p. 9.

Daily Variety, August 30, 2002, Josef Adalian, interview with Abrams, pp. 15-16.

Electronic Media, June 3, 2002, Leslie Ryan, interview with Abrams, p. 12.

Entertainment Weekly, June 13, 1997, Lisa Schwarzbaum, review of *Gone Fishin',* p. 42; September 11, 1998, review of *Felicity,* p. 48; September 10, 1999, review of *Felicity,* p. 114; October 15, 1999, Ken Tucker, review of *Felicity,* p. 59; October 19, 2001, interview with Abrams, p. 85; November 23, 2001, Ken Tucker, review of *Alias,* p. 30; February 7, 2003, Dan Snierson, review of *Alias,* p. 6.

Hollywood Reporter, September 13, 2001, Michael Rechtshaffen, review of *Joy Ride,* p. 9; October 4, 2002, "Scribe Abrams Defuses Kryptonite Web Reviews," p. 8; June 25, 2003, Nellie Andreeva, "Abrams on Hunt in ABC Series," pp. 1-2; September 3, 2003, Chris Marlow, interview with Abrams, p. 10.

Magazine of Fantasy and Science Fiction, June, 1992, Kathi Maio, review of *Forever Young,* pp. 58-61.

Newsweek, December 28, 1992, David Ansen, review of *Forever Young,* p. 58.

New York Times, December 16, 1992, Vincent Canby, review of *Forever Young,* p. B3, C17; October 5, 2001, A. O. Scott, review of *Joy Ride,* pp. E21, E23; November 18, 2001, Joyce Millman, review of *Alias,* p. AR34; September 29, 2002, Steve Vineberg, review of *Alias,* p. AR34.

Premiere, June, 1991, Rachel Abramowitz and John H. Richardson, review of *Regarding Henry,* pp. 58-59; October, 1992, review of *Forever Young,* pp. 99-100.

Record (Bergen County, NJ), May 3, 1996, Roger Ebert, review of *The Pallbearer,* p. 41; June 4, 1997, Gene Seymour, review of *Gone Fishin',* p. Y7.

Rocky Mountain News (Denver, CO), Lawrence Van Gelder, review of *Gone Fishin',* p. 11D.

Rolling Stone, January 7, 1993, Peter Travers, review of *Forever Young,* p. 51.

Seattle Times, May 31, 1997, review of *Gone Fishin',* p. F3.

Time, December 28, 1992, Richard Schickel and Richard Corliss, review of *Forever Young,* p. 65.

TV Guide, September 12, 1998, Matt Roush, review of *Felicity,* pp. 44-45.

Variety, December 7, 1992, Brian Lowry, review of *Forever Young,* p. 71; September 28, 1998, Ray Richmond, review of *Felicity,* p. 86; September 10, 2001, review of *Joy Ride,* p. 60; October 1, 2001, Phil Gallo, review of *Alias,* p. 46.

Wall Street Journal, October 5, 1998, Barbara D. Phillips, review of *Felicity,* p. A28.

ONLINE

Internet Movie Database, http://www.imdb.com/ (November 21, 2003), "Jeffrey Abrams."*

*　　*　　*

AITKEN, Rosemary 1942-
(Bessie Reynolds, Rosemary Rowe)

PERSONAL: Born January 22, 1942, in Penzance, England; daughter of Garfield Emmanuel Vivian (a pharmaceuticals company executive) and Clara Irene (a homemaker; maiden name, Williams) Rowe; married Thomas Gordon Aitken, 1964 (divorced, 1972); children: Vivienne Jane, Michael Richard. *Ethnicity:* "Caucasian." *Education:* Auckland Training College, LTCL (speech and drama), 1959, teaching diploma, 1963, diploma in educational management, 1974, LTCL TESOL, 1982; Sydney University, B.A., 1961; Victoria University, New Zealand, M.A. (with honors), 1962. *Religion:* "Protestant Christian."

ADDRESSES: Home—Gloucestershire, England. *Agent*—Dorian Literary Agency, Upper Thornehill, Church Road, St. Mary Church, Torquay, Devon, England. *E-mail*—raitken.wyenet.co.uk.

CAREER: Secondary teacher, Taumarunui, New Zealand, 1964-67; teacher-trainer and lecturer in higher education, Cheltenham, England, 1967-72, senior lecturer, 1972-87, tutor in charge of ESOL program, 1978-87; Trinity College, London, England, examiner and moderator, 1990—. Also consultant in English as a foreign language for schools in the United Kingdom, Dubai, and Singapore. Tutor in charge for the Quillen Postal Writing Course, 1990-2000.

MEMBER: Society of Authors, Crime Writers' Association, South and Midwales Writers, Historical Novel Society.

AWARDS, HONORS: English Language Society prize, 1978.

WRITINGS:

NOVELS; "CORNISH SAGA" SERIES

The Girl from Penvarris, Orion (London, England), 1995.
The Tinner's Daughter, Orion (London, England), 1996.

Cornish Harvest, Orion (London, England), 1999.
Stormy Waters, Severn House (Sutton, England), 2001.
The Silent Shore, Severn House (Sutton, England), 2001.
The Granite Cliffs, Severn House (Sutton, England), 2003.
Against the Tide, Severn House (Sutton, England), 2004.

MYSTERY NOVELS; "LIBERTUS" SERIES; AS ROSEMARY ROWE

The Germanicus Mosaic, Headline Books (London, England), 1999.
A Pattern of Blood, Headline Books (London, England), 2000.
Murder in the Forum, Headline Books (London, England), 2001.
The Chariots of Calyx, Headline Books (London, England), 2002.
The Legatus Mystery, Headline Books (London, England), 2003.

OTHER

Make Up Your Mind (teaching materials), Macmillan (London, England), 1979.
Teaching Tenses (teaching materials), Nelson (London, England), 1992.
Writing a Novel: A Practical Guide, Crowood (Ramsbury, England), 2004.

Contributor of numerous short stories, some under the name Bessie Reynolds, to publications such as *Bella, Women's Realm,* and *Chat.* Author of the "Skill of Listening Series." Also author of plays.

SIDELIGHTS: Rosemary Aitken has produced a number of fictional works of historical romance and mystery, grouped into two well-received series. She told *CA:* "I began writing seriously after an industrial accident forced me to abandon my lecturing career." Prior to her injury, Aitken's writing consisted largely of textbooks and teaching guides for English as a second language.

Aitken's "Cornish Saga" series begins with *The Girl from Penvarris.* Set in a small tin-mining town at the turn of the twentieth century, this book tells the story of Katie Warren, who goes to work in the "Big House" for the local gentry. Eventually, Katie finds herself attracted to George, one of the sons of the family, but his unscrupulous brother Robert gets her turned out of the house, and she is forced to find work in a strange town. By the time Katie and George meet again, both are married to other people, but they cannot deny their old attraction.

Other books in the "Cornish Saga" series follow the lives of Penvarris residents as the settled certainties of the nineteenth century give way to the upheavals of the twentieth century and World War I. *Cornish Harvest,* for example, tells the story of several Cornish families torn apart by the war. According to *Booklist* reviewer Catherine Sias, the book is a "melodramatic yet intelligent and socially conscious historical romance." *Stormy Waters* and *The Silent Shore* are set in the Edwardian era. In these books, sixteen-year-old Wilhelmina "Sprat" Nicholls and young Denzil Vargo must deal with family secrets, local prejudices, and the strange new ideas promoted by the suffragist movement. *Booklist* reviewer Maria Hatton noted that in *The Silent Shore,* the result is a "sweet and simple tale in which early twentieth-century England comes alive."

Class issues comes to the fore once again in *The Granite Cliffs.* The vicar's daughter, Victoria, occupies a strange and lonely social station, above the local miners but below the gentry. Hatton stated that when Victoria falls in love with a miner recovering from an accident, the stage is set for a "wonderfully evocative, socially sensitive tale."

Writing as Rosemary Rowe, Aitken has also produced a series of mysteries set in Roman-era Glevarus, the town that is now known as Gloucester. This series focuses on Libertus, a mosaicist who draws on his fascination with puzzles and patterns to untangle murder mysteries, generally at the behest of his wealthy benefactor, Marcus Septimus. In the first novel in the series, *The Germanicus Mosaic,* Libertus investigates the murder of a retired centurion. *Kliatt* reviewer Janet Julian called the novel "well written, full of lively details of Roman life." In *A Pattern of Blood,* which Julian termed "a satisfying presentation," Libertus must find the murderer of a wealthy cavalry officer.

BIOGRAPHICAL AND CRITICAL SOURCES:

PERIODICALS

Booklist, December 1, 1998, Catherine Sias, review of *Cornish Harvest,* p. 654; September 15, 2001, Maria Hatton, review of *Stormy Waters,* p. 202; February 15, 2002, Maria Hatton, review of *The Silent Shore,* p. 997; April 1, 2002, Maria Hatton, review of *The Granite Cliffs,* p. 1383.
Kliatt, March, 2002, Janet Julian, audiobook review of *The Germanicus Mosaic;* September, 2003, Janet Julian, audiobook review of *A Pattern of Blood.*

*   *   *

ANDERSEN, Dennis Alan

PERSONAL: Male. *Education:* Attended the University of Washington (graduate studies in Germanic languages and literature).

ADDRESSES: Home—410 W. Roy St., Seattle, WA 98119. *Office*—Bethany Lutheran Church, 7400 Woodlawn Ave. NE, Seattle, WA 98115 *Agent*—c/o Author Mail, University of Washington Press, P.O. Box 50096, Seattle, WA 98145.

CAREER: Lutheran minister and author. Bethany Lutheran Church, Seattle, WA, pastor. Formerly curator at University of Washington Libraries, Special Collections Division. Also served on the Seattle Landmarks Preservation Board, the Board of Governors of the Book Club of Washington, the Pacific Northwest Lutheran Historical Society, Board of Trustees of the Friends of the Seattle Public Library, and as president of the Lutheran Ecumenical Representatives Network, 2000—.

WRITINGS:

(With Jeffrey Karl Ochsner) *Distant Corner: Seattle Architects and the Legacy of H. H. Richardson,* University of Washington Press (Seattle, WA), 2003.

Also contributor to *Shaping Seattle Architecture: A Historical Guide to the Architects,* University of Washington Press (Seattle, WA) 1994.

SIDELIGHTS: Dennis Alan Andersen parlayed his long interest in architecture and his experience in working with photographs and architectural drawings at the University of Washington libraries into his first book, *Distant Corner: Seattle Architects and the Legacy of H. H. Richardson,* written with Jeffrey Ochsner, a professor of architecture at the University of Washington. The book chronicles the rebuilding of downtown Seattle after a fire in June, 1889, destroyed more than thirty blocks covering more than one hundred acres of the city. The massive rebuilding effort, most of which is today located in Seattle's Pioneer Square Historic District, began almost immediately after the fire. The designs of most of the new buildings bear the influence of architect H. H. Richardson, the originator of the Romanesque revival in the United States, who died three years prior to the fire. The book explores Richardson's far-reaching influence on the city's design. Containing over 200 black-and-white illustrations, *Distant Corner* begins with coverage of the city prior to the fire, includes details of the eighteen-month peak of the rebuilding effort, and ends with the financial panic of 1893, by which point rebuilding efforts had come to a halt. Peter S. Kaufman, writing in *Library Journal,* commented that Ochsner and Andersen "are perfectly qualified to write this historical scholarly study." In *Choice,* S. Schuyler found the book to be "a skillful examination of the diffusion of architectural taste" that "explains how the Romanesque Revival, so closely associated with Henry Hobson Richardson, became a national style in the aftermath of the architect's death." In addition to Richardson, the designs of Seattle architects William Boone, Elmer Fisher, John Parkinson, Charles Saunders, Edwin Houghton, Willis Ritchie, Emil DeNeuf, Warren Skillings, and Arthur Chamberlin are discussed.

BIOGRAPHICAL AND CRITICAL SOURCES:

PERIODICALS

Choice, September, 2003, D. Schuyler, review of *Distant Corner: Seattle Architects and the Legacy of H. H. Richardson,* p. 138.
Library Journal, May 1, 2003, Peter S. Kaufman, review of *Distant Corner,* pp. 111-112.

ONLINE

Seattle Public Library, http://www.spl.org/ (March 6, 2004), short biography of Dennis Alan Andersen.*

*   *   *

ANTIN, Steve
See ANTIN, Steven

*   *   *

ANTIN, Steven (Howard) 1961-
   (Steve Antin)

PERSONAL: Born February 17, 1961, in Portland, OR.

ADDRESSES: Agent—International Creative Management, 8942 Wilshire Blvd., Beverly Hills, CA 90211.

CAREER: Actor, producer, and screenwriter. Credited as both Steven and Steve Antin. Actor in films, including (as Hank Burke) *Sweet 16* (also known as *Sweet Sixteen*), Vestron Video, 1981; (as Rick) *The Last American Virgin,* Cannon Film Distributors, 1982; (as Troy Perkins) *The Goonies,* Warner Bros., 1985; (as Roscoe) *Penitentiary III,* Cannon Films, 1987; (as Bob Joiner) *The Accused,* Paramount, 1988; (as raider) *Survival Quest,* Metro-Goldwyn-Mayer/United Artists, 1989; (as himself) *Without You I'm Nothing,* MCEG Productions, 1990; (as the passenger) *Drive,* MEI, 1991; (as Monkey Zetterland; and producer, with others) *Inside Monkey Zetterland,* IRS Media, 1992; (as Dick Zetterland) *S.F.W.,* Gramercy Pictures, 1994; (as Zack Phillips) *It's My Party,* United Artists, 1996; and (as Kevin) *'Til There Was You,* Paramount, 1997.

Performed stunts for films, including (aerial wolf stunts; uncredited) *Wolfen,* 1981; (uncredited) *Breakin',* 1984; (as stunt basketballer) *Beat Street,* 1984; (as stunt break dancer; uncredited) *Breakin' 2: Electric Boogaloo,* 1984; (uncredited) *Teen Wolf,* 1985; (cabbage patch break dance stunts; uncredited) *Rappin',* 1985; (uncredited) *Teen Wolf Too,* 1987; (as aerial stunt dancer for Patrick Swayze) *Swayze Dancing,*

1988; (aerial wolf stunts; uncredited) *Curse of the Queerwolf,* 1988; (uncredited) *Dances with Wolves,* 1990; (dance stunts for Screech; uncredited) *Saved by the Bell: Hawaiian Style* (television movie), 1992; and (as stunt dancer) *Titans* (television movie), 2000. Also performed stunts (uncredited) for the television series *Titans,* 2000.

Played Detective Nick Savino in the television series *NYPD Blue,* American Broadcasting Companies, Inc. (ABC), 1993-98. Actor in television movies, including (as Paulie) "The Last Outpost" and (as American soldier) "The Last Soldier," *Vietnam War Story: The Last Days,* Home Box Office (HBO), 1989. Appeared in the television special *Can a Guy Say No?,* ABC, 1986. Guest star on television shows, including *Misfits of Science, Amazing Stories, 21 Jump Street, The Marshal,* and *Civil Wars.* Executive producer of the television series *Young Americans,* Warner Bros., Inc. (WB), 2000.

WRITINGS:

FILM SCREENPLAYS, UNLESS OTHERWISE NOTED

Gloria (adapted from a 1980 screenplay by John Cassavetes), Columbia, 1999.
(With others) *Young Americans* (television series), WB, 2000.
(With Laura Angélica Simón) *Chasing Papi,* Twentieth Century Fox, 2003.

Also author of, with John Boskovich, *Inside Monkey Zetterland,* 1992.

WORK IN PROGRESS: The Hit Factory, a film about "boy bands," for Columbia Pictures.

SIDELIGHTS: Steven Antin had been acting in Hollywood for twenty years before he turned to screenwriting in 1992. He both wrote and starred in the 1992 film, *Inside Monkey Zetterland,* a dark comedy about a struggling screenwriter of that name and his eccentric friends and family. "Quirks may not make the man, but they certainly make *Inside Monkey Zetterland,*" *Austin Chronicle* reviewer Marjorie Baumgarten wrote, noting the "wonderful characterizations" that went into the film.

Antin's next film, *Gloria,* stars actress Sharon Stone (of *Basic Instinct* fame) as Gloria, a middle-aged woman who has just been released from the Florida prison where she spent the past three years. (She was innocent, but she took the fall to protect her mobster boyfriend, Kevin.) When Gloria makes it back to New York, she finds Kevin only to discover that he has just killed a seven-year-old boy's entire family and is now going after the boy. The boy's father was a bookie for the mob, but he was skimming money from them and keeping records of their illegal gambling; the boy, named Nicky, is now in possession of that evidence. Gloria takes it upon herself to rescue Nicky. Comparing the 1999 version of *Gloria* to the 1980 film from which it was adapted, Richard von Busack of *Metro-Active* commented, "The plot points are stronger [in the later version], the bonding between Gloria and Nicky is made sweeter and a new ending has been cooked up."

Antin is also one of the authors of the screenplay for *Chasing Papi,* a film notable for being the first major Hollywood studio release to feature an entirely Latino cast. Mexican singer and soap opera star Eduardo Verstegui stars as a traveling businessman who has three different girlfriends, one each in Miami, New York, and Chicago. When the women all bump into each other in the man's Los Angeles home, they become "entangled in the kind of complications that ensue only in the goofiest romantic comedies," Ken Fox wrote on *TV Guide Online.* But despite the farce's unbelievable plot, "If you're in the mood for a couple of hours of carefree fun, *Chasing Papi* is well worth chasing down," Richard Horgan wrote on *FilmStew.com.*

BIOGRAPHICAL AND CRITICAL SOURCES:

PERIODICALS

Austin Chronicle (Austin, TX), November 19, 1993, Marjorie Baumgarten, review of *Inside Monkey Zetterland.*
Back Stage, August 20, 1993, Robert Hofler, interview with Antin, p. 9W.
Chicago Sun-Times, April 16, 2003, Roger Ebert, review of *Chasing Papi.*
Dayton Daily News (Dayton, OH), July 11, 2000, review of *Young Americans,* p. 3C.

Entertainment Weekly, July 14, 2000, Ken Tucker, review of *Young Americans,* p. 62.

Interview, August, 1993, Sofia Coppola, "Steve Antin: A Tinseltown Kid Looks Back (through a Camera)," p. 18.

Los Angeles Times, August 3, 2000, Steven Linan, interview with Antin, p. F7.

New York Times, February 12, 1986, John J. O'Connor, review of *Can a Guy Say No?,* pp. 29, C21; October 15, 1993, Stephen Holden, review of *Inside Monkey Zetterland,* p. C12; January 23, 1999, Lawrence Van Gelder, review of *Gloria,* p. B14.

People, November 22, 1982, review of *The Last American Virgin,* p. 30; October 24, 1988, Peter Travers, review of *The Accused,* p. 17; August 21, 1989, John Stark, review of *Vietnam War Story: The Last Days,* pp. 9-10.

Record (Bergen County, NJ), July 12, 2000, Kinney Littlefield, review of *Young Americans,* p. Y3; April 18, 2003, Roger Ebert, review of *Chasing Papi,* p. 6.

Seattle Times, January 25, 1999, John Hartl, review of *Gloria,* p. F3.

Star-Ledger (Newark, NJ), July 12, 2000, Alan Sepinwall, review of *Young Americans,* p. 35.

Variety, October 6, 1982, review of *The Last American Virgin,* pp. 14-15; September 9, 1987, review of *Penitentiary III,* pp. 16-17; May 2, 1990, review of *Without You I'm Nothing,* p. 287; November 4, 1991, David Stratton, review of *Drive,* p. 63; July 27, 1992, Emanuel Levy, review of *Inside Monkey Zetterland,* p. 60; January 25, 1999, Godfrey Cheshire, review of *Gloria,* p. 77.

Video Review, February, 1991, Rich Conaty, review of *Without You I'm Nothing,* pp. 56-57.

ONLINE

Chasing Papi, http://www.chasingpapi.com (June 23, 2003).

FilmStew.com, http://www.filmstew.com/ (June 24, 2003), Richard Horgan, review of *Chasing Papi.*

Internet Movie Database, http://www.imdb.com/ (May 23, 2003), "Steve Antin."

MetroActive, http://www.metroactive.com/ (June 24, 2003), Richard von Busack, review of *Gloria.*

MSN Entertainment, http://entertainment.msn.com/ (June 24, 2003), Paul Brenner, review of *Inside Monkey Zetterland.*

Reel.com, http://www.reel.com/ (June 24, 2003), Richard Horgan, review of *Chasing Papi.*

Salon.com, http://www.salon.com/ (January 29, 1999), Charles Taylor, review of *Gloria.*

TV Guide Online, http://www.tvguide.com/ (June 24, 2003), Ken Fox, review of *Chasing Papi.**

*   *   *

ARENA, Felice 1968-

PERSONAL: First name is pronounced "Fe-li-che;" born March 10, 1968, in Kyabram, Victoria, Australia. *Education:* Graduated from La Trobe University (Bendigo, Victoria, Australia).

ADDRESSES: Home—St. Kilda, Victoria, Australia. *Agent*—Booked Out Speakers Agency, P.O. Box 2321, Prahran, Victoria 3181, Australia. *E-mail*—felicearena@hotmail.com.

CAREER: Children's author. Formerly worked as an actor, starring in various musicals in London's West End; playing Marco Alessi in the Australian soap opera *Neighbours,* 1992; and appearing in numerous other television dramas. Presenter for children's television.

WRITINGS:

Dolphin Boy Blue, Collins (London, England), 1996.
Mission Buffalo, Collins (London, England), 1997.
Wish, Angus & Robertson (Pymble, New South Wales, Australia), 1999.
Bravo, Billy!, HarperCollins (Pymble, New South Wales, Australia), 2000.
Breakaway John, Angus & Robertson (Pymble, New South Wales, Australia), 2001.

"SPECKY MAGEE" SERIES; WITH GARRY LYON

Specky Magee, Angus & Robertson (Pymble, New South Wales, Australia), 2002.
Specky Magee and the Great Footy Contest, Puffin (Camberwell, Victoria, Australia), 2003.
Specky Magee and the Season of Champions, Puffin (Camberwell, Victoria, Australia), 2004.

"BOYZ RULE!" SERIES; WITH PHIL KETTLE

Yabby Hunt, MacMillan Education Australia (South Yarra, Victoria, Australia), 2003, published as *Crawfish Hunt,* Mondo (New York, NY), 2004.

Golf Legends, MacMillan Education Australia (South Yarra, Victoria, Australia), 2003, Mondo (New York, NY), 2004.

Test Cricket, MacMillan Education Australia (South Yarra, Victoria, Australia), 2003.

Bull Riding, MacMillan Education Australia (South Yarra, Victoria, Australia), 2003.

Basketball Buddies, MacMillan Education Australia (South Yarra, Victoria, Australia), 2003.

Bike Daredevils, MacMillan Education Australia (South Yarra, Victoria, Australia), 2003.

Rock Star, MacMillan Education Australia (South Yarra, Victoria, Australia), 2003.

Skateboard Dudes, MacMillan Education Australia (South Yarra, Victoria, Australia), 2003.

Camping Out, MacMillan Education Australia (South Yarra, Victoria, Australia), 2003.

Water Rats, MacMillan Education Australia (South Yarra, Victoria, Australia), 2003.

Gone Fishing, MacMillan Education Australia (South Yarra, Victoria, Australia), 2003.

Secret Agent Heroes, MacMillan Education Australia (South Yarra, Victoria, Australia), 2003, Mondo (New York, NY), 2004.

Park Soccer, MacMillan Education Australia (South Yarra, Victoria, Australia), 2003.

Tree House, MacMillan Education Australia (South Yarra, Victoria, Australia), 2003, Mondo (New York, NY), 2004.

Tennis Ace, MacMillan Education Australia (South Yarra, Victoria, Australia), 2003, Mondo (New York, NY), 2004.

Wet World, MacMillan Education Australia (South Yarra, Victoria, Australia), 2003, Mondo (New York, NY), 2004.

Battle of the Games, MacMillan Education Australia (South Yarra, Victoria, Australia), 2004.

Olympic Champions, MacMillan Education Australia (South Yarra, Victoria, Australia), 2004.

On the Farm, MacMillan Education Australia (South Yarra, Victoria, Australia), 2004.

Pirate Attack, MacMillan Education Australia (South Yarra, Victoria, Australia), 2004, published as *Pirate Ship,* Mondo (New York, NY), 2004.

Hit the Beach, Mondo (New York, NY), 2004.

Halloween Gotcha!, Mondo (New York, NY), 2004.

Race Car Dreamers, Mondo (New York, NY), 2004.

Rotten School Day, Mondo (New York, NY), 2004.

SIDELIGHTS: Felice Arena took a long detour between graduating from college as a certified elementary school teacher and beginning to write children's books. He had a successful career as an actor for many years, capped by the role of "Marco Alessi" on the popular Australian soap opera *Neighbours* and several starring roles in musicals in London's West End theater district. Arena left acting to become a full-time author and a popular guest speaker in schools. As critics have noted, his books appeal to reluctant readers, particularly young males. Partially because of his success at reaching this audience, Arena receives many requests by teachers, as he once commented, "to visit their classrooms and excite readers about learning."

Published in England, Arena's first book, *Dolphin Boy Blue,* features a story about a teenage boy who is a champion swimmer, as Arena was at that age. (At one point, Arena owned the under-fourteen record for the fifty meter butterfly in Victoria.) One summer vacation, thirteen-year-old Mickey befriends a dolphin named Dana. Mickey discovers that he swims better and faster as he and Dana slice through the ocean waves together, but then he must find the confidence to leave Dana behind and transfer his newfound skills to chlorinated racing lanes. "I concentrate on the feel-good factor," Arena told *Daily Telegraph* interviewer Liz Deegan. "I prefer to write about striving for your goals, achieving your dreams."

Arena partnered with his old school friend and former Melbourne Football Club star Garry Lyon to write a series of books about Specky Magee, a boy whose art-loving parents cannot comprehend his obsession with Australian Rules football. The books have proved to be a smash hit with Aussie youngsters. "I'm getting hundreds of letters from parents and teachers that say, 'My kids are reading again,' which is the biggest inspiration for me to continue writing," Arena said to Courtney Walsh of the *Herald Sun.*

Also focusing on a young male readership, Arena has teamed up with fellow Australian children's author Phil Kettle to create "Boyz Rule!," a popular series themed around boys' recreational interests. According to the Children's Book Council of Australia's quarterly journal *Reading Time,* the series is "of premier appeal to boys in the lower-middle primary school and would be a worthy inclusion in a reading program."

BIOGRAPHICAL AND CRITICAL SOURCES:

PERIODICALS

Daily Telegraph (Surry Hills, New South Wales, Australia), November 30, 1996, Liz Deegan, "Playing in the Write Arena," p. 93.

Herald Sun (Melbourne, Victoria, Australia), June 1, 2002, Eddie McGuire, "Showing the Right Stuff," p. 114; July 24, 2002, Courtney Walsh, "Taking Author at His Word," p. 12.

Mirror (London, England), June 29, 1996, review of *Dolphin Boy Blue,* p. 3.

Reading Time, February, 2004, review of "Boyz Rule!" series.

ONLINE

Felice Arena Home Page, http://www.felicearena.com/ (January 11, 2004).

*   *   *

ARLEDGE, Roone (Pinckney, Jr.) 1931-2002

PERSONAL: Born July 8, 1931, in Forest Hills, NY; died of cancer, December 5, 2002; son of Roone (a lawyer) and Gertrude (Stritmater; a homemaker) Arledge; married Joan Heise, December 27, 1953 (divorced, 1971); married; wife's name, Anne (divorced, 1983); married Gigi Shaw; children (first marriage): Elizabeth Ann, Susan Lee, Patrcia Lu, Roone Pinckney. *Education:* Columbia University, B.A., 1952.

CAREER: Television producer. Dumont Television Network, 1952-53; *The Shari Lewis Show,* National Broadcasting Company, Inc. (NBC), 1955-60; American Broadcasting Companies, Inc. (ABC), producer, network sports, 1960-61; *Wide World of Sports,* producer and creator, 1961; vice president in charge of sports, 1963-68; executive producer of all sports programs, 1964, 1968, 1974; president, ABC News,

1968-85; creator, *Monday Night Football,* 1969; creator, *Nightline,* 1980; president, ABC Sports Inc., 1977-85; group president, ABC News and Sports, 1985-1990; ABC News president, 1990-1998; chairman ABC news, 1998-2002. *Military service:* U.S. Army, 1953-54.

AWARDS, HONORS: Recipient of thirty-seven Emmy Awards, given by the National Academy of Television Arts and Sciences; two Christopher Awards; four George Foster Peabody Awards; Kennedy Family Award, 1972; National Football Foundation and Hall of Fame Award, 1972; Broadcast Pioneers Award; Gold Medal, International Radio and Television Society, 1983; Distinguished Service to Journalism Honor Medal, University of Missouri; John Jay Distinguished Professional Service Award, Columbia University; Distinguished Achievement Award, University of Southern California Journalism Association; Founders Award; Olympic Order, Medal of the International Olympic Committee; Grand Prize, Cannes Film Festival; Man of the Year, National Association of Television Program Executives; Man of the Year, *Football News;* Man of the Year, Ohio State University; Man of the Year, Gallagher Report; inducted into Academy of Arts and Sciences Hall of Fame, and U.S. Olympic Hall of Fame, both 1990; du Pont-Columbia Award, 1995; Lifetime Achievement Emmy, 2002 (first ever awarded).

WRITINGS:

Roone: A Memoir, HarperCollins (New York, NY), 2003.

SIDELIGHTS: Roone Arledge has been a significant pioneer and innovator in the world of television sports and news. *Life* magazine placed Arledge on their list of "One Hundred Most Important Americans of the Twentieth Century" and *Sports Illustrated* placed him third on their list (just behind Muhammad Ali and Michael Jordan) of forty individuals who have most impacted the world of sports in the last four decades. Arledge's career as a television executive for ABC spanned four decades. He is credited with creating *Monday Night Football,* including hiring Howard Cosell as an announcer. Arledge also created ABC's *Wide World of Sports, Nightline, 20/20,* and *Prime Time Live.* In the world of sports broadcasting, his ideas (and implementations) include instant replays, isolated cameras, slow motion, and stop action. He also introduced the first female and black news anchors to network television.

Arledge's memoir, *Roone,* was published posthumously. In the book he wrote about being called a legend, "I've been called that, much to my chagrin. Legends are the dead . . . and I'm very much alive despite the cane, still chairman of ABC News and working on these memoirs in my spare time." The cane Arledge referenced was the cancer that wreaked havoc in his body. In a review for the *Post-Gazette.com* Allan Walton stated, "Arledge has a lot to tell, and most of it is worthy of your attention . . . it's dotted with names, a bit of gossip and enough insight to give you a feel not just for the man, but for the industry." The book explores his friendships with people he hired, such as Barbara Walters, Peter Jennings, and Howard Cosell. It delves deep into the industry of television broadcasting and into Arledge's life itself.

When Arledge first began at ABC, the network was trailing in third place among the three television networks. Arledge had much success in helping to change the company's situation. He altered the style of sports and news coverage to create a more up-close and personal feel to the broadcasts. During his lifetime he won thirty-seven Emmys for his work in the television industry. He was also the first non-athlete to be appointed to the U.S. Olympic Hall of Fame, for his work in revamping the coverage of the Olympics on television. "Showing just how he did it, these well-crafted memoirs provide a beind-the-scenes look at prominent personalities, milestone events, and land-mark programs," wrote John Maxymuk in a review for *Library Journal.*

Arledge completely changed the face of television news and sports coverage forever. "Anyone who has watched television for the last thirty or so years will find it a remarkable memoir . . . not only is the book full of fascinating information, it's written in an im-mensely readable style," stated Ilene Cooper in *Booklist.* A reviewer for *Publishers Weekly* also com-mented, "In his long career as an executive at ABC-TV, Roone Arledge revolutionized sports and news broadcasting by emphasizing entertainment—and his posthumous memoir entertains as well."

BIOGRAPHICAL AND CRITICAL SOURCES:

BOOKS

Arledge, Roone, *Roone: A Memoir,* HarperCollins (New York, NY), 2003.
Contmeporary Theatre, Film, and Television, Volume 4, Gale Group (Detroit, MI), 1987.
Gunther, Marc, *The House That Roone Built: The Inside Story of ABC News,* Little, Brown (Boston, MA), 1994.
Newsmakers, Gale Group (Detroit, MI), 1992.

PERIODICALS

Booklist, May 1, 2003, Ilene Cooper, review of *Roone: A Memoir,* p. 1506.
Electronic Media, September 9, 2002, "NATAS makes the right call," p. 9.
Esquire, October, 1974, Sol Yurick, "That Wonderful Person Who Brought You Howard Cosell," pp. 152-154.
Library Journal, June 1, 2003, John Maxymuk, review of *Roone,* p. 134.
Los Angeles Times, June 6, 2003, Carmela Ciuraru, review of *Roone,* p. E22.
New York Times, February, 1980, Desmond Smith, "The wide world of Roone Arledge," pp. 153-158; December 29, 2002, Julian Rubinstein, "The emperor of the air," p. 36.
Playboy, October, 1976, "*Playboy* Interview: Roone Arledge," pp. 63-68.
Publishers Weekly, April 28, 2003, review of *Roone,* p. 61.

ONLINE

Museum of Broadcast Communications, http://www.museum.tv/archives/ (October 22, 2003), biogra-phy of Roone Arledge.
New York Metro, http://www.newyorkmetro.com/ (October 22, 2003), John Homans, review of *Roone.*
Post-Gazette.com, http://www.post-gazette.com/books/reviews/ (October 22, 2003), Allan Walton, review of *Roone.*

OBITUARIES:

PERIODICALS

Broadcasting & Cable, December 16, 2002, p. 30.
Daily Variety, December 6, 2002, p. 1.
Electronic Media, December 9, 2002, p. 6.
Entertainment Weekly, January 3, 2003, p. 26.
Maclean's, December 16, 2002, p. 17.
Newsweek, December 16, 2002, p. 43.
Sports Illustrated, December 16, 2002, p. 121.
Time, December 16, 2002, p. 21.
Washington Post, December 6, 2002, p. C1.

ONLINE

ABC News, http://www.abcnews.com/ (October 22, 2003).
Mediaweek, http://www.mediaweek.com/ (December 9, 2002).*

* * *

ARMSTRONG, David 1946-

PERSONAL: Born 1946, in Birmingham, England. *Education:* Attended University of Cardiff.

ADDRESSES: Home—Wales. *Agent*—c/o Author Mail, Allison & Busby, Bon Marche Centre, 241 Ferndale Rd., London SW9 8BJ, England.

CAREER: Has taught adult education at a college in Shropshire, England.

AWARDS, HONORS: Best First Crime Novel Award shortlist, Crime Writers' Association, for *Night's Black Agents.*

WRITINGS:

Night's Black Agents (novel), Crime Club (London, England), 1993.
Less than Kind (novel), HarperCollins (London, England), 1994.

Until Dawn Tomorrow (novel), HarperCollins (London, England), 1995.
Thought for the Day (novel), HarperCollins (London, England), 1997.
Small Vices (novel), Allison & Busby (London, England), 2001.
How NOT to Write a Novel (nonfiction), Allison & Busby (London, England), 2003.

Also author of poems, short stories, and plays. Contributor to periodicals, including *Daily Telegraph, Sunday Times,* London *Times, London Evening Standard,* and the *Manchester Evening News.*

SIDELIGHTS: Despite five published novels and a nomination for the Crime Writers' Association Best First Crime Novel Award, David Armstrong received little critical attention until he published *How NOT to Write a Novel.* A chronicle of his many setbacks and frustrations as a writer, Armstrong's only nonfiction title has outsold all his other books combined and attracted a following of writers and aspiring writers looking for the unvarnished truth about their chosen field. Humorous tips such as not crying in public when your publisher drops you and not visiting bookstores because your book either will not be carried or will not be selling are combined with hard truths about the vast oversupply of would-be authors, the extreme unlikelihood of "no-name" authors breaking into the big time, and the many frustrations of book tours. The underlying theme throughout is a message to would-be novelists: don't do it. Oddly enough, Armstrong himself emerges without the bitterness or anger one might expect. *Birmingham Post* reviewer Mike Ripley found Armstrong's book "a witty, quite endearing and very probably painfully honest guide to the trials and tribulations of an author so enthusiastic about the whole business of being a writer that he cheerfully suffers the slings and arrows of outrageous publishers and passes on the fruits of his decade of experience in useful tips to the aspiring author."

Prior to his newfound career as no-nonsense writer's guru, Armstrong was a writer of gritty crime novels. His first novel, 1993's *Night's Black Agents,* is set in the 1930s Midlands, a backwater town along a canal that is gripped by depression. When a barkeep pays a hit man to kill his wife's lover, the homicide inquiry sets into motion a series of events that brings out a number of buried secrets. This novel was shortlisted by the Crime Writers Association, which chose not to give out their Best First Crime Novel Award that year, to the outrage of many mystery fans and reviewers. Armstrong's next novel, *Less than Kind,* moves to the late 1960s and the rural Welsh borderlands, where Birmingham policeman John Munroe finds himself drawn into a world of fugitives and drug dealers lurking below the tranquil scenes of country life.

With *Until Dawn Tomorrow,* Armstrong introduces Birmingham Detective Inspector Frank Kavanaugh. Grieving over the recent separation from his wife, Kavanaugh finds himself drawn into the apparently motiveless murder of a local art teacher. Stymied by fruitless interviews and dead ends, he appears on the Crimewatch program and encounters a colleague working on a similarly baffling crime. Eventually, he finds himself on a trail that takes him to Wales and to the seedy side of London. Kavanaugh reappears in *Thought for the Day.* This time he is transferred to London and assigned to a kidnapping case. The missing advertising executive he is looking for, it turns out, has a shady past and a young mistress, and Kavanaugh's suspicions grow as more secrets come out. When another employee of the ad agency is murdered, Kavanaugh begins to wonder what is true and false in a world where exaggerated claims are business as usual. "Unfortunately, the ending is contrived and artificial . . . and does little justice to what is otherwise a fine novel," concluded *Sunday Times* reviewer Donna Leon.

Kavanaugh makes another appearance in *Small Vices,* which explores the way in which petty offenses can grow into serious crimes and how little betrayals can have huge consequences. Still separated from, but emotionally attached to, his wife, Kavanaugh has been having an affair with Detective Constable Jane Salt, "one of the most cleverly drawn characters in the book," according to Ripley in another *Birmingham Post* review. When Kavanaugh's investigation of a serial killer targeting prostitutes takes him to Birmingham, Salt remains on a London case involving a series of armed robberies, causing Kavanaugh to once again go through the pangs of separation. Eventually, he and Salt find themselves caught up in a tangled web that includes a radical eco-warrior and a drug czar coming under increasing suspicion for his own activities. "Armstrong knows is stuff . . . has interesting things to say and says them well," concluded Ripley in his review.

BIOGRAPHICAL AND CRITICAL SOURCES:

PERIODICALS

Birmingham Post (Birmingham, England), April 27, 2002, Mike Ripley, review of *Small Vices,* p. 48; July 5, 2003, Mike Ripley, review of *How NOT to Write a Novel,* p. 53.
Sunday Times (London, England), February 1, 1998, Donna Leon, review of *Thought for the Day,* Books section, p. 8.*

*   *   *

ASHLEY, Trisha

PERSONAL: Born in St. Helens, Lancashire, England; divorced. *Education:* Studied architectural glass at Swansea College of Art. *Hobbies and other interests:* Painting.

ADDRESSES: Home—North Wales. *Agent*—The Marsh Agency, 111 Dover St., London W1S 4LJ, England. *E-mail*—Trisha.Ashley@tesco.net.

CAREER: Novelist. Has worked for a stained-glass maker and a plumber.

WRITINGS:

NOVELS

Good Husband Material, Piatkus (London, England), 2000.
The Urge to Jump, Piatkus (London, England), 2001.
Every Woman for Herself, Piatkus (London, England), 2002, Thomas Dunne Books (New York, NY), 2003.
Singled Out, Piatkus (London, England), 2003, Thomas Dunne Books (New York, NY), 2004.
The Generous Gardener, Severn House (London, England), 2004, (Brooklyn, NY), 2005.

SIDELIGHTS: When British novelist Trisha Ashley had difficulty finding a publisher for her first book, her agent suggested that the problem was a lack of romance in the satirical comedy. After taking her agent's suggestion and revising the manuscript, Ashley sold the book—*Good Husband Material*—to Piatkus. The author has since published several other novels that feature decidedly unglamorous heroines who are in the midst of midlife crises but who maintain a humorous outlook on the difficulties of marriage, divorce, dating, and family ties.

Good Husband Material portrays Tish, a woman who is restless in her marriage to a seemingly perfect man and preoccupied with the rock musician who once treated her so badly. Her second book, *The Urge to Jump,* is the story of spinster novelist Sappho Jones, who is worried that the single life breeds eccentric behavior. A reviewer for the London *Times* called *The Urge to Jump* "enjoyable, if easily forgotten."

Every Woman for Herself is Ashley's first book to be published in the United States. In this story, protagonist Charlotte is deserted by her husband of more than twenty years, leaving her in need of a home and a job. When she returns to the Yorkshire village where her oddball father and siblings live, she finds romance with actor Mace North. *Booklist*'s Carol Haggas recommended *Every Woman for Herself* as an "uproarious coming-of-middle-age novel," calling it "truly laugh-out-loud funny." Similarly, a *Kirkus Reviews* writer enjoyed it as "shrewd but gentle satire . . . that never misses a beat" and said that the book was "wonderfully funny to boot."

Ashley told *CA:* "My readers are a marvellous bunch, ranging in age from sixteen to eighty-six (the ones I know about anyway), and I'm always amazed and delighted that so many of them take the time out of their busy lives to write and tell me what they think of my books.

"What we all share is a sense of humor, and while mine may be darker than most, it has helped me negotiate the trickier parts of my life, just as it helps the heroines of my books to find a way through their own difficulties. Although my books are romantic comedy, they also deal with painful issues, too: divorce, desertion, miscarriage, breast cancer, and other issues that are familiar in our own lives or those of close friends.

"Friendship is very important to me: all of my friends are other novelists or keen readers, and I have found a great generosity, a sharing of information and encouragement, among them.

"I think if you read my novels, you will quickly discover that I love literary biography and also the works of Jane Austin, the Brontës, John Milton, and Shakespeare. But so many influences go into the melting pot of becoming a writer, and I've always been a bookaholic who will read anything and everything. And literary snobbism makes me angry: if a novelist has an original writing voice and creates a brilliant world in their book, then I want to go there, whatever the genre.

"I wrote my first novel at eighteen, and I've written at least one a year since then. (That's a lot of unpublished novels!) Of course, most of the early ones were rubbish, and I was trying to write satire and failing to find a market for it—but writing was—and still is—a compulsion. I don't set out to write funny books either, but I do come from Lancashire, where a lively sense of humour, especially in adversity, is the norm!

"Which of my books is my favourite? Well, which one of your children do you prefer?"

BIOGRAPHICAL AND CRITICAL SOURCES:

PERIODICALS

Booklist, May 15, 2003, Carol Haggas, review of *Every Woman for Herself,* p. 1642.
Kirkus Reviews, April 1, 2003, review of *Every Woman for Herself,* p. 488.
Library Journal, July, 2003, Margaret Hanes, review of *Every Woman for Herself,* p. 119.
Times (London, England), October 20, 2001, review of *The Urge to Jump,* p. 19.

ONLINE

Trisha Ashley Web Site, http://www.geocities.com/trisha_ashley2002/ (June 21, 2004).

*　　*　　*

ASHWORTH, Robert A(rchibald) 1871-1959

PERSONAL: Born July 26, 1871, in Glasgow, Scotland; died March 8, 1959, in the United States; son of John W. and Emma (Gregson) Ashworth; married Mabelle Edgerton, 1902. *Education:* Columbia University, A.M., 1892, A.M., 1894; Union Theological Seminary, B.D., 1896.

CAREER: Ordained minister of Northern Baptist Convention, 1896; pastor of Baptist churches in Minerva, NY, 1896-98, Bridgeton, NJ, 1898-1900, Meriden, CT, 1900-11, Milwaukee, WI, 1911-21, and Yonkers, NY, 1921-33; National Conference of Christians and Jews, founding member, 1928, editorial secretary, 1933-c. 1955. Union Theological Seminary, lecturer in Baptist principles and polity, beginning 1931. Milwaukee Federation of Churches, president, 1912; affiliate of Federal Council of Churches; Conference on Faith and Order, delegate to international conferences, 1927, 1937; World Council of Churches, member of American Committee, c. 1938.

WRITINGS:

The Union of Christian Forces in America, American Sunday-School Union (Philadelphia, PA), 1915.
Being a Christian, Judson Press (Philadelphia, PA), 1924.

Editor of *Baptist,* 1921-30; contributing editor, *Christian Century,* beginning 1931.*

*   *   *

AVERY, Fiona Kai

PERSONAL: Female. *Education:* Graduate of Indiana University.

ADDRESSES: Agent—c/o Author Mail, Top Cow Productions, Inc., 10390 Santa Monica Blvd., Los Angeles, CA 90025.

CAREER: Writer, poet, archeologist, historian.

WRITINGS:

No Honor: Set 1, Volumes 1-4, Top Cow Productions (Los Angeles, CA), 2001.
(With Billy Tan and Steve Firchow) *Witchblade: Obakemono* (graphic novel), Top Cow Productions (Los Angeles, CA), 2002.

Also author of *The Lucky Strike* (movie screenplay), 2000. Author of comic book series *No Honor;* writer for television and comic book series, including *Crusade, Babylon 5, Spiderman, Tomb Raider, Witchblade,* and *XMen;* interviewer for periodicals, including *Starlog;* work represented in anthologies, including *The Year's Best Science Fiction,* St. Martin's Press (New York, NY), 2001.

ADAPTATIONS: A Showtime television pilot based on the *No Honor* series was filmed.

SIDELIGHTS: Fiona Kai Avery earned her break writing for the science fiction genre because of her background in archeology. Avery was writing for publications, and when she interviewed *Babylon 5* creator J. Michael Straczynski for *Starlog,* she asked him how he was going to handle the archaeology aspects of *Crusade.* Straczynski said he planned to hire consultants, and Avery immediately mailed him her resume. She was hired as a reference editor, and from there, she became a screenwriter.

In an interview with Mark A. Rivera for *Visi.com,* Avery responded to his question of how she views science fiction, sci-fi, and fantasy, by saying, "I believe that science fiction explores the impact of technology on people. . . . I think it's rare to find science fiction on television or the big screen today." Avery said that as she sees it, "if you took all the techno-babble and the neat futuristic elements out of the story, and you set the same story in the Bronze Age, and instead you were showing the impact of the stirrup or iron, or agriculture . . . you've got the same heart of the story, and it will have the same impact on your readers/ viewers. I guess because I am a historian and archaeologist, I use parallels when I write what will happen in a hypothetical future, and through those parallels I tend to tell stories that may have a universal appeal to an audience."

Avery told Rivera that she enjoys writing mystery, fantasy, and dark fantasy, and she said that has a number of completed, but as yet unpublished, stories and novels, as well as screenplays. Rivera asked for her point of view as a woman who writes science fiction. She replied, "I don't really think of myself as a 'woman' who writes science fiction. But I don't really think of myself as a 'woman' in life either. That would predispose me to think of others as 'men' or 'women' first, and I'm the type to look at someone as a person first, not their gender. . . . But I guess that some people feel this is a genre that's heavily male-oriented. If it's about space, or science, it must be for men. I don't really feel that way. But then, I grew up on this stuff too."

Avery's first graphic novel is *Witchblade: Obakemono.* While the comic and television series focused on police officer Sara Pezzini, the graphic novel is instead about the weaponry Sara uses and is set in feudal Japan. There is a woman, Shiori, who is given the opportunity to use an ancient sword to avenge the murder of her husband. In order to draw on its power, Shiori must go on a journey, and along the way, she is joined by other women, including a runaway, an archer, a priestess, and a chimneysweep. The women return to vanquish those who have taken over Shiori's homeland, justice is achieved, and the repentant are forgiven. *Library Journal*'s Steve Raiteri called *Witchblade* an "enjoyable, above-average mainstream comic."

BIOGRAPHICAL AND CRITICAL SOURCES:

PERIODICALS

Library Journal, November 1, 2002, Steve Raiteri, review of *Witchblade: Obakemono,* p. 64.
Publishers Weekly, September 30, 2002, review of *Witchblade,* p. 52.

ONLINE

Fiona Kai Avery Home Page, http://www.fionaavery. com/ (May 28, 2003).
Visi.com, http://www.visi.com/~wildfoto/reviews/ interview3.html (May 28, 2003), Mark A. Rivera, interview with Avery.*

B

BAER, Greg

PERSONAL: Married; wife's name, Donna; children: seven. *Education:* Earned M.D. degree.

ADDRESSES: Home—Georgia. *Agent*—c/o Author Mail, Gotham Books, 375 Hudson St., New York, NY 10014.

CAREER: Worked as ophthalmologist and eye surgeon; became full-time writer, teacher, and public speaker, including appearances at Unity churches. Guest on more than one hundred television and radio programs.

WRITINGS:

The Wart King: The Truth about Love and Lies, LA Press (Chattanooga, TN), 1997.
The Truth about Relationships: A Simple and Powerfully Effective Way for Everyone to Find Real Love and Loving Relationships, Blue Ridge Press (Rome, GA), published as *Real Love: A Simple and Powerfully Effective Way for Everyone to Find Unconditional Love and Loving Relationships,* Gotham Books (New York, NY), 2003.
The Wise Man: The Truth about Sharing Real Love, Blue Ridge Press (Rome, GA), 2003.

Author of other self-help books.

BIOGRAPHICAL AND CRITICAL SOURCES:

PERIODICALS

Library Journal, November 12, 2002, Margaret Cardwell, review of *Real Love: A Simple and Power-* *fully Effective Way for Everyone to Find Unconditional Love and Loving Relationships,* p. 88.
Publishers Weekly, November 4, 2002, review of *Real Love,* p. 73.

ONLINE

GregBaer.com, http://www.gregbaer.com/ (March 26, 2003).*

* * *

BAHAL, Aniruddha 1967-

PERSONAL: Born 1967, in India.

ADDRESSES: Home—Noida, India. *Agent*—c/o Author Mail, Farrar, Straus & Giroux, 19 Union Square West, New York, NY 10003.

CAREER: Investigative journalist and novelist. Worked for *India Today* and *Outlook;* cofounder and CEO of Tehelka.com; founder and editor and chief of Cobrapost.com.

AWARDS, HONORS: Bad Sex in Fiction Award, Literary Review, 2003, for the sexual encounters in *Bunker Thirteen.*

WRITINGS:

A Crack in the Mirror, Rupa and Company (Calcutta, India), 1991.
Bunker Thirteen, Farrar, Straus and Giroux (New York, NY), 2003.

SIDELIGHTS: Born in 1967, Aniruddha Bahal has made a name for himself in India as a muckraker and journalist determined to uncover the truth. Early in his career he worked as a reporter for *India Today* and *Outlook* and helped brake a story about match-fixing in international cricket. He went on to cofound and work as CEO of *Tehelka.com,* a news Web site which name means "sensation" in Hindi. In 2001 *Tehelka. com* gained fame when the group organized a sting to uncover politicians, senior bureaucrats and army officials accepting brides from arms dealers. They were able to capture the interactions on video and the scandal resulted in the resignation of BJP president Bangaru Laxman and defense minister George Fernandez. While the scandal gained fame and prestige for Bahal it also resulted in his short and wrongful imprisonment and the closing of *Tehelka.com,* due to loss of funding. He has since started a new news Web site called *Cobrapost.com.* He lives in Noida, India, near New Delhi.

In 1991 Bahal published his first work of fiction called *A Crack in the Mirror.* It was published in India and did not make much in sales. His second publication in 2003, *Bunker Thirteen,* has received much more attention. It is a spy thriller set in modern India about a journalist named MM who becomes involved in a tangled plot of intrigue, all the while seeking to satisfy his drug addictions and sexual desires. The story is told uniquely in the second person "you." David Wright for *Library Journal* wrote, "The second-person narration seems less calculated to grab the reader than to abstract the borderline sociopath narrator from his own relentless gamesmanship." However, a reviewer for *Publishers Weekly* found "Bahal's use of the second person heightens suspense and adds psychological depth." Jamie James of *Time International* found that the book "suffers from some common flaws of the thriller...yet on his first time out, Bahal has succeeded admirably at the genre's main requirement by creating a complex and compelling (if frequently repellent) protagonist." Frank Sennett of *Booklist* concluded, "MM proves wearisome after extended exposure, and Aniruddha tips off the book's big surprise too early. Even so, there's a lot of fresh, crackling action here for thrill junkies." *Bunker Thirteen* received the dubious honor of Literary Review's Bad Sex in Fiction award in 2003, for the sexual encounters depicted throughout the book.

BIOGRAPHICAL AND CRITICAL SOURCES:

PERIODICALS

Booklist, July, 2003, Frank Sennett, review of *Bunker Thirteen,* p. 1862.

Bookseller, December 12, 2003, "Literary Review's Bad Sex in Fiction Award," p. 29.
Kirkus Reviews, May 1, 2003, review of *Bunker Thirteen,* p. 621.
Library Journal, June 15, 2003, David Wright, review of *Bunker Thirteen,* p. 98.
M2 Best Books, December 4, 2003, "Bad Sex Award Goes to Indian Author."
Nation, August 18, 2003, Amitava Kumar, "Thieves Like Us," p. 46.
New York Times Book Review, June 22, 2003, James Buchan, "Old Nukes and Spooks," p. 8.
Publishers Weekly, April 28, 2003, review of *Bunker Thirteen,* p. 44.
Time International, July 7, 2003, Jamie James, "James Bond is a Choirboy," and "Troublemaker" (interview), p. 58.

ONLINE

Desi Journal, http://www.desijournal.com/ (October 22, 2003), Sudheer Apte, review of *Bunker Thirteen.*
South Asian, http://www.the-south-asian.com/ (October 22, 2003), Avinash Kalla, "Anifuddha Bahal-Creating Another *Tehelka.*"*

*   *   *

BAICKER-McKEE, Carol 1958-

PERSONAL: Born 1958, in CA; married; children: three. *Education:* Yale University, B.A.; University of Virginia, M.A., Ph.D.

ADDRESSES: *Home*—Mt. Lebanon, PA. *Office*—c/o Author Mail, Peachtree Publishers, Ltd., 1700 Chattahoochee Ave., Atlanta, GA 30318-2112.

CAREER: Child psychologist; writer; lecturer on child-rearing subjects.

WRITINGS:

Mapped Out!: The Search for Snookums, illustrated by Traci O'Very Covey, Gibbs Smith (Salt Lake City, UT), 1997.

Fussbusters at Home: Around-the-Clock Strategies and Games for Smoothing the Rough Spots in Your Preschooler's Day, Peachtree (Atlanta, GA), 2002.

Fussbusters on the Go: Strategies and Games for Stress-Free Outings, Errands, and Vacations with Your Preschooler, Peachtree (Atlanta, GA), 2002.

WORK IN PROGRESS: Further "Fussbuster" books.

SIDELIGHTS: Carol Baicker-McKee is a trained child psychologist who has based her books more on her experiences as a mother than on her clinical studies. Both *Fussbusters at Home: Around-the-Clock Strategies and Games for Smoothing the Rough Spots in Your Preschooler's Day* and *Fussbusters on the Go: Strategies and Games for Stress-Free Outings, Errands, and Vacations with Your Preschooler* combine practical tips with good humor to make a child's preschool years less stressful for busy parents. Baicker-McKee told *SouthCoastToday.com* that she got the idea for a series of "Fussbuster" books from her own adventures as a stay-at-home mom. "I've written the book that I would have wanted when my kids were little," she said.

Baicker-McKee has always been intimately involved with young children, first as an older sibling, then as a babysitter, and later as a student at Yale and the University of Virginia. She worked as a child psychologist until her three children were born and then quit to stay at home with them. Baicker-McKee found a support system among other mothers in her neighborhood, more or less pooling creative ideas for keeping their children amused and easing them into the major life transitions, such as preschool, elementary school, and family vacations. Some of these ideas have found their way into the "Fussbusters" books.

Library Journal correspondent Kay Hogan Smith praised *Fussbusters on the Go* for its "earthy sense of humor," noting that Baicker-McKee has introduced fun into such chores as taking daily errands, going to family events, and traveling long distances for vacations. Hogan Smith concluded that the book is both "practical and a joy to read."

Baicker-McKee's juvenile title *Mapped Out!: The Search for Snookums* is a book/puzzle in which youngsters must use detachable maps and other clues

to find a pet iguana named Snookums, who has been kidnapped. In her *School Library Journal* review of the work, Adele Greenlee suggested that *Mapped Out* would supply several hours of challenge, and that its readers "will likely feel a sense of pride in solving a clever, multifaceted puzzle."

Baicker-McKee lives in western Pennsylvania with her husband and three teenaged children.

BIOGRAPHICAL AND CRITICAL SOURCES:

PERIODICALS

Library Journal, October 1, 2002, Kay Hogan Smith, review of *Fussbusters on the Go: Strategies and Games for Stress-Free Outings, Errands, and Vacations with Your Preschooler,* p. 121.
School Library Journal, January, 1998, Adele Greenlee, review of *Mapped Out!: The Search for Snookums,* p. 108.

ONLINE

Peachtree Publishers, Ltd., http://www.peachtree-online.com/ (April 25, 2003), promotional material for the "Fussbusters" titles.
SouthCoastToday.com, http://www.s-t.com/ (August 6, 2002), Karen MacPherson, "Coping with Grumpy Kids: How to Chill Out Your Children."*

*   *   *

BAKER, Kyle 1965-

PERSONAL: Born 1965, in New York, NY; married; wife's name, Liz.

ADDRESSES: Agent—c/o Author Mail, DC Comics, 1700 Broadway, New York, NY 10019. *E-mail*—kylebaker@kylebaker.com.

CAREER: Writer and illustrator; director of animated films. Founder of Kyle Baker Publishing.

AWARDS, HONORS: Harvey Award for Best Graphic Album of Original Work, 1991, for *Why I Hate Saturn,* and 1999, for *You Are Here;* Eisner Award for Best Writer/Artist, Humor, 1999, for *You Are Here,* and 2000, for *I Die at Midnight* and "Letitia Lerner, Superman's Baby Sitter" (the latter, created with Elizabeth Glass, also won Best Short Story).

WRITINGS:

GRAPHIC NOVELS; SELF-ILLUSTRATED

The Cowboy Wally Show, Doubleday (New York, NY), 1988, Sixteenth Commemorative Edition, 2003.

Why I Hate Saturn, DC Comics (New York, NY), 1993.

You Are Here, DC Comics (New York, NY), 1999.

King David, Vertigo/DC Comics (New York, NY), 2002.

Undercover Genie: The Irreverent Conjurings of an Illustrative Aladdin, DC Comics (New York, NY), 2003.

OTHER

(Illustrator) Aaron McGruder and Reginald Hudlin, *Birth of a Nation: A Comic Novel,* Crown (New York, NY), 2004.

Also author of *I Die at Midnight, Truth, The Bakers, The New Baker, Break the Chain,* and *Kyle Baker, Cartoonist.* Contributor of "Letitia Lerner, Superman's Baby Sitter," created with Elizabeth Glass, to *Elseworlds Eighty-Page Giant.* Illustrator of weekly comic strip "Bad Publicity" for *New York* magazine. Contributor of cartoons to newspapers and magazines, including *Entertainment Weekly, ESPN, Esquire, Mad, New Yorker, New York Times, Rolling Stone, Spin, Vibe,* and *Village Voice.* Director of animated music video, "Break the Chain," based on comic book of the same name illustrated by Baker. Contributor of drawings to *9-11: The World's Finest Comic Book Writers and Artists Tell Stories to Remember,* edited by Paul Levitz and published by DC Comics in 2002, and to numerous other comic books. Writer and director of "Looney Tunes" animated theatrical shorts for Warner Bros., Inc.

WORK IN PROGRESS: A graphic novel biography of Nat Turner, leader of a nineteenth-century slave rebellion; a graphic novel titled *My Special Plan.*

SIDELIGHTS: Kyle Baker's graphic novels have covered subjects as diverse as an unscrupulous television performer, young New York hipsters, and the Bible's King David. His body of work includes "at least two graphic novel cult classics," according to a *Publishers Weekly* reviewer, those being *The Cowboy Wally Show* and *Why I Hate Saturn.* He also has illustrated numerous comic books written by others and has begun writing and directing animated short films. He produced a multimedia project with the comic *Break the Chain,* which he illustrated while sharing writing duties with rap artist KRS-One; it was sold with an audiocassette of KRS-One's music, and Baker directed a companion music video.

The Cowboy Wally Show, Baker's first graphic novel, is a send-up of the television industry. Cowboy Wally is an obnoxious, not-very-bright entertainer who nevertheless rises to fame and power as a TV host and executive, thanks to some underhanded schemes. *Quill and Quire* critic Paul Stuewe found the story only "intermittently effective," but *Booklist* contributor Ray Olson deemed it "desperately, mordantly, stomping-and-crying-ly funny."

Why I Hate Saturn takes a satirical look at the culture of young, trendy New Yorkers. The main character, Anne, is a gifted writer but is also maladjusted and misanthropic. The shooting of Anne's sister, by a former lover, sets in motion a series of bizarre experiences. This "clever" book "became an underground comics classic," reported a *Publishers Weekly* reviewer.

Baker's next graphic novel, *You Are Here,* is also set in New York City. Its protagonist, Noel Coleman, is a man with a lengthy criminal record, but he is being pursued by someone with a much worse record—a serial murderer—whose wife once had an affair with Noel. While trying to elude his would-be killer, Noel carries on a romance with an unconventional, free-spirited woman named Helen. Baker's drawings portray New York with "virtuoso comics draftsmanship," observed a *Publishers Weekly* commentator, adding that his story is "rip-roaringly entertaining."

The humor that some critics found in those titles is evident even in Baker's Bible-inspired effort, *King David.* His retelling of the tale of the shepherd who rose to become king of Israel "is funny and irreverent, and Bible study has never been so hip" a *Publishers Weekly* reviewer remarked. *Entertainment Weekly*'s Ken Tucker, meanwhile, noted that the novel is "sometimes slapstick-silly but always true to biblical narrative." It also remains true to its source by featuring frank portrayals of violence and sexuality; to *Bible Review* contributor Michael M. Homan, "This is precisely why Baker's *King David* succeeds where so many artistic re-creations (especially movies) of the Bible have failed." Homan called the novel "a hit of epic proportions" that will "help bring back the Bible—the uncut version—to pop culture."

BIOGRAPHICAL AND CRITICAL SOURCES:

PERIODICALS

Bible Review, December, 2002, Michael M. Homan, "Truth, Justice and the Judean Way," pp. 50-51.
Booklist, June 1, 1988, Ray Olson, review of *The Cowboy Wally Show,* p. 1635; October 1, 2003, Gordon Flagg, review of *Undercover Genie: The Irreverent Conjurings of an Illustrative Aladdin,* p. 309.
Entertainment Weekly, April 12, 2002, Ken Tucker, review of *King David,* p. 70; June 27, 2003, Tom Sinclair, review of *Undercover Genie,* p. 145.
Publishers Weekly, January 25, 1999, review of *You Are Here,* p. 74; September 9, 2002, review of *King David,* p. 45.
Quill and Quire, May, 1988, Paul Stuewe, review of *The Cowboy Wally Show,* p. 29.

ONLINE

Kyle Baker Home Page, http://www.kylebaker.com/ (December 31, 2003).*

*   *   *

BANGS, Nina

PERSONAL: Female. *Education:* Rutgers University, received degree in English literature. *Hobbies and other interests:* Horses and cats.

ADDRESSES: Home—Texas. *Agent*—c/o Author Mail, St. Martin's Press, 175 Fifth Ave., New York, NY 10027.

CAREER: Author. Has worked as an elementary school teacher for over twenty years.

AWARDS, HONORS: Dorothy Parker Award of Excellence Reviewer Choice Award, Reviewers International Organization, 2001, PRISM finalist, 2002, and Paranormal Excellence Award for Romantic Literature nomination, *Romantic Times,* all for *The Pleasure Master.*

WRITINGS:

ROMANCE FICTION

An Original Sin, Love Spell (New York, NY), 1999.
(With Madeline Baker, Ann Lawrence, and Kathleen Nance) *Paradise,* Leisure Books (New York, NY), 1999.
(With Lisa Cach, Thea Devine, and Penelope Neri) *Seduction by Chocolate,* Leisure Books (New York, NY), 2000.
(With Claudia Dain and Shirl Henke) *Unwrapped* (includes Bangs' "Man with a Golden Bow"), Love Spell (New York, NY), 2000.
The Pleasure Master, Love Spell (New York, NY), 2001.
(With Jenelle Denison and Erin McCarthy) *Men at Work,* Berkeley Publishing Group (New York, NY), 2001.
Night Games, Love Spell (New York, NY), 2002.
From Boardwalk with Love, Love Spell (New York, NY), 2003.
(With Cheryl Holt, Kimberly Raye, and Patricia Ryan) *Burning Up: Four Novellas of Erotic Romance* (includes Bangs' "The Flame"), St. Martin's (New York, NY), 2003.
Master of Ecstasy, Dorchester (New York, NY), 2004.

SIDELIGHTS: Nina Bangs is a grade-school teacher turned author who writes over-the-top romance novels involving science fiction and horror elements such as time travel and vampires. The female leads are often sexually unsatisfied women who find fulfillment in their unlikely encounters with men from the future or the past, either through time travel or in stories that are set in alternate times. In Bangs's debut novel, *An Original Sin,* Fortune MacDonald lives in the year 2300, when the male gender has become extinct. She finds herself transported back 300 years to the state of Texas, where she meets, oddly enough, a Scottish man named Leith who has been transported forward in time from the year 1700.

In another time-travel adventure, *The Pleasure Master,* a hairdresser named Kathy Bartlett finds herself in 1542 Scotland, where she becomes the object of a competition between three brothers who wish to hold the title of Pleasure Master.

In *Night Games,* Brian Byrne is from the year 2502, where sex has become a spectator sport performed in large arenas and broadcast to the world. When Brian decides to go on a vacation to 2002 Ireland, he meets a woman named Ally who has endured an unhappy marriage and is now writing a book about finding sexual satisfaction as a single woman.

Depending on how much of the premise they could believe, critics have both praised and ridiculed Bangs's time-travel books. On the Web site *Romance Reader,* for example, reviewer Kerry Keating was somewhat repulsed by the concept of a future in which sex is a spectator sport: "While it is obvious to me that the premise of *Night Games* is meant to be tongue-in-cheek," she wrote, "I couldn't get over the whole 'sex as sport' idea." On the other hand, Kathy Boswell, writing for *Sensual Romance Reviews* online, attested that she has "never been so glued to a book as I was to this one." In a *Romance Reader* review of *The Pleasure Master,* Cathy Sova had reservations about the many varying plot elements in the story, but concluded that the novel may satisfy "readers who are looking for something way beyond different."

In addition to time travel plot devices, Bangs, who knowingly introduces strange ideas into her romances, often for satirical effect, has also written a story about a woman from the future venturing into the past and meeting a vampire in *Master of Ecstasy.* In *From Boardwalk with Love,* she spoofs spy thrillers with an extra dash of sex and humorous scenes. In the latter story, Camryn O'Brian works for an agency called B.L.I.S.S. On an assignment to protect a wealthy man from assassination by an agent from the League of Violent Economic Revolutionaries (L.O.V.E.R.), Cam-

ryn travels to an island that is an oversized replica of the game Monopoly. There she falls in love with a millionaire's son, Jace. However, Camryn possesses a secret power that is dangerous to any man who tries to protect her. While *Romance Reader* critic Joni Richards Bodart noted that *From Boardwalk with Love* is an obvious satire of the James Bond spy thrillers, she found it annoying that Camryn is "an incompetent secret agent who can't shoot, has the ultimate weapon that almost never does what it's supposed to, and constantly has to be rescued from her mistakes." Nevertheless, the reviewer concluded that this spoof would be a "treat" for those who like Bond satires.

BIOGRAPHICAL AND CRITICAL SOURCES:

PERIODICALS

Booklist, February 1, 2003, John Charles, "B.L.I.S.S.ed Out!," p. 977; February 1, 2004, John Charles, review of *Master of Ecstasy,* p. 954.

ONLINE

All about Romance, http://www.likesbooks.com/ (November 8, 2003), Heidi L. Haglin, review of *From Boardwalk with Love;* Lori-Anne Cohen, review of *An Original Sin;* Jennifer Keirans, review of *The Pleasure Master.*
Nina Bangs Home Page, http://www.ninabangs.com/ (June 16, 2004).
Readers Read, http://www.readersread.com/ (November 8, 2003), review of *The Pleasure Master.*
Romance and Friends, http://www.romanceandfriends.com/ (May, 2001), Carla Hosom, review of *The Pleasure Master.*
Romance Reader, http://www.theromancereader.com/ (June 16, 2004), Joni Richards Bodart, review of *From Boardwalk with Love;* Diana Burrell, review of *An Original Sin;* Cathy Sova, review of *The Pleasure Master;* Kerry Keating, review of *Night Games.*
Sensual Romance Reader, http://sr.thebestreviews.com/ (August 22, 2001), Leslie Tramposch, review of *An Original Sin;* (November 11, 2002), Harriet Klausner, review of *Night Games;* (May 15, 2002), Kathy Boswell, review of *Night Games;* (March 27, 2003), Brenda Horner, "Three Contemporary Christmas Love Stories."*

BARTLEY, Robert L(eRoy) 1937-2003

OBITUARY NOTICE—See index for *CA* sketch: Born October 12, 1937, in Marshall, MN; died of complications from cancer, December 10, 2003, in Manhattan, NY. Journalist and author. Bartley was a Pulitzer Prize-winning editor who was best known as the former financial editor of the *Wall Street Journal.* He was a graduate of Iowa State University, where he completed his undergraduate work in 1959, and the University of Wisconsin, where he earned a master's in 1962 after serving a year in the U.S. Army Reserve as a second lieutenant. After a brief apprenticeship as a reporter at the *Grinnell Herald-Register* in Iowa, Bartley joined the *Wall Street Journal* staff in Chicago in 1962. This was followed by a year's stint in Philadelphia and six years in New York City as an editorial writer in the late 1960s. Bartley started writing editorials for the *Journal'*s Washington, D.C., office in 1970 and was promoted to editorial page editor two years later. He became editor of the *Journal* in 1979, remaining at that post until his retirement as editor emeritus in 2002 after having also served as vice president of the newspaper since 1983; in 2003 he was made vice president of Dow Jones, the corporate owner of the *Wall Street Journal.* During his tenure as editor, Bartley became somewhat controversial among his staff for his very conservative economic and political views, often using the editorial section of the paper to publish the opinions of conservative economic writers. Along with Bartley, writers such as Jude Wanniski and Robert B. Laffer believed in what became known as supply-side economics, favoring the tax cuts and less government regulation of businesses that became characteristic of the Reagan administration's policies. Liberal economists, along with many of the *Journal'*s staff, criticized Bartley's use of the editorial page to express his views on the economy. Bartley was also criticized for publishing his political opinions against Democratic vice presidential candidate Geraldine Ferraro, for accusing former Democratic presidential candidate Michael Dukakis of having a history of mental illness, and for his support of conservative judges to the Supreme Court. On the other hand, Bartley gained plaudits for his support of women's rights, especially in the area of promoting women writers and editors. Bartley's editorial writing earned him a Pulitzer Prize in 1980, and just before his death he was awarded the Presidential Medal of Freedom. He was also the author of *The Seven Fat Years: And How to Do It Again* (1992).

OBITUARIES AND OTHER SOURCES:

PERIODICALS

Chicago Tribune, December 11, 2003, Section 3, p. 14.
Los Angeles Times, December 11, 2003, p. B14.
New York Times, December 11, 2003, p. C12.
Times (London, England), December 17, 2003.
Washington Post, December 11, 2003, p. B6.

*   *   *

BARTRUM, Giulia

PERSONAL: Female. *Education:* Sydney University, B.A., 1961; Victoria University (New Zealand), M.A. (with honors), 1962; Auckland Training College, teaching diploma, 1963, diploma in educational management, 1974, LTCL TESOL, 1982.

ADDRESSES: Office—Department of Prints and Drawings, The British Museum, London WC1B 3DG, England.

CAREER: British Museum, London, England, assistant keeper of prints and drawings, 1979—.

AWARDS, HONORS: Catalogue of the Year Award, Art Newspaper/AXA Art Exhibiton, 2003, for *Albrecht Dürer and His Legacy: The Graphic Work of a Renaissance Artist.*

WRITINGS:

(Coeditor, with John Rowlands) *The Age of Dürer and Holbein: German Drawings, 1400-1550,* British Museum Publications (London, England), 1988.
German Renaissance Prints, 1490-1550, British Museum Publications (London, England), 1995.
(Editor) *Albrecht Dürer and His Legacy: The Graphic Work of a Renaissance Artist,* British Museum Publications (London, England), 2002.

SIDELIGHTS: A curator and assistant keeper of prints and drawings at the British Museum, Giulia Bartrum specializes in the work of German printmakers and artists in the northern Renaissance, especially the hugely influential Albrecht Dürer. Her published works come from the catalogs that accompany major exhibits of these prints and drawings, and these works constitute important resources for anyone seeking a deeper understanding of the life and influence of Renaissance artists and their work. In 1988 she assisted John Rowlands in putting together *The Age of Dürer and Holbein: German Drawings, 1400-1550,* a catalogue "replete with sound opinions," according to Christopher Wood, who reviewed it for *Speculum: A Journal of Medieval Studies.*

Bartrum provides her own take on the museum's vast collection of German etchings in *German Renaissance Prints: 1490-1550.* "For specialists in Renaissance prints, there are few surprises in Giulia Bartrum's book," asserted *Sixteenth Century Journal* reviewer Linda C. Hults. "However, for those students of art history or of Early Modern Europe who want an excellent scholarly introduction to this highly prolific and innovative period of German printmaking, with recent literature well represented in the essays and entries, Bartrum's book is a must." In addition to covering the influence of individual artists and regional schools, Bartrum offers an organizational structure and introductory essays that provide useful information on the wide use of engravings for Reformation propaganda, the importance of the Emperor Maximilian's patronage of this "lesser" art form, and the phenomenal landscape etchings of the Danube School. In addition, she covers some of the humbler etchings whose purpose was social satire or burlesque. "A particularly generous feature of the catalogue," adds *Renaissance Quarterly* contributor Jane Campbell Hutchison, "is the author's decision to call attention to areas in want of further research."

One name is practically synonymous with German printmaking of the northern Renaissance, and in *Albrecht Dürer and His Legacy: The Graphic Work of a Renaissance Artist,* Bartrum and her collaborators tell the remarkable story of this artistic giant, a story that in fact extends far beyond his own era and well into today. As with her other works, this one accompanied a major exhibition of the artist's prints, adding a great deal of background understanding to the works themselves. As *Times Literary Supplement* reviewer Theodore K. Rabb noted, "He is just the right artist to warrant the homage of an institution that is not a gallery but does have one of the world's great collections of drawings and prints, and the Museum has accordingly done him proud." Revered in his own time by artists and philosophers alike, Dürer was later eclipsed by the great Italian masters such as Michelangelo and Raphael, only to reemerge as a cultural icon for nineteenth-century German nationalists. "The enthusiastic reception the artist inspired, and the way that different generations have made him their own, is the central concern of the beautifully illustrated catalog," explained Rabb in his review. Thus the book covers a wide spectrum of pieces by Dürer's imitators and admirers, including reproductions on porcelain and even banknotes. It also provides an interesting look at the hardheaded business sense of this unusually practical artistic genius, who was willing to produce lesser but more profitable works, rather than tie himself to demanding patrons. In addition, it includes an essay by Nobel laureate Günter Grass on Dürer's haunting *Melancholia.*

BIOGRAPHICAL AND CRITICAL SOURCES:

PERIODICALS

Renaissance Quarterly, spring, 1997, Jane Campbell Hutchinson, review of *German Renaissance Prints, 1490-1550,* pp. 327-328.
Sixteenth Century Journal, fall, 1997, Linda C. Hultz, review of *German Renaissance Prints, 1490-1550,* pp. 853-855.
Speculum: A Journal of Medieval Studies, April, 1991, Charles Wood, review of *The Age of Dürer and Holbein: German Drawings 1400-1550,* pp. 471-475.
Times Literary Supplement, January 17, 2003, Thomas K. Rabb, "Bestseller of the Apocalypse," review of *Albrecht Dürer and His Legacy: The Graphic Work of a Renaissance Artist,* pp. 16-17.*

*   *   *

BATTLE, Richard V. 1951-

PERSONAL: Born September 15, 1951, in Sterling, IL; son of Billy and Martha (Matthews) Battle; married Laura Floyd (a homemaker), July 1, 1995; children: John William (deceased), Elizabeth Brooke. *Education:* University of Texas—Austin, B.B.A., 1973. *Religion:* Baptist.

ADDRESSES: Home—124 Lido, Austin, TX 78734; fax: 775-251-8681. *E-mail*—rbat1@attglobal.net.

CAREER: Burroughs Corp., Office Products Group, sales representative in Austin, TX, 1973-76, zone sales manager in Montgomery, AL, 1976-77; Bell & Howell Co., Microfilm Products Division, Austin, sales representative, 1977-86; Datatron Communication, Austin, sales representative, 1986-87; Bell & Howell Co., Austin, sales representative, 1987-88, western area sales manager, 1987-2001; KeyTrak, Austin, national sales manager, 2001—. Public speaker and trainer in leadership, personal development, volunteering, and sales techniques. Celebrity Golf Tournament, Inc., member of board of directors, 1981-86; John Ben Shepperd Public Leadership Forum, chair, 1986, member of board of directors, 1988-92, 1996—, board chair, 1990-91. *Military service:* Texas State Guard, 1989-99; became lieutenant colonel.

MEMBER: Greater Austin Chamber of Commerce (1983-88), Leadership Austin (1984-85), Keep Austin Beautiful (member of inaugural board of directors, 1985-86), Austin Jaycees (life member, 1980—, president, 1983-84), Muscular Dystrophy Association (member of advisory board, 1983-85), Alpha Kappa Psi (past president).

AWARDS, HONORS: Distinguished service award, Alpha Kappa Psi; Bell & Howell Co., named sales representative of the year for the southern United States, 1981, 1982, 1984, named sales manager of the year, 1991, 1992, 1996, 1997.

WRITINGS:

The Volunteer Handbook: How to Organize and Manage a Successful Organization, Volunteer Concepts (Austin, TX), 1988.
Surviving Grief by God's Grace, 1st Books Library (Bloomington, IN), 2002.

*   *   *

BAUER, Peggy 1932-2004

OBITUARY NOTICE—See index for *CA* sketch: Born March 2, 1932, in Riverside, IL; died in an automobile accident, March 23, 2004, in Sequim, WA. Photographer and author. Along with her husband, Erwin Bauer, Peggy Bauer was renowned as a wildlife photographer and writer. An alumna of Mount Holyoke College, she married Harry Politi not long after graduating and spent her early life raising a family. When she met Erwin Bauer in Nairobi in 1972, the two made a connection that would lead them both to divorce their first spouses and marry each other. Erwin was already a renowned photographer at the time, but Peggy learned quickly and the two became an inseparable team, traveling the world and taking pictures of exotic wildlife. Together, they collaborated on dozens of books, including *Photographing Wild Texas* (1985), *Wild Africa* (1992), and *The Last Big Cats: An Untamed Spirit* (2003). The husband-and-wife team were also active in conservation organizations and received writing and photography awards, most recently the 2000 Lifetime Achievement Award from the North American Nature Photography Association.

OBITUARIES AND OTHER SOURCES:

PERIODICALS

Seattle Post-Intelligencer, March 26, 2004, p. B1.
Washington Post, March 29, 2004, p. B5.

ONLINE

Joseph Van Os Photo Safaris, http://www.photosafaris.com/ (April 28, 2004).

*   *   *

BEARD, William R. 1946-

PERSONAL: Born December 21, 1946, in Lethbridge, Alberta, Canada; married Wendy Kersteen (a schoolteacher). *Education:* University of Alberta, B.A., 1967; University of California—Berkeley, M.A., 1969; King's College, London, Ph.D., 1974.

ADDRESSES: Office—Department of English and Film, University of Alberta, Edmonton, Alberta T6G 2E6, Canada. *E-mail*—william.beard@ualberta.ca.

CAREER: University of Alberta, Edmonton, Alberta, Canada, professor of English and film, 1976—.

MEMBER: Film Studies Association of Canada (member of executive board, 2000—).

WRITINGS:

Persistence of Double Vision: Essays on Clint Eastwood, University of Alberta Press (Edmonton, Alberta, Canada), 2000.

The Artist as Monster: The Cinema of David Cronenberg, University of Toronto Press (Toronto, Ontario, Canada), 2001.

(Editor, with Jerry White) *North of Everything: English Canadian Cinema since 1980,* University of Alberta Press (Edmonton, Alberta, Canada), 2002.

BIOGRAPHICAL AND CRITICAL SOURCES:

PERIODICALS

Choice, November, 2000, A. Hirsh, review of *Persistence of Double Vision: Essays on Clint Eastwood,* p. 541; February, 2002, T. Lindvall, review of *The Artist as Monster: The Cinema of David Cronenberg,* p. 1055.

Science-Fiction Studies, July, 2002, Suzie S. F. Young, review of *The Artist as Monster,* p. 298.

University of Toronto Quarterly, winter, 2001, Anne Lancashire, review of *Persistence of Double Vision,* p. 353.

*   *   *

BeauSEIGNEUR, James 1953-

PERSONAL: Born 1953, in Waltham, MA; married; wife's name, Geri; children: Faith, Abigail. *Education:* B.A.; also attended graduate school at Middle Tennessee State University and the University of Tennessee—Knoxville. *Politics:* Republican. *Religion:* Christian.

ADDRESSES: *Agent*—c/o Author Mail, Warner Books, 1271 Avenue of the Americas, New York, NY 10020.

CAREER: Novelist and writing consultant. Has also worked as a political science instructor, technical writer, political campaign manager, lobbyist, and newspaper publisher. *Military service:* Served in U.S. Army, including assignment as an intelligence analyst for the National Security Agency, 1976-1981.

WRITINGS:

In His Image (book one of "Christ Clone" trilogy), Selective House Publishers (Rockville, MD), 1997, Warner Books (New York, NY), 2003.

Birth of an Age (book two of "Christ Clone" trilogy), Selective House Publishers (Rockville, MD), 1997, Warner Books (New York, NY), 2003.

Acts of God (book three of "Christ Clone" trilogy), Warner Books (New York, NY), 2003.

Has written many newspaper and magazine articles, and published manuals *Military Avionics,* 1985, and *Strategic Defense,* 1986. Has written lyrics for published songs.

ADAPTATIONS: *In His Image* was adapted for audio cassette, read by Pete Bradbury, Recorded Books, 2001.

WORK IN PROGRESS: A collection of biographies.

SIDELIGHTS: James BeauSeigneur is a former U.S. Army intelligence analyst who now works as a writing consultant to the federal government. He once ran for U.S. Congress against Al Gore, but eventually left politics, seeking a more stable life for his family. Turning to technical writing for a regular income, he sought creative satisfaction in fiction writing. This pursuit resulted in the publication of the "Christ Clone" trilogy, a series of novels that blend science fiction and theology. The author describes his religious awakening during the early 1970s as starting amongst the hippie Christians who were known as "Jesus Freaks." He has said that he hopes that his fiction writing will connect non-Christians with the Gospel.

Originally self-published, the trilogy earned an enthusiastic following for its unusual blend of science, inside view of government, and apocalyptic speculation. The first installment, *In His Image,* introduces biochemist Harold Goodman and his former student, who is now a journalist, Decker Hawthorne. Goodman is part of a team testing the Shroud of Turin for authenticity. He discovers live skin cells in the cloth and uses them to secretly create a human clone. Only Hawthorne knows the origins of the scientist's "son" Christopher. When a plague kills millions of people and war in the Middle East escalates, the young man becomes an important negotiator. The later volumes in the trilogy are *Birth of an Age* and *Acts of God,* in which Christopher becomes a powerful figure in the United Nations and is revealed to be the Anti-Christ.

The first episode, however, leaves readers wondering if Christopher is in fact the son of Christ. A reviewer for *Publishers Weekly* noted that the author "warns his audience to read the entire trilogy before judging." Commenting on BeauSeigneur's creation, the writer said that he "awkwardly mixes religion, geopolitics and preposterous plot twists." A *Kirkus Reviews* contributor described the thriller as "silly, cheap, and fun: a garden-variety potboiler with a neat gimmick thrown in." *Booklist*'s John Mort credited the book's popularity to the fact that BeauSeigneur "knows how to write, deploying a tough, driving style in perfect cadence." Remarking on the timing of Warner's publication of the trilogy in 2003, he said, "the paranoia [BeauSeigneur] evokes is a perfect fit for these times of religious hatred and political terror." Jackie Alnor commented in a review for the *Christian Sentinel* that BeauSeigneur is "a compelling story-teller" and "writes with a sophistication that makes it very believable." She remarked that the trilogy "does not read preachy with gospel messages."

BIOGRAPHICAL AND CRITICAL SOURCES:

PERIODICALS

Booklist, January 1, 2003, John Mort, review of *In His Image,* p. 845.
Kirkus Reviews, December 1, 2002, review of *In His Image,* p. 1711; May 15, 2003, review of *Birth of an Age,* p. 694.
Publishers Weekly, January 6, 2003, review of *In His Image,* p. 38; June 9, 2003, review of *Birth of an Age,* p. 34.

ONLINE

Christian Fandom Home Page, http://www.swcp.com/christian-fandom/ (March, 2000), interview with James BeauSeigneur.

Christian Sentinel, http://cultlink.com/sentinel/ChristClone.htm (May, 2003), Jackie Alnor, review of "Christ Clone" trilogy.
Time Warner Bookmark, http://twbookmark.com/ (June 27, 2003), information on James BeauSeigneur.*

*   *   *

BECKER, Josh 1958-

PERSONAL: Born August 17, 1958.

ADDRESSES: Home—Santa Monica, CA. *Office*—Panoramic Pictures, 3315 Little Applegate Rd., Jacksonville, OR 97530.

CAREER: Director and screenwriter. Film credits include (as unit sound and lighting director) *The Evil Dead* (also known as *Book of the Dead* and *The Evil Dead, the Ultimate Experience in Grueling Horror*), New Line Cinema, 1981; (as director, cinematographer, and editor) *Stryker's War* (also known as *Thou Shalt Not Kill . . . Except*), Film World Distributors, 1985; (as director) *Lunatics: A Love Story,* RCA Home Video, 1991; (as director, camera operator, and editor) *Battle the Big Tuna* (documentary), 1991; (as camera operator) *Hawg Wild in Sturgis* (documentary), 1992; (as producer and director) *Running Time,* Panoramic Pictures, 1997; (as producer and director) *If I Had a Hammer,* Panoramic Pictures, 1999.

Actor in films, including (as Fake Shemp) *Evil Dead II* (also known as *Evil Dead 2: Dead by Dawn* and *Evil Dead II, the Sequel to the Ultimate Experience in Grueling Horror*), Rosebud Releasing, 1987; (as Fake Shemp) *Army of Darkness* (also known as *Army of Darkness, the Ultimate Experience in Medieval Horror, Army of Darkness: Evil Dead 3, Bruce Campbell vs. Army of Darkness, Captain Supermarket, Evil Dead 3,* and *The Medieval Dead*), Universal, 1993; (as Camper Steve) *Mosquito* (also known as *Blood Fever* and *Nightswarm*), Hemdale Home Video, 1995; and (uncredited, as voice of heroin dealer) *Running Time,* Panoramic Pictures, 1997.

Director of episodes of television stories, including *Real Stories of the Highway Patrol,* 1993; "A Fistful of Dinars," "Warrior . . . Princess . . . Tramp," "For

Him the Bell Tolls," "Blind Faith," "Fins, Femmes, and Gems," "In Sickness and in Hell," "If the Shoe Fits," "Kindred Spirits," and "Soul Possession," *Xena: Warrior Princess,* syndicated, 1996-2001; and "The Return of the Dragoon" and "The People's Dragoon," *Jack of All Trades,* syndicated, 2000. Unit director of the television movie *Hercules and the Amazon Women,* 1994; director of the television movie *Hercules in the Maze of the Minotaur,* syndicated, 1994.

WRITINGS:

SCREENPLAYS

(With Bruce Campbell, Sheldon Lettich, and Scott Spiegel) *Stryker's War* (also known as *Thou Shalt Not Kill . . . Except*), Film World Distributors, 1985.
(And lyricist) *Lunatics: A Love Story,* RCA Home Video, 1991.
(With Peter Choi) *Running Time,* Panoramic Pictures, 1997.
If I Had a Hammer, Panoramic Pictures, 1999.

Author, with others, of the episodes "Chariots of War" and "Locked Up and Tied Down," *Xena: Warrior Princess,* syndicated, 1995 and 1998 respectively. Also author of short stories, essays, and magazine articles.

SIDELIGHTS: Director and screenwriter Josh Becker got his start in cinema as a teenager in suburban Detroit. He made Super 8 home movies with other local teenagers who went on to become famous Hollywood figures, including director Sam Raimi (of *Spider-Man*), actor Bruce Campbell (of the *Evil Dead* films), and producer Rob Tapert (of *Xena: Warrior Princess*). Finally, in their twenties, the group decided to try making a "real" movie. The result was *The Evil Dead,* filmed on a shoestring budget in miserable weather. "Not quitting during the production of the first *Evil Dead*" was the hardest thing he ever did, Becker told *Whoosh!* interviewer Amy Murphy, but sticking with it paid off, as the film became a cult classic and launched Becker's and his friends' careers. Even after becoming successful, the group has often continued to work on projects together. Campbell has appeared in several of Becker's films, including *Stryker's War* (which Campbell also cowrote), *Lunatics: A Love Story*

(which was executive produced by Raimi and Tapert), and *Running Time,* and Becker has directed numerous episodes of the Tapert-produced series *Xena.*

BIOGRAPHICAL AND CRITICAL SOURCES:

PERIODICALS

Variety, September 30, 1987, review of *Thou Shalt Not Kill . . . Except,* p. 22; September 16, 1991, Daniel M. Kimmel, review of *Lunatics: A Love Story,* p. 88; January 5, 1998, Leonard Klady, review of *Running Time,* p. 80; January 17, 2000, Laura Fries, review of *Jack of All Trades,* p. 72.

ONLINE

Becker Films, http://www.beckerfilms.com (June 25, 2003).
Internet Movie Database, http://www.imdb.com/ (May 23, 2003).
Whoosh!, http://www.whoosh.org/ (June 8, 2003), Amy Murphy, "Inside the Head of Josh Becker."*

*   *   *

BELLOWS, Nathaniel 1972-

PERSONAL: Born 1972, in Boston, MA.

ADDRESSES: Home—New York, NY. *Office*—c/o Author Mail, HarperCollins, 10 E. 53rd St., 7th floor, New York, NY 10022.

CAREER: Writer of poetry and fiction; visual artist.

WRITINGS:

On This Day (novel), HarperCollins (New York, NY), 2003.

Poetry published in periodicals and literary journals, including *New York Times Book Review, New Republic, Paris Review,* and *Ploughshares.*

SIDELIGHTS: Nathaniel Bellows won some notice as a poet, with verse appearing in a variety of publications, before the publication of his first novel, *On This Day.* The novel, which some reviewers found informed by Bellows' poetic style, deals with two young-adult siblings trying to cope with life after the deaths of their parents. Warren, the narrator, is eighteen, and his sister, Joan, is twenty when their father dies of cancer, an event followed closely by their mother's suicide. Their inheritance allows the brother and sister a measure of financial independence, but they are not ready for emotional independence. Relying primarily on each other, they are resistant and suspicious when relatives and neighbors in their small Maine town reach out to them; meanwhile, their late father's business partner schemes to cut them out of their share in the family firm, a plant nursery. The siblings also have problematic love lives; Joan's boyfriend is noncommittal, and Warren falls for a woman who once worked for his father—then discovers that she was his father's lover as well.

"Poet Bellows brings a lyrical voice to his bittersweet first novel," commented *Booklist* contributor Margaret Flanagan, while *Ploughshares* critic Don Lee saw "poetic patience and eloquence" in the author's prose. Tanya Corrin, reviewing for the online publication *Bookreporter,* praised Bellows' style as "simple and honest" and his story as "compelling." Particularly, Corrin observed, he "demonstrates a profound grasp of the humor, hatred and intimate bond between brother and sister." Some other reviewers had similar compliments for the portrayal of the sibling relationship. For instance, Mary Elizabeth Williams, writing in the *New York Times Book Review,* observed that "Bellows has a warm sympathy for Warren and Joan's newfound isolation and a clear-eyed respect for the power of the bond between them," which he depicts as "deeply intimate without a hint of prurience."

Williams, though, found Warren somewhat deficient as a narrator-protagonist, explaining, "Warren lacks the charisma to carry his own story, and Bellows doesn't yet have the confident authority to make his hero's predicament sufficiently absorbing." Corrin thought the use of Warren as narrator contributed to the story's sometimes-slow pace, but she added, "We like Warren. His pain is poignant and real. We might miss this gift of intimacy with him if he were a more dynamic character or, rather, if the author was less honest about

the true nature of a shell-shocked teenage introvert." A *Publishers Weekly* reviewer described Warren as "a believable, beguiling voice" and the storytelling as "eloquent yet down-to-earth." Overall, the reviewer noted, "Bellows brings grace and grit to this debut novel."

BIOGRAPHICAL AND CRITICAL SOURCES:

PERIODICALS

Booklist, February 15, 2003, Margaret Flanagan, review of *On This Day,* p. 1046.
Kirkus Reviews, December 1, 2002, review of *On This Day,* p. 1711.
New York Times Book Review, April 27, 2003, Mary Elizabeth Williams, "Home Alone," p. 29.
Ploughshares, spring, 2003, Don Lee, review of *On This Day.*
Publishers Weekly, December 9, 2002, review of *On This Day,* pp. 58-59.

ONLINE

Bookreporter, http://www.bookreporter.com/ (October 13, 2003), Tanya Corrin, review of *On This Day.**

*   *   *

BERRY, Andrew

PERSONAL: Born in London, England. *Education:* Oxford University, degree in zoology; Princeton University, Ph.D. (evolutionary genetics); postgraduate work under Martin Kreitman at the University of Chicago.

ADDRESSES: Office—Museum of Comparative Zoology, Harvard University, 26 Oxford St., Cambridge, MA 02138; fax: 617-495-5667.

CAREER: Geneticist. Harvard University, Museum of Comparative Zoology, Cambridge, MA, research associate. Also worked as an instructor at Harvard University.

WRITINGS:

(Editor) *Infinite Tropics: An Alfred Russel Wallace Anthology,* Verso (New York, NY), 2002.
(With James D. Watson) *DNA: The Secret of Life,* Alfred A. Knopf (New York, NY), 2003.

Also author of screenplay, *DNA,* and contributor to numerous scientific and popular journals, including *Science, Gentetics,* the *New York Observer,* and the *London Review of Books.*

SIDELIGHTS: A geneticist with a special interest in the fruit fly, Andrew Berry was one of a team of graduate students who overturned a classic evolutionary assumption that the tiny chromosome 4 never varied across the entire fruit fly species. It was an impressive start for a career that has taken Berry to his affiliation with Harvard University and as a research associate at Harvard's Museum of Comparative Zoology.

In 2002, Berry compiled a group of writings from one of the most brilliant figures in the history of evolutionary science. *Infinite Tropics: An Alfred Russel Wallace Anthology* brings together the wide-ranging pieces produced by a man who independently discovered evolution but made the mistake of sending his ideas to his idol Charles Darwin, who thereupon rushed his own theory into print. While Wallace was denied the title of father of evolution, he continued to write extensively on a wide range of subjects, and Berry's collection "introduces the reader to his pioneering explorations in natural science and his critical insights into social issues," noted *Library Journal* reviewer H. James Birx. Lacking Darwin's wealth and connections, Wallace had to finance his own expeditions and overcome sometimes heartbreaking obstacles, as when he lost his entire record of studies on South American flora and fauna when his ship sunk on its way back to England. Still, Wallace seemed to have retained his enthusiasm and optimism throughout his long life, and Berry's collection illustrates his determined, often unconventional ideas and interests. As *New Scientist* reviewer Roy Herbert found, Wallace's "enjoyment of living and intellectual verve inform it all, from his thoughts on evolution and the science of biogeography, which he founded, to those on conservation, public education, and that most Victorian of interests, spiritualism."

Having reintroduced the writings of this Victorian genius, Berry next teamed with a legend of genetics to produce a chronicle of the most recent developments in evolutionary biology. With James D. Watson, codiscoverer of the double-helix model of DNA, Berry coauthored *DNA: The Secret of Life,* "an illuminating account of DNA and genetics from the nineteenth century to the present," according to Jon Beckwith in *American Scientist.* After a brief review of genetics from Gregor Mendel, the monk who first theorized the science of genetic inheritance, to Watson and Francis Crick's discovery of the double helix structure, the book describes the many ways genetics has revolutionized science. "What makes this text extraordinary is its accessibility even to readers with little background in biology," noted a reviewer for *Science News.* At the same time, the book confronts the fascinating, and sometimes disturbing, implications of this powerful knowledge, such as the use of genetic fingerprinting, genetically modified plants, and behavioral science based on genetic tampering. "If by his conclusion, a reader still adamantly opposes this or that technology, at least the stance won't be in the face of ignorance," observed *Booklist* reviewer Gilbert Taylor. Other subjects include the search for the genetic basis of various diseases, the use of DNA evidence in criminology, and the contribution of genetics to the study of human evolution. And "while the text is written in Watson's voice, credit must surely go to Berry as an able coauthor," commented a *Kirkus Reviews* contributor.

BIOGRAPHICAL AND CRITICAL SOURCES:

PERIODICALS

American Scientist, July-August, 2003, Jon Beckwith, "Double Take on the Double Helix," p. 1107.
Booklist, March 1, 2003, Gilbert Taylor, review of *DNA: The Secret of Life,* p. 125.
Kirkus Reviews, March 1, 2003, review of *DNA,* p. 372.
Library Journal, August, 2002, H. James Birx, review of *Infinite Tropics: An Alfred Russel Wallace Anthology,* p. 137; April 1, 2003, Rita Hoots, review of *DNA,* p. 125.
Natural History, February, 2002, Richard Milner, review of *Infinite Tropics,* p. 74.
Nature, April 25, 2002, Charlotte Sleigh, "Putting Evolution in Context," p. 790.

New Scientist, July 6, 2002, Roy Herbert, "Verve in Adversity," p. 57.

Science News, May 10, 2003, review of *DNA,* p. 303.*

*   *   *

BERTAGNA, Julie 1962-

PERSONAL: Born 1962, in Kilmarknock, Ayrshire, Scotland; married; husband's name, Riccardo (a banker); children: Natalie. *Education:* Glasgow University, M.A. (honours).

ADDRESSES: Home—Glasgow, Scotland. *Agent*—Caroline Walsh, David Higham Associates Ltd., 5-8 Lower John St., Golden Square, London W1F 9HA, England. *E-mail*—julie@juliebertagna.com.

CAREER: Freelance writer. Formerly worked as a magazine editor and a primary school teacher in Barmulloch, Glasgow, Scotland.

AWARDS, HONORS: Two Writer's Bursaries, Scottish Arts Council; Angus Award shortlist, for *The Spark Gap;* Children's Book Award, Scottish Arts Council, and Scottish Writers Project citation, Library Association, both for *Soundtrack;* Lancashire Children's Book of the Year Award, 2003, and Whitbread Children's Book Award shortlist, both for *Exodus.*

WRITINGS:

The Spark Gap, Mammoth (London, England), 1996.
The Ice-Cream Machine, illustrated by Guy Parker-Rees, Mammoth (London, England), 1998, illustrated by Chambers and Dorsey, Macmillan Children's (London, England), 2004.
Clumsy Clumps and the Baby Moon, illustrated by Anthony Lewis, Mammoth (London, England), 1999.
Soundtrack, Mammoth (London, England), 1999.
Dolphin Boy, illustrated by Chris Chapman, Mammoth (London, England), 1999.
Bungee Hero, illustrated by Martin Salisbury, Barrington Stoke (Edinburgh, Scotland), 1999.
Exodus, Young Picador (London, England), 2002.
The Opposite of Chocolate, Young Picador (London, England), 2003.

Author of columns for *Scotland on Sunday* newspaper, Edinburgh, Scotland.

ADAPTATIONS: The Ice-Cream Machine was adapted as a thirteen-part television series, in English and Gaelic, by SMG, 2004.

WORK IN PROGRESS: A sequel to *Exodus.*

SIDELIGHTS: Along with "Harry Potter" series author J. K. Rowling, Julie Bertagna is among the most prominent children's book authors to emerge from Scotland in recent memory. Her book *Exodus* was shortlisted for the prestigious Whitbread Children's Book Award and was a hit with both teenagers and adults, while her children's book *The Ice-Cream Machine* has been turned into a television series. Along the way, Bertagna has also written several other challenging, gritty novels about the lives of Scottish teens, including *The Spark Gap, Soundtrack,* and *The Opposite of Chocolate.*

Bertagna was inspired to write her first novel, *The Spark Gap,* by a group of eleven-year-old students she was teaching in a poor area of Glasgow, Scotland. The children were reluctant readers, and they were particularly frustrated because they could not find any books about contemporary Scottish children. Bertagna searched and, finding only one book that met that description, set out to write a story herself. *The Spark Gap* tells the stories of three homeless teenagers who live on the streets of Glasgow, in circumstances to which her students could easily relate. Making the story more appealing to her former class, Bertagna gave several of her actual students supporting roles in the tale.

Bertagna completed *The Spark Gap* in the months after her daughter, Natalie, was born, which made writing rather challenging. Bertagna laughed when she first heard Rowling's famous tale of writing the first "Harry Potter" novel while sitting in cafés with her child in another Scottish city, Edinburgh. "It's the easiest way to write," she told Gillian Bowditch of the *Sunday Times.* "As soon as the baby was asleep, I'd nip into a nice warm café and whip out my notebook. If I'd waited until I'd got the buggy home and unloaded, the baby would have woken up and I never would have written anything."

Bertagna's next book, *The Ice-Cream Machine,* was inspired by Natalie. Bertagna made up stories based on her own experiences with her uncles' ice cream vans as a child to entertain her daughter, and the stories eventually grew into a book. *The Ice-Cream Machine* stars Wendy and Wayne MacDonald as the children of an ice cream van owner—not just any ice cream van, but a magical one. The story reached a wider audience in 2004, when television adaptations of it in both English and Gaelic aired on British television.

Offering a change of pace, *Exodus* is a futuristic tale, set in 2099. Global warming has led to extensive flooding along the Scottish coast, and refugees from the low-lying Orkney and Hebrides Islands cluster on the hills around Glasgow. Affluent families live in shining, glass-enclosed towers built on the ruins of old Glasgow, but the refugees are not allowed to enter those buildings. One such refugee, a teenage girl named Mara, refuses to be so easily defeated. She sneaks inside the wall surrounding New Mungo and allies herself with the city's underclass, including the plastic-bag-clad Treenester tribe. Together, these dispossessed people steal vehicles and set off for a new land where they hope to find happiness.

Exodus is a book that asks big questions, as many reviewers and Bertagna herself have noted. As Anne Johnstone described the story in the *Herald,* "Bertagna explores the issue of what constitutes a fair and just society, examines how people exploit technology for good and ill, questions the invisibility of women in our political and cultural history, and takes a look at the way fear can undermine human rights and render a society oblivious to suffering." Bertagna told Bowditch, "It's difficult to write a book like *Exodus* because in a sense the injustice is so plain, but you also have to show the complexities of the issue. . . . There are no black and white answers. Nothing is clear cut."

Another book that tackles difficult issues and provides no easy answers is *The Opposite of Chocolate,* about fourteen-year-old Sapphire, whose life is turned upside down when she discovers that she is pregnant. The book was criticized by some for seeming to promote abortion, but Bertagna told *Evening Times* interviewer Sheila Hamilton that she was simply trying to make the story realistic. "Statistics show that nearly ninety percent of pregnant fourteen-year-olds go for an abortion," she explained. While unplanned pregnancy features prominently in the novel, Bertagna also

explores teen-parent strife, not only in Sapphire's house, but in her arsonist friend Gilbert's as well. Writing in the *Irish Times,* reviewer Robert Dunbar thought that *The Opposite of Chocolate* "searingly depicts friction between parent and adolescent at its darkest and most uncompromising."

BIOGRAPHICAL AND CRITICAL SOURCES:

PERIODICALS

Evening Times (Glasgow, Scotland), November 14, 2002, "Writer Tipped for Glory," p. 6; January 4, 2003, Sheila Hamilton, review of *Exodus,* p. 8.
Guardian (London, England), March 16, 1999, Lindsey Fraser, review of *Soundtrack,* p. 4; October 7, 2003, Lindsey Fraser, review of *The Opposite of Chocolate,* p. 55.
Herald (Glasgow, Scotland), August 8, 2001, Julie Bertagna, "Myth and Magic," p. 14; July 27, 2002, Anne Johnstone, interview with Bertagna, p. 12.
Irish Times (Dublin, Ireland), October 18, 2003, Robert Dunbar, review of *The Opposite of Chocolate,* p. 61.
Mail on Sunday (London, England), December 8, 2002, Artemis Cooper, review of *Exodus,* p. 68.
Observer (London, England), May 30, 1999, Stephen Pritchard, review of *Soundtrack,* p. 13.
Scotland on Sunday (Edinburgh, Scotland), November 17, 2002, Julie Bertagna, "Notebook: Doing a Gwyneth Paltrow after Making the Shortbread Shortlist," p. 4.
Scotsman (Edinburgh, Scotland), November 14, 2002, "Scottish Writer on Whitbread Shortlist," p. 5; December 20, 2003, Sharol Ward, review of *The Ice-Cream Machine* (television series), p. 4.
Sun (London, England), December 18, 2003, Yvonne Bolour, interview with Bertagna, p. 68.
Sunday Times (London, England), November 24, 2002, Gillian Bowditch, interview with Bertagna, p. 3.

ONLINE

Julie Bertagna Home Page, http://www.juliebertagna.com/ (January 11, 2004).*

*   *   *

BIERINGER, R(eimund) 1957-

PERSONAL: Born May 2, 1957, in Hamburg, Germany. *Education:* Catholic University of Louvain, Ph.D., 1988. *Religion:* Roman Catholic.

ADDRESSES: Office—Faculty of Theology, Catholic University of Louvain, Sint Michielsstraat 6, 3000 Louvain, Belgium. *E-mail*—reimund.bieringer@theo. kuleuven.ac.be.

CAREER: Catholic University of Louvain, Louvain, Belgium, professor of theology, 1990—.

WRITINGS:

(With J. Lambrecht) *Studies on 2 Corinthians,* Louvain University Press (Louvain, Belgium), 1994.
(Editor) *The Corinthian Correspondence,* Louvain University Press (Louvain, Belgium), 1996.
(Editor, with D. Pollefeyt and F. Vanneuville) *Anti-Judaism and the Fourth Gospel,* Westminster John Knox Press (Louisville, KY), 2001.
(Editor, with V. Koperski and B. Lataire) *Resurrection in the New Testament: Festschrift J. Lambrecht,* Uitgeverij Peeters (Dudley, MA), 2002.
(With Mary Elsbernd) *When Love Is Not Enough: A Theo-ethic of Justice,* Liturgical Press (Collegeville, MN), 2002.

* * *

BLOOM, Reginald
See STINE, Scott A.

* * *

BOEHMER, Ulrike 1959-

PERSONAL: Born August 9, 1959, in Ludwigshafen/ Rhein, Germany; daughter of Franz (a house painter) and Claire (Kalker) Boehmer; companion of Angela Radan (a psychologist). *Ethnicity:* "Caucasian." *Education:* Technische Hochschule Darmstadt, Staatsexamen, 1984; Boston College, M.A., 1995, Ph.D., 1997.

ADDRESSES: Home—76 Garfield St., No. 4, Cambridge, MA 02138. *Office*—Center for Health Quality, Outcomes, and Economic Research, Boston University, 200 Springs Rd., Bldg. 70, Bedford, MA 01730. *E-mail*—boehmer@bu.edu.

CAREER: Boston University, Boston, MA, instructor, 1997-2000, assistant professor at Center for Health Quality, Outcomes, and Economic Research, Bedford, MA, 2000—.

WRITINGS:

(With Ilse Kokula) *Die Welt gehört uns doch! Zusammenschluss lesbischer Frauen in der Schweiz der 30er Jahre,* eFeF-Verlag (Bern, Switzerland), 1991.
The Personal and the Political: Women's Activism in Response to the Breast Cancer and AIDS Epidemics, State University of New York Press (Albany, NY), 2000.

BIOGRAPHICAL AND CRITICAL SOURCES:

PERIODICALS

Library Journal, April 15, 2000, Barbara M. Bibel, review of *The Personal and the Political: Women's Activism in Response to the Breast Cancer and AIDS Epidemics,* p. 116.
NWSA Journal, fall, 2002, Rebecca Lovell Scott, review of *The Personal and the Political,* p. 215.

* * *

BOLING, Fredrick W. 1926-

PERSONAL: Born November 11, 1926, in Edmond, OK; son of Fred (a rancher and farmer) and Florence (Hargrave) Boling; married Wilma Cave (a social worker), June 4, 1950; children: Paul, Amy Boling-Blassingame, David, Mark. *Education:* Northeastern Oklahoma Agricultural and Mechanical College, A.A., 1947; attended University of Central Oklahoma, 1947-48; University of Health Sciences, D.O., 1952. *Politics:* Independent. *Religion:* Lutheran.

ADDRESSES: Agent—c/o Author Mail, Bighorn Publishing, 35 La Canada Way, Hot Springs, AR 71909. *E-mail*—fboling@cox-internet.com.

CAREER: Physician and writer. Practiced surgery in Wyoming for nine years.

MEMBER: American Academy of Surgeon Specialists (fellow), American Medical Association, Western Writers of America.

WRITINGS:

Incident at Crazy Woman Creek (historical Western novel), Bighorn Publishing (Hot Springs, AR), 2002.
Ridden Hard—Put Up Wet (Western short stories), Bighorn Publishing (Hot Springs, AR), 2002.
Wakan Man (historical Western novel), Bighorn Publishing (Hot Springs, AR), 2002.

Contributor to magazines, including *American Western* and *ReadWest Western.*

WORK IN PROGRESS: No Lesser Measure, a historical novel with a Civil War setting in Gettysburg, PA.

SIDELIGHTS: Fredrick W. Boling told *CA:* "I am a third-generation descendant of pioneers who homesteaded farms and ranches during the 1889 Oklahoma Land Rush. I have written historical Western novels, short stories, and magazine articles. I practiced general surgery in Wyoming for nine years, during which time I became a dedicated student of the state's historical background. My writings reflect my love for the rich heritage of our great American West."

*   *   *

BOWLING, Lewis 1959-

PERSONAL: Born July 28, 1959, in Oxford, NC; son of O. L., Jr. (a farmer) and Mary (a business owner) Bowling; children: Damien. *Education:* Louisburg College, A.A.; Appalachian State University, B.S.; U.S. Sports Academy, master's degree.

ADDRESSES: Home—1735 Bowling Rd., Stem, NC 27581. *E-mail*—lewis_bowling@yahoo.com.

CAREER: North Carolina Central University, Durham, NC, teacher of physical education, 1996—. Aerobics and Fitness Association of America, personal trainer certification examiner, 1999—.

WRITINGS:

(With others) *Lifetime Physical Fitness,* Kendall-Hunt Press (Dubuque, IA), 1999.
Granville County: Images of America, Arcadia Publishing (Charleston, SC), 2002.
Resistance Training: The Total Approach, Carolina Academic Press (Durham, NC), 2003.
Granville County Revisited, Arcadia Publishing (Charleston, SC), 2003.

Fitness columnist for *Durham Herald Sun.*

WORK IN PROGRESS: Research on exercise physiology and on exercise and sport history.

SIDELIGHTS: Lewis Bowling told *CA:* "To say I love to read is quite an understatement. I'm not sure what I would do without that faithful companion, a book. To think that just possibly I can write words that other people enjoy reading is very rewarding to me.

"Primarily I write about physical fitness. My resistance training book contains extensive details on different exercises, listing exercises with barbells, dumbbells, cables, bands, stability balls, medicine balls, plyometrics, and body weight movements. Also an entire chapter is devoted to weight training to improve sports performance. Research abstracts are included, such as one on the effects of creatine. A chapter on the history of resistance exercise, going back to the ancient Greeks, is also included. My goal in this book was to cover all aspects of weight training and to make the book somewhat unique. I made myself familiar with other books on the same topic, and I believe I succeeded in my goal.

"Two of my other books deal with the history of the county in which I grew up, Granville County, North Carolina. My goal was to make residents of Granville more aware and appreciative of their local history. Knowing your roots and being aware of people and events that preceded you and made what you have possible helps individuals to invest in their hometowns or counties. They better appreciate what they have at present and feel a sense of ownership, which usually translates into more active participation in the community."

BRACH, Tara

PERSONAL: Children: one son. *Education:* Ph.D. *Religion:* Buddhist.

ADDRESSES: Office—8129 Hamilton Spring Road, Bethesda, MD 20817.

CAREER: Clinical psychologist, educator, and lecturer. Meditation teacher, 1975—, psychotherapist, 1980—, clinical psychologist, 1994—. Founder of the Insight Meditation Community of Washington.

WRITINGS:

Radical Acceptance: Embracing Your Life with the Heart of a Buddha, Bantam Books (New York, NY), 2003.

SIDELIGHTS: In addition to her career as a clinical psychologist, Tara Brach has been a meditation teacher since 1975. She founded the Insight Meditation Community of Washington, D.C., one of the largest meditation centers on the East Coast. She is a lay Buddhist priest and lecturer who conducts workshops at the Omega Institute, Spirit Rock Center, the New York Open Center, and other meditation centers.

Her first book, *Radical Acceptance: Embracing Your Life with the Heart of a Buddha,* acknowledges an affliction she notices in her clinical patients and meditation students—deep feelings of unworthiness and inadequacy she feels can be fueled by the competitiveness of Western society. These feelings can paralyze a person's mental health and potential happiness. One of Brach's friends described it as "feeling that something is wrong with me is the invisible and toxic gas I am always breathing."

Brach presents her strategy of radical acceptance to combat the "trance of unworthiness." Her approach blends psychology and Buddhist practices, and *Library Journal* contributor Mark Woodhouse felt Brach's "tone is more logical and oriented toward psychology. While experienced practitioners will recognize her concepts, drawn largely from Insight Meditation, the language and methodology and the numerous case studies tend to blur the distinctions between clinical psychology and Buddhist practice."

Brach uses personal stories, case histories, Buddhist tales, meditations at the end of chapters, snippets of poetry, and exercises to learn compassion and acceptance to override extreme self-judgment. The exercises encourage consciousness of every moment, while accepting everything, to learn to perceive situations and feelings clearly. Another key to acceptance is learning to open up to compassion. Brach stresses that radical acceptance does not mean losing motivation for change. Brach includes success stories of those who have used the lessons and changed their thinking for the better. After learning to accept themselves, only then were they able to make the changes.

Radical Acceptace garnered praise from critics. In a review from *spiritualityhealth.com* Frederic and Mary Ann Brussat wrote, "The spiritual practices in *Radical Acceptance* arrive like manna from heaven." A *Publishers Weekly* reviewer agreed: "Garnishing her gentle advice and guided meditation with beautiful bits of poetry and well-loved dharma stories...Brach describes what it can mean to...belong to the world." The reviewer continued, "This is a consoling and practical guide that can help people find a light within themselves."

BIOGRAPHICAL AND CRITICAL SOURCES:

PERIODICALS

Library Journal, May 15, 2003, review of *Radical Acceptance: Embracing Your Life with the Heart of a Buddha,* p. 95.
Publishers Weekly, May 12, 2003, review of *Radical Acceptance,* p. 63.

ONLINE

Dharma, http://www.dharma.org/ (October 23, 2003), Adah Miller, review of *Radical Acceptance.*
Healing Outside the Margins, http://www.healing outsidethemargins.com/ (October 23, 2003), short bio.

Insight Meditation Community of Washington, D.C., http://www.imcw.org/ (October 23, 2003), book description and short bio.

Omega Institute, http://www.eomega.org/ (October 23, 2003), short bio.

Spirituality & Health, http://www.spiritualityhealth. com/ (October 23, 2003), Frederic and Mary Ann Brussat, review of *Radical Acceptance: Embracing Your Life with the Heart of a Buddha.**

*   *   *

BRAIKER, Harriet B. 1948-2004

OBITUARY NOTICE—See index for *CA* sketch: Born November 22, 1948, in Los Angeles, CA; died of respiratory failure as a complication from pneumonia, January 10, 2004, in Pasadena, CA. Psychologist and author. Braiker was best known for her popular books and lectures on stress management for women. An alumna of the University of California—Los Angeles, she did her undergraduate and graduate work there, finishing with a doctorate in 1975. During her early career, she taught psychology at the Windward School in Santa Monica, California, from 1972 to 1973, and was a clinical intern at San Fernando Valley Child Guidance Center for the next two years. She then joined the Rand Corp., where she researched the problems engendered by alcohol and drug abuse in studies for U.S. government agencies and the Air Force. After being fully licensed in 1980, she opened a private practice in Los Angeles. Braiker became interested in stress management in the 1980s, when news about Type A personalities in men—those who are workaholics—started to become a concern in America. Braiker believed, though, that stress in women was even more severe in many cases because of increasing pressure on women to not only be successful at work but also in the home as wives, mothers, and perfect hostesses. An article she published on the subject for *Working Woman* magazine in 1984 generated such a large reader response that she turned it into her first bestselling book, *The Type E Woman: How to Overcome the Stress of Being Everything to Everybody* (1986). This was followed by several more similar books, including *Getting Up When You're Feeling Down: A Woman's Guide to Overcoming and Preventing Depression* (1988) and *The Disease to Please: Curing the People-Pleasing Syndrome* (2001). Finding a wide audience and appearing on such televi-sion programs as *The Oprah Winfrey Show,* Braiker offered her expertise as director of the Praxis Training Group management consulting firm from 1985 to 1993 and, beginning in 1987, as senior vice president of the public relations firm Lexicon Communications. More recently, she published *The September 11 Syndrome: Anxious Days and Sleepless Nights* (2002) to help people get over the stress caused by the 2001 terrorist attacks.

OBITUARIES AND OTHER SOURCES:

PERIODICALS

Chicago Tribune, January 14, 2004, Section 1, p. 10.
Los Angeles Times, January 13, 2004, p. B10.
New York Times, January 21, 2004, p. A27.

*   *   *

BRASHEAR, Jean 1949-

PERSONAL: Born March 12, 1949, in Hereford, TX; daughter of Edward (in law enforcement) and Diane (in nursing; maiden name, Jowell) Roberson; married Ercel Brashear. *Ethnicity:* "Anglo."

ADDRESSES: Agent—c/o Author Mail, Harlequin Enterprises, P.O. Box 5190, Buffalo, NY 14240-5190. *E-mail*—jean@jeanbrashear.com.

CAREER: Novelist.

MEMBER: Romance Writers of America, Novelists Inc. (president, 2003).

WRITINGS:

ROMANCE NOVELS

Millionaire in Disguise, Harlequin (New York, NY), 2001.
What the Heart Wants, Harlequin (New York, NY), 2002.
The Healer, Harlequin (New York, NY), 2002.

The Good Daughter, Harlequin (New York, NY), 2003.
Real Hero, Harlequin (New York, NY), 2004.

Author of five other romance novels published by Harlequin (New York, NY), 1998-2001.

OTHER

Contributor to magazines, including *Romance Writers Report, Novelists Ink,* and *Good Life.*

WORK IN PROGRESS: Additional romance novels.

* * *

BROOK-SHEPHERD, (Frederick) Gordon 1918-2004
(Gordon Shepherd)

OBITUARY NOTICE—See index for *CA* sketch: Born March 24, 1918, in England; died January 24, 2004. Journalist, editor, and author. Brook-Shepherd was well known for his reportage of events behind and near the Iron Curtain, as well as his books about the Habsburg family of Austria. After studying history at Peterhouse, Cambridge, he passed the civil service exam not long before the beginning of World War II. With a working knowledge of German and French, he was recruited into British Intelligence, where he was a liaison between the British government and resistance movements in Europe, becoming a lieutenant colonel. After the war, he was hired by the London *Daily Telegraph* as a foreign correspondent, despite his lack of journalism experience. His knowledge of European politics was more than enough to compensate, however, and Brook-Shepherd found himself on the forefront of reporting such events as the Communist overthrow of Czechoslovakia and the 1956 Hungarian Uprising, as well as events in other areas of the world, such as the Suez Canal crisis. Moving on to the *Sunday Telegraph* in 1960, Brook-Shepherd became the newspaper's diplomatic editor, then assistant editor in 1965, and finally deputy editor in 1975. The reporter and editor also developed a successful career as an author, writing biographies, histories, and books on political events. Among these are *The Austrian Odyssey* (1957), *The Anschluss* (1963), *November 1918* (1981), and *Iron Maze: The Western Secret Services*

and the Bolsheviks (1998). A personal friend of the Archduke Otto, son of Emperor Karl of Austria, Gordon-Shepherd penned several well-received biographies about the Habsburgs, including *The Last Habsburg* (1968) and *The Last Empress: The Life and Times of Zita of Austria-Hungary, 1892-1989* (1991). His writings about Austria earned him praise in that country as well, and in 1979 he received its Officer's Cross of the Grand Decoration of Honour. His own country appointed him a Commander of the British Empire in 1987.

OBITUARIES AND OTHER SOURCES:

PERIODICALS

Daily Telegraph (London, England), January 30, 2004.
Times (London, England), February 20, 2004.

* * *

BROWN, Brooks 1981(?)-

PERSONAL: Born c. 1981; son of Randy and Judy Brown. *Education:* Graduated from Columbine High School, 1999.

ADDRESSES: Agent—c/o Lantern Books, 1 Union Square W., Suite 201, New York, NY 10003.

CAREER: Writer. Consultant on the film *Bowling for Columbine,* Dog Eat Dog Films, 2002.

WRITINGS:

(With Rob Merritt) *No Easy Answers: The Truth behind Death at Columbine,* Lantern Books (New York, NY), 2002.

SIDELIGHTS: Brooks Brown was a senior at Columbine High School in 1999 when two of his friends, Dylan Klebold and Eric Harris, went on a shooting rampage that killed twelve students and one teacher and wounded at least two dozen others. Brown was possibly the last person to speak to Harris on April 20, 1999, before the shooting spree began. Because of his contact with the killer, Brown was erroneously suspected by police and others of having been an accomplice in the crime. *No Easy Answers: The Truth behind Death at Columbine* is the first account written by one of the students of Columbine, someone who knew both the victims and the perpetrators of the murders. Brown's collaboration with journalist Rob Merritt includes first person recollections, journalism, and interviews.

Growing up in Littleton, Colorado, Brown was already a close friend of Klebold when Eric Harris moved to the area from Pennsylvania in the mid-1990s. Although friendly at first, he and Harris became estranged in high school, and Harris posted death threats against Brown on his Web site in 1998. Brown's parents brought the Web site to the attention of local law enforcement officials, but no action was taken. Brown and Harris reached a reconciliation of sorts during the winter of 1999, when they were in several classes together.

In *No Easy Answers*, Brown, as someone who knew both shooters well, discusses possible motivation for the rage that led to the attack. He describes the school culture as giving preferential treatment to "jocks," or sports stars, while subjecting individualists to unrelenting bullying, and he places much of the blame for the violence on the school and law enforcement officials who did nothing to relieve the situation. A *Publishers Weekly* reviewer noted that "too little time has elapsed since the shootings for Brown to have the perspective necessary to make this a definitive work." However, in *Booklist*, reviewer John Green described the volume as "gripping and provocative," calling it an "excellent choice for outsider teens wondering if there's a light at the end of the bullying tunnel."

BIOGRAPHICAL AND CRITICAL SOURCES:

PERIODICALS

Booklist, October 15, 2002, John Green, review of *No Easy Answers: The Truth behind Death at Columbine*, p. 367.
Publishers Weekly, September 30, 2002, review of *No Easy Answers*, p. 63.

ONLINE

ABC News.com, http://abcnews.go.com/ (April 20, 2000), "Columbine, One Year Later: Chat—Former Columbine Student Looks Back."

Denver Post Online, http://63.147.65.175/news/col0516g.htm (January 21, 2003), Kieran Nicholson, "Parents of Survivor Blast Sheriff as 'Coward.'"
Online Athens, http://www.onlineathens.com/ (October 24, 2002), Robert Weller, "Book Tells Story behind Columbine."*

*   *   *

BROWN, Lee Ann 1964-

PERSONAL: Born 1964, in Japan. *Education:* Brown University, B.A., M.F.A.

ADDRESSES: Home—New York, NY. *Office*—St. John's University, 101 Murray St., New York, NY 10007.

CAREER: Educator, poet, and filmmaker. St. John's University, New York, NY, assistant professor of English; Naropa Institute, Boulder, CO, member of writing and poetics program; founder and editor of Tender Buttons Press.

AWARDS, HONORS: New American Poetry Series Award for *Polyverse*.

WRITINGS:

Polyverse (poems), Sun & Moon Press (Los Angeles, CA), 1999.
The Sleep That Changed Everything (poems), Wesleyan University Press (Middletown, CT), 2003.

SIDELIGHTS: Lee Ann Brown is a poet, filmmaker, professor, and founder and editor of Tender Buttons Press. She was born in Japan but grew up in North Carolina. A contributor for *Publishers Weekly* considered Brown to be "the most credible candidate for Queen of the New York poetry scene" and felt that her second collection of poetry, *The Sleep That Changed Everything*, "should solidify her national reputation."

In her first collection of poetry, *Polyverse*, Brown works within many forms, styles, and voices, giving her book a sense of playfulness. She crosses boundaries to stretch forms and styles into constant reshaping and morphing. In an interview with Dannye Romine Powell for the *Charlotte Observer* Brown explained, "I want people to see language around them in daily conversation, on signs in the street, in popular culture as material to remake."

Her playfulness is displayed in the poem "Love," in which she takes a traditional love lyric and arranges the words to appear backward, reversed, and twisted in the first two parts. In the third part the same words read clearly, as a traditional love poem would, and the reader sees the first two parts as rearranged versions of the last. The effect is a course of confusion, from the first two parts, to clarity in the last part.

The title *Polyverse* suggests a celebration of "many," downplaying the concept of one big idea and one form, recognizing the many ways to arrive somewhere. Patrick Pritchett wrote in *American Book Review* that Brown reminds readers that "a poem, any poem, is the result of the author's collaboration with the polyphonic forces of language." To loosely tie together the three sections of Brown's collection of many, the theme of celebration of desire and pleasure runs throughout the book.

Brown again emphasizes the playfulness of language in the five sections of her second collection of poetry, *The Sleep That Changed Everything.* She uses a range of forms that includes prose poems, limericks, songs, ballads, and utterances. In addition to the witty, twist-and-turn on words she used in *Polyverse,* some of the poems use more straightforward language in this collection. She applies the straightforward style to her political poems that address the death of Matthew Sheppard, a gay teen who was beaten to death, and civil rights activist Harry Golden's idea of "vertical integration," which refers to everyone standing vertical until everyone is treated equally.

The last section of the book contains twelve poems about her grandmother's death and pays tribute to her. In the poem "Obba I Remember," Brown lists unrelated memories of her grandmother, reflecting how memory is not always coherent and orderly. A *Publishers Weekly* reviewer called *The Sleep That Changed Everything* "restorative" and "wonderfully wakeful." Ken Rumble concluded in the *Electronic Poetry Review,*

"Brown's relentless experimentation establishes her as a poet who blazes the trails poetic trends follow, even when those trails seem to lead back into the main at times."

BIOGRAPHICAL AND CRITICAL SOURCES:

PERIODICALS

American Book Review, March-April, 2000, Patrick Pritchett, review of *Polyverse,* pp. 18, 21.
Publishers Weekly, September 28, 1998, review of *Polyverse,* p. 96; February 17, 2003, review of *The Sleep That Changed Everything,* p. 72.

ONLINE

Charlotte Observer Online, http://www.bayarea.com/ (August 24, 2003), Dannye Romine Powell, interview with Brown.
Electronic Poetry Center, http://epc.buffalo.edu/ (October 24, 2003), short biography of Brown.
Electronic Poetry Review, http://www.poetry.org/ (October 24, 2003), Ken Rumble, review of *The Sleep That Changed Everything.*
Montserrat Review, http://www.themontserratreview. com/ (October 24, 2003), review of *The Sleep That Changed Everything.*
Poetry.org, http://www.poetry.org/ (October 24, 2003), Ken Rumble, review of *The Sleep That Changed Everything.* *

* * *

BURTON, Sandra 1941(?)-2004

OBITUARY NOTICE—See index for *CA* sketch: Born c. 1941, in Long Beach, CA; died February 27, 2004, in Bali, Indonesia. Journalist and author. Burton was a former correspondent for *Time* magazine who was most often remembered for her reportage in Asia. A graduate of Middlebury College, where she earned her bachelor's degree, her first journalism job came in 1963 with the *Hunterdon County Democrat* in New Jersey. A secretarial job at *Time* in 1964 led to a research position the following year, and in 1970 Burton was hired as a correspondent in Los Angeles for the Time-Life News Service. Increasingly more important positions followed, including being named Boston bureau chief from 1973 to 1976, followed by a lengthy post in Paris as a correspondent, and then bureau chief positions in Hong Kong from 1982 to 1986 and Beijing from 1988 until 1990. From 1990 to 1997 she continued to work for *Time* as a senior correspondent in Hong Kong; thereafter she was a freelance journalist for the magazine. Some of the most important events that Burton covered occurred while she was in Asia, including the assassination of Benigno Aquino Jr. in the Philippines and the Tiananmen Square massacre in China. Burton wrote about her experience in the Philippines in her book, *Impos-*

sible Dream: The Marcoses, the Aquinos, and the Unfinished Revolution (1989). At the time of her death, she was working on a biography of the nineteenth century rajah James Brook.

OBITUARIES AND OTHER SOURCES:

PERIODICALS

Chicago Tribune, March 1, 2004, Section 4, p. 10.
New York Times, March 2, 2004, p. A25.
Washington Post, March 1, 2004, p. B5.

C

CANTOR, Milton 1925-

PERSONAL: Born June 11, 1925, in New York, NY; *Education:* Columbia University, Ph.D., 1954.

ADDRESSES: Office—History Department, Herter Hall, University of Massachusetts, 161 Presidents Dr., Amherst, MA 01003-9312. *E-mail*—mcantor@history. umass.edu.

CAREER: University of Massachusetts—Amherst, member of faculty of history department, beginning 1963, professor, 1973-2002, professor emeritus, 2002—. University of Kiel, Fulbright lecturer, 1960-61; University of Warwick, senior lecturer, 1981-82. Historian for National Foundation for Infantile Paralysis. *Labor History,* managing editor, 1963.

WRITINGS:

(Editor, with Howard H. Quint and Dean Albertson) *Main Problems in American History,* Dorsey Press (Homewood, IL), 1964, 4th edition, 1978.

(Editor) *Black Labor in America,* Negro Universities Press (Westport, CT), 1969.

Max Eastman ("United States Authors" series), Twayne Publishers (New York, NY), 1970.

(Editor) *Hamilton,* Prentice-Hall (Englewood Cliffs, NJ), 1971.

(Editor, with Howard H. Quint) *Men, Women, and Issues in American History,* Dorsey Press (Homewood, IL), 1975, revised edition, 1980.

(Editor, with Bruce Laurie) *Class, Sex, and the Woman Worker,* Greenwood Press (Westport, CT), 1977.

The Divided Left: American Radicalism, 1900-1975, Hill and Wang (New York, NY), 1978.

(Editor) *American Workingclass Culture: Explorations in American Labor and Social History,* Greenwood Press (Westport, CT), 1979.

(Editor, with Henry Steele Commager) *Documents of American History,* 10th edition, Prentice-Hall (Englewood Cliffs, NJ), 1988.

Contributor of category essays to *Words That Make America Great,* compiled by Jerome Agel, Random House (New York, NY), 1997.

SIDELIGHTS: Historian Milton Cantor has specialized in American labor and social history. For Twayne's "United States Authors" series, he wrote *Max Eastman,* a brief study of the radical poet and editor (1883-1969) who promoted women's suffrage and vehemently opposed U.S. intervention in World War I. Cantor also wrote *The Divided Left: American Radicalism, 1900-1975.* Cantor has edited or coedited several major works, including *Main Problems in American History,* which has gone into three subsequent editions since its initial publication in 1964.

In 1988, Cantor collaborated with editor Henry Steele Commager on the tenth edition of Commager's *Documents of American History.* This work, which collects important primary documents relating to the creation and development the United States, is widely regarded as one of the best reference works in its field. Cantor has also contributed essays to Jerome Agel's book

Words That Make America Great, which collects not only well-known speeches and documents, but also such unexpected pieces as comedian George Carlin's "Seven Dirty Words" routine. A *Booklist* reviewer observed that Cantor's "well-written" introductions to each section "are valuable by themselves as an overview of each topic and a survey of critical issues in American history."

A member of the department of history at University of Massachusetts—Amherst since 1963, Cantor became a full professor in 1973. Although he officially retired in 2002, he continues to teach.

BIOGRAPHICAL AND CRITICAL SOURCES:

PERIODICALS

Booklist, March 15, 1997, review of *Words That Make America Great,* p. 1262.
Library Journal, April 1, 1997, Grant A. Fredericksen, review of *Words That Make America Great,* p. 105.*

*   *   *

CARDOSO, Rafael
   See DENIS, Rafael Cardoso

*   *   *

CARROLL, Cathryn

PERSONAL: Female.

ADDRESSES: Office—World around You, Laurent Clerc National Deaf Education Center, Gallaudet University, 800 Florida Ave. N.E., Washington, DC 20002; fax: 202-651-5340. *E-mail*—cathryn.carroll@gallaudet.edu.

CAREER: Gallaudet University, Washington, DC, managing editor at National Deaf Education Network and Clearinghouse, Laurent Clerc National Deaf Education Center.

WRITINGS:

(With Susan M. Mather) *Movers and Shakers: Deaf People Who Changed the World; Twenty-six Tales of Genius, Struggle, Perseverance, and Heroism,* DawnSignPress (San Diego, CA), 1997.
(With Catherine Hoffpauir Fisher) *Orchid of the Bayou: A Deaf Woman Faces Blindness,* Gallaudet University Press (Washington, DC), 2001.

Editor, *World around You.*

BIOGRAPHICAL AND CRITICAL SOURCES:

PERIODICALS

Publishers Weekly, February 19, 2001, review of *Orchid of the Bayou: A Deaf Woman Faces Blindness,* p. 84.*

*   *   *

CHANT, Sylvia (H.) 1958-

PERSONAL: Born December 24, 1958, in Dundee, Scotland; daughter of Stuart (a senior lecturer in microbiology) and June (a legal secretary) Chant; married Andrew McInally (a furniture designer), May 14, 1992 (divorced, December 2, 1994); married Chris Mogridge (a financial analyst and triathlete), January 2, 2002. *Education:* King's College, Cambridge, B.A. (geography; honors), 1981; University College London, Ph.D, 1984.

ADDRESSES: Office—London School of Economics, Department of Geography and Environment, S515, St. Clements Bldg., Houghton St., London WC2A 2AE, England. *E-mail*—s.chant@lse.ac.uk.

CAREER: Liverpool University, Liverpool, England, lecturer in geography and Latin American studies, 1987-88; London School of Economics, London, England, lecturer in geography, 1988-95, reader in geography, 1995-2002, professor of development geography, 2002—. University of London, associate fellow at the Institute of Latin American Studies; Universidad Complutense de Madrid, Madrid, Spain, visiting professor in gender studies, 2001. Acted as consultant to World Bank, United Nations Development Program, ILO, Economic Commission of Latin Americas (ECLA), Commonwealth Secretariat, UNU-WIDER LEAD International (Rockeller), UNICEF-Ecuador, and Womankind Worldwide. Also editorial advising board member of *International Development Planning Review, Singapore Journal of Tropical Geography, Journal of Migration Studies,* and *Critical Business.*

MEMBER: Society for Latin American Studies.

AWARDS, HONORS: Nuffield Social Science Research Fellowship, 1994-95; finalist, National Book Award for Social Science (Philippines), 1995, for *Women of a Lesser Cost: Female Labour, Foreign Exchange, and Philippine Development;* Leverhulme Major Research Fellowship, 2003-06.

WRITINGS:

(With Caroline O. N. Moser) *The Role of Women in the Execution of Low-Income Housing Projects: Training Module,* United Nations Centre for Human Settlements (Nairobi, Kenya), 1986.

(With Lynne Brydon) *Women in the Third World: Gender Issues in Rural and Urban Areas,* Rutgers University Press (New Brunswick, NJ), 1989.

Women and Survival in Mexican Cities: Perspectives on Gender, Labour Markets, and Low-Income Households, Manchester University Press (New York, NY), 1991.

(Editor) *Gender and Migration in Developing Countries,* John Wiley (New York, NY), 1992.

(With Cathy McIlwaine) *Women of a Lesser Cost: Female Labour, Foreign Exchange, and Philippine Development,* Pluto (London, England), 1995.

Gender, Urban Development, and Housing (volume two of the "Habitat II" series), United Nations Development Programme (New York, NY), 1996.

Women-Headed Households: Diversity and Dynamics in the Developing World, St. Martin's Press (New York, NY), 1997.

(With Cathy McIlwaine) *Three Generations, Two Genders, One World: Women and Men in a Changing Century,* Zed Press (London, England), 1998.

(With Matthew Gutmann) *Mainstreaming Men into Gender and Development: Debates, Reflections, and Experiences,* Stylus Publications (Herndon, VA), 2000.

(With Nikki Craske) *Gender in Latin America,* Rutgers University Press (New Brunswick, NJ), 2003.

Contributor of chapters to books and of articles to scholarly journals.

WORK IN PROGRESS: Gender, Generation, and Poverty: Exploring the Feminisation of Poverty in Africa, Asia, and Latin America, for Edward Elgar (Cheltenham, England); research for *Intergenerational and Household Dimensions of Poverty in the Gambia, Philippines, and Costa Rica.*

SIDELIGHTS: Geography professor Sylvia Chant has focused her research efforts on women in developing countries, publishing the results of her studies in a number of volumes. In *Women and Survival in Mexican Cities: Perspectives on Gender, Labour Markets, and Low-Income Households,* Chant examines the links between the household structures of women employed in the workforce outside of the home. In doing so, she provides "intriguing glimpses into the way in which households expand or contract in response to surrounding pressures," noted *Economic Development and Cultural Change* reviewer M. Patricia Fernandez Kelly. "This book should have wide appeal not only to students of Mexico and Latin America but, perhaps more significantly, to those interested in a comparative approach to the relationship between household, gender, and labor markets," Kelly added. Likewise, *Sociology* reviewer Sue Szabo applauded the "comprehensive and excellent overview of literature on women's employment and household structure," although she felt that the small sample size diminished the study's statistical validity. "Ultimately," Szabo concluded, "the book will stand as a significant contribution to filling the gap which . . . exists between the literature on women's work and development and that of the effects of economic change on household form."

Chant presents another look at female-run families in *Women-Headed Households: Diversity and Dynamics in the Developing World,* a "meticulously researched analysis of women-headed households [that] brings into focus important issues for policy and research in the developing, as well as the (post-) industrialised world," to quote Ruth Pearson, writing for the *European Journal of Development Research.* Chant examines a large body of data and stresses the need to study the age of the head of household, as well as the class, ethnic, and racial make-up of the rest of the household. "A striking feature of the book is the way it points up the very different political and policy debates in advanced and developing countries," Pearson remarked. In developed countries, the social role and influence of the lone mother is of particular importance, while in developing countries many lifestyle issues have no relevance in the face of making sure women have a way to earn a living.

Chant's book *Gender in Latin America,* written in association with Nikki Craske and shortly to be published in Spanish for publication by Ciesas del Occidente (Guadalajara, Mexico), provides an overview of continuity and change in Latin American gender relations over the last three decades. In a review for *Contemporary Sociology,* Nancy Lopez heralds the book as a "major contribution to the growing literature that moves from examining gender as 'women' to 'gender as process,' which includes men and women conjointly."

As she told *CA,* Chant passionately enjoys writing about gender and development issues, particularly where she is able to draw on her own primary research with women and men at the grassroots and is able to give ample space to their own voices and stories. For this reason, the favorite of her own books is *Women-Headed Households,* which documents the experiences of women in Mexico, Costa Rica, and the Philippines who, for one reason or another, have ended up raising children without the support of co-resident husbands or partners. Chant's main aims with her writing, as she expressed to *CA,* "are to enrich the experiences of her students, to inspire and engage her fellow scholars, and to sensitise policymakers to the needs and interests of disadvantaged women in developing countries."

BIOGRAPHICAL AND CRITICAL SOURCES:

PERIODICALS

Ahfad Journal, June, 2001, Badri Balghis, review of *Mainstreaming Men into Gender and Development: Debates, Reflections, and Experiences,* p. 70.
Contemporary Sociology, 2004, Nancy Lopez, review of *Gender in Latin America,* pp. 294-296.
Economic Development and Cultural Change, April, 1993, M. Patricia Fernandez Kelly, review of *Women and Survival in Mexican Cities: Perspectives on Gender, Labour Markets, and Low-Income Households,* pp. 671-673.

European Journal of Development Research, December, 1998, Ruth Pearson, review of *Women-Headed Households: Diversity and Dynamics in the Developing World,* pp. 187-188.
Journal of Contemporary Asia, January, 1998, Herb Thompson, review of *Women of a Lesser Cost: Female Labour, Foreign Exchange, and Philippine Development,* pp. 130-133.
Latin American Research Review, 2001, Susan Tiano, review of *Women-Headed Households,* pp. 183-203.
Sociology, February, 1992, Sue Szabo, review of *Women and Survival in Mexican Cities,* pp. 139-140.

*   *   *

CHUPACK, Cindy 1973(?)-

PERSONAL: Born c. 1973, in Tulsa, OK; married (divorced). *Education:* Graduated from Northwestern University (journalism).

ADDRESSES: Home—New York, NY, and Los Angeles, CA. *Agent*—c/o Home Box Office, 1100 Avenue of the Americas, New York, NY 10036.

CAREER: Writer. *Coach,* television series producer, 1989; *A Whole New Ballgame,* television series scriptwriter, 1995; *Everybody Loves Raymond,* Columbia Broadcasting System, Inc. (CBS), television series scriptwriter, 1996-98; *Sex and the City,* Home Box Office (HBO), scriptwriter and executive producer, 1998-2004; *Madigan Men,* television series executive producer, 2000.

AWARDS, HONORS: WGA and Emmy Award nominations for *Sex and the City* episodes, including "Evolution," "Attack of the Five-Foot Ten-Inch Woman," "Just Say Yes," "Plus One Is the Loneliest Number," and "I Love a Charade."

WRITINGS:

The Between Boyfriends Book: A Collection of Cautiously Hopeful Essays, St. Martin's Press (New York, NY), 2003.

Contributor to periodicals, including *New York Woman, Allure, Slate, Harper's Bazaar,* and *Glamour.* Author of "Dating Dictionary," a monthly column in *Glamour.* Also scriptwriter for series pilot of *Madigan Men,* 2000.

SIDELIGHTS: For writer Cindy Chupack, best known for her scriptwriting credits for HBO's hit series *Sex and the City,* there is "no such thing as a bad date, only good material," as she told Cynthia Littleton of *Hollywood Reporter.* The Oklahoma native left her home state for journalism school at Northwestern University, then departed for New York City to try her hand at advertising. However, a piece she wrote for a magazine caught the attention of a television producer, and soon she was penning episodes for television series such as *A Whole New Ballgame* and *Everybody Loves Raymond.* She joined the *Sex and the City* team in its second season and wrote over a dozen scripts for the series, in addition to acting as an executive producer. "From the moment I pitched my first freelance [*Sex and the City*] episode, I loved the process—the way they work at HBO and the way they were dealing with women in a more honest and complicated way than I'd ever seen before," Chupack further related to Littleton. Chupack explained her writing process for *Sex and the City* on the *HBO* Web site: "nothing really comes together for me until I figure out the question [in the main character's, Carrie's, newspaper column], because that basically becomes the theme of the episode, and that's the filter through which we try to see each character's story." Chupack further observed, "I know I'm on track when the question is something I truly want the answer to."

Chupack branched out into book publishing with *The Between Boyfriends Book: A Collection of Cautiously Hopeful Essays,* which deals with territory Chupack has mined for her television writing: single women, dating, relations between the sexes, and splitting up. The collection of humorous dating and relationships essays, which had previously appeared in magazines during the 1990s and early 2000s, was praised by a critic for *Kirkus Reviews,* who called it "a wry, upbeat tour of the dating scene for women currently considering reentry." Themes and chapters vary from "The Breakup" and "The Year Ahead" to "Your New Boyfriend." Rachel Collins, writing in *Library Journal,* observed that Chupack "gives the gals without guys advice from the front lines of the dating scene."

Caitlin Flanagan, on the other hand, reviewing Chupack's book in *Atlantic Monthly,* found it "slight, glib, clever to a point, and exceedingly pleased with itself." *Entertainment Weekly*'s Clarissa Cruz was more positive, however, commenting that Chupack's "breezy observations . . . are as hilarious as they are true." Andrea Sachs, writing in *Time,* also had praise for this "witty" debut book, which "captures the sometimes angst-ridden world of single women," while *People*'s Michelle Tauber commended Chupack's "stiletto wit."

Writing on her author Web site, Chupack observed, "I'd like to think the reason I've been successful writing about relationships (if not in actual relationships) is that I still believe in love, and I believe deep down all of us do."

BIOGRAPHICAL AND CRITICAL SOURCES:

PERIODICALS

Atlantic Monthly, December, 2003, Caitlin Flanagan, review of *The Between Boyfriends Book: A Collection of Cautiously Hopeful Essays,* p. 133.
Entertainment Weekly, August 15, 2003, Clarissa Cruz, review of *The Between Boyfriends Book,* p. 80.
Glamour, June, 2002, Leslie Robarge, "What's Next on *Sex and the City*?," p. 178.
Hollywood Reporter, December 10, 2002, Cynthia Littleton, "Writer Chupack Gets 'Sex,' More in New HBO Deal," pp. 1-2.
Kirkus Reviews, June 1, 2003, review of *The Between Boyfriends Book,* p. 787.
Library Journal, May 1, 2003, Rachel Collins, review of *The Between Boyfriends Book,* p. 139.
People, September 8, 2003, Michelle Tauber, review of *The Between Boyfriends Book,* p. 47.
Time, August 11, 2003, Andrea Sachs, review of *The Between Boyfriends Book,* p. 65.

ONLINE

Boston Herald Online, http://www.theedge.bostonherald.com/ (August 28, 2003), Raakhee P. Mirchandani, "The Breaking Point: 'The Between Boyfriends Book' Dumps on How Men End Relationships."
Cindy Chupack Home Page, http://www.betweenboyfriends.com/ (June 25, 2004).
HBO Web site, http://www.hbo.com/ (June 18, 2004), "Cindy Chupack."*

CLANCY, Flora Simmons

PERSONAL: Female; children: Raphael. *Education:* Pratt Institute, B.F.A., 1964; Yale Unversity, Ph.D., 1980.

ADDRESSES: Office—Department of Art and Art History, University of New Mexico, Albuquerque, NM 87131. *E-mail*—flora@unm.edu.

CAREER: Colgate University, Hamilton, NY, lecturer, 1973-78; University of New Mexico, Albuquerque, 1979—, currently professor of art history. Contributor to symposia on Mayan art and architecture.

AWARDS, HONORS: Dumbarton Oaks junior fellowship, 1978-79; National Endowment for the Humanities fellowship, 1982-83; Dumbarton Oaks fellowship, 1986-87; National Endowment for the Humanities summer institute fellowships, 1991 and 1993.

WRITINGS:

Maya: Treasures of an Ancient Civilization, photographs by Stuart Rome, H. N. Abrams (New York, NY), 1985.
(Editor, with Peter D. Harrison) *Vision and Revision in Maya Studies,* University of New Mexico Press (Albuquerque, NM), 1990.
Pyramids, Smithsonian Books (Washington, DC), 1994.
Sculpture in the Ancient Maya Plaza: The Early Classic Period, University of New Mexico Press (Albuquerque, NM), 1999.

Contributor of scholarly articles to periodicals.

SIDELIGHTS: Flora Simmons Clancy is a scholar of the art and architecture of the Mayan civilization of Mexico and Central America. Clancy has written about the sculptures and construction of Mayan pyramids and other remaining artistic treasures of that ancient civilization. To quote K. A. Dixon in a *Choice* review of *Sculpture in the Ancient Maya Plaza: The Early Classic Period,* Clancy has made "an important addition to Maya studies" through her writings and presentations. In an *American Antiquity* review of *Vision and Revision in Maya Studies,* Aleksandar Boʻk-

oviċ called the book a "very useful summary of the work in the last decade, but also a book that can pose questions for future research." Boʻkoviċ concluded that the work "is without any doubt the best book on Maya studies."

BIOGRAPHICAL AND CRITICAL SOURCES:

PERIODICALS

American Antiquity, July, 1993, Aleksandar Boʻkoviċ, review of *Vision and Revision in Maya Studies,* pp. 591-592.
Antiquity, December, 1994, George Stuart, review of *Vision and Revision in Maya Studies,* p. 867.
Choice, February, 1992, C. L. Riley, review of *Vision and Revision in Maya Studies,* p. 932; November, 1999, K. A. Dixon, review of *Sculpture in the Ancient Maya Plaza: The Early Classic Period,* pp. 582-583.
Journal of Interdisciplinary History, autumn, 1992, David Webster, review of *Vision and Revision in Maya Studies,* pp. 431-433.
Latin American Research Review, summer, 1993, Barbara Tedlock, review of *Vision and Revision in Maya Studies,* p. 154.

ONLINE

Columbia University, http://www.mcah.columbia.edu/westnon/clancy.html/ (October 23, 2003), Flora Simmons Clancy, "Shield Jaguar and the French Academy."*

*   *   *

CLAUSEN, Lowen

PERSONAL: Male. *Education:* Attended the University of Washington.

ADDRESSES: Office—2208 Northwest Market St., Ste. 505, Seattle, WA 98107. *E-mail*—totheauthor@lowenclausen.com.

CAREER: Writer and business owner. Police officer for thirteen years in the Seattle, WA, police department.

WRITINGS:

First Avenue: A Novel, Watershed Books (Seattle, WA), 1999.
Second Watch, New American Library (New York, NY), 2003.

SIDELIGHTS: Lowen Clausen was a Seattle, Washington, police officer for thirteen years. His first novel, *First Avenue,* uses the author's inside knowledge of police work in Seattle. *First Avenue* features officer Sam Wright, a loner with a pretty routine life. However, Sam's existence is shaken up when he is sent to investigate the death of a baby that he was certain he had seen earlier in the week with its mother. A reviewer for *Publishers Weekly* claimed that "Clausen debuts with a strong effort" and goes on to say that Sam is a "well-develped, intriguing protagonist."

Clausen's second novel, aptly titled *Second Watch,* features detectives Katherine Murphy and Grace Stevens. Together they must unravel a case of two separate child murders—both bodies found in garbage bins. In a review for the *Mystery Reader,* Andy Plonka noted, "*Second Watch* has much to offer beyond the emotionally charged plot of interrupting a child pornography scheme. The author . . . clearly displays his knowledge of Seattle and the workings of a police department." A reviewer for *Publishers Weekly* stated, "The second novel from former Seattle police officer Clausen is equal parts police procedural and character study, and the two halves are balanced to perfection."

BIOGRAPHICAL AND CRITICAL SOURCES:

PERIODICALS

Publishers Weekly, November 20, 2000, review of *First Avenue,* p. 52; February 17, 2003, review of *Second Watch,* p. 62.

ONLINE

A Novel View, http://www.anovelview.com/book reviews/second_watch/ (October 26, 2003), review of *Second Watch.*

Lowen Clausen Web site, http://www.lowenclausen. com (October 26, 2003).
Mystery Reader, http://www.mysteryreader.com/ clausen-second.html (October 26, 2003), Lesley Dunlap, review of *First Avenue;* http://www. mysteryreader.com/clausen-first.html (October 26, 2003) Andy Plonka, review of *Second Watch.**

*   *   *

COBAIN, Kurt (Donald) 1967-1994

PERSONAL: Born February 20, 1967, in Hoquiam, WA; died, April 8, 1994, in Seattle, WA; son of Donald (a car mechanic) and Wendy Cobain; married Courtney Love, February 24, 1992; children: Frances Bean.

CAREER: Lead singer, songwriter, and guitarist for rock band Nirvana. Recorded albums *Bleach,* Sub Pop, 1989; *Nevermind,* Geffen/DGC, 1991; and *In Utero,* Geffen/DGC, 1993.

WRITINGS:

Journals, Riverhead Books (New York, NY), 2002.

SIDELIGHTS: Grunge rocker Kurt Cobain courted fame but was not prepared for the effects of stardom. As the lead singer of the band Nirvana, his albums went multi-platinum but he worried that his listeners were no different from the people who had sneered at him in high school. Depression and an undiagnosed stomach ailment led Cobain to "self-medicate" using heroin and to make several attempts at suicide. In 1994, after escaping a drug treatment center, he killed himself with a shotgun. He has since been heralded by some critics as a music icon. When a selection of entries from Cobain's diaries were published as *Journals,* the book thrilled some and troubled others, who found the public airing of private thoughts shameful. The writings reveal the musician's loves and hates, fears and pains, and ultimate inability to cope with his life.

Growing up in the small logging town of Aberdeen, Washington, Cobain was a happy child until his parents divorced when he was seven. The ensuing years were full of uncertainty and anger, as he was shifted from one home to another. Music became an outlet for his emotions, and in 1985 Cobain decided to drop out of school and form a band with his friend Krist Novoselic, who played bass. In 1987 they began playing as Nirvana and moved to Seattle. Their first album, a low-budget recording titled *Bleach,* was filled with harsh, punk-influenced cuts as well as Cobain's more melodic "About a Girl." Word-of-mouth popularized the album and attracted the attention of major record companies. With a new drummer, Dave Grohl, the band signed with DGC Records and released *Nevermind* in 1991. The album features Nirvana's best-known song, "Smells Like Teen Spirit."

Nevermind was considered the first "alternative" rock album to reach number one on the pop music charts. It made the band members millionaires and catapulted Cobain into the public eye. This new role conflicted with his self-image as an outsider whose songs included criticism of the exploitation of women and gay-bashing. During this tumultuous period, Cobain married punk-rocker Courtney Love, who was pregnant with his child; the birth of his daughter Frances Bean would be one of the brightest points in his life. But Cobain's dependence on heroin, painful medical condition, and growing fears that he was artistically bankrupt fed his despair. Following the release of *In Utero,* he nearly died in Rome from an overdose of tranquilizers in early March of 1994. The band's tour was cancelled and Cobain returned to the United States. After escaping from a drug treatment center, he killed himself on April 8, 1994, leaving a loving but tortured note to his wife and child.

The sale of Cobain's journals, which he began in the late 1980s and included some twenty spiral notebooks, was controversial. It earned Love some $4 million and was viewed by some as supporting her own drug habit. The resulting book was a full-color, facsimile of a portion of his writings. The cover includes a note that Cobain made warning someone, most likely a girlfriend, not to read what was inside; another encourages the reader to go ahead, so that they might figure him out. The contents include his often bitter commentary on the music industry, fame, musical influences, politics, his health, drug use, and family life.

The act of reading such private thoughts without permission troubled a number of reviewers. Writing for *Powell's Books,* Adrienne Miller said, "eighty percent of this book made me feel as if I were examining someone's dirty underwear." What she did gain from the book was the perception that "one thing is clear . . . nobody achieves Cobain-level fame unless he wants it." Jeremy Fenton wrote for the *Northern Rivers Echo* that "interpreting a person's life from journals left behind is a dangerously misguided exercise." He warned that "Kurt Cobain was as contradictory as they come" and judged that "as a stand-alone document it is for fans alone." *Library Journal*'s Rachel Collins suggested that the book needs to be read in conjunction with a biography, noting "no one involved with the project provides any context, and this absence is keenly felt."

In a review for *Nation,* Alex Abramovich considered at length the impressions made by *Journals.* He explained, "what Cobain tries hardest to communicate in his journals is his own inability to communicate, and he seems to recognize, in his own spiritual exhaustion, an exhaustion of the language itself." Abramovich found the writing far grimmer than any of Cobain's songs, of which he said, "Even at their darkest, Nirvana's songs were filled with light. But Cobain's *Journals,* which consist essentially of the same rhetoric we find in his songs, pull off the difficult trick of making his words sound mundane again—they never break through the darkness." The distaste he felt for the invasion of Cobain's privacy was, however, mitigated by this thought: "But Cobain is dead, and a better question may be not what he would have thought of the *Journals*' publication but whether a book like the *Journals* could have saved the life of someone like Cobain, had he read it in time."

BIOGRAPHICAL AND CRITICAL SOURCES:

BOOKS

Newsmakers, Issue 4, Gale (Detroit, MI), 1994.

PERIODICALS

Library Journal, December 2002, Rachel Collins, review of *Journals,* p. 129.
Nation, December 9, 2002, Alex Abramovich, review of *Journals,* p. 28.

ONLINE

Northern Rivers Echo, http://echonews.com/ (April 29, 2003), Jeremy Fenton, review of *Journals.*

Observer Online, http://www.observer.co.uk/ (October 20, 2002), Barney Hoskyns, "Rock's Last Great Star."

Powell's Books, http://www.powells.com/review/ (November 13, 2002), Adrienne Miller, review of *Journals.**

*   *   *

COCKS, Nancy L.

PERSONAL: Female.

ADDRESSES: Office—50 Wynford Dr., Toronto, Ontario M3C 1J7, Canada.

CAREER: Writer, teacher, deputy warden, and Presbyterian minister on the Isle of Iona, Scotland.

WRITINGS:

"ADVENTURES OF FERGIE THE FROG" SERIES

Fearless Fergie, illustrated by Michael Leveille, Novalis (Toronto, Ontario, Canada), 1996.

Fergie Feels Left Out, illustrated by Michael Leveille, Novalis (Toronto, Ontario, Canada), 1996.

Fergie Goes Moose Hunting, illustrated by Michael Leveille, Novalis (Toronto, Ontario, Canada), 1996.

Fergie Hogs the Lily Pad, illustrated by Michael Leveille, Novalis (Toronto, Ontario, Canada), 1996.

Fergie Fails a Test, illustrated by Michael Leveille, Novalis (Toronto, Ontario, Canada), 1997.

Fergie, Frog Scout, illustrated by Michael Leveille, Novalis (Toronto, Ontario, Canada), 1997.

Fergie Loses a Friend, illustrated by Michael Leveille, Novalis (Toronto, Ontario, Canada), 1997.

Welcome Home, Fergie, illustrated by Michael Leveille, Novalis (Toronto, Ontario, Canada), 1997.

OTHER

Growing Up with God: Using Stories to Explore a Child's Faith and Life, Novalis (Toronto, Ontario, Canada), 2003.

SIDELIGHTS: Nancy L. Cocks is a Presbyterian minister and the author of the popular children's series "Fergie," along with her latest work for parents, *Growing Up with God: Using Stories to Explore a Child's Faith and Life.* The "Adventures of Fergie the Frog" series stars a seven-year-old frog called Fergie. He lives in the swamp with his mother, father, and brother, and he is always getting into something. The series is designed so that each book illustrates a lesson in Christianity. Cocks believes that stories are important to children and can help them explore their faith and fears about life.

In her book *Growing Up with God: Using Stories to Explore a Child's Faith and Life,* Cocks notes "we can help children grow up trusting God to be at the center of their lives by telling children stories that speak to their genuine concerns and by listening to stories that children long to tell." Part one of the book contains the author's theories behind using stories to convey God to children and part two contains actual stories by Cocks. In a review for *Library Journal,* John Moryl stated that "part three comprises indexes of faith themes, life situations, feelings explored in the stories, and biblical references, making the work easy for parents and educators to use."

BIOGRAPHICAL AND CRITICAL SOURCES:

BOOKS

Cocks, Nancy L., *Growing Up with God: Using Stories to Explore a Child's Faith and Life,* Novalis (Toronto, Ontario, Canada), 2003.

PERIODICALS

Canadian Book Review Annual, Volume 13, 1997, review of "Fergie" series, pp. 467-468.

Library Journal, May 1, 2003, John Moryl, review of *Growing Up with God: Using Stories to Explore a Child's Faith and Life,* p. 118.

Presbyterian Record, May, 1997, review of *Adventures of Fergie the Frog,* pp. 44-45.*

*   *   *

COHEN, Allen 1940-2004

OBITUARY NOTICE—See index for *CA* sketch: Born April 23, 1940, in New York, NY; died of liver cancer, April 29, 2004, in Walnut Creek, CA. Editor and author. Cohen was a poet who was also well known as the founding editor of the underground newspaper *San Francisco Oracle*. A graduate of Brooklyn College of the City University of New York, he earned a B.A. there in 1963. Moving to San Francisco, he worked at the Psychedelic Shop for several years before cofounding the *Oracle* in 1966. The paper published the works of such noted writers as Allen Ginsberg and Ken Kesey and announced cultural events such as 1967's "Human Be-In." It was also the *Oracle* that declared the summer of 1967 the "Summer of Love." After the newspaper closed its doors in 1968, Cohen lived in a commune near Mendocino, California, and wrote poetry. Among his collections are *Childbirth Is Ecstasy* (1970), *Reagan Poems* (1981), and *Book of Hats* (1992). In the 1990s, he occupied his time by giving poetry readings and working as a substitute teacher in Oakland, California. After the terrorist attacks in 2001, Cohen edited an anthology with Clive Matson titled *An Eye for an Eye Makes the Whole World Blind: Poets on 9/11* (2002), which won the 2003 Natural Literary Award from the Oakland chapter of PEN.

OBITUARIES AND OTHER SOURCES:

PERIODICALS

Chicago Tribune, May 8, 2004, Section 2, p. 11.
Los Angeles Times, May 7, 2004, p. B15.

*   *   *

CONN, Didi 1951-

PERSONAL: Original name, Didi Bernstein; born July 13, 1951, in Brooklyn, NY; daughter of Leonard (a clinical psychologist) and Beverly Bernstein; married David Shire (a composer); children: Daniel.

ADDRESSES: Agent—William Morris Agency, 151 South El Camino Dr., Beverly Hills, CA 90212-2775.

CAREER: Actress. Actress in films, including (as voice of Raggedy Ann) *Raggedy Ann and Andy,* Twentieth Century-Fox, 1977; (as Laurie Robinson) *You Light Up My Life,* Columbia, 1977; (as Donna DeVito) *Almost Summer,* Universal, 1978; (as Frenchy) *Grease,* Paramount, 1978, re-released, 1998; (as title role)

Violet, 1981; (as Frenchy) *Grease II,* Paramount, 1982; (as actress) "Mutual Orgasms," *Funny,* Original Cinema, 1988; (as Stacy Jones) *Thomas and the Magic Railroad,* Destination Films, 2000; (as Patrice) *Shooting Vegetarians,* Cineblast Productions, 2000; and (as waitress) *Frida,* Miramax, 2002. Appeared on the recording *Grease* (original soundtrack), Paramount, 1991.

Actress in television series, including *Happy Days,* c. 1975; *Keep on Truckin',* American Broadcasting Companies, Inc. (ABC), 1975; (as Helen) *The Practice,* ABC, 1976; (as voice) *The Scooby-Doo and Scrappy-Doo Show* (animated), ABC, 1980; (as voice of Cup Cake) *Fonz and the Happy Days Gang* (animated), ABC, 1980-1982; (as Denise Stevens Downey) *Benson,* ABC, 1981-1985; (as voice) *Bad Cat* (animated), ABC, 1984; (as additional voices) *The New Jetsons* (animated), syndicated, 1985; and (as Stacy Jones) *Shining Time Station,* Public Broadcasting Service (PBS), 1990-1993. Actress in television movies, including (as television actress) *Genesis II,* Columbia Broadcasting System, Inc. (CBS), 1973; (as Julie Evans) *Murder at the Mardi Gras,* CBS, 1978; and (as Eve Harris) *Three on a Date,* ABC, 1978. Executive producer of the television movie *We'll Always Be Together!,* ABC, forthcoming.

Guest star on television programs, including *$20,000 Pyramid* (game show), ABC, 1978, 1979, and 1981; (as Patty Maloney) "Sleeping Dogs," *Hotel,* ABC, 1985; (as Dinah Roswell) *Cagney & Lacey,* CBS, 1987; (as Wanda) "All That Glitters," *Highway to Heaven,* National Broadcasting Company, Inc. (NBC), 1987; (as Birdy Belker) "Ghost Rider," *Highway to Heaven,* NBC, 1987; (as Ms. Tressman) "He Ain't Guilty, He's My Brother," *L.A. Law,* NBC, 1994; *Saturday Night Live,* NBC, 1998; "Revenge Is Sweet," *Oz,* 2001; *The Montel Williams Show,* 2001; and (as housekeeper) *Romeo,* 2003; also appeared as guest player, *Body Language,* CBS; and as guest panelist, *The Match Game/Hollywood Squares Hour,* NBC.

Appeared in television specials, including (as receptionist) "Working," *American Playhouse,* PBS, 1982; *Circus of the Stars, Number Seven,* CBS, 1982; (as Stacy Jones) *Shining Time Station,* PBS, 1989; (as herself and Frenchy) *VH-1 Where Are They Now: Grease,* VH1, 1998; (as herself and Frenchy) *VH1's Behind the Music: Grease,* VH1, 2000; and *Grease: After They Were Famous.* Also appeared in television programs, including (as Nurse Jackie Morse) *Handle with Care* (pilot), CBS, 1977; (as Cal) *The Magic Show,* 1983; and (as voice) *The Adventures of Don Coyote and Sancho Panda,* 1990.

Actress in stage productions, including (as understudy for the role of Grandma Kurnitz) *Lost in Yonkers,* Richard Rodgers Theatre, New York, NY, between 1991 and 1993; (as Debbie Wastba) *The Primary English Class,* Minetta Lane Theatre, New York, 1998; (as lamplighter and ghost of Christmas past) *A Christmas Carol,* Theatre at Madison Square Garden, New York, 1999; (as Smeraldina) *The Green Bird,* Cort Theatre, New York, 2000; made Broadway debut as Bella, *Lost in Yonkers;* appeared in *Consequence, Hello, I Love You, The Lesson,* and *The Vagina Monologues,* all New York; in *Danny and the Deep Blue Sea,* Los Angeles, CA; and in *Anything Goes, Birdbath, Enter Laughing, It Had to Be You,* and *Room Service,* all regional productions.

WRITINGS:

Mommy, Give Me a Drinka Water (recording; for children), Ambassador, 1995.
Frenchy's "Grease" Scrapbook: We'll Always Be Together!, Hyperion (New York, NY), 1998.

SIDELIGHTS: Actress Didi Conn's career is still defined for many by a role she played over a quarter-century ago: Frenchy in the hit John Travolta/Olivia Newton-John musical romance *Grease.* When the film was re-released on its twentieth anniversary in 1998, Conn put together a book, *Frenchy's "Grease" Scrapbook: We'll Always Be Together!,* to commemorate the event. Conn wrote about her own memories of making the film, and she tracked down the other actors and actresses, asking them for their memories, behind-the-scenes snapshots, and information about where they are now. "Tracking everyone down was work," Conn told syndicated reporter Terry Lawson, "But it was worth it just to talk to people I hadn't seen in years." There was one person who it wasn't hard to find: Newton-John and Conn became best friends on the set and have remained so ever since.

Humorously, in the book, the actors were asked where they thought their characters would be twenty years later. For example, Jeff Conaway (recently of *Babylon*

5), who played Kenickie, thought that Kenickie would be married to his high school sweetheart Rizzo, and that they would have "kids screaming all over the place." But Stockard Channing (recently of *West Wing*), who played Rizzo, declared that she would be divorced from Kenickie by now, because they had a "dysfunctional relationship."

BIOGRAPHICAL AND CRITICAL SOURCES:

BOOKS

Conn, Didi, *Frenchy's "Grease" Scrapbook: We'll Always Be Together!,* Hyperion (New York, NY), 1998.

PERIODICALS

Buffalo News (Buffalo, NY), March 28, 1998, Terry Lawson, "A Pink Lady, Still in the Pink," p. C8.
Daily Herald (Arlington Heights, IL), July 26, 2000, Stacey Cara Cohen, review of *Thomas and the Magic Railroad,* p. 2.
Entertainment Weekly, January 10, 1992, Ken Tucker, review of *Shining Time Station,* pp. 78-79.
Fresno Bee (Fresno, CA), March 26, 1998, Terry Lawson, "Didi Untangles Mystery of *Grease* Appeal," p. E2.
Hollywood Reporter, October 11, 2002, Frank Scheck, review of *Say Goodnight Gracie,* p. 56.
Los Angeles Magazine, July, 1980, Dick Lochte, review of *Division Street,* pp. 246-248.
Milwaukee Journal Sentinel (Milwaukee, WI), July 26, 2000, Sue Pierman, review of *Thomas and the Magic Railroad,* p. 12.
Mirror (London, England), July 3, 1998, Thomas Quinn, "Slick Back and Enjoy: As *Grease* Returns, Didi Conn (aka Frenchy) Tells Thomas Quinn What the Original Cast Are Up to Twenty Years On," p. 4.
News & Record (Piedmont Triad, NC), April 3, 1998, "The *Grease* Cast: Where Are They Now?," p. D4, Terry Lawson, "For Actress, 'Grease' Is Still the Word," p. D4.
New York, April 13, 1987, John Simon, review of *Consequence,* p. 104.
New York Times, June 4, 1982, "Gene Wilder's Plans Include Gilda Radner," pp. 20, C12; March 30, 1987, Mel Gussow, review of *Consequence,* pp. 15, C12; November 17, 1998, Peter Marks, review of *The Primary English Class,* p. E12.

Record (Bergen County, NJ), March 27, 1998, Terry Lawson, "Her Chance to Be Frenchy Again: *Grease* Reunion," p. 40; July 26, 2000, Roger Ebert, review of *Thomas and the Magic Railroad,* p. Y2.

Rocky Mountain News (Denver, CO), March 27, 1998, Robert Denerstein, review of *Grease* (re-release), p. 9D.

San Francisco Chronicle, March 27, 1998, Edward Guthman, review of *Grease* (re-release), p. D1.

Seattle Times, July 26, 2000, John Hartl, review of *Thomas and the Magic Railroad,* p. E8.

Star-Ledger (Newark, NJ), June 5, 1998, Bette Spero, "Dance: Greasers," p. 41.

TV Guide, October 5, 1996, James Kaplan, review of *Shining Time Station,* p. 43.

Variety, March 11, 1996, Jeremy Gerard, review of *The Green Bird,* p. 54.

ONLINE

Internet Movie Database, http://www.imdb.com/ (May 23, 2003), "Didi Conn."

Playbill, http://www.playbill.com/ (June 2, 2003), "Celebrity Buzz: Who's Who: Didi Conn."*

*   *   *

CONWAY, Martha

PERSONAL: Female. *Education:* Attended University of California—Berkeley.

ADDRESSES: Home—San Francisco, CA. *Agent*—Matt Williams, The Gernet Co., 136 East 57th. St., New York, NY 10022. *E-mail*—twelvebliss@yahoo.com.

CAREER: Author; writes a regular column for the Web site *Enterzone.*

AWARDS, HONORS: Fellowship, California Arts Council, 1997, for creative writing.

WRITINGS:

12 Bliss Street, St. Martin's Minotaur (New York, NY), 2003.

Author of the hyper-fiction *Girl Birth Water Death,* 1993. Stories have been published in the *Iowa Review, Epoch,* the *Quarterly, Carolina Quarterly, Massachusetts Review, Puerto del Sol,* and other journals. Contributor to the anthology *Coffeehouse: Writings from the Web.*

WORK IN PROGRESS: All Her Favorite Fruit, a novel.

SIDELIGHTS: Martha Conway is the author of the novel *12 Bliss Street.* In the work, Nicola, a thirty-one-year-old Web designer, is having a bad day. She has just received an eviction notice, has to put up with a terrible boss, and the guy she regularly flirts with seems nice but is really a serial killer. After attending her nightly exercise class, Nicola is kidnapped by the teens Dave and Davette. She figures out that the brains behind the kidnapping is her ex-husband, who is trying to get money out of her to pay off his loan sharks. Nicola decides to take matters into her own hands to outwit her captors and fix the problems in her life. *Books and Bytes* contributor Harriet Klausner claimed, "*12 Bliss Street* is a funny upbeat chick-lit mystery." A *Kirkus Reviews* contributor claimed, "Short-story writer Conway's jump to novel length is as lean and sexy as her cardio-kickboxing heroine."

BIOGRAPHICAL AND CRITICAL SOURCES:

PERIODICALS

Kirkus Reviews, May 1, 2003, review of *12 Bliss Street,* p. 644.

ONLINE

Bookloons, http://www.bookloons.com/ (October 26, 2003), Hillary Williamson, review of *12 Bliss Street.*

Books and Bites, http://www.booksnbytes.com/ (October 26, 2003), Harriet Klausner, review of *12 Bliss Street.*

Martha Conway Home Page, http://www.marthaconway.com (October 26, 2003).

Mystery Ink, http://www.mysteryinkonline.com/ (October 26, 2003), Elyse Dinh-McCrillis, review of *12 Bliss Street.*

Mystery Reader, http://www.themysteryreader.com/ (October 26, 2003), Jennifer Monahan Winberry, review of *12 Bliss Street.*

Sunset Beacon, http://www.sunsetbeacon.com/ (February 25, 2004), Jonathan Farrell, "First-Time Author Sets Stage in Sunset, Ocean Beach.*"

* * *

COOPER, Polly Wylly 1940-

PERSONAL: Born June 4, 1940, in Savannah, GA; daughter of John Cummings (an attorney) and Polly (maiden name, Chisholm; later surname, Brooks) Wylly; married Timothy S. B. Cooper, August 18, 1961; children: Jennifer, Julian. *Education:* Mount Vernon Junior College, B.A.; attended Jordanhill Training College (Glasgow, Scotland), and Redland Training College (Bristol, England); earned elementary education degree. *Religion:* Episcopal.

ADDRESSES: Home—519 Parkersburg Rd., Savannah, GA 31406; fax: 912-354-1375.

CAREER: Potter and gallery owner. Crabettes (music group), founding member.

WRITINGS:

A Visitor's Guide to Savannah, Wyrick and Co. (Charleston, SC), 1995.
Savannah Safari Walking Tour, privately printed, 1998.
Savannah Movie Memories, privately printed, 2000.
Isle of Hope, Wormsloe, and Bethesda, Arcadia Publishing (Charleston, SC), 2002.
Images of America: Beaufort, South Carolina, Arcadia Publishing (Charleston, SC), 2003.

* * *

COX, Julian

PERSONAL: Male. *Education:* Attended the University of Manchester and the University of Wales.

ADDRESSES: Office—J. Paul Getty Museum, 1200 Getty Center Dr., Los Angeles, CA 90049-1679.

CAREER: National Library of Wales, Aberystwyth, Wales, department of prints, drawings, and photographs, curator; National Museum of Photography, Film & Television, Bradford, CA, curator and interpreter; J. Paul Getty Museum, Los Angeles, CA, associate curator of photographs, 1992—.

WRITINGS:

(With Colin Ford) *Julia Margaret Cameron: The Complete Photographs,* contributions by Lukitsh and Philippa Wright, J. Paul Getty Museum (Los Angeles, CA), 2003.
Spirit into Matter: The Photographs of Edmund Teske, J. Paul Getty Museum (Los Angeles, CA) 2004.

SIDELIGHTS: Julian Cox, a curator at the J. Paul Getty Museum, is coauthor, with Colin Ford, of *Julia Margaret Cameron: The Complete Photographs.* Julia Margaret Cameron (1815-1879) became a photographer at the age of forty-eight, and concentrated mainly on potraits. In *Julia Margaret Cameron* Cox and Ford provide pictures of all 1,222 of Cameron's photographs, along with essays about the photographer and her work. "A highly worthy investment for all serious art and photography collections," commented Carolyn Kuebler in a *Library Journal* review. A *Publishers Weekly* contributor claimed, "This book is a necessary expense for any Victorianist or early photography buff."

BIOGRAPHICAL AND CRITICAL SOURCES:

PERIODICALS

Biography, summer, 2003, Judith Thurman, Frederick Kaufman, "Cameron, Julia Margaret," p. 520.
Booklist, March 1, 2003, Donna Seaman, review of *Julia Margaret Cameron: The Complete Photographs,* p. 1139.
Library Journal, May 1, 2003, Carolyn Kuebler, review of *Julia Margaret Cameron,* p. 109.
New York Times, April 27, 2003, Frederick Kaufman, "Cupid, Circe, and Jesus," p. 24.
Publishers Weekly, January 27, 2003, review of *Julia Margaret Cameron,* p. 252.
Times Literary Supplement, March 21, 2003, Claire Tomalin, "Don't Smile for the Camera," pp. 16-17.

ONLINE

J. Paul Getty Museum, http://www.getty.edu/ (October 26, 2003), review of *Julia Margaret Cameron.*
National Museum of Photography, Film, and Television, http://www.nmpft.org/uk/ (February 10, 2004), "An International Conference, Speaker Biographies.*"

* * *

CRANE, Harry 1914-1999

PERSONAL: Born April 23, 1914, in Brooklyn, NY; died of cancer, September 13, 1999, in Beverly Hills, CA; married; children: Barbara, Stephanie.

CAREER: Comedy writer for popular television shows of the 1950s; creator (with Joe Bigelow) of the series *The Honeymooners.*

WRITINGS:

Air Raid Wardens (screenplay), Metro-Goldwyn-Mayer, 1943.
The Harvey Girls (screenplay), Metro-Goldwyn-Mayer, 1946.
Song of the Thin Man (screenplay), Metro-Goldwyn-Mayer, 1947.

Comedy writer for television series, including *Cavalcade of Stars,* DuMont Network, 1951; *The Honeymooners,* Columbia Broadcasting System, Inc. (CBS), 1955-56; *The Jackie Gleason Show; Celebrity Roast;* and for special presentations, including the Academy Awards, Emmy Awards, and Golden Globe Awards broadcasts; writer for comedians such as Jimmy Durante, the Marx Brothers, Jerry Lewis, Milton Berle, and the duo Abbott and Costello; joke writer for other entertainers, including Frank Sinatra, Red Skelton, Perry Como, Dinah Shore, and Bing Crosby.

OBITUARIES:

PERIODICALS

Chicago Tribune, September 15, 1999, obituary by Associated Press, section 2, p. 10.
Los Angeles Times, September 15, 1999, obituary by Myrna Oliver, p. A22.
New York Times, September 20, 1999, obituary by Nick Ravo, p. A15.
Washington Post, September 17, 1999, p. B6.*

* * *

CREED, William S.

PERSONAL: Born in Detroit, MI; son of William and Mae (Card) Creed; married Jeanetta Imbler (divorced); children: Debra Creed Bazzo, William S., Jr., Lori Creed Powell. *Ethnicity:* "Caucasian." *Education:* Attended Wayne State University. *Politics:* Republican. *Religion:* Baptist. *Hobbies and other interests:* Sailing.

ADDRESSES: Office—64155 Van Dyke Ave., Suite 270, Washington, MI 48095. *E-mail*—wscreed@comcast.net.

CAREER: Writer. Formerly served as a member of a city council. *Military service:* Served in U.S. Air Force.

WRITINGS:

Comes the End: A Futuristic Thriller, House of Stuart Publishing, 2003.

Also author of *G.I. in Germany: A Guide to Servicemen and Their Families.*

WORK IN PROGRESS: The Final Day.

* * *

CROYDEN, Margaret

PERSONAL: Female. *Education:* Attended Hunter College, New York University, and Oxford University.

ADDRESSES: Home—New York, NY. *Agent*—c/o Author Mail, Faber & Faber, 19 Union Square W., New York, NY 10003.

CAREER: New Jersey City University, Jersey City, NJ, former professor of English literature; Columbia Broadcasting System, Inc. (CBS), former host of *Camera Three; New York Theatre Wire,* commentator and reviewer; theater critic; lecturer and speaker.

AWARDS, HONORS: Lifetime Achievement Award, New York League of Professional Theatre Women, 2003.

WRITINGS:

Lunatics, Lovers, and Poets: The Contemporary Experimental Theatre, McGraw-Hill (New York, NY), 1974.
In the Shadow of the Flame: Three Journeys, Continuum (New York, NY), 1993.
Conversations with Peter Brook: 1970-2000, Faber & Faber (New York, NY), 2003.

Contributor of articles to publications such as the *New York Times, Village Voice, American Theater, Antioch Review, Texas Quarterly,* and the *Transatlantic Review.*

SIDELIGHTS: In *Lunatics, Lovers, and Poets: The Contemporary Experimental Theatre,* theater critic Margaret Croyden discusses the contemporary experimental theater groups of the 1960s, including the Living and Open Theaters, Jerszy Grotowski, Peter Brook, Kaprow, Schechner's Performance Group, the Bread and Puppet Theater, and more. *Christian Science Monitor* contributor Barbara Nell Hymes noted, "Here is a rewarding book for the theater buff willing to persevere through some of the mazes of avant garde playmaking."

In her second book, *In the Shadow of the Flame: Three Journeys,* Croyden provides a look at three of her personal experiences in life. The first journey is to Poland to take part in an experimental theater group's exercise in a forest. The second journey is a visitation with the Hindu guru Baba Muktananda. The final journey is to Israel where Croyden talks to a spiritual teacher. In each journey Croyden overcomes part of her past and learns more about herself. A *Publishers Weekly* contributor claimed, "It is a mysterious and sometime dark chronicle, but it is one with a rare honesty and with a beauty that comes through."

In *Conversations with Peter Brook: 1970-2000,* Croyden has compiled thirty years worth of interviews with theater and film director Peter Brook. Croyden and Brook discuss his major works throughout the fourteen interviews that make up the book. A *Publishers Weekly* contributor concluded that in *Conversations with Peter Brook,* "Croyden shows how the craft of journalism can rise to the level of art itself by challenging an artist to reveal himself."

BIOGRAPHICAL AND CRITICAL SOURCES:

PERIODICALS

American Theatre, September, 2003, review of *Conversations with Peter Brook: 1970-2000,* p. 83.
Booklist, April 15, 2003, Jack Helbig, review of *Conversations with Peter Brook,* p. 1438.
Christian Science Monitor, April 17, 1974, Barbara Nell Hymes, review of *Lunatics, Lovers, and Poets: The Contemporary Experimental Theatre,* p. F5.
Kirkus Reviews, November 1, 1973, review of *Lunatics, Lovers, and Poets,* p. 1234.
Library Journal, April 1, 2003, Minnesota Schwartz, review of *Conversations with Peter Brook,* p. 102.
Los Angeles Times, March 13, 1994, Susan Salter Reynolds, review of *In the Shadow of the Flame: Three Journeys,* p. 6.
New Age Journal, May, 1994, Lisa Horvitz, review of *In the Shadow of the Flame,* p. 120.
New Yorker, July 7, 2003, Leo Carey, "Giving Direction," p. 17.
Publishers Weekly, October 11, 1993, review of *In the Shadow of the Flame,* p. 38; April 7, 2003, review of *Conversations with Peter Brook,* p. 61.
Sewanee Review, January, 1977, John Rees Moore, "Perspectives on Modern Drama," pp. 167-180.
Virgina Quarterly Review, summer, 1974, review of *Lunatics, Lovers, and Poets,* p. R107.

OTHER

New York Theatre Wire, http://www.nytheatre-wire.com/ (February 10, 2004), "Lifetime Achievement Award to Margaret Croyden."
Theater Mania, http://ibs.theatermania.com/ (October 26, 2003), Charles Wright, review of *Conversations with Peter Brook.* *

D

da CRUZ, Vera 1910-2002

PERSONAL: Born 1910; died May 29, 2002. *Education:* Trained as a midwife in Birmingham, England, and Hampshire, England. *Hobbies and other interests:* Gardening, needlework.

CAREER: Royal Hampshire Hospital, Hampshire, England, midwife, beginning 1936; worked as a tutor at Queen Charlotte's Hospital, London, England, and in Leeds, England; also worked abroad, including service as a hospital matron in Abu Dhabi and the United Arab Emirates and as a trainer in Kuwait. Central Midwives Board, member, 1969-72, and examiner.

MEMBER: Royal College of Midwives (member of council, 1957-78; vice president, 1973).

WRITINGS:

(Author of revisions) *Baillière's Midwives' Dictionary,* 4th edition, Baillière, Tindall & Cox (London, England), 1962, 6th edition (with Margaret E. Adams), Baillière Tindall (London, England), 1976.
(Author of revision) Mary Mayes, *Handbook of Midwifery,* 7th edition, Baillière, Tindall & Cassell (London, England), 1967.
C.M.B. Questions and How to Answer Them, Faber (London, England), 4th edition, 1969, 5th edition, 1977.

OBITUARIES:

PERIODICALS

Times (London, England), August 8, 2002.

ONLINE

RCM Midwives Journal Online, http://www.midwives.co.uk/ (January 2, 2003).*

*   *   *

DAHL, Curtis 1920-2004

OBITUARY NOTICE—See index for *CA* sketch: Born July 6, 1920, in New Haven, CT; died April 5, 2004, in Norton, MA. Educator and author. Dahl was an English professor emeritus at Wheaton College in Norton, Massachusetts. Educated at Yale, he earned his doctorate there in 1945. After working for two years at the publishing house Dodd, Mead & Co. in New York City, he joined the faculty at the University of Tennessee in 1946. He next accepted a post as an assistant professor at Wheaton College in 1948, rising to professor of English in 1958 and Samuel Valentine Cole Professor of English in 1966; Dahl retired in 1991. A former president of the New England College English Association and the New England American Studies Association, he was the author of *Robert Montgomery Bird* (1963) and was an editor and contributor to several other scholarly books. His last publication was *Around the World in 500 Days: The Circumnavigation of the Merchant Bark Charles Stewart, 1883-1884, Recounted with Zest and Detail* (1999), which he edited.

OBITUARIES AND OTHER SOURCES:

PERIODICALS

Chronicle of Higher Education, May 7, 2004, p. A44.

DALLAS, Roland

PERSONAL: Male.

ADDRESSES: Office—*Foreign Report,* Jane's Information Group, Sentinel House, 163 Brighton Rd., Coulsdon, Surrey CR5 2YH, England.

CAREER: Journalist. *Foreign Report,* England, editor, 1982—; former Reuters correspondent.

WRITINGS:

The Economist Pocket Africa ("*Economist* Economic Surveys" series), Hamish Hamilton (London, England), 1994.
Pocket Latin America: Profiles, Facts, and Figures about Latin America ("*Economist* Economic Surveys" series), Profile Books (London, England), 1994.
Pocket Middle East and North Africa ("*Economist* Economic Surveys" series), Profile Books (London, England), 1995.
King Hussein: A Life on the Edge, (London, England), 1998, Fromm International (New York, NY), 1999.

SIDELIGHTS: British journalist Roland Dallas has been the editor of the world affairs newsletter *Foreign Report* since 1982. Dallas has written a number of guides as part of a series created by the *Economist,* and he has also penned a biography of the late king of Jordan.

In *King Hussein: A Life on the Edge,* Dallas documents Hussein's long reign, from his rise to the throne in 1953 until his death from cancer in 1999. He was known as a peacemaker, and over the decades, any acts of force used by Hussein appeared tame in comparison to those employed by many of Jordan's neighbors. Although there have been other biographies of Hussein, Dallas's was the first published after his death.

Charles Tripp wrote in the *Times Literary Supplement* that "Hussein's death and the succession of his son, Abdullah, raise questions about the future of Jordan. Having ruled over the kingdom for more than forty-five years, Hussein's imprint on the political life of Jordan has been a powerful one. The mark of the autocrat is strong, and . . . there is a feeling that the whole apparatus exists on the late king's sufferance."

At the age of eighteen, Hussein took over for his incapacitated father. He was a moderate who kept open channels with Israel, the Palestinians, and other Arab countries, and who was aided by the United States and Britain, as well as Israel, because Hussein was perceived as being a buffer to Egypt, Syria, and Saudi Arabia. Dallas describes Hussein's rule as a "quasi-democracy." Hussein married his fourth wife, American Lisa Halaby, whom he named Queen Noor, in 1978. A *Publishers Weekly* contributor called the biography "astute, dramatic," and interesting "for the light it sheds on conflict among the Arabs—especially the strife between the king and PLO leader Yasser Arafat, who, after 1967, set up a Palestinian state-within-a-state in Jordan." *Library Journal*'s Ruth K. Baacke called *King Hussein* "a clearly written, objective, and focused account of Hussein's complex life."

BIOGRAPHICAL AND CRITICAL SOURCES:

PERIODICALS

Booklist, August, 1999, Mary Carroll, review of *King Hussein: A Life on the Edge,* p. 1980.
Library Journal, September 15, 1999, Ruth K. Baacke, review of *King Hussein,* p. 90.
Publishers Weekly, August 9, 1999, review of *King Hussein,* p. 333.
Times Literary Supplement, February 12, 1999, Charles Tripp, review of *King Hussein.**

*   *   *

DAVEY, H. E.

PERSONAL: Male. *Education:* Trained in the *shin-shin-toitsu-do* form of Japanese yoga in the United States and Japan; also studied the art of brush writing with Kobara Ranseki. *Hobbies and other interests:* Sports cars.

ADDRESSES: Office—Center for Japanese Cultural Arts, Sennin Foundation, Inc., 1053 San Pablo Ave., Albany, CA 94706.

CAREER: Teacher of Japanese arts, including martial arts, yoga, and calligraphy. Sennin Foundation, Inc., Albany, CA, president; also founder and director of Center for Japanese Cultural Arts. Kokusai Budoin, councilor at headquarters in Tokyo, Japan, director of U.S. branch, and teacher of *nihon jujutsu* and *kobudo.* Art work in the form of brush writing is exhibited annually in Japan.

MEMBER: Shudokan Martial Arts Association (member of board of directors), Tempu Society.

AWARDS, HONORS: Numerous awards for brush writing.

WRITINGS:

The Way of the Universe, Sennin Organization Headquarters (Berkeley, CA), 1985.
Unlocking the Secrets of Aiki-jujutsu, Masters Press (Indianapolis, IN), 1997.
Brush Meditation: A Japanese Way to Mind and Body Harmony, Stone Bridge Press (Berkeley, CA), 1999.
(With Ann H. Kameoka) *The Japanese Way of the Flower: Ikebana as Moving Meditation,* Stone Bridge Press (Berkeley, CA), 2000.
Japanese Yoga: The Way of Dynamic Meditation, Stone Bridge Press (Berkeley, CA), 2001.
Living the Japanese Arts and Ways: Forty-five Paths to Meditation and Beauty, Stone Bridge Press (Berkeley, CA), 2003.

Contributor of articles and art work to periodicals, including *Karate Kung-Fu Illustrated, Furyu: Budo Journal of Classical Japanese Martial Arts and Culture, Journal of Asian Martial Arts, Body Mind Spirit, Yoga Journal, Hokubei Mainichi, Nichibei Times, Gendo, Excellence—About Porsche, Porsche Panorama,* and *Miata.* Editor of *Michi Online: Journal of Japanese Cultural Arts.*

BIOGRAPHICAL AND CRITICAL SOURCES:

PERIODICALS

Publishers Weekly, October 28, 2002, review of *Living the Japanese Arts and Ways: Forty-five Paths to Meditation and Beauty,* p. 66.

ONLINE

Michi Online: Journal of Japanese Cultural Arts, http://www.michionline.org/ (spring, 2000), Dave Lowry, review of *Brush Meditation: A Japanese Way to Mind and Body Harmony.*
Spirituality and Health: Spiritual Practices for Human Being, http://www.spiritualityhealth.com/ (January 21, 2003), Frederic Brussat and Mary Ann Brussat, review of *The Japanese Way of the Flower: Ikebana as Moving Meditation.**

*   *   *

DEARIE, John

PERSONAL: Born in Corpus Christi, TX; married Stefanie, 2001. *Education:* Attended University of Notre Dame and Columbia University School of International and Public Affairs.

ADDRESSES: Home—Wappingers Falls, NY. *Office*—Financial Services Volunteer Corps, 10 East 53rd St., 24th Floor, New York, NY 10022. *Agent*—Alice Martell, Martell Agency, 545 Madison Ave., 7th Floor, New York, NY 10022.

CAREER: Writer and finance professional. Federal Reserve Bank of New York, held various positions in Banking Studies, Foreign Exchange, and Policy and Analysis for nine years; Financial Services Forum, vice president and chief policy officer; Financial Services Volunteer Corps (FSVC), managing director.

WRITINGS:

Love and Other Recreational Sports, Viking (New York, NY), 2003.

Speechwriter for New York Federal Reserve Bank presidents E. Gerald Corrigan and William J. McDonough.

SIDELIGHTS: John Dearie arrived in New York City for a job on Wall Street and spent the next fifteen years as a young single professional enjoying city life.

In addition to his career as a novelist, Dearie is the managing director of the Financial Services Volunteer Corps (FSVC), a non-profit organization that recruits senior executives to volunteer on technical assistance missions to developing countries. He and wife Steffanie have left Manhattan to live in nearby Wappingers Falls, NY. His writing experience includes short stories and speech writing. Taking Mark Twain's advice to "write what you know," his first novel, *Love and Other Recreational Sports,* is a romantic romp that reveals what men really think about women, relationships, sex, and commitment along the way to true love and happiness.

Main character Jack Lafferty is good looking, thirty-five, a successful Wall Street banker, and unhappy in love when his fiancée cheats on him three weeks before their wedding. After swearing off both women and drink, he meets Sarah Mitchell—the woman everyone says is his perfect mate. An embittered Jack goes to great lengths to avoid Sarah. When he finally realizes the truth of his love, Sarah is no longer available. How this relationship evolves, or rather does not, is the heart of this contemporary romantic tale of a modern guy giving up on love and the surprises that follow his vow of abstinence.

"*Love and Other Recreational Sports* isn't a fictional map into the psyches of men," stated reviewer April Umminger in *USA Today.* "If anything, this light-hearted read revives the rules of dating." Harriet Klausner of the *Best Reviews* considers Jack to be a "great character whose lack of self deprecating humor and overall depressing outlook over his love life makes him seem real." A reviewer for *Publishers Weekly* credited Dearie with "an eye for amusing details and [described] the book as a spirited ode to New York City."

When asked about how men relate to women, Dearie told Umminger that "relationships are one of the only ways that men can show their vulnerability without risking their masculinity. There's a common misperception that all men do is grunt at each other when they get together. I wanted to show that there is emotion and feeling beneath the surface. It's like a type of code, but it's there between men." About his first novel, Dearie said, "We've been hearing an awful lot in recent years about single, young, professional women. I had to ask myself, 'Where are the guys?' One of my main reasons for writing this was to give voice to the male experience."

BIOGRAPHICAL AND CRITICAL SOURCES:

PERIODICALS

Library Journal, June 1, 2003, Elizabeth Mellett, review of *Love and Other Recreational Sports,* p. 164.
People, August 4, 2003, Dan Jewel, review of *Love and Other Recreational Sports,* p. 41.
Publishers Weekly, April 14, 2003, review of *Love and Other Recreational Sports,* p. 46.

ONLINE

Best Reviews, http://thebestreviews.com/ (March 28, 2004), Harriet Klausner, review of *Love and Other Recreational Sports.*
USA Today, http://www.usatoday.com/ (March 28, 2004), April Umminger, review of *Love and Other Recreational Sports.**

*   *   *

DENIS, Rafael Cardoso 1964-
(Rafael Cardoso)

PERSONAL: Born June 4, 1964, in Rio de Janeiro, Brazil; son of Roger (a physician) and Nadya (a translator; maiden name, Cardoso) Denis. *Education:* Johns Hopkins University, B.A., 1985; Universidade Federal do Rio de Janeiro, M.A., 1991; Courtauld Institute of Art (London, England), Ph.D., 1995.

ADDRESSES: Agent—c/o Author Mail, Editora Record, Rua Argentina 171, Rio de Janeiro, Brazil 20921-380. *E-mail*—rafaelcd@dsg.puc-rio.br.

CAREER: Universidade do Estado do Rio de Janeiro, Rio de Janeiro, Brazil, adjunct professor, 1996-2000; Pontifícia Universidade Católica, Rio de Janeiro, assistant professor, 2000—.

WRITINGS:

(Editor, with Colin Trodd, and contributor) *Art and the Academy in the Nineteenth Century,* Rutgers University Press (Piscataway, NJ), 2000.

Uma introdução à história do design, Editora Edgard Blücher, 2000.

A maneira negra (fiction), Editora Record (Rio de Janeiro, Brazil), 2000.

Controle remoto (novel), Editora Record (Rio de Janeiro, Brazil), 2002.

Some writings appear under the name Rafael Cardoso.

BIOGRAPHICAL AND CRITICAL SOURCES:

PERIODICALS

Victorian Studies, autumn, 2001, Joy Sperling, review of *Art and the Academy in the Nineteenth Century,* p. 135.

*   *   *

DENT, David J.

PERSONAL: Male. *Education:* Morehouse College, B.A. (political science), 1981; Columbia University, M.S. (journalism), 1982.

ADDRESSES: Office—New York University, Department of Journalism, Arthur Carter Hall, 10 Washington Pl., New York, NY 10003; fax: 212-995-4148. *E-mail*—dd2@nyu.edu.

CAREER: Journalist, educator, and author. Has worked as a television reporter for the American Broadcasting Companies, Inc. (ABC); New York University, New York, NY, associate professor of journalism and mass communication. Contributing correspondent to *Black Entertainment Television News;* has also appeared as a commentator on *Court TV.*

AWARDS, HONORS: Award of Excellence, National Association of Black Journalists, 1990, for television news series "Brothers in Arms"; Freedom Forum Foundation Grant for Journalists in Education, 1990; Teaching Fellowship for Outstanding Broadcast Journalism Professors, Poynter Institute for Media Studies, 1992; Griot Award, New York Association of Black Journalists, 1992, for "The New Black Suburbs"; Golden Dozen Award for Excellence in Teaching and

Service, New York University, 1993; Journalism Award for Excellence in Reporting, Print/Minority Audience, Lincoln University, 1993.

WRITINGS:

In Search of Black America: Discovering the African American Dream, Simon & Schuster (New York, NY), 2000.

Contributor to *New York Times, Washington Post, Vibe, Black Renaissance, Playboy, Essence, Black Enterprise,* and *Christian Science Monitor.*

SIDELIGHTS: When journalist David J. Dent was assigned to write an article about the "black rage" that resulted in riots in Brooklyn, New York, in 1991, he decided to do his research by hanging out on a Brooklyn street corner frequented by black youths. Instead of being confronted with angry young men, however, Dent discovered conversations about sports, values, money, music, women, and careers. "They were not victims waiting for Jesse Jackson and Louis Farrakhan . . . to rescue them," wrote Dent in his book, *In Search of Black America: Discovering the African American Dream.* "Nor did they possess a blind optimism and belief in the purity of American meritocracy in the vein of Shelby Steele or Thomas Sowell. Their views were harsh, masculine and real."

Dent realized he had discovered a part of black culture seldom seen in mainstream media. He began a four-year voyage of discovery across the nation to investigate the lifestyles and attitudes of what he calls the "secluded spaces of black culture in America"— African Americans of the middle and upper-middle classes. During 350 hours of interviews, he talked to business people, artists, bounty hunters, bowlers, teachers, and preachers, avoiding celebrities and hostile, inner-city youths most commonly portrayed to the general public.

Of these efforts, Amy Alexander wrote in *Black Issues Book Review:* "Dent plumbs the hopes and dreams of many blacks who have 'made it' economically, but whose spirits are still dampened by white racism and discrimination on some level or another. To his credit, Dent does a fabulous job of telling their stories." A

Publishers Weekly reviewer also commented, "Candid and consistently engaging, Dent's work contributes to a better understanding of the role of race in American life."

BIOGRAPHICAL AND CRITICAL SOURCES:

BOOKS

Dent, David J., *In Search of Black America: Discovering the African American Dream,* Simon & Schuster (New York, NY), 2000.

PERIODICALS

Black Issues Book Review, July 2000, Amy Alexander, review of *In Search of Black America: Discovering the African American Dream,* p. 52.
Booklist, February 15, 2000, Mary Carroll, review of *In Search of Black America,* p. 1058.
Essence, February 2000, review of *In Search of Black America,* p. 60.
Library Journal, January 2000, Stephen L. Hupp, review of *In Search of Black America,* p. 139.
Publishers Weekly, December 6, 1999, review of *In Search of Black America,* p. 60.
Rocky Mountain News (Denver, CO), February 20, 2000, Laurence Washington, "Search Offers Clear View of Black America," p. 3E.*

*   *   *

DEWAR, Margaret
See QUINTON, Ann

*   *   *

DIAMOND, John 1907-2004

OBITUARY NOTICE—See index for *CA* sketch: Born April 30, 1907, in Leeds, England; died April 3, 2004, in Little Chalfont, Buckinghamshire, England. Politician, accountant, and author. Diamond was a Labour Party member of Parliament and later Social Democratic Party leader who held important governmental posts in which he influenced the British economy.

After attending Leeds Grammar School, he passed qualifying exams to become a chartered accountant in 1931 and set up his own firm, John Diamond & Co. Though he had not originally intended to do so, he became involved in politics and in 1945 won the Blackley, Manchester, seat under the Labour Party ticket. He lost the election in 1951, working as chair and managing director of a chain of theaters until reentering Parliament when he won the Gloucester seat in 1957. Here he remained until 1970, during which time served in the late 1960s as chief secretary to the Treasury and, from 1968 to 1970, as member of the Cabinet. Gaining the title of Baron in 1970, Diamond joined the House of Lords that year. Here he served as royal chairman of the Royal Commission on the Distribution of Income and Wealth in the late 1970s, and of the Industry and Parliament Trust from 1976 to 1982. When the Social Democratic Party was formed, Diamond left the Labour Party and led the SDP until 1988. But when the SDP gradually merged back into the Labour Party, Diamond left the House of Lords and, somewhat reticently, returned to his old party in 1995. Throughout his career, Diamond was admired by politicians of all political persuasions for his knowledge of finances, his organization and discipline, and his courtesy. He managed to avoid most political divisiveness in government, up until his years with the SDP. Diamond was the author of several books on economics, including *Public Expenditure in Practice* (1975), *Lower Incomes* (1978), and *Fifth Report on the Standing Reference* (1979).

OBITUARIES AND OTHER SOURCES:

PERIODICALS

Independent (London, England), April 6, 2004, p. 35.
Times (London, England), April 5, 2004, p. 25.

*   *   *

DINELLO, Paul

PERSONAL: Male. Education: Attended DePaul University.

ADDRESSES: Agent—c/o Author Mail, Hyperion Editorial Dept., 77 West 66th St., 11th Fl., New York, NY 10023.

CAREER: Comedian, actor, writer. Worked for All-state Insurance Co. and at the Chicago Mercantile Exchange; performed with Second City. Actor in the plays *Stitches, Jackie's Kosher Khristmas,* and *Jackie's Valentine's Day Massacre,* and in films, including *When; Plump Fiction,* Rhino Films; *Straight Talk,* Hollywood Pictures; *The Howard Beach Story* (television movie), National Broadcasting Company, Inc. (NBC); and *The Untouchables* (television), Paramount.

WRITINGS:

(With Amy Sedaris and Stephen Colbert) *Wigfield: The Can-Do Town That Just May Not,* photographs by Todd Oldham, Hyperion (New York, NY), 2003.

Creator (and actor), with Amy Sedaris and Stephen Colbert, of the series *Exit 57* and *Strangers with Candy,* both for Comedy Central. Dinello, Sedaris, and Colbert also adapted *Wigfield: The Can-Do Town That Just May Not* as a performance piece, and they adapted *Strangers with Candy* as a 2003 film.

SIDELIGHTS: Paul Dinello and Amy Sedaris first tried out for Second City in 1988. They were both accepted and found themselves on tour with Stephen Colbert, who would complete the trio that went on to success with such Comedy Central series as *Exit 57* and *Strangers with Candy.* Dinello and Colbert, known to many for his contribution as a correspondent on *The Daily Show,* did not hit it off immediately, but something clicked between them when they wrote a Christmas show for McDonald's employees. The three traveled with Second City for two years, creating their zany characters and off-the-wall skits.

By 1994, they were in New York City, where they created *Exit 57.* The successful series was followed by *Strangers with Candy,* in which Sedaris plays Jerri Blank, a forty-six-year-old woman who returns to high school where she corrupts the youngsters while wearing outdated clothing. Dinello plays art teacher Mr. Jellineck, and Colbert is Mr. Noblet, a history teacher with a passion for Hummel figurines. The show is a satire of the after-school specials of the 1970s, but in this case, it is about making the wrong choices, rather than the right ones. The creators planned to push the limits even further with the film adaptation.

Dinello and Sedaris had also once done a stage bit about a worm and decided to write a book featuring that character. They pitched it to Hyperion, but the idea of a children's book about a worm in the bottom of a tequila bottle was not approved. Instead the publisher accepted their concept of a book about a town called Wigfield.

Colbert, who was asked to collaborate, had visited the town of Jefferson, West Virginia, while doing a story about eccentrics for *The Daily Show.* It was the perfect inspiration for the book, a town that consisted of a stretch of strip clubs and used car parts stores that had been incorporated as a tax shelter. In the fictional town, murders are commonplace, toxic waste abounds, the police chief is an arsonist, one mayor is a mentally challenged fudgeaholic, while another is a stripper, and all of the members of the town council own porn shops. The town is located at the base of a dam that the government wants to destroy to save the salmon.

Designer and photographer Todd Oldham put the three in costumes to create multiple characters, images of which are included in the book. Colbert, as Russell Hokes, a highway line painter who is writing his first book, narrates and also plays two woman who appear mostly naked. Dinello is Lenare Degrout, the town taxidermist, and Sedaris plays various roles, including Mrs. Grimmet, poetry-writing teen Carla Port Hollinger, and Cinnamon the stripper.

Book reviewer Steve Wilson called *Wigfield: The Can-Do Town That Just May Not* "smart and often hysterical," adding that "not since the authors' sitcom *Strangers with Candy* has sleaze been so hilarious." A *Publishers Weekly* reviewer called it "one of those rare works of satire that combine creative form, uproariously funny text, and a painfully sharp underpinning of social criticism."

The authors adapted the book to a stage show that is part book review, part performance, and took it on the road. They donned the freaky costumes created by Oldham, and by using wigs, various voices, and makeup, portrayed the characters of the book. Jacki Lyden, of National Public Radio's *Weekend Edition,* said that "this play about a fictitious backwoods crossroad mines the same territory as *Our Town,* or *Spoon River Anthology,* or as—Dare we say it?—Lake Wobegon always does."

BIOGRAPHICAL AND CRITICAL SOURCES:

PERIODICALS

Book, May-June, 2003, Steve Wilson, review of *Wigfield: The Can-Do Town That Just May Not,* p. 76.

Boston Globe, June 13, 2003, Christopher Muther, review of *Wigfield,* p. C1.

Chicago Sun-Times, April 27, 2003, Darel Jevens, "Wigging Out" (interview), p. 1.

Los Angeles Times, July 27, 2003, Diane Haithman, review of *Wigfield* (stage show) and interview, p. E37.

Publishers Weekly, April 28, 2003, review of *Wigfield,* p. 46.

ONLINE

Weekend Edition, http://www.npr.org/ (May 31, 2003), Jacki Lyden, interview with Dinello, Sedaris, and Colbert.*

*   *   *

DOBIE, Kathy

PERSONAL: Female.

ADDRESSES: Agent—c/o Author Mail, Dial Press, Bantam Dell Publishing Group, Random House, 1745 Broadway, New York, NY 10019.

CAREER: Writer.

WRITINGS:

The Only Girl in the Car: A Memoir, Dial Press (New York, NY), 2003.

Contributor to periodicals and Web sites, including *Village Voice, Harper's, Vibe, Tikkun, Salon.com,* and *Pacific News Service.*

SIDELIGHTS: Kathy Dobie is a respected writer who published an account of her teen years in the 1960s in *The Only Girl in the Car: A Memoir.* Dobie also wrote about this period of her life in *Harper's* in 1996. Both her article and her memoir relate her longing for sexual relations from a young age and her loss of virginity at fourteen years old.

Dobie grew up in Hamden, Connecticut, in a large, loving Catholic family. Her father was an administrator at Yale University in nearby New Haven, and her mother was a homemaker. Dobie was the third child and eldest girl and helped with the care of her younger siblings.

In the *Harper's* article, she wrote, "When I was in my teens, my mother told me that I didn't seem to like being held or touched as a child—I cringed, I grew stiff—so she and my father made a decision not to. They would wait until I came to them. And they waited and waited. For it seems the touch I wanted wasn't familial, wasn't even 'loving.' That affection was for good little girls, and it made me feel like an imposter, made me lonelier."

Dobie's first infatuation came in fourth grade, with the kind of boy she was destined to be drawn to. He had a shaved head and wore Nazi insignias and a trench coat. "He was my ally in a world that seemed increasingly cold," Dobie remembered. Her lust was fed by the large pornography collections of a family for which she babysat. While on a family vacation, she sat in the rear window of the motor home and flirted with the male drivers of cars and trucks that passed by. Two of them followed the family to a campground but left in a huff when the child who had promised more turned out to be merely a tease.

But Dobie's sexuality was obvious to the men and boys who saw her, including her father's own friends. When she made the decision to lose her virginity, she sat on her front lawn with her dog, wearing a halter top, hiphugger jeans, and platform shoes until a man came along who would relieve her of it. She was fourteen. But Dobie wanted boys her own age, and she began to frequent the Teen Center, just blocks from her house, and hang out with the bad boys who congregated there. She was often the only girl in the car. These boys had girlfriends who wouldn't give them sex, and Dobie soon became the one to satisfy their needs, infuriating the girls and gaining her a reputation as a promiscuous teen.

She was warned of the danger she was inviting, particularly by a group of black friends, but Dobie did not heed the warnings. She became a frequent partner of a boy she calls Joey, a handsome, motorcycle-jacket wearing young hood who worked in his father's gas station. On the night around which the memoir revolves, Dobie and Joey were in his car with three other boys, along with a bottle of gin and a case of beer. They stopped the car, and the three got out so that Dobie and Joey could have sex. But when they were finished, Joey told her he wanted them to see how good she was.

"It doesn't matter what was said," Dobie wrote in the article, "only that it came out of Joey's mouth and that no other world existed for me that night—just those boys, that car in the snowy woods. That was the moment when everything that had been said about me became real, when I gave up."

News of that episode quickly spread, and the kids at the Teen Center screamed insults at her and were intent on beating her up. The director drove her home before that happened, and Dobie never returned. Instead, she took mature men for lovers, and at sixteen she worked in the kitchens at Yale, unloading trucks, cleaning, and cooking to save enough to move to New York. She was again the only girl on the crew. But in her hometown, she suffered taunts and threats for years after the incident.

In her article, Dobie writes of men who were kind to her, of a Yale student she loved but with whom she never had sex. "A grizzled, gray-haired biker guessed something about me," she wrote, "and when we pulled out of my parents' driveway, he stopped the bike, turned to me, and said, 'Kath, you've got to hold on to me or you'll fall off the bike. I don't know what the boys did to you, but I'm not going to do anything, okay?' And he would sweep me far away from Hamden and into farm fields. After all our rides, we went to his rented room and drank tea."

Rebecca Denton reviewed the book for *BookPage* online, noting that "What's striking about the book is that Dobie . . . delves so honestly and fearlessly into a young girl's sexual experiences and attitudes. She doesn't shy away from the image she presents of herself as a reckless, eager teen with no regard for reputation or restraint."

In an online review for *Charlotte Observer,* Courtney Devores felt that Dobie's memoir should be discussed in light of the fact that many of the same double standards that existed during Dobie's girlhood continue to exist today. "While she admittedly chose her sexually curious path," said Devores, "she was undoubtedly punished for it in a way a boy her age would never be."

Philly.com's Carole Goldberg wrote that "this is a cautionary tale, a dizzying mixture of sunshine and shadows, lyrical and tough-minded. Dobie beautifully evokes the closeness of family life and the restlessness that drives some teenagers to fight free, no matter the cost. Her memoir explains the sexual education of Kathy D. in a way that earns the utmost respect, the very thing she lost that night in that car full of boys."

BIOGRAPHICAL AND CRITICAL SOURCES:

BOOKS

Dobie, Kathy, *The Only Girl in the Car: A Memoir,* Dial Press (New York, NY), 2003.

PERIODICALS

Booklist, March 15, 2003, Kristine Huntley, review of *The Only Girl in the Car: A Memoir,* pp. 1257-1258.
Harper's August, 1996, Kathy Dobie, "The Only Girl in the Car: A Remembrance of Promiscuity," pp. 42-49.
Kirkus Reviews, December 15, 2002, review of *The Only Girl in the Car,* p. 1818.
Library Journal, February 15, 2003, Nancy R. Ives, review of *The Only Girl in the Car,* pp. 138-139.
People, March 17, 2003, Arion Berger, review of *The Only Girl in the Car,* p. 45.
Publishers Weekly, December 9, 2002, review of *The Only Girl in the Car,* p. 70.
Women's Review of Books, June, 2003, Leora Tanenbaum, review of *The Only Girl in the Car,* pp. 6-8.

ONLINE

BookPage, http://www.bookpage.com/ (July 1, 2003), Rebecca Denton, review of *The Only Girl in the Car.*

Charlotte Observer, http://www.charlotte.com/ (June 27, 2003), Courtney Devores, review of *The Only Girl in the Car.*

Philly.com, http://www.philly.com/ (March 12, 2003), Carole Goldberg, review of *The Only Girl in the Car.*

Salon.com, http://www.salon.com/ (March 19, 2003), Laura Miller, review of *The Only Girl in the Car.**

*   *   *

DOLIN, Eric Jay

PERSONAL: Married, wife's name, Jennifer; children: Lily, Harrison. *Education:* Brown University, B.A., 1983; Massachusetts Institute of Technology, Ph.D. *Religion:* Jewish. *Hobbies and other interests:* Stamp collecting.

ADDRESSES: Home—Marblehead, MA. *Agent*—c/o Author Mail, University of Massachusetts Press, P.O. Box 429, Amherst, MA 01004.

CAREER: Independent scholar and freelance writer. National Marine Fisheries Service, fishery-policy analyst. Also worked for the U.S. Environmental Protection Agency as environmental consultant and program manager.

AWARDS, HONORS: American Association for the Advancement of Science Writing Fellow, *Business Week;* Pew Research Fellow, Harvard Law School; Knauss Sea Grant Fellow, U.S. National Oceanic and Atmospheric Administration.

WRITINGS:

The U.S. Fish and Wildlife Service ("Know Your Government" series), Chelsea House Publishers (Langhorne, PA), 1989.

(Editor, with Lawrence E. Susskind and J. William Breslin) *International Environmental Treaty Making,* Program on Negotiation at Harvard Law School (Cambridge, MA), 1992.

(With Bob Dumaine) *The Duck Stamp Story: Art, Conservation, History,* Krause Publications (Iola, WI), 2000.

(Author of text) *Smithsonian Book of National Wildlife Refuges,* photography by John Hollingsworth and Karen Hollingsworth, Smithsonian Institution Press (Washington, DC), 2003.

Snakehead: A Fish Out of Water, Smithsonian Books (Washington, DC), 2003.

Political Waters: The Long, Dirty, Contentious, Incredibly Expensive but Eventually Triumphant History of Boston Harbor; A Unique Environmental Success Story, University of Massachusetts Press (Amherst, MA), 2004.

Has published numerous articles on environmental topics in journals, magazines, and newspapers.

WORK IN PROGRESS: A history of whaling in America, for Norton.

SIDELIGHTS: Eric Jay Dolin is a writer with a passion for the conservation of wildlife. In 2003 Dolin authored a book about America's unique national wildlife refuge system. The Smithsonian Institute published the book on the occasion of the refuges' centennial celebration. Dolin has written other books and numerous articles on topics relating to nature and the environment, among them a book on the extensive environmental cleanup of Boston Harbor.

Dolin's book *The U.S. Fish and Wildlife Service* was published in 1989 as part of an extensive series of books called "Know Your Government." It explains about the Fish and Wildlife Service's history and its purpose as a federal agency. For instance, the agency has in the past launched a successful recovery program for the whooping crane.

The Duck Stamp Story: Art, Conservation, History, published in 2000, chronicles one of the most successful conservation programs in history. In the 1930s Congress adopted the Migratory Bird Hunting Stamp Act. Since then the federal government has been able to add five million acres to the national wildlife refuge system by revenues from the sale of duck stamps. The book is also a reference source for readers interested in the value of their stamps.

The research and writing of *The Duck Stamp Story* launched Dolin's interest in the refuges and led to the creation of the *Smithsonian Book of National Wildlife*

Refuges. The 258-page book, filled with pictures by *National Geographic* photographers John and Karen Hollingsworth, tells how Pelican Island Reserve was established in 1903 by President Theodore Roosevelt as the nation's first refuge, launching a system that today consists of 538 sanctuaries overseen by the U.S. Fish and Wildlife Service. Providing a detailed history of the system of national wildlife refuges, the book also chronicles the many challenges and struggles the system has had to face over the years. Robert Engel wrote in *Environment* that the *Smithsonian Book of National Wildlife Refuges* is not only "a handsome coffee table book" but also "an informative history" whose analysis is thorough. Nancy Moeckel, reviewing the book for *Library Journal,* called it "an outstanding book" that "undoubtedly will serve the purpose of educating the public and garnering more support from them."

In *Snakehead: A Fish Out of Water,* Dolin documents a near ecological disaster that took place in Maryland in 2002. A local resident dumped a couple of large northern Chinese snakehead fish into a backwash gravel pond in Crofton, Maryland. The fish is a carnivorous predator that not only eats every other fish in its area but is also capable of migrating over relatively long stretches of land. By the time the Maryland Department of Natural Resources poisoned the pond, the fish had already reproduced on a large scale. Apart from the snakehead's discovery and elimination, Dolin also looks at media reactions. Adrian Barnett, reviewing *Snakehead* in *New Scientist,* lauded the book's "fine combination of wildlife biology, interviews and news material."

BIOGRAPHICAL AND CRITICAL SOURCES:

PERIODICALS

Booklist, April 15, 2003, Nancy Bent, review of *Smithsonian Book of National Wildlife Refuges,* p. 1430.

Book Report, January-February, 1990, Sister Alma Marie Walls, review of *The U.S. Fish and Wildlife Service,* p. 64-65.

Environment, January-February, 2004, Robert E. Engel, review of *Smithsonian Book of National Wildlife Refuges,* p. 43.

Library Journal, March 1, 2003, Nancy Moeckel, review of *Smithsonian Book of National Wildlife Refuges,* p. 113.

Los Angeles Times, November 4, 2003, David Lukas, review of *Smithsonian Book of National Wildlife Refuges,* section F, p. 9.

New Scientist, Volume 80, number 2422, 2003, Adrian Barnett, "Attack of the Killer Fish," p. 54.

Post-Standard (Syracuse, NY), August 17, 2000, J. Michael Kelly, "The Stamp of Approval," section D, p. 8.

Publishers Weekly, February 17, 2003, review of *Smithsonian Book of National Wildlife Refuges,* p. 67.

Voice of Youth Advocates, Volume 12, number 3, 1989, Joel Shoemaker, review of *The U.S. Fish and Wildlife Service,* p. 170.*

*   *   *

DOLNICK, Barrie 1960-

PERSONAL: Born June 17, 1960. *Education:* University of Wisconsin, degree in business administration.

ADDRESSES: Agent—c/o Author Mail, Harmony Books, 1745 Broadway, New York, NY 10019. *E-mail*—execmystic@aol.com.

CAREER: Writer, consultant, astrologer, and tarot card reader. Worked in marketing in London, England, and New York, NY; founder of Executive Mystic Services, 1993.

WRITINGS:

Simple Spells for Love: Ancient Practices for Emotional Fulfillment, Harmony Books (New York, NY), 1994.

Simple Spells for Success: Ancient Practices for Creating Abundance and Prosperity, Harmony Books (New York, NY), 1996.

(With Julia Condon and Donna Limoges) *Sexual Bewitchery: And Other Ancient Feminine Wiles,* illustrated by Julia Condon, Avon Books (New York, NY), 1998.

The Executive Mystic: Psychic Power Tools for Success, HarperBusiness (New York, NY), 1998.

(With Donald Baack) *How to Write a Love Letter: Putting What's in Your Heart on Paper,* Harmony Books (New York, NY), 2000.

Simple Spells for Hearth and Home: Ancient Practices for Creating Harmony, Peace, and Abundance, Harmony Books (New York, NY), 2000.

(Illustrator) Vivienne Flesher, *Zodiac Memory Book of Days,* Galison Books, 2001.

Instructions for Your Discontent: How Bad Times Can Make Life Better, foreword by Sarah Ban Breathnach, Simple Abundance Press/Scribner (New York, NY), 2003.

Minerva Rules Your Future: Goddess-Given Advice for Smart Moves at Work, Harmony Books (New York, NY), 2003.

WORK IN PROGRESS: Astrobabe: The Planetary Powers of Romance; Dreambabe: Understanding Dreams—and Using Them to Make Your Dreams Come True; Karmababe: Deciphering Your Karmic Code for Your Best Possible Life.

SIDELIGHTS: As a child, Barrie Dolnick was told she had psychic powers, an idea she rejected for many years before she investigated alternative methods of achieving happiness and success. In the meantime, she earned a business degree and spent years in marketing in both London and New York City. Finding her life unfulfilling, Dolnick responded to a friend's suggestion that she meet with a respected metaphysics teacher, which she did, changing Dolnick's life forever. She effectively blended her business skills with astrology, tarot card reading, and other occult and nontraditional methods in assisting hundreds of clients through her Executive Mystic Services.

Dolnick has also written a number of bestsellers, including *Simple Spells for Love: Ancient Practices for Emotional Fulfillment.* The book offers "recipes for romance," noted Ralph Novak in *People,* and as Patricia Monaghan commented in *Booklist,* there are "excellent chapters" that address how one's own self-esteem transfers to others and how one should allow time between relationships. Monaghan also pointed out Dolnick's observation that love often comes in unexpected ways.

Dolnick shows that spells are not just for love with her *Simple Spells for Success: Ancient Practices for Creating Abundance and Prosperity.* The volume includes forty spells, and each chapter begins with a

personal story. The author proposes that although readers should set goals, they would be wise not make them too rigid. She writes that it is belief in a greater energy that creates success. *Rapport*'s Lisa McKevitt said that the book "is well-penned, easy-to-follow, and pleasing to the eye, as well. And the premise hits a note of truth."

The office supplies list in *The Executive Mystic: Psychic Power Tools for Success* consist of spells, amulets, herbs, feng shui, crystals, dream interpretation, the use of tarot and astrology, and understanding the influence of the moon and the colors that one wears. The volume includes chapters on power animals, psychic dreamscapes, and zodiac archetypes. Of this work, Jilly Welch wrote in a review for *People Management* that Dolnick's views are that "properly harnessed energy can help people visualize successes, enhance their self-confidence, protect them from the office's 'emotional toxicity,' and relate their job to a wider concept of fate and meaning." Welch noted that many of Dolnick's suggestions are "rooted in a common-sense understanding of people's motivation and feelings that deserve more attention in a business world that is too locked in to capitalist ideas of success and happiness." But Welch added that such terms as "the seeing eye" and "karma" would be more acceptable to the business world if they were called by their more mainstream names, intuition and emotional responsibility, respectively.

In *Minerva Rules Your Future: Goddess-Given Advice for Smart Moves at Work,* Dolnick suggests that business people invoke the deity in times of need, which *Library Journal* contributor Graham Christian saw as "appealing . . . especially for those who are not comfortable putting Jesus in that role." The book instructs the reader on using the sun and moon signs to understand talents of which they are unaware and drawing on the essential elements of earth, fire, air, and water for strength and direction.

Dolnick has written other books that advise on the writing of love letters and using spells to enhance the place in which one lives. She continues to write her self-improvement books for those who wish to improve their lives, loves, and careers.

BIOGRAPHICAL AND CRITICAL SOURCES:

PERIODICALS

Across the Board, April, 1998, Matthew Budman, review of *The Executive Mystic: Psychic Power Tools for Success.*

Booklist, February 15, 1995, Patricia Monaghan, review of *Simple Spells for Love: Ancient Practices for Emotional Fulfillment,* p. 1037; February 15, 1996, Barbara Jacobs, review of *Simple Spells for Success: Ancient Practices for Creating Abundance and Prosperity,* p. 971; February 1, 1998, David Rouse, review of *The Executive Mystic,* p. 885.

Library Journal, May 1, 2003, Graham Christian, review of *Minerva Rules Your Future: Goddess-Given Advice for Smart Moves at Work,* p. 122.

People, February 13, 1995, Ralph Novak, review of *Simple Spells for Love,* p. 36.

People Management, November 26, 1998, Jilly Welch, review of *The Executive Mystic.*

Rapport, April, 1996, Lisa McKevitt, review of *Simple Spells for Success,* pp. 18-21.

ONLINE

Barrie Dolnick Home Page, http://www.barriedolnick.com/ (March 9, 2004).

Weekend Edition Sunday, http://www.npr.org/ (February 11, 2001), Liane Hansen, interview with Dolnick.*

* * *

DUBOSE, Lou(is H.) 1948-

PERSONAL: Born March 3, 1948; married Jeanne Goka. *Education:* Earned a master's degree in Latin American studies.

ADDRESSES: Home—Austin, TX. *Office*—Texas Observer, 307 West 7th St., Austin, TX 78701.

CAREER: Austin Chronicle, Austin, TX, politics editor; *Texas Observer,* Austin, editor, 1987—.

WRITINGS:

(With Molly Ivins) *Shrub: The Short but Happy Life of George W. Bush,* Random House (New York, NY), 2000.

(With Molly Ivins) *Bushwhacked: Life in George W. Bush's America,* Random House (New York, NY), 2003.

(With Jan Reid and Carl Cannon) *Boy Genius: Karl Rove, the Brains behind the Remarkable Political Triumph of George W. Bush,* PublicAffairs (New York, NY), 2003.

(With Jan Reid) *The Hammer,* PublicAffairs (New York, NY), 2004.

Contributor to periodicals, including *Nation, Texas Monthly, Washington Post, Globe and Mail, Liberty, Texas,* and *Vindicator.*

SIDELIGHTS: A longtime editor at the *Texas Observer,* which covers the Texas state legislature, Lou Dubose had a front row seat to observe the rise of George W. Bush. He has parlayed that into studies of Bush's performance, both as governor and president, and a biography of his chief political strategist Karl Rove. More recently, Dubose has turned his attention to House Majority Leader Tom DeLay, another Texan driving much of the national agenda of the Republican Party.

At the start of the 2000 presidential campaign, Dubose teamed up with well-known liberal columnist Molly Ivins to write *Shrub: The Short but Happy Political Life of George W. Bush.* While many Americans at least knew Bush's name, thanks to his father, few were aware of his record as governor of Texas, and the authors set out to correct this, focusing on Bush's legislative proposals and administrative regulations in areas such as pollution control, educational reform, and worker safety. As political scientist Brendan O'Connor explained in the *Australian Journal of Politics and History,* "It is this concern for the details of governing that is the driving force behind Ivins and Dubose's *Shrub.* They suggest the best way to judge a politician is by closely examining their record. This is underdone in much current political journalism." Both Ivins and Dubose are proud liberals, and like political biographies throughout history, this one drew divergent reactions from different sides of the political spectrum. For John Nichols, writing in the liberal *Progressive,* "Molly Ivins and Lou Dubose have written the best damn book of the 2000 election season. . . . This tale of the presumptive Republican Presidential nominee's political foibles is so thoroughly reported, so well written, and so consistently convincing that a casual reading could turn even the most radical critic of the Vice President into a rabid Al Gore partisan." In contrast, Charlotte Hays concluded in the conservative *National Review* that "the book is so predictable that it doesn't really lay a glove on Bush. Indeed, ambivalent conservatives will find it a convincing brief for Bush." A more neutral view came from *Booklist* contributor Mary Carroll, who said, "No tabloid-style revelations here; just solid (though partisan) analysis of governance issues that should become important as campaign 2000 continues."

Dubose and Ivins followed up with a study of Bush's first years as president: *Bushwhacked: Life in George W. Bush's America.* This time, the authors interspersed stories of ordinary Americans with a look at the policies of the Bush administration, showing the impact of the latter on the former. "Using an old journalistic tactic, Ivins and Dubose cut repeatedly between descriptions of the rich, cosseted men in the Bush circle—born into vast wealth—and the straightforward, irrefutable stories of poor people hammered yet further since Bush came to power," noted *New Statesman* contributor Johann Hari. *Booklist* contributor Ilene Cooper commented that "unlike some partisan books on both sides . . . these authors have another agenda. . . . [T]hey show what the Bush domestic program has meant to individual citizens in particular and the populace in general."

While policy lies at the heart of *Shrub* and *Bushwhacked,* pure politics is the theme of *Boy Genius: Karl Rove, the Brains behind the Remarkable Political Triumph of George W. Bush,* which Dubose wrote in conjunction with Jan Reid and Carl Cannon. The authors "offer smart political judgments and lovely anecdotes, particularly in their appropriately irreverent chapters on Texas' political whackiness," according to veteran political journalist E. J. Dionne in the *American Prospect.* But that is not all. They also offer a portrait of a uniquely talented political consultant, who saw Bush's potential long before the future

president himself did and who has done much to shape the fortunes of the Republican Party and the entire national agenda. As Dionne noted later in that same review, "what makes Rove interesting is not his ruthlessness but rather his strategic vision and ability to execute. When Rove began plying his trade in Texas, it was a Democratic state. When he left for Washington in 2000, Republicans, most of them former clients of Rove's firm, controlled almost everything." *Boy Genius* describes, according to the authors, the curious, but highly effective, partnership between Rove, a self-described nerd and political wonk, and Bush, the intellectually lazy frat boy with the famous name and outgoing personality. While Rove engineered the hardball tactics and political dirty tricks, Bush largely stayed above the fray. Their partnership has continued into the White House, where Rove has the kind of power rarely given to political operatives, a not entirely benign state of affairs, according to Dubose and his fellow authors.

BIOGRAPHICAL AND CRITICAL SOURCES:

PERIODICALS

American Prospect, July 17, 2000, Jeff Danziger, review of *Bushwhacked: Life in George W. Bush's America,* p. 46; April, 2003, E. J. Dionne, review of *Boy Genius: Karl Rove, the Brains behind the Remarkable Political Triumph of George W. Bush,* p. 52.

Australian Journal of Politics and History, December, 2001, Brendan O'Connor, review of *Shrub: The Short but Happy Life of George W. Bush,* p. 594.

Booklist, February 15, 2000, Mary Carroll, review of *Shrub,* p. 1050; October 1, 2000, Candace Smith, review of *Shrub,* p. 367; August, 2003, Ilene Cooper, review of *Bushwhacked,* p. 1923.

Business Week, March 13, 2000, "Company Man?"

Economist, February 22, 2003, "The Limits of Spin; American Politics."

Kirkus Reviews, August 1, 2003, review of *Bushwhacked,* p. 1004.

Library Journal, March 1, 2000, Michael A. Genovese, review of *Shrub,* p. 110; October 15, 2000, Sally G. Waters, review of *Shrub,* p. 125.

Los Angeles Times Book Review, March 14, 2004, Mark Hertsgaard, "Chapter and Verse on the Need for Regime Change," p. 4.

Mother Jones, September-October, 2003, Colleen O'Brien, review of *Bushwhacked,* p. 96.

National Review, April 17, 2000, Charlotte Hays, "This Bush Has Thorns."

New Statesman, January 12, 2004, Johann Hari, review of *Bushwhacked,* p. 55.

New York Review of Books, February 24, 2000, Lars-Erik Nelson, "Legacy," p. 4; May 1, 2003, Elizabeth Drew, "The Enforcer," p. 14.

New York Times Book Review, February 18, 2000, Michiko Kakutani, "Books of the Times; A Texas-Style Bashing: Double-Teaming 'Dubya,'" p. 53; March 5, 2000, Peter Applebome, "Heir Apparent?," p. 30.

Progressive, May, 2000, John Nichols, review of *Shrub,* p. 41.*

Publishers Weekly, February 7, 2000, review of *Shrub,* p. 79; August 4, 2003, review of *Bushwhacked,* p. 68.

Times Literary Supplement, November 3, 2000, James Bowman, "Not as Thick as He Pretends?"

*   *   *

DYNES, Wayne R. 1934-

PERSONAL: Born August 23, 1934, in Fort Worth, TX. *Education:* University of California, B.A., 1956; New York University, Institute of Fine Arts, Ph.D., 1969; attended Warburg Institute of the University of London.

ADDRESSES: Office—Hunter College, City University of New York, 695 Park Ave., New York, NY 10021.

CAREER: Vassar College, Poughkeepsie, NY, lecturer, 1967-68, assistant professor, 1969-70, adjunct associate professor, 1974-75; University of Pennsylvania, Philadelphia, PA, visiting associate professor, 1971, adjunct professor, 1972-74, associate professor, 1974-85; Hunter College of the City University of New York, New York, NY, professor of art history, 1986—; Columbia University, New York, NY, visiting adjunct professor, 1992.

MEMBER: Gay Task Force of the American Library Association, Gay Academic Union (founder).

AWARDS, HONORS: Woodrow Wilson Fellowship, 1956-57; University Fellowship, 1957-58; Fulbright fellow, University of London, 1963-65.

WRITINGS:

Palaces of Europe, Paul Hamlyn (London, England), 1969.

The Illuminations of the Stavelot Bible, Garland (New York, NY), 1978.

(With others) *Explorations in the Arts,* Holt (New York, NY), 1985.

Homolexis: A Historical and Cultural Lexicon of Homosexuality, GAU (New York, NY), 1985.

(With Marshall Neal Myers) *Hieronymus Bosch and the Canticle of Isaiah,* Cabirion Press (New York, NY), 1987.

Homosexuality: A Research Guide, Garland (New York, NY), 1987.

(Editor, with others) *Encyclopedia of Homosexualtiy,* Garland (New York, NY), 1990.

(With Stephen Donaldson) *Major Lines of Investigation in Gay/Lesbian Studies,* GAU (New York, NY), 1992.

Author of numerous journal articles.

"STUDIES IN HOMOSEXUALITY" SERIES; WITH STEPHEN DONALDSON

Asian Homosexuality, Garland (New York, NY), 1992.

Ethnographic Studies of Homosexuality, Garland (New York, NY), 1992.

History of Homosexuality in Europe and America, Garland (New York, NY), 1992.

Homosexual Themes in Literary Studies, Garland (New York, NY), 1992.

Homosexuality and Government, Politics, and Prisons, Garland (New York, NY), 1992.

Homosexuality and Homosexuals in the Arts, Garland (New York, NY), 1992.

Homosexuality and Medicine, Health, and Science, Garland (New York, NY), 1992.

Homosexuality and Psychology, Psychiatry, and Counseling, Garland (New York, NY), 1992.

Homosexuality and Religion and Philosophy, Garland (New York, NY), 1992.

Homosexuality in the Ancient World, Garland (New York, NY), 1992.

Homosexuality: Discrimination, Criminology, and the Law, Garland (New York, NY), 1992.

Lesbianism, Garland (New York, NY), 1992.

Sociology of Homosexuality, Garland (New York, NY), 1992.

SIDELIGHTS: Wayne R. Dynes told *CA:* "In the present intellectual climate of relativism and nihilism, I remain a rationalist, committed to weighing and improving ideas, always comparing them with empirical data, so that human knowledge, which is a unity, may advance ever closer to the truth. Only this unceasing quest for truth can establish a firm foundation for social justice."

BIOGRAPHICAL AND CRITICAL SOURCES:

PERIODICALS

Sex Roles: A Journal of Research, October, 1993, Frank Y. Wong, a review of *Ethnographic Studies of Homosexuality,* p. 565.

E

ECHEVARRIA, Jana 1956-

PERSONAL: Born March 1, 1956, in American Falls, ID; daughter of Charles and Joanne (Monroe) Echevarria; married William E. Ratleff, October 1, 1983 (marriage ended, August 10, 1994); married Charles S. Vose, May 16, 2003; children: (first marriage) Paige Ann, Dillon Edward. *Education:* California State University—Long Beach, B.A., 1978, M.S., 1984; University of California—Los Angeles, Ph.D., 1993. *Politics:* Democrat. *Religion:* Christian. *Hobbies and other interests:* Sports, travel.

ADDRESSES: Home—7030 Seawind Dr., Long Beach, CA 90803. *Office*—Department of Educational Psychology, California State University—Long Beach, 1250 Bellflower Blvd., Long Beach, CA 90840. *E-mail*—jechev@csulb.edu.

CAREER: California State University—Long Beach, Long Beach, professor of bilingual special education, 1992-2003, department chair, 2002—. SIOP Institute, writer and consultant; National Center for Learning Disabilities, member of professional advisory board.

MEMBER: American Educational Research Association, Teachers of English to Speakers of Other Languages, Council for Exceptional Children.

WRITINGS:

(With R. McDonough) *Instructional Conversations in Special Education Settings: Issues and Accommodations,* National Center for Research on Cultural Diversity and Second Language Learning (Washington, DC), 1993.

Instructional Conversations: Understanding through Discussion Training Manual, National Center for Research on Cultural Diversity and Second Language Learning (Washington, DC), 1995.

(With A. Graves) *Sheltered Content Instruction: Teaching Students with Diverse Abilities,* Allyn & Bacon (Boston, MA), 1998, 2nd edition, 2003.

(With A. Pickett and L. Safarik) *A Core Curriculum and Training Program to Prepare Paraeducators to Work with Learners Who Have Limited English Proficiency,* National Resource Center for Paraprofessionals in Education (New York, NY), 1998.

(With M. E. Vogt and D. Short) *Making Content Comprehensible for English Language Learners: The SIOP Model,* Allyn & Bacon (Boston, MA), 2000.

Contributor to books, including *Schools and the Culturally Diverse Student: Promising Practices and Future Directions,* edited by A. Ortiz and B. Ramirez, Council for Exceptional Children (Reston, VA), 1988; *Promoting Learning for Culturally and Linguistically Diverse Students,* edited by R. Gersten and R. Jimenez, Wadsworth Publishing (New York, NY), 1998; and *Observational Research in U.S. Classrooms: New Approaches for Understanding Cultural and Linguistic Diversity,* edited by H. Waxman, R. Tharp, and S. Hilberg, Cambridge University Press (Boston, MA), in press. Contributor to periodicals, including *Learning Disabilities Research and Practice, Intervention in School and Clinic, Special Edge, Bilingual Research Journal, Science Teacher,* and *Issues in Teacher Education.*

WORK IN PROGRESS: School Reform and Standards-Based Education: Where Does It Leave English

Language Learners?; research on the effects of the Sheltered Instruction Observation Protocol (SIOP) Model on student achievement.

SIDELIGHTS: Jana Echevarria told *CA:* "I have always been drawn to helping students who are at risk for school failure, either because of their learning differences or because of cultural or linguistic diversity, or both. My career began in special education, where I realized that teachers benefit from new ideas and approaches, especially those that are scientifically validated through research. I also was interested in bilingual populations and taught bilingual classes and English as a second language. The two disciplines came together through an interdisciplinary master's degree in bilingual special education and subsequently when I began teaching at a university that had a program to prepare special education teachers to work effectively with language-minority students. After a couple years in teacher preparation, I wrote a training manual for teachers that discussed effective practices. That is how my writing career began.

"After I received my doctorate, I was better equipped for scholarly writing, and I learned that I really enjoyed writing; it was more than something to do to receive tenure. I continued writing for scholarly journals and then wanted to write a book that incorporated the materials I had developed for the courses I taught. I wrote my first textbook in 1998.

"The research a colleague and I conducted resulted in an observation protocol for qualifying how well teachers implement the model of instruction for English learners that we developed. The book we wrote to illustrate the model of teaching that is effective for English learners appealed to teachers, administrators, and teacher trainers; we just completed the second edition. Interestingly, I believe part of the appeal is that it is written in language that is understandable, rather than a more scholarly voice. So, my writing has come full circle—after I learned scholarly writing, the most popular publication is the one that is more user-friendly.

"I enjoy the feeling that I've made a contribution to enhancing the teaching and learning process for students who are in the greatest need of assistance in our schools."

ELEB, Monique 1945-

PERSONAL: Born 1945, in Casablanca, Morocco; married Jean-Louis Cohen (an architectural historian).

ADDRESSES: Home—Paris, France. *Agent*—c/o Author Mail, Monacelli Press, 902 Broadway, Eighteenth Floor, New York, NY 10010. *E-mail*—monique.eleb@wanadoo.fr.

CAREER: Writer and educator. Ecole d'Architecture Paris-Malaquais, Paris, France, currently professor of psychology and sociology, director of Architecture, Culture, and Society Research Center, and director of the doctoral program on architecture and urbanism.

WRITINGS:

(With Anne Marie Châtelet and Thierry Mandoul) *Penser l'habité: le logement en questions, PAN 14,* P. Mardaga (Liege, Belgium), 1988.

(With Anne Debarre-Blanchard) *Architectures de la vie privée. Maisons et mentalités, XVIIe-XIXe siècles,* Aux Archives d'architecture moderne (Brussels, Belgium), 1989.

L'apprentissage du "chez-soi": le Groupe des maisons ouvrières, Paris, avenue Daumesnil, 1908, Editions Parenthèses (Marseille, France), 1994.

(With Anne Debarre-Blanchard) *L'invention de l'habitation moderne: Paris, 1880-1914. Architectures de la vie privée,* Hazan (Paris, France) and Archives d'architecture moderne (Brussels, Belgium), 1995.

(With husband, Jean-Louis Cohen) *Casablanca: mythes et figures d'une aventure urbaine,* Hazan (Paris, France), 1998, translation published as *Casablanca: Colonial Myths and Architectural Ventures,* Monacelli Press (New York, NY), 2002.

(With Jean-Louis Violeau) *Entre voisins: dispositiv architectural et mixité,* Epure (Paris, France), 2000.

(With husband, Jean-Louis Cohen) *Paris architecture, 1900-2000,* Éditions Norma (Paris, France), 2000, translation published as *Paris Architecture, 1900-2000,* Gingko Press, 2001.

Also author of *A deux chez soi,* 2002, and (with husband, Jean-Louis Cohen) *Les mille et une villes de Casablanca,* Art Creation Realisation, 2003.

WORK IN PROGRESS: A book on L.A. café life, for Editions de L'Imprimeur; a book on Paris café life.

SIDELIGHTS: Monique Eleb is a French psychologist and sociologist who specializes in domestic architecture. She has written a number of books on Parisian architecture, as well as on that of her native Casablanca. Two of her books have been published in English.

Eleb's 1989 book *Architectures de la vie privée. Maisons et mentalités, XVIIe-XIXe siècles* chronicles the history of Parisian domestic planning from the seventeenth to the late nineteenth century, a period during which, for example, the apartment house arrived as an architectural type. Her volume *L'invention de l'habitation moderne: Paris, 1880-1914. Architectures de la vie privée* picks up where the other book left off and covers the thirty-four years before World War I. This period is not particularly known for richness of invention in French architecture, but Eleb challenges that notion and argues that it was, in many ways, a very innovative time period. It was during the early twentieth century that modern notions of living comfort were incorporated into exterior and interior architectural planning. Barry Bergdoll, who reviewed *L'invention de l'habitation moderne* in *Burlington* magazine, commended Eleb for bridging "two well-known periods; the mid-nineteenth century Haussmannian city and the great concern of the modern movement in the 1920s with housing and domesticity."

Eleb collaborated with her husband, Jean-Louis Cohen, on *Casablanca: mythes et figures d'une aventure urbaine,* published in English as *Casablanca: Colonial Myths and Architectural Ventures.* The book deals with the city's architecture and city planning from 1900 to the 1960s. It portrays a unique effort of architects and urban planners to blend different cultures while at the same time trying to ensure adequate living conditions for all classes. David Soltesz found in *Library Journal* that the book's major themes "could have been more coherently developed" amidst a mountain of data, but he still called it "a feast for serious students of North Africa, urban planning and trends in twentieth century architecture."

BIOGRAPHICAL AND CRITICAL SOURCES:

PERIODICALS

Burlington, Volume 139, number 1129, 1997, Barry Bergdoll, review of *L'invention de l'habitation*

moderne: Paris, 1880-1914. Architectures de la vie privée, p. 270.
Houses, November, 2001, Julie Oliver, review of *Paris Architecture, 1900-2000,* p. 70.
Library Journal, May 1, 2003, David Soltesz, review of *Casablanca: Colonial Myths and Architectural Ventures,* p. 108.*

*   *   *

ELEVELD, Mark

PERSONAL: Male.

ADDRESSES: Office—EM Press, 305 Brooks Ave., Joliet, IL 60435.

CAREER: Teacher, publisher, editor, and freelance writer. Joliet West High School, Joliet, IL, English teacher; University of St. Francis, IL, philosophy instructor; EM Press, Joliet, cofounder and copublisher; press agent for poet Marc Smith, 1993-1996.

MEMBER: Midland Authors Society (Chicago, IL; board member).

WRITINGS:

(Editor) *The Spoken Word Revolution: Slam, Hip-Hop, and the Poetry of a New Generation* (includes audio CD), introduction by Billy Collins, Sourcebooks MediaFusion (Naperville, IL), 2003.

SIDELIGHTS: In addition to teaching at the high school and university levels, Mark Eleveld is a freelance writer and book reviewer who also wrote press releases for poet Marc Smith during the 1990s. Smith is the founder of the poetry slam that began with Chicago, Illinois, venues in the 1980s and encouraged poetry for all. Eleveld, also a champion of spoken-word poetry, collaborated with Smith and poet laureate Billy Collins on a collection of work by fifty performance poets titled *The Spoken Word Revolution: Slam, Hip-Hop, and the Poetry of a New Generation.* The book also provides a history of the art and its evolution.

In an interview with Marie Lecrivain for *PoeticDiversity.org,* Eleveld said, "I wanted to document some of the history of the current movement while these people are still alive. I always found it ironic that contemporary or modern poetry classes usually end in the late fifties. . . . I wanted to mend some fences between people and 'scenes' that might not have been associated in the past. Having the U.S. poet laureate, Guggenheim president, Iowa Writers Workshop professor, Pulitzer Prize winner, Carnegie professor of the year, etc., next to Slammers, next to performance artists, next to youth—an interesting coming together of voices that have never been paired together like that before."

The Spoken Word Revolution is divided into six sections, titled "The Beat Remnants," "Hip-Hop," "Performance Art," "Competitive Poetry/Taos," "Slam," and "Youth Speaks." It comes with a CD that begins with the introduction by Collins, followed by a piece by Quincy Troupe, accompanied by guitar, in the "Beat" section. A *Publishers Weekly* reviewer felt that the printed text is "secondary" to the CD, which includes twenty of the poets found in the book on forty-six cuts. The critic concluded by saying that this collection "heralds spoken word's further entry into the marketplace, a presence that should spread logarithmically over the coming years."

BIOGRAPHICAL AND CRITICAL SOURCES:

PERIODICALS

Publishers Weekly, April 28, 2003, review of *The Spoken Word Revolution: Slam, Hip-Hop, and the Poetry of a New Generation,* p. 63.

ONLINE

Mark Eleveld Home Page, http://www.em-press.com/ (February 28, 2004).
PoeticDiversity.org, http://www.poeticdiversity.org/ (February 28, 2004), Marie Lecrivain, interview with Mark Eleveld.*

*　　*　　*

ELIZONDO, Virgil P. 1935-

PERSONAL: Born August 25, 1935, in San Antonio, TX. *Education:* St. Mary's University (San Antonio, TX), bachelor's degree, 1959; attended Assumption Seminary, beginning 1959; Ateneo de Manila University, M.A., 1969; Institut Catholique, Paris, France, two doctorates.

ADDRESSES: Office—Mexican American Cultural Center, Assumption Seminary, 3000 West French Pl., San Antonio, TX 78228.

CAREER: Ordained Roman Catholic priest, 1965; Assumption Seminary, San Antonio, TX, dean of students, beginning 1969, organizer of Mexican American Cultural Center, 1972—. San Fernando Cathedral, rector and presenter of the weekly televised mass *Misa de las Américas.*

MEMBER: Padres Asociados para Derechos Religiosos, Educativos, y Sociales (founding member).

AWARDS, HONORS: Laetare Medal, University of Notre Dame, 1997.

WRITINGS:

A Search for Meaning in Life and Death, East Asian Pastoral Institute (Manila, Philippines), 1971, published as *The Human Quest: A Search for Meaning through Life and Death,* Our Sunday Visitor (Huntington, IN), 1978.
Christianity and Culture: An Introduction to Pastoral Theology and Ministry for the Bicultural Community, Our Sunday Visitor (Huntington, IN), 1975.
Mestizaje: The Dialectic of Cultural Birth and the Gospel; A Study in the Intercultural Dimension of Evangelization, three volumes, Mexican American Cultural Center, Assumption Seminary (San Antonio, TX), 1978.
(With Angela Erevia) *Our Hispanic Pilgrimage,* Mexican-American Cultural Center, Assumption Seminary (San Antonio, TX), 1980.
La Morenita, evangelizadora de las Américas, Liguori Publications (Liguori, MO), 1981.
Galilean Journey: The Mexican-American Promise, Orbis Books (Maryknoll, NY), 1983, revised edition, 2000.
The Future Is Mestizo: Life Where Cultures Meet, Meyer-Stone Books (Oak Park, IL), 1988, revised edition, University Press of Colorado (Boulder, CO), 2000.

Guadalupe, Mother of the New Creation, Orbis Books (Maryknoll, NY), 1997.

(With Timothy M. Matovina) *Mestizo Worship: A Pastoral Approach to Liturgical Ministry,* Liturgical Press (Collegeville, MN), 1998.

(With Timothy M. Matovina) *San Fernando Cathedral: Soul of the City,* Orbis Books (Maryknoll, NY), 1998.

Beyond Borders: Writings of Virgilio Elizondo and Friends, edited by Timothy M. Matovina, Orbis Books (Maryknoll, NY), 2000.

(With Bernard J. Lee, William V. D'Antonio, and others) *The Catholic Experience of Small Christian Communities,* Paulist Press (New York, NY), 2000.

EDITOR

(With Norbert Greinacher) *Women in a Men's Church,* Seabury Press (New York, NY), 1980.

(With Norbert Greinacher) *Tensions between the Churches in the First World and the Third World,* Seabury Press (New York, NY), 1981.

(With Norbert Greinacher) *Churches in Socialist Societies of Eastern Europe,* Seabury Press (New York, NY), 1982.

(With Norbert Greinacher) *Church and Peace,* Seabury Press (New York, NY), 1983.

(With Claude Geffré and Gustavo Gutiérrez) *Difference Theologies, Common Responsibility: Babel or Pentecost?,* T. and T. Clark (Edinburgh, Scotland), 1984.

(With Leonardo Boff) *The People of God Amidst the Poor,* T. and T. Clark (Edinburgh, Scotland), 1984.

(With Norbert Greinacher) *The Transmission of the Faith to the Next Generation,* T. and T. Clark (Edinburgh, Scotland), 1984.

(With Leonardo Boff) *Option for the Poor: Challenge to the Rich Countries,* T. and T. Clark (Edinburgh, Scotland), 1986.

(With Leonardo Boff) *Convergences and Differences,* T. and T. Clark (Edinburgh, Scotland), 1988.

(With Leonardo Boff) *1492-1992: The Voice of the Victims,* Trinity Press International (Philadelphia, PA), 1990.

Way of the Cross: The Passion of Christ in the Americas, translated by John Drury, Orbis Books (Maryknoll, NY), 1992.

(With Leonardo Boff) *Any Room for Christ in Asia?,* Orbis Books (Maryknoll, NY), 1993.

(With Leonardo Boff; and contributor) *Ecology and Poverty: Cry of the Earth, Cry of the Poor,* Orbis Books (Maryknoll, NY), 1995.

(With Sean Freyne) *Pilgrimage,* Orbis Books (Maryknoll, NY), 1996.

Editor of the book series "Concilium."

BIOGRAPHICAL AND CRITICAL SOURCES:

BOOKS

Religious Leaders of America, 2nd edition, Gale (Detroit, MI), 1999.

PERIODICALS

Houston Chronicle, March 15, 1997, "Texas Priest to Get Notre Dame Medal," p. 3.

National Catholic Reporter, May 16, 1997, Sally Cunneen, review of *Guadalupe: Mother of the New Creation,* p. 13.

Review of Politics, summer, 1998, John Francis Burke, "U.S. Hispanic Theology and the Politics of Border Crossings: 'We Hold These Truths' from La Frontera," p. 563.*

*   *   *

ELLENBERG, Jordan S. 1971-

PERSONAL: Born 1971, in Potomac, MD; married Tanya Schlam. *Education:* Harvard University, B.A. (mathematics; summa cum laude), 1993, Johns Hopkins University, M.A. (fiction); Harvard University, Ph.D. (mathematics), 1998.

ADDRESSES: Office—Dept. of Mathematics, Princeton University, 808 Fine Hall, Washington Rd., Princeton, NJ 08544 *E-mail*—ellenber@math.princeton.edu.

CAREER: Mathematician and writer. Princeton University, Princeton, NJ, instructor, 1998-2001, assistant professor, 2001—.

AWARDS, HONORS: International Mathematical Olympiad awards, gold medals, 1987 and 1989, silver medal, 1988; first place, U.S.A. Mathematical Olympiad, 1989; Science Service, Inc./Westinghouse Electric Corporation scholarship, 1989; Barry M. Goldwater scholarship, 1991-92; National Science Foundation graduate fellow, 1994-97; National Science Foundation postdoctoral fellowship (declined), 1998; NSA Young Investigator grant, 2001.

WRITINGS:

The Grasshopper King (novel), Coffee House Press (Minneapolis, MN), 2003.

Author of the column "Do the Math" for *Slate* online; contributor to scientific journals and to periodicals, including *Boston Book Review* and *Boston Phoenix.*

SIDELIGHTS: Jordan S. Ellenberg's parents are both statisticians, and their math prodigy son went on to teach the subject at Princeton University. On his Princeton home page, Ellenberg explains that his field "is arithmetic algebraic geometry: my specific interests include rational points on varieties, Galois representations attached to varieties and their fundamental groups, non-abelian Iwasawa theory, counting arithmetic objects, automorphic forms, Hilbert-Blumenthal abelian varieties, Q-curves, curves of low genus, Serre's conjecture, the ABC conjecture, and Diophantine problems related to all of the above."

On his personal home page, Ellenberg talks about his scientific interests, but also about his writing, beginning with his debut novel, *The Grasshopper King,* which was called a "very strange and over-the-top but amusing novel" by *Booklist* contributor Elsa Gaztambide. The story is set on the campus of Chandler State University, where the only claim to fame is the university's Gravinics Department. Researchers here study the most difficult language on earth, one in which a four-word sentence can have thousands of meanings, depending on subtleties. Graduate student Sam Grapearbor is given the task of watching Stanley Higgs, a professor who has not talked for more than a dozen years but who is the preeminent scholar on the work of Gravinian poet Henderson, a literary figure and genius who lives in a fictional Soviet republic.

Sam and his girlfriend, Julia, go to Higgs's home every day, where tape recorders are placed at the ready in the event that Higgs decides to speak. A *Publishers Weekly* reviewer found this plot element reminiscent of works by Tom Robbins and Kurt Vonnegut, Jr. The critic felt that the "distinct tenderness" and "mutual craziness" seen in the relationship between Higgs and his wife, Ellen, reflect "an unconventional but oddly appealing model of married life." Mahinder Kingra also reviewed the novel for the *Baltimore City Paper Online,* saying that "Sam's self-deprecating narration is witty and satisfyingly melancholic, Ellenberg's characters are genuinely likable, and there is an undercurrent of conspiracies and machinations that keeps the narrative moving forward."

BIOGRAPHICAL AND CRITICAL SOURCES:

PERIODICALS

Booklist, April 1, 2003, Elsa Gaztambide, review of *The Grasshopper King,* p. 1376.
Kirkus Reviews, February 1, 2003, review of *The Grasshopper King,* p. 159.
Library Journal, March 15, 2003, Josh Cohen, review of *The Grasshopper King,* p. 114.
Publishers Weekly, April 7, 2003, review of *The Grasshopper King,* p. 47.
Washington Post, June 29, 2003, Kit Reed, review of *The Grasshopper King,* p. T13.

ONLINE

Baltimore City Paper Online, http://www.citypaper.com/ (April 23, 2003), Mahinder Kingra, review of *The Grasshopper King.*
Hybridmagazine.com, http://www.hybridmagazine.com/ (March 9, 2004), review of *The Grasshopper King.*
Jordan Ellenberg Home Page, http://www.math.princeton.edu/ (March 9, 2004).*

*   *   *

ENG, David L.

PERSONAL: Male. *Education:* Columbia University, B.A., 1990; University of California—Berkeley, M.A., 1992, Ph.D., 1995.

ADDRESSES: Office—Department of English and Comparative Literature, Columbia University, 1150 Amsterdam Ave., New York, NY 10027. *E-mail*—dle8@columbia.edu.

CAREER: Columbia University, New York, NY, teacher of English and comparative literature.

AWARDS, HONORS: Lambda Literary Award, 1998, for *Q & A: Queer in Asian America.*

WRITINGS:

(Editor, with Alice Y. Hom) *Q & A: Queer in Asian America,* Temple University Press (Philadelphia, PA), 1998.

Racial Castration: Managing Masculinity in Asian America, Duke University Press (Durham, NC), 2001.

(Editor, with David Kazanjian) *Loss: The Politics of Mourning,* University of California Press (Berkeley, CA), 2003.

BIOGRAPHICAL AND CRITICAL SOURCES:

PERIODICALS

Amerasia Journal, spring, 1999, Amy Sueyoshi, review of *Q & A: Queer in Asian America,* p. 194.

Choice, October, 2001, D. N. Mager, review of *Racial Castration: Managing Masculinity in Asian America,* p. 294.

GLQ: Journal of Lesbian and Gay Studies, December, 2000, Mun-Hou Lo, review of *Q & A,* p. 609.

Journal of Homosexuality, May, 2000, Mary K. Bloodsworth, review of *Q & A,* p. 159.

Journal of the History of Sexuality, January, 2001, Clive Moore, review of *Q & A,* p. 129.

Lambda Book Report, May, 1999, Kitty Tsui, review of *Q & A,* p. 17.

Library Journal, October 1, 1998, Richard Violette, review of *Q & A,* p. 122.

Signs, winter, 2001, Caroline Chung Simpson, review of *Q & A,* p. 555.

*   *   *

ESQUITH, Rafe 1954-

PERSONAL: Born June 2, 1954, in Los Angeles, CA; son of Joseph (a social worker) and Claire Esquith; married Barbara Tong (a nurse), 1991; children: four stepchildren. *Education:* Earned degree in social work from University of California—Los Angeles, 1981.

ADDRESSES: Home—Los Angeles, CA. *Office*—Hobart Elementary, Hobart Shakespeareans, 980 South Hobart Blvd., Los Angeles, CA 90006. *Agent*—Lavin Agency, 77 Peter St., Fourth Fl., Toronto, Ontario M5V 2G4, Canada. *E-mail*—willpower6@aol.com.

CAREER: Educator and author. Hobart Elementary School, Los Angeles, CA, teacher, 1985—.

AWARDS, HONORS: Walt Disney National Outstanding Teacher of the Year Award, 1992; Professional Achievement Award, University of California—Los Angeles, 2000; Use Your Life Award, Oprah Winfrey, 2000; National Medal of Arts, National Endowment for the Arts, 2003; Officer of the Most Excellent Order of the British Empire, Queen Elizabeth; As You Grow Award, *Parents* magazine; Leavey Award for Excellence in Private Enterprise Education, Freedoms Foundation; Sigma Beta Delta Fellowship, Johns Hopkins University; Weingart Foundation grant; Joseph Drown Foundation grant.

WRITINGS:

There Are No Shortcuts (memoir), Pantheon Books (New York, NY), 2003.

SIDELIGHTS: Rafe Esquith is a fifth-and sixth-grade teacher at Hobart Elementary School, an institution located in one of the poorest neighborhoods of central Los Angeles. Over ninety percent of Esquith's students come from impoverished Asian and Hispanic immigrant families, and many of them do not speak English as a first language. Yet Esquith's students, known as the "Hobart Shakespeareans," perform at Shakespeare festivals at home and abroad every year. They also consistently score in the top five to ten percent nationally on standardized tests. Esquith, who has garnered many teaching awards, was the first teacher to be honored with the National Medal of Arts. His first book, *There Are No Shortcuts,* is about his life as a teacher.

The title of Esquith's book is an allusion to how he has made his students so successful. The secret is hard work, to which, in Esquith's opinion, there is no alternative. The standards he sets for the children are high. His fifth-graders study and rehearse one Shakespeare play for the entire school year, while at the same time receiving a well-rounded education. In order to make time for math, history, sports, computers, and music instruction, Esquith extends the school day by three hours, and he offers college-preparation tutoring on Saturdays. Most of his young students turn out to be eager to study. As a result, the children have made headlines appearing at the Globe Theatre in London, opening for the Royal Shakespeare Company, and performing at the World Shakespeare Congress. Many of Esquith's former students have found their way into top colleges, and often return to Hobart School to raise funds or help tutoring.

There Are No Shortcuts also criticizes public schools for being too bureaucratic and too concerned with standardization. Esquith offers advice and warnings for aspiring teachers, talking about his own teaching mistakes and what he sees as central issues in education. Critics offered mostly positive opinions on the book. A *Kirkus Reviews* contributor likened the book to its author's teaching style: "freethinking, demanding, encouraging, at times bumptious." Scott Walter, while recommending the book in *Library Journal,* noticed a "self-righteous indignation at those who have failed to see the logic behind his methods." In *Booklist,* Vanessa Bush commented, "With anecdotes that are alternately amusing and disheartening, Esquith details the joys and frustrations of teaching and offers valuable insights to parents and teachers alike."

BIOGRAPHICAL AND CRITICAL SOURCES:

BOOKS

Esquith, Rafe, *There Are No Shortcuts,* Pantheon Books (New York, NY), 2003.

PERIODICALS

Booklist, April 1, 2003, Vanessa Bush, review of *There Are No Shortcuts,* p. 1359.
Education Week, November 8, 2000, Kathleen Kennedy Manzo, "Honors from Oprah."
Kirkus Reviews, February 15, 2003, review of *There Are No Shortcuts,* p. 283.
Library Journal, April 1, 2003, Scott Walter, review of *There Are No Shortcuts,* p. 112.

People, February 12, 2000, Christina Cheakalos and Karen Grigsby Bates, "Child's Play."
Policy Review, March-April, 1996, Nina H. Shokraii, "Raising the Bar."
Teacher, May, 2003, David Ruenzel, "Pay Your Dues, Then Rebel," interview with Esquith.
Time, April 24, 2000, "This Teacher Works Six Days a Week: Rafe Esquith Has Immigrant Students Learning Shakespeare in the Fifth Grade," p. 8.*

*   *   *

ESTRIDGE, Robin 1920-
(Philip Loraine, Robert York)

PERSONAL: Born 1920.

ADDRESSES: Home—CA and France. *Agent*—Rochelle Stevens, 2 Terrets Pl., Upper St., London NI 1Q2, England.

CAREER: Author. Has worked as a journalist in London, England, and as a dishwasher in Paris, France. *Military service:* Served in the Royal Navy.

WRITINGS:

NOVELS

The Future Is Tomorrow, Davies (London, England), 1947.
The Publican's Wife, Davies (London, England), 1948.
Meeting on the Shore, Davies (London, England), 1949.
Return of a Hero, Davies (London, England), 1950, published as *Sword without Scabbard,* Morrow (New York, NY), 1950.
The Olive Tree, Morrow (New York, NY), 1953.
A Cuckoo's Child, Davies (London, England), 1969.
(Under pseudonym Robert York) *The Swords of December,* Scribner (New York, NY), 1978.
(Under pseudonym Robert York) *My Lord the Fox,* Constable (London, England), 1984.

NOVELS; UNDER PSEUDONYM PHILIP LORAINE

White Lie the Dead, Hodder & Stoughton (London, England), 1950, published as *And to My Beloved Husband—,* Mill (New York, NY), 1950.

Exit with Intent: The Story of a Missing Comedian, Hodder & Stoughton (London, England), 1950.

The Break in the Circle, Mill (New York, NY), 1951, published as *Outside the Law,* Pocket Books (New York, NY), 1953.

The Dublin Nightmare, Hodder & Stoughton (London, England), 1952, published as *Nightmare in Dublin,* Mill (New York, NY), 1952.

The Angel of Death, Mill (New York, NY), 1961.

Day of the Arrow, Mill (New York, NY), 1964, published as *The Eye of the Devil,* Fontana (London, England), 1966, published as *13,* Lancer (New York, NY), 1966.

W.I.L. One to Curtis, Random House (New York, NY), 1967.

The Dead Men of Sestos, Random House (New York, NY), 1968.

A Mafia Kiss, Random House (New York, NY), 1969.

Photographs Have Been Sent to Your Wife, Random House (New York, NY), 1971.

Voices in an Empty Room, Collins (London, England), 1973, Random House (New York, NY), 1974.

Ask the Rattlesnake, Collins (London, England), 1975, published as *Wrong Man in the Mirror,* Random House (New York, NY), 1975.

Lions' Ransom, Collins (London, England), 1980.

Sea-Change, Collins (London, England), 1982, St. Martin's (New York, NY), 1983.

Death Wishes, St. Martin's (New York, NY), 1983.

Loaded Questions, Collins (London, England), 1985, St. Martin's (New York, NY), 1986.

Last Shot, St. Martin's (New York, NY), 1986.

Crackpot, Crime Club (London, England), 1993.

In the Blood, Crime Club (London, England), 1994.

Ugly Money, Crime Club (London, England), 1996.

SCREENPLAYS

Author of numerous screenplays, including (with John Gilling) *House of Darkness,* 1948; *A Day to Remember,* 1953; (with George Tabori) *The Young Lovers* (also known as *Chance Meeting*), 1954; (with John Baines) *Simba,* 1955; *Above Us the Waves,* 1955; *Checkpoint,* 1956; (with Hammond Innes) *Campbell's Kingdom,* 1957; *Dangerous Exile,* 1957; *North West Frontier* (also known as *Flame over India*), 1959; *Escape from Zahrain,* 1962; (with Arthur Hoerl) *Drums of Africa,* 1963; (with Denis Murphy) *Eye of the Devil,* 1966; *The Boy Cried Murder,* 1966; and *Permission to Kill,* 1975.

SIDELIGHTS: Robin Estridge is best known as the author of crime novels under the pseudonym Philip Loraine, including *Lions' Ransom,* the occult-tinged *Voices in an Empty Room,* and the spy story *Sea-Change.* Recognized for creating well-rounded characters, he is known for setting his stories in a wide variety of locations, including California, Vienna, Africa, San Francisco, and Sicily.

BIOGRAPHICAL AND CRITICAL SOURCES:

PERIODICALS

Publishers Weekly, November 19, 1982, review of *Sea-Change,* p. 63; October 28, 1983, review of *Death Wishes,* p. 61; November 15, 1985, review of *Loaded Questions,* p. 47; October 31, 1986, review of *Last Shot,* p. 59.*

*   *   *

EVANS, Mary Anna

PERSONAL: Female. Married; children: three. *Education:* Degrees in physics and chemical engineering.

ADDRESSES: *Home*—8321 SW 23rd Place, Gainesville, FL 32607. *E-mail*—maryannaevans@yahoo.com.

CAREER: Mystery writer. Has also worked as an environmental consultant, university administrator, community college instructor, and a roustabout on an offshore natural gas platform.

AWARDS, HONORS: Patrick D. Smith Florida Literature Award, Florida Historical Society, 2004, and finalist for Benjamin Franklin Award for mystery and suspense, both for *Artifacts.* 2004

WRITINGS:

Artifacts, Poisoned Pen Press (Scottsdale, AZ), 2003.

WORK IN PROGRESS: *Relics,* a sequel to *Artifacts.*

SIDELIGHTS: After a number of jobs and a budding career as an environmental consultant, Mary Anna Evans decided to spend more time at home with her three children and put her talents and interests to use in writing a novel. The result was *Artifacts,* a mystery set around an old Floridian plantation house named Joyeuse. Once owned by a freed slave named Cally, the home is now in the possession of her great-great granddaughter Faye Longchamp, an archeology student. When Faye finds herself unable to pay the higher property taxes, she decides to dig for artifacts on the property and sell them on the black market. What she finds instead is the skull of a murdered woman, which she decides not to report for fear that this will expose her own illegal activities. Alternatively, Faye decides to investigate on her own. Faye soon finds herself on the trail of a killer who is still very much alive and determined to prevent anyone from uncovering the crime. As other bodies start turning up and several of Faye's fellow students disappear from an archeology dig, Faye realizes the past is catching up with her. A *Kirkus Reviews* contributor called the novel a "capably written debut with perhaps too much history and not enough mystery for its high body count." More enthusiastically, *Booklist* reviewer Barbara Bibel commended Evans for introducing "a strong female sleuth in this extremely promising debut . . . weaving past and present together in a multilayered, compelling plot."

BIOGRAPHICAL AND CRITICAL SOURCES:

PERIODICALS

Booklist, May 1, 2003, Barbara Bibel, review of *Artifacts,* p. 959.

Kirkus Reviews, April 1, 2003, review of *Artifacts,* pp. 507-508.

Publishers Weekly, April 7, 2003, review of *Artifacts,* p. 49.*

F

FABIJANCIC, Tony 1966-

PERSONAL: Born 1966, in Edmonton, Alberta, Canada; son of Josip Fabijancic; mother, a college instructor; married; children: two. *Ethnicity:* "Canadian, of Croatian and German background." *Education:* St. Francis Xavier, B.A. (English); University of Victoria, M.A. (English); University of New Brunswick, Ph.D. (English). *Politics:* "Left." *Hobbies and other interests:* Visual art and sports such as soccer, hockey, and track.

ADDRESSES: Office—Sir Wilfred Grenfell College, Memorial University of Newfoundland, University Dr., Corner Bank, Newfoundland A2H 6P9, Canada. *E-mail*—afabijan@swgc.mun.ca.

CAREER: Educator. Sir Wilfred Grenfell College, Memorial University of Newfoundland, Corner Bank, Newfoundland, Canada, associate professor of contemporary literature.

WRITINGS:

(And photographer) *Croatia: Travels in Undiscovered Country,* University of Alberta Press (Edmonton, Alberta, Canada), 2003.

Contributor of academic, fiction, travel, and other articles and photographs to periodicals, including *Mosaic, Antigonish Review, University of Toronto Quarterly, West Coast Line, Brunswickan, Western Star,* and *Globe and Mail.*

WORK IN PROGRESS: A collection of short stories; a scholarly work about urban space, vision, and modernity; essays about Joseph Cornell and David Lynch; a historical novel set in Bosnia.

SIDELIGHTS: Tony Fabijancic is a Canadian professor of English. He is also of Croatian descent, the son of a man who immigrated to Canada from Yugoslavia in 1964, and who maintained his relationship with his home country by taking his family back for holidays and visits. Fabijancic continued traveling to Croatia to learn more about its people, history, and what its future might hold, and he published an account of his visits as *Croatia: Travels in Undiscovered Country.*

Fabijancic begins on the Adriatic island of Pag, then visits the capital city of Zagreb. He concludes in Istria, along the way concentrating on the rural areas and their inhabitants, particularly the peasants in the north and the fishermen in the south. Little-known towns as well as familiar tourist spots, like Dubrovnik, are visited. Throughout these travels, the people he meets discuss such matters as how the events of 1991 have changed their lives, what it felt like to have neighbors become enemies, and changing attitudes toward tradition.

Fabijancic reflects on his family's history and his own life as he writes of military struggles, landmarks, and figures important to the history of Croatia. *M2 Best Books* critic Peter Haswell noted that some of the regions discussed are not included in the map that is located near the front of the book, but he did say that *Croatia* is "a very enjoyable read."

In *Library Journal,* Mirela Roncevic noted that with the influx of European and North Americans, the larger population centers of Croatia are becoming more influenced by Western-style capitalism and populated by many Croatians who would like to become players in the cultures and economies of Europe and the United States. Roncevic said that although the book represents only a part of Croatian life, it "tries to capture what is left of rural Croatia," and that "these personal (but never biased) essays fully encapsulate the country's essence" without letting the politics interrupt the overall rhythm of the narrative.

Fabijancic observes the feelings of many Croatians, including some of the young, who are content with the old way of life. He writes that in Herzegovina, there are those who have hope that some day all the people of the former Yugoslavia will again live together in peace.

Fabijancic "foregoes the usual blend of ethnography, historical writing, and travel journalism in this short, sweet examination of Croatian culture," according to *Quill & Quire*'s Andrew Kett. Cindy Appel wrote in *CelebrityCafe.com,* "Open up *Croatia* and start reading. You'll be engulfed in more than a world—it's a frame of mind, a mood, a sensation. It's the next best thing to being there."

BIOGRAPHICAL AND CRITICAL SOURCES:

PERIODICALS

Library Journal, July, 2003, Mirela Roncevic, review of *Croatia: Travels in Undiscovered Country,* p. 111.
M2 Best Books, September 17, 2003, Peter Haswell, review of *Croatia.*
Quill & Quire, January, 2003, Andrew Kett, review of *Croatia,* pp. 29-30.

ONLINE

CelebrityCafe.com, http://www.thecelebritycafe.com/ (June 24, 2003), Cindy Appel, review of *Croatia.*

FARR, Diane

PERSONAL: Born in CA; daughter of J. Wesley Farr (a minister).

ADDRESSES: Agent—Irene Goodman, Irene Goodman Literary Agency, 80 Fifth Ave., Suite 1101, New York, NY 10011.

CAREER: Writer.

WRITINGS:

ROMANCE NOVELS

Fair Game, Signet (New York, NY), 1999.
The Nobody, Signet (New York, NY), 1999.
Falling for Chloe, Signet (New York, NY), 2000.
Once upon a Christmas, Signet (New York, NY), 2000.
Duel of Hearts, Signet (New York, NY), 2002.
The Fortune Hunter, Signet (New York, NY), 2002.
Under the Wishing Star, Signet (New York, NY), 2003.
Under a Lucky Star, Signet (New York, NY), 2004.

WORK IN PROGRESS: The Mistletoe Test, for Signet (New York, NY).

BIOGRAPHICAL AND CRITICAL SOURCES:

PERIODICALS

Booklist, April 1, 2002, Maria Hatton, review of *The Fortune Hunter,* p. 1311; September 15, 2002, Maria Hatton, review of *Duel of Hearts,* p. 213.
Publishers Weekly, September 9, 2002, review of *Duel of Hearts,* p. 48.

*   *   *

FAVREAU, John
   See FAVREAU, Jon

*   *   *

FAVREAU, Jon 1966-
   (John Favreau)

PERSONAL: Born October 19, 1966, in Queens, NY; son of Charles (a special education teacher) and Madeleine (an elementary school teacher) Favreau;

married Joya Tillem, November 24, 2000; children: Max. *Education:* Studied acting at Improv Olympic and Second City (Chicago, IL).

ADDRESSES: Agent—Endeavor, 9701 Wilshire Blvd., 10th floor, Beverly Hills, CA 90212.; manager: Sweet Mud Group, 280 S. Beverly Dr., Suite 207, Beverly Hills, CA 90212; publicist: I/D PR, 3859 Cardiff Ave., 2nd floor, Culver City, CA 90232.

CAREER: Actor in films, including (as Chicago taxi driver) *Folks!,* Twentieth Century-Fox, 1992; (as uncredited extra) *Hoffa,* 1992; (as D-Bob) *Rudy,* TriStar, 1993; (as Gutter) *PCU* (also known as *PCU Pit Party*), Twentieth Century-Fox, 1994; (under the name John Favreau; as Elmer Rice) *Mrs. Parker and the Vicious Circle* (also known as *Mrs. Parker and the Round Table*), Fine Line, 1994; (as Assistant) *Batman Forever* (also known as *Forever*), Warner Bros., 1995; (as Zerkov) *Notes from the Underground,* Renegade Films, 1995; (as Straker) *Just Your Luck* (also known as *Whiskey Down*), PolyGram Video, 1996; (as Mike Peters; and producer, with others) *Swingers,* Miramax, 1996; (as Ezra Good) *Dogtown,* Stone Canyon Entertainment, 1997; (as Gus Partenza) *Deep Impact,* Paramount, 1998; (as Kyle Fisher) *Very Bad Things,* PolyGram, 1998; (as title role) *Rocky Marciano,* Metro-Goldwyn-Mayer/United Artists, 1999; *To the Moon,* Paramount, 1999; *Marshall of Revelation,* 1999; (as Adam Levy) *Love & Sex,* Behaviour Entertainment, 2000; (as Daniel Bateman) *The Replacements* (also known as *Scabs*), Warner Bros., 2000; (as Bobby Ricigliano; and producer) *Made,* Summit Entertainment, 2001; (as Franklin "Foggy" Nelson) *Daredevil,* Twentieth Century Fox, 2003; (as John; and executive producer) *The Big Empty,* 2003; (as doctor) *Elf,* New Line Cinema, 2003; (as Leo) *Something's Gotta Give,* 2003; (as Ron Roth) *Wimbledon,* 2004; and (as himself) *In Search of Ted Demme,* in production. Appeared in videos, including *Making It in Hollywood,* 2002, and *Beyond Hell's Kitchen: Making "Daredevil,"* 2003.

Actor in television series, including (as Peter Becker, a recurring role) *Friends,* National Broadcasting Company, Inc. (NBC), 1996; (as voice of Jealousy) *Hercules* (animated; also known as *Disney's Hercules*), American Broadcasting Companies, Inc. (ABC) and syndicated, 1998; (as voice of Crumford Lorak, a recurring role) *Buzz Lightyear of Star Command*

(animated), Disney Channel, 2000; and (as host) *Dinner for Five,* IFC, 2001. Actor in television movies, including (as Terry) *Persons Unknown,* Home Box Office (HBO), 1996; and (as title role) *Rocky Marciano,* Showtime, 1999. Actor in television pilots, including (as Alan) *Meant for Each Other,* Columbia Broadcasting System, Inc. (CBS), 1995; (as Terry Bianculli) *Desert Breeze,* Fox, 1996. Appeared in television specials, including (as Paul Metsler) *Grandpa's Funeral,* Showtime, 1994; "Hot New Trends," *The 1998 VH1 Fashion Awards,* VH1, 1998; and (as himself) *Daredevil: From the Comic to the Big Screen,* 2003. Guest star on television series, including *Seinfeld,* (as Dr. Tim Carney) *Chicago Hope, The Larry Sanders Show,* (as Douglas Lund) *Tracey Takes On . . .,* Late Show with David Letterman, The Late Late Show with Tom Snyder, The Daily Show, Dilbert,* (as himself) *The Sopranos, The Late Late Show with Craig Kilborn,* and *Mad TV.*

Director of films, including *Made,* 2001; *Elf,* New Line Cinema, 2003; and *Date School,* in production. Executive producer of the television series *Dinner for Five,* IFC, 2001. Director of television movies, including *Life on Parole,* 2002; and *Bad Cop, Good Cop,* Fox. Producer and director of the television pilot *Hollywood Tales,* Fox, 1997; executive producer and director of the television pilot *Smog,* UPN, 1999. Directed episodes of the television series *Undeclared,* Fox.

AWARDS, HONORS: Named most promising actor, Chicago Film Critics Association, 1997, for *Swingers.*

WRITINGS:

SCREENPLAYS

Swingers, Miramax, 1996.
Hollywood Tales (television pilot), Fox, 1997.
To the Moon, Paramount, 1999.
Marshall of Revelation, 1999.
Smog (television movie), UPN, 1999.
Made, Summit Entertainment, 2001.
(With Gary Tieche) *The First $20 Million Is Always the Hardest* based on the novel by Po Bronson) Twentieth Century-Fox, 2002.

Also wrote the screenplay for the television movie *Bad Cop, Good Cop,* Fox.

SIDELIGHTS: When actor Jon Favreau first turned to writing screenplays, he never expected to make a career out of it. With his guy-next-door looks, Favreau was having trouble winning substantial film roles, so with his unwanted free time he wrote a screenplay with a starring role designed for himself and with supporting roles written for some friends who were also actors. Several producers liked the screenplay and offered large sums of money for it, but they all wanted to cast a bigger-name actor as the star. Finally, Favreau sold the screenplay to director Doug Liman for $1000 and a promise that Liman would cast Favreau and his friends.

That screenplay became *Swingers,* a modest hit and cult favorite. Favreau's character is a struggling actor and comedian who leaves his lover in New York and comes to Los Angeles to try to make it in show business. While waiting for his big break, he and his friends hang out, chase girls, and analyze their lives. *Time* reviewer Richard Corliss noted that the "multiple-buddy movie" has been done numerous times before, but *Swingers* "smartly . . . spiffs up a tired formula." Favreau's screenplay is "exuberantly witty," Owen Gleiberman declared in *Entertainment Weekly,* and the interplay between the shy, neurotic Favreau and his cocksure friend, played by Vince Vaughn, was widely praised.

Several years later, Favreau and Vaughn teamed up again in another Favreau-written buddy film, *Made.* The two play an odd-couple pairing, with Favreau as the quiet, honest one and Vaughn as an obnoxious loud-mouth. In this film, the two are small-time gangsters who feud constantly while trying to complete a job under the direction of a mobster played by Sean "P. Diddy" Combs. "These two have major chemistry with each other," wrote *People*'s Leah Rozen.

In 2001, Favreau told *Back Stage West* interviewer Jamie Painter Young, "I was never going to get a part like I had in *Swingers.* . . . A movie like that wouldn't get made. But in making it, I created some opportunities as an actor. The irony is that in me attempting to showcase my ability as an actor, I ended up becoming a studio-approved writer. And the opportunities that have opened themselves up to me based on that were so much more interesting than the acting opportunities."

BIOGRAPHICAL AND CRITICAL SOURCES:

BOOKS

Newsmakers, Issue 3, Gale (Detroit, MI), 2002.

PERIODICALS

Back Stage West, October 17, 1996, Jamie Painter, interview with Favreau, pp. 6-7; July 12, 2001, Jamie Painter Young, interview with Favreau, p. 10.

Cosmopolitan, November, 1996, Guy Flatley, review of *Swingers,* p. 26.

Entertainment Weekly, November 1, 1996, Owen Gleiberman, review of *Swingers,* pp. 44-45; December 27, 1996; May 23, 1997, Eric Richter, review of *Swingers,* p. 68; June 1, 2001, Ann Limpert, interview with Favreau, p. 93; July 20, 2001, Owen Gleiberman, review of *Made,* p. 45.

Interview, June, 1998, Peter Berg, interview with Favreau, pp. 106-108.

Jet, July 16, 2001, Sylvia Flanagan, review of *Made,* p. 64.

Los Angeles Times, July 13, 2001, Kevin Thomas, review of *Made,* p. F6.

New York Times, October 18, 1996, Janet Maslin, review of *Swingers,* pp. B3, C3; May 30, 1997, review of *Swingers,* pp. B24, D18; May 13, 2001, Ariel Swartley, review of *Made,* p. MT24; July 13, 2001, Elvis Mitchell, review of *Made,* pp. B10, E12.

People, November 25, 1996, Dan Jewel, interview with Favreau, pp. 115-116; July 23, 2001, Leah Rozen, review of *Made,* p. 33.

Premiere, August, 2001, review of *Made,* p. 93; February, 2002, Howard Karren, review of *Made,* pp. 76-77.

Rolling Stone, August, 2001, Peter Travers, review of *Made,* p. 70.

Sight and Sound, July, 1997, Peter Matthews, review of *Swingers,* pp. 55-56.

Time, October 21, 1996, Richard Corliss, review of *Swingers,* p. 80.

US Weekly, September 4, 2000, Irene Zutell, interview with Favreau, pp. 88-90; July 23, 2001, Andrew Johnston, review of *Made,* p. 63.

Variety, September 9, 1996, Todd McCarthy, review of *Swingers,* p. 119; July 16, 2001, Joe Leydon, review of *Made,* p. 19.

Vogue, November, 1996, John Powers, review of *Swingers,* p. 160.

ONLINE

Internet Movie Database, http://www.imdb.com/ (November 21, 2003), "Jon Favreau."

PopMatters, http://www.popmatters.com/ (November 29, 2003), Cynthia Fuchs, interview with Favreau.*

FISHER, Rhoda Lee 1924-2004

OBITUARY NOTICE—See index for *CA* sketch: Born October 10, 1924, in Chicago, IL; died of complications from uterine cancer, March 21, 2004, in Medina, OH. Psychologist, educator, and author. Fisher gained wide recognition for her advice on child rearing, about which she wrote in her popular book *What We Really Know about Child Rearing: Science in Support of Effective Parenting*. Her initial area of study was in music education, and she earned her bachelor's in the subject from De Paul University in 1946; she then went on to earn a Ph.D. in psychology from the University of Chicago in 1956. During the 1950s, she had a private practice in Houston, Texas, while also working at the Jewish Vocational Service from 1950 to 1952 and as a psychologist for the Medical College in Houston from 1952 to 1954. During the 1960s, she was a researcher at the State University of New York's Upstate Medical School in Syracuse from 1961 to 1964, an instructor there from 1962 to 1968, and a research psychologist for Syracuse Public Schools from 1963 to 1968. Around this time, she also published her first book, *The Family* (1964). Going into private practice in 1968, her next work was *What We Really Know about Child Rearing* (1976; second edition, 1986), a book inspired by her realization that many of the then-available advice books on the subject were not supported by hard scientific data. Her interest in child psychology also led to the unique study *Pretend the World Is Funny and Forever: A Psychological Analysis of Clowns, Comedians and Actors* (1981), which won a *Psychology Today* award in 1981. For this book, she interviewed such comedians and Sid Caesar and Jackie Mason, forming a theory she called "schlemiel children," using humor to deal with family pressures. Remaining in private practice until 2003, Fisher was the author of one other book, *The Psychology of Adaptation to Absurdity: Tactics of Make-Believe* (1993), and she was a contributor to the 1997's *From Placebo to Panacea: Putting Psychiatric Drugs to the Test.*

OBITUARIES AND OTHER SOURCES:

PERIODICALS

Chicago Tribune, March 30, 2004, Section 3, p. 9.
New York Times, March 27, 2004, p. A15.

FISHMAN, Steve 1955-

PERSONAL: Born August 3, 1955. *Education:* Attended Brown University, until 1976.

ADDRESSES: Agent—c/o Author Mail, Free Press, Simon & Schuster, 1230 Avenue of the Americas, New York, NY 10020.

CAREER: Journalist. Worked for *Norwich Bulletin,* Norwich, CT, and *Miami Herald,* Miami, FL; stringer for *Christian Science Monitor,* the Associated Press, and *Newsweek;* editor for United Press International.

AWARDS, HONORS: Rotary Foundation fellowship; Inter-American Press Association fellowship; President's Award, American Medical Association; three-time winner of the Best Magazine Story Award, American Society of Journalists and Authors.

WRITINGS:

A Bomb in the Brain: A Heroic Tale of Science, Surgery, and Survival, Scribner (New York, NY), 1988.
Karaoke Nation; or, How I Spent a Year in Search of Glamour, Fulfillment, and a Million Dollars, Free Press (New York, NY), 2003.

Contributor to periodicals, including the *New York Times* (magazine), *Rolling Stone, Health, Details, GQ, New York, Vogue,* and *Success.*

SIDELIGHTS: In 1983 journalist Steve Fishman was twenty-eight and in Nicaragua when a genetic malformation in his brain caused him to quickly return to New York. His mother put him in the care of a team of neurosurgeons who examined him, scanned his brain, and performed an angiogram and brain surgery to repair the damage that had resulted from the hemorrhaging of a blood vessel. Fishman survived, but approximately one year later he developed epilepsy, which caused another set of problems and forced him to make adjustments in his life. His *A Bomb in the Brain: A Heroic Tale of Science, Surgery, and Survival* is a memoir of this period and a source of information about the various conditions that require brain surgery, how it is performed, and the intense emotions that

Fishman observed in the surgeons who perform procedures that are sometimes as much about intuition as they are about medical knowledge. He writes of watching the videotape of his operation by Dr. Eugene S. Flamm and the operations of others, including one during which Flamm could not find the source of bleeding and nearly lost his self-control.

"It is in the telling of his own story, an adventure with just the scent of a Ulysses about it, that Fishman pays his dues here in this literary tour de force," wrote Robert H. Williams in the *Washington Post*. Williams noted that although the book is a chronology, "every time the chronology demands some explanation, Fishman stops and gives a complete chapter on the history of neuroradiology, the history of neurosurgery, the biography of the titanic figure of a brain surgeon who wears open-heeled clogs in the operating room and shouts obscenities at tumor, staff, and patient as he wields long-handled knives in the pursuit of the physiological devils that cloud men's minds." *Psychology Today* reviewer Marjory Roberts called Fishman "a wonderful writer with powerful insights. He is also a fine reporter, though at times his thorough accounts of doctors past and present threaten to crowd out his own tale. But the juxtaposition serves a purpose. In weaving his story with theirs, Fishman shows that it is the ultimate business of both doctor and patient to preserve life. And the worlds they inhabit seem less distant when we peer beyond the technology of medicine and into the lives of those who pioneer the inexact science of healing."

Fishman's second book is also about him, but this time it concerns his time as an Internet entrepreneur during the 1990s dot.com boom. In *Karaoke Nation; or, How I Spent a Year in Search of Glamour, Fulfillment, and a Million Dollars,* Fishman details how, without the benefit of any business experience, he pursued the idea of a hip-hop karaoke Web site that would make him rich. He started with three thousand dollars in seed money from *New York* magazine to help him create his karaoke community. He was advised in this endeavor by big names in the world of hip hop, such as Russell Simmons of Def Jam records, as well as by a promoter, a lawyer, and others, but no one else offered to invest their money, nor did Fishman ever get an actual commitment, and so he sold and "became a thousandaire, not a millionaire," as Abby Ellin commented in the *New York Times. Boston Globe* commentator Tom Ehrenfeld further noted that

in losing the company, Fishman gained the time to write the book: "Which is a good thing: He is a terrific writer with a smart take on the insanity around him."

BIOGRAPHICAL AND CRITICAL SOURCES:

BOOKS

Fishman, Steve, *A Bomb in the Brain: A Heroic Tale of Science, Surgery, and Survival,* Scribner (New York, NY), 1988.
Fishman, Steve, *Karaoke Nation; or, How I Spent a Year in Search of Glamour, Fulfillment, and a Million Dollars,* Free Press (New York, NY), 2003.

PERIODICALS

Booklist, April 15, 2003, David Siegfried, review of *Karaoke Nation; or, How I Spent a Year in Search of Glamour, Fulfillment, and a Million Dollars,* p. 1434.
Boston Globe, May 18, 2003, Tom Ehrenfeld, review of *Karaoke Nation,* p. D2.
Houston Chronicle, November 15, 1992, Jane E. Brody, review of *A Bomb in the Brain: A Heroic Tale of Science, Surgery, and Survival,* p. 12.
Kirkus Reviews, April 1, 2003, review of *Karaoke Nation,* p. 520.
Library Journal, May 1, 2003, Stacey Marien, review of *Karaoke Nation,* p. 131.
New York Times, July 13, 2003, Abby Ellin, review of *Karaoke Nation,* Section 3, p. 5.
Psychology Today, December, 1988, Marjory Roberts, review of *A Bomb in the Brain,* p. 68.
Toronto Star, January 11, 2004, Nick Krewen, review of *Karaoke Nation,* p. D14.
Washington Post, January 31, 1989, Robert H. Williams, review of *A Bomb in the Brain,* p. Z9.

ONLINE

Mediabistro.com, http://www.mediabistro.com/ (May 16, 2003), Eric Messinger, interview with Steve Fishman.*

*   *   *

FITZGERALD, Carol 1942-

PERSONAL: Born August 18, 1942, in Pittsburgh, PA; daughter of Edward A. (an accountant) and Catherine (a homemaker; maiden name, McKay) Bloch; married John M. McKee (marriage ended); married Jean

Fitzgerald (in business; a retired naval officer), December 19, 1984; children: (first marriage) John M., Jr., James S. *Ethnicity:* "English-American." *Education:* Attended University of Florida, 1960-61, Louisiana State University, 1963, and studied in Mexico; University of Mississippi, B.A., 1964. *Politics:* Independent. *Religion:* Roman Catholic. *Hobbies and other interests:* Travel, collecting books, cultural events.

ADDRESSES: Home—2100 South Ocean Ln., Apt. 706, Fort Lauderdale, FL 33316; fax: 954-463-9509. *E-mail*—riversgal@aol.com.

CAREER: Broward County Commission, Broward County, FL, commission aide, 1978-2001; Broward County Library System, administrative coordinator for the director, 2001—. Cleveland Clinic Hospital, Fort Lauderdale, FL, trustee, 1987-98, chair, 1988-90, vice chair of executive board, 1990-97; Light of the World Clinic, director, 1996—.

MEMBER: Fellowship of American Bibliophilic Societies (trustee, 1998—), Fontaneda Society (director), Grolier Club, Book Club of California.

AWARDS, HONORS: Grant from Book Club of California, 2003.

WRITINGS:

The Rivers of America: A Descriptive Bibliography, Oak Knoll Press (New Castle, DE), 2001.

Author of foreword to reprint, *The Connecticut,* by Walter Hard, Massachusetts Audubon Society (Lincoln, MA), 1998.

WORK IN PROGRESS: Series Americana, 1940-1980: A Descriptive Bibliography and History (tentative title).

SIDELIGHTS: Carol Fitzgerald told *CA:* "While 'The Rivers of America' series was my first interest among series on Americana, it is not alone. Many other such series were begun, starting in 1940, including 'American Folkways,' 'American Lakes,' and 'Seaports.'

There are more than a dozen such series, valued for their literary quality and their contributions to American history, but there is no single, comprehensive history of them, a work that would include bibliographical descriptions of individual volumes and biographies of their authors, editor, and illustrators. I am well along in the research and writing of such a work, following the pattern established in my first book, with the intention of producing the definitive annotated bibliography of the most important and respected of such series.

"I am an independent scholar, motivated primarily by a desire to preserve the history of various 'series Americana' and their contributing authors, illustrators, editors, and publishers. The series in which I have the strongest interest are 'The Rivers of America,' 'American Folkways,' 'American Lakes,' 'American Trails,' 'Mainstream of America,' and 'Regions of America.' I have been encouraged in my work by Dr. John Y. Cole, director of the Center for the Book at the Library of Congress; Dr. Alexander C. McLeod, clinical professor of medicine emeritus at Vanderbilt University; Dr. Thomas D. Clark, Commonwealth Historian Laureate of Kentucky; and my husband and editor, Jean.

"When I began to collect 'The Rivers of America,' I soon discovered that there was no comprehensive listing of the sixty-five titles in the series, and that some contributors to the series were already forgotten, despite the undisputed excellence of the series itself. As I state in the foreword of my book, my early research on the series led me to a diverse group of talented and accomplished men and women—the series authors, illustrators, and editors—some of them household names, others essentially forgotten.

"I resolved to develop a descriptive bibliography of the series that would also tell the stories of the men and women who had brought it to life. Eventually, after considerable research and extensive correspondence, I was able to develop a biographical sketch of every one of the sixty authors, fifty-three illustrators, and eight principal editors. This was truly a labor of love, ten years in the making, much of the early years spent in research in various libraries, not on the Internet, which for me at least was just coming on the scene.

"I am well along on my second book, working title *Series Americana, 1940-1980: A Descriptive Bibliography and History,* researching the history of a given series title by title, author by author, and so forth. As my research develops, I write a rough draft of the related chapter or section. When I have finished the research for a given series, I assemble and rewrite all the drafts, pulling them into a coherent whole. This process, which is surely not unusual, was established as I wrote my first book, and it works well for me. My primary motivation is unchanged: to preserve the histories of these distinctively American series and the memory of their authors, illustrators, editors, and publishers.

"A collateral value of my work, I believe, is that the finished product, the descriptive bibliography of one or more series, becomes a useful reference work for book collectors and booksellers. With its precise, accurate bibliographical descriptions, *The Rivers of America: A Descriptive Bibliography* permits ready and certain identification of any of the 400-odd printings in the series and their dust jackets. My next book will limit technical bibliographical descriptions to the first edition, first printing of each title in each series, but for most users it will serve the same purpose.

"I have been fortunate to work in a fascinating period of American history, encompassing the Great Depression, World War II, and the postwar boom in population and publishing. The authors, editors, and illustrators of these diverse series Americana produced several hundred volumes of distinctively American literature that in many ways stand alone, separate from other American literature and worthy of preservation and respect."

BIOGRAPHICAL AND CRITICAL SOURCES:

PERIODICALS

Choice, February, 2002, review of *The Rivers of America: A Descriptive Bibliography.*
Firsts, November, 2001, review of *The Rivers of America.*

*   *   *

FLEMING, Daniel B(arry), Jr. 1931-

PERSONAL: Born November 28, 1931, in St. Marys, WV; son of Daniel B. and Ruth (Sayer) Fleming; married Beverly Browne, June 29, 1963; children: Kathy, Elizabeth, Susan. *Education:* West Virginia University,

B.A. (political science), 1953, M.A. (political science), 1954; George Washington University, Ed.D., 1970.

ADDRESSES: Home—615 Piedmont St., Blacksburg, VA 24060-4924. *Office*—Virginia Tech, 306 War Memorial Hall, Blacksburg, VA 24061. *Agent*—c/o Author Mail, Vandamere Press, P.O. Box 17446, Clearwater, FL 33762.

CAREER: Marietta, OH, school system, high school teacher, 1957-64; Fairfax County, VA, school system, social studies superintendent, 1964-70; Virginia Polytechnic Institute, Blacksburg, VA, assistant professor of education, 1970-92, professor emeritus.

MEMBER: National Council for the Social Studies, Social Science Education Consortium.

AWARDS, HONORS: Fulbright fellow; Congressional fellow.

WRITINGS:

(With Paul C. Slayton, Jr.) *Virginia History and Government: 1850 to the Present,* Silver Burdett Co. (Morristown, NJ), 1986.
Kennedy vs. Humphrey, West Virginia, 1960: The Pivotal Battle for the Democratic Presidential Nomination, McFarland (Jefferson, NC), 1992.
. . . *Ask What You Can Do for Your Country: The Memory and Legacy of John F. Kennedy,* Vandamere Press (Clearwater, FL), 2002.

Author of five textbooks; contributor of articles to professional journals.

SIDELIGHTS: Daniel B. Fleming, Jr.'s . . . *Ask What You Can Do for Your Country: The Memory and Legacy of John F. Kennedy* reaches back to a decades-old tragedy, the assassination of the president on November 22, 1963. For readers too young to remember the moment, this book offers the recollections of those who will never forget it. It is a fitting tribute to the leader who is memorialized by people from all walks of life within its covers. Politicians, journalists, civil rights leaders, actors, artists, Peace Corps volunteers, the Secret Service men who guarded him, and Keith Clark, the soldier who played taps at Arlington National Cemetery during the funeral, recall Kennedy. Some remember his life and others his death.

Contributors include Myrlie Evers (wife of Medgar), former President Gerald Ford, John Glenn, Barry Goldwater, William Fulbright, Margaret Chase Smith, Margaret Truman (daughter of former President Harry Truman), Evelyn Lincoln (Kennedy's secretary), former President Jimmy Carter, and Lena Horne. Psychic Jeanne Dixon, who predicted that Kennedy would die in Dallas and begged his friends to prevent him from going, also adds her thoughts. The pilot of Air Force One tells of how they ripped seats out of the plane so that the body of the president could ride with the passengers rather than in the cargo hold.

Library Journal's Michael A. Genovese wrote that Fleming "does a fine job of bringing to life . . . [Kennedy's] meaning for a generation of Americans." A *Publishers Weekly* contributor noted that the book is "filled with admiration and fondness for Kennedy, and with curiosity about what his presidency might have meant for the country had he lived."

BIOGRAPHICAL AND CRITICAL SOURCES:

PERIODICALS

Library Journal, November 1, 2002, Michael A. Genovese, review of . . . *Ask What You Can Do for Your Country: The Memory and Legacy of John F. Kennedy,* pp. 99-100.
Publishers Weekly, November 25, 2002, review of . . . *Ask What You Can Do for Your Country,* p. 55.*

*   *   *

FLEMING, Keith 1960(?)-

PERSONAL: Born c. 1960; *Education:* Graduated from University of Chicago, 1984.

ADDRESSES: Home—Providence, RI. *Agent*—c/o Author Mail, HarperCollins Publishers, 10 East 53rd St., 7th Floor, New York, NY 10022.

CAREER: Writer, editor, and journalist. Served as editor of *Chicago Literary Review.*

WRITINGS:

The Boy with a Thorn in His Side: A Memoir, Morrow (New York, NY), 2000.
Original Youth: The Real Story of Edmund White's Boyhood, Green Candy Press (San Francisco, CA), 2003.

SIDELIGHTS: In the mid 1970s, at the age of sixteen, writer Keith Fleming went to New York City to live with his uncle, prominent gay novelist Edmund White. Fleming's parents had just divorced, and he faced a rough future of being institutionalized for little more than teenage rebelliousness and his emotional reaction to the crumbling of the life he had known. White "rescued me," Fleming wrote in the *Guardian.* "It was the defining moment of my life: my experience as the heterosexual ward of a gay uncle was even weirder than one might imagine."

Fleming describes his years with White in *The Boy with a Thorn in His Side: A Memoir.* Though at the time White was struggling financially, and the milieu of mid-70s gay Manhattan did not make much accommodation for a teenage boy, Fleming was welcomed, loved, treated with respect, and reminded of his own worth. Immediately after arriving, White sent him to a dermatologist to treat his severe acne; he also sent him to the barber and the dentist and changed Fleming's wardrobe to fit in better with his environment. White then sent him to a pricey private school, financed in part by the advance from one of the writer's best-known works, *The Joy of Gay Sex.* White provided Fleming with the most normal life he possibly could, even while continuing to pursue his own lifestyle. "Uncle Ed continued to lead the life of a dandy, equally at home with leather bars and the Lincoln Center," Fleming commented in the *Guardian* article. "Many a school night would find me doing my homework at the kitchen table and my uncle, in leather jacket and jeans, saying good night as he headed out for a wild night downtown" at any of a number of gay nightspots. "And yet," observed Adam Goodheart in *New York Times Book Review,* "improbably enough, Fleming found in his Uncle Eddie the first really trustworthy parent, and the first happy family life, that he'd ever had." Fleming "tells his story with humor and compassion, all the while informing the national debate about the definition of a family," observed Ron Ratliff in *Library Journal.* Sheryl Fowler, writing in *School Library Journal,* remarked favorably on the book's "strong and affecting narrative," while *Lambda Book Report* critic Kevin W. Reardon called it a "first-rate coming-of-age memoir."

In *Original Youth: The Real Story of Edmund White's Boyhood,* Fleming examines the childhood and teen years of the man who became his surrogate parent. Writing "with a biographer's zeal and an intimate's insight," noted Reardon, Fleming "reinterprets the formative years between White's parents' divorce when he was seven years old and White's first contact with gay subculture during his freshman year at the University of Michigan." He finds parallels to his own youth in White's childhood. White had also been threatened with institutionalization as a teen, though in the context of 1950s America, where homosexuality was considered a mental disorder and institutional "treatment" a common practice. While White struggled with his own sexual impulses, he also had to deal with a dysfunctional family in the form of his emotionally distant, self-centered father and needy, emotionally manipulative mother. Even in his youth, however, White was drawn to writing, composing plays and novels while still a boy.

Fleming fills in the details of White's youth through interviews with friends and associates, his own mother (White's older sister), and White himself. "Keith's wonderful biography of my early years will set a new standard, I'm sure," White remarked in an interview on the *Green Candy Press* Web site. "I think he takes a sympathetic but objective look at my youth." Nancy R. Ives, writing in *Library Journal,* called the book "An intimate biography about an important man of letters" and "a valuable contribution to literature collections." And Felice Picano and Jeff Reys remarked in the *Advocate* that Fleming's work "substantially raises the criterion by which gay literary criticism must now be judged."

BIOGRAPHICAL AND CRITICAL SOURCES:

PERIODICALS

Advocate, December 9, 2003, Felice Picano and Jeff Reys, "Play Grounds," review of *Original Youth: The Real Story of Edmund White's Boyhood,* p. 90.

Booklist, November 15, 2003, Ray Olson, review of *Original Youth,* pp. 563-564.
Guardian (Manchester, England), January 15, 2000, Keith Fleming, "My Life with Uncle Ed; At Sixteen, Keith Fleming Was Rescued from a Psychiatric Ward by His Uncle, the Writer Edmund White. Fleming, a Heterosexual, Was Raised in New York's Wild Gay 70s Scene, and Learned Unexpected Lessons about Life, Love, and Art," p. 1.
Lambda Book Report, December, 2003, Kevin W. Reardon, "Proustian Detail," pp. 31-32.
Library Journal, April 15, 2000, Ron Ratliff, review of *The Boy with a Thorn in His Side: A Memoir,* p. 110; December, 2003, Nancy R. Ives, review of *Original Youth,* pp. 117-118.
New York Times Book Review, May 21, 2000, Adam Goodheart, "Uncle Ed," p. 12.
Publishers Weekly, February 21, 2000, review of *The Boy with a Thorn in His Side,* p. 72; November 24, 2003, review of *Original Youth,* pp. 55-56.
School Library Journal, February, 2001, Sheryl Fowler, review of *The Boy with a Thorn in His Side,* p. 145.

ONLINE

Green Candy Press Web Site, http://www.greencandypress.com/ (April 1, 2004), interview with Edmund White and Keith Fleming.*

*   *   *

FORD, Susan 1957-

PERSONAL: Born July 6, 1957, in Washington, DC; daughter of Gerald R. (Thirty-eighth president of the United States) and Betty Ford; married Chuck Vance (a Secret Service agent; divorced); married Vaden Bales (a lawyer), 1990; children: two daughters, three stepsons. *Education:* Studied photography with Ansel Adams; attended University of Kansas (studied photojournalism).

ADDRESSES: Home—Corrales, NM. *Agent*—c/o Author Mail, Thomas Dunne Books, St. Martin's Press, 175 Fifth Ave., New York, NY 10010.

CAREER: Writer, photographer, spokesperson. National Breast Cancer Awareness Month spokesperson in the 1990s; Betty Ford Center, board member.

WRITINGS:

(With Laura Hayden) *Double Exposure: A First Daughter Mystery,* Thomas Dunne Books (New York, NY), 2002.

(With Laura Hayden) *Sharp Focus: A First Daughter Mystery,* Thomas Dunne Books (New York, NY), 2003.

Also contributor to *Seventeen.* Ford's photographs have appeared in *Newsweek* and *Ladies' Home Journal,* and other magazines and newspapers through the Associated Press.

SIDELIGHTS: Susan Ford, daughter of President Gerald R. Ford, turned the years she spent in the White House in the 1970s to good use in two mysteries which are set at 1600 Pennsylvania Avenue. Teaming up with novelist and scriptwriter Laura Hayden, Ford—whose married name is Susan Ford Bales—merged memories of her time in Washington with her early career as a photographer to come up with a behind-the-scenes look at life in the White House that has been compared to the mystery series of other presidential "First Children," such as Margaret Truman and Elliot Roosevelt. Ford in fact began her writing career while still a teenager, writing a column for *Seventeen* magazine on life in the White House.

It took more than two decades for Ford to return to writing, however, after pursuing a career in photojournalism, and then as spokesperson for the National Breast Cancer Awareness Month. Living in New Mexico, and with one of her two daughters going off to college, Ford decided to finally mine the material she had gathered as a young daughter of the president. Collaborating with Hayden, she published *Double Exposure: A First Daughter Mystery* in 2002. In the tale, Elliot Cooper, a widower, becomes president and is accompanied by his twenty-five-year-old aspiring photojournalist daughter Eve Cooper into the White House. Eve moves from Denver to Washington and shares the White House with an aunt, who serves as the stand-in First Lady; her teenage brother, Drew; her father; and assorted Secret Service men. When the White House photographer, Michael Cauffman, finds a body in the Rose Garden during a photo shoot one snowy day, and further discovers a photo on the corpse's body depicting sexual shenanigans in the

Lincoln Bedroom, things grow tense at the White House. The corpse—of a man who apparently died of a heart attack—is the twin brother of White House chief usher, Burton O'Connor; the man photographed in an uncompromising position is an advertising executive, Roger Stansfield. This constellation of events could badly compromise the president, for allegations soon arise that the president accepted tobacco lobby money via Stansfield. Thereafter, it is a race against the clock by Eve, her Secret Service contingent, and Cauffman to keep this from turning into a major scandal and ruining her father's first term in office.

Ford's debut as a novelist "offers some pleasant glimpses behind the scenes at the White House," a critic for *Kirkus Reviews* noted. This same writer also felt, however, that "the underlying mystery defies common sense." A similar view was shared by a reviewer for *Publishers Weekly,* who felt that Ford got off to a "shaky start" with this mystery, but that the author's "insider knowledge" was put to good use to "provide an authentic view of life in the White House fishbowl." Rex E. Klett, writing in *Library Journal,* also praised the "insider's view" that Ford provides in her book. Indeed, several parallels exist between Ford and her protagonist: both experienced the "fishbowl" aspect of life in the White House; both are photojournalists; both know the workings of the Secret Service firsthand (Ford's first husband was one of her father's Secret Service agents); and both stood in for an absent mother. In Ford's case, however, it was not death but breast cancer that sidelined her mother. "I had to apologize to my mother," Ford told Carrie Seidman of the *Albuquerque Tribune Online.* "'Sorry, you're dead. Don't take it personally.'"

Ford continued her collaboration with Hayden on the 2003 addition to the series, *Sharp Focus: A First Daughter Mystery.* In this outing, Eve takes a glider ride only to learn that moments later another glider has been involved in a fatal crash. This sets her and the Secret Service to wondering if there is someone stalking the president's daughter. Such questions are proven moot once someone starts shooting at Eve. In order to stop the mayhem, Eve must figure out what connection she has to a passenger who died aboard the second glider. A critic for *Publishers Weekly* found more to like in this second novel, noting that the authors "nicely blend action, suspense, humor and a little romance."

BIOGRAPHICAL AND CRITICAL SOURCES:

PERIODICALS

Detroit Free Press, May 8, 2002, review of *Double Exposure: A First Daughter Mystery.*
Independent Living, March-April, 1994, Nancy Lee Norman, "A Champion for Women's Health: Susan Ford Bales Is Committed to Promoting the Need for the Early Detection of Breast Cancer," pp. 42-43.
Kirkus Reviews, January 15, 2002, review of *Double Exposure,* p. 76.
Library Journal, March 1, 2002, Rex E. Klett, review of *Double Exposure,* p. 144.
New York Times, August 6, 1975, William Farrell, "Susan Ford Finds a 'Superneat' Job"; June 6, 1978, Judy Klemesrud, "Susan Ford Tries Life on Her Own."
New York Times Upfront, October 2, 2000, "A Teen in the White House," p. 2S18.
Publishers Weekly, February 4, 2002, review of *Double Exposure,* pp. 55-56; May 12, 2003, review of *Sharp Focus: A First Daughter Mystery,* p. 47.
USA Today, April 18, 2002, Deirdre Donahue, "A 'First Daughter' Tries Mystery for First Book," p. D4.

ONLINE

AEI Speakers Bureau, http://www.aeispeakers.com/ (March 23, 2004).
Albuquerque Tribune Online, http://www.abqtrib.com/ (August 29, 2003), Carrie Seidman, "First Daughter Has Second Mystery Novel."
Presidents' Children Web site, http://www.presidents children.com/ (March 23, 2004).
St. Martin's Press Web site, http://www.stmartins.com/ (March 23, 2004).*

*   *   *

FOWLER, Will 1922-2004

OBITUARY NOTICE—See index for *CA* sketch: Born August 29, 1922, in Jamaica, NY; died of prostate cancer, April 14, 2004, in Burbank, CA. Journalist, publicist, and author. A colorful journalist who worked for the *Los Angeles Examiner* in the 1940s, Fowler later became involved with television and penned acclaimed books and a hit Broadway play. The son of the famous newspaperman Gene Fowler, who had many Hollywood connections, the young Fowler grew up knowing such renowned actors and writers as W. C. Fields, John Barrymore, and William Faulkner. He developed an early love of music and became a talented pianist while still attending Beverly Hills High School. After serving in the U.S. Coast Guard, he joined the *Examiner* in 1944 as a reporter. A few years later, in 1947, he gained attention as the first reporter on the scene of the Black Dahlia murder in which a young woman named Elizabeth Short was cut in two. This and other stories of his reporter days were later recounted in his 1991 book, *Reporters: Memoirs of a Young Newspaperman.* Fowler left the newspaper business in 1952 to exercise other writing talents. For a year he wrote for *The Red Skelton Show,* and he also wrote songs, including 1959's "He's So Married," which was performed by Doris Day. He also penned a biography about his well-known father, *The Young Man from Denver* (1962). During much of the 1950s, Fowler worked for American Airlines as a public relationship representative before returning to television as director of news and public affairs for KTTV from 1959 to 1960; he also worked for Twentieth Century-Fox television as a publicist for series such as *Daniel Boone* and *Twelve O'Clock High.* Interested in the stage, as well, Fowler wrote the off-Broadway play *Julius Castro* (1961) and the Broadway sensation *Barrymore* with William Luce. *Barrymore,* which earned its star, Christopher Plummer, a Tony Award, ran from 1996 to 1997. Other books by Fowler include *The Ping-Pong Table* (1966) and the autobiography *The Second Handshake* (1980).

OBITUARIES AND OTHER SOURCES:

PERIODICALS

Los Angeles Times, April 15, 2004, p. B13.
New York Times, April 17, 2004, p. A13.
Washington Post, April 19, 2004, p. B7.

*   *   *

FRALEY, Tobin 1951-

PERSONAL: Born August 9, 1951; married Rachel Perkal.

ADDRESSES: Home—Illinois. *Agent*—c/o Author Mail, Chronicle Books, 85 Second St., Sixth Fl., San Francisco, CA 94105.

CAREER: Writer and woodcarver. Restorer and collector of wooden carousel animals.

WRITINGS:

The Carousel Animal, Zephyr Press (Berkeley, CA), 1983.
(With Carol Bialkowski) *Carousels: The Myth, the Magic, and the Memories,* Willitts Designs (Petaluma, CA), 1991.
The Great American Carousel: A Century of Master Craftsmanship, Chronicle Books (San Francisco, CA), 1994.
A Humbug Christmas (children's book), Humbug Publishing (Kansas City, MO), 1998.
Carousel Animals: Artistry in Motion, Chronicle Books (San Francisco, CA), 2002.

SIDELIGHTS: Tobin Fraley is the author of several books on old-fashioned carousels. He is trained in wood-carving and the restoration of carousel animals and comes from a family of amusement park owners. Aside from authoring several books pertaining to carousels, he has also written a children's book, *A Humbug Christmas,* about a little creature called Humbug that runs around causing trouble at Christmas time.

Fraley's first book, *The Carousel Animal,* published in 1983, informs readers about the origins of the word "carousel" and contains a large number of photographs of carousel animals made by various craftsmen. Mark Stevens, reviewing the book in *Newsweek,* called it "a lovely, concise and reasonably priced collection."

The Great American Carousel: A Century of Master Craftsmanship focuses on the history of carousels in America. The popularity of wooden carousels was at its high point around the turn of the twentieth century. The onset of World War I started the slow decline of the once-flourishing carousel industry, which in the 1940s came to an end. In the 1960s a new generation started to restore vintage carousel animals, leading to a renewed interest in old wooden carousels. A reviewer writing in *American Craft* called *The Great American Carousel* an "informative and nostalgic account of the rise and decline and revival of the amusement park merry-go-round."

Fraley's 2002 publication, *Carousel Animals: Artistry in Motion,* is about the craftsmen who built wooden carousel animals. The heyday of the carousel coincided with a surge of immigrants from Europe, many of whom were highly skilled woodworkers. Fraley provides selected biographical sketches and maintains that these woodcarvers were, in fact, artists, as they trained professionally for many years. Reviewer Margaret Todd Maitland commented in an article for *Ruminator Review* that "Fraley is not completely convincing as he struggles with the fine points of aesthetic theory in his attempt to differentiate between a craftsperson and an artist. But his rather pedestrian prose brightens in the chapters on the creators themselves."

BIOGRAPHICAL AND CRITICAL SOURCES:

PERIODICALS

American Craft, Volume 54, issue 6, 1994, review of *The Great American Carousel: A Century of Master Craftsmanship,* p. 22.
Los Angeles Times Book Review, December 4, 1983, review of *The Carousel Animal,* pp. 8-9.
Newsweek, December 12, 1983, Mark Stevens, review of *The Carousel Animal,* p. 100.
Rocky Mountain News, December 7, 2002, review of *Carousel Animals: Artistry in Motion,* section D, p. 1.
Ruminator Review, winter, 2002-2003, Margaret Todd Maitland, review of *Carousel Animals,* p. 14.
St. Louis Post-Dispatch, December 13, 1999, Mikal Harris, "Toys for Tots Puts Good 'Humbug' Back into the Christmas Season," p. 1.
Time, December 12, 1983, review of *The Carousel Animal,* p. 104.
Tribune Books, December 4, 1994, review of *The Great American Carousel,* p. 8.
Washington Post Book World, November 6, 1994, review of *The Great American Carousel,* p. 12; November 10-16, 2002, Dennis Drabelle, review of *Carousel Animals,* p. 9.*

*   *   *

FRANKLIN, Allan (David) 1938-

PERSONAL: Born August 1, 1938, in Brooklyn, NY; son of Charles (in real estate) and Helen (a homemaker; maiden name, Cohen) Franklin; married Cynthia Betts (a homemaker), March 12, 1994. *Education:* Columbia College, A.B., 1959; Cornell University, Ph.D., 1965.

ADDRESSES: Home—1911 Mariposa, Boulder, CO 80302. *Office*—Department of Physics, UCB 390, University of Colorado, Boulder, CO 80309-0390. *E-mail*—Allan.Franklin@colorado.edu.

CAREER: Princeton University, Princeton, NJ, research associate, 1965-66, instructor, 1966-67; University of Colorado, Boulder, assistant professor, 1967-73, associate professor, 1973-82, professor of physics, 1982—. Visiting professor and lecturer at various institutions, including City University of New York, 1974-75; University of Campinas, Brazil, 1982; and University of London, 1982-92.

MEMBER: American Physical Society (chairman, forum on history of physics), History of Science Society, Philosophy of Science Association (executive board).

AWARDS, HONORS: Center for Philosophy of Science senior research fellow, University of Pittsburgh, 1986; Dibner Institute for the History of Science and Technology, senior resident fellow, 1994, 1999; Miegunyah Distinguished Fellow, University of Melbourne, 2000; American Physical Society centennial speaker.

WRITINGS:

The Principle of Inertia in the Middle Ages, Colorado Associated University Press (Boulder, CO), 1976.

The Neglect of Experiment, Cambridge University Press (New York, NY), 1986.

Experiment, Right or Wrong, Cambridge University Press (New York, NY), 1990.

The Rise and Fall of the Fifth Force: Discovery, Pursuit, and Justification in Modern Physics, American Institute of Physics (New York, NY), 1993.

Can That Be Right? Essays on Experiment, Evidence, and Science, Kluwer Academic Publishers (Boston, MA), 1999.

Are There Really Neutrinos? An Evidential History, Perseus Books (Cambridge, MA), 2000.

Selectivity and Discord: Two Problems of Experiment, University of Pittsburgh Press (Pittsburgh, PA), 2002.

No Easy Answers: Science and the Pursuit of Knowledge, University of Pittsburgh Press (Pittsburgh, PA), 2005.

Also contributor to numerous academic journals, including *Physical Review, American Journal of Physics,* and *Journal of the History of Ideas.*

SIDELIGHTS: As *Isis* contributor Michael Riordan explained, "Few scholars have written more about experimentation than Allan Franklin, who has been analyzing its role in physics for more than two decades." Riordan asserted that though "social constructivists" feel that "scientific knowledge is socially conditioned," Franklin claims that "experiments can and do yield valid, objective knowledge about nature."

In *The Neglect of Experiment,* Franklin disputes the conception that science is primarily theory-driven rather than experiment-driven. After laying out the views of such theorists as Thomas Kuhn, Paul Feyerabend, and Willard Quine, Franklin describes and defends the role that experiments have played in confirming various hypotheses. In the *American Historical Review,* Robert Kargon stated that "Franklin does more in this fine book. . . . He challenges historians and philosophers to examine real and not 'mythical' experiments, and, above all, he prescribes a new agenda for the philosophy of science." According to Kargon, "This new agenda calls for philosophical appraisal of what scientists actually do."

Franklin modified his position somewhat in *Experiment, Right or Wrong.* Still, his primary purpose in the book is to defend science from the charge that it acts unreasonably in accepting certain theories and discarding others. Franklin looks at experimental evidence that was ultimately rejected after a theory it seemed to support was found to be false. For Franklin, scientists have by and large rejected experimental evidence, not because it did not fit a preconceived theory but because competing evidence proved stronger or the results had to be reinterpreted in light of a better theory.

The Rise and Fall of the Fifth Force: Discovery, Pursuit, and Justification in Modern Physics explores a particularly interesting example of physicists reacting to an experiment that seemed to overthrow an established scientific paradigm. In January of 1986, a group of physicists announced that they had discovered a fifth force in nature, slightly weaker than gravity but also affected by interacting masses. This came as quite a shock to the scientific community and seemed at first to overturn a number of assumptions of Newtonian physics. Scientists undertook a number of experiments hoping to confirm or refute the novel hypothesis, until, as Allan Franklin's book chronicles, the preponderance of the evidence gradually turned against the theory in the early 1990s. "What makes this book unique," observed *Science* reviewer George T. Gillies, "is the way it opens windows on the methods by which scientific inquiry proceeds by introducing the reader to historical analysis techniques."

In *Selectivity and Discord: Two Problems of Experiment,* Franklin acknowledges that biases do indeed slip in when it comes to weighing and evaluating data, but he argues that experiment and empirical research still underlie true science. Once again using a series of case studies, Franklin probes the actual justifications for accepting or rejecting certain data, claiming that these decisions are in practice based on reasonable, rational, and scientifically valid criteria. Riordan notes that Franklin attempts to understand the "ambiguities that must be resolved if scientific knowledge is to be trusted."

BIOGRAPHICAL AND CRITICAL SOURCES:

PERIODICALS

American Historical Review, June, 1990, Robert Kargon, review of *The Neglect of Experiment,* p. 778.
British Journal for the Philosophy of Science, March, 1994, J. E. Tiles, review of *Experiment, Right or Wrong,* p. 341.
Isis, September, 2003, Michael Riordan, review of *Selectivity and Discord: Two Problems of Experiment,* p. 565.
Science, May 13, 1994, George T. Gillies, review of *The Rise and Fall of the Fifth Force: Discovery, Pursuit, and Justification in Modern Physics,* p. 1001.

ONLINE

Allan Franklin Home Page, http://spot.colorado.edu/ (June 10, 2004).

*   *   *

FREEHLING, William W(ilhartz) 1935-

PERSONAL: Born December 26, 1935, in Chicago, IL; son of Norman and Edna (Wilhartz) Freehling; married Natalie Paperno, January 27, 1961 (divorced, April, 1970); married Alison Goodyear, June 19, 1971;

children: (first marriage) Alan, Deborah; (second marriage) Alison, William. *Education:* Harvard University, A.B., 1958; University of California—Berkeley, M.A., 1959, Ph.D., 1964.

ADDRESSES: Home—3500 Huntertown Rd., Versailles, KY 40383-9198. *Office*—Dept. of History, University of Kentucky, 1715 Patterson Office Tower, Lexington, KY 40506-0027 *Agent*—c/o Author Mail, Oxford University Press, 198 Madison Ave., New York, NY 10016. *E-mail*—wwfree0@uky.edu.

CAREER: Historian, educator, Civil War scholar. University of California—Berkeley, teaching fellow, 1961-63; Harvard University, Cambridge, MA, instructor, 1963-64; University of Michigan, assistant professor, 1964-67, associate professor, 1967-70, professor of history, 1970-72; Johns Hopkins University, Baltimore, MD, professor of history, 1972-91; State University of New York—Buffalo, Thomas B. Lockwood professor of history, 1991-94; University of Kentucky—Lexington, professor of history, Otis A. Singletary chair in humanities, 1994—.

MEMBER: American Antiquarian Society, Society of American Historians, American Historical Association, Southern History Association, Organization of American Historians, Phi Beta Kappa.

AWARDS, HONORS: Allan Nevins History Prize, 1965; Bancroft History Prize, 1967; National Humanities Foundation fellow, 1968; Guggenheim fellow, 1970; American Antiquarian Society/National Humanities Foundation fellow, 1990; Owsley History Prize, 1991, for *The Road to Disunion,* Volume 1: *Secessionists at Bay.*

WRITINGS:

Prelude to Civil War: The Nullification Controversy in South Carolina, 1816-1836, Harper & Row (New York, NY), 1966, Oxford University Press (New York, NY), 1992.
(Editor) *The Nullification Era: A Documentary Record,* Harper & Row (New York, NY), 1967.
(Editor) Willie Lee Rose, *Slavery and Freedom,* Oxford University Press (New York, NY), 1982.

The Road to Disunion, Volume 1: *Secessionists at Bay, 1776-1854,* Oxford University Press (New York, NY), 1990.
(Editor, with Craig M. Simpson) *Secession Debated: Georgia's Showdown in 1860,* Oxford University Press (New York, NY), 1992.
The Reintegration of American History: Slavery and the Civil War, Oxford University Press (New York, NY), 1994.
(With others) *A Place Not Forgotten: Landscapes of the South from the Morris Museum of Art,* University of Kentucky Art Museum (Lexington, KY), 1999.
The South vs. The South: How Anti-Confederate Southerners Shaped the Course of the Civil War, Oxford University Press (New York, NY), 2001.

SIDELIGHTS: Historian William W. Freehling has published a number of books that focus on the Civil War period, including *The Road to Disunion,* Volume 1: *Secessionists at Bay, 1776-1854.* The volume is a history of the period leading up to the Civil War, beginning with the first Missouri Compromise in 1820, then the gag rule controversy of 1835-36, the annexation of Texas in 1845, the Compromise of 1850, and the Kansas-Nebraska Act of 1854. Freehling emphasizes that positions on slavery in the antebellum South varied by location, with those of Southerners closer to the nonslaveholding states being more moderate than those of Southerners further south.

Bertram Wyatt-Brown wrote in the *New York Review of Books* that Freehling "has freshly and usefully clarified the division in the South between the proslavery ideology of the Lower South—based on the profitable exploitation of blacks in growing cotton, sugar, and rice—and the ambivalent views of the upper South states, where the slave economy was not expanding and the economy based on free labor was growing. Indeed, the division he explores helps to explain the differing dates of secession of the slave states after Lincoln's election." In fact, South Carolina, Mississippi, Florida, Alabama, Georgia, Louisiana, and Texas left the Union during the winter of 1860-1861, before Lincoln was inaugurated. Following the assault on Fort Sumter on April 14, Virginia, Arkansas, Tennessee, and North Carolina reluctantly followed.

The slave states that stayed in the Union were Delaware, Maryland, Kentucky, and Missouri. These four plus West Virginia kept from the Confederacy

more than half of the slave states' factory capacity, thirty-seven percent of the corn, twenty percent of the livestock, and nearly thirty percent of the people. They were home to 250,000 troops that joined Lincoln's army, and to that was added another 100,000 (mostly from Tennessee) from the Upper South slave states. The South was at a disadvantage by reason of these numbers.

Wyatt-Brown wrote that Freehling "is most concerned with ambivalence toward slavery in the Upper South for two reasons. First, he sees the difficulties over emancipation in Virginia and Maryland as a portent of things to come: the loosening of the Upper South's ties to the Lower South as new, free-labor interests and industries developed, particularly in the Chesapeake Bay region. Second, for most of the antebellum decades, the delusion of emancipation in a far distant future made more difficult the secessionists' hope of uniting the South in bellicose defense of slavery."

The Reintegration of American History: Slavery and the Civil War is a collection of eleven of Freehling's articles and essays. *American Historical Review*'s Robert McColley wrote that the book is "a satisfying distillation of the chief subjects that have engaged a major historian over most of a long and fruitful career." *New York Times Book Review*'s Tom Chaffin described as "standouts" Freehling's two essays about the Founding Fathers' attitude toward slavery and nineteenth-century expansionism.

Michael O'Brien reviewed the volume in the *Times Literary Supplement,* saying that Freehling "is concerned that American history has become balkanized and myopic. . . . What we need, he counsels, is to tell history as an accessible story, whose centre might be political history, because 'all regions, classes, sexes, and ethnics eventually seek political power, whether to control the American mainstream or to separate from it.' Hence we should acknowledge 'two integrating imperatives,' that 'the history of one American group must be related to other groups, and that a fragment of American history must be related to the larger whole, chronologically and topically.'"

Booklist reviewer Gilbert Taylor called *The South vs. The South: How Anti-Confederate Southerners Shaped the Course of the Civil War* "a masterful account of the South's internal 'house divided.'" "Concerning fugitive slaves," noted Christine Dee for *H-Net* online, "Freehling suggests their nonviolent resistance undermined slavery before the war, especially in the Border States. During the war, they were agents in their own emancipation, the author maintains, successfully negotiating Northern whites' desire to destroy the cornerstone of the Confederacy and whites' fear of black violence. Blacks, by assuming the roles of the 'nonviolent runaway and cooperative soldiers,' played a significant part in anti-Confederate efforts."

Joan Waugh reviewed the volume in *Civil War History,* saying that "Freehling's analysis of Lincoln's leadership is enlightening. Lincoln managed to hold onto the loyal slaveholding states by stressing the importance of preserving white liberties and treading lightly on the slavery issue. He recognized the vital importance of uniting all whites behind the war effort, even if it meant delaying emancipation indefinitely. As the war ground on, however, Lincoln pressed for emancipation and black soldierhood as a powerful addition to the northern military capacity. Freehling has no illusions about Lincoln's lackluster commitment to racial equality." Freehling feels that the Union couldn't have won the war without the help of both Southern whites and blacks.

In *The South vs. The South,* Freehling discusses events of the war that include the Fifty-fourth Massachusetts Regiment's assault on Fort Wagner, Grant's siege of Vicksburg, and the Massacre at Fort Pillow. Dee noted that "by measuring the role anti-Confederates played in the war, Freehling reminds us of the importance of the western theater in both emancipation and the ultimate defeat of the Confederacy." The book originated with a series of lectures given at the University of Texas. The text is enhanced by maps of important battles and places.

BIOGRAPHICAL AND CRITICAL SOURCES:

PERIODICALS

American Historical Review, October, 1995, Robert McColley, review of *The Reintegration of American History: Slavery and the Civil War,* pp. 1299-1300.

Booklist, March 1, 2001, Gilbert Taylor, review of *The South vs. The South: How Anti-Confederate Southerners Shaped the Course of the Civil War,* p. 1222.

Civil War History, June, 2002, Joan Waugh, review of *The South vs. The South,* p. 167.

Journal of Southern History, November, 1994, Donald A. DeBats, review of *Secession Debated: Georgia's Showdown in 1860,* pp. 811-812; May, 2003, William Blair, review of *The South vs. The South,* p. 432.

Kirkus Reviews, July 15, 1990, review of *The Road to Disunion,* Volume 1: *Secessionists at Bay, 1776-1854,* pp. 979-980.

Library Journal, March 15, 2001, Kathleen M. Conley, review of *The South vs. The South,* p. 94.

Los Angeles Times Book Review, September 23, 1990, Leonard Bushkoff, review of *The Road to Disunion,* pp. 1, 13.

Newsweek, January 4, 1982, Jim Miller, review of *Slavery and Freedom,* p. 59.

New York Review of Books, October 10, 1991, Bertram Wyatt-Brown, review of *The Road to Disunion,* pp. 35-39.

New York Times Book Review, January 24, 1982, Robert F. Durden, review of *Slavery and Freedom,* pp. 8-9; September 30, 1990, Robert V. Remini, review of *The Road to Disunion,* pp. 22-24; June 12, 1994, Tom Chaffin, review of *The Reintegration of American History,* pp. 22-23.

Publishers Weekly, February 12, 2001, review of *The South vs. The South,* p. 197.

Times Literary Supplement, August 19, 1994, Michael O'Brien, review of *The Reintegration of American History,* pp. 8-9.

ONLINE

Civil War News, http://www.civilwarnews.com/ (January 22, 2003), Richard McMurry, review of *The South vs. The South.*

H-Net, http://www.2.h-net.msu.edu/ (February, 2002), Christine Dee, review of *The South vs. The South.**

*   *   *

FRIEDLANDER, Shems

PERSONAL: Male. *Religion:* Sufi Muslim.

ADDRESSES: Home—Cairo, Egypt. *Office*—Apple Center for Graphic Communications, American University in Cairo, P.O. Box 2511, 113 Sharia Kasr

El Aini, Cairo, Egypt. *Agent*—c/o Author Mail, Parabola, 656 Broadway, New York, NY 10012. *E-mail*—shems_f@aucegypt.edu.

CAREER: Visual artist, educator, poet, filmmaker, and Islamic scholar. Parsons School of Design, New York, NY, professor of editorial communication, advertising, and design, 1987-88; American University, Cairo, Egypt, began in 1992, became senior lecturer in journalism and mass communication and founding director of the Apple Center for Graphic Communications, 1994—. Sony Gallery, chair of international advisory board; worked in New York, NY, as a designer and art director for various publications, including *Look.* Has had several photography and painting exhibitions, including ones in New York and Cairo.

AWARDS, HONORS: Thirty New York Art Directors Club awards; Sony Video Filmmaker Award, 2001, for *Rumi: The Wings of Love.*

WRITINGS:

The Whirling Dervishes, Being an Account of the Sufi Order Known as the Mevlevis and Its Founder the Poet and Mystic Mevlana Jalalu'ddin Rumi, music section by Nezih Uzel, Macmillan (New York, NY), 1975, with new foreword by Annemarie Schimmel, State University of New York Press (Albany, NY), 1992, reprinted as *Rumi and the Whirling Dervishes: Being an Account of the Sufi Order Known as the Mevlevis and Its Founder the Poet and Mystic Mevlana Jalalu'ddin Rumi,* Parabola Books (New York, NY), 2003.
Submission: Sayings of the Prophet Muhammad, hadith notations by Al-Hajj Shaikh Muzaffereddin, Harper and Row (New York, NY), 1977.
Ninety-Nine Names of Allah: The Beautiful Names, calligraphy by Hamid al-Amidi, Arabic and Turkish translation by Tevfik Topuzoglu, Harper and Row (New York, NY), 1978.
When You Hear Hoofbeats, Think of a Zebra: Talks on Sufism, Perennial Library (New York, NY), 1987.
Sunlight, Poems, and Other Words, Safina Books (Cairo, Egypt), 1997.
Rumi: The Hidden Treasure, Fons Vitae (Louisville, KY), 2001.

Writer, producer, and director of documentary film *Rumi: The Wings of Love,* c. 2002. Contributor of articles, photographs, and design to periodicals, including *Geo, Digital Press,* and *Middle East Insight.*

WORK IN PROGRESS: The Circles of Remembrance (film).

SIDELIGHTS: Shems Friedlander is a visual artist and Islamic scholar who began photographing whirling dervishes in 1973 while he was working on his first book, *The Whirling Dervishes, Being an Account of the Sufi Order Known as the Mevlevis and Its Founder the Poet and Mystic Mevlana Jalalu'ddin Rumi,* which remains in print. (A dervish is a member of a Muslim ascetic religious sect.) Friedlander, himself a Mevlevi dervish, became a lecturer at American University in Cairo, Egypt, after a successful career in New York as a designer, art director, and teacher. His own work, both photography and paintings, has been displayed in exhibitions. At American University, he founded the Apple Center for Graphic Communications with a 200,000 dollar grant from Apple Computers, Inc.

Friedlander's study of the legendary thirteenth-century Muslim poet Rumi is an introduction to the poet's life, philosophy, and poetry as well as a history of the Sufis. A *Publishers Weekly* contributor reviewed the 2003 Parabola edition, commenting that Friedlander's black and white photographs, historical illustrations, and "splendid color cover photo of whirling dancers capture the longing, the rapture, and the God-graced mindfulness of the Sufis in contemplation, at prayer and at dance."

When You Hear Hoofbeats, Think of a Zebra: Talks on Sufism is an instructional on living from the perspective of the Sufi Muslims. The title indicates that it is necessary to think in new ways; for example, when one hears hoofbeats, they are not necessarily being made by horses. Friedlander writes of the importance of friendship, patience, and helpfulness and notes that, according to Sufism, the teachings of Allah must be practiced daily. *Kliatt* reviewer Ruth R. Woodman described the book as "excellent reading for all those interested in understanding Islam and Sufism."

BIOGRAPHICAL AND CRITICAL SOURCES:

PERIODICALS

Booklist, May 15, 1987, Sheila E. McGinn-Moorer, review of *When You Hear Hoofbeats, Think of a Zebra: Talks on Sufism,* p. 1389.

Kliatt, September, 1987, Ruth R. Woodman, review of *When You Hear Hoofbeats, Think of a Zebra,* p. 53.

Library Journal, May 1, 2003, Graham Christian, review of *Rumi and the Whirling Dervishes: Being an Account of the Sufi Order Known as the Mevlevis and Its Founder the Poet and Mystic Mevlana Jalalu'ddin Rumi,* p. 122.

Publishers Weekly, June 16, 2003, review of *Rumi and the Whirling Dervishes,* p. 67.

Religious Studies Review, January, 1993, Glenn Yocum, review of *The Whirling Dervishes, Being an Account of the Sufi Order Known as the Mevlevis and Its Founder the Poet and Mystic Mevlana Jalalu'ddin Rumi* (1992 edition), p. 89.

Whole Earth Review, winter, 1985, review of *Submission: Sayings of the Prophet Muhammad,* p. 41.

ONLINE

Al-Ahram Weekly Online Web site, http://weekly.ahram.org.eg/ (June 27, 2002), Nur Elmessiri, interview with Friedlander.

Rumi Society Web site, http://www.rumisociety.org/ (June 29, 2004).

*   *   *

FRISBIE, Charlotte J(ohnson) 1940-

PERSONAL: Born December 20, 1940, in Hazleton, PA; married Theodore R. Frisbie (an anthropologist); children: Elizabeth Boardman, Jennifer Alison. *Education:* Smith College, B.A. (cum laude), 1962; Wesleyan University (Middletown, CT), M.A., 1964; University of New Mexico, Ph.D., 1970. *Hobbies and other interests:* Quilting, knitting.

ADDRESSES: Home—5923 Quercus Grove Rd., Edwardsville, IL 62025. *Office*—c/o Department of Anthropology, Box 1451, Southern Illinois University—Edwardsville, Edwardsville, IL 62026-1451. *E-mail*—cfrisbie@siue.edu.

CAREER: Anna State Hospital, Anna, IL, social worker, 1968-70, coordinator of Aftercare Program, 1970; Southern Illinois University—Edwardsville, Edwardsville, IL, assistant professor, 1970-73, associate professor, 1973-77, professor of anthropology, 1977-98, professor emeritus, 1999—, chair of anthropology program, 1973-75, 1985-87, 1992-96. Indiana University, guest speaker, 1992; Laurentian University, distinguished lecturer, 1993; Colorado College, guest faculty, 1994; organizer and presenter of workshops and seminars; public speaker. Conducted extensive field research among the Navajos, beginning 1963. Wheelwright Museum, trustee, 1977-80, member of national advisory board, 1980-87; member of American Museum of Natural History and Museum of New Mexico; consultant to Smithsonian Institution, National Park Service, and U.S. Fish and Wildlife Service. Navajo Studies Conference, member of steering committee, 1984-2000, member of board of directors, 2000—; Music Research Institute, member of national academic advisory board, 1985—. Eden Village (retirement community), member of board of directors, 1986—; also works as church organist; volunteer with Senior Fit Program and Faith in Action.

MEMBER: American Anthropological Association (fellow), Society for Ethnomusicology (member of council, between 1973 and 1988; member of board of directors, 1979-81, 1984-90; president, 1987-89), American Association of University Professors (chair of Faculty Welfare Committee, 1977-78; member at large of executive committee, 1981-82), American Ethnological Society, Arizona Archaeological and Historical Society, Northern Arizona Society of Science and Art, Phi Beta Kappa, Sigma Xi, Lambda Alpha.

AWARDS, HONORS: American Philosophical Society grant, 1971-72; Weatherhead resident scholar, School of American Research (Santa Fe, NM), 1976; grants from Wheelwright Museum, 1976, and National Endowment for the Humanities, 1983-84, 1990; awards from Navajo Studies Conference, 1995 and 1998, for contributions to the preservation and dissemination of information pertaining to Navajo culture; grants from National Science Foundation and American Association of University Women.

WRITINGS:

Kinaaldá: A Study of the Navaho Girl's Puberty Ceremony, Wesleyan University Press (Middletown, CT), 1967, reprinted with new preface, University of Utah Press (Salt Lake City, UT), 1993.

Music and Dance Research of Southwestern United States Indians: Past Trends, Present Activities, and Suggestions for Future Research, Information Coordinators (Detroit, MI), 1977.

(Editor, with David P. McAllester) *Navajo Blessing-way Singer: The Autobiography of Frank Mitchell (1881-1867),* University of Arizona Press (Tucson, AZ), 1978, new edition (with introduction by Frisbie), University of New Mexico Press (Albuquerque, NM), 2003.

(Editor and contributor) *Southwestern Indian Ritual Drama,* University of New Mexico Press (Albuquerque, NM), 1980, revised edition, Waveland Press (Prospect Heights, IL), 1989.

(Editor, with David M. Brugge, and contributor) *Navajo Religion and Culture: Selected Views; Papers in Honor of Leland C. Wyman,* Museum of New Mexico Press (Santa Fe, NM), 1982.

(Editor and contributor) *Explorations in Ethnomusicology: Essays in Honor of David P. McAllester,* Information Coordinators (Detroit, MI), 1986.

Navajo Medicine Bundles or Jish: Acquisition, Transmission, and Disposition in the Past and Present, University of New Mexico Press (Albuquerque, NM), 1987.

(Editor) *Tall Woman: The Life Story of Rose Mitchell, a Navajo Woman, c. 1874-1977,* University of New Mexico Press (Albuquerque, NM), 2001.

Contributor to books, including *Issues of Feminism: A First Course in Women's Studies,* edited by Sheila Ruth, Houghton Mifflin and Co. (Boston, MA), 1980; *Ethnography of Musical Performance,* edited by Norma McLeod and Marcia Herndon, Norwood Editions (Norwood, PA), 1980; *Comparative Musicology and Anthropology of Music: Essays on the History of Ethnomusicology,* edited by Bruno Nettl and Philip V. Bohlman, University of Chicago Press (Chicago, IL), 1991; *Washington Matthews: Studies of Navajo Culture, 1880-1894,* edited by Katherine Spencer Halpern and Susan Brown McGreevy, University of New Mexico Press (Albuquerque, NM), 1997; and *Diné Bíkéyah: Papers in Honor of David M. Brugge,* edited by Meliha S. Duran and David T. Kirkpatrick, Archaeological Society of New Mexico, 1998. Author of album liner notes. Contributor of articles and reviews to periodicals, including *Visual Anthropology, American Ethnologist, American Indian Culture and Research Journal, Anthropological Linguistics, Ethnohistory, American Anthropologist, Medical Anthropology Quarterly, Anthropology and Humanism Quarterly,*

American Antiquity, and *Journal of Man. American Indian Quarterly,* member of editorial advisory board, 1977—, guest editor, 1980; newsletter editor, Society for Ethnomusicology, 1972-76.

WORK IN PROGRESS: Research on women and the Society for Ethnomusicology, 1952-61; research on the history of the Quercus Grove community.

SIDELIGHTS: Charlotte J. Frisbie told *CA:* "I guess all of my writing has been academic or academically related. I've done a lot of research in Navajo studies, women's studies, and ethnomusicology, and am interested in a broad number of issues. I've written books and articles, and I've also done jacket blurbs for presses, reviews of books and records, compact discs, and films, liner notes for one album, and I've edited several collections that were published both in book and journal format.

"I love to read and always have. I always have a book to read, and my idea of a real vacation is to have the chance to put my feet up with a good book and no interruptions. I read all kinds of things, and every now and then I make a plan which results in my exploring new authors, checking up on developments in certain genres, or catching up on the latest works of somebody I like. There are a number of areas that I am determined to keep up with professionally, so that kind of reading is always ongoing. When I really want to relax, I read mysteries, preferably ones with a female sleuth and female author. I also enjoy Native American authors. My professional network shares ideas about what to read, and since I know my friends' tastes, I usually know whether or not I'd like something they have suggested. I also reread classics every now and then, always finding something new to ponder. I am not one to go see the movie instead of reading the book.

"I write because I'm interested in the topics I'm researching. I get excited and want to tell others about what I've learned. I write letters because I'm interested in talking with friends. I also frequently will be asked to write things for groups that need reports, since I enjoy writing and know how to do it. I had hoped to able to write every day once I retired, but so far it hasn't turned out that way. People have often said I should write children's stories or mysteries myself, but I have no idea where I'd get the time, at least right now."

FÜSSEL, Stephan 1952-

PERSONAL: Born March 24, 1952, in Hildesheim, Germany; married; wife's name, Rita; children: Daniela, Matthias, Benedikt. *Education:* University of Göttingen, Ph.D., 1983, Habilitation, 1991.

ADDRESSES: Office—Institut für Buchwissenschaft, Johannes Gutenberg-Universität, D-55099 Mainz, Germany. *E-mail*—fuessel@mail.uni-mainz.de.

CAREER: University of Regensburg, Regensburg, Germany, assistant professor of communications, 1983-89; Johannes Gutenberg University of Mainz, Mainz, Germany, professor of communications, 1991—. Director of the Institute of Book and Culture Studies, 1991—; director of the Institute of Reading and Media, 1996—; director of the Institute of the History of the Book.

MEMBER: International Gutenberg Society (board member, 1992—), Willibald Pirckheimer Society for Renaissance and Humanist Studies (vice president, president), Society for Humanism Studies (president, 1989—), Society of Book History (president, 1991—).

WRITINGS:

(With Joachim Knape and Alfred Lindner) *Hans Sachs: Katalog zur Ausstellung,* Arbeitsstelle für Renaissanceforschung des Seminars für Deutsche Philologie der Universität (Göttingen, Germany) 1976.

Die Geschichte der Volksbibliothek Göttingen: 80 Jahre Stadtbibliothek Göttingen, 1897-1977 ("Arbeiten zur Geschichte des Buchwesens in Niedersachsen" series, Heft 1), Göttinger Hochschulschriften-Verlag (Göttingen, Germany), 1977.

(With Joachim Knape, Alfred Lindner, and Julia Aeffner) *Hans Sachs: Katalog zur Ausstellung in der Kunstsammlung der Universität Göttingen 4. bis 22. Februar 1976,* Gratia-Verlag (Göttingen, Germany), 1979.

Riccardus Bartholinus Perusinus: Humanistische Panegyrik am Hofe Kaiser Maximilians I ("Saecula Spritualia" series, 16), Verlag Valentin Koerner (Baden-Baden, Germany), 1987.

(With Sabine Doering and Carola Staniek) *Georg Joachim Göschen, 1752-1828: Dokumente zur Verlagsgeschichte aus den Beständen des Deutschen Buch-und Schriftmuseums Leipzig* (Catalog of an exhibition held in the Deutschen Buch-und Schriftmuseum of the Deutsche Bücherei Leipzig, September-November, 1992 and in the Deutsche Bibliothek, Frankfurt am Main, December, 1992-February, 1993), Die Deutsche Bibliothek (Leipzig, Germany), 1992.

Die Welt im Buch: Buchkünstlerischer und humanistischer Kontext der Schedelschen Weltchronik von 1493 ("Kleiner Druck der Gutenberg-Gesellschaft" series, No. 111), Gutenberg-Gesellschaft (Mainz, Germany), 1996.

(With Ulrich Everling and Bert Rürup) *Die Buchpreisbindung: Aus europarechtlicher, ökonomischer und kulturhistorischer Sicht,* Verlag der Buchhändler-Vereinigung (Frankfurt am Main, Germany), 1997.

Verlagsbibliographie Göschen 1785 bis 1838 ("Georg Joachim Göschen, ein Verleger der Spätaufklarung und der deutschen Klassik" series, Bd. 2), W. de Gruyter (Berlin, Germany, and New York, NY), 1998.

Georg Joachim Göschen, Bd. 2, Verlagsbibliographie Göschen 1785 bis 1838, W. de Gruyter (Berlin, Germany), 1998.

Studien zur Verlagsgeschichte und zur Verlegertypologie der Goethe-Zeit ("Georg Joachim Göschen, ein Verleger der Spätaufklarung und der deutschen Klassik" series, Bd. 1), W. de Gruyter (Berlin, Germany), 1999.

Johannes Gutenberg, Rowohlt (Reinbek bei Hamburg, Germany), 1999.

Gutenberg und seine Wirkung, Insel (Frankfurt am Main, Germany), 1999.

Günter Grass, Das Treffen in Telgte, Reclam (Stuttgart, Germany), 1999.

Georg Joachim Göschen, Bd. 1, Studien zur Verlagsgeschichte und zur Verlegertypologie der Goethe-Zeit, W. de Gruyter (Berlin, Germany), 1999.

Gutenberg und seine Wirkung, Insel (Frankfurt am Main, Germany), 1999, translation by Douglas Martin published as *Gutenberg and the Impact of Printing,* Ashgate (Aldershot, England), 2004.

Gutenberg-Jahrbuch, Jg. 75, 2000, Schmidt (Mainz, Germany), 2000.

(With Weimar Herzogen and Anna Amalia) *Hartmann Schedel: Nuremberg Chronicle,* Taschen America (New York, NY), 2001.

(Author of introduction and appendix) Hartmann Schedel, *Liber chronicarum (Chronicle of the World:*

The Complete and Annotated Nuremberg Chronicle of 1493) (text in German with introduction and appendix in English, translated from the Latin), Taschen (Cologne, Germany, and London, England), 2001.

(With Helmut Hiller) *Wörterbuch des Buches,* sixth edition, Klostermann (Frankfurt am Main, Germany), 2002, first published, 1954.

(With Klaus Arnold and Franz Fuchs) *Venezianisch-deutsche Kulturbeziehungen in der Renaissance,* Harrassowitz (Wiesbaden, Germany), 2003.

The Book of Books. The Luther Bible of 1534: A Cultural-Historical Introduction, Taschen (Cologne, Germany, and London, England), 2003.

EDITOR

Aby M. Warburg, *Mnemosyne: Beitr. zum 50. Todestag von Aby M. Warburg* ("Gratia" series, Heft 7), Gratia-Verlag (Göttingen, Germany), 1979.

(With Hans Joachim Kreutzer) *Historia von D. Johann Fausten: Text des Druckes von 1587. Kritische Ausgabe. Mit den Zusatztexten der Wolfenbütteler Handschrift und der zeitgenössischen Drucke,* Reclam (Stuttgart, Germany), 1988.

Die Folgen der Entdeckungsreisen für Europa: Akten des interdisziplinären Symposions ("Pirckheimer-Jahrbuch" series, Bd. 7), H. Carl (Nuremberg, Germany), 1992.

Deutsche Dichter der frühen Neuzeit (1450-1600): Ihr Leben und Werk, E. Schmidt (Berlin, Germany), 1993.

(With Gert Hübner and Joachim Knape, and contributor) *Artibus: Kulturwissenschaft und deutsche Philologie des Mittelalters und der frühen Neuzeit. Festschrift für Dieter Wuttke zum 65. Geburtstag,* Harrassowitz (Wiesbaden, Germany), 1994.

500 Jahre Schedelsche Weltchronik: Akten des interdisziplinären Symposions vom 23/24. April 1993 in Nürnberg ("Pirckheimer-Jahrbuch" series), H. Carl (Nuremberg, Germany), 1994.

Hans Sachs im Schnittpunkt von Antike und Neuzeit: Akten des interdisziplinären Symposions vom 23./ 24. September 1994 in Nürnberg ("Pirckheimer-Jahrbuch" series), H. Carl (Nuremberg, Germany), 1995.

(With Volker Honemann) *Humanismus und früher Buchdruck: Akten des interdisziplinären Symposions vom 5.-6. Mai 1995 in Mainz* ("Pirckheimer-Jahrbuch" series), H. Carl (Nuremberg, Germany), 1996, 1997.

Repertorium der Verlagskorrespondenz Göschen (1783 bis 1828) ("Georg Joachim Göschen, ein Verleger der Spätaufklärung" series, Bd. 3), W. de Gruyter (Berlin, Germany, and New York, NY), 1996.

(With Jan Pirozynski) *Der polnische Humanismus und die europäischen Sodalitäten: Akten des polnisch-deutschen Symposiums vom 15.-19. Mai 1996 im Collegium Maius der Universität Krakau,* Harrassowitz (Wiesbaden, Germany), 1996.

Im Zentrum: Das Buch, 50 Jahre Buchwissenschaft in Mainz ("Kleiner Druck der Gutenberg-Gesellschaft" series, No. 112), Gutenberg-Gesellschaft (Mainz, Germany), 1997.

50 Jahre Frankfurter Buchmesse 1949-1999, Suhrkamp (Frankfurt, Germany), 1999.

(With Klaus A. Vogel) *Deutsche Handwerker, Künstler und Gelehrte im Rom der Renaissance: Akten des interdisziplinären Symposions vom 27. und 28. Mai 1999 im Deutschen Historischen Institut in Rom,* Harrassowitz (Wiesbaden, Germany), 1999.

(With Georg Jäger, Hermann Staub, and Monika Estermann) *Der Börsenverein des Deutschen Buchhandels 1825-2000: Ein geschichtlicher Aufriss,* Buchhändler-Verein (Frankfurt, Germany), 2000.

Register 1987-2000, Gutenberg-Gesellschaft (Mainz, Germany), 2000.

Hartmann Schedel, *Schedel'sche Weltchronik,* Taschen (Cologne, Germany), 2001.

Martin Luther, *Die Luther-Bibel von 1534, Kolorierte Faksimileausgabe, 2 Bde. u. Begleitband,* Taschen (Cologne, Germany), 2002.

Gutenberg-Jahrbuch 2002, Harrassowitz (Wiesbaden, Germany), 2002.

Kaiser Maximilian I, *Die Abenteuer des Ritters Theuerdank,* Taschen (Cologne, Germany), 2003, published in English as *The Adventures of the Knight Theuerdank,* Taschen America (New York, NY), 2003.

Editor of and contributor to the annual *Gutenberg-Jahrbuch,* 1995—; editor of *Pirckheimer-Jahrbuch;* editor, with Severin Corsten and Günther Pflug, *Lexikon des gesamten Buchwesens;* editor, with Joachim Knape, *Poesis & Pictura: Festschrift für Dieter Wuttke.*

SIDELIGHTS: German communications professor Stephan Füssel has published widely on early printing, bookselling, and publishing, from the 1500s to modern times, as well as on the future of communications. He is best known as editor of and contributor to the *Gutenberg-Jahrbuch,* a position he has held since

1995. The yearbook was first published in 1926 by the Gutenberg Society and is considered the leading scientific yearbook on Gutenberg research, art history research, and the history of printing and the book. Each issue contains essays by an international roster of writers, publishing in English, French, Spanish, Italian, and German. Füssel also serves as editor of *Pirckheimer-Jahrbuch* and has edited numerous books in German in addition to his writings.

An example of Füssel's work on early authors and books is his *Riccardus Bartholinus Perusinus: Humanistische Panegyrik am Hofe Kaiser Maximilians I,* a study of the sixteenth-century Italian humanist poet Ricardo Bartolini, who glorified the intervention of Emperor Maximilian I in the Bavarian war of succession in his most famous epic, the *Austrias.* As a panegyrist, Bartolini also wrote poems for Giovanni di Medici on his election as pope, for Charles V on his election as Habsburg emperor, and for Pope Leo X. He wrote in detail about the Diet of Augsburg. Füssel's study of Bartolini concludes with a complete list of the poet's works and their location in European libraries. In a review of the book for *Sixteenth Century Journal,* Eckhard Bernstein concluded, "Füssel has immeasurably increased our knowledge of Bartolini, producing what might very well be the definitive study of Emperor Maximilian's most important Neo-Latin panegyrist."

Füssel coedited and contributed to the fifteen-essay collection *Artibus: Kulturwissenschaft und deutsche Philologie des Mittelalters und der frühen Neuzeit,* which honored medieval and early modern philology professor Dieter Wuttke on his retirement in 1994. Füssel's essay discusses the cooperation of Renaissance humanist authors and printers, using the case of Joachim Vadian. In a review of the book for *Renaissance Quarterly,* Susan C. Karant-Nunn observed that the essays "reflect the philological and literary concerns that ... are a major wellspring of Renaissance scholarship in Germany."

Füssel coedited a new edition of the sixteenth-century Faustus legend, *Historia von D. Johann Fausten: Text des Druckes von 1587.* The editors received praise from reviewers for replacing the author's preface, adding supplementary texts, correcting printing mistakes, providing text notes and valuable extracts from other authors used in compiling the *Historia,* and for Füssel's meticulous justification of his editorial policy in light of the old syntax and typefaces. John L. Flood, in *Modern Language Review,* said the new edition "contains practically everything one needs to acquire a thorough familiarity with the first literary manifestation of the Faust theme." He called the volume a "generally splendid edition" that could "correct the balance and help the *Historia . . .* achieve the place it deserves as a work of truly seminal importance in German, indeed world literature." Frank Baron, reviewing the work for the *German Quarterly,* found that the editors had made the work far more accessible compared with the earlier edition. Although he said he felt the editors should have included still more background extracts, including a reference to Faustus's twenty-four-year pact with the devil, Baron concluded that the new edition "redirects attention to the narrative that inspired the modern Faust tradition."

The annual volumes of the *Gutenberg-Jahrbuch* are generally considered praiseworthy by reviewers. John L. Flood, reviewing the 1996 yearbook for the *Times Literary Supplement,* commented favorably on Füssel's article, "Gutenberg Goes Electronic," in which he compares the technical impact of the Gutenberg press on the fifteenth century with the advent of electronic publishing in the twentieth. Reviewing the 2000 yearbook, which commemorated the 600th anniversary of Gutenberg's birth, Flood called Füssel's essay on incunabula studies of the past one hundred years "important" and an "informative survey." The following year, Flood praised Füssel's essay on Gutenberg prize winner Joseph M. Jacobson's development of "digital ink" and "digital paper," a small device that can store electronic texts downloaded from the Internet and can be reused to contain hundreds of books. Flood found the 2002 yearbook to be "full of contributions of exceptional interest," especially essays about Gutenberg's forty-two-line Bible and physician and humanist scholar Hartmann Schedel's *Nuremberg Chronicle.*

Füssel wrote the introduction and appendix for *Liber chronicarum (Chronicle of the World: The Complete and Annotated Nuremberg Chronicle of 1493),* an annotated reprint edition of Schedel's famous work. L. K. Hanson, in a review for the Minneapolis *Star Tribune,* called the book "a wonderfully illustrated mish-mash of history, religion, fact and opinion from a great urban center, in a world on the edge of massive change."

BIOGRAPHICAL AND CRITICAL SOURCES:

PERIODICALS

German Quarterly, fall, 1989, Frank Baron, review of *Historia von D. Johann Fausten: Text des Druckes von 1587,* pp. 522-523.

Modern Language Review, April, 1990, John L. Flood, review of *Historia von D. Johann Fausten,* pp. 500-502.

Renaissance Quarterly, winter, 1996, Susan C. Karant-Nunn, review of *Artibus: Kulturwissenschaft und deutsche Philologie des Mittelalters und der frühen Neuzeit,* p. 840.

Sixteenth Century Journal, winter, 1988, Eckhard Bernstein, review of *Riccardus Bartholinus Perusinus: Humanistische Panegyrik am Hofe Kaiser Maximilians I,* pp. 724-725.

Star Tribune (Minneapolis, MN), January 16, 2002, L. K. Hanson, "Visual Books: An Illuminating Look at Early Books; Two Volumes Are Part of Western Visual Heritage" (review of *Liber chronicarum [Chronicle of the World: The Complete and Annotated Nuremberg Chronicle of 1493]*), section E, p. 3.

Times Literary Supplement, June 6, 1997, John L. Flood, "The Electronic Galaxy" (review of *Gutenberg-Jahrbuch 1996*), p. 36; June 9, 2000, John L. Flood, "Man of that Millenium" (review of *Gutenberg-Jahrbuch 2000*), p. 30; September 6, 2002, John L. Flood, "Electric Paper" (review of *Gutenberg-Jahrbuch 2001*), p. 32; January 17, 2003, John L. Flood, "From B42 to the Censors of Taiwan" (review of *Gutenberg-Jahrbuch 2002*), p. 25.

ONLINE

Gutenberg University Web site, http://www.gutenberg-gesellschaft.uni-mainz.de/eghome.htm (May 28, 2004), *Gutenberg-Jahrbuch.*

Taschen Web site, www.taschen.com (May 28, 2004), "Stephan Füssel."*

G

GARDNER, Leonard 1934-

PERSONAL: Born 1934, in Stockton, CA.

ADDRESSES: Home—Northern California. *Agent*—c/o Author Mail, University of California Press, 2120 Berkeley Way, Berkeley, CA 94720.

CAREER: Writer; worked briefly as a boxer.

AWARDS, HONORS: National Book Award nomination, 1969, for *Fat City*.

WRITINGS:

Fat City (novel; also see below), Farrar, Straus and Giroux (New York, NY), 1969, University of California Press (Berkeley, CA), 1996.
Fat City (screenplay; adapted from his book of the same name), Columbia TriStar, 1972.

Contributor to journals, including *Paris Review, Esquire,* and *Southwest Review.*

ADAPTATIONS: Fat City was adapted as a film in 1972, directed by John Huston and released by Columbia TriStar.

SIDELIGHTS: Although he has written only one novel, Leonard Gardner has earned enduring literary fame for his book's depiction of the boxing world in mid-twentieth century Stockton, California. *Fat City,* which Gardner later adapted as a screenplay, was named in *Sports Illustrated* as one of the hundred best sports books of all time.

Fat City is set among the shabby tenements and seedy bars of Gardner's home town of Stockton. Its characters are has-beens and never-weres who still cling to their dreams of achieving glory in the ring, despite the ravages of alcohol, loneliness, and bruising bouts. The plot follows the efforts of Billy Tully, an alcoholic ex-boxer, to nurture the career of a new young fighter. "I wanted to show boxing as it really is," Gardner told an interviewer for *Life* magazine, "not an exciting piece of entertainment but as the sport of the poorest element of our society."

Critical reception of the novel was emphatically positive. In the *New York Times Book Review* Patricia T. O'Connor praised it for its "detached and lyrical" tone, as well as the extraordinary accuracy of its setting. In a *Los Angeles Times* review quoted on the *University of California Press* Web site, Keith S. Felton wrote that "Gardner's careful characterizing eye gleans apt images to build the stark reality of human beings on the aimless loose." Novelists such as Joan Didion, Joyce Carol Oates, and Denis Johnson hailed *Fat City* as a masterpiece. In a later piece for *Salon. com* Johnson described reading the novel at age eighteen or nineteen and being profoundly influenced: it was "so precisely written and giving such value to its words that I felt I could almost read it with my fingers, like Braille," he noted, adding that he was so excited by the book that he discussed it constantly with another aspiring writer. "We talked about every paragraph of *Fat City* one by one and over and over," he wrote, "the way couples sometimes reminisce about each moment of their falling in love." The novel was nominated for a National Book Award in 1969.

The film version of *Fat City*, however, did not attract as much popular enthusiasm as the book. Nevertheless, it earned great acclaim from critics, who suggested that its refusal to sugarcoat its story may have affected viewers' enjoyment. Many movie critics consider *Fat City* to be John Huston's finest film. *Guardian* contributor Derek Malcolm included it on his list of the hundred greatest movies, considering it Huston's best cinematic achievement.

BIOGRAPHICAL AND CRITICAL SOURCES:

PERIODICALS

Atlantic Monthly, September, 1969.
Commonweal, December 26, 1969.
Guardian (Manchester, England), August 24, 2000, Derek Malcolm, "John Huston: *Fat City.*"
Life, August 29, 1969.
New York Times Book Review, December 28, 1986, Patricia T. O'Conner, review of *Fat City,* p. 28.
Sports Illustrated, December 16, 2002, "The Top One Hundred Sports Books of All Time," p. 130.
Washington Post Book World, September 7, 1969.

ONLINE

Salon.com, http://www.salon.com/ (June 23, 2003), Denis Johnson, "Personal Best: *Fat City* by Leonard Gardner."
University of California Press, http://www.ucpress.edu/books/ (June 23, 2003), "Leonard Gardner, *Fat City.*"*

*   *   *

GARDNER, Michael R. 1942-

PERSONAL: Born November 19, 1942, in Philadelphia, PA; married Theresa Lennon; children: two daughters. *Education:* Graduate of the College at Georgetown University, 1964, and Georgetown University Law School, 1977.

ADDRESSES: Home—Washington, DC. *Agent*—c/o Author Mail, Southern Illinois University Press, P.O. Box 3697, Carbondale, IL 62902-3697.

CAREER: Attorney and author. Bracewell and Patterson (law firm), partner, 1977-82; Akin, Gump, Strauss, Hauer, and Feld (law firm), Washington, DC, partner, 1982-89; The Law Offices of Michael R. Gardner, P.C., Washington, DC, communications policy lawyer, 1990—. College of Georgetown University, Washington, DC, adjunct professor, 1992-2000. United States Ambassador to the International Telecommunication Union (ITU) Plenipotentiary Conference, Nairobi, Kenya, 1982; United States Telecommunications Training Institute (USTTI), founder and pro bono chair, 1982—; served on Presidential Commissions of Presidents Richard Nixon, Gerald Ford, Ronald Reagan, and George H. W. Bush, including President's Committee for Mental Retardation, Council of the Administrative Conference of the United States, Board of Directors of the Pennsylvania Avenue Development Corporation of Washington, DC, and International Cultural Trace Center Commission.

AWARDS, HONORS: Conde Naste Award, Georgetown College, 1990; Chairman of the College Board of Advisors' Award, Georgetown University, 1996; Henry Adams Book Prize, Society for History in the Federal Government, 2003, for *Harry Truman and Civil Rights: Moral Courage and Political Risks.*

WRITINGS:

Harry Truman and Civil Rights: Moral Courage and Political Risks, forewords by George M. Elsey and Kweisi Mfume, Southern Illinois University Press (Carbondale, IL), 2002.

SIDELIGHTS: Michael R. Gardner is an attorney and a founder and chairperson of the United States Telecommunications Training Institute (USTTI), a nonprofit joint venture between ranking officials of the federal government and leaders of the communications industry. USTTI's goal is to share advances in technology and communications globally by providing communications training to people in developing countries. Since 1982, the USTTI has graduated 6,633 men and women who are now working to make modern communication a reality for their fellow citizens in 165 developing countries.

Gardner is also the author of an award-winning study, *Harry Truman and Civil Rights: Moral Courage and Political Risks.* Gardner had served on commissions during the terms of four presidents and also taught at Georgetown University, and his interest in presidential history is apparent in this volume, which offers a unique and uncommon perspective on Truman as a champion of civil rights. As Gardner notes, Truman was the first president to have an integrated inaugural during a period when the nation's capitol continued to be segregated and was the first president to accept a speaking invitation from the National Association for the Advancement of Colored People (NAACP). During his seven years as president, Truman named the first black judge to the federal bench, ended segregation in the federal civil service and armed forces, desegregated Washington's public swimming pools, and, in 1953, delivered the commencement address at the historically black Howard University.

Michael S. Neiberg reviewed the book in *American Studies International,* noting that Gardner contends that Truman's commitment came from his personal experiences with prejudice in Missouri and the racist attitudes, including those of his mother, that he witnessed there. However, Neiberg called Truman's stance "more like a middle ground than a freshly blazed trail," noting that several of his key reversals of segregation were implemented just months before the 1948 election. Gardner maintains in the book that Truman opposed "the unholy alliance of Southern Democrats and conservative Republicans, risking his chance at the presidency in order to accomplish what was 'morally right.'"

In reviewing *Harry Truman and Civil Rights* for *H-Net Reviews* online, Peter M. Carrozzo stated that "Gardner's main contribution is to present a story that has been often overlooked by historians who credit other presidents for civil rights. To demonstrate the social impact of Truman's accomplishments, Gardner includes statements from people who were involved or affected." Carrozzo also noted, "An excellent source that Gardner uses with skill is the biography of White House butler Alonzo Fields. Fields's fond depiction of his friend Harry Truman speaks volumes about the President's true feelings."

Political Science Quarterly's Kevin J. McMahon found that Gardner "presents a forceful case for why Harry Truman deserves recognition as one of history's great champions of civil rights." The reviewer called the book "a captivating story. And Gardner tells it well."

Gardner told *CA:* "Growing up as I did in the nation's capital in the 1940s and 1950s, I saw firsthand how Washington, D.C., was an apartheid city in every respect. While I had little direct appreciation of the Truman Presidency during those early years, I was keenly aware of the racist environment that dominated Washington, D.C.

"While attending the College of Georgetown University in the early 1960s, I had the good fortune to work for Eunice Kennedy Shriver and to observe members of the Kennedy family. Subsequently, in the 1970s through my extensive work with Texas Governor John B. Connally, I was exposed to many of the Johnson and Nixon Administration officials with whom Connally worked. I also worked closely with the Reagan Administration in the 1980s. Based on the various relationships with several of the leading political forces of the 1960s, 70s, and 80s, I became aware of the considerable mythology that had taken root in this country about which president was the real pioneer of federal civil rights reform.

"Based on my lifelong interest in modern American presidents and my firsthand knowledge of the pervasive segregation in the Washington, D.C., of my youth, I determined to document the largely unheralded actions of Harry Truman as he tenaciously challenged segregationists in the Congress and throughout much of the country. After seven years of research that included extensive discussions with several key people who worked closely with Harry Truman in the White House, *Harry Truman and Civil Rights: Moral Courage and Political Risks* was published with forewords by Truman historian and former Truman White House staffer George Elsey, and NAACP president Kweisi Mfume. Importantly, for future presidential scholars and students of this country's ongoing civil rights struggle, *Harry Truman and Civil Rights* documents the fact that neither Franklin Delano Roosevelt, nor Harvard-educated John F. Kennedy, nor the great legislator Lyndon Johnson launched the modern federal civil rights movement; it was our plain talking, high-school educated, thirty-third President from a rural Missouri background—Harry Truman—who forever altered the racial landscape in American as he labored to ensure that all Americans enjoy the full protection of a colorblind Constitution."

BIOGRAPHICAL AND CRITICAL SOURCES:

PERIODICALS

American Studies International, October, 2002, Michael S. Neiberg, review of *Harry Truman and Civil Rights: Moral Courage and Political Risks,* p. 100.

Library Journal, March 1, 2002, William D. Pederson, review of *Harry Truman and Civil Rights,* p. 118.

Political Science Quarterly, fall, 2002, Kevin J. Mc-Mahon, review of *Harry Truman and Civil Rights,* p. 535.

Ruminator Review, spring, 2003, Sharon Kinney Hanson, review of *Harry Truman and Civil Rights,* p. 47.

ONLINE

Foreword Online Web site, http://www. forewordmagazine.com/ (June 2, 2004), Karl Helicher, interview with Gardner.

H-Net Reviews Web site, http://www.h-net.org/ (June 2, 2004), Peter M. Carrozzo, review of *Harry Truman and Civil Rights.*

*   *   *

GERSTMANN, Evan

PERSONAL: Male. *Education:* Oberlin College, B.A., 1983; University of Michigan, J.D., 1986; University of Wisconsin—Madison, M.A., 1992, Ph.D., 1996.

ADDRESSES: Office—Department of Political Science, Loyola Marymount University, Loyola Blvd. at West 80th St., Los Angeles, CA 90045. *E-mail*—egerstma@lmumail.lmu.edu.

CAREER: Loyola Marymount University, Los Angeles, CA, assistant professor of political science.

WRITINGS:

The Constitutional Underclass: Gays, Lesbians, and the Failure of Class-Based Equal Protection, University of Chicago Press (Chicago, IL), 1999.

BIOGRAPHICAL AND CRITICAL SOURCES:

PERIODICALS

Choice, November, 1999, review of *The Constitutional Underclass,* pp. 620-621.*

*   *   *

GIBSON, Eleanor Jack 1910-2002

PERSONAL: Born December 7, 1910, in Peoria, IL; died December 30, 2002, in Columbia, SC; daughter of William A. and Isabel (Grier) Jack; married James J. Gibson (a psychology professor), September 17, 1932 (died, 1979); children: James J., Jean Grier. *Education:* Smith College, B.A., 1931, M.A., 1933; Yale University, Ph.D. (psychology), 1938.

CAREER: Psychologist. Smith College, Northampton, MA, instructor; Cornell University, Ithaca, NY, research associate, 1949-66, Susan Linn Sage Professor of Psychology, 1966-79. Visiting professor, Massachusetts Institute of Technology, 1973, University of California—Davis, 1978, University of Pennsylvania, 1984, University of South Carolina, 1987, University of Connecticut, 1988, Emory University, 1988-90, Center for Advanced Behavioral Studies, University of Minnesota, and the Salk Institute.

AWARDS, HONORS: Honorary degrees from Smith College, Rutgers University, Trinity College, Bates College, University of South Carolina, Emory University, Middlebury College, Columbia University, State University of New York—Albany, Miami University, and Yale University; Century Psychology Series Award, 1967; Distinguished Scientific Contribution Award, American Psychological Association (APA), 1968; G. Stanley Hall Medal, APA, 1971; Guggenheim fellow, 1972-73; Wilbur Cross Medal, Yale University, 1973; Howard Crosby Warren Medal, 1977; Montgomery fellow, Dartmouth College, 1985; Gold Medal, American Psychological Foundation, 1986; National Medal of Science, 1992. Gibson's lab at Cornell was named in her honor, and one of the department's events was renamed the Eleanor J. and James J. Gibson Lecture.

WRITINGS:

(With Richard D. Walk) *A Comparative and Analytical Study of Visual Depth Perception,* American Psychological Association (Washington, DC), 1961.

Principles of Perceptual Learning and Development, Appleton-Century-Crofts (New York, NY), 1969.

(With Harry Levin) *The Psychology of Reading,* MIT Press (Cambridge, MA), 1975.

An Odyssey in Learning and Perception (part of "Learning, Development, and Conceptual Change" series), MIT Press (Cambridge, MA), 1991.

(With Anne D. Pick) *An Ecological Approach to Perceptual Learning and Development,* Oxford University Press (New York, NY), 2000.

Perceiving the Affordances: A Portrait of Two Psychologists, L. Erlbaum Associates (Mahwah, NJ), 2002.

Contributor to journals, including *Psychological Science.*

SIDELIGHTS: Eleanor Jack Gibson was a pioneer in the study of perceptual development in children. Her "visual cliff" experiment, first conducted in 1960, is still pictured in some psychology books today. The cliff was a table upon which a sheet of plate glass lay and extended beyond the table's actual edge. When babies were placed on the table and coaxed by their mothers or offered a favorite toy to entice them to crawl out onto the clear glass, nearly all of them withdrew. Gibson showed how the infant's depth perception helps prevent injuries and falls.

Gibson began the study of psychology under teachers who included Kurt Koffka, Fritz Heider, and James Gibson, whom she would later marry. She was an exceptional student in spite of many obstacles, particularly gender discrimination. She and James married in 1932, and they had two children, to whom Gibson devoted much of her time. When she decided to pursue her postgraduate studies at Yale, she was initially rejected, and when she was accepted, she was refused use of the university's laboratories, cafeterias, and libraries, and admission to Freudian seminars. At one point, she was wrongfully accused of incompetence, and the director of the laboratory later published her work under his name.

When James was offered a position at Cornell, Gibson became his research associate, as rules against nepotism were firmly enforced at the time. When they received a large grant, she was able to begin her study of perceptual learning, and they formulated their first theory in 1955. The papers they published two years later became the basis for his ecological theory.

During the 1950s, Gibson and Richard D. Walk first tested the visual cliff theory with baby animals, and in 1961 they published *A Comparative and Analytical Study of Visual Depth Perception.*

In 1965, rules about the employment of family members changed, and Gibson was awarded an endowed chair as a professor of psychology. She and James became the first married couple on the Cornell campus.

James died in 1979, and Gibson, who had been able to establish her infant study laboratory just a few years earlier, devoted more of her research to ecological psychology and the concept of affordance, or how objects can be used by a person. In 1982, she was invited to teach in Beijing, China.

Gibson continued to publish, and among her later volumes is *An Odyssey in Learning and Perception,* a collection of her research articles and new essays "in which Gibson complements her scientific vision with the wisdom of hindsight," noted Nancy McCarell in *American Journal of Psychology.* Gibson also includes essays by opponents of her theories, including Leo Postman and Richard Gregory. "Throughout her commentary," wrote McCarell, "Gibson's intellectual honesty forms the ground against which her intellectual determination figures boldly."

An Ecological Approach to Perceptual Learning and Development, written with Anne D. Pick, advances Gibson's theories on the development of perception in the human child from birth through the toddler years, beginning with communication, through recognizing and acting on objects, and concluding with locomotion.

Near the end of her life, Gibson wrote *Perceiving the Affordances: A Portrait of Two Psychologists.* The book, unlike her others, is not academic, but rather a presentation of scientific observations interspersed with personal anecdotes. In addition to covering her own research, she writes about her husband's influence, his research, and the development of his theories. The birth of her grandchildren and the death of her husband are also discussed.

F. Averill and D. M. Bernad reviewed the volume for *Cognitive Systems Research,* noting that "the postscript finds Gibson reflecting back on her life thus far. She explores the nature versus nurture question, suggesting that genes and the environment both contribute to the development of an individual. The reader is left with one last piece of wisdom elucidating the analogy of affordances with life: the environment affords us with the opportunity to make choices that result in the most personal satisfaction and success."

Gibson touches on concepts that include optical flow, depth perception, object constancy, and locomotion, according to Averill and Bernad, who said her discussion of these topics renders the volume "generally enjoyable because it gives the reader a greater understanding of the Gibsons' theories." Furthermore, they found the social perspective of Gibson's life to be worth reading, including the number of scientific achievements she accomplished while developing her field, notable not only in and of itself, but also for having occurred in a time of great discrimination against women.

Averill and Bernad concluded by saying that "although she confesses that she put her career on hold in order to raise her children and support her husband's professional development, she never lost her focus and desire to pursue her own questions. Such determination is the mark not simply of a brilliant woman, but more importantly, a brilliant scientist."

Gibson died on December 30, 2002, in Columbia, South Carolina, at the age of ninety-two.

BIOGRAPHICAL AND CRITICAL SOURCES:

BOOKS

Gale Encyclopedia of Psychology, Gale (Detroit, MI), 2001.
Pick, Anne D., editor, *Perception and Its Development: A Tribute to Eleanor J. Gibson,* L. Erlbaum Associates (Hillsdale, NJ), 1979.

PERIODICALS

American Journal of Psychology, summer, 1993, Nancy McCarell, review of *An Odyssey in Learning and Perception,* pp. 273-278.
Cognitive Systems Research (McGill University), September 6, 2002, F. Averill and D. M. Bernad, review of *Perceiving the Affordances: A Portrait of Two Psychologists.*
Contemporary Psychology, April, 1976, Jonathan Baron, review of *The Psychology of Reading,* pp. 261-263.
Development Psychology, September, 1992, Herbert L. Pick, Jr., "Eleanor J. Gibson: Learning to Perceive and Perceiving to Learn," pp. 787-794.
Journal of Reading, January, 1977, Richard L. Allington, review of *The Psychology of Reading,* pp. 339-340.
Modern Language Journal, November, 1977, Olga K. Garnica, review of *The Psychology of Reading,* pp. 387-388.
New Scientist, November 14, 1992, Stuart Sutherland, review of *An Odyssey in Learning and Perception,* p. 45.
Science, May 22, 1970, Wendell R. Garner, review of *Principles of Perceptual Learning and Development,* pp. 958-959.

OBITUARIES:

PERIODICALS

New York Times, January 4, 2003, p. A12.

ONLINE

Cornell Chronicle, http://www.news.cornell.edu/ (January 16, 2003).*

*   *   *

GINNA, Robert Emmett, Jr. 1927(?)-

PERSONAL: Born c. 1927. *Education:* Attended University of Rochester, received degree, 1948; Harvard University, M.A. (art history), 1950.

ADDRESSES: Home—Jaffrey Center, NH; and Sag Harbor, NY. *Agent*—c/o Author Mail, Random House, 1745 Broadway, New York, NY 10019.

CAREER: In early career, worked as a reporter and editor for magazines, including *Horizon, Life,* and *Scientific American;* cofounder of *People* magazine; Little, Brown (publisher), New York, NY, editor in chief, 1977-80; Harvard University, Cambridge, MA, member of faculty teaching writing and filmmaking, 1988-2002. Film producer, including for movies *Young Cassidy,* 1965, *The Last Challenge,* 1967, *Before Winter Comes,* 1969, *Brotherly Love,* 1970, and *Ireland Moving. Military service:* Served in the U.S. Navy during World War II, until 1946.

WRITINGS:

The Irish Way: A Walk through Ireland's Past and Present, Random House (New York, NY), 2003.

SIDELIGHTS: The son of Irish immigrants, Robert Emmett Ginna, Jr., has long been interested in the history of Ireland, and during his career as a filmmaker, he made the documentary *Ireland Moving* about his ancestral land. Much later, after a long career as a writer, editor, and university instructor, Ginna went back to Ireland when he was seventy-eight and took a long walking tour of the country to find out how the land had changed in recent years. His experiences during this adventure are recorded in his 2003 book, *The Irish Way: A Walk through Ireland's Past and Present.* "I wanted to have a way to write about Ireland as it is today and how it got that way," he is quoted as saying on the *University of Rochester* Web site. He found during his trip that although Ireland has become a modern country in many ways, its history and charm are still surviving: "Ireland's past is very palpable. . . . I tried to weave the past into the present because the past is so crucial to understanding the present." He added that "in many ways the 'soul' of the Irish—the love of talk and the love of sport and the quiet love of life—that has not changed."

In his book, Ginna describes the landscape and atmosphere of Ireland that he experienced while traveling through the center of the island, avoiding for the most part the large cities and coastlines that draw American tourists. He records conversations he had with people ranging from ordinary pub customers and farmers to industry moguls and castle-owning gentry. While some reviewers enjoyed Ginna's portrait of Ireland, others found it somewhat lacking in depth. For instance, some reviewers complained that Ginna takes what everyone tells him at face value, including optimistic views of business people, and that the author never finds anything critical or incisive to say. "It makes for a monotonous, somewhat narrow view of a vibrant, culturally rich country," stated a *Publishers Weekly* critic, who suggested that readers looking for information about modern life in Ireland "should look elsewhere." And a *Washington Post* writer found the interviews with Irish "captains of industry . . . dutiful and uninspiring, with the captains speaking in full paragraphs about how business is doing." However, other reviewers were entertained by *The Irish Way.* For example, *Wilson Quarterly* contributor Terence Winch stated that Ginna "has a sharp eye and a sure feel for the castles, forts, great houses, monasteries, and other places that contain so much vivid Irish history," and added that the author "is also gifted at resurrecting the memory of a select crew of departed luminaries."

BIOGRAPHICAL AND CRITICAL SOURCES:

PERIODICALS

Kirkus Reviews, May 1, 2003, review of *The Irish Way: A Walk through Ireland's Past and Present,* p. 655.

Library Journal, July, 2003, Janet Ross, review of *The Irish Way,* p. 111.

Publishers Weekly, May 19, 2003, review of *The Irish Way,* p. 61.

Washington Post, July 4, 2003, "Walking on Eire: The Gentleman's Tour."

Wilson Quarterly, autumn, 2003, Terence Winch, review of *The Irish Way,* p. 122.

ONLINE

Random House, http://www.randomhouse.com/ (April 5, 2004).

University of Rochester Web site, http://www.rochester.edu/ (April 5, 2004), "A Walk through Fire," author comments from Ginna*

GLENER, Doug

PERSONAL: Male. *Education:* Vassar College, B.A.

ADDRESSES: Office—Catalyst Creative Services, 283 Countryhaven Rd., Encinitas, CA 92024. *E-mail*—doug.glener@sbcglobal.net.

CAREER: Writer.

MEMBER: Self-Realization Fellowship.

WRITINGS:

(With Sarat Komagiri) *Wisdom's Blossoms: Tales of the Saints of India,* Shambhala (Boston, MA), 2002.

SIDELIGHTS: Doug Glener and Sarat Komagiri are coauthors of *Wisdom's Blossoms: Tales of the Saints of India.* The book presents twenty-six stories of Indian saints, martyrs, and other religious figures throughout Indian history. The figures in the stories represent Hindu, Buddhist, Muslim, Sikh, and Jain traditions, and the stories have been passed on through Indian oral traditions. Glener and Komagiri emphasize the universal values that unite these traditions, rather than the differences among them, and they shape each story for dramatic effect, ending in an inspirational or moral insight. Each story is also illustrated by a drawing of one of the saints. The tales emphasize nonviolence and individual renunciation, as well as charity, courage, pacifism, purity of heart, truthfulness, generosity, gentleness, patience, forgiveness, and the pursuit of wisdom. In *Publishers Weekly,* a reviewer praised the authors' "accessibility and coherence of style." Frederic and Mary Ann Brussat wrote in *Spirituality and Health* online, "These stories are good medicine for those who want to walk the path of devotion."

Glener holds a B.A. in English from Vassar College. He is a member of the Self-Realization Fellowship, an international society devoted to teaching meditation.

BIOGRAPHICAL AND CRITICAL SOURCES:

PERIODICALS

Library Journal, October 1, 2002, review of *Wisdom's Blossoms: Tales of the Saints of India,* p. 104.
Publishers Weekly, October 21, 2002, review of *Wisdom's Blossoms,* p. 70.

ONLINE

Spirituality and Health, http://www.spiritualityhealth.com/ (April 30, 2003).*

*   *   *

GLOCK, Allison

PERSONAL: Born in WV; children: two daughters.

ADDRESSES: Home—New Jersey. *Agent*—c/o Author Mail, Alfred A. Knopf Publicity, 1745 Broadway, New York, NY 10019.

CAREER: Writer.

WRITINGS:

Beauty before Comfort: A Memoir, Alfred A. Knopf (New York, NY), 2003.

Contributor to periodicals, including *GQ.*

SIDELIGHTS: Allison Glock's first book, *Beauty before Comfort: A Memoir,* is a tribute to her maternal grandmother, who died in 2002, and has been described by a *Kirkus Reviews* contributor as "a memoir as elemental as its subject: pulsing, fetching, leaving a strong afterglow." In the book Glock writes that Aneita Jean Blair was born in Chester, West Virginia, in a pottery-making community that relied on the clean clay from the shores of the Ohio River. The pottery factories provided the sole source of work, and the families were poor. As Aneita reached puberty, she began to realize she could use her beauty to her benefit: she began collecting boys, then men, searching for the one who could give her more than life in the little town. However, she eventually married Donald Thornberry, a potter, and remained in West Virginia.

Tony Earley noted in the *New York Times Book Review* that between puberty and marriage, "the possibility of securing for themselves Jeannie Blair's delectable (and prominently displayed) favors at least gave the otherwise down-on-their-luck men of the northern West Virginia panhandle something to hope for." The couple had three daughters, and Aneita was an unconventional mother, always taken with her good looks and beauty, advice about which she passed on to her daughters. Earley said that her story "varies only in its particulars from who knows how many other tales of beauty and talent blooming furiously in some American backwater, witnessed only by people who, possessing no other resources, grind it up to ameliorate their own anonymous hungers. We mistake the tale of the starlet discovered in the drugstore as the archetypal American story, when it's the story, most often untold, of the beauty who goes undiscovered, the voice that goes unheard, that comes closer to getting right who we actually are."

Los Angeles Times reviewer Merle Rubin wrote that "there's more to this memoir than a celebration of one woman's narcissism. It is also a vivid evocation of the imperiled natural beauty of this region of mines and potteries, the hardships of the Depression, and the charms of small-town life as well as its shibboleths, petty snobberies, and sheer boredom. Glock writes with enormous zest, and her book is a delight to read: funny, forceful, down-to-earth."

BIOGRAPHICAL AND CRITICAL SOURCES:

BOOKS

Glock, Allison, *Beauty before Comfort: A Memoir,* Alfred A. Knopf (New York, NY), 2003.

PERIODICALS

Booklist, May 1, 2003, Elsa Gaztambide, review of *Beauty before Comfort: A Memoir,* p. 1568.
Kirkus Reviews, March 1, 2003, review of *Beauty before Comfort,* p. 360.
Library Journal, August, 2003, Gene Shaw, review of *Beauty before Comfort,* p. 96.
Los Angeles Times, June 9, 2003, Merle Rubin, review of *Beauty before Comfort,* p. E10.
New York Times Book Review, August 10, 2003, Tony Earley, review of *Beauty before Comfort,* p. 14.
People, May 12, 2003, Joyce Cohen, review of *Beauty before Comfort,* p. 47.
Publishers Weekly, March 3, 2003, review of *Beauty before Comfort,* p. 61.*

GODDARD, Tariq 1975-

PERSONAL: Born 1975, in London, England. *Education:* Attended King's College London, and University of Warwick.

ADDRESSES: Agent—c/o Author Mail, Sceptre, 338 Euston Road, London NW1 3B4 England.

CAREER: Writer.

AWARDS, HONORS: Homage to a Firing Squad was shortlisted for Whitbread First Novel Award, 2002.

WRITINGS:

Homage to a Firing Squad, Sceptre (London, England), 2002.
Dynamo, Sceptre (London, England), 2003.

WORK IN PROGRESS: War Pigs, a novel.

SIDELIGHTS: Novelist Tariq Goddard, according to a reviewer in the *Guardian,* "sets his novels in periods of extreme political turmoil, and then populates them with characters who lack any passion for politics." This juxtaposition is evident in Goddard's first novel, *Homage to a Firing Squad,* set during the Spanish Civil War. In the novel, four young men head out in a car to find and assassinate the politician Don Rojo. However, none of them have experience in assassination, and to complicate matters, three of them are in love with Don Rojo's daughter. In addition, as they head toward Don Rojo's hacienda to kill him, he lies in bed, considering killing himself.

As they travel down the dark and rainy Tibidabo road, with the war raging around them, the would-be assassins meet amorous barmaids, crises, road blocks, and the man who ordered them to assassinate Don Rojo. When they finally get to Don Rojo's hacienda, they converge with two other assassins and two of Don Rojo's daughters in what the publisher described as "a surreal and bullet-ridden climax." *Homage to a Firing Squad* was shortlisted for the 2002 Whitbread First Novel Award.

Goddard's second book, *Dynamo,* is set during Stalin's Russia in the late 1930s. Europe is heading toward World War II, and Stalin rules with an iron grip, killing anyone who displeases him and setting impossible production goals for factories and laborers. The novel features two rival soccer teams, Spartak and Dynamo; Dynamo is run by the Soviet secret police, and Spartak represents ordinary workers. On the eve of a critical game, the star striker for Spartak takes to his bed, threatening Spartak's winning streak. In addition the secret police threaten the manager and trainer of Spartak, telling them that if they don't lose the game to Dynamo, they and their teammates will be harassed, imprisoned, and perhaps even killed. These men are forced to choose between their honor as athletes and their own safety. A *Guardian* reviewer noted, "It is an extraordinary moment, brimming with symbolism: individualism versus collectivism, passion versus discipline; the workers versus the secret police."

BIOGRAPHICAL AND CRITICAL SOURCES:

PERIODICALS

Guardian (Manchester, England), June 21, 2003, review of *Dynamo.*

ONLINE

Spoiled Ink, http://www.spoiledink.com/ (February 22, 2004), Sean Merrigan, interview with Tariq Goddard.*

*   *   *

GOYER, David S. 1966-

PERSONAL: Born 1966. . *Education:*University of Southern California Film School, B.A., 1988.

ADDRESSES: Office—c/o Author Mail, D.C. Comics, 1700 Broadway, Seventh floor, New York, NY 10019-5905. *Agent*—Phil Raskind, Endeavor, 9701 Wilshire Blvd., Tenth floor, Beverly Hills, CA 90212.

CAREER: Comics writer, novelist, short story writer, screenwriter, producer, and television series creator.

WRITINGS:

COMICS

(With James Robinson) *Justice Be Done: JSA,* D.C. Comics (New York, NY), 2000.
(With Geoff Johns) *A Burning Hate,* D.C. Comics (New York, NY), 2001.
(With others) *JSA: Darkness Falls,* D.C. Comics (New York, NY), 2002.
(With Geoff Johns) *JLA, JSA: Virtue and Vice,* D.C. Comics (New York, NY), 2002.
(With Geoff Johns) *JSA: The Return of Hawkman,,* D.C. Comics (New York, NY), 2002.
(With James Robinson) *Starman: A Starry Knight,* D.C. Comics (New York, NY), 2002.
(With James Robinson and Chuck Dixon) *The Justice Society Returns!,* D.C. Comics (New York, NY), 2003.
(With Leonard Kirk) *JSA: Stealing Thunder,* D.C. Comics (New York, NY), 2003.

SCREENPLAYS

Death Warrant, Metro-Goldwyn-Mayer/United Artists, 1990.
(And associate producer) *Kickboxer 2: The Road Back,* Trimark, 1991.
Demonic Toys,, Paramount, 1992.
Arcade, Full Moon Entertainment, 1993.
(With Ted Elliott and Terry Rossio) *Robert A. Heinlein's The Puppet Masters,* Buena Vista, 1994.
The Crow: City of Angels, (also known as *The Crow II*), Miramax, 1996.
Blade, New Line Cinema, 1998.
Dark City, New Line Cinema, 1998.
(And coproducer) *Mission to Mars,* 2000.
(And executive producer) *Blade 2,* New Line Cinema, 2002.
(And director) *ZigZag,* Franchise Classics, 2002.
(And director and producer) *Blade: Trinity,* New Line Cinema, 2004.

TELEPLAYS

(And executive producer) *Sleepwalkers,,* National Broadcasting Company, Inc. (NBC), 1997.

Also author of television specials including *Nick Fury: Agent of SHIELD*, 1998; *Origins of "Blade:" A Look at Dark Comics*, 1998; *La Magra*, 1998; *Blood Tide*, 1998; *Blood Pact: The Making of "Blade II,"* 2002; *Night Bites: Women and Their Vampires*, 2003. Author of "Dream of Doom" episode for *Perversions of Science*, Home Box Office (HBO), 1997. Writer and executive producer of the television series *Fearsum* (originally titled *FreakyLinks*).

NOVELS

(With Frank Lauria, Lem Dobbs, and Alex Proyas) *Dark City*, St. Martin's Press (New York, NY), 1998.

WORK IN PROGRESS: Current projects expected in 2005 include *Batman Begins* and *Ghost Rider*.

SIDELIGHTS: David S. Goyer is a prolific writer with projects that range from comic books to screenplays. Goyer is also well known for his work on the popular movie series "Blade." In an interview with Reg Seeton at the *Ugo Web site*, Goyer noted that his start as a screenplay writer was "fortunate"; his first manuscript was produced as the Jean-Claude Van Damme film "Death Warrant."

In this interview, Goyer also told Seeton that "Blade" was an interesting project because he was attempting to make a movie about what was originally a minor comic book character. "We didn't have the burden of a canon [that] we had to adhere to." Called an "edgy fantasy" by *Variety* reviewer Joe Leydon, "Blade" has been followed by two sequels: "Blade II" and "Blade: Trinity."

Dark City, produced in 1998, is another movie that Goyer is well known for. In the film, John Murdoch finds himself in a hotel room, with no memory of how he got there, only to learn that he is wanted under suspicion of multiple murders. At the same time, Murdoch is being chased by strange men who have the ability to alter reality at will. According to Todd McCarthy in a *Variety* review, the movie "trades in such weighty themes as memory, thought control, human will and the altering of reality, but is engaging mostly in the degree to which it creates and sustains a visually startling alternate universe."

Goyer's comic writing career began in 2000 when D.C. Comics published *Justice Be Done: JSA*. (JSA stands for Justice Society of America.) Goyer also reintroduced an old comic book character in *JSA: The Return of Hawkman*. Bill Radford of the Colorado Springs *Gazette* wrote, "The fact that it has taken nearly two years to bring back the winged warrior shows the challenge DC faced in reviving a character whose history had become a tangled nightmare." In 2003, after completing fifty-one issues, Goyer chose to take a hiatus from comic writing.

Goyer wrote and directed the 2002 film *ZigZag*, which explores the relationship between an autistic teen and his dying social worker. *Hollywood Reporter*'s Frank Scheck commented that the film's "familiar material is enlivened by reasonably clever plot twists and strong performances." Joe Leyden in a *Variety* review found that "Goyer infuses heart and vigor into material that could have come off as overly familiar at best, sappily improbable at worst."

BIOGRAPHICAL AND CRITICAL SOURCES:

PERIODICALS

Gazette (Colorado Springs, CO), April 5, 2001, Bill Radford, "Hawkman to Make Long-Delayed Return."
Hollywood Reporter, June 21, 2002, Frank Scheck, review of *ZigZag*, p. 46; August 11, 2003, Chris Gardner, "Meditating," p. 55.
Library Journal, May 1, 2003, Steve Raiteri, review of *JLA, JSA: Virtue and Vice*, p. 96.
Publishers Weekly, April 28, 2003, review of *JLA/JSA: Virtue and Vice*, p. 51; January 26, 2004, review of *The Justice Society Returns!*, p. 233.
Variety, October 27, 1997, Tony Scott, review of *Sleepwalkers*, p. 32; February 23, 1998, Todd McCarthy, review of *Dark City*, p. 73; March 20, 2002, Joe Leydon, review of *Blade II*, p. 12; April 11, 2002, Joe Leydon, review of *ZigZag*, p. 12.

ONLINE

IMDb Web site, http://www.imdb.com./ (July 2, 2004), "Biography for David S. Goyer."
Underground Online, http://www.ugo.com/ (July 2, 2004), interview by Reg Seeton.*

GREEN, Angela 1949(?)

PERSONAL: Born c. 1949. Married; children: two. *Education:* Attended Kings College.

ADDRESSES: Home—South Nutfield, England. *Agent*—c/o Author Mail, Peter Owen Publishers, 73 Kenway Rd., London SW5 0RE, England.

CAREER: Writer. Worked in marketing and as a public relations consultant.

WRITINGS:

Cassandra's Disk, Peter Owen Publishers (London, England), 2002.
The Colour of Water, Peter Owen Publishers (London, England), 2003.

SIDELIGHTS: Angela Green became a writer after first enjoying a career in marketing and public relations. *Times Literary Supplement* contributor Margaret Stead wrote that her debut novel, *Cassandra's Disk,* "uses Greek myth as a springboard for a contemporary fiction that blends the real with the fantastical. The novel also takes the form of a metafictional puzzle, Borges-style."

The story opens with Englishwoman Cassandra Byrd writing the story of her life on a laptop as she waits in a mental institution on the island of Ithaca for cancer to claim her. Cassandra had been the first born of twins, a dark, homely child whose fair and lovely sister, Helen, was her mother's favorite. Cassandra carries her childhood behavior of the "Big, Bad Baby" into adulthood, and although the twins are in a constant state of rivalry, they are also bound to each other. It is their classicist father, Feargal, who exerts a tender influence on the twins, but after he dies, their mother marries a man who sexually abuses Helen. Cassandra kills him, and the girls, now fifteen, are taken in by a wealthy Greek actress and former lover of their father.

Helen becomes an actress, and Cassandra a photographer in the style of Diane Arbus. Helen has no trouble attracting men, while Cassandra seduces hers, and in the end Cassandra wants only one man, the famous war photographer who has married her sister. A *Kirkus*

Reviews contributor wrote that in *Cassandra's Disk,* "there are lingering questions of identity throughout, but the probing coexists with flashier, fleshier passages."

A *Publishers Weekly* reviewer said that "the narrative is significantly enlivened by Cassandra's brassy style, and Green keeps the dramatic developments coming at a brisk clip." *Spectator*'s Patrick Skene Catling called *Cassandra's Disk* an "exceptionally clever, vivacious account of sibling rivalry."

BIOGRAPHICAL AND CRITICAL SOURCES:

PERIODICALS

Kirkus Reviews, October 15, 2002, review of *Cassandra's Disk,* p. 1504.
Publishers Weekly, November 4, 2002, review of *Cassandra's Disk,* p. 61.
Spectator, October 26, 2002, Patrick Skene Catling, review of *Cassandra's Disk,* p. 49.
Times Literary Supplement, July 26, 2002, Margaret Stead, review of *Cassandra's Disk,* p. 23.

ONLINE

Angela Green Home Page, http://www.angelagreen.com/ (November 16, 2003).*

*   *   *

GREEN, Richard Lancelyn (Gordon) 1953-2004

OBITUARY NOTICE—See index for *CA* sketch: Born July 10, 1953, in Bebington, Cheshire, England; died March 27, 2004, in London, England. Collector and author. During his lifetime, Green amassed one of the largest existing collections of manuscripts and memorabilia related to the fictional detective Sherlock Holmes, about whom he also published extensively. Becoming interested in Holmes and his creator, Sir Arthur Conan Doyle, at the young age of eleven when he attended his first meeting of the Sherlock Holmes Society, Green quickly became obsessed with this subject. Attending Bradford College from 1966 to 1971, and earning a master's degree from University

College, Oxford, in 1975, Green would hold a number of different jobs in his lifetime, including as an editor, researcher, and even as a surveyor's assistant, but his principal focus remained Sherlock Holmes. He collected books and original manuscripts by Doyle, as well as writings by other authors relating to Holmes, and memorabilia that included simulated artifacts once "owned" by the characters, such as Dr. Watson's army revolver and a copy of the notice announcing the end of the Red-Headed League. Green managed to earn an income from his obsession by editing works such as *Arthur Conan Doyle on Sherlock Holmes* (1981) and Doyle's *The Adventures of Sherlock Holmes* (1993), as well as collaborative efforts with John Michael Gibson that include *My Evening with Sherlock Holmes* (1981) and *The Unknown Conan Doyle: Uncollected Stories* (1982). In 1984, Green earned an Edgar Allan Poe Award, with Gibson, for his 1983 work *A Bibliography of A. Conan Doyle*. The chair of the Sherlock Holmes Society of London from 1996 to 1999, Green had hopes of writing an authoritative, three-volume biography on Doyle, but his plans were frustrated by his inability to gain access to the author's private papers, which remained inaccessible to the public because of rights disputes. Nevertheless, Green's substantial archives of research material will likely become a useful resource to Doyle scholars for many years to come.

OBITUARIES AND OTHER SOURCES:

PERIODICALS

Daily Post (London, England), April 12, 2004, p. 11.
Independent (London, England), April 8, 2004, p. 34.

*　　*　　*

GREENING, John 1954-

PERSONAL: Born 1954.

ADDRESSES: Home—Huntingdonshire, England. *Agent*—c/o Cargo Press, The Sea House, Coverack, Helston, Cornwall TR12 6SA, England.

CAREER: Poet and teacher.

AWARDS, HONORS: Society of Authors grant.

WRITINGS:

COLLECTIONS OF POEMS

Westerners, Hippopotamus Press (Surrey, England), 1984.
The Tutankhamun Variations, Bloodaxe Books (Newcastle upon Tyne, England), 1991.
Fotheringhay and Other Poems, Rockingham Press (Ware, England), 1995.
The Bocase Stone, Dedalus (Dublin, Ireland), 1996.
Nightflights: New and Selected Poems, Rockingham Press (Ware, England), 1999.
Gascoigne's Egg, Cargo Press (Cornwall, England), 2000.
Omm Sety, Shoestring Press (Nottingham, England), 2001.

Also author of texts included in six songs called *Falls,* premiered by the Dunedin Consort in 2000 at Wigmore Hall, United Kingdom. Contributor of poems to literary magazines and anthologies.

SIDELIGHTS: John Greening is a poet who writes about the intimate relationship between everyday life and historical worlds. He has composed poems about Egypt, the Norse gods, polar exploration, and various historical figures. As noted by reviewer Tim Dooley in *Times Literary Supplement,* "Greening's poems can offer lyrical graces as well as psychological or political perspectives."

Greening found much of the inspiration for his work through his travels in Germany, the United States, and Egypt. His book of poems *The Tutankhamun Variations,* for example, combines views of historical archeological expeditions in Egypt with impressions gathered by Greening when he visited the country as a young man. His travels to the United States and Canada led him to Niagara Falls, which in turn served as the inspiration for Greening's *Falls,* an unaccompanied choral work with six songs focusing on the stories and folklore surrounding the famous water falls.

In 1984, Greening's first collection of poems, titled *Westerners,* was published. The book includes six poems on artifacts in Egyptian museums, poems about

Cleopatra, and a long mythic poem. Writing in *Times Literary Supplement,* Michael Hulse noted that the "poems of the present are never far removed from a sense of the past." He mentioned that Greening does not avoid sociological and political comment, including acerbic observations about wealth and privilege. Hulse also praised Greening for his "highly developed sense of the suggestiveness of human history."

Greening focuses on Egypt and an Antarctic expedition in *The Tutankhamun Variations.* The book features the notion of a sequence as a compositional device. In his book, Greening includes twenty-three poems based on such varied topics as a 1922 expedition to Egypt, the London Tutankhamun Exhibition that took place in 1972, and the poet's own experience when he traveled in Egypt in the late 1970s. Nearly half of the book focuses on the excavation of a boy pharaoh's tomb. Another major sequence is titled "The Winter Journey" and is based on three members of Robert Scott's Antarctic expedition of 1911 in their quest to collect an emperor penguin's egg. "A nostalgia for Britain's empire riddles the work, and yet its *Masterpiece Theater* costume drama has a surreal tilt," wrote Mark Jarman in the *Southern Review.* Dooley commented in *Times Literary Supplement,* "Images of burial and bringing to light, of childhood and the attribution of value recur in poems clogged with historical detail or private reminiscence."

In *Nightflights: New and Selected Poems,* Greening provides a retrospective of his poems prior to 1999 in addition to some new works. Writing in *Times Literary Supplement,* Neil Powell pointed out "notable successes among the newly collected poems" which end the book. He particularly praised the poem "The Twilight of Birds," which he said benefited from more "attentive writing" than some of the earlier works.

In *Gascoigne's Egg,* Greening provides a series of poems that mingle the accident of the airship R101 (a dirigible that crashed on October 5, 1930, into a hillside near Beauvais in France, killing everybody on board) with the memories of George Gascoigne, a sixteenth-century English Renaissance poet who once owned an estate that included the site where the airship was built. In his poems, Greening explores how the past and present intertwine and provides a look at the flight's disastrous outcome due to hubris.

In 2002, *Omm Sety* was published. Once again, Greening returns to the setting of Egypt, this time to write about historical figure Dorothy Eady, who took the

name Omm Sety, which means "mother of Sety," after the birth of her and her Egyptian husband's son. Eady was convinced that she had lived a previous life in Egypt as a priestess in a temple and had been King Sety's forbidden lover. When Eady's marriage ended, she stayed in Egypt as an archeologist and further pursued her lover from the past. In his thirty-five-page poem, Greening counterpoises matching free verse stanzas, all spoken by Omm Sety, with metrical verse representing King Sety speaking from the other world. The two worlds are often juxtaposed on opposite pages. Writing in *Critical Survey,* John Haynes commented on Greening's ability to show great variety in his metrical verse, using everything from octosyllabic couplets to full pentameter. Haynes noted, "A short review cannot cover all the facets of this wonderfully rich poem, for example the Jungian and Egyptian mythological undercurrent about the deep impersonality, or the linking of Ozimandias with Oz, the slangy shortening of Soiris, and then to the Emerald City of Oz and another Dorothy also concerned with 'home.'" Haynes also remarked that "Greening unveils no avuncular trickster" who tried to "explain it all," and noted, "The poem ends in unflinching solitude."

BIOGRAPHICAL AND CRITICAL SOURCES:

PERIODICALS

Critical Survey, January, 2002, John Haynes, review of *Omm Sety,* pp. 126-28.
Southern Review, spring, 1994, Mark Jarman, "Diversity Comes to British Poetry," pp. 393-408.
Times Literary Supplement (London, England), October 12, 1984, Michael Hulse, review of *Westerners,* p. 1169; December 20, 1991, Tim Dooley, review of *The Tutankhamun Variations,* p. 8; November 12, 1999, Neil Powell, review of *Nightflights: New and Selected Poems,* p. 26.*

* * *

GREGG, Hubert (Robert Harry) 1914-2004

OBITUARY NOTICE—See index for *CA* sketch: Born July 19, 1914, in London, England; died March 29, 2004, in Eastbourne, East Sussex, England. Composer, actor, director, broadcaster, and author. In addition to being well known as the host of the British Broadcasting Corporation (BBC) music request program *Hubert Gregg Says Thanks for the Memory* for over three decades, Gregg was the author of popular World War II-era songs, a director of plays, an actor, and an author of novels, plays, and nonfiction. After attending St. Dunstan's College on a scholarship, he attended the Webber-Douglas School of Singing and Dramatic Art from 1933 to 1936 because his parents could not afford to send him to university. Gregg, however, proved to be an acting talent, and during the 1930s performed with the Birmingham Repertory Company in various play productions. When World War II ensued, he joined the Lincolnshire Regiment but instead of fighting was tapped as a broadcaster, speaking in German for propaganda programs against the Nazis. While in the army, Gregg also wrote the popular songs "I'm Going to Get Lit Up (When the Lights Go Up Again in London)" (1940) and "Maybe It's Because I'm a Londoner" (1944), which helped British morale and became tunes that are still remembered today. After the war, Gregg returned to stage work, directing versions of Agatha Christie's *The Mousetrap* and *The Hollow,* as well as acting in productions of *Caesar and Cleopatra* and *The Cocktail Party.* In 1952, he wrote the song "Elizabeth" in honor of Queen Elizabeth II's coronation, but his main interest turned from song writing to writing musicals, as well as to broadcasting work for the BBC. He was a costar in the BBC-TV series *From Me to You* in 1956, and during the late 1960s was a presenter on BBC-Radio's *A Square Deal.* In the 1970s and early 1980s, Gregg was host of such series as *Hubert Gregg at the London Theatre, I Call It Genius,* and *I Call It Style,* but his most successful program was *Hubert Gregg Says Thanks for the Memory,* which debuted in 1972 and featured popular songs from the first half of the twentieth century. In addition to all these activities, Gregg had acting roles in films such as *Doctor at Sea* (1955), *Simon and Laura* (1955), and the 1973 Disney animated feature, *Robin Hood.* Furthermore, he was the author of numerous plays such as *Cheque Mate* (1957) and *Who's Been Sleeping . . .?* (1965), the novels *April Gentlemen* (1951) and *A Day's Loving* (1974), and the nonfiction books *Agatha Christie and All That Mousetrap* (1980) and *Thanks for the Memory: A Personal Spotlight on Special People in Entertainment* (1983). For his many contributions to the arts, Gregg was named a Member of the British Empire in 2002.

OBITUARIES AND OTHER SOURCES:

BOOKS

Gammond, Peter, *The Oxford Companion to Popular Music,* Oxford University Press (Oxford, England), 1991.

PERIODICALS

Independent (London, England), March 31, 2004, p. 35.
Los Angeles Times, April 1, 2004, p. B11.
Times (London, England), March 31, 2004.
Washington Post, April 3, 2004, p. B6.

H

HAINSWORTH, Peter (R. J.)

PERSONAL: Male.

ADDRESSES: Office—Lady Margaret Hall, Oxford University, Oxford OX2 6QA, England.

CAREER: Lady Margaret Hall, Oxford University, Oxford, England, professor.

WRITINGS:

(Editor and author of notes, with T. Gwynfor Griffith) *Selected Poems of Petrarch,* Manchester University Press (Manchester, England), 1971.

(Editor, with Michael Caesar) *Writers and Society in Contemporary Italy: A Collection of Essays,* St. Martin's Press (New York, NY), 1984.

Petrarch the Poet: An Introduction to the "Rerum Vulgarium Fragmenta," Routledge (New York, NY), 1988.

(Editor and contributor, with V. Lucchesi, C. Roaf, David Robey, and J. R. Woodhouse) *The Languages of Literature in Renaissance Italy,* Oxford University Press (New York, NY), 1988.

(Editor, with David Robey) *The Oxford Companion to Italian Literature,* Oxford University Press (New York, NY), 2002.

SIDELIGHTS: Peter Hainsworth is an Oxford University professor who specializes in Italian literature of the Renaissance period. He has coedited several books on the subject, including the comprehensive *The Oxford Companion to Italian Literature,* and is the author of *Petrarch the Poet: An Introduction to the "Rerum Vulgarium Fragmenta."* The latter work, which evaluates what is considered by many modern academics to be among the most significant poetic works in Western literature, has been highly praised by critics, who noted that it is the first scholarly work of its kind to place Petrarch's work within the context of his entire literary output. The book is also a thorough critical analysis of Petrarch's style, structure, and themes.

According to the Hainsworth, one goal of *Petrarch the Poet* is to introduce readers to Italian poetry. Jennifer Petrie wrote in *Medium Aevum* that Hainsworth's study is a helpful discussion of Petrarch's concern for what the author calls "the nature of poetry in the post-Dantesque era." *Choice* contributor C. Kleinhenz praised the work for, among other assets, the author's ability to discuss "with great critical acumen some of the basic complex themes of the collection." Janet L. Smarr concluded in *Renaissance Quarterly* that "all in all the book provides a good array of basic information in clear form for the student and enough insightful analysis of detail for the scholar."

The Languages of Literature in Renaissance Italy is a collection of essays coedited by Hainsworth. The book also contains one of Hainsworth's essays on Petrarch, which Brian Richardson described as "a subtle examination of Petrarch's use of metaphor" in a *Notes and Queries* review. According to John Barnes in the *Times Literary Supplement,* the essays examine the "language and style [of Italian writers] from the age of Dante to the High Renaissance."

Hainsworth also coedited *The Oxford Companion to Italian Literature,* which contains 2,400 entries covering "almost every writer of reputation active over a period of about nine centuries, together with a generous number of General Entries," as Masolino D'Amico noted in another *Times Literary Supplement* review. D'Amico declared this reference source to be "as complete, reliable and useful as any such enterprise could be."

BIOGRAPHICAL AND CRITICAL SOURCES:

PERIODICALS

Choice, February, 1989, C. Kleinhenz, review of *Petrarch the Poet: An Introduction to the "Rerum Vulgarium Fragmenta,"* p. 945.

Medium Aevum, spring, 1990, Jennifer Petrie, review of *Petrarch the Poet,* pp. 170-171.

Modern Language Review, April, 1991, Conor Fahy, review of *The Languages of Literature in Renaissance Italy,* pp. 487-488.

Notes and Queries, June, 1989, Brian Richardson, review of *The Languages of Literature in Renaissance Italy,* pp. 230-231.

Renaissance Quarterly, autumn, 1989, Janet L. Smarr, review of *Petrarch the Poet,* pp. 546-549.

Times Literary Supplement, September 23, 1988, John Barnes, "Ancient and Modern Revised," review of *The Languages of Literature in Renaissance Italy,* p. 1055; August 18, 1989, Rachel Jacoff, "Doing and Undoing," p. 900; January 31, 2003, Masolino D'Amico, "Dante to Fellini," review of *The Oxford Companion to Italian Literature,* pp. 10-11.*

* * *

HAKALA, Dee 1958-

PERSONAL: Born February 13, 1958, in Sacramento, CA; daughter of Leland and Sharon (maiden name, Gardner; later surname, Swan) Dast; married Keith Hakala (an engine testing specialist), October 5, 1984; children: Zachary, Jeremy. *Ethnicity:* "White." *Education:* Attended college. *Religion:* United Methodist.

ADDRESSES: Home—3024 Long Grove Ln., Aurora, IL 60504. *Office*—C.H.O.I.C.E.S. VVV with De, Inc., c/o C. Dupuis, 1215 South Post Oak Rd., Sulphur, LA 70663; fax: 630-375-9274. *Agent*—David Black, David Black Literary Agency, 156 Fifth Ave., New York, NY 10010-7002. *E-mail*—DeeVVV@aol.com.

CAREER: Lake Charles Memorial Hospital, Lake Charles, LA, developer, instructor, and program director of exercise programs, 1991-93; MWR Sports, Governors Island, NY, program director, fitness instructor, and personal trainer, 1993-94; Advanced Health and Fitness Club, Detroit, MI, program director, fitness instructor, and personal trainer, 1998-99; Young Women's Christian Association, Aurora, IL, program director, 2001—. C.H.O.I.C.E.S. VVV with De, Inc., president and chief executive officer; New Face of Fitness (exercise and well-ness program), founder; Rush Copley Healthplex, personal trainer and fitness instructor; public speaker on fitness and exercise topics. American Council on Exercise, certified fitness instructor, 1991—, certified personal trainer, 1993—; certified by Aerobics and Fitness Association of America, 1995—; American College of Sports Medicine, certified health and fitness trainer, 1996—; American Red Cross, certified lifeguard, 2001. Laubach Literacy Volunteer Service, tutor, 1989-93; Women's Commission of Southwest Louisiana, member, 1992-93; P.L.A.Y., creator, facilitator, and volunteer teacher of activities courses, 1994-97.

MEMBER: International Association of Fitness Professionals (IDEA; master member), American College of Sports Medicine, Aquatic Exercise Association, Southwest Louisiana Coast Guard Wives Club (president, 1989-92).

AWARDS, HONORS: Nike Fitness Innovation Award, 1994, for New Face of Fitness; award from Delaware Governor's Council on Lifestyle and Fitness, 1998; Healthy People 2000 Award (Lima, OH), 1999.

WRITINGS:

(With Micheal D'Orso) *Thin Is Just a Four Letter Word: Living Fit for All Shapes and Sizes,* Little, Brown (Boston, MA), 1997.

WORK IN PROGRESS: Hungry Heart (tentative title), a sequel to *Thin Is Just a Four Letter Word.*

SIDELIGHTS: Dee Hakala told *CA:* "Writing has been a creative outlet for me since I was in elementary school. Poetry, plays, stories, and daily journal entries filled my school and college days. One of my dreams was to write a book. Thanks to assistance from Nike, Black, Inc., and Micheal D'Orso, that dream became reality.

"Writing is my form of therapy. I equal it to a musician who is inspired and makes music. My grandmother was a poet. My father wrote some pretty intense pieces, too.

"My first book is honest, and I know it has helped thousands—including me!"

BIOGRAPHICAL AND CRITICAL SOURCES:

PERIODICALS

Nutrition Health Review, summer, 1996, review of *Thin Is Just a Four Letter Word: Living Fit for All Shapes and Sizes,* p. 22.

ONLINE

Dee Hakala, New Face of Fitness Home Page, http://www.deehakala.com/ (December 16, 2003).

*   *   *

HALL, Sarah 1974-

PERSONAL: Born 1974, in Cumbria, England. *Education:* Graduated from Aberystwyth University (English and art history); St. Andrews University, M.Litt. (creative writing).

ADDRESSES: Home—NC and Europe. *Agent*—c/o Editorial Department, Faber and Faber Ltd., 3 Queen Sq., London WC1N 3AU, England.

CAREER: Novelist and poet. Has taught at St. Andrews University in the undergraduate creative writing program.

AWARDS, HONORS: Commonwealth Writers Prize for Best First Book and Betty Trask Award, both 2003, both for *Haweswater;* Orange Prize nomination, 2004, for *The Electric Michelangelo.*

WRITINGS:

Haweswater (novel), Faber and Faber (London, England), 2002.
The Electric Michelangelo (novel), Faber and Faber (London, England), 2004.

Also contributor of poems to various publications.

SIDELIGHTS: English poet and novelist Sarah Hall won two awards for her first novel, *Haweswater,* and has drawn critical acclaim for her second, *The Electric Michelangelo.* A serious writer by age twenty, Hall had poetry published by the late 1990s and turned to writing novels soon after. She moved to the United States in 1999 and divides her time between North Carolina and Europe. Hall's favorite form of writing is poetry, which is evident, claim critics, in the lilting prose of her novels.

Based on a true event, *Haweswater* is the story of the village of Mardale in northern England's Cumbrian Valley. The valley is destroyed when it is flooded in a 1936 reservoir project designed to bring water to city dwellers. Benedicte Page, writing for *Bookseller,* called *Haweswater* a "striking rural tragedy." Central to the story is a devastating romance between Manchester City Waterworks representative Jack Liggett, who delivers the bad news to Mardale residents, and eighteen-year-old Mardale farm girl Janet Lightburn, a strong, unsentimental woman whose life is inextricably tied to her environment.

Stephen Knight, in a review for the *Times Literary Supplement,* observed that the water is the true main character of the story. Knight noted that "lives are governed by [water's] metaphors, and, in the end, swamped by it." Fiona Hook observed in a review for the London *Times* that "the clean, freezing water, teeming with life, that pervades the valley in pools and rivulets is a metaphor for Hall's own style." Knight praised Hall's use of pauses throughout the text, which make the story "a series of vignettes," and found her phonetic dialogue yet another means of slowing the reader to the story's pace.

Hall's second novel, *The Electric Michelangelo,* was born out of Hall's fascination with folk art and tattooing. She told Mark Thwaite of the *Ready Steady*

Book Web site that the issues associated with tattooing, "the human body, the mysterious urge to ornament, identity, symbolism, commemoration of life's experiences through art," compelled her to write about it. In an interview with *Bookseller* writer Benedicte Page, Hall noted that "Tattooing is a record of life, because you commemorate events with a picture, so your skin becomes a kind of history."

The Electric Michelangelo is set in the northern England seaside town of Morecambe (near the author's own childhood home) and on New York's Coney Island. The novel's protagonist, Cy Parks, born in 1907 Morecambe, lives with his mother, who runs a seedy vacation resort and haven for pregnant teens. Cy becomes an apprentice to acclaimed tattoo artist Eliot Riley, a foul-mouthed alcoholic who nevertheless passes on his art and vocation. Cy sails to New York after Riley's death and takes up his practice among the freak show booths on Coney Island. Cy falls in love with Grace, a European immigrant circus performer who hires him to tattoo black-rimmed green eyes all over her body. The palpable facts of pain and suffering are the book's true themes, from the consumptive guests at the Parks's boarding house to scenes in which Riley and Grace are assaulted by fanatics. The pain caused by the tattoo needle is also an undercurrent in the novel.

Manchester *Guardian* contributor Jem Poster wrote that "Hall certainly knows how to shock, but the shock is an essential part of a serious artistic and—in the best sense—moral enterprise." Poster called the novel "a work of unusual imaginative power and range." Michelene Wandor, writing in the London *Sunday Times,* praised Hall's "muscular, glinting prose." *Financial Times* reviewer Lilian Pizzichini remarked, "her gorgeously embellished prose compels the narrative. . . . If we only see tantalising glimpses of lives, their jagged shards, it is their very fragmentation that is the point."

BIOGRAPHICAL AND CRITICAL SOURCES:

PERIODICALS

Bookseller, November 21, 2003, Benedicte Page, "Recorded on the Skin: Sarah Hall's Second Novel Explores the Mysterious Art of the Tattooist," p. 26.

Daily Mail (London, England), March 26, 2004, Hephzibah Anderson, review of *The Electric Michelangelo,* p. 56.
Financial Times, April 17, 2004, Lilian Pizzichini, review of *The Electric Michelangelo,* p. 33.
Guardian (Manchester, England), March 27, 2004, Jem Poster, "Written in Skin: Jem Poster Traces a Tattoo Artist's Compelling Journey," p. 27.
Sunday Times (London, England), August 4, 2002, Tom Deveson, "The Danger of a Stranger," p. 45; May 16, 2004, Michelene Wandor, review of *The Electric Michelangelo,* p. 52.
Times (London, England), June 22, 2002, Fiona Hook, "Force of Nature," review of *Haweswater,* p. 14; June 7, 2003, review of *Haweswater,* p. 18.
Times Literary Supplement, June 28, 2002, Stephen Knight, "A Land of Beck and Scree," p. 23.

ONLINE

Arvon Foundation Web site, http://www.arvon foundation.org/ (May 28, 2004), "Sarah Hall Award recipient listing."
Commonwealth Writers, http://www.commonwealth writers.com (May 28, 2004), "Commonwealth Writers Prize 2003."
Ready Steady Book, http://www.readysteadybook.com/ (May 28, 2004), Mark Thwaite, "Interview with Sarah Hall, Author of *The Electric Michelangelo.*"*

*   *   *

HANNA, Edward B. 1935-

PERSONAL: Born October 24, 1935, in New York, NY; son of Lee J. (a journalist) and Hannah (a homemaker; maiden name, Burd) Blumberg; married Marcia Freeman Hanna (in magazine publishing), May 22, 1966 (died, July 5, 1998); children: Leigh Jessica. *Education:* Attended University of Colorado, 1953-55. *Politics:* "None." *Hobbies and other interests:* Archaeology, history.

ADDRESSES: Agent—c/o Author Mail, Carroll & Graf Publishers, 245 West 17th St., 11th Floor, New York, NY 10011-5300. *E-mail*—edwbhanna@members. authorsguild.net.

CAREER: American Broadcasting Companies, Inc. (ABC), New York, NY, producer and writer for *ABC News,* 1960-63, correspondent, 1963-65; National Broadcasting Company, Inc. (NBC), New York, NY, executive producer for *NBC News,* 1975-79; Public Broadcasting Service, New York, NY, executive producer, 1975-79. *Military service:* U.S. Army, 1955-58.

MEMBER: Authors Guild, Authors League of America, Mystery Writers of America.

AWARDS, HONORS: George Foster Peabody Broadcasting Awards, Henry W. Grady School of Journalism and Mass Communications, University of Georgia, 1971, 1972, 1973, and 1974, for documentary news programs.

WRITINGS:

The Whitechapel Horrors (mystery novel), Carroll & Graf Publishers (New York, NY), 1992.

BIOGRAPHICAL AND CRITICAL SOURCES:

PERIODICALS

Publishers Weekly, August 24, 1992, review of *The Whitechapel Horrors,* p. 65.

*   *   *

HANSEN, Drew D. 1964(?)-

PERSONAL: Born c. 1964, in Merrill, WI. *Education:* Harvard, A.B. (summa cum laude), 1995; Oxford University, B.A. (theology), 1997; Yale Law School, J.D., 2000.

ADDRESSES: *Home*—Seattle, WA. *Office*—Susman Godfrey Attorneys at Law, Suite 3100, 1201 Third Ave., Seattle, WA 98101-3000. *E-mail*—dhansen@susmangodfrey.com.

CAREER: Called to the bar of Washington State, 2000; teaching assistant to Professor Drew S. Days, III; law clerk to Honorable Pierre N. Leval, U.S. Court of Appeals for the Second Circuit, 1999-2000; Susman Godfrey Attorneys at Law, Seattle, WA, currently associate attorney.

AWARDS, HONORS: Rhodes Scholar, Oxford University, 1996-97; Judge William E. Miller Prize, 2000; named a "Rising Star," *Washington Law and Politics,* 2003, 2004; Colby Townsend Prize, 1999.

WRITINGS:

The Dream: Martin Luther King, Jr., and the Speech that Inspired a Nation, Ecco (New York, NY), 2003.

Contributor of articles to newspapers and professional journals, including *USA Today, Seattle Post-Intelligencer, Wayne Law Review,* and *Yale Law Journal.* Former editor, *Yale Law Journal.*

SIDELIGHTS: Drew D. Hansen is a graduate of theology from Oxford University and holds a doctorate of jurisprudence from Yale. A practicing lawyer in Seattle, Hansen explores the origins and legacy of the "I Have a Dream" speech by Martin Luther King, Jr., in his 2003 book, *The Dream: Martin Luther King, Jr., and the Speech that Inspired a Nation.* As Hansen noted in an article for *USA Today,* King's speech, delivered during the 1963 March on Washington for Jobs and Freedom, "is justly famous for its lyricism, its musical delivery and its unforgettable visions of an America free of racism." King's speech has become over the four decades since it was first enunciated, "one of America's sacred texts—the oratorical equivalent of the Declaration of Independence," according to Hansen.

It was the iconic quality of the speech that drew Hansen to it and ultimately led to publication of *The Dream.* Steve Neal, reviewing the book in the *Chicago Sun-Times,* felt that it "does much to explain why this speech was so important." In his book, Hansen first sets the scene for American race relations in the early 1960s. At the time King gave his speech, about two-thirds of the African-American population of the United States resided in the South, where segregationist laws still held sway. Thus, King directed his speech at finding equality for those people who were disenfranchised and forced to lead separate lives at schools and in other spheres of public life. Hansen goes on to provide a behind-the-scenes look at the preparation not only of King's speech, but also of the march itself with its spectacle of a quarter of a million people gathered in front of the Lincoln Memorial. King's speech was covered by all three major television networks and "sparked nothing less than the second American Revolution," according to Neal. Not a bad result for a speech that took only four days to write, as Hansen tells his readers.

Cameron McWhirter, writing in the *Atlanta Journal-Constitution,* commented that Hansen "places the speech in historical context and shows how over time the speech was transformed to overshadow King the man." McWhirter also wrote that "Hansen argues persuasively" that many of King's later achievements in seeking equality in the North "have been largely forgotten." The book also found praise from Vernon Ford in a *Booklist* review, which concluded: "Readers interested in the moral issues tied to the civil rights struggle will enjoy Hansen's analysis." Similarly, a reviewer for *Publishers Weekly* commended *The Dream* as "serious, scholarly and engaged," and a critic for *Kirkus Reviews* dubbed Hansen's book a "studied anatomy of one bold moment of extemporaneous triumph."

BIOGRAPHICAL AND CRITICAL SOURCES:

PERIODICALS

Atlanta Journal-Constitution, August 3, 2003, Cameron McWhirter, review of *The Dream: Martin Luther King, Jr., and the Speech that Inspired a Nation,* p. E4.
Booklist, July, 2003, Vernon Ford, review of *The Dream,* pp. 1850-1851.
Chicago Sun-Times, August 27, 2004, Steve Neal, review of *The Dream,* p. 51.
Kirkus Reviews, May 1, 2003, review of *The Dream,* p. 657.
Library Journal, June 1, 2003, Thomas J. Davies, review of *The Dream,* p. 140.
New Republic, September 29, 2003, David J. Garrow, review of *The Dream,* p. 28.
Publishers Weekly, June 9, 2003, review of *The Dream,* p. 49.
USA Today, August 27, 2003, Drew D. Hansen, "King's Dreams for Demise of Racism, Poverty Continue Today," p. A11.

ONLINE

Stanford University, Black Community Services Center Web Site, http://www.stanford.edu/dept/BCSC/mlk. html/ (January 14, 2004).
Susman Godfrey Web site, http://www.susmangodfrey. com/ (March 27, 2004).*

HANSEN, G. Eric 1938-

PERSONAL: Born November 25, 1938, in Milwaukee, WI. *Education:* Lawrence College, B.A. (summa cum laude); Fletcher School of Law and Diplomacy, Tufts University, M.A., M.A.L.D., Ph.D.

ADDRESSES: Home—250 B Red Rock Way, San Francisco, CA 94131. *Office*—School of Economics and Business Administration, Saint Mary's College of California, Moraga, CA 94575.

CAREER: Wellesley College, Wellesley, MA, faculty member, 1963-64; Massachusetts Institute of Technology, Cambridge, faculty member, 1964-69; Haverford College, Haverford, PA, faculty member, 1969-73; San Francisco State University, San Francisco, CA, faculty member, 1973-77; Saint Mary's College of California, Moraga, professor of international political economy, 1977—, director of graduate business programs, 1979-89, and associate dean of School of Economics and Business Administration.

MEMBER: Phi Beta Kappa.

AWARDS, HONORS: Younger Humanist fellow, National Endowment for the Humanities.

WRITINGS:

The Culture of Strangers: Globalization, Localization, and the Phenomenon of Exchange, University Press of America (Lanham, MD), 2002.

Also author of *Culture and Commerce: The Development of Business Values* (monograph), 1998. Contributor to books, including *The Essential Nature of the College,* edited by Mel Anderson, (Moraga, CA), 1988; and *Contemporary Issues in Business and Society,* edited by Karen Paul, Edwin Mellen Press (Lewiston, NY), 1993. Contributor to periodicals, including *American Political Science Review, Journal of Politics, Orbis, Pacific Affairs,* and *Educational Perspectives.*

*   *   *

HANZO, L(ajos) 1952-

PERSONAL: Born May 18, 1952, in Szarvas, Hungary; son of Lajos and Klara (Vamos) Hanzo; married December 3, 1977; wife's name, Rita; children: Lajos II. *Education:* Earned B.Eng., 2000.

ADDRESSES: Office—Department of Electronics and Computer Science, University of Southampton, Highfield, Southampton SO17 1BJ, England; fax: +44-023-8059-4508. *E-mail*—lh@ecs.soton.ac.uk.

CAREER: Telecommunications Research Institute, Budapest, Hungary, staff member, 1976-87; University of Southampton, Southampton, England, professor of communications.

MEMBER: Institute of Electrical and Electronics Engineers, IEE.

WRITINGS:

(With Raymond Steele) *Mobile Radio Communications: Second and Third Generation Cellular and WATM Systems,* 2nd edition, Wiley Publishing Group (New York, NY), 1999.

(With W. Webb and T. Keller) *Single-and Multi-Carrier Quadrature Amplitude Modulation: Principles and Applications for Personal Communications, WLANs, and Broadcasting,* Wiley Publishing Group (New York, NY), 2000.

(With Peter Cherriman and Jurgen Streit) *Wireless Video Communications: Second to Third Generation Systems and Beyond,* Wiley Publishing Group (New York, NY), 2001.

(With F. Clare, A. Somerville, and Jason P. Woodward) *Voice Compression and Communications: Principles and Applications for Fixed and Wireless Channels,* Wiley Publishing Group (New York, NY), 2001.

(With T. H. Liew and B. L. Yeap) *Turbo Coding, Turbo Equalisation, and Space-Time Boding for Transmission over Fading Channels,* Wiley Publishing Group (New York, NY), 2002.

(With C. H. Wong and M. S. Yee) *Adaptive Wireless Transceivers: Turbo-Coded, Turbo-Equalised, and Space-Time Coded CDMA, TDMA, and OFDM Systems,* Wiley Publishing Group (New York, NY), 2002.

(With J. S. Blogh) *Third-Generation Systems and Intelligent Wireless Networking: Smart Antennas and Adaptive Modulation,* Wiley Publishing Group (New York, NY), 2002.

(With M. Münster, B. J. Choi, and T. Keller) *OFDM and MC-CDMA for Broadband Multi-user Communications, WLANs, and Broadcasting,* Wiley Publishing Group (New York, NY), 2003.

HARPER, Lila Marz 1955-

PERSONAL: Born May 27, 1955, in Los Angeles, CA; daughter of Harold George (a high school biology teacher and geologist) and Sally (a botanist and self-employed nursery operator; maiden name, Spiegel) Marz; married James Dale Harper (a professor of mathematics), December 23, 1975; children: Artemus Samuel, Sara Katherine. *Ethnicity:* "Russian Jew/German." *Education:* Humboldt State University, B.A., 1976, graduate study, 1976-78; attended University of Oregon, 1979-84; St. Cloud State University, M.A., 1987; University of Oregon, Ph.D., 1996.

ADDRESSES: Office—Department of English, Central Washington University, 400 East Eighth Ave., Ellensburg, WA 98926-7558; fax: 509-963-1561. *E-mail*—harperl@cwu.edu.

CAREER: Central Washington University, Ellensburg, instructor in English, 1989—. Field bibliographer for Modern Language Association of America and Modern Humanities Research Association, 1996—.

MEMBER: North American Society for the Study of Romanticism, Modern Language Association of America, American Society for Eighteenth-Century Studies, United Faculty of Central American Federation of Teachers and National Education Association (vice president).

AWARDS, HONORS: Citation for "outstanding academic book," *Choice,* 2001, for *Solitary Travelers: Nineteenth-Century Women's Travel Narratives and the Scientific Vocation.*

WRITINGS:

Solitary Travelers: Nineteenth-Century Women's Travel Narratives and the Scientific Vocation, Fairleigh Dickinson University Press (Madison, NJ), 2001.

(Editor) Edwin Abbott, *Flatland* (critical edition), Wesleyan University Press (Middletown, CT), 2003.

Author of instructor's manuals. Contributor to reference books. Contributor to periodicals, including *Extrapolation, George Eliot-George Henry Lewes Studies,* and *Journeys: International Journal of Travel and Travel Writing.*

WORK IN PROGRESS: Research on the travel accounts of Mary Wollstonecraft and Gilbert Imlay; research on Darwin.

SIDELIGHTS: Lila Marz Harper told *CA:* "My family's concern for the natural world, my working-class immigrant background, and the experiences of the women in my family drive me and commit me to scholarship. The difficulties women faced professionally in the past link with my experiences and what I see today.

"Because of my parents' intellectual drives and my ethnic, non-Christian background, I have always felt like an outsider trying to understand why we organize information and see the world the way we do. Studying nineteenth-century and eighteenth-century literature and science helps me make sense of the modern or post-modern culture. It is like there are puzzles around me that I try to figure out, wondering how did professions form the way they did and what have women done in the past to keep intellectually alive.

"I write when I can, often setting aside projects for months during the school year while I teach and balancing projects with family and union commitments, somehow holding and mulling over ideas until I get the chance to write them down. I think working on adjunct contracts and constantly 'multi-tasking' gives me some empathy for women writers of the eighteenth and nineteenth centuries. I understand the barriers—both physical and emotional—and respect the achievements of those who did manage to write despite them."

*   *   *

HARPHAM, Wendy S(chlessel) 1954-

PERSONAL: Born October 18, 1954, in New York, NY; married Ted Harpham (a professor), December 30, 1979; children: Rebecca, Jessica, William. *Education:* Cornell University, B.S. (with honors), 1976; University of Rochester School of Medicine and Dentistry, M.D., 1980. *Hobbies and other interests:* Playing violin, watching high school volleyball.

ADDRESSES: Office—P.O. Box 835574, Richardson, TX 75083-5574. *E-mail*—harpham@comcast.net.

CAREER: Writer, public speaker, and physician. Physician in private practice of internal medicine, beginning 1983. Host, ACS Cancer Survivors Network; speaker, consultant, and patient advocate.

MEMBER: American College of Physicians, various Texas and U.S. medical associations, National Coalition for Cancer Survivorship.

AWARDS, HONORS: Natalie Davis Spingarn Writer's Award, National Coalition for Cancer Survivorship, 1998; Governor's Award for Health, Office of Governor George Bush, 2000; Ellen Glesby Cohen Leadership Award, Lymphoma Research Foundation, 2001; Outstanding Service Award, Leukemia and Lymphoma Society, 2002.

WRITINGS:

Diagnosis: Cancer. Your Guide through the First Few Months, Norton (New York, NY), 1992, published as *Diagnosis Cancer: Your Guide to the First Months of Health Survivorship,* 2003.
After Cancer: A Guide to Your New Life, HarperCollins (New York, NY), 1995.
When a Parent Has Cancer: A Guide to Caring for Your Children, HarperCollins (New York, NY), 1997.
(With Laura Harpham) *The Hope Tree: Kids Talk about Breast Cancer,* illustrated by David McPhail, Simon & Schuster (New York, NY), 2001.

Contributor to books, including *Principles and Practices of Supportive Oncology,* Lippincott, 1997. Contributor to professional journals and periodicals, including *Ca, Ladies' Home Journal, Medical Economics,* and *Postgraduate Medicine.* Member of editorial board, *CURE* magazine.

WORK IN PROGRESS: Happiness in a Storm.

SIDELIGHTS: Wendy S. Harpham developed a passion for writing and public speaking when she was no longer able to practice internal medicine after being diagnosed with non-Hodgkin's lymphoma. She has since published a series of inspirational books that focus on the coping and healing processes following cancer diagnosis and treatment, including *Diagnosis:*

Cancer. Your Guide through the First Few Months, After Cancer: A Guide to Your New Life, When a Parent Has Cancer: A Guide to Caring for Your Children, and *The Hope Tree: Kids Talk about Breast Cancer.*

Harpham demonstrates her unique perspective as both doctor and patient, in her books. In *When a Parent Has Cancer* she also demonstrates her strength as a mother of three who was forced to deal not only with her own disease, but also with its affect on her family. The book blends together her own experiences—grappling with the fear of diagnosis, right up through the sickness she felt while undergoing treatment—along with advice from other parents undergoing similar ordeals. Her strength is evident, as she manages the responsibilities of parenting throughout the many stages her illness—which happily has gone into remission. Writing in the Bergen County, New Jersey, *Record,* Michael Precker called the book "A straightforward mix of advice," while in the *Journal of the American Medical Association,* Sylvia M. Ramos maintained that *When a Parent Has Cancer* "should help give children and their parents a context within which to deal with life after cancer and to 'find the courage to face the future honestly, with love and hope.'"

On the other side of diagnosis, *The Hope Tree* was written to help children cope with a mother's breast cancer. Using animal characters, many sensitive issues are discussed. The sons and daughters of women suffering from this common cancer, who often feel "stifled by the chaos and fear experienced by the family," will "greatly benefit from the discussions this book should stimulate and the comfort it provides," praised Mary R. Hofmann in a *School Library Journal* review.

Harpham told *CA:* "In 1983, I opened a solo practice of internal medicine with a mission to help others through the synergy of science and caring. When illness made it impossible to practice clinical medicine, and forced me to redefine my career, writing and speaking became different but equal passions, and ways to reach more people than I ever could in my medical office."

BIOGRAPHICAL AND CRITICAL SOURCES:

PERIODICALS

American Medical News, December 7, 1992, Wayne Hearn, "Drawing on Experience to Help Cancer Patients Cope," p. 42.

Booklist, February 15, 1997, Kathryn Carpenter, review of *When a Parent Has Cancer: A Guide to Caring for Your Children,* p. 974.
Journal of the American Medical Association, March 25, 1998, Sylvia M. Ramos, review of *When a Parent Has Cancer,* p. 961.
Library Journal, May 15, 1992, Janet M. Coggan, review of *Diagnosis: Cancer. Your Guide through the First Few Months,* p. 110; August, 1994, Janet M. Coggan, review of *After Cancer: A Guide to Your New Life,* p. 114; February 15, 1997, Mary J. Jarvis, review of *When a Parent Has Cancer,* p. 156.
New York Times, September 28, 1994, Jane E. Brody, "A Doctor Who Survived Cancer Uses Her Experiences to Help Guide Other Patients," p. C10; February 12, 1997, Jane E. Brody, "Children Need Special Help When a Parent Has Cancer," p. B12.
Publishers Weekly, June 22, 1992, review of *Diagnosis: Cancer,* p. 59; December 10, 2001, review of *The Hope Tree: Kids Talk about Breast Cancer,* p. 73.
Record (Bergen County, NJ), March 3, 1997, Michael Precker, review of *When a Parent Has Cancer,* p. H1.
Rocky Mountain News, July 4, 1996, "War on Cancer Got Stuck, and There's No Will to Unglue I," p. A42.
School Library Journal, October, 2001, Mary R. Hofmann, review of *The Hope Tree,* p. 127.

*   *   *

HARRIS, William V. 1938-

PERSONAL: Born September 13, 1938, in Nottingham, England; son of K. W. F. (an architect) and Elizabeth Harris; married Silvana Patriarca, November 30, 1988; children: Neil. *Education:* Oxford University, B.A., M.A., D.Phil. *Politics:* Socialist.

ADDRESSES: Office—Department of History, 624 Fayerweather Hall, Columbia University, New York, NY 10027. *E-mail*—wvh1@columbia.edu.

CAREER: Columbia University, New York, NY, Shepherd Professor of History.

MEMBER: Academia Europaea, Archaeological Institute of America, American Philological Association, Century Association.

AWARDS, HONORS: Fellow, American Academy of Arts and Sciences; James Henry Breasted Prize, American Historical Association, 2003.

WRITINGS:

Rome in Etruria and Umbria, Oxford University Press (New York, NY), 1971.
War and Imperialism in Republican Rome, Oxford University Press (New York, NY), 1979.
Ancient Literacy, Harvard University Press (Cambridge, MA), 1989.
Restraining Rage: The Ideology of Anger Control in Classical Antiquity, Harvard University Press (Cambridge, MA), 2002.

WORK IN PROGRESS: Another book on a topic from Roman history.

BIOGRAPHICAL AND CRITICAL SOURCES:

PERIODICALS

Library Journal, February 1, 2002, Clay Williams, review of *Restraining Rage: The Ideology of Anger Control in Classical Antiquity,* p. 114.

*   *   *

HEFER, Hayim (Baruch) 1925-

PERSONAL: Born October 29, 1925, in Sosnowice, Poland; son of Isachar Feiner and Rivka Hertzberg; married Ruth Morhy-Levy; children: Miryam. *Education:* Attended the Hebrew University of Jerusalem. *Religion:* Jewish.

ADDRESSES: Home—53 Arlozoroff St., Tel Aviv, Israel.

CAREER: Writer, translator. Former columnist for *Yediot Ahronot.* El-Hamam Satirical Theater, cofounder, 1960. Worked for the Consul for Cultural Affairs for the West Coast.

MEMBER: Hebrew Writers Association, Israeli Arts Council for Theater and Film.

AWARDS, HONORS: Sokolov Prize for Outstanding Journalism, 1969, for column in *Yediot Ahronot;* Israel Prize for Song-Writing, 1983.

WRITINGS:

Milim la-manginot, Hotsa at Amikamn (Tel Aviv, Israel), 1961.
The Megilla of Itzik Manger (play), produced on Broadway, 1969.
To Live Another Summer, to Pass Another Winter (play), produced on Broadway, 1971.
(With Dan Ben-Amotz) *Tel-Aviv ha-ketanah: hizayon,* Sifre Metsi'ut (Tel Aviv, Israel), 1980.
Af milah ra ah, Zemorah-Bitan (Tel Aviv, Israel), 1998.

Author of screenplays, including *The Rooster,* or *The Boys Will Never Believe It,* 1971; *Tevie and His Seven Daughters; The Trial of the Stubborn; Hot Line to Damascus; Kazabian; On a Narrow Bridge,* 1985. Author of *Sefer ha-pizmonim shel Hayim Hefer,* 1981. Hefer is also the author of over a thousand song lyrics.

SIDELIGHTS: Hayim Hefer was born in Poland, but relocated to Israel in 1936. He told *CA:* "In 1943 I joined the Palmach, the commandos of the Israeli underground army, and was instrumental in bringing the illegal immigrants in from Syria and Lebanon. In 1948, during the Israeli War of Liberation, I formed the Chizbatron, the first Israeli Army entertainment troupe, and wrote most of their material." He is the author of song lyrics, musicals, plays, screenplays, newspaper columns, and books.

BIOGRAPHICAL AND CRITICAL SOURCES:

PERIODICALS

New York Times, October 22, 1971, Clive Barnes, review of *To Live Another Summer, to Pass Another Winter.*

*   *   *

HEHN, Paul N. 1927-

PERSONAL: Born April 8, 1927, in New York, NY; married, 1956; children: three children. *Education:* University of Oregon, A.B., 1950; Columbia University, M.A., 1954; New York University, Ph.D., 1961.

ADDRESSES: *Office*—Department of History, SUNY Brockport, 350 New Campus Dr., Brockport, NY 14420.

CAREER: Wilkes College, Wilkes-Barre, PA, instructor in history and political science, 1959-61; Temple University, Philadelphia, PA, instructor in history, 1961-63; Ohio University, Athens, assistant professor, 1963-66; University of Dayton, Dayton, OH, assistant professor, 1966-68; State University of New York, Brockport, assistant professor, 1968-80, associate professor, beginning 1980, became professor emeritus. *Military service:* Served in World War II.

MEMBER: American Historical Association, American Association for Advanced Slavic Studies.

WRITINGS:

The German Struggle against Yugoslav Guerrillas in World War II: German Counter-Insurgency in Yugoslavia, 1941-1943, Columbia University Press (New York, NY), 1979.
A Low Dishonest Decade: The Great Powers, Eastern Europe, and the Economic Origins of World War II, 1930-1941, Continuum Books (New York, NY), 2002.

SIDELIGHTS: Paul N. Hehn specializes in the history of central Europe, the Balkans, and Russia. In *A Low Dishonest Decade: The Great Powers, Eastern Europe, and the Economic Origins of World War II, 1930-1941,* he makes a case for the importance of economic considerations in planting the seeds of this conflict. Companies in Western Europe and the United States were willing to do business with Nazi Germany; they were driven not only by the profit motive but also by the belief that Adolf Hitler's aggression could be limited, or perhaps turned only against the Soviet Union. But when the Nazi regime sent its armies west as well as east, it was a regime that had been strengthened, according to Hehn, by the Western powers. He supports his argument with numerous quotes from political and economic leaders of the period.

In playing up the role of economics, the book does not take into account the importance of other factors, such as Hitler's racist worldview, observed a *Publishers*

Weekly critic, who nevertheless found Hehn's thesis "compelling." Hehn, the reviewer added, takes into account not only the accepted reasons, but also "the failures, hypocrisies, greed, and venality of England, France, and the United States, and powerfully argues for their role in bringing on WWII."

BIOGRAPHICAL AND CRITICAL SOURCES:

PERIODICALS

Publishers Weekly, October 21, 2002, review of *A Low Dishonest Decade: The Great Powers, Eastern Europe, and the Economic Origins of World War II, 1930-1941,* p. 62.*

*   *   *

HENREY, Madeleine 1906-2004
(Mrs. Robert Henrey, Robert Henrey)

OBITUARY NOTICE—See index for *CA* sketch: Born August 13, 1906, in Paris, France; died April 25, 2004, in Normandy, France. Author. Henrey was a prolific author best known for her autobiographical stories about her childhood and adult experiences in France and England, including the popular *The Little Madeleine* (1951). Born in the industrial section of Paris, her father died when she was still a teenager, and she subsequently moved with her mother to London. In England, Henrey was educated at a convent and then worked in various jobs ranging from manicurist to store worker to secretary. She met her husband, Robert, while she was a manicurist, and the couple moved to Normandy, where they lived on a farm until Adolph Hitler's invading forces compelled them to flee to England in 1940. Henrey soon after that began publishing books about her experiences, with the first being *A Farm in Normandy* (1941); these were written under either her husband's name, Robert Henrey, or as Mrs. Robert Henrey. Sometimes, her husband edited or collaborated on the books, and the pen name was her way of acknowledging that and the life they shared together. Over the next four decades, Henrey would publish over thirty books, including *A Journey to Gibraltar* (1943), *The Siege of London* (1946), *Madeleine Grown Up* (1952), *Her April Days* (1963), *Julia: Reminiscences of a Year in Madeleine's Life as* a *London Shop Girl* (1971), *Green Leaves* (1976), and *The Golden Visit* (1979). Having moved back to the farm in Normandy in 1964, Henrey spent the rest of her life there, even after the death of her husband in 1982.

OBITUARIES AND OTHER SOURCES:

PERIODICALS

Guardian (London, England), April 30, 2004, p. 31.
Times (London, England), May 4, 2004, p. 26.

*   *   *

HENREY, Mrs. Robert
    See HENREY, Madeleine

*   *   *

HENREY, Robert
    See HENREY, Madeleine

*   *   *

HERSHENHORN, Esther 1945-

PERSONAL: Born December 15, 1945, in Philadelphia, PA; daughter of Samuel (a businessman) and Vivian (a teacher) Chairnoff; children: Jonathan. *Education:* Attended the University of Pennsylvania.

ADDRESSES: Home—Chicago, IL. *Agent*—c/o Author Mail, Holiday House, 425 Madison Ave. #12, New York, NY 10017. *E-mail*—esthersh.aol.com.

CAREER: Writer and educator. Previously worked as an elementary school teacher in Illinois.

MEMBER: Society of Children's Book Writers and Illustrators (regional advisor, 1994—).

AWARDS, HONORS: Sydney Taylor Book Award for Younger Readers, Association of Jewish Libraries, 2003, for *Chicken Soup by Heart;* Best Books selec-

tion, Bank Street College of Education, 2003, for *The Confe$$ion$ and $ecret$ of Howard J. Fingerhut,* and 2004, for *Fancy That;* Children's Crown Award nominee, National Christian Schools Association, 2004-2005, for *The Confe$$ion$ and $ecret$ of Howard J. Fingerhut.*

WRITINGS:

There Goes Lowell's Party, illustrated by Jacqueline Rogers, Holiday House (New York, NY), 1998.
Illinois: Fun Facts and Games, GHB Publishers, 2000.
The Confe$$ion$ and $ecret$ of Howard J. Fingerhut, illustrated by Ethan Long, Holiday House (New York, NY), 2002.
Chicken Soup by Heart, illustrated by Rosanne Litzinger, Simon & Schuster (New York, NY), 2002.
Fancy That, illustrated by Megan Lloyd, Holiday House (New York, NY), 2003.

SIDELIGHTS: Along with being a writer of picture books and novels for young readers, Esther Hershenhorn is active in teaching writing as well. She coaches children's book writers through the classes she teaches at an artists residency program, at Chicago's Newberry Library, and at the University of Chicago's Writer's Studio. Before she taught writers, she was an elementary school teacher. Her desire to teach shows in the books she writes; in *There Goes Lowell's Party,* for example, Hershenhorn provides a list of twenty-nine rain proverbs from the Ozark tradition, many of which have been proven to be scientifically accurate. In *The Confe$$ions and $ecret$ of Howard J. Fingerhut,* Hershenhorn uses a name poem—a poem that takes each letter of a person's name and gives it a descriptive word—to describe her main character, giving him traits ideal for becoming an entrepreneur. Hershenhorn once commented: "I spend my days doing what I love and loving what I do: writing picture book texts, teaching 'Writing for Children' classes, and helping writers of all ages discover and tell their stories."

Though dedicated to teaching, Hershenhorn knew from early on that she wanted to write for children. She told Cynthia Leitich Smith in an interview on the *Children's Literature Resources* Web site, "At age six I can remember thinking, while I played library or school with my friends, 'Someday my name will be on a book like this.' I kept that dream a secret and shared it with no one."

Hershenhorn's first title, *There Goes Lowell's Party,* describes how Lowell looks forward to his birthday when all his family will gather for a party. But when his birthday finally arrives, Ozark Mountains weather lore shows that they should expect rain. Lowell Piggott worries that his party may not go as planned, but in spite of the rain, the family gathers together to celebrate his birthday. Hazel Rochman of *Booklist* noted that "teachers might like to use this comedy to spark a nature unit."

Hershenhorn described Lowell Piggott as a character "who knows jest as sure as snakes crawl, that even iffen red skies and loud geese and leafbacks mean rain, and even iffen that rain brings floods, mudslides, and twisters, his Ozark Mountain kin are smart enough and love him enough, that they'll do what they have to do to get to his birthday party! The Library of Congress classified the book under 'Rain and rainfall—fiction, Storms—fiction, Birthdays—fiction, and Ozark Mountains—fiction.' I would add a fifth category: 'Faith and Hope.'"

In writing her first middle-grade novel, *The Confe$$ion$ and $ecret$ of Howard J. Fingerhut,* Hershenhorn credits an editor at Holiday House with helping her give her book a "successful, character-based plotline. Howie's 'Howieness' leads to escalating scenes of calamity and disaster until Howie's 'Howieness' saves him and the day." The author admitted that "crucial to this telling was my understanding—finally—of how the character's physical plotline (what he wants) and emotional plotline (why he wants what he wants) must intersect at that crucial moment so the character is different for making the journey. Crucial too was my willingness to dig deep, to remember how *I* felt when walking in Howie's shoes. What did I want then and why did I want it?"

Narrator Howie Fingerhut, in *The Confe$$ion$ and $ecret$ of Howard J. Fingerhut,* explains how to start up a business, one that is sure to win him first place in the H. Marion Muckley Junior Businessperson of the Year contest. In fact, he is so certain that he will win the contest that he is keeping a journal of the experience, which he hopes to sell to a publisher as a how-to business book for kids. In his lawn care business, Howie rakes, shovels, and plants, despite difficulties he encounters along the way and competition provided by his classmates. A writer for *Kirkus Reviews* praised *The Confe$$ion$ and $ecret$ of Howard J. Fingerhut,*

saying, "no one will be able to resist its spirit," and a reviewer for *Publishers Weekly* noted that readers would "undoubtedly deem his $illy mi$adventure$ amu$ing."

Hershenhorn once commented on her thoughts about creating a story: "I believe that cooking up a story is just like cooking chicken soup. Take one full-bodied idea, back-burner it in the recesses of your mind, add a little of this, add a little of that. Season it, stir it, simmer it some more. Then reduce it, refine it, and serve it up . . . with love. In the case of my picture book *Chicken Soup by Heart,* I simmered a Chicago newspaper article titled 'The Great Chicken Soup Debate.' The article's author sought the ingredients for the 'World's Best Chicken Soup.' I simmered that story idea for months, savoring chicken soup while reading every chicken soup book ever written. I read recipes for clear broths, creamed soups and gumbos, for tortilla soup, cock-a-leekie, and mulligatawny. I read about roasters and broilers and capons. I studied medical reports likening chicken soup to penicillin. Before long, I cooked up a character, Rudie Dinkins, who shared his beloved babysitter, Mrs. Gittel, with eight little misters and misses in his Brooklyn apartment house. I cooked up a problem—Mrs. Gittel had the flu!—and eight loving chefs cooking Mrs. Gittel chicken soup. Of course, each chef cooked the chicken soup his or her family's way. In its final reduction, the story of friendship belonged to Rudie and Mrs. Gittel. Mrs. Gittel's secret chicken soup ingredient—three very nice stories about her soon-to-be soup-eaters—proved good for the cook and good for the soup-eater, not to mention for the writer who loves sharing it with readers."

In *Chicken Soup by Heart,* which won the Sydney Taylor Book Award for Younger Readers, Rudie Dinkins decides to take care of his sitter, Mrs. Gittel, when she has the flu. Whenever Rudie is sick, Mrs. Gittel makes chicken soup for Rudie, so Rudie and his mother together make soup for Mrs. Gittel, using the sitter's secret ingredient: nice stories about the "soon-to-be soup eater." Hershenhorn explained in her interview with Smith, "I loved cooking up this story, though I'm the first to admit my own chicken soup is not a threat to Mrs. Gittel's—the recipe for which is included on the back page [of the book]." Joy Fleishhacker of *School Library Journal* commented, "Hershenhorn's folksy telling is as comfortable as a grandmother's embrace," and in a review for *Booklist,*

GraceAnne A. DeCandido praised, "love and care radiate from the pages."

While attending a folk art show in the Chicago area, Hershenhorn met a young artist with a sign that read "Limner and Fancy Painter." The man explained to the author that before the advent of photography, artists traveled about America painting people's portraits, as well as signs and walls and harpsichord covers. Finding the information an inspiration for her next book, Hershenhorn immediately began looking for material about these traveling artists. One year later, finally ready to write the story, she phoned the young man she met at the show, only to learn his disastrous fate proved to be that of his nineteenth-century models: dissatisfied with their images, customers refused to pay him. "Right then and there," Hershenhorn once commented, "I saw my story!"

Fancy That is a Christmas story, featuring young Pippin, whose parents have died, leaving him and his sisters to fend for themselves. Pippin takes up work as a limner, or a traveling painter, to earn money. But despite his efforts, his paintings end up being too accurate and his customers refuse to pay him. Coming home in defeat, he is delighted to find that while he was gone, his sisters started a crafts business and have managed to raise enough money to keep them out of the poor house. "Hershenhorn tells a spirited story about an unusual subject in appealing, colloquial language," wrote Gillian Engberg in her *Booklist* review. A reviewer for *Publishers Weekly,* complimenting the "sonorous prose," claimed that "Hershenhorn and Lloyd's collaboration is an unqualified success," while a critic for *Kirkus Reviews* noted, "this tongue-in-cheek piece of Americana will delight a wide range of readers and listeners."

Besides teaching and writing, Hershenhorn visits schools, sharing her passion for writing. As she shared with Smith in her interview, she tells young writers that "everyone has a story worth telling. Period. And no two stories are the same. The writer's job is to figure out the best way to tell it so it resonates with the readers."

Hershenhorn once commented that her characters—Pippin, Lowell, Howie, and Rudie—hold a place in her heart as if they were family. "I enjoy sharing their stories at schools, libraries, bookstores, and fairs."

She also shares with young readers her favorite childhood books—"the Little Golden Books fairy tales, with their happy-ever-after endings; 'the orange true books' that were actually the books in the 'Childhoods of Famous Americans' series; Nancy Drew, of course; and Hans Christian Andersen's *The Ugly Duckling.*"

A voracious reader, she knew as a youngster that she wanted her name on the cover of a children's book. However, as she once commented, "my writer's journey took longer than I'd expected, with stops for teaching, newspaper writing, mothering, and learning the craft. To my delight and surprise, however, my story, with its twists and turns, encourages others to tell their tales."

About her career, Hershenhorn noted, "When folks ask what I do, I say I'm in the hope business, bringing children's books to the hands and hearts of readers."

BIOGRAPHICAL AND CRITICAL SOURCES:

PERIODICALS

Booklist, March 15, 1998, Hazel Rochman, review of *There Goes Lowell's Party,* p. 1248; September 1, 2002, GraceAnne A. DeCandido, review of *Chicken Soup by Heart,* p. 120; September 15, 2003, Gillian Engberg, review of *Fancy That,* p. 245.
Kirkus Reviews, April 1, 2002, review of *The Confe$$ion$ and $ecret$ of Howard J. Fingerhut,* p. 492; September 1, 2003, review of *Fancy That,* p. 1124.
Publishers Weekly, March 11, 2002, review of *The Confe$$ion$ and $ecret$ of Howard J. Fingerhut,* p. 72; September 20, 2003, review of *Fancy That,* p. 104.
School Library Journal, March, 1998, Carolyn Noah, review of *There Goes Lowell's Party,* p. 180; May, 2002, Laura Reed, review of *The Confe$$ion$ and $ecret$ of Howard J. Fingerhut,* p. 116; November, 2002, Joy Fleishhacker, review of *Chicken Soup by Heart,* p. 124; November, 2003, Beth Tegart, review of *Fancy That,* p. 96.

ONLINE

Cynthia Leitich Smith's Children's Literature Resources, http://www.cynthialeitichsmith.com/ (May-June, 2002), "Interview with Children's Book Author Esther Hershenhorn."

Esther Hershenhorn Home Page, http://www.esther hershenhorn.com/ (April 15, 2004).

Society of Children's Book Writers and Illustrators Illinois Chapter, http://www.scbwi-illinois.org/ (February 9, 2004), "Esther Hershenhorn."

*   *   *

HIGHTOWER, Scott 1952-

PERSONAL: Born 1952, in TX. *Education:* University of Texas—Austin, B.A., 1973; Antioch University of Ohio, M.Ed., 1977; Columbia University, M.F.A., 1994.

ADDRESSES: Home—New York, NY. *Office*—Lincoln Center Campus, Fordham University, New York, NY 10023.

CAREER: Fordham University, New York, NY, poet in residence at Lincoln Center Campus. Worked as junior high school and high school teacher; also taught at Gallatin School of Individualized Study, New York University, and at Gay Men's Health Crisis.

AWARDS, HONORS: Academy of American Poets Prize, 1994.

WRITINGS:

Tin Can Tourist (poetry), Fordham University Press (New York, NY), 2001.

Contributor of poetry to periodicals, including *AGNI, Barrow Street, Gulf Coast, New England Review, Ploughshares, Salmagundi, Southwest Review,* and *Yale Review.* Contributing editor, *Journal.*

BIOGRAPHICAL AND CRITICAL SOURCES:

PERIODICALS

American Poet, spring, 2002, review of *Tin Can Tourist,* p. 57.*

HILLS, Denis (Cecil) 1913-2004

OBITUARY NOTICE—See index for *CA* sketch: Born November 8, 1913, in Birmingham, England; died April 26, 2004, in Richmond, Surrey, England. Educator, journalist, adventurer, and author. Hills led a remarkable career in the military and as a traveling teacher who journeyed around the world, but he gained the most fame when he was imprisoned and threatened with death by Ugandan dictator Idi Amin. Educated at Lincoln College, Oxford, he was a better athlete than student, yet he still obtained a master's degree with honors in 1935. He briefly worked for the *Birmingham Post* as a freelance journalist in central Europe, then traveled to Poland to edit an anti-Nazi publication and teach English in Warsaw. Along the way, he became fluent in several languages, including German and Polish. With the invasion of Poland by the Nazis and Russians in 1939, Hills escaped to Romania, where he worked for the British Council, and then to Cairo, Egypt, where he enlisted in the King's Own Royal Regiment in 1940. He remained in the army until 1950, rising to the rank of major and serving in the Middle East, Austria, Germany, and Italy. With the end of the war, Hills had the unpleasant assignment of assisting the Soviet government in repatriating Russians and Ukrainians who had worked with Germany against Joseph Stalin; he knew that sending these people back to Russia would mean certain death or imprisonment at the hands of the Communist government, so Hills put up what bureaucratic barriers he could to prevent this from happening, though many were sent back despite his efforts. It was also Hills who was in the unique position of convincing Italian authorities to allow 1,200 Polish Jews aboard the *La Spezia* to leave Europe for Palestine, a journey that was immortalized in Leon Uris's book *Exodus.* After leaving the military, Hills resumed his teaching career, lecturing in history and economic theory at the University of Mainz for three years and then moving to Turkey, where he taught in Ankara until 1963. Next, Hills moved to Uganda, where he taught English literature at Makarere University and National Teachers' College in Kampala. Hills was disgusted when Idi Amin seized power in a 1971 military coup and murdered thousands of civilians. He wrote about this event in his 1975 book, *The White Pumpkin,* which labeled Amin a "village tyrant," among other disparaging phrases. Amin, of course, discovered this and promptly imprisoned Hills, threatening him with a death sentence. When the dictator received letters of appeal from Queen Elizabeth II and British Prime

Minister Harold Wilson, along with a formal apology and retraction from Hills and a visit from the British Foreign Secretary, his ego was satisfied and he released Hills. Now an international celebrity, Hills's career as a writer was assured, but he still enjoyed teaching and traveled next to Rhodesia to teach English and environmental studies for two years. He would later return to Uganda to teach, as well as to Kenya, while also working for British, Canadian, and Rhodesian television and radio stations as a journalist. In 1985, Hills was back in Poland, where he butted heads with the Communist government and was expelled from the country once by the police. As if these adventures were not enough, Hills was an avid mountain climber and bicyclist who once biked from the Arctic Circle all the way south to Greece. All of these adventures lent themselves well to being recorded in Hills many books, including *My Travels in Turkey* (1964), *The Last Days of White Rhodesia* (1981), *Return to Poland* (1988), and his autobiography, *Tyrants and Mountains: A Reckless Life* (1992). In 1992, Hills also received an honorary doctorate in literature from Birmingham University.

OBITUARIES AND OTHER SOURCES:

PERIODICALS

Daily Post (Liverpool, England), May 3, 2004, p. 11.
Guardian (London, England), May 4, 2004, p. 23.
Independent (London, England), May 11, 2004, p. 34.
Los Angeles Times, May 3, 2004, p. B11.
Times (London, England), May 3, 2004, p. 23.

*   *   *

HOGAN, Linda 1947-

PERSONAL: Born July 16, 1947, in Denver, CO; daughter of Charles and Cleona (Bower) Henderson; married Pat Hogan (divorced); children: Sandra Dawn Protector, Tanya Thunder Horse. *Ethnicity:* "Tribal affiliation is Chickasaw." *Education:* University of Colorado—Boulder, M.A., 1978. *Hobbies and other interests:* Gardening and Native Science.

ADDRESSES: Home—P. O. Box 141, Idledale, CO 80453. *Office*—CB 226, English Department, University of Colorado, Boulder, CO 80309.

CAREER: Has worked variously as a nurse's aide, dental assistant, waitress, homemaker, secretary, administrator, teacher's aide, library clerk, freelance writer, and researcher; poet-in-schools for states of Colorado and Oklahoma, 1980-84; workshop facilitator in creative writing and creativity, 1981-84; Colorado College, Colorado Springs, assistant professor in TRIBES program, 1982-84; University of Minnesota—Twin Cities, Minneapolis, associate professor of American and of American Indian studies, 1984-89; University of Colorado, Boulder, professor of English, 1989—.

MEMBER: Writers Guild, Authors Guild, PEN, American Academy of Poets.

AWARDS, HONORS: Five Civilized Tribes Playwriting Award, 1980, for *A Piece of Moon;* short fiction award, *Stand Magazine,* 1983; Western States Book Award honorable mention, 1984; fellow, Colorado Independent Writers, 1984, 1985; National Endowment for the Arts grant, 1986; American Book Award, Before Columbus Foundation, 1986, for *Seeing Through the Sun;* Guggenheim fellowship, 1990; Colorado Book Award, 1993, for *The Book of Medicines;* Lannan Foundation Award, 1994; Pulitzer Prize finalist, for *Mean Spirit;* National Book Critics Circle Award finalist, and Oklahoma Book Award, both for *The Book of Medicines.*

WRITINGS:

POETRY

Calling Myself Home, Greenfield Review Press (Greenfield, NY), 1979, reprinted, with stories added, as *Red Clay: Poems and Stories,* Greenfield Review Press, 1991.
Daughters, I Love You, Loretto Heights Women's Research Center (Denver, CO), 1981.
Eclipse, American Indian Studies Center, University of California (Los Angeles, CA), 1983.
Seeing through the Sun, University of Massachusetts Press (Amherst, MA), 1985.
Savings, Coffee House Press (Minneapolis, MN), 1988.
The Book of Medicines, Coffee House Press (Minneapolis, MN), 1993.

OTHER

A Piece of Moon (three-act play), produced in Stillwater, OK, 1981.

That Horse (short fiction), Pueblo of Acoma Press, 1985.

(Editor, with Carol Buechal and Judith McDaniel) *The Stories We Hold Secret,* Greenfield Review Press, 1986.

Mean Spirit (novel), Atheneum (New York, NY), 1990.

Dwellings: A Spiritual History of the Living World (essays), Norton (New York, NY), 1995.

Solar Storms (novel), Scribner (New York, NY), 1995.

(Editor, with Brenda Peterson and Deena Metzger) *Between Species: Women and Animals,* Ballantine (New York, NY), 1997.

Power (novel), Norton (New York, NY), 1998.

(Editor, with Brenda Peterson) *Intimate Nature: The Bond between Women and Animals,* Fawcett Columbine, 1998.

(Editor, with Brenda Peterson) *The Sweet Breathing of Plants: Women Writing on the Green World,* North Point Press (New York, NY), 2001.

The Woman Who Watches over the World: A Native Memoir, Norton (New York, NY), 2001.

(With Brenda Peterson) *Sightings: The Gray Whale's Mysterious Journey,* National Geographic (Washington, D.C.), 2002.

(Editor, with Barbara FitzGerald) *Between Poetry and Politics: Essays in Honour of Edna McDonagh,* Columba Press (Dublin, Ireland), 2003.

(Editor, with Brenda Peterson) *Face to Face: Women Writers on Faith, Mysticism, and Awakening,* North Point Press (New York, NY), 2004.

Also author of screenplays *Mean Spirit* and *Aunt Moon,* both 1986, and of the television documentary *Everything Has a Spirit.* Guest editor of *Frontiers,* 1982. Contributor to anthologies, including *I Tell You Now,* edited by Brian Swann, University of Nebraska Press, 1987.

SIDELIGHTS: Linda Hogan, a member of the Chickasaw tribe, draws on her Native-American heritage in both fiction and verse. Noted for novels, short stories, and poems that are characterized by a combination of a strong female perspective, a deep theological insight, and a sensitivity to the natural world that has been called uniquely Native American, Hogan has been honored with numerous awards. Her 1994 novel, *Mean Spirit,* was a finalist for both the Pulitzer Prize and the National Book Critics Circle Award. Of her poetry in particular, essayist Laurel Smith wrote in *Contemporary Women Poets* that Hogan "combines lyrical and political elements . . . that prompt us to reconsider the ways we know our world and ourselves." In a *Booklist* review of Hogan's *Solar Storms,* Donna Seaman commented "Hogan writes beautifully and with great wisdom in any literary form."

Hogan's first novel, *Mean Spirit,* depicts murder in a community of Osage Indians living in Oklahoma during the oil boom of the early 1920s. The discovery of oil has enriched the Osage, but it has also attracted the attention of unscrupulous white oil barons. The murder of Grace Blanket, owner of a large plot of oil-rich land—committed in front of both her daughter Nora and Nora's friend, Rena Graycloud—proves to be the first link in a chain of events designed to deprive the Osage of their territory. The escalating violence and bloodshed bring federal police officer Stace Red Hawk from Washington to Oklahoma to investigate, but to solve the mystery, he first has to overcome government corruption and cultural prejudice.

In *Mean Spirit,* commented a critic in *Publishers Weekly,* Hogan "mines a rich vein of Indian customs and rituals, and approaches her characters with reverence, bringing them to life with quick, spare phrases." Joseph A. Cincotti, reviewing the novel for the *New York Times Book Review,* stated that Hogan "has an eye for detail, and [for] the Native American rituals and customs" depicted in the book. *School Library Journal* contributor Lynda Voyles called *Mean Spirit* "thought-provoking and unsettling."

Hogan's 1995 novel, *Solar Storms,* recounts the dislocation and suffering of Native Americans through the spiritual journey of Angel Jensen, a seventeen-year-old Native-American girl with unexplained facial scars that symbolize the fragmentation and enduring affliction of her people. Angel leaves a foster home in Oklahoma to revisit her birthplace in a town near the border lakes of Minnesota. There she encounters her great-grandmother, Agnes Iron, her great-great-grandmother, Dora Rouge, and a Chickasaw friend named Bush, who help Angel reconstruct her lost ancestral origins and early life. Together the women embark on a canoe voyage to join a protest against the construction of a hydroelectric power plant that threatens to destroy tribal lands. Despite its setting in the 1970s, the lesson of Hogan's work is an allegory representing the destruction by more powerful foreign cultures of the lands belonging to indigenous peoples around the globe. "Hogan has the spiritual depth to bring us through all the suffering to some glimpsing understanding of the Holy," wrote Bettina Berch in *Belles Lettres.* Reviewing the novel in the *New York Times Book Review,* Maggie Garb noted that Hogan's "sensuous descriptions of the sights, smells and sounds of the natural world are tempered by heart-wrenching depictions of rural poverty." Though in *World Literature Today,* Robert L. Berner felt that the last five chapters took away from the abstract quality of the narrative, he conceded that the work was an "extraordinary, almost mythical narrative." In an article for *Women's Review of Books,* Heid E. Erdrich praised, "Hogan's Native-American female characters wear their scars and wounds, their history, tender side out, and are no less beautiful or peaceful for them." *Los Angeles Times Book Review* contributor Susan Heeger described *Solar Storms* as "stunning," a book through which it is learned that true humanity depends on connections "to family, friends, nature, the whole of life—rather than lording it over the rest of creation," and Joe Staples in *American Indian Quarterly* considered the novel "a work of depth and beauty."

Power, published in 1998, tells the story of sixteen-year-old Omishito, a member of the Taiga tribe of southern Florida. While trying to search for her own identity, especially in relation to the traditions of her tribe, Omishito witnesses her Aunt Ama killing a sacred Florida panther. Though this is taboo in their tribe and illegal due to the panther's status on the federal endangered species list, Aunt Ama believed that by hunting it, she would invoke powerful forces that would help bring the panther back. Omishito is called to both to court and in front of her tribe to describe what she witnessed, and through the experience, the young woman asks many questions about what is right and what is wrong, and about whether someone can be both at the same time. *Power* is "one of those books that transports you to a different state of mind," according to Jacqueline Shea Murphy in *Women's Review of Books.* Bill Ott of *Booklist* considered the book "beautifully written, highly dramatic, and thought provoking," and a writer for *Publishers Weekly* commented on Hogan's "lyrical, almost mystical use of language." In an article for *Horizons,* a reviewer praised, "Hogan's poetic penchant spills over into her novel writing. . . . [She] has the remarkable ability to make urbanites stop and smell the roses. She does not waste or rush through descriptions of the natural world; she forces readers to visualize the beauty which likely surrounds them daily but may be overlooked." Murphy concluded, "[The] sense of clarity and simplicity, that feeling that you are

awake and alive in the world, glancing up, for a flash of a second, into the eye of the hurricane around you, is what *Power* communicates."

Although Hogan published her first novel in 1990, she has been writing poetry since the 1970s. Her first collection, *Calling Myself Home,* according to Smith, "introduc[es] ideas of identity and community that continue to be compelling elements in all her writing." Including works about the quest for one's origins, Hogan weaves together strong characters with images of the landscape that sustains them, and includes several works about members of her own family. The poet also deals with birth and metamorphosis in such poems as "Celebration: Birth of a Colt" and "The River Calls Them," about tadpoles' transition into frogs.

In *Eclipse,* published in 1983, Hogan retains the perspective established in *Calling Myself Home* and based in her Chickasaw heritage and her faith in female strength. Containing poems confronting such areas of concern as nuclear armaments and advancing the causes of Native Americans that were previously published in *Daughters, I Love You, Eclipse* also includes poems that attempt to reconnect readers with the natural world, honoring each of the four winds, the sky father, and the mother earth. "Hogan crafts phrases of common speech and weaves the lines in natural idioms," noted Kenneth Lincoln in the book's foreword. "The verses carry the muted voices of talk before sleep, quieting the world, awaiting the peace of home. . . . Her poems offer a careful voicing of common things not yet understood, necessary to survival."

Hogan's 1993 poetry collection, *The Book of Medicines,* invokes the therapeutic power of rhyme to treat the psychic damage inflicted by human conquest over nature and other people. Drawing on Native-American folklore, ritual, and female spirituality, Hogan's incantations address profound manifestations of illness, grief, and the failure of science in the modern world. In one poem, "The Alchemists," she contrasts ancient attempts to transmute lead into gold with a contemporary physician's effort to heal the sick. Robyn Selman describes Hogan's work as "ecopoetry" in her essay in the *Voice Literary Supplement,* particularly as the poems in this volume "take as their subject the very elements of life—fire, air, earth, and water—set into motion with bears, fishes, and humans." Carl L. Bankston noted in the *Bloomsbury Review,* "Hogan's fine sense of rhythm weaves through images of nature and of humankind's uneasy place in nature. These are dreamlike images that draw on Native-merican legends of the time before time when the First People were at once animals and people." As Robert L. Berner concluded in *World Literature Today,* "*The Book of Medicines* is a significant step, indeed a giant stride, in the development of a major American poet."

Hogan's *Dwellings: A Spiritual History of the Living World* is a collection of seventeen essays that explore the interconnectedness of nature, religion, and myth. Alternating between storyteller and poet, Hogan relates the universality of minor occurrences in daily life, especially as reflected in the essential relationship between humans and various creatures, including bats, wolves, and birds of prey at a rehabilitation center for wildlife. A writer for *Publishers Weekly* wrote that Hogan "successfully couples a poet's appreciation of phrasing and rhythm with Native American sensibilities and stories." Heid E. Erdrich observed in the *Women's Review of Books,* "Hogan's sense of mystery impels these essays, whose topics range from Hiroshima to the space probe *Voyager* to humor in captive primates," and noted that "*Dwellings* reads like a correspondence . . . with a partculary intelligent, well-read, poetic, spiritual, and earthy friend." The title of the collection alludes to its central theme, that of home and shared existence. According to Liz Caile in the *Bloomsbury Review,* "By honoring all creatures, we grow stronger and more content—that is the message of this book."

Hogan has also edited a number of books, several of them with Brenda Peterson. She and Peterson together compiled works of women authors on the theme of women relating to the natural environment. *Intimate Nature: The Bond between Women and Animals* and *The Sweet Breathing of Plants: Women Writing on the Green World* feature such well known women authors as Terry Tempest Williams, Ursula K. Le Guin, Susan Orlean, Isabel Allende, and Zora Neal Hurston. A. M. Wilborn, reviewing *The Sweet Breathing of Plants* for *E* magazine called the book "an entrhalling look at ecology" while a *Publishers Weekly* critic wrote, "Not merely for nature lovers, this provocative collection ranks with the best anthologies of women's writing." Peterson and Hogan edited *Face to Face: Women Writers on Faith, Mysticism, and Awakening* as a third book in this series of collections.

Peterson and Hogan also worked together on a project where they followed the migration of the gray whales from Baja California up to the Arctic Ocean. The book, *Sightings: The Gray Whales' Mysterious Journey,* covers the history both of the gray whales and the people who interact with them, and presents such issues as aboriginal whaling rights. Nancy Bent, in *Booklist,* noted that *Sightings* has "Hogan's more philosophical musing . . . juxtaposed with Peterson's more reporterly presentation" and proclaimed it "an unbeatable combination of a thrilling subject and good writing."

In 2001, Hogan published her first memoir, *The Woman Who Watches over the World: A Native Memoir.* Called a "complex, sensitive book" by Edna M. Boardman in a review for *Kliatt, The Woman Who Watches over the World* is not only the story of Hogan's own history, but also the story of Native-American demoralization throughout U. S. history. Tales of Hogan's family life are mixed with essays on nature, mythology and mysticism, traditions, and love. "Hogan's memories spill out," wrote a critic for *Publishers Weekly,* continuing, "the smallest detail can evoke a whole history." A reviewer for *Booklist* considered the book a "beautifully rendered, cathartic, and ultimately transcendent narrative." Donna Seaman, in an earlier *Booklist* review, wrote, "The anguish of her personal experiences and the sorrows of the decimated tribal world are palpable," and in a *Library Journal* review, Sue Samson commented that *The Woman Who Watches over the World* "goes a long way toward explaining Native Americans today."

Hogan once told *CA:* "My writing comes from and goes back to the community, both the human and the global community. I am interested in the deepest questions, those of spirit, of shelter, of growth and movement toward peace and liberation, inner and outer. My main interest at the moment is in wildlife rehabilitation and studying the relationship between humans and other species, and trying to create world survival skills out of what I learn from this."

AUTOBIOGRAPHICAL ESSAY:

Linda Hogan contributed the following autobiographical essay to *CA:*

Daily I have been watching the first opening of green buds into the leaves of the bee balm tree, as I call it for want of a better name. Soon it will be warm, and

Linda Hogan

the window will be open, the sound of honey bees thick in the tree, the sweet smell of blossom in the window. How many generations of bees have been coming to this tree? I wonder that not just about the bees, but about myself, how many generations I hold, from ancestral wanderings and journeys, miseries and moments of joy, loves, and disappointments. I think it is a miracle I slipped through history, a Chickasaw who was carried in some woman's body over the Trail of Tears, part of a world, a historical part, that defined me.

It is a question held from the beginning.

I was born in Denver, in 1947, to a carpenter and a housewife. My father, an American Indian, a Chickasaw, had come from Oklahoma to work as a ranch hand. My mother, from a farm family in Nebraska, worked as a housekeeper for a doctor's family. They met. They ate dime tamales. They won a jitterbug contest. They drank nickel glasses of wine. My father won a wedding ring set in a poker game and proposed.

They were married for sixty years. My mother still wears the rings, worn thin.

*

After my older sister was born, there was the first disappearance of our father to war. My mother and sister stayed in Nebraska, California, and once lived next door to a turkey farm. I know nothing of this time, except for a few family photos, but believe I lived part of my infancy by that turkey farm in Colorado.

I was conceived when my father returned from WWII. I was one of the war babies, divisions of cells within an egg, beginning on one of the nights of celebration that America was back on course again. America was in the right. My father was proud of being in the army.

Nine months later, I was born with black hair and sideburns and frequent visitations from an uncle who had a great affinity for me because I was going to be the new Indian in the family. I looked like a Chickasaw. My dark eyes and sideburns were testament to that. And he, Uncle Wesley, spent years of his life introducing me to the American Indian world, until I was an adult and worked at the Denver Indian Center. It was important to him to keep the life in it, whether it was traveling to Colorado Springs to take me to powwows in Manitou or having me serve turkey at the Denver Indian Center Thanksgiving and Christmas powwows, then held in school gyms. We danced together. He spoke Chickasaw to me and teased me mercilessly. In Oklahoma, years later, we, my parents included, went to all the family reunions, mixed-bloods, some of us, some women in braids. Our identity, our relations, were important. Now the family is greatly diminished by the deaths of my aunts and uncles and father.

*

During the Relocation Act of the 1950s, a time when Indians were moved off reservations and sent to cities, my Uncle Wesley, a man named Richard Tallbull, and a Bureau of Indian Affairs (BIA) employee named Helen Peterson formed an organization called "The White Buffalo Council," which remained in existence for many years. They helped to feed and house and find jobs for the different tribal members who were put on buses and sent to Denver. Indians came from everywhere. The idea was to send a person or family as far from home as possible. Choctaws ended up in Chicago, Navajos in California, Cherokees in San Francisco.

My uncle had gone to Denver earlier than that and worked for the railroad. My father followed. They were a close family and traveled long distances to be together. The brothers would travel to see us frequently. My Uncle James was so much like my father that when my father came home from the Korean War, I thought he was Uncle James. On learning he was not, I went to a closet and cried. I didn't know my father, though later in our lives we became close, traveling together, interviewing Chickasaw elders in Oklahoma, returning to our historical sites and those important to our own familial history.

When I look back at the influences in my life, aside from my uncle who helped define my identity, my paternal grandmother was the greatest influence. Not in terms of my identity as an American Indian, but because she had a kindness and a compassion that was palpable. It was felt beyond the boundaries of her skin, because she loved in a world where love was a rare commodity, as if no one had time for it, or patience. And she seemed to love all equally, all of us, and there were many, and even the large land tortoise that came to her door. When I was at her house, my special joy was to get up early in the morning. Her day began around four. And I would brush her long hair that had never been cut.

We came from another America. When I was a girl, my grandparents still used horses and wagon. A photograph of my grandfather riding into the town of Gene Autry, Oklahoma, to get water in milk cans is on the cover of my first book, *Calling Myself Home,* now renamed with stories added, *Red Clay.* I somehow thought this was wondrous and magical, living in the old days for part of the year. But, of course, it was a hard life. And reflecting on it now, my family, which once had land and been ranchers, had fallen into deep poverty because of land foreclosures and dishonest policies in Oklahoma, policies designed to disinherit the Chickasaws from their land allotments. Our family Indian allotments under the Dawes Act are now the Ardmore Airpark.

Because of the closeness of our Native family and the telling of stories and history, this became my life. It was as if I had lived through the Depression, the foreclosures, the horse traders, the classroom my grandfather shared with Jesse and Frank James at the Harley Institute, an Indian boys school. As a child, I listened. My sister and I walked the land and sat at the *tanque* where there were fish and turtles and talked about Indian princesses. We were as steeped in stereotypes as the rest of America. We had watched Western movies at the drive-in theaters. I remember us finding beads and believing they belonged to the old chiefs, which had been our relatives. The beads we found were actually plant fossils common to that area, ancient land, of Oklahoma.

I listened as an adult, as well. We would go from place to place dropping in on Oklahoma relatives, even though I told my father this is no longer done as in the old days of which they always spoke. But at each place there were stories, or at least there was gossip.

In our other world, in Colorado, I grew up in a silent household. My father, when I was four or five, left for the Korean War. My mother took in ironing and baby-sat in order to support us. We didn't read, the only book being a large family Bible from my mother's more affluent side of the family in McCook, Nebraska. When I visited that side of our family, I spent much time on the carpet with the open Bible, looking at the pictures and all the saved added things, postage cards, cards from soldiers, pieces of lace, and the history of births and deaths. It was what I had and knew of my mother's life. She, in all her silences, was very interesting to me. I watched her. I asked her questions. I hid in places and observed her. I searched her clothing and shoes. I recall moments at her family's home in Nebraska, watching the wind blow the curtains in the early morning, listening to the doves outside where my white grandfather had a large garden with tomatoes and deep purple eggplants. Those were blissful moments.

When television arrived, I was more interested in being outdoors than in watching those first shows, except at night when I laid at the foot of my bed to watch whatever was on while I was supposed to be sleeping, and of course, I watched my mother who was ironing, always ironing. Ten cents a shirt, I remember. She worked so hard to take care of us girls.

But outdoors was my school. While other writers talk about the teachers who influenced them, the education they had, the books that illumined their writing lives, I watched the insects, the birds, and hid in the doghouse when planes flew over, being a military child very aware of bombs because of the printed materials that were given to us and not to civilians. Instructions: In case we were bombed, we were to boil our clothes and bathe our bodies. Hide under a desk or table to avoid injury. We were as deluded as the others, believing the propaganda, that this would save us from an atomic bomb.

So, I watched life. I watched the ants move their eggs and disappear quickly into the earth, the newly hatched spiders leaving trees, the sun on their strands of silk. My father once took me to an underpass to see barn swallows flying back and forth from mud to their clay nests, intricate art, all of them returning at dusk, disappearing quickly into their beautifully crafted nests. Chewing roofing tar for lack of gum, I followed beetles. My friends and I sucked on rhubarb stalks and made jewelry out of tree branches, dolls out of hollyhocks, and followed bees to their hidden shelters, looking on the ground for pieces of honeycomb that had fallen or been thrown out of the hive. I watched blue robin eggs, waiting for them to open. What an abundance of life everywhere I looked.

I look back now, at this age, not at any of the unhappiness I suffered, not on the emotions I contained that I would never have known how to express in those days. I have written the difficulties already in my memoir, *The Woman Who Watches over the World.* Perhaps it is my age, but I am looking back on those moments of happiness. I want to remember rolling around in piles of autumn leaves. The man next door, the only man who wasn't at war on our street, coming by the army blanket tent I made with a friend. He gave us fudgesicles and other treats. There were choices to be made in the candy shop: long black licorice or the short round ones? There was a dump near our house, a place of great finds. Furniture. Old dolls. Rusted cars we could sit in and pretend to drive. At home I sat at the end of my bed and pulled on the cloth that curtained our closet, pretending to be riding a horse, holding the reins. All the rest of my family were rodeo people. I longed to be a barrel racer. I dressed in cowboy boots and hats. I even wore a fringed vest, all this to my sister's dismay! There were also the nights out playing in our pajamas, hide and seek, with cousins and friends.

I remember one day, later, after we moved to Colorado Springs near the army base, Ft. Carson, where my father had been transferred. I was sitting at the door, peaceful in the sun, clean and wearing white, and felt a moment of spiritual strength, coming for no reason at all, unsought. It would be something, after that, I would want to open again. After that one moment of feeling awake, I would seek it out. Through acts of attention, through silence, solitude, yoga, and writing. And these are the ways it still comes to me, that being awake. Perhaps this was the early stirrings of whatever that great something was that would bring me to words and the attention that creates writing.

Then there were the teen years. Bruce Orndoff came to my house on his horse to take me riding into the woods. That was happiness! My friend, Janie, and I drove around singing. Always singing. We sang together in chorus. In madrigal chorus. Folk songs in a beatnik coffee house, La Chat Noir. She is a serious opera singer still. I joined a community chorus. Another friend, Linda, and our boyfriends went to toboggan, none of us wealthy enough to have the proper attire. I was wearing plastic shoes in snow. We sat in the car with the heater on, frozen, laughing, drying out, the smell of her wet wool scarf strong in my memory.

I worked then in a nursing home, from after school until late at night. My father was medically disabled by heart disease and discharged from the army. I wanted clothes, money, eventually a car. It meant I had to work. Looking back, it was a blessing of my birth, being born without a family of money. (Nevertheless, when people ask me what I want for my birthday, I say, a rich father and a trust fund.) Even now, the active army personnel either have extra work or are in an income bracket eligible for food stamps. Our income, disability, was even less than before.

I was quiet, chatty only in Oklahoma with my cousins and other loved ones. Beyond that, I only spoke out in defense of the world. I grew up around much cruelty to animals. I fought it, and I would fly out of bed and run out the door in record time, wearing pajamas, to save a kitten, but the rest of time I could barely speak. And I was protective of my brother. He was my special one, the love I could create in my family. Eight years younger than I was, I even wanted to take him on dates when I was older.

In Sunday school when I was twelve I suddenly spoke out and asked why I felt God more when I was with a tree than when sitting there in the folding chair hear-

Linda Hogan and her brother, Larry

ing about Shadrach and Abednego and the fiery furnace. The Bible was full of lessons on how not to behave as a human. And if people really loved Jesus, why didn't they just act like him? That was how I felt, even though our family Bible had been my most precious item, and I traced my finger across the etchings in it for hours.

I never aspired to be a writer, never thought to assert my Native identity, but I was firm on this tree fact and the Sunday school teacher said we were in the house of God, and I knew I was different if I felt God when I sat under a tree, smelling the fresh earth, the blades of grass, the small flowers blooming. I even argued. God permits that in other religions. Perhaps this was a defining moment, though it would take years to ripen, the beginning of a greater spirit for a dispirited child. I didn't know I would one day write and that this would be my source, my breath, my God. And that there would follow again those moments of being awake and sitting beneath trees, feeling their spirit, writing there.

*

In the meantime, I had jobs. From my father's side were Indian cowboys and while I had wanted nothing more than to be a barrel racer and ride in the rodeo

parade, it was not going to be my world. They, after all, were legends, having won ribbons, money, jackpots, being wild bronc riders and bull riders, but my skills were poor. We only had horses once, and for a short while. So I worked as a waitress, a dental assistant, and numerous other jobs that paid little. By then I had given up on the rodeo and taken to my second practical choice: figure skating. I'd wanted to ice skate all my childhood, and we could never afford it, so as soon as I graduated from high school, all my earnings went to skating, to gliding along the ice, to lessons, private, to custom skates with amazing blades, and even to dresses made by a woman who had been a skater, but developed a disease called lupus and began making dresses for skaters since she could no longer skate. My favorite dress was black with white trim across the chest. Then I had a dance partner. We learned the dances. I threw myself into it seriously, from five-thirty in the morning "patching," watching Peggy Fleming with her perfect figures, to nighttimes of free-skating. Afterwards there was still energy for beer and dancing.

During this time I now worked as a dental assistant, and I loved my job. The dentist, Dr. Pitcher, was the first person who thought I was intelligent. He taught me to read x-rays, do lab work, and I even cleaned the teeth of my friends and family during the lunch hour. It was important that he thought I was intelligent. It was the first time anyone had thought so. It was what later influenced me to return to school, that and moving to California where I stayed for a brief time with my Uncle James, my father's brother, my Aunt Corrine, and cousins. My cousin was in school at the university; he had interesting friends, and they talked about things I wanted to think about. I began to take night classes in vocabulary and reading. I would later, because of this, go to a junior college, then to the university. I wanted to be a biology major, but all the classes were in the daytime when I worked. My first degree, instead, was in psychology. I wanted to be a counselor.

*

Of all the writers I know, I am the one who never intended it. It never would have been expected by anyone, least of all myself. I was working as a teacher's aide in Maryland, having gone there with my husband, Pat. He was doing post-graduate work at the University of Maryland. His friends from Oregon sent him a book of Rexroth poems. I worked as a teacher's aide. One day I picked up the book and read some of the poems. It was then that poetry chose me. I began writing. I wrote to find words to say what couldn't be said in ordinary language. I wrote for the feel of it. This was what kept me writing and later what kept me in school. I returned to school part-time. I took not only a poetry workshop from Rod Jellema, but decided to study literature. The first class that was significant to me, other than the poetry class, was Proletariat Literature.

I read the underwords of America. I call them that because the stories are there, of working people, by working people, people of color. Carlos Bulosan, a Philipino fruit picker, wrote a book about his life, *If You Want to Know What We Are.* There was Meridel LeSueur, Tillie Olson. Meridel's work has been particularly valuable because of its beauty, Tillie's because of its craft and commitment. I could understand the literature of poor people, workers. I had worked for less that minimum wage. I had grown up with people who were poor, one family from Nicaragua next door and me not knowing about the war, drunks across the street, people fighting, and then, too, people like my father with the nicest house, trying always to assert his dignity and his pride.

And then later, in American Literature [class], I read [William] Faulkner's *Go Down Moses.* I had the benefit of a professor telling me about it, teaching me to understand this book, which I bought for my father. I read in it about the Chickasaw man Sam Fathers and I thought, "I am a Chickasaw. If he can write about us, so can I." And that was when I turned toward my own self and people, my own words, to further represent us. Searching for other references he might have had about us, I found a description of a Chickasaw woman ill a purple turban, proud, taking money for the land she was forced to leave, and I knew what was ahead for her, weeping, humiliation, death. Chickasaw Trail of Tears. Perhaps that woman carried a cell of mine in her body.

I decided I was going to write about us, and we were a far cry from that. My first book, *Calling Myself Home,* like that of many Indians, was on identity. Not knowing there were others, not having seen their work from earlier in the century. Even when I went to school later, I did not find the writings of Wendy Rose, Scott Momaday, or Simon Ortiz. When I researched Indian

literature, I found ceremonies, oral traditions, materials from ethnologists, and journals of travelers.

Even while researching other areas, I graduated in creative writing, and by then my first book of poems was published by writer and publisher Joe Bruchac at Greenfield Review Press, a great champion of American-Indian literature. That book, the one having to do with Oklahoma and my Chickasaw world, changed my life. I was not really prepared to deal with what followed. I was asked to give readings. I was looked at closely, for Indian identity, I discovered, is a complex thing. I was not dark enough for some people. Being of mixed heritage was the focus of the book, and it was one of the first contemporary books of poems by many mixed-blood writers to follow, but there is, even among us, a question of "realness" and this can be directly traced to politics and the genocide of ways of thought. There is a rich heritage, from earlier times, of mixed-blood writers. There were Darcy McNickle, Zitkala Sa (Gertrud Simmons Bonnin), and others from earlier times. Even Osceola was a mixed blood and Eastern-educated Indian. And there were Wendy Rose, Leslie Silko, and others I did not know, whose books were obscure and in anthropology sections of bookstores, instead of with the other literature.

*

I was first a poet, and I think of it as my first language, if silence wasn't my first language. Looking back, I can say that, younger, I was a poet of heart, even before I had words, but there was pain associated with not having a means to express, and I will always be thankful I found words and beyond that. Poetry says what can't be said in ordinary language. Perhaps, also, it is most in touch with the earth, its rhythms, its dry lands, oceans, profusions and dominions of life, and also the fault lines, storms, the surprise of emotion. It also brings about the need for balance. So, it is no surprise that poetry with its silences and underpoems was my first love.

It brings in something beyond the human mind and thought. It comes from somewhere else. I can't say where. I can't point it out on a map or tell its location in the human psyche. The secret of it is its beauty and surprise and magnetic draw. It is a sacred contract of words between us and something else. For me, that something else is nature. Some Native languages do not even have a word for nature because the human is inseparable from the natural world.

Poetry is a search. It wants to make a map, but it is a map only the poem knows. You have to follow it or you will lose it. If remaining humble and in the service of the poem, magic can happen.

A way of being in the world. This is what it is, this writing, and the life of it, so calm. If I could write only poetry I would be so happy.

But as I have added essays and fiction to my world, I find my approach to language is the same, that the way I go about writing in other genres is the same approach as to a poem.

*

In 1978, my husband Pat and I adopted two children, Tanya and Sandra. I was delighted by the adoption. It was my dream come true, and family was important to me. There was much elation on my part as I prepared for the two girls to come into our home. It took six months, a short pregnancy. They were older children, five and ten. We did not have their histories. Their records have been "lost." As it turned out, neither of them were bonded, or attached, as they now call it, and they had already a life's history of troubles, from physical abuse to sexual abuse to malnutrition. Nevertheless, I had so much love to give, and I believed love and care would win out over all things. And yet, it didn't. The world began to seem darker then than it ever did as we struggled through life with children in pain, one child violent and dangerous, another hurting herself and unable to speak.

I wanted to write a novel about adoption, about their histories. I finished it, and never published it. At that time, I did somehow manage to write the book of poems, *Eclipse,* from University of California Indian Studies Press. The middle section of the book centered on my daughters, my love for them, and for the politics of those days in the early '80s.

When I was young and people asked me what I wanted to be when I grew up, I said "a grandmother." Now I am one. It seems so long ago now. I look back as a

grandmother to those years of stress with my daughters. The tension and added burdens contributed to an already fragile marriage. In 1982 my husband and I separated. At that time I taught in an all-Indian program at Colorado College in Colorado Springs during the summer and put together other teaching jobs in various places during the school year. Then in 1984 I accepted a job teaching Native-American studies, on which I had written much, and American studies, at the University of Minnesota.

Thinking I would remain there, I bought a house. It had stained glass windows in the little living room, two bedrooms. I thought we were wealthy! I had a desk in my bedroom and continued to write poetry. I also wrote essays and short stories. But after the first school year, I realized something was not working at the University. I was young, inexperienced at politics, and I couldn't pinpoint it at the time, but when I look back I can say only that I was treated very badly. There was great resentment toward me. I was the only Native professor in a program which didn't exist except in name. And I was also in American studies. I didn't have the experience to fight it, and even if I had, I wouldn't have been able to put my energy there. The despair and stress of my job made me sick, and I finally had to leave. I wasn't even able to stay long enough to thank the people who *were* kind. After the second year, I left. I left my house. On leave, my daughter and I returned to our small town in Colorado, and I tried to heal. Still writing. By then I had written *Seeing Through the Sun,* which received an American Book Award from the Before Columbus Foundation. Now I worked on fiction, short stories, published in small journals, and wrote, slowly, *Mean Spirit,* which became, to my surprise, a Pulitzer finalist, and received an Oklahoma Book Award.

My friend, Gary Holthaus, once said that writing doesn't heal, but sometimes healing comes through writing. And I felt this to be the truth. The writing, my life in the mountains. *Mean Spirit* contained family history, Osage history, and events that were true in Oklahoma Indian Territory. It was also fictionalized, even the landscape, and it was because I could do things with fiction that I couldn't do with only history. It was necessary for a book that contained such painful truths.

I taught again, at the University of Colorado. This time I taught in the creative writing program. It was exciting to inspire the minds and hearts of newer writers. I loved the work. There were problems there, too, but they seemed like nothing in comparison to Minnesota. I could never have complained. Later, after I was gone, I looked back at the amount of bias that existed there. In the whole history of the University, I was only the second woman of color to ever be a full professor.

*

Being a Native woman has been the single most significant part of my life, my identity, and of my work. It creates a direction I cannot help but follow. It used to bother me that Euro-American writers could write about anything, including us, and no one would be bothered, while we are confined to write about who we are, and our work was believed to be true, anthropological, even when it was fiction. And yet, being Native opens a world. It opens *to* a world. It gives me reason to understand why the most urgent theme for me has been the natural world, the physical world, the great without. The spiritual is in the air around us. We are never alone, we are never without some life force about us, on a tundra, in the sand dunes, in a prison. And I am only a small part of it, a humble being in a world large and full. Knowing this and seeking out this awareness is what has allowed me to become a writer and a thinker, and in demand as a public speaker.

*

A writer grows into their life and work. It is a mystery. A person's writing comes from some other place and like the natural world it is larger than the person.

It helps reveal the world. One afternoon I watched the fascinating life of ants and later I thought, if anyone asked me what I did, they would think I had done nothing. But I had done a great amount of work and ant society is extremely intelligent. In Australia there is a Green Ant Dreaming. For Navajos there is a Red Ant Chantway. Their significance is acknowledged by people of the earth. In the bush, advancing fires are predicted because certain ants protect their hills with reflective quartz ahead of time, knowing what humans don't know. The way the animals and insects knew about Chernobyl before the humans did. The bees remained in their hives. The animals fled.

Creature life is part of my autobiography. I live with other creations, mountains lions now, deer, fox, horses,

yesterday even vultures. And there have been wasps in my houses. For fifteen years I lived with several generations of wasps. It was my old home. They lived in the ceiling areas above my office. I felt it was an enchanted office. No screens. Once, the blue dragonflies drifted in and out as well as the wasps. These are as important as a human relationship, the relationships and connections with the world. They are connections and relationships with the divine.

There are so many voices and language from this world. There is nothing meaningless or without worth. I honor the cultures of the others and the often ignored. This includes animal cultures. It is told now by science that elephants communicate over a hundred miles, and we can't hear their subsonic voices. Whales make a sound that stuns squid into motionlessness. Prairie dogs have a grammar and ability to describe, their own language. Now as I pass by their villages I watch them killed as development after development goes up. Those who have studied their language find they have syntax and structure. Finally, it was in National Geographic, which made it true. Researchers found that they even describe people walking by, a thin man, a short woman.

Dwellings: A Spiritual History of the Natural World, a book of essays, is a book about this world, the plants, animals I have observed and worked with in eight years of volunteer work in wildlife rehabilitation, six of those years with raptors. It is about where I live and what I have seen or known of this world, and the ancestral spirits that dwell behind us all.

*

After writing *Mean Spirit* and *Dwellings,* the hydroelectric development at James Bay up in Hudson Bay was evolving. I heard about it first at the American Indian Community House in New York. I was shocked by what I heard. The city of New York was so dismayed by the damage to the Native people in the region and to the environment that they canceled their contract for energy with Hydro Quebec. I began working on *Solar Storms,* which was not only about James Bay but also about adoption and about the child of my oldest adopted daughter, a child I wanted desperately to adopt, but was not well enough, was single, and not financially stable. So I wrote the book for her and for the land and the people of the far north. One of the consequences of the book was that I dedicated it to this granddaughter, and the woman who adopted my granddaughter called me, and we were reunited, that child I had so bonded with when she was an infant. We are still in touch.

*

Until now, the novels were based on factual history, fictionalized. Their focus and impetus was toward healing ourselves, our land, our spiritual lives. Similar circumstances brought about the novel, *Power.* I was on a Native working group for the reauthorization of the Endangered Species Act, and I mentioned the Florida panther. It created a polarization of people in the room. I didn't know then about the killing of an endangered Florida panther by a Seminole man, the chief of the tribe, and that there had been a four year attempt to bring charges against him. In fact, I don't believe I knew anything about the Florida panther. It was as if something spoke those words through me.

Disturbed by the incident, I went to Florida to read the court records and find out what happened for myself. I decided to write an article about this case for a legal journal. I felt that the cat was sacred, that there was no circumstance which should allow for its death, particularly considering their diseased conditions, their fight for health and the continuation of their species.

Caught in a storm, sitting it out in the car, I heard the words of the main character, Omishto, begin to speak, and I knew this for what it was, the voice, the inner world that begins as a story. I listened. I had heard these people of the air speak before and knew I had to honor them and write down what they said. And so began *Power,* told by Omishto. She was young but wise. She had important choices to make. It is not the story of the true event. It is fiction. And it is about what if; what if the story the man tried to bring into court at the last minute had been true, that it was a religious act. But, of course, it hadn't been.

The Book of Medicines was my next book of poetry, from Coffee House Press, the press which also published *Savings,* and I felt it was the strongest I had written so far. It was truly about the history of the Americas as much as a book of poems of the heart and world. It was a finalist for the National Book Critics Circle.

About this time, I had a riding accident. My life was going well. I taught at the University of Colorado. My writing was moving along well. I was traveling up and down the West Coast following gray whales with my friend Brenda Peterson, preparing to write the book, *Sightings: The Mysterious Journey of the Gray Whale.* I had bought an old uninhabited cabin and some land walking distance from where I lived, so I finally had space for a horse. One was for sale in my town. I was going to buy him. I went for my first ride one happy Saturday morning, and I was inexperienced, and he was a problem horse, Big Red, but they didn't tell me this. He was "hot-blooded." They were afraid of him. I had an accident I do not remember. Someone found my body in the road. I woke up three weeks later in a hospital for brain and spinal cord injuries. I had numerous fractures and injuries, some of them healed by then. My first memory was of the doctor watching me leave in an ambulance. I was being transferred to another hospital. It has been five and a half years and I still remember none of it. I wrote still, even during times I do not remember writing or being, and I wrote about the accident in my memoir, *The Woman Who Watches over the World.* My memory problems, along with other brain injury left-overs, still persist.

There are things in a life that are junctures, corners turned that one can never step back to again and this accident was one of those things. It changed my life forever. Nothing has yet settled back into place, although it is beginning to.

Because of this accident, I later had to sell my house, and I moved to the little, dilapidated cabin. One day Colorado Horse Rescue called me and said they thought they had a horse for me. Considering they had a two year waiting list, I felt fortunate. Having had three fractures in my pelvis, I was still unable to walk without crutches. I went to look at the horse. She was terribly underweight, limping, her head tilted to one side. She was a miserable little horse, I realize now. The woman said, "This is the one we were thinking about, a companion horse. She can't run. She isn't for riding."

I took her for a walk, a prerequisite, frustrating as it was with crutches. She pulled away and one of my crutches fell. She looked at me, my crutch, and came back to walk at my side. I adopted her. Kelly. How could I not? She was thoughtful and aware. Before I knew it, the next day, a cowgirl in a horse trailer came and put Kelly inside it, commenting all the while on what a beautiful Arab she was, this little mess. She closed the door and began driving. Kelly looked out the window of the burgundy trailer as I followed them to her little place at Lori's house, watching my car behind the trailer all the way, as if to make sure I would not leave. Ted and Lori. Horse lovers, both. With many rescued horses there, including a blind one.

I visited Kelly daily, taking apples and carrots. I walked her down the road to fresh grass. Eventually she gained weight and began to shine. One day I went out and Kelly was running! At first I felt joy. Then dismay as I thought, Oh no, she's not supposed to run. What if I can't handle her?

*

At my new dilapidated cabin, the work began. Ongoing work. The siding was roofing from the '30s and it had a built-in working '30s refrigerator with a tiny ice cube tray. I didn't discover until winter that it was truly a summer cabin, made of fiber board, of materials once used for a temporary ice hockey rink, but that first summer, what joy. The cottage windows opened inward. I opened the windows wide and in my room was a painted bird house. The wasps built a home inside it. We were compatible. We kept the same hours. I closed the windows in the evenings after they settled in for the night. They woke up in the warmth of day and the windows were open. If I slept too long one would come wake me up to open the window. I placed hyssop inside my room and hummingbirds flew in and out.

Gratefully, hypnotically, beautiful nature insisted its way into my new life and brought healing. It still does, even when I write fiction, or an essay, or a book about the journey of the gray whale.

I think about the coincidences of lives, how I ended up with Kelly. In a way she laid claim to me in the same way writing does. Then, at Ted and Lori's, there was a blue horse, a mustang. Young, pregnant, she looked at me constantly. One day I saw the foal moving inside her. I began to spend time with her. No one else did. She was a pitiful horse, as well, with only a piece of cloth in a corner of a fence for a shelter, even

in winter. Carrots. Apples. Walks to grass. I began to feel attached to her. One day I knew by intuition that she was going to foal. I went home, packed my dog and car for the night, and returned to spend the night. It was a long night as she thrashed in pain, and we ran from side to side to avoid being kicked by her hooves. In the end, she could not give birth. She was taken away to the hospital, the dead foal removed and no one could pay the bill. I asked the vet, "Do you take MasterCard?" I laugh at this sometimes, buying a wild horse with a charge card. A very expensive horse. Now she lives with me, too. She also stands outside my window, a stubborn little thing, the wilderness still in her, hooves like stone. In pasture, in a herd across the way from where I live, even though she was young, she became the dominant mare. Kelly, now thirty, has her own days of running and returns of youthfulness. Recently she jumped over a stone wall, surprising me. There are also our town horses. They roam loose. Sometimes they are in the road as I drive home at night. Standing.

As Chickasaws, we had our own breed of horse. Stolen and lost along our Trail of Tears to Oklahoma, experts now say that the American quarter horse is the outcome of our ponies bred with larger ones. The Chickasaw ponies possessed so many good qualities that they were sought after all along the Mississippi River. We lived at a major trade center and sold the horses far and wide. They were so short in the neck it was said that they had to get down on knees to eat. They worked. They raced. They were good to ride and had endurance. I believe this may have been my own attraction to the mustang. She is blue corn, an Indian horse. The letters "U.S." are frozen into the side of her neck followed by symbols, as are all the wild horses, rounded up. She had a broken pelvis from the round up, thinks the vet. It doesn't show in her movement. After she lost the foal she cried on the way back to her paddock and for weeks looked for it.

AFFINITY: Mustang

> Tonight after the sounds of day
> have given way
> she stands beneath the moon,
> a gray rock shining.
> She matches the land,
> belonging.
>
> She has a dark calm face,
> her hooves like black stone
> belong to the earth

the way it used to be,
long grasses
as grass followed rain
or wind laid down the plains of fall
or in winter now when
her fur changes and becomes snow
or her belly hair turns
the color of red water willows
at the creek,
her legs black as trees.

These horses
almost a shadow,
broken.

When we walk together
in the tall grasses, I feel her
as if I am walking with mystery,
with beauty and fierce powers,
as if far a while we are the same animal
and remember each other from before.

Or sometimes I sit on earth
and watch the wind blow her mane and tail
and the waves of dry grasses
all one way
and it calls to mind
how I've came such a long way
through time
to find her.

Same days I sing to her
remembering the Kiowa man
who sang to cover the screams
of their ponies killed by the Americans
the songs I know in my sleep.

Same nights, hearing her outside,
I think she is to the earth
what I am to her,
belonging.

Sometimes it seems as if we knew each other
from a time before our journeys here
In secret, I sing to her, the old songs
the ones I speak in my sleep.

But last night it was her infant that died
after the kinship and movement
of so many months
Tonight I sit on the straw
and watch as the milk streams from her nipples
to the ground. I clean her face.

Linda Hogan and Misty

I've come such a long way through time
to find her and
It is the first time
I have ever seen a horse cry.

Sing then, the wind says,
Sing.

*

I have watched wasps, whales, their mappings, and have realized their sentience. It is the same with the horses. They have a great intelligence. They require much of me. Part of that requirement is that I am conscious, awake.

*

By some act of fortune, I was invited, around 1993, before my accident, to participate in the Native Science dialogues in Canada, a group of indigenous and

Western thinkers that was started by physicist David Bohm. This was another life-changing event for me, sitting in a room with others who understood, understand, the absolute intelligence of those who came before us, our ancestors, their knowledge, from astronomy to agriculture to mathematics. I realized more than ever that my work was to give Indian people and characters dignity, to reveal the intelligence of our people, and to honor this world we first people inhabited.

I am a traditionally-minded Indian. The European-shaped mind is different. I remember being in Rome seeing Europa, America, and America was snakes and a black panther larger than life, attacking a European man. The wildness of it, the way it was portrayed, a world, a continent, needing to be subdued and conquered, contributed to our tragic histories. Looking back to European history at the time of invasions, I see how so many losses came about. As a writer I have to look into the depths of time before this history and the knowledge that was there before invasion. Now science speaks of dark matter. Native peoples have spoken of dark matter for tens of centuries. The Navajo have a concept of holy wind, meaning the air is alive and even breath is part of wind. Dark matter tells us even more completely that the air around us is full. Also the wholeness of a life is based on balance and harmony. I look often to the Navajo philosophy because it is so intelligent a knowledge system. The traditional knowledge has not been overlaid by European knowledge as it has so seemingly in other traditions, although looking to the stories, songs, and ceremonies, we find it must still exist.

I know this, that there is no lifeless cosmos, no lifeless stone. So I listen to the stones. They all have their stories and most have stories about them. There is nothing without its worth. So I listen. Sometimes Americans call us oral cultures, but my cousin Sakej, responsible for my first and my ongoing education, says we are listening cultures. Not just listening to stories, either, though they are of utmost significance.

*

Listening. With my poetry, I try to listen, not to speak. And its creation is uniquely its own. I just listen to the world. And I watch. I think of Nobel laureate Barbara McClintock listening to corn plants, knowing them

intimately, learning gene transposition in this manner and receiving recognition from the scientific community, who had a different manner of study. There again is the importance in understanding our place in the world, the kind of knowledge humans carry, the humble creatures we are in this small planet in the universe. Sometimes I think of this process, like all processes at work, as magic. Where it comes from is a mystery. The first image, word, and then the unfolding that sometimes takes years for one poem to become whole. The stories.

*

I'd like to return to the circumstances of *Sightings: The Mysterious Journey of The Gray Whale,* and its origins: One day, working on the anthology *Intimate Nature: The Bond between Women and Animals,* I was kayaking with Brenda Peterson, and we were having a wonderful day watching spinner dolphins when we heard a breath behind us. It was a humpback, so close, so large, all we could do was watch and cry and say, "My God," knowing we were seeing something sacred from the ocean realm. She looked at us, we at her. We were so close.

We left the whale after a while, worried that we were bothering her, and watched her from land. Several hours later, she gave birth and a tiny spume erupted from the water, a small whale surfaced with the mother, sleek, then they headed away. This poem is to Brenda who took me to dolphins and whales:

WHALE RISING

> Breath. Behind us.
> Milk creature, she has navigated the world
> by whale map, this ancient mother,
> and we see ourselves
> inside the large dark eyes
> that takes our human measure,
> and there is nothing to hide behind,
> history unspeakable.
>
> What moves the waves we cannot see,
> nor can we know what moves a whale
> to rise upward to the daughters of her enemies
> except for faith in air,
> and we sit in the boat for hours now,

blown by mystery that, like all mystery,
could sink or drown us,
but it doesn't.

Beneath water is the blue, infinite
light from the bottom of ocean.
No one returns from there unchanged
by everything larger, that dark eye
that fixed us in its gaze, the clouds
behind us, the wind-breath of a stormy world,
the exquisite smell of fish and krill
from inside a great life.

I want you to know they are beautiful,
the songs from beneath this world,
rising up from water
as we sit in the boat,
held in the fold of its song,
lost in the mist of its breath.

*

Not long after this we received a call from elder women of a Northwest tribe wanting to talk to us about their protest of a whale hunt. As it turned out, we wrote a series for the *Seattle Times* on the Makah whale hunt. But who could not have done it after looking into the eye of the whale?

*

This took me to the world not only of politics, global, national, and Native, but of cetaceons. I had already been in the world of American Indian politics, having worked at the Denver Indian Center and done some work for my own tribe, so I knew what I was in for, and I felt old enough and courageous enough to take it on. As I said earlier, I am traditional. I have a traditional mind and feel there needs to be an ethical voice.

Then, too, I had to learn science. I began my self-education in marine biology and Native history along the West Coast. I tell people I should have a degree in marine biology for all the research I did, but together we wrote this book and for many years we followed the journey of the whales. I studied the ocean environment while she, more extroverted, did the above ground work, interviews, recent events, and stories. I again chose the beneath, the small, the hidden: I

studied the ocean floor, plankton, diatoms, kelp forests, the Indian and European history of the coast, the prehistory and the tragedy of the whaling industry. Here is a brief excerpt: *The life of a gray whale consists of the small and minute. If you could see diatoms with the naked eye, they would look like houses of crystal, boxes with exquisite patterns. Their formation is one of the mysteries of the earth. Beautiful, shapely, at times some of them form a film over the bodies of gray whales and make the skin of the whale shine luminescent in the dark so that its passages north are covered in beauty in a floating world both delicate and powerful.*

The opportunity to follow the migration of whales and their ancient history as land animals having evolved into the ocean was a journey of many kinds. We followed whales from Baja to the Bering Sea. We recounted the relationship of tribes to whale, but also the biology and world beneath the sea. I wanted early in my life to be a biologist or a veterinarian, to look at the secrets of life. Yet, as a writer I have been able to do this. I live with a Horse Rescue horse and a wild mustang. I've worked in the magnificent presence of eagles, hawks, owls, even once a fawn. I have given showers to young swans shot by duck hunters, healing in wildlife clinics. After many years I still love this work, its own diversity from a woman diverse. Writing means taking risks and searching my way into them, trying to have them come out right, knowing there is a chance it may not.

At the same time there is the rest of life. Living is a large thing. Someone once said, "What are you most proud of?" and I said working with birds. They meant my writing, but I had spent eight years working with wildlife, and the last six was with raptors. That was what I felt best about in my life. Though it was not something they expected, at the time, it was where I felt I offered the most to the world, gave the most.

But now, from the feedback I receive, I think it is the writing. I learned, in large part teaching myself, how to write in order to convey the intelligence and suffering of the world, to pass on the love of life in all its forms, word by word, sentence by sentence.

*

All of the American landscape is "storied" land. I think writer and ethnobotanist Gary Nabhan now uses this word, also. But the land and its stories are known by those who lived here for at least ten thousand years, in some places thirty. In the north where the names of towns and places have been overlaid with European names, they are taking back the traditional ones. I like it: The Place Where the White Crow Walked, The Creator's Elbow. The land has great amounts of information and scientific knowledge attached to it by the First Nations peoples who had treaties with the land and animals.

I think of my work, in part, as a return to this. It is the creation of true, unseen bonds, filaments of connection with the world, revelations. I come from America in a way many American writers don't. I want to carry, without diminishing, without appropriating, our knowledge into the present world. For the sake of life and the future. I still carry the cells of those dispossessed Chickasaws who touched the trees, saying good-bye on the night before their leaving.

*

Because of this, my work rises out of the American earth and water. It is rooted in traditional indigenous traditions, and I try to open this world of indigenous philosophy and knowledge into the pages of a book. With this language I want to reestablish the bonds that have been broken. Those that are spiritual, those that are compassionate.

As an American-Indian writer, my work comes from the magnificence of this continent, the earth, the language of the land, largely unheard, too often overlooked by the new people on this continent who have a worldview that does not show humans in place with the rest of nature. Whose world, even here, is still based on a European Venus, Mars, astronomy from only one mythology laid down upon even the universe. The oldest literatures are not nearly as old as the indigenous literatures, some known to be twenty thousand years old. And part of the sadness of this is that we have all been wounded by Western philosophy and a culture that has feared or hated the natural world, or at least not known and understood it, and too often has yet to hear the voice of the land. But I can also see the fear that arrived with the Europeans, the wilderness they no longer had, the power of the land, the threat, even imagined, of the animal world.

*

I believe if I have any success in my work it has to do with that traditional mind, because I hope it adds one

new dimension in our vision of the world, our awareness, even our own constellations of swimming ducks, snake, buffalo. There are many dimensions in this world. More than three. And dimensions, as we know, are many, varied, significant. One day, I was at a conference on medicinal plants at the birthplace of Chief Seattle and went walking along the water of the island.

Dimensions

> How is it decided
> who among us has hands,
> gill slits, who will gather up
> a small thing
> waiting too far from the ocean
> to be alive or return
> with the kelp and its bulbs of gold,
> and the creature we see almost through,
> see in the light of morning
> among the many baleful closures of the ocean.
>
> How is it decided
> who will gather up the small thing
> seemingly lifeless
> and return it to water as its grave
> only to watch it slowly open;
> jelly fish like a pulse,
> a robe of orange splendor
> in the finery of ocean creation.
>
> I see the wave, with a curve of light,
> the force of it, one after another,
> not wondering if it is the ocean.
> I see the infinite pastures of the water
> some with the newly born, some
> with the just as newly gone.
>
> Here is a place of sliding worlds,
> the birthplace of Chief Seattle
> whose people he said would always be
> among those with bodies.
> And how is it decided who has dominion
> of the flesh
> to pass through unseen
> or on its way to being
> spirit,
> forgetting the brief distances in time
>
> I don't know who lives here,
> if they are happy
> in that slide of cells

that created and birthed them
or who is it that decided who has hands,
who can speak
who is light?

*

As it has turned out in my life, my writing is larger than I am, and I have to grow into it. I am the root. It is the trunk, the flowers, the leaves. I am still a beginning, still growing into it. I have always followed the writing, rather than using my mind, my thought. I consider the mind as something that contains lesser knowledge than the rest of me. Knowledge isn't the right word. Knowing, I should say. "Truthing," my cousins calls it. We are just humans. We are humble. In our own place. Only a part of all the rest. With writing there is a way to make a balance between the head and the heart, to put it in place. I am able to convey what we thought, and to learn what we knew, as well as knowing the new world, new systems of thought.

Whatever is inside me that beckons me to write is the wind in the trees, the green light and shadows on the road. It is looking in the eyes of my grandchildren. The long light of summer, the brief light of winter, the life that resides in matter, the opening of leaf, the earth rich with turtles laying eggs, lizards and egrets. Not only the five senses, but the feeling of the land itself, as if there is cellular knowledge and understanding and exchange with the world: *Tonight I walk. I am watching the sky. I think of the people who came before me and how they knew the placement of stars in the sky, watched the moving sun long and hard enough to witness how a certain angle of light touched a stone only once a year. Without written records, they knew the gods of every night, the small fine details of the world around them and of immensity above.*

Walking, I can almost hear the redwoods beating. And the oceans are above me here, rolling clouds heavy and dark, considering snow. On the dry, red road, I pass the place of the sunflower, that dark and secret location where creation took place. I wonder if it will return this summer, if it will multiply and move up to the other stand of flowers in a territorial struggle.

It's winter and there is smoke from the fires. The square, lighted windows of houses are fogging over. It is a world of elemental attention, of all things working

together, listening to what speaks in the blood. Whichever road I follow, I walk in the land of many gods, and they love and eat one another. Walking, I am listening to a deeper way. Suddenly all my ancestors are behind me. Be still, they say. Watch and listen. You are the result of the love of thousands. (From *Dwellings: A Spiritual History of the Natural World*)

BIOGRAPHICAL AND CRITICAL SOURCES:

BOOKS

Contemporary Women Poets, St. James Press (Detroit, MI), 1997.

Cotelli, Laura, *Winged Words: American Indian Writers Speak,* University of Nebraska Press (Lincoln, NE), 1990.

Dictionary of Literary Biography, Volume 175: *Native American Writers of the United States,* Gale (Detroit, MI), 1997.

Hogan, Linda, *Eclipse,* foreword by Kenneth Lincoln, American Indian Studies Center, University of California (Los Angeles, CA), 1983.

This Is about Vision: Interviews with Southwestern Writers, University of New Mexico Press (Albuquerque, NM), 1990.

PERIODICALS

American Indian Quarterly, summer, 1998, Joe Staples, review of *Solar Storms,* p. 397.

Belles Lettres, January, 1996, Bettina Berch, review of *Solar Storms,* p. 13.

Bloomsbury Review, November-December, 1993, Carl L. Bankston, review of *The Book of Medicines;* September-October, 1995, Liz Caile, review of *Dwellings: A Spiritual History of the Living World.*

Booklist, August, 1995, Donna Seaman, review of *Dwellings,* p. 1914; September 15, 1995, Donna Seaman, review of *Solar Storms,* p. 142; May 1, 1998, Donna Seaman, review of *Power,* p. 1501; January 1, 2000, Bill Ott, review of *Power,* p. 987; December 15, 2000, Donna Seaman, review of *Power,* p. 787; February 1, 2001, Donna Seaman, review of *The Sweet Breathing of Plants: Women Writing on the Green World,* p. 1031; May 15, 2001, Donna Seaman, review of *The Woman Who Watches over the World: A Native Memoir,* p. 1723; January 1, 2002, review of *The Woman Who*

Watches over the World, p. 756, p. 763; August, 2002, Nancy Bent, review of *Sightings: The Gray Whales' Mysterious Journey*, p. 1902.

Choice, June, 1986, p. 1508; April, 1989, p. 1328.

E, January-February, 2002, A. M. Wilborn, review of *The Sweet Breathing of Plants*, p. 60.

English Journal, March, 1994, p. 100.

Explorations in Sights and Sounds, summer, 1985.

Herizons, fall, 1999, review of *Power*, pp. 34-35.

Journal of Ethnic Studies, spring, 1988, pp. 107-117.

Kirkus Reviews, June 15, 1995, p. 835; August 15, 1995, p. 1132.

Kliatt, July, 2002, Edna M. Boardman, review of *The Woman Who Watches over the World*, p. 35.

Library Journal, January, 1998, Joan S. Elbers, review of *Intimate Nature: The Bond between Women and Animals*, p. 132; January 1, 2001, Sue O'Brien, review of *The Sweet Breathing of Plants*, p. 150; June 1, 2001, Sue Samson, review of *The Woman Who Watches over the World*, p. 174.

Los Angeles Times, November 4, 1990, p. B3.

Los Angeles Times Book Review, July 30, 1995, p. 6; January 21, 1996, Susan Heeger, review of *Solar Storms*, p. 2.

Ms., March-April, 1994, p. 70; November-December, 1995, p. 91.

New York Times Book Review, February 24, 1991, Joseph A. Cincotti, review of *Mean Spirit*, p. 28; November 26, 1995, Maggie Garb, review of *Solar Storms*, p. 19.

Publishers Weekly, August 3, 1990, review of *Mean Spirit*, pp. 63-64; June 26, 1995, review of *Dwellings*, p. 101; August 28, 1995, review of *Solar Storms*, p. 104; December 1, 1997, review of *Intimate Nature*, p. 42; April 20, 1998, review of *Power*, p. 48; January 1, 2001, review of *The Sweet Breathing of Plants*, p. 81; May 21, 2001, review of *The Woman Who Watches over the World*, p. 92.

School Library Journal, April, 1991, Lynda Voyles, review of *Mean Spirit*, pp. 153-154.

Studies in American Indian Literature, spring, 1994, pp. 83-98; fall (special Hogan issue), 1994.

Voice Literary Supplement, November, 1993, Robyn Selman, review of *The Book of Medicines*, p. 8.

Washington Post, December 6, 1990, p. D3.

Women's Review of Books, February, 1996, Heid E. Erdrich, review of *Dwellings* and *Solar Storms*, p. 11; July, 1998, Jacqueline Shea Murphy, review of *Power*, pp. 41-42.

World Literature Today, spring, 1994, Robert L. Berner, review of *The Book of Medicines*, pp. 407-408; fall, 1996, Robert L. Berner, review of *Solar Storms*, p. 1007.

HOPKINS, (Morris) Keith 1934-2004

OBITUARY NOTICE—See index for *CA* sketch: Born June 20, 1934, in London, England; died of cancer March 8, 2004, in Cambridge, England. Historian, sociologist, educator, and author. Hopkins uniquely combined his knowledge of sociology with the discipline of history to form theories about life in ancient Rome. Studying the classics at King's College, Cambridge, he completed his master's degree in 1961, and was working on a doctorate before deciding to leave university to accept a post at Leicester University as a junior lecturer. He quickly moved on to the London School of Economics, which assigned him to a post in Hong Kong. One result of his time in China was his editorship of the 1971 book *Hong Kong: The Industrial Colony*. Hopkins also studied population density in London, and the combination of his sociological research in China and London helped broaden his views on his main field of interest: Roman history. Moving on to Brunel University at the London School of Economics in 1972, he was a professor of sociology there and also, in 1981, was named dean of studies. Continuing his research at the Institute of Classical Studies in London around the same time, Hopkins found success with his next publication, the two-volume *Sociological Studies in Roman History* (1978, 1983). In these two books, *Conquerors and Slaves* and *Death and Renewal*, Hopkins devised startling theories about Roman Senate membership and other aspects of Roman life. Hopkins would later become controversial for drawing on fictional narrative by Roman authors such as Apeuleius and the fables of Aesop to speculate on Roman culture, but he drew even greater criticism from historians for his *A World Full of Gods: The Strange Triumph of Christianity* (1999) in which he created his own fictional narrative to discuss classical history. Retiring from teaching in 2000, Hopkins remained active in academia as vice provost for King's College from 2001 until his death. He was, at the time, working on a book about the Colosseum.

OBITUARIES AND OTHER SOURCES:

PERIODICALS

Chicago Tribune, March 16, 2004, Section 2, p. 12.

Los Angeles Times, March 16, 2004, p. B11.

New York Times, March 15, 2004, p. A23.

Times (London, England), March 25, 2004.

HOPPER, Kim

PERSONAL: Male. *Education:* Earned Ph.D.

ADDRESSES: Office—Nathan S. Kline Institute for Psychiatric Research, 140 Old Orangeburg Rd., Orangeburg, NY 10962; fax: 845-398-5510. *E-mail*—Hopper@nki.rfmh.org.

CAREER: Nathan S. Kline Institute for Psychiatric Research, Orangeburg, NY, research scientist; Columbia University School of Public Health and Law, New York, NY, lecturer.

WRITINGS:

(With Ellen Baxter) *Private Lives/Public Spaces: Homeless Adults on the Streets of New York City,* Community Service Society, Institute for Social Welfare Research (New York, NY), 1981.
(With others) *One Year Later: The Homeless Poor in New York City, 1982,* Community Service Society, Institute for Social Welfare Research (New York, NY), 1982.
(With Jill Hamberg) *The Making of America's Homeless: From Skid Row to New Poor,* Community Service Society, Institute for Social Welfare Research (New York, NY), 1984.
(With Baxter and Dan Salerno) *Hardship in the Heartland: Homelessness in Eight U.S. Cities,* Community Service Society, Institute for Social Welfare Research (New York, NY), 1984.
(With Mervyn Susser and William Watson) *Sociology in Medicine,* 3rd edition, Oxford University Press (New York, NY), 1985.
(Editor with others) *Recovery from Schizophrenia: An International Perspective,* PsychoSocial Press (Madison, CT), 2003.
Reckoning with Homelessness, Cornell University Press (Ithaca, NY), 2003.
(With Ernest Cook) *Conservation Finance Handbook,* 2004.

Contributor to *New York Review of Books.*

BIOGRAPHICAL AND CRITICAL SOURCES:

PERIODICALS

City Limits, July-August, 2003, Bob Roberts, review of *Reckoning with Homelessness.*

Library Journal, March 15, 2003, review of *Reckoning with Homelessness.*
Washington Post Book World, April 6, 2003, review of *Reckoning with Homelessness.*

ONLINE

Mental Help Net, http://mentalhelp.net/ (June 5, 2003), Diana Pederson, review of *Reckoning with Homelessness.**

*   *   *

HUFF, Brent 1961-

PERSONAL: Born 1961.

ADDRESSES: Home—2203 Ridgemont Dr, Los Angeles, CA 90046.

CAREER:

Actor, director, and screenwriter. Director of films, including *One Hundred Mile Rule.* Actor in films, including (as Keith) *Coach,* Crown International Pictures, 1978; (as Willard) *The Perils of Gwendoline in the Land of the Yik Yak* (also known as *Gwendoline* and *The Perils of Gwendoline*), Samuel Goldwyn Company, 1984; (as Steve Gordon) *Nine Deaths of the Ninja,* Cannon Films, 1985; (as Sam Black) *Deadly Passion,* 1986; (as Tommy Roth) *Armed Response* (also known as *Jade Jungle*), Cintel Films, 1986; (as Zar) *Stormquest,* 1987; (as Morgan) *Cop Game,* 1988; *Strike Commando 2,* 1989; (as Sam Wood) *Born to Fight,* 1989; *Sulle tracce del condor* (also known as *Condor*), 1990; (as Parker Parks) *Falling from Grace,* Columbia, 1992; (as Red) *We the People,* 1994; (as Tinkercrank) *Tinkercrank,* 1995; (as Long John) *Oblivion 2: Backlash* (also known as *Backlash: Oblivion 2*), Full Moon, 1996; *Final Justice,* 1996; (as Agent Adams) *Dead Tides,* Live Entertainment, 1997; (as Till) *Scorpio One,* 1997; (as Bobby Joe) *Girls' Night,* 1998; *Defiance* (short film), 1998; (as Callin) *The Bad Pack,* Avalanche Home Entertainment, 1998; (as Randall Garrett) *Hitman's Run,* Avalanche Home Entertainment, 1999; (as Officer Mack) *Hot Boyz,* Artisan Entertainment, 1999; (as David Anderson)

Hijack (also known as *The Last Siege*), Hallmark Entertainment, 1999; (as Miss Illinois local pageant host) *Beautiful,* Destination Films, 2000; (as Mack) *Submerged,* New City Releasing, 2000; and (as Shane) *Final Exam,* 2003.

Actor in made-for-television movies, including (as Samuels) *Summer Fantasy,* National Broadcasting Company, Inc. (NBC), 1984; (as Georg) *Tierarztin Christine,* 1993; (as Werner Sternbach-Stolze) *Das Paradies am Ende der Berge,* 1993; (as Birnbaum) *Der Blaue Diamant* (also known as *Hunt for the Blue Diamond*), 1993; (as Tilden) *I Spy Returns,* Columbia Broadcasting System, Inc. (CBS), 1994; *Der schwarze Fluch—Todliche Leidenschaften,* 1994; and (as Lawrence Brendt) *Hollywood Confidential,* UPN, 1997. Played Adam Burns and Inferno in the television series *Black Scorpion,* 2001; guest starred as Steve "Psycho" Kessick in the television series *Pensacola: Wings of Gold,* syndicated, 1998-99.

WRITINGS:

SCREENPLAYS

(With Douglas L. Walton) *The Bad Pack,* Avalanche Home Entertainment, 1998.

Also author of *We the People,* 1994; *Final Justice,* 1996; *Defiance* (short film), 1998; with Adrian Fulle and Douglas L. Walton, *Power Play,* 2002; and, with Titus Llangort, Robert Tiffe, and Douglas L. Walton, *Face of Terror,* 2003.

BIOGRAPHICAL AND CRITICAL SOURCES:

BOOKS

Contemporary Theatre, Film and Television, Volume 37, Gale (Detroit, MI), 2002.

PERIODICALS

Hollywood Reporter, October 8, 2002, Marilyn Moss, review of *One Hundred Mile Rule,* p. 94.
Interview, September, 1985, "Actors, Agents, Atmosphere," pp. 56-80.

New York Times, January 27, 1985, Janet Maslin, review of *Gwendoline,* pp. 22, 30.
Rolling Stone, March 5, 1992, Peter Travers, review of *Falling from Grace,* p. 78.
Variety, February 22, 1984, review of *Gwendoline,* p. 18; June 26, 1985, review of *Deadly Passion,* p. 18; October 8, 1986, review of *Armed Response,* p. 21; February 24, 1992, Amy Dawes, review of *Falling from Grace,* pp. 247-248.

ONLINE

American Cinema International, http://new.aci-americancinema.com/ (April 11, 2003), synopsis of *Face of Terror.*
Cold Fusion Video Reviews, http://www.coldfusion video.com/ (April 11, 2003), Nathan Shumate, review of *The Bad Pack.*
Fort Lauderdale International Film Festival, http://www.fliff.com/ (April 11, 2003), synopsis of *One Hundred Mile Rule.*
Hollywood.com, http://www.hollywood.com/ (April 11, 2003), information about *The Bad Pack.*
Internet Movie Database, http://www.imdb.com/ (April 10, 2003), "Brent Huff."
Minneapolis/Saint Paul International Film Festival, http://www.ufilm.org/ (April 11, 2003), synopsis of *One Hundred Mile Rule.*
United Film Partners, Inc., http://www.unitedfilm partners.com/ (April 11, 2003), information about *We the People.**

*   *   *

HUSER, Glen 1943-

PERSONAL: Born February 1, 1943, in Elk Point, Alberta, Canada; son of Harry (a carpenter and craftsman) and Beatrice (a teacher; maiden name, Daily) Huser; children: Casey Lawrence Huser (deceased). *Ethnicity:* "Norwegian/Irish-American." *Education:* Vancouver School of Art, second year qualification, 1965; University of Alberta, B.Ed. (with distinction), 1970, M.A., 1988.

ADDRESSES: Home—6012 Ada Blvd., Edmonton, Alberta T5W 4N9, Canada. *E-mail*—glenh@planet.eon. net.

CAREER: Teacher, educational consultant, and writer. Teacher at Rosslyn and Highlands Schools, 1962-65; McArthur School, 1967-69; and librarian, Holyrood, Lendrum, Homesteader, Kirkness, and Overlanders Schools, 1970-88. Learning Resources, Edmonton Public Schools, consultant, 1988-96; Concordia College, student teaching advisor, 1997-98; University of Alberta, sessional instructor, 1997-98, 1999-2000, and 2003-2004; Oz New Media/Education-on-line, language arts resource writer, 2000-01. Writer-in-residence, Mee-Yah-Noh Elementary School, 2001-02, and Virginia Park Elementary School, 2003-04. Leader of workshops and conference sessions at various schools and education conventions.

MEMBER: Children's Literature Roundtable (executive member, 1979-99), Young Alberta Book Society (president, 1990-95), Writers' Guild of Alberta.

AWARDS, HONORS: Edmonton Journal Literary Awards, 1974, for short fiction, 1979, for poetry, and 1980, for one-act play; Wilfrid R. May scholarship for career development, 1986; Award of Merit, Learning Resources Council ATA (Greater Edmonton Regional); Staff Service Award, Edmonton Public Schools, 1996, for services provided by the *Magpie* editorial committee; Governor General's Literary Award (for text), Canada Council, 2003, for *Stitches.*

WRITINGS:

Grace Lake (for adults), NeWest Press (Edmonton, Alberta, Canada), 1990.
Touch of the Clown, Groundwood (Toronto, Ontario, Canada), 1999.
Jeremy's Christmas Wish, illustrated by Martin Rose, Hodgepog (Vancouver, British Columbia, Canada), 2000.
Stitches, Groundwood (Toronto, Ontario, Canada), 2003.

Contributor of short stories to anthologies, including *Boundless Alberta,* NeWest Press (Edmonton, Alberta, Canada), 1993, and periodicals, including *Dandelion* and *Prism International;* contributor to "Nelson Mini-Anthology" series for teens. *Magpie* (a magazine of student writing and graphics), initiator and managing editor, 1978-96; *Edmonton Journal,* Edmonton, Alberta, Canada, reviewer of children's books, 1982-2001; Hodgepog Books, editor for the series "Novels for Beginning Readers," 1996-99.

SIDELIGHTS: Glen Huser once commented: "I believe that, almost from the time I was able to hold a pencil, I was drawing pictures, and, once the school in the hamlet where I began my education revealed the treasures unlocked through literacy, I was reading and writing stories. My dad was an artist and skilled craftsman (woodwork, metal engraving, scrimshaw on bone); my mother wrote poetry and stories and has maintained a diary since she was a teenager; an aunt (more, in age, like an older sister), lived in a nest of paper, crayons, and watercolors, to which all children were invited. Although I never realized it at the time, how blessed I was to grow up in such an environment!

"When my family moved to Edmonton in 1959, I finished high school and began the studies that would secure me a job as a teacher. But my loves remained drawing, painting, and writing. Other loves were plays and films, to which I now had access. Every spare moment I had, when I wasn't reading or drawing, I was lost in the cheap seats of local theaters or the dark balconies of second-run movie palaces, discovering all the films I'd missed growing up in Ashmont where, for most of my life, movies were shown once a week, on Saturday night, by a traveling projectionist at the Legion Hall. Often I'd rush home from a double feature to watch the midnight movie on television— another addition to my cultural life since moving to the city. Once I began teaching, I wangled myself a second job with a local magazine as their film critic.

"Watching films, I secretly longed to be Anthony Perkins or Robert Redford. The photograph at the top of my movie column was a recurring reminder that mine was not a face to launch a film, though, and I found myself thinking of that other dream: the dream of becoming a writer. It was a dream that settled over me whenever I was stirred by something I read, books such as Steinbeck's *East of Eden* or Carson McCullers' *The Heart Is a Lonely Hunter.* As I returned to university to complete my education degree, I sought out creative writing options, and, in the early 1970s, I enrolled in a course taught by the great Canadian novelist W. O. Mitchell. It was a course that changed my life. Through what he termed a 'free fall' method, Mitchell taught us to plumb our own life experiences for material that we could eventually transform into fiction. It was a system that worked for me. Before long, my writing was winning competitions and my short stories were appearing in Canadian literary magazines.

"My first novel, *Grace Lake,* drew on my own experiences attending summer church camps as a teenager.

When I crafted *Touch of the Clown,* a novel for young adults, I drew on my knowledge, gleaned over years of teaching, in which, sadly, I had encountered a few children growing up in situations of neglect and abuse. At the same time, *Touch of the Clown* paid homage to a caring artist modeled somewhat on a personal friend, Nion, who had starred as a clown in Stratford, Halifax's Neptune Theater, and Edmonton's Citadel. The father in the book is an old movie fanatic. Guess where that came from!"

Touch of the Clown is the story of two sisters named after old movie stars, twelve-year-old Barbara Stanwyck Kobleimer and six-year-old Olivia de Havilland. Their two caretakers, their father and grandmother, spend their days drinking and watching movies on the VCR, leaving Barbara to care for Livvy and the house. Barbara's life improves when the girls meet Cosmo Farber, an actor who is teaching a clowning workshop for teenagers. Cosmo gives the girls books to read, talks Barbara into taking his clown class, and provides a sympathetic ear for her to talk about her problems. The constant stream of old movies in her home provides Barbara with much material to work with, and with Cosmo's help, she shines in the workshop. However, Cosmo is dying of AIDS, and when Barbara's father finds out that she is taking the workshop, he beats her because of it; but with her newfound strength, Barbara reports her father, and she and Livvy are taken into foster care. "Young teens will find it easy to sympathize with Barbara, to admire her loyalty and acceptance of responsibility, and to root for her as she tries to find a space for herself," Betty McDougal commented in *Resource Links.* Other reviewers praised Huser's writing style. Paula E. Kirman wrote in the *Edmonton Journal* that Huser "has created a novel that is realistically moving in simple, elegant prose," while *Voice of Youth Advocates* contributor Julie Roberts termed it "a beautifully-written story with a heartwarming conclusion that will satisfy its readers."

Huser continued: "My love for drama and film is also evident in my next book, *Jeremy's Christmas Wish,* a holiday novel for younger readers. In this story, a wealthy eight-year-old's Yuletide boredom is allayed by watching horror movies and, eventually, playing the part of the scary Christmas-Yet-to-Come in a version of Dickens's *A Christmas Carol* put on by newfound friends in a harum-scarum family from the other side of the tracks.

"In *Stitches,* my next young adult novel, teenaged Travis pursues a passion for puppetry and sewing that sets him at odds with a group of school bullies who have dogged his heels since fifth grade. Once again, I brought my own love of literature and drama to the story—this time by interweaving elements from *Peter Pan* and a *Midsummer Night's Dream* into the plot. Other, darker elements came from current newspaper headlines and accounts of the tragic dimensions of bullying that still exist in our society."

Stitches "might . . . be called an 'issues' novel, but it's one in which character, feeling, and social ill are fully realized," wrote Dierdre Baker in the *Toronto Star.* Travis endures endless harassment from other children in his school and small rural town because of his typically feminine hobbies. However, he and his motley band of supporters do not fall into stereotypical roles, and while the increasing brutality of the attacks on Travis supply "the book with tension and a conscience, the real story is the friendship between the two outsiders and their marshaling of forces within themselves, each other, and their families to keep going," wrote Roger Sutton in *Horn Book.* The other outsider, Travis's best friend, is Chantelle, who suffers from medical conditions that have warped her face and body. Other supporters include Chantelle's older brothers, who, despite generally being cut from the same macho mold as Travis's tormenters, have no problem with the effeminate boy; Travis's aunt Kitaleen, with whom he lives; and two caring teachers. Writing in *Resource Links,* critic Elaine Rospad thought that Huser "has captured the thoughts, feelings, and actions of young people as they move through the teen years."

"What advice might I give to aspiring writers?" Huser once asked. "I would urge you to practice writing, as W. O. Mitchell had us doing, from our own experience and from the heart. Write often and with full sensory detail. What do you remember? What do you recall seeing, hearing, touching, tasting, smelling? Bring your own passions and preoccupations to your writing (as I do with film, drama, and our heritage of literature in my own writing). No one knows these passions better than you. And, lastly—read. Read widely from books on a shelf where you can envision your own books being placed one day. By reading widely, you will learn style and pacing and ways of developing character and setting, ways of allowing plot to unfold. The books you love will prove to be the best of all creative-writing schools."

BIOGRAPHICAL AND CRITICAL SOURCES:

PERIODICALS

Edmonton Journal (Edmonton, Alberta, Canada), April, 1999, Paula E. Kirman, review of *Touch of the Clown.*

Horn Book, November-December, 2003, Roger Sutton, review of *Stitches,* p. 748.

Junior Library Guild, April-September, 1999, review of *Touch of the Clown,* p. 43.

Quill & Quire, March, 1999, Annette Goldsmith, review of *Touch of the Clown.*

Resource Links, June, 1999, Betty McDougal, review of *Touch of the Clown,* p. 23; February, 2004, Elaine Rospad, review of *Stitches,* p. 34.

School Library Journal, December, 2003, Lisa Prolman, review of *Stitches,* p. 152.

Toronto Star (Toronto, Ontario, Canada), October 26, 2003, Dierdre Baker, review of *Stitches.*

Voice of Youth Advocates, October, 1999, Julie Roberts, review of *Touch of the Clown.*

*   *   *

HUTCHINSON, Timothy A. 1960-

PERSONAL: Born November 18, 1960, in St. Paul, MN; married Jennifer Sturm (a high school teacher and administrator), April 4, 1992; children: Victoria, Alexander, Brittany, Vanessa. *Ethnicity:* "Caucasian."

ADDRESSES: Agent—c/o Author Mail, Riverstone Publishing, P.O. Box 270852, St. Paul, MN 55127. *E-mail*—contact@americanyouth.net.

CAREER: Writer. Also works as emergency medical technician.

WRITINGS:

Battlescars (autobiography), Riverstone Publishing (St. Paul, MN), 2003.

Author of articles on the prevention of teen violence.

WORK IN PROGRESS: Books about preventing violence; ghost-writing a biography of a millionaire; research on the school shooting in Columbine, CO.

SIDELIGHTS: Timothy A. Hutchinson told *CA:* "I was stopped on the way to attacking my high school with an assault rifle, then spent years on the wrong side of the law, always one step from prison or the grave. My first book, *Battlescars,* is the shocking true story of my battle against gangs, firearms, drugs, the Ku Klux Klan, and more. In it I detail all the violence that surrounded me, all the hate that consumed me, and how I turned it all around and survived. Fortunately I am now happily married with children, an emergency medical technician credited with saving two lives, and an expert on teen violence."

I-J

IAGNEMMA, Karl 1972-

PERSONAL: Born October 19, 1972, in MI. *Education:* University of Michigan, B.S., 1994, Massachusetts Institute of Technology, M.S., 1997, Ph.D. (mechanical engineering), 2001.

ADDRESSES: Office—Department of Mechanical Engineering, Massachusetts Institute of Technology, 77 Massachusetts Ave., Cambridge, MA 02139-4307. *E-mail*—kdi@mit.edu.

CAREER: Massachusetts Institute of Technology, Cambridge, MA, research scientist.

AWARDS, HONORS: Paris Review Discovery Prize; Pushcart Prize; *Playboy* college fiction prize; Massachusetts Cultural Council artist grant.

WRITINGS:

On the Nature of Human Romantic Interaction (short stories), Dial (New York, NY), 2003.

Work anthologized in *Best American Short Stories.* Contributor of stories to *Tin House, SEED, One Story,* and *Zoetrope.*

WORK IN PROGRESS: A novel about a nineteenth-century scientific expedition.

SIDELIGHTS: Karl Iagnemma's collection of short stories, *On the Nature of Human Romantic Interaction,* tells of characters who are involved in scientific pursuits and who hope to use scientific methods to further their understanding of personal relations. Iagnemma himself combines the role of an academic research scientist—he specializes in robotics—with that of a writer of literary fiction. "These disparate aspects of his personality work together; he seamlessly blends the lyrical and the precise to create gemlike little portraits of individuals," according to Barbara Hoffert in *Library Journal.*

All of the stories in *On the Nature of Human Romantic Interaction* demonstrate the impossibility of applying scientific precision to human emotions. In the collection's title story, Joseph, an engineering school dropout, hopes to marry his ex-advisor's daughter, a woman engaged in sexual relationships with several men and not interested in changing her ways. Joseph works out a mathematical equation he hopes will explain to him the nature of his romantic relationship, but the equation ultimately fails him. In "The Phrenologist's Dream" a nineteenth-century phrenologist tours the Midwest, examining the skulls of the rural folks he meets, convinced that the shape of a person's skull holds the key to that person's personality. When he falls in love with a bald woman, she makes him rethink his theory of human nature in an unsuspected manner. Both of these stories, Jim Holt wrote in the *New York Times,* are "richly imagined and laced with delicate ironies." Speaking of the collection as a whole, James Klise, writing in *Booklist,* called the works "intelligent, quirky, and suspenseful." A critic for *Kirkus Reviews* found that "Iagnemma's prose is always lively, well suited to the quirky characters and odd subjects he tends toward."

Iagnemma explained in a statement posted at his Web site: "Many people view science as a chilly, rational exploration of facts, but scientific discovery is often shaped by emotion. Jealousy, fear, and desire can play as much a role in research as quiet contemplation. I wanted to write about people who long to uncover the mysteries of science, which are so often entangled with their own lives and the lives of people around them."

BIOGRAPHICAL AND CRITICAL SOURCES:

PERIODICALS

Booklist, April 15, 2003, James Klise, review of *On the Nature of Human Romantic Interaction,* p. 1449.
Kirkus Reviews, March 1, 2003, review of *On the Nature of Human Romantic Interaction,* p. 335.
Library Journal, April 1, 2003, Barbara Hoffert, review of *On the Nature of Human Romantic Interaction,* pp. 132-133.
New York Times, May 18, 2003, Jim Holt, review of *On the Nature of Human Romantic Interaction.*
Publishers Weekly, April 21, 2003, review of *On the Nature of Human Romantic Interaction,* p. 40.

ONLINE

Karl Iagnemma Home Page, http://www. karliagnemma.com/ (October 1, 2003).*

*   *   *

INGRAM, Heather E(lizabeth) 1969-

PERSONAL: Born 1969, in Canada. *Education:* Simon Fraser University, B.A. (business administration); University of British Columbia, degree in education.

ADDRESSES: Home—Gibsons, British Columbia, Canada. *Agent*—c/o Author Mail, Greystone Books, Douglas & McIntyre Publishing Group, Suite 201, 2323 Quebec St., Vancouver, British Columbia V5T 4S7, Canada.

CAREER: Educator, office administrator, and author. Chatelech High School, Sechelt, British Columbia, Canada, math, business, and accounting teacher, 1994-99; worked as a math tutor and an office administrator for a British Columbia environmental consulting firm. Has appeared on radio and television shows, including *Oprah.*

WRITINGS:

Risking It All: My Student, My Lover, My Story, Greystone Press (Toronto, Ontario, Canada), 2003.

SIDELIGHTS: In 1999 British Columbia secondary school mathematics teacher Heather E. Ingram, age twenty-nine, became a celebrity of sorts when news broke that she had been having a sexual relationship with a seventeen-year-old student. While Ingram's ethical judgment was quickly called into question, the Canadian criminal courts had their say also, and in March of 2000, she was sentenced to ten months under house arrest after being convicted of sexual exploitation. Ingram, who has ended her teaching career and returned to work in business administration, decided to publish her account of the relationship, and in 2003 *Risking It All: My Student, My Lover, My Story* appeared on bookstore shelves.

Risking It All met with a mixed response from critics. In its tell-all prose, the book attracted those interested in the soap-opera aspects of the case, from the beginnings of the relationship between teacher and student—both Ingram and her student agree that she was not the initiator in the relationship—to the public outcry, trial, and aftermath. For others, however, the book proved problematic. "Pushing between the lines of her plain, business-teacher prose," Vivian Moreau noted in a review for the Toronto *Globe and Mail,* ". . . it's also easy to see that Ingram was an emotionally troubled young woman who craved intimacy enough to believe that she could find it with a boy four months shy of his eighteenth birthday." Confused as to why Ingram published *Risking It All,* Moreau continued: "She learned as a beaten dog avoids an upraised hand, to avoid the media. This book will do nothing but bring the hounds back to her door." For the abusee's part, the publicity has sparked a career as a budding rap star, and by 2003, at age twenty-one, he had petitioned to have his true name released to the public to help push sales of his gangsta rap single *Teacher Scandal.* Ingram was also reported to be assisting her former accounting student in writing his own book about the affair. A 2003 appearance by the obviously still-friendly couple on the *Oprah* daytime talk show sparked discussion that a movie deal would follow.

BIOGRAPHICAL AND CRITICAL SOURCES:

BOOKS

Ingram, Heather, *Risking It All: My Student, My Lover, My Story,* Greystone Press (Toronto, Ontario, Canada), 2003.

PERIODICALS

Globe and Mail (Toronto, Ontario, Canada), July 26, 2003, Vivian Moreau, "A Minor Infraction?"
Maclean's, May 19, 2003, Sharon Doyle Deiedger, "The Teacher's Lesson," p. 56.
National Post, (British Columbia, Canada), March 11, 2000; May 30, 2000.*

*   *   *

JACK, Malcolm Roy 1946-

PERSONAL: Born December 17, 1946, in England; son of Iain Ross and Alicia Maria (Eça de Silva) Jack. *Education:* University of Liverpool, B.A. (honors), 1967; London School of Economics, University of London, Ph.D., 1974.

ADDRESSES: Office—Public Bill Office, House of Commons, London SW1A 0AA, England. *E-mail*—malcolm.jack@btinternet.com.

CAREER: House of Commons, London, England, clerk, 1967—; House of Commons, Ways and Means Committee, private secretary to chairman, 1977-80; Agriculture Select Committee, clerk, 1980-88; House of Commons, clerk of supply, 1989-91, clerk of standing committees, 1991-95, secretary to House of Commons Commission, 1995-2001, clerk of the journals, 2001-02, clerk of legislation, 2003.

MEMBER: Beckford Society (chairman, 1996—), Johnson Club (secretary, 1998—), Highgate Literary and Scientific Institute.

AWARDS, HONORS: Hong Kong Government Scholar, 1964-67.

WRITINGS:

The Social and Political Thought of Bernard Mandeville, Garland Publishers (New York, NY), 1987.
Corruption and Progress: The Eighteenth-Century Debate, AMS Press (New York, NY), 1989.
(Editor, with Anita Desai) *The Turkish Embassy Letters of Lady Mary Wortley Montagu,* University of Georgia Press (Athens, GA), 1993.
(Editor) *Vathek and Other Stories: A William Beckford Reader,* Pickering (London, England), 1993.
(Editor) *Episodes of Vathek,* Dedalus (Cambridge, England), 1994.
William Beckford: An English Fidalgo, AMS Press (New York, NY), 1996.
Sintra: A Glorious Eden, Carcanet Press (Manchester, England), 2001.

WORK IN PROGRESS: Research for a book on Lisbon earthquake of 1755.

SIDELIGHTS: While working his way up the career ladder of the Parliamentary hierarchy, becoming Clerk of Legislation for the House of Commons in 2003, Malcolm Roy Jack has also earned a reputation as a solid historian of eighteenth-century British and Portuguese politics and personalities. After publishing *The Social and Political Thought of Bernard Mandeville,* an appraisal of the prominent eighteenth-century economic theorist and author of *The Fable of the Bees,* Jack followed up with *Corruption and Progress: The Eighteenth-Century Debate,* an analysis of one of the thorniest issues for Mandeville and other political thinkers of his era. "The Focus of this highly readable volume by Malcolm Jack is the eighteenth-century 'corruption debate' whose central paradox as formulated by Jack was that 'material progress entails moral decline,'" explained *Eighteenth Century Studies* contributor Kathleen Szantor. In addition to Mandeville, Jack focuses on Jean-Jacques Rousseau and Scottish philosopher Adam Ferguson, all of who wrestled with the hope for a utopian future of material prosperity for all and the ancient fear that such prosperity inevitably leads to moral decline. Jack elaborates on the divergent approaches of these three men, with Mandeville an unabashed proponent of progress, even if meant encouraging humanity's selfish passions, and Rousseau searching for a way out of this conundrum through re-education that stresses community, with Ferguson coming down in the middle between these two positions. Not everyone was pleased with the results. "It is an unfortunate, but not fatal flaw in Jack's otherwise valuable monograph that he seems to have slighted the [economic] dimension of Scottish moral theory," wrote Ronald Hamowy in *Eighteenth Century Scottish Studies*. Still, "Jack's rekindling of the debate is timely as present-day political and economic conditions worldwide give rise alternately to optimism and pessimism concerning progress," concluded Kathleen Szantor in her review.

In later works, Jack has gone further afield, covering two of the more exotic personalities of the era. In 1993, he coedited *The Turkish Embassy Letters of Lady Mary Wortley Montagu* with Anita Desai. Denounced in her time by Alexander Pope as a "Lewd Lesbia," Lady Montagu is seen today as one of the best female poets and most skillful essayists of her era. From 1716 to 1718, she was stationed with her husband at the court of the "Sublime Porte" in Istanbul, the exotic capital of the Ottoman Empire. Jack's and Desai's selections cover this remarkable period in Lady Montagu's eventful life. "As well as the obvious value of the letters for their wealth of historical, social, and cultural detail, the Turkish Embassy Letters are of great interest for what they reveal of Mary Wortley Montagu's reactions to finding herself in a country which would have seemed entirely alien . . . to her contemporary correspondents," noted *Review of English Studies* contributor Harriet Devine Jump.

That same year, Malcolm Jack edited *Vathek and Other Stories: A William Beckford Reader*, a collection of tales by another controversial figure from the era. A few years later he published a biography of the author, titled *William Beckford: An English Fidalgo*. Bisexual and a dabbler in black magic, Beckford was an early Romantic and a pioneer of Gothic novels. In 1784, he was accused of sodomizing a sixteen-year-old boy and fled to Portugal, where he lived in self-imposed exile from English society as an unofficial "Fidalgo," or Portuguese gentleman, having affairs with both men and women, while developing aesthetic and architec-

tural ideals that he put into practice in Portugal, and later in England after he returned to his native country. In addition to his stories, Beckford's literary reputation rests on a series of rather sanitized travel journals from his travels in Portugal and Spain, and in trying to bring Beckford to life, Jack focuses on this period in Beckford's dramatic life. "Unfortunately . . . Malcolm Jack writes at times like a tremulous Victorian maiden aunt, never quite bringing himself to say what he so evidently wants to, which is that Beckford was very queer indeed," according to a *Times Literary Supplement* reviewer. However, *Eighteenth Century Studies* reviewer Kevin Berland found that "Jack presents a compelling vision of the force of Beckford's charismatic presence and imagination."

Jack has also published an appreciation of Beckford's primary refuge in Portugal, titled *Sintra: A Glorious Eden*. For centuries, Sintra has housed the palaces and pleasure domes of Portuguese royalty, and with its mix of Celtic, Roman, and Arabic influences, it remains one of the most treasured spots for travelers and residents alike. "Jack's own enchantment with the town is strong enough to convince us that this remarkable spot will somehow survive Lisbon's insidious suburban creep northwards," concluded *Times Literary Supplement* reviewer Jonathan Keates.

BIOGRAPHICAL AND CRITICAL SOURCES:

PERIODICALS

Eighteenth Century Scottish Studies, 1992, Ronald Hamowy, review of *Corruption and Progress: The Eighteenth-Century Debate*, pp. 14-15.
Eighteenth Century Studies, autumn, 1992, Kathleen Szantor, review of *Corruption and Progress*, pp. 202-205; spring, 2000, Kevin Berland, review of *William Beckford: An English Fidalgo*, pp. 457-460.
Review of English Studies, May, 1996, Harriet Devine Jump, review of *The Turkish Embassy Letters of Lady Mary Wortley Montagu*, p. 304.
Times Literary Supplement, January 9, 1998, review of *William Beckford*, p. 27; December 20, 2002, Jonathan Keates, review of *Sintra: A Glorious Eden*, p. 27.

JAMES, (Darryl) Dean

PERSONAL: Born in MS. *Education:* Received B.A. and M.A. (both in history) from Delta State University; Rice University, Ph.D. (medieval history), 1986; University of North Texas, M.A. (library science).

ADDRESSES: Office—Murder by the Book, 2342 Bissonnet St., Houston, TX 77005.

CAREER: Writer. Houston Academy of Medicine-Texas Medical Center Library, Houston, TX, worked as librarian and director of cataloging; Murder by the Book (mystery book store), Houston, general manager, 1996—.

AWARDS, HONORS: Macavity Award, Mystery Readers International, and Agatha Award for best nonfiction, both for the first edition of *By a Woman's Hand: A Guide to Mystery Fiction by Women.*

WRITINGS:

"SIMON KIRBY-JONES" MYSTERY SERIES

Posted to Death, Kensington Books (New York, NY), 2002.
Faked to Death, Kensington Books (New York, NY), 2003.
Decorated to Death, Kensington Books (New York, NY), 2004.

WITH JEAN SWANSON

By a Woman's Hand: A Guide to Mystery Fiction by Women, Berkley Books (New York, NY), 1991, revised edition, Berkley Prime Crime (New York, NY), 1996.
Killer Books: A Reader's Guide to Exploring the Popular World of Mystery and Suspense, Berkley Prime Crime (New York, NY), 1998.
The Dick Francis Companion, Berkley Prime Crime (New York, NY), 2003.

OTHER

(Editor, with Jan Grape and Ellen Nehr) *Deadly Women,* Carroll and Graf (New York, NY), 1998.
Cruel as the Grave, Silver Dagger Mysteries (Johnson City, TN), 2000.

Closer than the Bones, Silver Dagger Mysteries (Johnson City, TN), 2001.
Death by Dissertation, Silver Dagger Mysteries (Johnson City, TN), 2004.
(Editor, with Claudia Bishop) *Death Dines In* (anthology), Berkley Prime Crime (New York, NY), 2004.

Work represented in anthologies, including *Malice Domestic 7,* Avon Books, 1998; *Canine Crimes,* Ballantine, 1998; *A Canine Christmas,* Ballantine, 1999; and *Magnolias and Mayhem,* Silver Dagger Mysteries, 2000.

ADAPTATIONS: Works adapted for audio include *Faked to Death.*

SIDELIGHTS: Dean James is a Mississippi native who relocated to Houston, Texas. There, after working as a librarian at the Texas Medical Center, he became the manager of the well-known mystery book store Murder by the Book. James's first works were several nonfiction books written with Jean Swanson, a librarian at the University of Redlands in California. Their first collaboration, *By a Woman's Hand: A Guide to Mystery Fiction by Women,* profiles women writers from 1977—the year Marcia Muller's first "Sharon McCone" mystery, *Edwin of the Iron Shoes,* was published. The writers featured in the volume are modern; consequently, "Golden Age" writers like Agatha Christie and Dorothy Sayers are not included. Writers are listed alphabetically by all names under which they have written and are indexed by regional setting, type of detective, series character, and author. Included is information on award winners as well as other pertinent information. *Choice* reviewer L. O. Rein commented on the fact that at the end of each chapter, James and Swanson include a listing of authors of similar works. This feature, claimed Rein, "will be invaluable to casual readers and students alike."

James and Swanson next wrote *Killer Books: A Reader's Guide to Exploring the Popular World of Mystery and Suspense.* This volume is similar to their first but focuses on both male and female writers. It includes essays arranged within chapters focusing on plot content or hero subgenres, such as historical mysteries, legal thrillers, psychological mysteries, police officers, amateur sleuths, or private eyes. Each category includes between fifteen and thirty authors, mainly contemporary, whose heroes are profiled and whose series are examined. James and Swanson also include trivia, such as which mysteries have musical themes and which authors like to fish. *The Dick Francis Companion* is their third collaboration.

James has written a number of mystery novels for Silver Dagger Mysteries, an imprint of Overmountain Press. The second, *Closer than the Bones,* is set in Mississippi and follows retired schoolteacher Ernestine Carpenter through the investigation of the death of Sukey Lytton, a young woman writer whose revealing manuscript is now missing. Suspects include the six proteges of Mary Tucker McElroy, matriarch of Idlewild, who has invited the young writers to assist with her memoir, and each of the six has a secret that may have been included in the missing novel. The last guest to arrive is a literary agent who has found the manuscript. A *Publishers Weekly* reviewer noted that "before long, bodies lie draped about like antimacassars."

Death by Dissertation is set in Houston. As the novel opens, Ph.D. candidate Andy Carpenter finds fellow student Charlie Harper lying on a couch in the library, dead from a violent blow to the head. A *Publishers Weekly* critic called Andy "an appealing narrator" and noted that his investigation includes explorations into rumors about kinky and gay sex, plagiarism, intellectual theft, and blackmail. James also collaborated with Claudia Bishop to edit *Death Dines In,* a collection of sixteen short stories, including those by the editors, all of which involve food.

The first installment of James's "Simon Kirby-Jones" mystery series is *Posted to Death,* which a *Publishers Weekly* reviewer felt "is sure to revolutionize the traditional British cozy and win the hearts of fans everywhere." Simon Kirby-Jones is a gay, American writer, born in Mississippi, who became a vampire while living in Houston, and who now lives in the English town of Snupperton Mumsley. He is able to go out during the day with the help of a pill that negates sunshine's side effects. Simon is a best-selling author writing under female pseudonyms, including Daphne Deepwood and Dorinda Darlington. Eager to become part of the community, he joins the fundraising committee of St. Ethelwold's Church. Following an argument about the choice of which play should be staged to raise funds, town postmistress and busybody

Abigail Winterton is found murdered. Enthusiastic about helping the attractive Inspector Robin Chase, Simon searches out the killer and ultimately uncovers the secrets of the little village. Other romantic possibilities include bookstore owner Trevor Chase. *Houston Chronicle* reviewer Amy Rabinovitz commented that "the setting and characters are as high camp as anything in *The Rocky Horror Picture Show,* but underneath the loving mockery is a worthy and cozy village mystery you can really sink your teeth into."

Reviewing the book in *Lambda Book Report,* Therese Syzmanski pointed out that James "has skillfully created a charming mystery whose language fairly dances across the page. His clever wit shines from the properly British dialogue, to the very names of his characters, all of which are aptly named and quite English. For instance, the Lady Prunella Blitherington has a distinct tendency to, well, blither. On and on."

The second book in the series, *Faked to Death,* finds Simon and his young aide, Sir Giles, at a crime writers' conference, where the featured speaker claims to be Simon's nom de plume Dorinda Darlington. Nina, their literary agent-in-common, seems to be behind the scam, but it is the Dorinda imposter who is killed, flattened by an urn pushed from a terrace. *Library Journal*'s Rex Klett called the book "great entertainment."

Detective Robin Chase again directs a murder investigation in *Decorated to Death,* with help from Simon. In the book Zeke Harwood, the pompous host of a room-makeover television series, is found dead in the locked drawing room of Lady Prunella Blitherington. In planning the makeover of Prunella's drawing room, Zeke had suggested that the room be painted red, which led to a huge argument between Zeke and Prunella, and which was caught on tape. Simon discovers that Prunella may not be the only one who had an ax to grind with Zeke. He also realizes that his own urge to suck blood is returning, in spite of medication he takes to control it. A *Publishers Weekly* contributor wrote that "as in an elaborate and fun game of Clue, all the pieces come neatly together." In *Library Journal,* Klett called this outing "great fun."

BIOGRAPHICAL AND CRITICAL SOURCES:

PERIODICALS

Booklist, June 1, 1994, review of *By a Woman's Hand: A Guide to Mystery Fiction by Women,* p. 1868;

June 1, 1998, Bill Ott, review of *Killer Books: A Reader's Guide to Exploring the Popular World of Mystery and Suspense,* p. 1707; May 15, 2004, review of *Death Dines In,* p. 1600.

Choice, December, 1994, L. O. Rein, review of *By a Woman's Hand,* p. 582.

Denver Post, April 7, 2002, Tom and Enid Schantz, review of *Posted to Death,* p. EE2.

Houston Chronicle, February 12, 1995, review of *By a Woman's Hand,* p. 24; June 2, 2002, Amy Rabinovitz, review of *Posted to Death,* p. 21.

Kirkus Reviews, January 15, 2002, review of *Posted to Death,* p. 77; February 1, 2003, review of *Faked to Death,* p. 189; April 1, 2004, review of *Death Dines In,* p. 300.

Lambda Book Report, May, 2002, Therese Syzmanski, review of *Posted to Death.*

Library Journal, April 1, 1998, Denise Johnson, review of *Killer Books,* p. 89; March 1, 2003, Rex Klett, review of *Faked to Death,* p. 122; April 1, 2004, Rex Klett, review of *Decorated to Death,* p. 126.

Publishers Weekly, April 30, 2001, review of *Closer than the Bones,* p. 60; March 4, 2002, review of *Posted to Death,* p. 59; March 3, 2003, review of *Faked to Death* (audio), p. 57; March 15, 2004, review of *Decorated to Death,* p. 58; April 12, 2004, review of *Death by Dissertation,* p. 42; April 19, 2004, review of *Death Dines In,* p. 43.

School Library Journal, February, 1999, Peggy Bercher, review of *Killer Books,* p. 140.*

*   *   *

JANKEN, Kenneth Robert 1956-

PERSONAL: Born January 31, 1956, in Los Angeles, CA; married; children: two. *Education:* Hunter College of the City University of New York, B.A., 1987, M.A., 1987; Rutgers University, Ph.D., 1991. *Hobbies and other interests:* Baseball.

ADDRESSES: Office—Department of African and Afro-American Studies, University of North Carolina—Chapel Hill, Chapel Hill, NC 27599-3395. *E-mail*—krjanken@email.unc.edu.

CAREER: Educator and writer. University of North Carolina—Chapel Hill, assistant professor, 1991-97,

associate professor of African and Afro-American studies, 1997—, adjunct professor of history, member of faculty advisory board, Office of Undergraduate Research.

MEMBER: Organization of American Historians.

AWARDS, HONORS: Institute of Arts and Humanities fellow, 1994; National Endowment for the Humanities fellow, 1997.

WRITINGS:

Rayford W. Logan and the Dilemma of the African-American Intellectual, University of Massachusetts Press (Amherst, MA), 1993.

White: The Biography of Walter White, Mr. NAACP, New Press (New York, NY), 2003.

Contributor of articles to professional journals.

SIDELIGHTS: Kenneth Robert Janken, an associate professor at the University of North Carolina—Chapel Hill, is the author of the biographies *Rayford W. Logan and the Dilemma of the African American Intellectual* and *White: The Biography of Walter White, Mr. NAACP.*

Rayford W. Logan and the Dilemma of the African American Intellectual examines the life of the Howard University professor who worked tirelessly to end segregation. Among Logan's achievements were "Education for Citizenship," a voter education program for southern blacks, and Executive Order 8802, an anti-discrimination document that he coauthored. "Janken argues that Logan longed for fame as a civil rights leaders, like that of W. E. B. du Bois, even more than recognition as a professional historian," observed Jeffrey C. Stewart in the *Washington Post Book World.* Janken also notes that Logan grew frustrated in his efforts to gain such recognition from black and white leaders alike. As Sterling Stuckey wrote in the *African American Review,* "Janken appears to have confirmed what troubled Logan greatly, that he did not receive the credit deserved from his involvement in help to make as well as write history." "Logan's struggle to balance his hatred of white racism and his longing for white recognition . . . comes through poignantly here," Stewart remarked.

Walter White, the subject of Janken's 2003 work *White*, served as executive secretary of the National Association for the Advancement of Colored People (NAACP) from 1931 until his death in 1955. An exceptionally light-skinned African American, White was able to use his physical appearance to his advantage, often posing as a reporter to get information from white racists. During his years with the NAACP, White oversaw tremendous growth in the organization, championed civil rights, and helped spark the Harlem Renaissance. He is perhaps best remembered for bringing national attention to the lynching of African Americans. "This elegantly written and comprehensive biography, the first major work on its subject, is a model of nuanced scholarship and popular history," wrote a critic in *Publishers Weekly.*

BIOGRAPHICAL AND CRITICAL SOURCES:

PERIODICALS

African American Review, spring, 1996, Sterling Stuckey, review of *Rayford W. Logan and the Dilemma of the African American Intellectual,* pp. 125-127; winter, 2003, Carol Anderson, review of *White: The Biography of Walter White, Mr. NAACP,* pp. 664-666.

American Historical Review, February, 1995, Louis B. Harlan, review of *Rayford W. Logan and the Dilemma of the African American Intellectual,* p. 247.

Choice, R. A. Fischer, review of *Rayford W. Logan and the Dilemma of the African American Intellectual,* p. 988.

Ebony, April, 2003, pp. 23-25.

Journal of African American History, summer, 2003, Brian Daugherity, review of *White,* pp. 317-319.

Journal of American History, December, 1994, Willard B. Gatewood, review of *Rayford W. Logan and the Dilemma of the African American Intellectual,* pp. 1360-1361.

Journal of Southern History, February, 1995, Jacqueline Goggin, review of *Rayford W. Logan and the Dilemma of the African American Intellectual,* pp. 172-173.

Kirkus Reviews, June 1, 1993, review of *Rayford W. Logan and the Dilemma of the African American Intellectual,* p. 699.

Library Journal, June 1, 1993, Gary Williams, review of *Rayford W. Logan and the Dilemma of the African American Intellectual,* p. 142; April 1, 2003, Anthony Edmonds, review of *White,* p. 110.

New Republic, September 29, 2003, David J. Garrow, "The Party of Freedom—The Golden Age of Civil Rights," p. 28.

Publishers Weekly, May 31, 1993, review of *Rayford W. Logan and the Dilemma of the African American Intellectual,* p. 37; March 24, 2003, review of *White,* p. 72.

Washington Post Book World, August 8, 1993, Jeffrey C. Stewart, "Historian, Teacher, and Activist," pp. 1, 6.

ONLINE

Library of Congress Web site, http://www.loc.gov/ (February 25, 2003), "Kenneth Janken."

New Press Web site, http://www.thenewpress.com/ (April 16, 2004).

University of North Carolina—Chapel Hill Web site, http://www.unc.edu/ (April 16, 2004), "Kenneth R. Janken."*

*			*			*

JOHNSON, Victoria 1958-

PERSONAL: Born 1958, in Ruston, LA; married; children: one daughter. *Education:* Attended Eastern Washington University and Kinman Business University.

ADDRESSES: Home—Portland, OR. *Office*—Victoria Johnson International, P.O. Box 1744, Lake Oswego, OR 97035. *Agent*—AIE Speakers Bureau, 214 Lincoln St., Ste. 113, Boston, MA 02134. *E-mail*—info@victoriajohnson.com.

CAREER: Fitness trainer and educator, entrepreneur, consultant, lecturer, and author. Owner and president, Victoria Johnson International, a marketing, management, and consulting company; owner of a distribution and sales company marketing health and fitness products. Star and producer of more than twenty-four dance fitness video programs; executive producer and host of *Celebrity Health and Fitness* television program.

WRITINGS:

(With Megan V. Davis) *Victoria Johnson's Attitude: An Inspirational Guide to Redefining Your Body,*

Your Health, and Your Outlook, Penguin (New York, NY), 1993.

Body Revival: Lose Weight, Feel Great, and Pump Up Your Faith, Health Communications (Deerfield Beach, FL), 2002.

Contributor to periodicals such as *Northwest Woman* and *Essence,* and to volumes such as *Health and Healing for African-Americans,* edited by Sheree Crute, Rodale Press (Emmaus, PA), 1997.

SIDELIGHTS: Fitness trainer and health advocate Victoria Johnson is the producer and star of more than two dozen dance videos designed to help viewers get in shape. Johnson uses her expertise in exercise, anatomy, and nutrition to train fitness instructors, physical education teachers, personal trainers, and other fitness professionals. A frequent lecturer and speaker, Johnson has traveled the country offering insight and instruction in losing weight, becoming fit, and maintaining a healthy, happy lifestyle. Her company, Victoria Johnson International, provides marketing and management consulting and distributes health and fitness products.

But this trim fitness queen did not always have model qualities. Born in Ruston, Louisiana, Johnson was one of eleven children in a family of migrant farm workers. When she was young, the family relocated to the Yakima Valley, in central Washington state, where Johnson grew up. "When you are migrant workers, the only time you come together with the family is around dinner," Johnson commented in an interview with Kristi Watts on the *Christian Broadcasting Network* Web site. "Every night we would have a huge dinner of fried chicken, red beans, and rice." The family "would get together and laugh and tell jokes," Johnson continued. "That's when I felt comfortable, so I started to associate food with comfort."

Fried foods and sugared desserts and drinks contributed to Johnson's weight problem as a child. "When I was younger, almost all the food I ate was fried," she related in an interview with Bev Bennett in *Chicago Sun-Times.* "And if it didn't have sugar, I didn't have it." During the summers, Johnson indulged in rich, high-calorie foods and gained weight; then, when school started again, she starved and purged herself to lose the weight so that she could be on the school dance team. She developed bulimia, and "the results of the stuff-and-starve regime took her body years to overcome," Bennett remarked.

From being an overweight child, Johnson became an overweight adult, at one time carrying 175 pounds on a body only five-feet, three-inches tall. She came to the abrupt realization that something was wrong when she passed out while teaching an aerobics class. She developed type II diabetes, high blood pressure, and discovered her arteries were beginning to clog. "I was having blackouts because I was going into mini-diabetic comas," she said in an interview with Neela Sakaria on the *Bookwire* Web site. "Here I was teaching aerobics, I was a certified instructor, I had my own training company," she related to Sakaria. "I knew all about dieting, weight training. But for some reason, I wasn't walking my talk." From there, Johnson took up a regimen of sensible diet, exercise, and nutrition counseling. It took her almost four years, but she lost the excess weight, "and it hasn't come back," she commented in the interview with Bennett.

Johnson took her health and weight loss message to a much wider audience as the producer and star of more than two dozen dance exercise videos. *Victoria's Power Shaping Workout,* for example, provides "easy-to-follow routines, effective exercises, and cheerful encouragement," wrote Lynn Voedisch in *Chicago Sun-Times.*

She has also offered her expertise and inspiration in books. *Victoria Johnson's Attitude: An Inspirational Guide to Redefining Your Body, Your Health, and Your Outlook* explores how she became overweight and how she achieved her fitness and weight goals. She advocates a diet high in nutrition along with high-energy workouts, as well as achieving personal control and discipline. Johnson stresses setting goals and taking tangible action based on those goals. "Having a positive attitude and sheer determination when trying to seek personal fulfillment" is a key message of this "upbeat and inspirational fitness book," remarked Jeanette Lambert in *Kliatt. Victoria Johnson's Attitude* "is the perfect book for someone wanting to improve their health and tired of diets that don't work," commented a reviewer in *Skanner.*

Johnson's religious faith has consistently been an integral component of her health and fitness philosophy. "She contends that we acquire extra weight because we're trying to fill a spiritual void," remarked Molly Martin in a profile of Johnson in the *Seattle Times.* In the *Bookwire* Web site interview, Johnson observed that "Weight is a result of what we're doing.

It's a [by-product] of our habits, thoughts, desires, and actions. So I learned to separate what I was eating, thinking, doing." This process led Johnson to write *Body Revival: Lose Weight, Feel Great, and Pump Up Your Faith.* In the book, "I start from the inside and have you work on that, and then I have you work on the outside," Johnson said in the interview with Sakaria. "I teach you to go inside and really truly figure out . . . what is going on." From there, Johnson remarked, readers can take control of their bodies to lose the weight they want. "We have a divine purpose," Johnson said in the interview with Sakaria, "each of us—we cannot trade that for food."

BIOGRAPHICAL AND CRITICAL SOURCES:

PERIODICALS

Chicago Sun-Times, January 24, 1992, Lynn Voedisch, "Gonna Make You Sweat," video review of *Victoria's Power Shaping Workout,* p. 59; July 22, 1993, Bev Bennett, "Fitness Expert Suggests Healthy Change to Blacks," interview with Victoria Johnson, p. 7.
Essence, September, 1993, Portia Hawkins-Bond, review of *Victoria Johnson's Attitude: An Inspirational Guide to Redefining Your Body, Your Health, and Your Outlook,* pp. 34-36; October, 1996, Joy Duckett Cain, "Victoria Johnson: Work That Body!," p. 54.
Houston Post, February 17, 1994, Deborah Mann Lake, "No Excuses," section D, p. 1.
Kliatt, September, 1993, Jeanette Lambert, review of *Victoria Johnson's Attitude,* p. 34.
Peoria Journal-Star, October 6, 2002, Shannon Countryman, "Gear Up Girls—It's a Women's Show," B4.
Recorder, March 20, 1993, Connie Gaines Hayes, "Exercise Key to Training Heart and Mind: Keeping Off the Pounds Leads to Happy, Healthy Life," B7.
Seattle Times, September 8, 2002, Molly Martin, "The Spirit Moves: For This Portland Fitness Pro, Working on the Outside Begins with Working on the Inside," p. 8.
Skanner, February 24, 1993, "Ex-Diet Diva Offers Realistic Take on Fitness," review of *Victoria Johnson's Attitude,* p. 7.
Tribune (Chicago, IL), April 19, 1992, Lisa Twyman Bessone, "Muscle Ballet: A Workout for a Longer, Leaner Line," video review of *Dance Step Formula,* p. 64.
Women's Sports and Fitness, January, 1992, Lisa Paul, "Funky Fitness," p. 68.

ONLINE

Bookwire Web site, http://www.bookwire.com/ (August 15, 2002), Neela Sakaria, interview with Victoria Johnson.
Christian Broadcasting Network Web site, http://www.cbn.com/ (August 21, 2002), Kristi Watts, interview with Victoria Johnson.
Victoria Johnson Home Page, http://www.victoriajohnson.com/ (June 30, 2004).*

* * *

JOHNSTONE, Nick 1970-

PERSONAL: Born June 11, 1970; married; wife's name, Anna.

ADDRESSES: Office—Guardian/Observer, 119 Farringdon Rd., London EC1R 3ER, England.

CAREER: Journalist and author. Writer for the *Guardian* and *Observer* newspapers, London, England.

WRITINGS:

Radiohead: An Illustrated Biography, Omnibus Press (London, England), 1997.
Patti Smith: A Biography, Omnibus Press (London, England), 1997.
Melody Maker History of Twentieth-Century Popular Music, Bloomsbury (London, England), 1999.
Abel Ferrara: The King of New York, Omnibus Press (London, England), 1999.
Sean Penn: A Biography, Omnibus Press (London, England), 2000.
A Head Full of Blue (autobiography), Bloomsbury (London, England), 2002.

SIDELIGHTS: Nick Johnstone is a writer for the *Guardian* and *Observer* newspapers in England and author of numerous biographies of musicians and actors. He has been especially noticed for his 2002 autobiography, *A Head Full of Blue.* Johnstone grew up in Surrey, England, in a fairly typical middle-class family. When he was ten, his family moved to

Buckinghamshire. He hated school and was depressed much of the time. At fourteen, he got drunk for the first time, which led to ten years of heavy drinking. By his late teens, Johnstone's depression had reached the point where the only outlet (besides alcohol) was self-mutilation. He began cutting himself at the age of eighteen and continued for the next four years. Johnstone wrote about his cutting in a column for the *Observer.* "Nothing made the pain go away like the soft, calculated sweep of a razor blade across my skin," he recalled. "Between the ages of eighteen and twenty-two, I cut my arms. It was a miraculous antidote to a long-term clinical depression that refused to lift. It worked better than anything else: the prescriptions for anti-depressants that my GP kept throwing at me, the psychiatrist he referred me to, the recreational drugs I took with my friends, the merry-go-round of alcohol abuse. On a quest to fix myself, I tried it all. And nothing healed me the way cutting did."

At the age of twenty-four, Johnstone stopped drinking. He gives Alcoholics Anonymous (AA) some of the credit for his newfound sobriety, although as an atheist he found some of the Christian-oriented sayings a bit troubling, and he felt there was a general lack of friendliness at AA. However, he credits much of his ability to stay sober to exercising, taking anti-depressant medication, and seeing a hypnotherapist. He taught himself self-hypnosis, which he used in place of alcohol. "Today the scars are still there," he remarked in his *Observer* article. "I haven't cut myself in ten years. I am proud of conquering my addiction to cutting. Just as I am proud of conquering my addiction to alcohol. I attribute stopping cutting to eighteen months of counseling. I was taught to express myself, to identify feelings, moods. To get angry, to speak my mind, to vent. To articulate. I learned about emotions, coping, surviving."

In a *Guardian* article from December, 2003, Johnstone wrote, "This will be my ninth sober Christmas. It is the first I have looked forward to since I stopped drinking. It is about time. For too long, I have dreaded the festive season as a time when I have felt like a steak tartare tossed into shark-infested waters. Like any recovering alcoholic, one of the biggest lessons of my sobriety has been learning to have fun without a one hundred degree proof bloodstream. For the first few years, I was the cliched uptight, shy, stiff, tongue-tied, wet blanket in the corner, a picture of chemical deprivation checking my watch every thirty seconds to

see if I was any closer to escaping whatever bash I was trapped at. Slowly, things have become easier."

Julie Burchill, writing in the *Guardian,* was not impressed by Johnstone's autobiographical work, however. "Writers have always had problems," she wrote. "That's probably a lot of the reason they become writers. . . . [So] they shoot their bolt in a 'memoir' and sit back smugly to listen to the oohs and aahs of the paying public. . . . A junkie proper may burgle you to feed his habit—but a recovery-junkie will bore you to within an inch of your life in order to feed his." Other critics were much more kind. Mark Stangate, for instance, commented in the Glasgow *Herald:* "Even though we know where this is going, Johnstone makes the journey entertaining. He's an instantly likeable guide. And a damn fine writer." London *Times* writer James Hopkin called *A Head Full of Blue* "a breathless and often brutal account of his talent for intoxication," and John Sutherland wrote in the *Sunday Times,* "*A Head Full of Blues* makes painful reading. There was no joy in Johnstone's drinking. He cut his arms with razors, abused his girlfriends . . . and permanently ruined his stomach." Sutherland added, "At thirty, with most of his life before him, Johnstone was clean and sober. Let's hope he makes it."

BIOGRAPHICAL AND CRITICAL SOURCES:

BOOKS

Johnstone, Nick, *A Head Full of Blue,* Bloomsbury (London, England), 2002.

PERIODICALS

Booklist, March 1, 2000, Mike Tribby, review of *Melody Maker History of Twentieth-Century Popular Music,* p. 1186.
Evening Post (Wellington, New Zealand), May 17, 2002, Ruth Nichol, review of *A Head Full of Blue,* p. 7.
Guardian (Manchester, England), October 29, 1999, review of *Melody Maker History of Twentieth-Century Popular Music;* March 23, 2002, Julie Burchill, review of *A Head Full of Blue;* December 9, 2003, Nick Johnstone, "Blue Notes."

Herald (Glasgow, Scotland), February 23, 2002, Mark Stangate, review of *A Head Full of Blue,* p. 13.

Library Journal, March 15, 2000, Heather McCormack, review of *Melody Maker History of Twentieth-Century Popular Music,* p. 87.

Observer (London, England), February 9, 2003, Oliver Robinson, review of *A Head Full of Blue,* p. 18; February 23, 2003, Nick Johnstone, "Sharp Practice."

Sunday Times (London, England), March 3, 2002, John Sutherland, review of *A Head Full of Blue,* p. 41.

Times (London, England), February 22, 2002, James Hopkin, review of *A Head Full of Blue,* p. 17.*

*   *   *

JONES, Tobias 1972-

PERSONAL: Born 1972, in Somerset, England. *Education:* Graduated from Jesus College, Oxford (English and history).

ADDRESSES: Home—Parma, Italy. *Agent*—c/o Editorial Department, Faber and Faber Ltd., Three Queen Square, London WC1N 3AU, England.

CAREER: London Review of Books, London, England, member of editorial department; *Independent on Sunday,* staff writer; freelance journalist, 1999—; Worked as a framer and seller of antiquarian maps at a bookshop in Bloomsbury, England.

WRITINGS:

The Dark Heart of Italy: Travels through Time and Space across Italy, Faber and Faber (London, England), published as *The Dark Heart of Italy: An Incisive Portrait of Europe's Most Beautiful, Most Disconcerting Country,* 2003, North Point Press (New York, NY), 2004.

Contributor of essays and articles to periodicals, including *Wallpaper, Prospect, Vogue,* the *Guardian,* and the *Independent on Sunday.*

SIDELIGHTS: English journalist Tobias Jones imigrated to Parma, Italy, in 1999 and came to love the country too much to leave. In *The Dark Heart of Italy:*

Travels through Time and Space across Italy (published in the United States with the subtitle *An Incisive Portrait of Europe's Most Beautiful, Most Disconcerting Country*), Jones delves deeply into the neo-Fascist, conservative, and Mafia influence on Italy after World War II. Jones covers the massive government corruption scandal of the early 1990s and the succession to power of wealthy soccer club owner Silvio Berlusconi, the media mogul who became prime minister. Critics described Jones's treatment of the subject as evenhanded. John Foot, in the Manchester *Guardian,* stated, "Jones does not simply demonise [Berlusconi] but tries to understand him and why millions of Italians voted for him." On the other hand, *Times Literary Supplement* writer Martin Clark found that Jones "exaggerates the clash between Berlusconi's supporters and opponents."

In *The Dark Heart of Italy,* Jones writes about the terrible state of Italian television since Berlusconi, whom he refers to as the "'owner' of Italy," took control of the airwaves. He also writes about Italian football, the proliferation of illegal building, church history and scandals, subtle nuances of the language, and the Italian people's respect for the beautiful and the sensual. Jones also comments about a bureaucracy that results in every Italian spending an average of 7,000 minutes a year standing in lines. A *Publishers Weekly* contributor noted, "Jones must now be admitted to the company of writers . . . who seem to understand Italy and the Italians better than the natives do themselves."

Spectator reviewer Caroline Moorehead applauded Jones's description of a nation where "the prime minister feels himself to be above the law," and where "protesters are quickly dispersed with bullets." *Library Journal* reviewer Joseph S. Carlson concluded that *The Dark Heart of Italy* is a book that should be read by "anyone attempting to dig beneath the surface of what makes modern Italy run."

BIOGRAPHICAL AND CRITICAL SOURCES:

PERIODICALS

Contemporary Review, July, 2003, review of *The Dark Heart of Italy: Travels through Time and Space across Italy,* p. 63.

Economist, February 15, 2003, review of *The Dark Heart of Italy.*

CONTEMPORARY AUTHORS • Volume 226   **JOY**

Guardian (Manchester, England), January 11, 2003, John Foot, "Dress Properly and Don't Pay Taxes: John Foot Takes the Via Storia to Unravel the Alarming Mixture of Wealth, Corruption and Xenophobia that Italians Confront under Berlusconi's Rule," p. 12.

Kirkus Reviews, April 15, 2004, review of *The Dark Heart of Italy,* p. 376.

Library Journal, April 15, 2004, Joseph S. Carlson, review of *The Dark Heart of Italy,* p. 112.

New Statesman, January 20, 2003, James Eve, "La Sporca Vita," p. 48.

Publishers Weekly, April 19, 2004, review of *The Dark Heart of Italy,* p. 48.

Spectator, January 25, 2003, Caroline Moorehead, "Bosoms, Football and Money," p. 49.

Times (London, England), January 11, 2003, "An Italian Job Well Done," p. 16.

Times Literary Supplement, February 14, 2003, Martin Clark, "Judge Not," p. 4.

ONLINE

University of Cambridge Web site, http://www.cam.ac.uk/ (May 28, 2004), Tobias Jones biography.*

*   *   *

JOY, Camden 1963(?)-

PERSONAL: Born c. 1963.

ADDRESSES: Agent—c/o Author Mail, Highwater Books, 5944 Rue Waverly, Montreal, Quebec, Canada H2T 2Y3; c/o Author Mail, TNI Books, 2442 Northwest Market, #357, Seattle, WA 98107.

CAREER: Author. Has worked as a receptionist, word processor, and legal secretary; worked for fourteen years as a musician, singer, and song writer.

WRITINGS:

The Greatest Record Album Ever Told (also see below), Verse Chorus Press (Portland, OR), 1995.

The Greatest Record Album Singer That Ever Was (also see below), Verse Chorus Press (Portland, OR), 1996.

The Last Rock Star Book; or, Liz Phair: A Rant (novel), Verse Chorus Press (Portland, OR), 1998.

Boy Island (novel), Quill (New York, NY), 2000.

Hubcap Diamondstar Halo (novella), Highwater Books (Montreal, Quebec, Canada), 2001.

Camden Joy, Highwater Books (Montreal, Quebec, Canada), 2002.

Pan (novella), Highwater Books (Montreal, Quebec, Canada), 2002.

Lost Joy (includes *The Greatest Record Album Ever Told, The Greatest Record Album Singer That Ever Was,* and *The Greatest Record Album Band That Ever Was*), TNI Books (Seattle, WA), 2002.

Palm Tree 13 (novella), Highwater Books (Montreal, Quebec, Canada), 2003.

Also author of numerous tracts and manifestos about music; contributor to periodicals, including *Village Voice, Boston Phoenix, SF Weekly, Puncture, Swim,* and *Greatest Hits.* Musical recordings include *Fallen Highways,* 1989, *Holy Water,* 1990, and *Interrogation Songs,* 1990.

SIDELIGHTS: A musician and songwriter who played with underground bands in the 1980s and 1990s, Camden Joy gained sudden attention in the music world in the mid-1990s for what could be called a binge of guerilla postering in New York City. Initially begun as a way of promoting his band, the posters he created evolved into a kind of street art containing comments and observations about various rock stars and bands, sometimes venturing into humorous or wry remarks on society such as "Advertocracy Rock Teaches Youth Tobacco and Tattoos. This Ain't Rock and Roll, This Is Genocide." The posters, which were often torn down by passers-by within days or even hours of being put up, gained Joy a kind of cult following, and the manifestos and tracts he published at the same time gained fans among music critics who compared his writing style to the likes of Hunter S. Thompson and Frank O'Hara. Although he does not consider himself a genuine rock critic—he told *Smokebox* interviewer John Richen, "I just rarely have very fixed beliefs. This is why I know myself to be a terrible 'music critic.' I change my mind a lot"—nevertheless, his passion for music is genuine. Joy tries to convey this passion in his essays, tracts, and fiction writing.

Joy's explorations into writing actually began with what he calls "faux-religious" tracts about Al Green and Frank Black, he told Richen. These pieces were

173

later published in *The Greatest Record Album Ever Told* and *The Greatest Record Album Singer That Ever Was,* which were later reprinted in *Lost Joy.* Joy's interest in old-style printing then led to the posters. By 1997, however, he felt he had run out of new things to say, so he left New York for Boston. Soon after, his first novel, *The Last Rock Star Book; or, Liz Phair: A Rant,* was published. The book offers a blend of fiction and reality about a down-and-out writer, also named Camden Joy, who accepts an assignment to write a biography about feminist rocker Liz Phair, whose album *Exile in Guyville* was a favorite of Joy's.

After releasing two acclaimed albums, Phair went underground, and in Joy's book he imagines a trip to Chicago to discover the person behind the music. But the novel is not really about Phair so much as it is an "ode to squandered youth and perfect pop songs," remarked a *Publishers Weekly* reviewer. Joy muses about the nature of rock music and the tension between fame and musical creativity. Although the critic felt that this first novel contains few genuine insights, the *Publishers Weekly* reviewer praised Joy as "a spectacularly energetic writer."

Joy was actually working on writing *The Last Rock Star Book* at the same time as his *Boy Island,* which was released in 2000. As with the former novel, *Boy Island* was inspired by Joy's fascination with a singer—in this case, David Lowery, the frontman for Cracker and the disbanded Camper Van Beethoven. The author, in fact, tagged along with Lowery's band for three weeks. At first, Lowery was suspicious of Joy, thinking that the young man was some kind of obsessed groupie or stalker. But when the singer confronted Joy, the writer explained he wanted to do a book about Cracker. Flattered, Lowery helped Joy out by providing names and contact information of people to interview. When the book eventually came out as a novelization instead of a nonfiction work, however, Lowery was upset to the point of seeking a lawsuit. *Boy Island,* which is about a touring rock group featuring Lowery and others by name, contains fictional scenes that the musician felt were slanderous. For example, the band members play a game called "tonnage" in which they add up the combined weights of the women they have slept with. This game was never played by Lowery and his Cracker band mates. But despite the threat of legal action, the only result of Lowery's ire was that the publisher changed the book's disclaimer to indicate that it was a work of fiction.

Originally, Joy had intended to write an objective work of nonfiction about Cracker, but he felt that the text was too dry, so it evolved into a novel. The main character, also named Camden Joy, is a drummer touring as part of a new band formed by Lowery. The members of the group have all agreed to join the tour for various reasons ranging from a desire to relive old times to a need to find musical success. For the character Joy, it becomes a journey in which he discovers his identity as a homosexual. Along the way, the characters philosophize and rant about the current music scene. While critics found parts of *Boy Island* to be admirable, many felt it fell short of capturing the experience of a band tour. For example, *Booklist* contributor George Needham felt Joy illustrates well the feelings of "isolation and . . . boredom" during a tour, but he misses "the exhilaration of performance," which is the reason musicians do what they do. Mark Athitakis, writing in the *New York Times Book Review,* said, "While there's no denying Joy's ear for dialogue and passion for music, he can't overcome the conventions of the genre."

Joy followed up *Boy Island* with three novellas that are one-hundred-percent fictional. *Hubcap Diamondstar Halo, Pan,* and *Palm Tree 13* are "about Camden Joy's fictional life in fictional bands," reported Katia Dunn in the *Portland Mercury.* As with the other books, the main theme in these stories is the "relationship between music and real life." While Dunn was somewhat disappointed that these novellas show Joy to have evolved into "a normal fiction writer," she still maintained that he remains a "pioneer in his time."

About his fiction writing, Joy told Richen: "I'm trying to accomplish several things in my writing. Polemics don't interest me, except as a character flaw. I think of myself as a storyteller. I want to evoke a place, a scene, a plot, or an identity which is suggested to me by a certain piece of favorite music. I want to testify to the slipperiness of self, the uncertainties of being. . . . I want to remind people that what is good about music is its unspeakable mystery, how it plugs directly into our consciousness, establishing a whole world inside the listener's head."

BIOGRAPHICAL AND CRITICAL SOURCES:

PERIODICALS

Booklist, February 15, 2000, George Needham, review of *Boy Island,* p. 1081.

New York Times Book Review, March 26, 2000, Mark Athitakis, review of *Boy Island,* p. 21.

Publishers Weekly, February 23, 1998, review of *The Last Rock Star Book; or, Liz Phair: A Rant,* p. 51; March 6, 2000, review of *Boy Island,* p. 85.

ONLINE

Camden Joy's Web site, http://www.camdenjoy.com/ (April 7, 2004).

Fine Print Magazine, http://www.fineprintmag.com/ (April 7, 2004).

Metro . . . Active, http://www.metroactive.com/ (January 18, 1999), Katy Radditz, "A Fan's Note."

Miami New Times, http://www.miaminewtimes.com/ (June 1, 2000), Robert Wilonsky, "Stalker Fiction."

Portland Mercury, http://www.portlandmercury.com/ (May 16, 2002), Katia Dunn, "Camden Joy: Reading Frenzy."

Salon.com, http://www.salon.com/ (February, 1997), Sarah Vowell, "Joy Division: Filling in the Gaps with Poster Boy Camden Joy."

Smokebox, http://www.smokebox.net/ (October, 2002), John Richen, "Smokebox Interview: Camden Joy on Liz Phair and Lost Joy."

Splendid Ezine, http://www.splendidezine.com/ (November 25, 2002), "An Interview with Camden Joy."*

*   *   *

JULIUS, Anthony (Robert) 1956-

PERSONAL: Born July 16, 1956; son of Morris and Myrna Julius; married Judith Bernie, 1979 (divorced, 1998); married Dina Rabinovitch, 1999; children: (first marriage) Max Yoram, Laura Yael, Chloe Anna, Theo Raphael; (second marriage) Elon Lev. *Education:* Jesus College, B.A. (with honors); University College of Law, Ph.D.

ADDRESSES: Office—Mishcon de Reya, Summit House, 12 Red Lion Sq., London WC1R 4QD, England. *E-mail*—anthony.julius@mishcon.co.uk.

CAREER: Attorney. Mishcon de Reya, London, England, 1981—, partner, 1984—, head of litigation, 1987—. Diana, Princess of Wales, Memorial Fund, trustee, 1997—, chairman, 1997-99, vice president, 2002—.

MEMBER: Institute of Jewish Policy Research (chairman of law panel, 1997—).

WRITINGS:

T. S. Eliot: Anti-Semitism and Literary Form, Cambridge University Press (New York, NY), 1995, reprinted with new preface, Thames and Hudson (New York, NY), 2003.

Idolizing Pictures: Idolatry, Iconoclasm, and Jewish Art, Thames and Hudson (New York, NY), 2001.

Transgressions: The Offences of Art, University of Chicago Press (Chicago, IL), 2002.

Book reviewer for English papers, including the *Guardian, Observer,* and *Sunday Telegraph.*

SIDELIGHTS: Anthony Julius is a litigation lawyer who represented Diana, Princess of Wales, in her divorce and became trustee of her memorial fund following her death. He has also written several books, including *T. S. Eliot: Anti-Semitism and Literary Form.* Julius studies how Eliot's anti-Semitism was central to his thought and how it inspired him. He writes that Eliot was "able to place his anti-Semitism at the service of his art." Eliot's dislike of Jews was evident in a number of his early poems, claims Julius. Among those Julius examines for anti-Semitic elements are "Gerontion," "Sweeney among the Nightingales," "Burbank with a Baedeker: Bleistein with a Cigar," "Dirge," "A Cooking Egg," and "The Waste Land."

R. F. Fleissner wrote in *Contemporary Review,* "So is the fact that a few Jews are cited in Eliot's poetry, and not admittedly in complimentary ways, sufficient evidence that he was of two minds? If so, on the same grounds, we would have to condemn great writers like Chaucer, Shakespeare, and Dickens. No doubt the close association with Ezra Pound constitutes a major factor (Pound having eventually confessed to having been anti-Semitic, as is well known), but it is also widely recognized that Eliot wrote Pound a strong letter deploring the latter's anti-Semitism."

ANQ reviewer Randy Malamud wrote, "I think that probably many, if not all, teachers and scholars of Eliot who read Anthony Julius's acclaimed and infamous book on Eliot's anti-Semitism will feel, as I do, that it will markedly affect how we teach and write about T. S. Eliot. Some will dismiss Julius's arguments and rhetoric as too far-reaching, finding them too subversive of Eliot's stature; too unfairly and too widely destructive of Eliot's poetic, his integrity, his aesthetic; too full of calumny; too subjective; and excessive." Malamud said he did not think the book "is any of these things, but I understand why readers might adjudicate Julius's argument in that way. Perhaps most productively, the book should spark vigorous and intellectually fruitful discussion among those who support and those who reject this work, along with fence-sitters."

Malamud wrote that "Julius's triumph is having set out, masterfully, the terms on which the issue of Eliot's distasteful relationship to Jewish culture—too often ignored, repressed, trivialized, or otherwise overlooked—must be confronted. To my mind, Julius irrefutably demonstrates that Eliot's readers must address his anti-Semitism much more vigorously than they have done in the past."

"Julius makes great efforts to sustain an appreciation of Eliot's talents as a poet," wrote Gregory Jay in the *Journal of English and Germanic Philology,* "even as he documents and explicates that poetry's expert manipulation of odious anti-Semitic cliches."

In *Idolizing Pictures: Idolatry, Iconoclasm, and Jewish Art,* Julius brings a new interpretation to Jewish law and the Second Commandment prohibition against Jews producing "any graven image." Judith Flanders noted in the *Times Literary Supplement* that his solution "seems almost simple: work out a theory whereby you declare that the biblical prohibitions actively encourage art, just art of a very specific nature. According to Julius, the Second Commandment doesn't just forbid figurative art, it also compels the observant Jew to iconoclasm, to idol-smashing. Thus, if your art is satirical enough, if it attempts to topple that which is respected, revered (loosely, 'idolized'), your creative bent can be welcomed by the religious."

Transgressions: The Offences of Art is Julius's tome on modern transgressive art, or art that depends on sensationalism, such as the depiction of blood, excrement, cruelty, or carnage. Julius refers to the shock value of such images as Robert Mapplethorpe's self-portrait in which a bullwhip protrudes from his anus.

Transgressive art has been evident since the Renaissance but has had more significant representation since the middle of the nineteenth century when it was employed by Edouard Manet, to a degree that now seems tame in comparison to such images as Andres Serrano's *Piss Christ* (1987), in which a crucifix is submerged in urine.

Arthur C. Danto noted in the *Times Literary Supplement* that "the issue with transgressive art was always one of whether it was right that it be supported by public funds, a matter that would be settled by default if the art were genuinely considered criminal. When the *Sensation* show opened at the Brooklyn Museum, Mayor Giuliani's objections to Chris Ofili's 'flinging dung' (the mayor's language) at an image of the Holy Virgin Mary (the artist's language) were to do with whether the transgressing art should be supported by taxpayers who might find it morally repugnant." The Brooklyn Museum falls under municipal authority, the only museum in New York that does, and transgressive art has been shown at private galleries without objection.

Judith Shulevitz wrote in the *New York Times Book Review* that the book "will, or ought to, make it impossible for art critics and curators ever again to utter the word 'transgressive' in a tone of unqualified admiration or to make fun of the 'taboos' of bourgeois society. Julius's rehabilitation of taboo is the most novel part of his thesis, in fact. In his definition, taboo, like art, can serve as a rebuke to reason."

Spectator reviewer Nigel Spivey wrote that "with admirable pleading energy, he [Julius] differentiates three particular modes of transgression—art that defies the rules of art, art that challenges the values of its audience, art that undermines the state—and he manages to present his case in an assize of secular deliberation. 'Decency' here bulks plain as an elephant. But the lure of the naughty, the drag of nastiness, will not go away. We have to check it out."

Art in America critic Carter Ratcliff wrote that although Julius "acknowledges that not all art of the past century and a half makes its point by breaking the rules, he argues that the tactics of transgression have been 'hegemonic' since the middle of the nineteenth century—so much so that, from Manet's time until our own, artists tend not to be taken seriously unless they manage to offend at least one segment of the audience."

BIOGRAPHICAL AND CRITICAL SOURCES:

PERIODICALS

ANQ, summer, 1998, Randy Malamud, review of *T. S. Eliot: Anti-Semitism and Literary Form,* p. 51.

Art in America, July, 2003, Carter Ratcliff, review of *Transgressions: The Offences of Art,* p. 19.

Contemporary Review, December, 1999, R. F. Fleissner, review of *T. S. Eliot.*

Guardian, June 7, 2003, review of *T. S. Eliot.*

Journal of English and Germanic Philology, January, 1998, Gregory Jay, review of *T. S. Eliot,* p. 149.

Library Journal, April 15, 2003, Savannah Schroll, review of *Transgressions,* p. 81; September 1, 2003, Denise J. Stankovics, review of *T. S. Eliot,* p. 166.

New Republic, July 29, 1996, James Wood, review of *T. S. Eliot,* p. 30.

New York Times Book Review, March 23, 2003, Judith Shulevitz, review of *Transgressions,* p. 27.

Notes and Queries, June, 1997, Frank McCombie, review of *T. S. Eliot,* p. 287.

Observer (London, England), January 28, 2001, Lisa Jardine, review of *Idolizing Pictures: Idolatry, Iconoclasm, and Jewish Art,* p. 19.

Publishers Weekly, April 9, 2001, review of *Idolizing Pictures,* p. 67.

Spectator, October 26, 2002, Nigel Spivey, review of *Transgressions,* p. 49.

Times Literary Supplement, April 13, 2001, Judith Flanders, review of *Idolizing Pictures,* p. 20; November 1, 2002, Arthur C. Danto, review of *Transgressions,* p. 7.*

K

KAISER, Ken 1945-

PERSONAL: Born 1945. *Education:* Attended umpire school.

ADDRESSES: Home—Rochester, NY. *Agent*—c/o St. Martin's Press, Publicity Dept., 175 Fifth Ave., New York, NY 10010.

CAREER: Western Carolinas League, Minor League baseball umpire; American League, Major League baseball umpire, 1977-99. Worked as a bar bouncer, bank teller, and as the professional wrestler "Hatchet Man."

AWARDS, HONORS: Sporting News poll, voted Most Colorful Umpire in the American League, 1986.

WRITINGS:

(With David Fisher) *Planet of the Umps: A Baseball Life from behind the Plate,* Thomas Dunne Books (New York, NY), 2003.

SIDELIGHTS: Ken Kaiser is one of America's best-known baseball umpires. Kaiser has umpired two World Series, one Major League All-Star Game, and eight playoff games. Kaiser's autobiography, *Planet of the Umps: A Baseball Life from behind the Plate,* written with biographer David Fisher, tells not only of his twenty-three years in the major leagues but of his ten years in the minors and his off-season jobs as a professional wrestler, bar bouncer, and bank teller. In *Planet of the Umps,* humorous stories abound. A *Publishers Weekly* contributor noted that every page contains "a lively and energetic style [and] at least one great story"

In his youth, Kaiser had no particular ambition. However, the life-changing experience of going to umpire school helped him find his calling. Struggling to make ends meet in the minor leagues, Kaiser worked at various jobs in the off season, including dressing in a black hood and carrying an ax in his wrestling gig as the "Hatchet Man." Kaiser relates stories about umpiring when Michael Jordan played baseball and of being behind the plate when pitcher Gaylord Perry had his 300th win for the Seattle Mariners on May 6, 1982. According to *Ballplayers, Hank Aaron to Jim Lyttle: Baseball's Ultimate Biographical Reference,* Kaiser once ripped a dugout phone from the wall when suspended manager Billy Martin called to direct players, telling Martin, "You're disconnected, Billy!"

Planet of the Umps discusses unions, salaries, and umpires' true feelings about players, managers, and fans. Kaiser also touches on rules about illegal pitchers' motions and the disastrous Major League labor dispute that cost him his job and his six-figure income in 1999. Carolyn T. Hughes noted in the *New York Times Book Review* that, despite all of the controversy, "Kaiser keeps things positive over all." Wes Lukowsky of *Booklist* stated that *Planet of the Umps* is "an enjoyable insider's view of baseball"

BIOGRAPHICAL AND CRITICAL SOURCES:

BOOKS

Ballplayers, Hank Aaron to Jim Lyttle: Baseball's Ultimate Biographical Reference, edited by Mike Shatzkin, Idea Logical Press (New York, NY), 1990.

Kaiser, Ken, and Fisher, David, *Planet of the Umps: A Baseball Life from behind the Plate,* Thomas Dunne Books (New York, NY), 2003.

PERIODICALS

Booklist, June 1, 2003, Wes Lukowsky, review of *Planet of the Umps: A Baseball Life from behind the Plate,* p. 1727.

Library Journal, May 1, 2003, Catherine Collins, review of *Planet of the Umps,* p. 124.

New York Times Book Review, June 29, 2003, Carolyn T. Hughes, review of *Planet of the Umps,* section 7, p. 16.

Publishers Weekly, April 14, 2003, review of *Planet of the Umps,* p. 56.

ONLINE

Baseball Library, http://www.baseballlibrary.com/ (May 28, 2004), Ken Kaiser biography.

South Atlantic League Web site, http://www. southatlanticleague.com/ (May 28, 2004), Ken Kaiser biography.*

*   *   *

KAPLAN, Dana Evan 1960-

PERSONAL: Born October 29, 1960. *Education:* Yeshiva University, B.A. (magna cum laude); State University of New York—Albany, M.A. (medieval Jewish history); University System of New Hampshire—Plymouth, M.Ed.; Tel Aviv University, Ph.D. (modern Jewish history).

ADDRESSES: Agent—Sandy Choron, March Tenth, Inc., 4 Myrtle St., Haworth, New Jersey 07641. *E-mail*—DanaKaplan@aol.com.

CAREER: Kaplan Centre for Jewish Studies and Research, University of Cape Town, South Africa, research associate and lecturer, 1994-97; Center for Jewish Studies, University of Wisconsin, Milwaukee, research scholar, 1997-2000; University of Missouri, Kansas City, Oppenstein Brothers Assistant Professor of Judaic and Religious Studies, 2000-03; visiting research scholar at the University of Miami's Sue and Leonard Miller Center for Contemporary Jewish Studies and Institute for Cuban and Cuban-American Studies, 2002—. Congregation B'nai Israel, Albany, GA, rabbi, 2001—.

MEMBER: Association for Jewish Studies, American Academy of Religion, American Historical Association, American Studies Association, Latin American Jewish Studies Association, Latin American Studies Association, American Association of University Professors, Semitics Society (Jewish Studies Division; South Africa), South African Academy of Religion, Southern Jewish Historical Society, Midwest Jewish Studies Association.

AWARDS, HONORS: State University of New York—Albany fellowship, 1984-86; Tel Aviv University research fellow, 1988-94, Mazer scholar, 1989-90; Forchheimer Foundation fellow, 1990-94; Union of American Hebrew Congregations Sisterhood scholar, 1990-94; Lowenstein-Weiner fellowships, American Jewish Archives, 1994-95, 1999; Ethel Marcus Memorial fellowship, American Jewish Archives, 1995-96; Wisconsin Society for Jewish Learning fellowships, 1997, 1998; Milwaukee Bureau of Jewish Education fellowship, 1998; University of Wisconsin—Milwaukee fellowships, 1998-2000; Tulane University Southern Jewish History Conference travel grant, 2000; Meriwether Lewis fellow, University of Missouri—Kansas City, 2001-02.

WRITINGS:

(Editor) *Contemporary Debates in American Reform Judaism: Conflicting Visions,* Routledge (New York, NY), 2001.

(Editor) *Platforms and Prayer Books: Theological and Liturgical Perspectives on Reform Judaism,* Rowman & Littlefield (Lanham, MD), 2002.

American Reform Judaism: An Introduction, Rutgers University Press (New Brunswick, NJ), 2003.

Contributor of over sixty articles to periodicals. General editor, *Cambridge Companion to American Judaism,* 2005.

WORK IN PROGRESS: A history of Jews in Cuba after Fidel Castro's 1959 revolution; a history of conversion to Judaism in the United States in the nineteenth century; an analysis of contemporary American Judaism; a reader of the primary sources on contemporary American Judaism.

SIDELIGHTS: Dana Evan Kaplan is a Jewish studies scholar whose research interests include American Jewish history, Reform Judaism, intermarriage, and conversion, as well as the Jewish experience in South Africa and Cuba. He was born in Manhattan, New York, and moved to Waterbury, Connecticut, when he was fourteen. He studied in Israel for several years and worked for a short time in Australia and a longer period in South Africa. His three published books have all dealt with Reform Judaism, but in his future work, Kaplan looks to include books on a number of other areas in Jewish studies.

His major work to date has been *American Reform Judaism: An Introduction,* published in 2003. In this book, Kaplan provides an overview of the Reform movement from its nineteenth-century European beginnings to the present time, with the stress on contemporary developments. He notes changes in services, challenges to Reform education, the impact of intermarriage, women's equality, gay and lesbian relationships, and speculates on the future of the movement. Kaplan notes that the recent trend toward returning to traditional beliefs and practices often clashes with Classical Reform, which is a more flexible approach that serves contemporary Jews, causing Reform to move "in two directions at the same time." *Booklist* contributor George Cohen called the volume "an expansive examination of the religion." A *Publishers Weekly* contributor felt that although Kaplan focuses on Reform Judaism, "his astute reasoning has value for all religious groups that struggle with maintaining their established beliefs in the face of the demands and challenges posed by modernity." In a *Dallas Morning News* review, Harriet P. Gross called *American Reform Judaism* "the book American Jews have been waiting for—whether they know it or not!" *Reform Judaism* magazine named it "a significant Jewish book," and the magazine's Bonny V. Fetterman

called it "essential reading for everyone concerned with the future of Reform Judaism." Writing in *Choice,* Alan Avery Peck thought that "the book's strength is Kaplan's determination to question why, in the historical context, the movement took the directions it did and, more importantly, to reflect on the impact each development had on Reform's current and future viability."

Published in 2001, Kaplan's first book was an edited collection on articles titled *Contemporary Debates in American Reform Judaism: Conflicting Visions.* According to the author, this was a groundbreaking collection of essays that took a hard look at the Reform movement today. Opening essays describe and evaluate interpretations of the then latest census data for Reform Jews, the problem of building a cohesive religious community, the competition in the "spiritual marketplace," and why people join or do not join a Reform synagogue. Other contributors examine a host of controversial issues, including patrilineal descent, outreach, intermarriage, gender issues (including women rabbis), gay and lesbian participation, the 1999 vote on the New Pittsburgh Platform, and others.

Kaplan's other book is *Platforms and Prayer Books: Theological and Liturgical Perspectives on Reform Judaism,* a collection of twenty essays in which he explores American Reform Judaism's response to social and theological change. "Like any such volume, some essays would have been better excluded," noted R. Langer in *Choice,* "but the aggregate is impressive." The volume includes historical essays dealing with abstract themes such as exclusivity, pluralism, and collective idenity. There are also liturgical studies, including an article on the first Reform prayer book in the United States and the role of meditation in Progressive Judaism. There is a section of comparative studies which, in particular, has an essay explaining the theological differences between Reconstructionalism and Reform. The final essay deals with autonomy and authority in Jewish texts.

Kaplan told *CA:* "I was interested in writing from a young age. Both my mother and my aunt worked in publishing and encouraged my interest. I particularly remember that during high school my aunt and I would analyze essays and books and discuss what was successful. At the same time, I was very interested in what even then was clearly a changing Jewish community. I wondered how things had gotten the way they were and what might happen in the future. I think I have been at least partially pleasantly surprised. I had expected that the rising intermarriage rate combined with the low-intensity religious involvement of most American Jews would severely diminish American Judaism. That may yet come to be the case, but if so, it is happening much slower that I expected.

"I was also interested in how Judaism was practiced in other countries, Although my family was Reform, my parents had sent me to an Orthodox Zionist day school in Manhattan. The teachers were constantly stressing how we should feel loyal to Israel, and how that even though that wasn't a dual loyalty problem, our historical roots had to take precedence over our recent comfortable sojourn in the United States. I studied in Israel and was actually very disappointed. The teachers had led me to believe that we would be welcomed with open arms. But I found the Israelis to be very arrogant and completely disinterested in the American Jewish issues that fascinated me. This was, of course, very understandable, but it upset me at the time. I think this was also a factor in my writing in that I wanted to understand American Judaism and how and why it differed from the Judaism I encountered in Israel.

"Once I left Israel, I stayed interested in various Diaspora communities. I served as a student rabbi in Australia for two four-month periods in the Northern Hemisphere in summers of 1992 and 1993. I never wrote about my experiences, but I read a lot and started the intellectual process which must precede any thoughtful writing. I lived in South Africa from 1994-1997. It was there that I began writing seriously about contemporary Jewish affairs. I arrived in August, 1994, just a few months after the historic election that brought Nelson Mandela to power. I thought that there was a need for a religiously progressive voice to interpret events and to suggest a way forward, so I began writing for both popular and academic publications on Judaism in the new South Africa. Later, I became interested in Fidel Castro's Cuba, and it is possible that I may write about other Diaspora communities in the future.

"When I was in graduate school, I asked one of my professors in medieval Jewish history if he felt that every Jewish topic had been covered. He told me no, that he had plenty of material. The only limitation he had was time. In contemporary Jewish studies, this is even more true. There are all sorts of articles talking about the proliferation of Jewish studies works. This is true, but there are many areas that have barely been touched on. I try to pick subjects that have an intrinsic importance but which are also likely to attract a readership. I would hope to model myself after those who have been both serious intellectuals as well as communal leaders and popular writers.

"I would hope that my books will help people to understand contemporary Judaism. I don't have an ideological agenda that I am trying to push, at least not consciously. I try to write in a readable way that I hope people will find enjoyable. I avoid unnecessary big words and try to convey my ideas in a simple, straightforward manner. But I'm still very much an academic-style writer. I recently collaborated with a journalist on an article on the Jews of Cuba for a national Jewish magazine. I am amazed at the questions that she asked me. 'What color was his coat? What kind of table cloth did they have?' I'm not used to thinking in such concrete terms. For me, there are certain central intellectual questions which I'm trying to answer or at least raise. But I hope to learn more about this descriptive writing as well. You want to be able to guide the reader gently into the story and help him or her engage with the ideas without scaring them off. I believe the books and articles that I publish can make a contribution to Jewish life and intellectual discourse, and that can happen only if people read my work."

BIOGRAPHICAL AND CRITICAL SOURCES:

PERIODICALS

Booklist, June 1, 2003, George Cohen, review of *American Reform Judaism: An Introduction,* p. 1713.

Choice, April, 2003, R. Langer, review of *Platforms and Prayer Books: Theological and Liturgical Perspectives on Reform Judaism;* February, 2004, A. J. Avery-Peck, review of *American Reform Judaism.*

Dallas Morning News, August 6, 2003, Harriet P. Gross, review of *American Reform Judaism.*

Publishers Weekly, May 12, 2003, review of *American Reform Judaism,* p. 63.

Reform Judaism, winter, 2003, Bonny V. Fetterman, "Significant Jewish Books, in Search for a Usable Past," pp. 54-55.

ONLINE

Dana Evan Kaplan Home Page, http://www.dana
kaplan.com/ (March 8, 2004).

* * *

KARL, Frederick R(obert) 1927-2004

OBITUARY NOTICE—See index for *CA* sketch: Born
April 10, 1927, in New York, NY; died of kidney
disease, April 30, 2004, in New York, NY. Educator
and author. Karl was an English professor, literary
critic, and biographer best known for his scholarly
works on Joseph Conrad. After serving in the U.S.
Navy from 1944 to 1946, he completed a bachelor's
degree at Columbia College in 1948; this was followed by a master's from Stanford University in 1949
and a doctorate from Columbia University in 1957. He
joined the faculty at the City College of the City
University of New York in 1957, where he remained
until 1982, when he became an English professor for
New York University. Karl retired from teaching in
2000. Fascinated by Conrad's life and career since his
days in graduate school, Karl contacted the author's
estate and obtained publication rights for his writings.
Thanks to this foresight, he was later able to edit, with
Laurence Davies, the three-volume *The Collected Letters of Joseph Conrad* (1983-88); he also wrote the
biography *Joseph Conrad: The Three Lives* (1979).
Karl was highly regarded for his literary guides, too,
which included such works as *The Contemporary
English Novel* (1962), *A Century of Fiction: The British Novel in the Nineteenth Century* (1965), and *American Fictions, 1940-1980: A Comprehensive History
and Critical Evaluation* (1983), as well as for his
biographies of other literary figures, including *C. P.
Snow: The Politics of Conscience* (1963), *William
Faulkner, American Writer: A Biography* (1989), and
George Eliot, Voice of a Century: A Biography (1995).
The former cochair of the New York University
seminar on biography writing and editor of the
"Biography and Source Studies" series from 1995 to
2003, Karl had just completed a collection of essays
about biography writing at the time of his death; it
will be published posthumously.

OBITUARIES AND OTHER SOURCES:

PERIODICALS

Los Angeles Times, May 10, 2004, p. B9.

New York Times, May 6, 2004, p. A26.
Times (London, England), May 19, 2004, p. 27.
Washington Post, May 13, 2004, p. B6.

* * *

KAUFFMAN, Donna 1960(?)

PERSONAL: Born c. 1960, in Washington, DC; married Mark Jean (in law enforcement); children: (first
marriage) two sons; (second marriage) one stepson.
Hobbies and other interests: "Soccer mom," hiking
the Blue Ridge Mountains, driving in the country.

ADDRESSES: Home—P.O. Box 541, Ashburn, VA
20146-0541. *Agent*—Bantam Dell Publishing Group,
Random House, Inc., 1745 Broadway, New York, NY,
10019. *E-mail*—donna@donnakauffman.com; dm
kauffman@aol.com.

CAREER: Romance novelist. Previously worked as a
hairdresser and competitive bodybuilder.

MEMBER: Romance Writer's Association, Washington
Romance Writers (board member; past president).

AWARDS, HONORS: RIO Dorothy Parker Award for
best paranormal, for *The Legend MacKinnon;* Reviewers Choice Award, Romance Communications, for *The
Legend of the Sorcerer* and *The Legend MacKinnon;*
National Readers Choice Award for best erotic
romance, for *Her Secret Thrill;* lifetime achievement
award, Washington Romance Writers, 2001.

WRITINGS:

Illegal Motion, Bantam (New York, NY), 1993.
Black Satin, Bantam (New York, NY), 1994.
Tango in Paradise, Bantam (New York, NY), 1994.
Bounty Hunter, Bantam (New York, NY), 1994.
Wild Rain (spin-off from *Black Satin*), Bantam (New
York, NY), 1995.
Bayou Heat, Bantam (New York, NY), 1996.
Tease Me, Bantam (New York, NY), 1998.
Her Secret Thrill, Harlequin (New York, NY), 2001.
His Private Pleasure (spin-off from *Her Secret Thrill*),
Harlequin (New York, NY), 2002.

Sean (spin-off from *Men of Courage* anthology; also see below), Harlequin (New York, NY), 2003.
Jingle Bell Rock, Kensington Brava (New York, NY), 2003.
Against the Odds (spin-off from *His Private Pleasure*), Harlequin (New York, NY), 2003.
Merry Christmas Baby, Kensington Brava (New York, NY), 2004.

NOVELS; "THREE MUSKETEERS" SERIES

The Three Musketeers: Surrender the Dark, Bantam (New York, NY), 1995.
The Three Musketeers: Born to Be Wild, Bantam (New York, NY), 1996.
The Three Musketeers: Midnight Heat, Bantam (New York, NY), 1996.

NOVELS; "DELGADO'S DIRTY DOZEN" SERIES

Santerra's Sin, Bantam (New York, NY), 1996.
Silent Warrior, Bantam (New York, NY), 1997.
Light My Fire, Bantam (New York, NY), 1997.
Dark Knight, Bantam (New York, NY), 1998.

ANTHOLOGIES

(With others) *Yours 2 Keep,* Bantam (New York, NY), 1999.
(With Lori Foster and Janelle Denison) *I Love Bad Boys,* Kensington Brava (New York, NY), 2002.
Men of Courage, Harlequin (New York, NY), 2003.
(With Lori Foster and Janelle Denison) *Bad Boys on Board,* Kensington Brava (New York, NY), 2003.
(With Lori Foster and Janelle Denison) *Bad Boys, Next Exit,* Kensington Brava (New York, NY), 2004.

PARANORMAL NOVELS

The Legend MacKinnon, Bantam (New York, NY), 1999.
The Legend of the Sorcerer, Bantam (New York, NY), 2000.
Your Wish Is My Command, Bantam (New York, NY), 2000.

The Royal Hunter, Bantam (New York, NY), 2001.
The Charm Stone, Bantam (New York, NY), 2002.

CONTEMPORARY ROMANCE NOVELS

The Big Bad Wolf Tells All (formerly titled *The Last Bridesmaid*), Bantam (New York, NY), 2003.
The Cinderella Rules, Bantam (New York, NY), 2004.
Dear Prince Charming, Bantam (New York, NY), 2004.

OTHER

Also author of *Walk on the Wild Side, In the Heat of the Night,* and *Carried Away,* all published by Harlequin.

WORK IN PROGRESS: Articles in anthologies, including *Men of Courage 2,* Harlequin (New York, NY), 2005, and *Velvet, Leather, and Lace,* Harlequin (New York, NY), 2005.

SIDELIGHTS: Romance novelist Donna Kauffman has either won or been nominated for an award for nearly every book she has published. She wrote her first romance novel, *Illegal Motion,* while pregnant with her second child. According to Sarah Schafer of the *Washington Post,* when Kauffman is confronted with the frequently asked question of when she intends to "write a real book," her response is simply that "It's entertainment . . . that's what I want to do," and jokes that country singer Willie Nelson is not ever asked about writing an opera. "Besides," Kauffman added, "romance books are a billion-dollar business. Who has to defend that?"

Kauffman described to Schafer that her first book was published through an "accidental" meeting with an editor while attending a writers conference in Harpers Ferry, West Virginia. The editor was frightened by a noise in the spooky old hotel the group was staying in and "came barreling into" Kauffman in the hallway. Kauffman helped the woman trace the noise to a handyman simply doing his duty; the editor helped her publish her book. The women became fast friends, and the editor ultimately became deputy vice publisher with Bantam.

Kauffman's books almost always receive favorable reviews. Reviewing for *Romance Reader,* Ellen Hestand commented after reading *Tease Me* that the book and the author "are both gems in my book," and called the story a "sexy, funny, good-timing romp that nevertheless packs a few emotionally intense punches . . . and doesn't sacrifice quality for laughs." Judi McKee, also a reviewer for *Romance Reader,* noted that Kauffman's characters are believable, real-world types and praised the way in which Kauffman builds a "real sexual tension" between them. "The relationship heats up at a believable pace, with a nice blend of action and insight into the characters' thoughts," commented McKee. Similarly, *Romance Reader* contributor Linda Mowery liked the fact that in *Walk on the Wild Side,* Kauffman's characters "seem normal, more like you and me, with fears and doubts about finally giving up autonomy and letting another person matter deeply."

The Legend of MacKinnon was Kauffman's first paranormal romance and could almost be said to be three novels in one. "Somehow, she wove the combination of six main characters and the various paranormal threads into a cohesive, if busy, whole," wrote Susan Scribner for *Romance Reader.* Duncan MacKinnon is a tall, 300-year-old Scottish ghost who, when spooking Maggie the mortal heroine for the first time, wears nothing but a kilt. Of the several challenges faced by Kauffman in this book, it was important, she told Schafer, for the heroine "to have reactions we would have." In order to make the entire story believable, she traveled to Scotland to complete her background research.

Kauffman's subsequent paranormals were also well received. A reviewer for *Kirkus Reviews* commented that *The Big Bad Wolf Tells All,* the story of a "been-there, done-that babe [who] falls for Mr. Nice Guy," is a "wisp of a story deftly spun to novel length—with a zippy style to keep it going." Of *The Charm Stone,* an intergenerational romance between a young South Carolina surfer girl and (again) a 300-year-old Scottish ghost, a *Publishers Weekly* reviewer wrote that the book is a good balance of romance and humor and that its "charm lies . . . in its playful plot, lively Scottish island setting, appropriately funny writing style, and eccentric cast of characters." Regarding *Royal Hunter,* Maria Hatton of *Booklist* commented that readers "are in for a great adventure."

BIOGRAPHICAL AND CRITICAL SOURCES:

PERIODICALS

Booklist, September 15, 2000, Nina Davis, review of *Santerra's Sin,* p. 225; September 15, 2001, Maria Hatton, review of *The Royal Hunter,* p. 204; May 1, 2003, Beth Leistensnider, review of *The Big Bad Wolf Tells All,* p. 1579.
Entertainment Weekly, June 13, 2003, review of *The Big Bad Wolf Tells All,* p. 100.
Kirkus Reviews, April 1, 2003, review of *The Big Bad Wolf Tells All,* pp. 496-497.
Library Journal, May 1, 2003, review of *The Big Bad Wolf Tells All,* p. 154.
Publishers Weekly, August 6, 2001, review of *The Royal Hunter,* p. 66; July 8, 2002, review of *The Charm Stone,* p. 37; May 26, 2003, review of *The Big Bad Wolf Tells All,* p. 48.
Washington Post, September 9, 1999, Sarah Schafer, "Author Profits from Her Passion; Sterling Woman Finds Her Happily Ever After Writing Romance Novels," interview with Donna Kauffman, V5.

ONLINE

AuthorsontheWeb.com Web site, http://www.authorsontheweb.com/ (February, 2004), "Chick Lit Author Roundtable."
Donna Kauffman Home Page, http://www.donnakauffman.com (July 10, 2004).
Romance Reader Web site, http://www.theromancereader.com/ (July 10, 2004), Susan Scribner, review of *The Royal Hunter;* Irene Williams, review of *Your Wish Is My Command;* Susan Scribner, review of *The Charm Stone;* Susan Scribner, review of *The Big Bad Wolf Tells All;* Susan Scribner, review of *The Royal Hunter;* Irene Williams, review of *In the Heat of the Night;* Ellen Hestand, review of *Tease Me;* Judi McKee, review of *Carried Away;* Linda Mowery, review of *Walk on the Wild Side;* Susan Scribner, review of *The Legend of the Sorcerer.**

*   *   *

KAUFMAN, Victor S(cott) 1969-

PERSONAL: Born February 27, 1969, in Slidell, LA; son of Burton Ira (a historian and college dean) and Diane Beatrice (a college archivist; maiden name, Kallison) Kaufman. *Ethnicity:* "Caucasian." *Education:*

Kansas State University, B.A. (cum laude), 1991; Ohio University, M.A., 1994, Ph.D., 1998. *Politics:* Democrat. *Religion:* Jewish. *Hobbies and other interests:* Travel, power lifting.

ADDRESSES: Home—1349 Brittany Dr., Apt. H, Florence, SC 29501. *Office*—Department of History, Francis Marion University, Box 100547, Florence, SC 29501-0547; fax: 843-661-1555. *E-mail*—vkaufman@ fmarion.edu.

CAREER: Ohio University, Athens, instructor in history, 1997; Virginia Polytechnic Institute and State University, Blacksburg, instructor in history, 1997-98; Kennesaw State University, Kennesaw, GA, instructor in history, 1998-99; Southwest Missouri State University, Springfield, lecturer in history, 1999-2001; Francis Marion University, Florence, SC, assistant professor of history, 2001—. Georgia State University, instructor, 1998-99.

MEMBER: Society for Historians of American Foreign Relations, American Association of University Professors, Phi Beta Kappa, Phi Alpha Theta, Phi Kappa Phi, Golden Key.

AWARDS, HONORS: Moody grant, Lyndon Baines Johnson Foundation, 1996; Eisenhower Presidential Library grant, 1999.

WRITINGS:

Confronting Communism: U.S. and British Policies toward China, University of Missouri Press (Columbia, MO), 2001.

Contributor to periodicals, including *English Historical Review, Journal of Contemporary History, Journal of American-East Asian Relations, China Quarterly,* and *Historian.*

WORK IN PROGRESS: The Pig War: The United States, Britain, and the Balance of Power in the Pacific Northwest, 1846-1872, for Lexington Books (Lexington, MA); a contribution to *SHAFR Guide to American Foreign Relations since 1600.*

SIDELIGHTS: Victor S. Kaufman told *CA:* "Having a father in the field of history and being surrounded by academicians all of my life influenced me to pursue a career as a history professor. Doctors Chester Pach and John Lewis Gaddis, with whom I took graduate classes, strengthened a burgeoning interest in U.S. foreign policy during the Cold War and, along with my father, moved me to work on Anglo-American policy toward communist China during that period of history. While I retain an interest in Cold War diplomacy, my current topic was inspired by, of all things, a bike ride. While riding bicycles with some friends in Seattle, I heard a story about a war that nearly started over a pig. I thought they were just joking. I began to do research into the subject and found out that, not only was it true—and that it was called, appropriately enough, the Pig War—but this subject had not been examined from a diplomatic standpoint, even though there were some very significant issues involved, especially that of the balance of power in the Pacific Northwest. Sometimes inspiration comes when one least expects it, and I can attest that this is true."

*   *   *

KELLY, Saul 1957-

PERSONAL: Born 1957; son of Dr. John Barrett (a professor) and Valda Elizabeth (Pitt) Kelly; married Judith Elizabeth Nicola Liddell-King, 1993 (divorced, 2003); children: Jacob. *Education:* London School of Economics and Political Science, B.A., 1980, Ph.D., 1995. *Hobbies and other interests:* Tennis, rugby.

ADDRESSES: Office—Defence Studies Department, Joint Services Command and Staff College, Faringdon Rd., Watchfield, Swindon, Wiltshire SN6 8TS England. *E-mail*—skelly@jscsc.org.

CAREER: King's College London (at Joint Services Command and Staff College), England, lecturer in defence studies, 2001—. Previously worked as research associate, International Boundaries Research Unit, University of Durham, and research fellow, University of Westminster.

MEMBER: London Library, Libyan Society, Royal Geographical Society (fellow).

WRITINGS:

(Editor, with Anthony Gorst) *Whitehall and the Suez Crisis,* Frank Cass (Portland, OR), 2000.

(With Charles Douglas-Home) *Dignified and Efficient: The British Monarchy in the Twentieth Century,* Claridge (London, England), 2000.

Cold War in the Desert: Britain, the United States, and the Italian Colonies, 1945-52, St. Martin's (New York, NY), 2000.

The Lost Oasis: The Desert War and the Hunt for Zerzura, J. Murray (London, England), 2002, Westview (Boulder, CO), 2003.

Contributor of essays to books, including Jonathan Hollowell, editor, *Anglo-American Relations in the Twentieth Century,* Macmillan (London, England); and Kent Fedorowich and Martin Thomas, editors, *The Politics of Colonial Retreat: Decolonization and International Diplomacy, 1940-75,* Frank Cass (London, England).

WORK IN PROGRESS: A study of the role of the British Embassy in Washington on Anglo-American relations; SOE in the Middle East and an account of the intelligence war in the Middle East from 1939-45.

SIDELIGHTS: Saul Kelly's scholarship centers upon the Cold War in the Middle East and on British espionage efforts in the North African desert during the Second World War. *Whitehall and the Suez Crisis,* which he edited with Anthony Gorst, consists of twelve essays profiling "key Whitehall warriors" who—sometimes against their better judgment—helped to deal with the Suez Crisis. In the *International History Review,* Howard Dooley called the work "a groundbreaking book about the workings of the machinery of the British government during the Suez Crisis." Dooley praised the contributors for concerning themselves with "the actions and problems of the civil servants in the back rooms who did not set policy but had to implement it and pick up the pieces afterwards." *Spectator* contributor Donald Cameron Watt felt that, taken together, the essays in the book "give a remarkably consistent picture." Watt also commended the essays as "carefully crafted perceptive studies." In his review, Dooley concluded by calling *Whitehall and the Suez Crisis* "a book full of plums, and rounded out by a fine bibliographic essay."

The late Charles Douglas-Home was at work on a book about the British monarchy when he died. Kelly finished the work and published it as *Dignified and Efficient: The British Monarchy in the Twentieth Century.* The book explores the monarchy from a political perspective and evaluates the performance of those kings and queens who reigned in the United Kingdom during the twentieth century. In his *Times Literary Supplement* review of *Dignified and Efficient,* John Grigg concluded: "Between them, Charles Douglas-Home and Saul Kelly have made a good contribution to the vast literature on the British monarchy. Their study of an ever-fascinating subject is both thoughtful and readable."

Kelly's *The Lost Oasis: The Desert War and the Hunt for Zerzura* tells the true story of the adventuresome explorer/spy who is featured in the novel *The English Patient.* Kelly's book describes the membership and objectives of the Zerzura Club, an international group of desert-lovers who began exploring the uncharted North African desert in the 1930s and then worked as spies for their respective governments or allegiances during World War II. One of these members, Lazlo Almasy, was portrayed in fiction as "the English Patient" by author Michael Ondaatje. In the *Times Literary Supplement* professor Hew Strachan felt that Kelly's "scholarly detective work clearly reveals how signals and human intelligence work off each other, and how 'spy stories' need once again to be reintegrated into the dominant narrative." *Spectator* reviewer Justin Marozzi observed: "Kelly's history of the early exploration of the Libyan desert and the swashbuckling operations of Bagnold and Almasy during the war is a fascinating read, packed with detail. Deserts, war and espionage are a potent trio from a literary point of view."

BIOGRAPHICAL AND CRITICAL SOURCES:

PERIODICALS

Booklist, March 15, 2003, Michele Leber, review of *The Lost Oasis: The Desert War and the Hunt for Zerzura,* p. 1272.

Choice, December, 2000, review of *Cold War in the Desert: Britain, the United States, and the Italian Colonies, 1945-52,* p. 757.

English Historical Review, September, 2000, Michael Dockrill, review of *Whitehall and the Suez Crisis,* p. 1037.

Geographical, September, 2002, "Recommended Reading on Africa," p. 56.

History: Review of New Books, fall, 2003, Richard A. Voeltz, review of *The Lost Oasis,* p. 29.

International History Review, September, 2001, Howard Dooley, review of *Whitehall and the Suez Crisis,* pp. 717-719; December, 2001, Scott L. Bills, review of *Cold War in the Desert,* pp. 977-978.

Publishers Weekly, March 31, 2003, review of *The Lost Oasis,* p. 51.

Spectator, April 1, 2000, Donald Cameron Watt, "Cock-up and Cover-up," review of *Whitehall and the Suez Crisis,* p. 58; June 8, 2002, Justin Marozzi, "Strange Exploits of the Zerzura Club," review of *The Lost Oasis,* p. 46.

Times Literary Supplement, December 22, 2000, John Grigg, "Stirred but Not Shaken," review of *Dignified and Efficient: The British Monarchy in the Twentieth Century,* p. 8; October 18, 2002, Hew Strachan, "The End of the Beginning," review of *The Lost Oasis,* p. 14.

ONLINE

Cairo Times, http://www.cairotimes.com/ (June 24, 2003), Steve Negus, "The Mother of All Conspiracies."

*   *   *

KELSAY, Michael 1957-

PERSONAL: Born December 18, 1957, in Huntington, WV; son of Don and Karen (Harvey) Kelsay; married Mary Fullington, November 1, 1996. *Education:* University of Kentucky, B.A., 1990; McNeese State University, M.A. and M.F.A., both 1993.

ADDRESSES: Home—P.O. Box 423, Lexington, KY 40588-0423. *Agent*—Witherspoon Associates, 235 East 31st St., New York, NY 10016. *E-mail*—m.kelsy@ insightbb.com.

CAREER: Writer.

AWARDS, HONORS: Emily Clark Balch Award, *Virginia Quarterly Review,* 1993, for a short story, "I'll Sleep When I'm Dead"; Al Smith fellowship, Kentucky Arts Council, 1995.

WRITINGS:

Too Close to Call (novel), University Press of Mississippi (Jackson, MS), 2001.

Basketball in Kentucky: Great Balls of Fire (documentary miniseries), broadcast by Kentucky Educational Television, 2002.

Contributor to periodicals, including *Virginia Quarterly Review.*

WORK IN PROGRESS: A novel.

*   *   *

KENNEY, Padraic (Jeremiah) 1963-

PERSONAL: Born March 29, 1963; married, wife's name, Iza; children: Maia, Karolina. *Education:* Harvard College, A.B. (Slavic languages and literature; magna cum laude), 1985; University of Toronto, M.A. (history), 1986; University of Michigan, Ph.D. (history), 1992.

ADDRESSES: Office—Department of History, Box 234, University of Colorado, Boulder, CO 80309-0234. *E-mail*—padraic.kenney@colorado.edu; kenneyp@ colorado.edu.

CAREER: University of Colorado, Boulder, assistant professor, 1992-99, associate professor, 1999-2003, professor of history, 2003—, associate chair and director of undergraduate studies, department of history.

MEMBER: American Association for the Advancement of Slavic Studies, Polish Studies Association.

AWARDS, HONORS: American Council of Learned Societies fellowship, 1991-92; research grant, International Research and Exchanges Board, 1993; awards from the University of Colorado, including the Twentieth-Century Humanist fellowship, 1996; research fellowship, Woodrow Wilson International Center for Scholars, 1997; Outstanding Academic Book, *Choice,* 1997, and AAASS/Orbis Book Prize, 1998, both for *Rebuilding Poland: Workers and Com-*

munists, 1945-1950; Heldt Prize, Association of Women in Slavic Studies, 1999, for "The Gender of Resistance in Communist Poland"; research fellowship, German Marshall Fund of the United States, 1999-2000; Fulbright lecturer, Poland, 2002-03; grant, Deutcher Akademiker Austausch Dienst, Goethe Institute (Berlin, Germany), 2003.

WRITINGS:

Rebuilding Poland: Workers and Communists, 1945-1950, Cornell University Press (Ithaca, NY), 1997.
A Carnival of Revolution: Central Europe, 1989, Princeton University Press (Princeton, NJ), 2002.
(Editor, with Gerd-Rainer Horn) *Transnational Moments of Change: Europe 1945, 1968, 1989,* Rowman and Littlefield (Lanham, MD), 2004.

Work represented in books by others, including *The Establishment of Communist Regimes in Eastern Europe: A Reassessment,* edited by Norman Naimark and Leonid Gibianskii, Westview (Boulder, CO), 1997, and *Cultures and Nations of Central and Eastern Europe,* edited by Zvi Gitelman, Lubomyr Hajda, John-Paul Himka, and Roman Solchanyk, Harvard Ukrainian Research Institute (Cambridge, MA), 2000. Author of "The Gender of Resistance in Communist Poland," *American Historical Review,* April, 1999. Contributor of articles, essays, and reviews to journals, including *American Historical Review, Slavic Review, Contemporary European History, H-Net Reviews* (online), *East European Politics and Societies, Labor History,* and *Journal of Cold War Studies;* contributor to periodicals, including the *Boston Globe.* Serves on the editorial boards of journals, including *Slavic Review,* and academic series, including Ohio University Press's "Polish-American Studies" series.

WORK IN PROGRESS: Editor, with Max Paul Friedman, *Partisan Histories: The Past in Contemporary Global Politics,* Palgrave, 2005.

SIDELIGHTS: Padraic Kenney is a professor of history whose teaching areas include modern Eastern and Central Europe, Poland, and comparative communism. His first book, *Rebuilding Poland: Workers and Communists, 1945-1950,* benefits from archival material that has been made available since the fall of communism in East and Central Europe. Robert A. Berry

wrote in *Europe-Asia Studies* that the book "is a pioneering effort to understand the dynamics of the early communist period at the level of the factory workers seeking to rebuild the state and to achieve dignity within it, as well as of the party cadres attempting to translate ideology into acceptance and power."

Kenney studies the struggle between the workers and the communists in two cities during this period. Lodz and its solidly united working-class population, which had been the center of the textile industry in prewar Poland, survived the war nearly unscathed. Wroclaw was an industrial town in the newly acquired west, and the traditional German population was replaced, for the most part, with Polish peasants, who lacked experience or the social structure of Lodz. Consequently, Lodz workers were more effective in their use of strikes in fulfilling their demands, but the Wroclaw workers, most of them single, also gained ground, in part because they had a lower degree of loyalty or pressure to remain either in the area or with any individual company.

During these years the state industry, the unions, and the workers felt the loss of their "moral community." In 1947 female textile workers in Lodz went on strike when they were told to work multiple looms. Eighteen factories were idled before the women were locked out. These strikers had stood up as women and mothers in the past, protesting working hours, shortages, and lack of child care. The workers of Wroclaw did not have the advantage of solidarity that protected the Lodz workers, and the Polish Workers' Party (PPR) was able to sign up most of them because the workers thought membership was necessary in order to obtain a job.

The state could not raise productivity through repression, however, and during the Stalinist revolution of 1948-1950 a system of rewards was instituted in which workers competed by producing more. In the end the system was not a permanent solution. Competition and tactics to "fix" documented production caused problems among employees, and the older workers resisted the changes. In 1949 wage reform was instituted that also eliminated the bonuses, but the state was unable to take away many of benefits that had been appropriated to the workers, and eventually the state was bankrupted by high labor costs.

Douglas Selvage wrote for *H-Net Reviews* online that Kenney "succeeds in demonstrating that Polish workers were not 'helpless victims' of the communist state. They did influence communist policies and their application; they did 'turn the system to their own advantage and lessen its crueler aspects.' More importantly, they maintained their antagonistic class identity, rooted in prewar traditions."

In *A Carnival of Revolution: Central Europe, 1989,* Kenney argues that the Iron Curtain (the ideological barrier between the communist countries and the Western world) did not fall solely because of the efforts of the United States or Soviet leader Mikhail Gorbachev's perestroika, but that the groundwork for the bloodless revolutions was laid by "broad social unrest on dozens of stages." Kenney was a graduate student researcher in Poland in the 1980s, and saw first-hand how the efforts of underground rock musicians, artists, guerrilla theater, and protestors fed dissent, along with the traditional grassroots peace movements in Poland and Hungary and the environmental movement in Czechoslovakia. This revolutionary carnival lasted from the spring of 1986, with demonstrations after the Chernobyl nuclear accident, until the Velvet Revolution in Prague. Kenney chose his title because the revolution was "joyous" and a mixture of "anarchism, nationalism, liberalism, conservatism, and postmaterialism in idiosyncratic ways." Ben Ehrenreich wrote in *Mother Jones* that "Kenney's careful account returns history to its rightful owners, the thousands who risked what little security they had to sneak a little joy into their lives."

American Historical Review's David Ost wrote that *A Carnival of Revolution* "should be a treasure chest for historians for years to come. . . . It is still too soon to explain what 1989 was all about, but this book contains important pieces of the puzzle, which is why it will be a crucial reference for a long time to come."

BIOGRAPHICAL AND CRITICAL SOURCES:

BOOKS

Kenney, Padraic, *A Carnival of Revolution: Central Europe, 1989,* Princeton University Press (Princeton, NJ), 2002.

PERIODICALS

American Historical Review, June, 1998, Robert E. Blobaum, review of *Rebuilding Poland: Workers and Communists, 1945-1950,* p. 929; June, 2003, David Ost, review of *A Carnival of Revolution: Central Europe, 1989,* pp. 941-942.

Choice, July-August, 1997, P. W. Knoll, review of *Rebuilding Poland,* p. 1857; November, 2002, J. Granville, review of *A Carnival of Revolution,* p. 532.
Europe-Asia Studies, January, 1998, Robert A. Berry, review of *Rebuilding Poland,* p. 161.
International History Review, December, 2002, John J. Kulczycki, review of *A Carnival of Revolution,* pp. 977-978.
Library Journal, June 1, 2002, Marcia L. Sprules, review of *A Carnival of Revolution,* p. 170.
Mother Jones, July-August, 2002, Ben Ehrenreich, review of *A Carnival of Revolution,* p. 73.
Slavic Review, fall, 1997, Richard D. Lewis, review of *Rebuilding Poland,* pp. 563-564.
Slavonic and East European Review, April, 2001, George Sanford, review of *Rebuilding Poland,* p. 367.
Social History, January, 1999, Andrew Port, review of *Rebuilding Poland, p. 103.*
Times Literary Supplement, January 31, 2003, John Gray, review of *A Carnival of Revolution,* p. 27.

ONLINE

H-Net Reviews Web site, http://www.h-net.msu.edu/ (June 5, 2004), Douglas Selvage, review of *Rebuilding Poland: Workers and Communists, 1945-1950.**

*   *   *

KENNY, Lorraine Delia 1961-

PERSONAL: Born February 21, 1961, in NY. *Education:* University of Chicago, B.A. (with honors), 1984; University of California—Santa Cruz, Ph.D., 1996.

ADDRESSES: Office—American Civil Liberties Union, 125 Broad St., New York, NY 10004. *E-mail*—lkenny@aclu.org.

CAREER: Visual Studies Workshop, Rochester, NY, intern, 1984-85, assistant editor, 1985-86, subscriptions coordinator, 1985-87, associate editor, 1987-89; National Council for Research on Women, New York, NY, coordinating editor, 1994-96; freelance copy editor and proofreader, 1996-97; Sarah Lawrence College, Bronxville, NY, member of anthropology guest faculty, 1997-2000; American Civil Liberties Union, New York, NY, public education coordinator for Reproductive Freedom Project, 2000—. University of California—Santa Cruz, instructor, 1992, 1993; La-Guardia Community College of the City University of New York, adjunct assistant professor, 1996, 1997; New School for Social Research, adjunct assistant professor at Eugene Lang College, 1997; also speaker at Free University of Amsterdam and University of California—Berkeley; workshop coordinator.

AWARDS, HONORS: Grant from New York State Council on the Arts, 1987; Woodrow Wilson fellowship, 1994-95; Significant University Press Title citation, *Choice*, 2001, for *Daughters of Suburbia: Growing Up White, Middle Class, and Female.*

WRITINGS:

Daughters of Suburbia: Growing Up White, Middle Class, and Female, Rutgers University Press (Piscataway, NJ), 2000.

Contributor to books, including *Racing Research, Researching Race: Methodological Dilemmas in Critical Race Studies,* edited by Franie Winddance Twine and Jonathan W. Warren, New York University Press (New York, NY), 2000. Contributor of articles and reviews to periodicals, including *American Anthropologist. Afterimage,* assistant editor, 1985-86, associate editor, 1987-89; managing editor, *Socialist Review,* 1993; coordinating editor, *Issues Quarterly* and *Women's Research Network News,* 1994-96.

WORK IN PROGRESS: Research on reproductive rights.

*   *   *

KEVELSON, Roberta 1931-1998

PERSONAL: Born November 4, 1931, in New York, NY; died November 28, 1998; daughter of Barney Kahan and Helen (Peiros) Cohen; married Seymour Kevelson, September 23, 1950 (divorced, 1980); children: Lorin, Kenneth. *Education:* Goddard College, B.A., 1969, M.A., 1974; attended Brown University, 1978; postdoctoral study at Yale University, 1979-80. *Religion:* Jewish.

CAREER: Bristol Women's Center, executive director, 1972-74; Bristol Textile Museum, president, 1972-75; Pennsylvania State University, University Park, assistant professor of philosophy, 1981, executive director of Center of Semiotic Research, 1984, associate professor, 1986, distinguished professor, 1987; writer. University scholar at Cambridge University, 1986, and University of New Mexico, 1992; visiting scholar at University of Virginia, 1988-89, and College of William and Mary, 1991.

MEMBER: International Association of Law and Semiotics, American Philosophical Association, Semiotic Association of America, Greater Philadelphia Philosophy Consortium (member of board of directors).

WRITINGS:

Style, Symbolic Language Structure, and Syntactic Change: Intransitivity and the Perception of It in English, Peter de Ridder (Lisse, Netherlands), 1976.

Charles S. Peirce's Method of Methods, University of Texas Press (Austin, TX), 1983, new edition, J. Benjamins (Philadelphia, PA), 1987.

(Editor) *Law and Semiotics,* Plenum (New York, NY), 1987-89.

The Law as a System of Signs, Plenum (New York, NY), 1988.

Peirce, Paradox, Praxis: The Image, the Conflict, the Law, Mouton de Gruyter (New York, NY), 1990.

(Editor) *Peirce and Law: Issues in Pragmatism, Legal Realism, and Semiotics,* Peter Lang (New York, NY), 1991.

(Editor) *Law and Aesthetics,* Peter Lang (New York, NY), 1992.

Peirce's Esthetics of Freedom: Possibility, Complexity, and Emergent Value, Peter Lang (New York, NY), 1993.

(Editor) *Codes and Customs: Millennial Perspectives,* Peter Lang (New York, NY), 1994.

Peirce, Science, Signs, Peter Lang (New York, NY), 1995.

(Editor) *Spaces and Significations,* Peter Lang (New York, NY), 1996.

Peirce's Pragmatism: The Medium as Method, Peter Lang (New York, NY), 1998.

(Editor) *HiFives: A Trip to Semiotics,* Peter Lang (New York, NY), 1998.

Peirce and the Mark of the Gryphon, St. Martin's Press (New York, NY), 1999.

Also author of *Inlaws/Outlaws: A Semiotics of Systemic Interaction, "Robin Hood" and the "King's Law,"* 1977, and *The Inverted Pyramid: An Introduction to a Semiotics of Media Language,* 1977. Editor of series *Worldmaking/Signmaking,* 1995. Editor-in-chief of *Law and Semiotics,* 1987-89, *Semiotics and the Human Sciences,* and *Criticism of Institutions.* Member of editorial board of *Journal of Philosophy and Rhetoric* and *International Journal of Law and Semiotics.*

SIDELIGHTS: Roberta Kevelson was a philosopher who specialized in the study of semiotics and the law. Among her writings is *The Law as a System of Signs,* a 1988 publication exploring the notion of legal semiotics. In this work, Kevelson discussed C. S. Peirce's notion of rhetorical approaches to analyzing and expressing signs related to law, and she noted the extent of Peirce's influence in the field of legal semiotics. "The recurrent theme [in *The Law as a System of Signs*] is that of origin and firstness," contended Peter Goodrich in his *Contemporary Sociology* review. "Such firstness is to be understood both literally and figuratively." Goodrich described *The Law as a System of Signs* as "lyrically written and on occasion poetic in its insights," but he found the book "more commendable than recommendable." He claimed that "Kevelson does not state clearly the object of the new discipline," but he also conceded that the book can be "commended . . . for its ambition and its range of theoretical and historical reference." *Choice* reviewer P. K. Moser, meanwhile praised the book as "well written."

BIOGRAPHICAL AND CRITICAL SOURCES:

PERIODICALS

Choice, June, 1978, review of *Inlaws/Outlaws: A Semiotics of Systemic Interaction, "Robin Hood" and the "King's Law,"* p. 539; July-August, 1978, review of *The Inverted Pyramid: An Introduction to a Semiotics of Media Language,* p. 681; July-August, 1988, P. K. Moser, review of *The Law as a System of Signs,* pp. 1707-1708.

Contemporary Sociology, November, 1989, Peter Goodrich, review of *The Law as a Systems of Signs,* pp. 926-928.*

KINGSLAND, Rosemary 1941-

PERSONAL: Born 1941, in India; married Gerald Kingsland (deceased); children: Roddick, Rory, Redmond (sons).

ADDRESSES: Home—London, England. *Agent*—c/o Author Mail, Crown Publishers, 299 Park Ave., New York, NY 10171-0002. *E-mail*—rosekingsland@aol.com.

CAREER: Novelist, journalist, ghostwriter, and screenwriter. Has also worked as an independent olive-oil maker and merchant.

WRITINGS:

Just a Gigolo (film novelization), Corgi (London, England), 1979.
A Saint among Savages, Collins (London, England), 1980.
Hussy (film novelization), Sphere (London, England), 1980.
Treasure Islands, Angus & Robertson (London, England), 1980.
After the Ball Was Over, Viking (New York, NY), 1985.
Cassata, Viking (New York, NY), 1987.
Savage Seas, TV Books (New York, NY), 1999.
Hold Back the Night: Memoirs of a Lost Childhood, a Warring Family, and a Secret Affair with Richard Burton, Century (London, England), 2003, published as *The Secret Life of a Schoolgirl,* Crown Publishers (New York, NY), 2003.

Collaborator and ghostwriter on volumes such as *Behind the White Ball,* Random House (London, England), 1998, the autobiography of snooker player Jimmy White; *The Antiques Buyer,* Orion, 1999, written with David Dickinson; and *David Dickinson: What a Bobby Dazzler,* BBC Consumer Publishing (London, England), 2003, autobiography of British television personality and antiques expert David Dickinson.

SIDELIGHTS: Journalist, novelist, and screenwriter Rosemary Kingsland was born in the Himalayan mountains of India in 1941. With the turmoil of Indian independence and the end of the days of the British raj, Kingsland's family left the life of relative privilege they had enjoyed in India and went to England, where they endured poverty and severe internal conflicts. "Her womanizing, spendthrift father and neurotic, dependent mother argued constantly and bitterly," noted Nancy P. Shires in *Library Journal*. At age fourteen, in an episode half schoolgirl fantasy, half storybook romance, Kingsland met renowned actor Richard Burton and engaged in a brief but intense affair with him.

Kingsland recounts in great detail her affair with Burton in her highly controversial but closely scrutinized autobiography, *The Secret Life of a Schoolgirl*, originally published in England as *Hold Back the Night: Memoirs of a Lost Childhood, a Warring Family, and a Secret Affair with Richard Burton*. Kingsland met the twenty-nine-year-old Burton at a cafe. Soon after, he seduced her in a friend's flat, and the two rendezvoused many times over the next year. Kingsland's affair with Burton was aided by her unpleasant, neglectful home life, which allowed her to be absent from home for extended periods and not missed.

Even when Burton found out her age—he originally thought she was about seventeen—he continued the relationship. A pregnancy and abortion ensued. The young Kingsland was devastated when she learned that Burton was married and also carrying on another affair with actress Claire Bloom. Eventually, Burton moved to Switzerland to escape taxes, and the affair with Kingsland ended as abruptly as it had begun.

The story might have remained safely untold with Kingsland if she hadn't confided in an old friend while the two rode out a tornado during her stay in Tennessee. Her friend encouraged her to write the story, and Kingsland agreed. Afraid that the writing would be difficult and painful, instead Kingsland found it "liberating," remarked Raakhee P. Mirchandani in *Boston Herald*. "The trigger to write this book was definitely my relationship with Richard," she told Mirchandani. "But the book turned out to be more than that, and in the end I made peace with my father."

Kingsland's "beautifully written memoir is a description of, on the one hand, a family life of drudgery and, on the other, her account of a secret, guilty affair with Burton," remarked Catherine Jones in the *Western*

Mail (Cardiff, Wales). "Kingsland brings Burton alive; his remarkable voice, his heavy drinking, his bitterness toward his father who abandoned him after his mother's death when he was a toddler, his uneasy relationship with his foster father, Philip Burton, who pushed him socially upward," wrote Deirdre Donahue in *USA Today*. "Kingsland's ability to convey her acceptance, forgiveness, and knowledge that to be human is to be weak, frail, and yet sometimes utterly marvelous makes *The Secret Life of a Schoolgirl* a profoundly satisfying read," Donahue concluded.

In the years after her episode with Burton, Kingsland began her career in writing and publishing. At age twenty she worked for a news agency on London's Fleet Street, and later, "I was publishing magazines, including one on film, called *Premier*," she recalled on the *Rosemary Kingsland* home page. She became the wife of Gerald Kingsland and the mother of three sons, Roddick, Rory, and Redmond. The family moved frequently, Kingsland reported on her home page. In the early 1970s they went to Tuscany to make wine and olive oil. She later left Italy and was commissioned to write *A Saint among Savages*, for which she spent about a year in the Ecuadorian Amazon rain forest. She started writing for television, then wrote novelizations of two movies (*Hussy* and *Just a Gigolo*) before moving to the United States and settling near Nashville, Tennessee. There she wrote two novels, *After the Ball Was Over* and *Cassata*. By 1990 she had returned to Wales, where she wrote documentaries for television. After she moved to London to care for her terminally ill mother, she became a ghostwriter. She also wrote her autobiography, *The Secret Life of a Schoolgirl*, during this period.

A Saint among Savages tells the story of Rachel Saint, a Christian missionary who lived for almost twenty years among the Wagrani, or Auca, of Ecuador. It is notable that she chose to spend so long among a violent tribe which had earlier killed her brother, one of five missionaries slain while trying to make initial contact with the tribe. That Saint "should be moved to befriend and live among them seems the extreme of Christian charity," observed Trevor Allen in *Contemporary Review*. Along with the widow of another slain missionary, and aided by a local Auca woman, Dayuma, Saint lived and worked among the Auca until her own poor health forced her to leave. "There have been many books about primitive Amazon tribes, rarely one with an arresting a story as this," commented Allen.

Kingsland's 1985 novel, *After the Ball Was Over,* is a "bouncy but slight comic novel" set in Jamalpur, India, where the populace is preparing for the year's most anticipated social event, the Railway Apprentices' Ball, noted a *Publishers Weekly* reviewer. Meanwhile, the "townful of quite horrid English households, rotten in the core," along with local drunkards, fornicators, murderers, psychopaths, and a man-eating tiger, go about their business, remarked a *Kirkus Reviews* critic. Mary Ellen Quinn, writing in *Booklist,* called it "an entertaining if inconsequential novel."

Savage Seas, a nonfiction companion book to the Public Broadcasting Service series of the same name, explores in depth the relationship of the seas to the earth and to planetary cycles. Divided into six sections, the book covers the effects of the oceans' tides, waves, and currents; the influence that oceans have on terrestrial weather; cold zones in the world's oceans; equipment and methods for deep-sea diving and exploration; legendary and actual "sea monsters" and creatures of the deep; and survival techniques for disasters and accidents at sea. "*Savage Seas* is a wonderful introduction to the different seas and oceans on our planet," commented Richard Sumrall on the *Lincoln Daily News* Web site. "The writing is lively," Sumrall continued, "and captures the reader's attention from beginning to end."

BIOGRAPHICAL AND CRITICAL SOURCES:

BOOKS

Kingsland, Rosemary, *Hold Back the Night: Memoirs of a Lost Childhood, a Warring Family, and a Secret Affair with Richard Burton,* Century (London, England), 2003, published as *The Secret Life of a Schoolgirl,* Crown Publishers (New York, NY), 2003.

PERIODICALS

Albuquerque Journal, July 11, 1999, David Steinberg, review of *Savage Seas,* F6.

Booklist, August, 1985, Mary Ellen Quinn, review of *After the Ball Was Over,* p. 1631; July, 2003, Michelle Kaske, review of *The Secret Life of a Schoolgirl,* p. 1856.

Books & Bookmen, April, 1980, Geoffrey Moorhouse, review of *A Saint among Savages,* pp. 34, 36.

Boston Herald, August 3, 2003, Raakhee P. Mirchandani, "Brit Writer: I Was Burton's Teen Lover," p. 10.

Contemporary Review, April, 1980, Trevor Allen, review of *A Saint among Savages,* p. 223.

Daily Telegraph (London, England), May 8, 2004, Isobel Shirlaw, review of *Hold Back the Night: Memoirs of a Lost Childhood, a Warring Family, and a Secret Affair with Richard Burton.*

Entertainment Weekly, July 25, 2003, Michael Sauter, review of *The Secret Life of a Schoolgirl,* p. 75.

Kirkus Reviews, June 15, 1985, review of *After the Ball Was Over,* pp. 547-548; March 1, 1987, review of *Cassata,* pp. 327-328; May 1, 2003, review of *The Secret Life of a Schoolgirl,* pp. 659-660.

Library Journal, August, 1985, review of *After the Ball Was Over,* p. 117; August, 2003, Nancy P. Shires, review of *The Secret Life of a Schoolgirl,* p. 96.

New York Post, August 6, 2003, "Richard Burton's Real-Life Lolita Reveals All," p. 45.

Publishers Weekly, June 21, 1985, review of *After the Ball Was Over,* p. 97; March 27, 1987, review of *Cassata,* pp. 36-37; May 19, 2003, review of *The Secret Life of a Schoolgirl,* p. 61.

School Library Journal, November, 2003, Susanne Bardelson, review of *The Secret Life of a Schoolgirl,* p. 173.

Sunday Times (London, England), July 27, 2003, review of *Hold Back the Night,* p. 47.

Times Literary Supplement, May 16, 1980, Paul Henley, review of *A Saint among Savages,* p. 564.

USA Today, July 31, 2003, Deirdre Donahue, "'Schoolgirl' Has a Secret: A Lusty Affair with Burton; Author's Memoir Goes Far Beyond a Scandal Story," D5.

Washington Post Book World, October 13, 1985, Wendy Law-Yone, review of *After the Ball Was Over,* p. 13; July 31, 2003, Jonathan Yardley, "A Schoolgirl and Her Secret Tutor," C2.

Western Mail (Cardiff, Wales), August 9, 2003, Catherine Jones, interview with Rosemary Kingsland, p. 4.

WWD, July 10, 2003, Samantha Conti, "London's Living Lolita," p. 4.

ONLINE

Elle Magazine Web site, http://www.elle.com/ (June 30, 2004), review of *The Secret Life of a Schoolgirl.*

Independent (London, England) Web site, http://www. enjoyment.independent.co.uk/ (April 23, 2003), David Thomson, review of *The Secret Life of a Schoolgirl.*

Johnson County Library Web site (Kansas), http:// www.jocolibrary.org/ (June 30, 2004), Leslie Loftus, review of *The Secret Life of a Schoolgirl.*

Lincoln Daily News Web site, http://www.lincoln dailynews.com/ (January 31, 2001), Richard Sumrall, review of *Savage Seas.*

Northern Express Web site, http://www.northern express.com/ (June 30, 2004), Nancy Sundstrom, review of *The Secret Life of a Schoolgirl.*

Rosemary Kingsland Home Page, http://www.rosemary kingsland.com (June 30, 2004).*

*   *   *

KISSING, Steve 1963-

PERSONAL: Born 1963, in Cincinnati, OH; married; children: two daughters. *Religion:* Catholic. *Hobbies and other interests:* Fly-fishing.

ADDRESSES: Home—8440 Lynnehaven Dr., Cincinnati, OH 45236-1416. *Office*—HSR Business to Business, 300 East Business Way, Suite 500, Cincinnati, OH 45241. *Agent*—Linda Roghaar, Linda Roghaar Literary Agency, Inc., Amherst, MA 01002.

CAREER: Writer, advertising copywriter, and editor. HSR Business to Business (advertising firm), Cincinnati, OH, associate creative director.

AWARDS, HONORS: American Advertising Federation and the Society of Professional Journalists awards.

WRITINGS:

Running from the Devil: A Memoir of a Boy Possessed, Crossroad Publishing (New York, NY), 2003.

Also a contributing editor to *Cincinnati* magazine.

WORK IN PROGRESS: Another memoir that describes the demons Kissing has run away from as an adult.

SIDELIGHTS: An award-winning advertising copywriter, Steve Kissing turned to the memoir format for his first published book, the 2003 title *Running from the Devil: A Memoir of a Boy Possessed.* Kissing applies tongue-in-cheek and laugh-out-loud humor in this personal tale of a young Catholic boy growing up in Cincinnati who experiences seizures (they were later diagnosed as a form of epilepsy) and believes he is being possessed by the devil. Begun as a magazine piece for the *Cincinnati* magazine in the year 2000, Kissing's autobiography grew to book length once he received positive reader response on his article.

When he was in the fifth grade, Kissing, a self-confessed "Prince of Dorkness," began having mild seizures and hallucinations in which the teacher's pencil holder grew to the size of a shovel and a film strip became a tuba. Convinced that the devil was after his very soul, Kissing fought back. Too frightened or timid to ask for help, he battled this personal demon on his own, turning to long-distance running to exorcize the beast. He also began a regimen of praying that would make most cloistered priests seem indolent by comparison. Along with this basic story line, Kissing introduces real characters from his past: a grandfather fond of gargling with bleach, a mother who liked to try out new hairstyles on her children, a father who ran backwards, and an uncle who gave bread instead of candy for Halloween. In the memoir, Kissing re-creates the 1970s with references to leisure suits, Transcendental Meditation, and Afro hairstyles. Kissing's private battle went on for eight years until Kissing finally discovered the physical problem causing his hallucinations.

"I worked hard to keep the story as true as possible," Kissing told Tim Bete in an interview for the *University of Dayton Erma Bombeck Writers' Workshop* Web site, "at least as it concerned the major details as well as the small ones that were likewise important. I chose not to worry about whether some old girlfriend's eyes were really blue or green, or whether some wacky event happened in the sixth grade or seventh. I let memory dictate these things."

Critics responded warmly to Kissing's humorous yet poignant tale. *America* contributor James Martin thought the book "might be the oddest and yet most enjoyable Catholic memoir you will read this year." Martin further noted that while *Running from the Devil* "is, essentially, about a painful topic, Mr. Kissing's unfailing sense of humor, his affection for his faith and his self-deprecating manner make it an enjoyable and even inspiring book." Similarly, a reviewer for *Publishers Weekly* found it a "bizarre and humorous memoir." For this same critic, the thing that "makes this a compelling story is that readers live inside the mind of a Catholic over-achiever." Jim Knippenberg, writing in the *Cincinnati Enquirer Online,* felt that "Kissing tells his tale with wry and merciless self-mockery," and further praised the "oddball characters" that populate the pages of this memoir. And Mary Prokop, reviewing the debut book in *Library Journal,* commented, "Not only is Kissing's story truly riveting, he is also a talented writer with a great sense of humor."

Kissing noted to Bete that childhood provides a rich vein of material for writers. "Experience has taught me that we all have plenty of weird and unusual and embarrassing experiences in our past, particularly in our childhoods."

BIOGRAPHICAL AND CRITICAL SOURCES:

PERIODICALS

ADWEEK (Midwest edition), October 14, 2003, Trevor Jansen, "HSR Reorders Management Ranks."

America, June 23, 2003, James Martin, review of *Running from the Devil: A Memoir of a Boy Possessed,* p. 2.

Library Journal, May 1, 2003, Mary Prokop, review of *Running from the Devil,* p. 121.

Publishers Weekly, April 28, 2003, review of *Running from the Devil,* p. 67.

ONLINE

Cincinnati Enquirer Online, http://www.enquirer.com/ (May 13, 2003), Jim Knippenberg, "'Running' Memoir of West-Side Boyhood."

Running from the Devil Web site, http://www.runningfromthedevil.com/ (October 30, 2003).

University of Dayton Erma Bombeck Writers' Workshop Web site, http://www.humorwriters.org/SteveKissing.html/ (October 30, 2003), Tim Bete, "An Interview with the Prince of Dorkness."*

KLAM, Matthew 1964-

PERSONAL: Born 1964; married; wife's name, Lara (a psychologist). *Education:* Attended University of New Hampshire and Hollins College.

ADDRESSES: Home—Washington, DC. *Agent*—c/o Author Mail, Random House, 299 Park Ave., New York, NY 10171-0002. *E-mail*—MattKlam@aol.com.

CAREER: Journalist and author of short fiction. Teacher of creative writing at St. Albans School, American University, and Stockholm University.

AWARDS, HONORS: O. Henry Award, for "Royal Palms;" *New York Times* Book of the Year citation, and *Los Angeles Times* Book of the Year finalist, both 2000, both for *Sam the Cat, and Other Stories;* Giles Whiting Foundation Award for emerging writers, 2001; Robert Bingham/PEN Award; National Endowment for the Arts grant.

WRITINGS:

Sam the Cat, and Other Stories, Random House (New York, NY), 2000.

Contributor of short fiction to periodicals, including *Harper's, New Yorker, Washington Post Magazine,* and *New York Times Magazine.*

SIDELIGHTS: In the short-story collection *Sam the Cat, and Other Stories,* Matthew Klam takes a clear-eyed, ironic look at modern love and tormented men. The title story of the collection, "Sam the Cat," is about a lonely man searching for love in an attempt to find comfort in his life. At a bar, Sam's eyes follow a pair of attractive legs from the floor up, and he becomes convinced that this is the woman he has been looking for. But when the head belonging to the legs turns, Sam finds himself staring into the face of another man. "There Should be a Name for It" finds a couple learning to reconcile with the superficiality of the emotions underlying their marriage. Klam's O. Henry Award-winning story "Royal Palms" finds the story's narrator sitting on a Caribbean beach as his marriage flounders. Klam's stories, which previously were published in the *New Yorker,* serve as a "reminder that the wealth of the American upper middle class, and the suburban materialism of its lifestyle is not old news," noted Lorrie Moore in her *New York Review of Books* appraisal of *Sam the Cat, and Other Stories.* Rather, Moore continued, in his fiction Klam addresses an affluence that "is unprecedented, socially and globally isolating in a manner that is new, overwhelming, and sinister to those looking on." Dubbing the collection "smart" and "absorbing," *New York Times Book Review* contributor D. T. Max commented: "If Matthew Klam's first story collection is to be believed . . . this is an awful time to be a young man."

A contributor to *Publishers Weekly* noted that in *Sam the Cat, and Other Stories* "Klam demonstrates his mastery of the fine art of irony, exposing the nerve endings of his complex, often tormented, sometimes funny, characters while allowing the reader to make his or her own judgments." In a review for *Booklist,* Nancy Pearl wrote that, "At their best . . . the stories truthfully convey our conflicted feelings about those we supposedly love the most. Klam's characters are all vividly and vocally both neurotic and depressed. . . . Even readers who are themselves neurotic and depressed will want to reach into the stories and shake these annoying characters until they snap out of whatever is dragging them down—which speaks to how successfully Klam brings them to life."

BIOGRAPHICAL AND CRITICAL SOURCES:

PERIODICALS

Booklist, May 15, 2000, Nancy Pearl, review of *Sam the Cat, and Other Stories,* p. 1728.

Harper's Bazaar, May, 2000, Katherine Dieckmann, review of *Sam the Cat, and Other Stories,* p. 118.

New York Review of Books, November 16, 2001, Lorrie Moore, review of *Sam the Cat, and Other Stories,* p. 32.

New York Times Book Review, June 11, 2000, D. T. Max, review of *Sam the Cat, and Other Stories,* p. 38; June 17, 2000, Scott Veale, review of *Sam the Cat, and Other Stories,* p. 28.

Publishers Weekly, April 24, 2000, review of *Sam the Cat, and Other Stories,* p. 59.

US, June 5, 2000, Melanie Rehak, review of *Sam the Cat, and Other Stories,* p. 55.

Wall Street Journal, June 30, 2000, Ken Bensinger, review of *Sam the Cat, and Other Stories,* p. W9.

Washington Post Book World, July 16, 2000, James Hynes, review of *Sam the Cat, and Other Stories,* p. 5.

ONLINE

Matthew Klam Web site, http://www.matthewklam.com (February 21, 2004).*

*   *   *

KLEH, Cindy (L.) 1959-

PERSONAL: Born March 14, 1959, in San Francisco, CA; daughter of Thomas Robert (an ophthalmologist) and Louise (Travers) Kleh; married Kimo Kaanapu, August 9, 1986 (divorced, 1994). *Ethnicity:* "White." *Education:* University of Hawaii—Manoa, B.A., 1982. *Politics:* "Green-leaning." *Religion:* Buddhist. *Hobbies and other interests:* Snowshoeing, mountain biking, inline skating, high-altitude hiking and backpacking, yoga, dance, meditation.

ADDRESSES: Home and office—584 Montezuma Rd., No. 5, Dillon, CO 80435. *E-mail*—ckleh63193@aol.com.

CAREER: Summit Outdoors, San Francisco, CA, columnist, 1993-98; *Ten Mile Times,* San Francisco, writer, 1999-2001; freelance writer, 2000—. Worked as a bartender, tour guide in Hawaii, and teacher of snowboarding techniques.

WRITINGS:

Snowboarding Skills: The Back-to-Basic Essentials for All Levels, Firefly Books (Buffalo, NY), 2002.

Work represented in anthologies, including *When in Doubt, Go Higher: Mountain Gazette Anthology,* edited by M. John Fayhee, Mountain Sports Press (San Francisco, CA), 2002. Author of "Riding High," a weekly column in *Summit Outdoors,* 1993-98. Contributor to periodicals, including *Mountain Gazette.*

WORK IN PROGRESS: Research on "the state of the hippie in the year 2003" and "the end of the ski bum era."

SIDELIGHTS: Cindy Kleh told *CA:* "I grew up in northern Vermont in a skiing family of six. Even my mom gave in and learned to ski when she was forty-five. I started in 1964 on wooden skis with cable bindings and lace-up leather boots. I attended college in Honolulu, where I learned to surf and scuba dive. I worked for Ski Hawaii for two years, helping with tours to the top of Mauna Kea (nearly 14,000 feet in elevation) on the Big Island. I missed skiing and visited my older sister and her family, who owned a bed-and-breakfast in Keystone, Colorado, each spring break. I finally decided I would rather live in the mountains and vacation in Hawaii. I moved to Colorado in 1985 and learned to snowboard the same year.

"I began my writing career with a snowboarding column, 'Riding High,' for *Summit Outdoors* magazine. I expanded my stories to all sports, writing about backpacking, rafting, wakeboarding, inline skating, and mountain biking (and more).

"I have been tending bar for the last twenty years, finding many of my best story ideas from bar patrons (and then they tip me!).

"I taught snowboarding at Keystone Resort for three winters. I thoroughly enjoyed empowering people through snowboarding, especially kids. I have witnessed entire lives turned around by learning to snowboard. The confidence overflows into all aspects of people's lives.

"Snowboarding is extremely easy to learn, but the first day(s) can be demoralizing and painful. After years of dealing with beginners, I began to see how much the mind could make or break the experience. I've always strived to make the learning process less intimidating and easier on the ego. I've also gained enormous amounts of patience in dealing with others' fears and failures. I was even more excited than my students when they succeeded.

"I expanded my teaching knowledge by becoming certified to teach by the Association of American Snowboard Instructors. My most inspiring teaching experience was with the Snowboard Outreach Society, which brings inner-city and/or 'at risk' youth to mountain resorts to learn to snowboard, with help from Vail Resorts, which donates all equipment, instructors, and lift tickets for five consecutive weekends.

"When I started teaching snowboarding, I also started competing, qualifying for the United States of America Snowboard Association Nationals, 1999-2003. I was covering many snowboard competitions for local papers and figured it would be more fun and less cold to compete than just to watch from the sidelines. I got interviews with the competitors while waiting in the starting gates with them.

"Thinking about competition kept me in shape all summer and made me more critical of my own technique. I forced myself to work on my carving and control. I wove yoga and meditation into my winning strategies, experimenting with the power of the mind over the power of the nerves. I have won three bronze, four silver, and two gold medals in the Women's Legend class (ages forty to forty-nine), competing in giant slalom, slalom, and boardercross categories.

"While writing *Snowboarding Skills: The Back-to-Basic Essentials for All Levels,* I constantly kept in mind the reader's well being. A mind-set of compassion made the writing process flow (usually)."

BIOGRAPHICAL AND CRITICAL SOURCES:

PERIODICALS

Booklist, December 15, 2002, Gillian Engberg, review of *Snowboarding Skills: The Back-to-Basic Essentials for All Levels,* p. 749.
School Library Journal, January, 2003, Michael Mc-Cullough, review of *Snowboarding Skills,* p. 176.

*   *   *

KLEINDIENST, Kris 1953-

PERSONAL: Born March 25, 1953; companion of Jay Steele (a poet). *Education:* Degree in women's studies.

ADDRESSES: Office—3631 Bellerive Blvd., St. Louis, MO 63116; fax: 314-367-3256. *E-mail*—kriski@ primary.net.

CAREER: Left Bank Books, St. Louis, MO, co-owner, 1977—; writer; political activist. Booksellers advisory board member for *Paris Review.*

AWARDS, HONORS: Hedgebook residency, 1997; Lambda Literary Award for nonfiction, 1999, for *This Is What Lesbian Looks Like: Dyke Activists Take on the Twenty-first Century.*

WRITINGS:

(Editor) *This Is What Lesbian Looks Like: Dyke Activists Take on the Twenty-first Century,* Firebrand (Ithaca, NY), 1999.

Also columnist for newspaper *Vital Voice.*

SIDELIGHTS: Kris Kleindienst is a writer and co-owner of Left Bank Books in St. Louis, Missouri. She is the editor of *This Is What Lesbian Looks Like: Dyke Activists Take on the Twenty-first Century,* a collection of essays by more than twenty activists who voice a wide range of viewpoints about the lesbian movement. Represented by such writers as Dorothy Allison, Victoria Brownworth, Leslie Feinberg, Jewell Gomez, Minnie Bruce Pratt, Mattie Richardson, and many others, *This Is What Lesbian Looks Like* covers many aspects of the gay/lesbian/bisexual/transgender movement.

Subjects included in the essays are racism, homophobia, ageism, transgendered individuals trying to fit into the lesbian community, parenting, and sexuality. "Among the appealing new voices is Surina Kahn's, as she recalls how, as a Pakistani teenager, she thought the best way to assimilate herself in America was to vote Republican," wrote a *Publishers Weekly* reviewer. In the *Berkeley Women's Law Journal,* Jennifer V. Stroffe commented, "From beginning to end, *This Is What Lesbian Looks Like* takes the reader on a journey through both the triumphant and trying experiences of individuals that helped to shape the queer community into what it is today. . . . Kris Kleindienst has put together a remarkable collection of works that is sure to inspire the activist in us all."

BIOGRAPHICAL AND CRITICAL SOURCES:

PERIODICALS

Berkeley Women's Law Journal, 2000, Jennifer V. Stroffe, review of *This Is What Lesbian Looks Like: Dyke Activists Take on the Twenty-first Century,* p. 357.

Booklist, December 15, 1999, Whitney Scott, review of *This Is What Lesbian Looks Like,* p. 743.
Lambda Book Report, January, 2000, Kerry Lobel, review of *This Is What Lesbian Looks Like,* p. 16.
Library Journal, January, 2000, Debra Moore, review of *This Is What Lesbian Looks Like,* p. 140.
Publishers Weekly, December 13, 1999, review of *This Is What Lesbian Looks Like,* p. 75.
Women's Review of Books, July, 2000, Sherri Paris, review of *This Is What Lesbian Looks Like,* p. 12.*

*　　　*　　　*

KNEEBONE, Geoffrey (Thomas) 1918-2003

OBITUARY NOTICE—See index for *CA* sketch: Born February 24, 1918, in London, England; died September 30, 2003. Mathematician, educator, and author. Kneebone, a former University of London professor, was the coauthor of the "Semple and Kneebone" books that are now considered classics in the field. Educated at the University of London, he earned three degrees there, including a Ph.D. in 1943. After teaching at Westfield College at the University of London for three years, he joined the Bedford College faculty, which is also at the University of London. At Bedford, he was a lecturer in mathematics from 1947 to 1964, a reader in the foundation of mathematics from 1964 to 1975, and a reader in mathematics from 1976 until his retirement in 1983. Kneebone is best known for the two books he wrote with J. G. Semple: *Algebraic Projective Geometry* (1952) and *Algebraic Curves* (1959). After his interests shifted from geometry to logic, he also wrote *Mathematical Logic and the Foundations of Mathematics* (1963) and, with B. Rotman, *The Theory of Sets and Transfinite Numbers* (1966).

OBITUARIES AND OTHER SOURCES:

PERIODICALS

Time (London, England), October 20, 2003, p. 28.

*　　　*　　　*

KONZAK, Burt 1946-

PERSONAL: Born April 28, 1946, in New York, NY; son of Anshel (a construction worker) and Rachel (a singer and music teacher; maiden name, Anbinder) Konzak; married Françoise Boudreau (a university professor); children: Sonya, Mélina. *Education:* Harpur College, State University of New York—Binghamton, B.A., 1967; State University of New York—Binghamton, M.A., 1971; University of Toronto, Ph.D., 1977. *Hobbies and other interests:* Swimming, scuba diving, bicycling, classical music, mountain climbing.

ADDRESSES: Home—50 Poplar Plains Crescent, Toronto, Ontario M4V 1E8, Canada. *E-mail*—boudreau@ glendon.yorku.ca.

CAREER: Toronto Academy of Karate and Judo, Toronto, Ontario, Canada, director and founder, 1970—; University of Toronto, assistant professor in the School of Physical and Health Education, 1973-94, instructor of "Zen Buddhism and the Martial Arts," 1974-77; University of Guelph, Guelph, Ontario, Canada, instructor in sociology, 1980-81. Research associate at the Center for Comparative Political Research, State University of New York—Binghamton, 1969-70; research assistant at Harvard University, Cambridge, MA, 1970. Guest lecturer at colleges and universities in the United States and Canada. Teaches martial arts, self-defense, self-confidence, and fitness through workshops and demonstrations to schools, businesses, and other groups around the world.

AWARDS, HONORS: Ford Foundation fellowship; Gold Seal Award, Canadian Children's Book Centre, for *Noguchi the Samurai; Storytelling World* Award, 2004, for *Samurai Spirit: Ancient Wisdom for Modern Life.*

WRITINGS:

Noguchi the Samurai, illustrated by Johnny Wales, Lester (Toronto, Ontario, Canada), 1994.
Girl Power: Self-Defence for Teens, Sports Books (Toronto, Ontario, Canada), 1999.
Samurai Spirit: Ancient Wisdom for Modern Life, Tundra Books (Plattsburgh, NY), 2002.

Contributor of numerous articles to scholarly and popular journals.

WORK IN PROGRESS: A second book of samurai stories and philosophy.

SIDELIGHTS: A former university professor, Burt Konzak has been studying Asian philosophy and martial arts for decades. Using his experience, he has distilled some of what he has learned into several books for children and young adults, including *Noguchi the Samurai,* a picture book for young children, *Girl Power: Self-Defence for Teens,* a practical how-to book for teenage girls about how to handle dangerous situations, and *Samurai Spirit: Ancient Wisdom for Modern Life,* an inspirational book containing a mix of traditional Japanese samurai folklore and stories about Konzak's own life.

Konzak once commented: "Writing is and always has been a liberating experience for me. The act of writing gives me insights into the world and people around me. It enriched my adolescence, made university into a formidable experience, and provided me with insights that I never knew were really in my head. The act of writing shook them out.

"Yet it was as a father that writing really became one of the center points of my life. Of course, I always wrote out detailed plans for my classes and research projects. In fact I always had written plans for just about everything. But now, as a father, I turned my writing toward what was to become three books that reflected the different stages of my children's lives: a children's book, a book for teens, and a book for young adults. I was speaking to a general audience, but I was also speaking to my own kids. I was saying things which in my heart I considered really important and that I believed needed to be said, to my children and to others, expressed in both fiction and nonfiction.

"When I finished my book *Samurai Spirit: Ancient Wisdom for Modern Life,* much to my surprise, as I read the final manuscript, I realized that I had finally written a book I had long planned on writing as a University of Toronto professor of Asian philosophy: a book on Buddhist ethics. Only this book was not for a very limited scholarly audience. It was for anyone with an interest in Asian wisdom. Buddhist ethics were expressed through the stories and legends of the ancient samurai, detailed with philosophical and historical commentary. This book was dedicated to and written for my children, who, I knew, needed to know these ideals to become the type of dignified and powerful adults that I truly wanted them to become (and that I believe every parent would like their children to become). *Samurai Spirit* was serious stuff, but full of mystery and adventure that anyone, young or old, would find fascinating to read." *Samurai Spirit* has been translated into Danish and further translations are being negotiated into Dutch, Swedish, and French. In 2004, it received the *Storytelling World Award*.

Samurai Spirit also received a positive review from *School Library Journal* contributor Vicki Reutter, who thought that Konzak "succeeds in drawing the connection between this ancient philosophy and daily life." Margot Griffin of the *Toronto Star* called the book's tales "inpiring," while *Resource Links* reviewer Lori Lavallee found that *Samurai Spirit*'s "strength lies in its introduction to Japanese history and culture, particularly of the warrior class."

Konzak continued, "My earlier book, *Girl Power: Self-Defence for Teens,* is a completely new approach to self-defence. It teaches the fundamentals of self-defence, physical fitness, and how to avoid dangerous situations and to deflate them should they occur. For a truly strong woman or man, physical technique is the absolute last resort to a violent encounter. Running away or avoiding danger in the first place are far better alternatives." Reviewers noted how important it is for teenage girls to be able to defend themselves, and *Journal of Asian Martial Arts* contributor Elisa Hendrey thought that Konzak did an excellent job of conveying that information to girls in the text, recommending that parents, school libraries, and martial arts schools should invest in a copy. "*Girl Power,* written as it is in such an engaging manner and designed with a contemporary look that has teen appeal, may well inspire many of its readers," observed Hendry, to begin classes in the martial arts.

Konzak once commented, "*Noguchi the Samurai* is a children's samurai story full of action and samurai ethics with beautiful paintings by Johnny Wales. It received fabulous reviews all across Canada and was the recipient of the Gold Seal Award from the Canadian Children's Book Centre. In this book, an elderly master-samurai outwits a violent attacker and saves the passengers on a boat from harm without even lifting his sword from the scabbard." Writing for the *Toronto Star*, Margot Griffin remarked that *Noguchi the Samurai* "will help empower [a child] with the self-confidence she needs to deal with life's bullies by using her brain against their brawn."

"I have also published scholarly works in the fields of ethics, Asian philosophy, and mental health in my capacity as a University of Toronto professor where I taught for over twenty-five years," Konzak once commented. "I was the recipient of a Ford Foundation fellowship as well as many other academic awards and have been a guest lecturer at Stanford University, the University of Calgary, Guelph University, Tokyo University, and conferences and workshops in Japan, Mexico, Europe, Israel, Canada, and the United States.

"My university teaching and my writing and research are of course related in theme. Yet my major material for writing comes from the art form at the center of my life: the Asian martial arts. I started my own *dojo* (training hall) when I was a Ph.D. student in 1970. Since then, I have been featured on the covers of many of the world's major martial arts magazines and have been written about in *National Geographic World* as well as dozens of other newspapers and magazines. I have traveled the world teaching and demonstrating martial arts.

"My wife and children are great martial artists and have shared this passion in their own lives. They have all been intimately involved in my three books, as in every aspect of my life from family dinner to training together at the *dojo*. Presently my two daughters, Sonya and Mélina, are in university. My wife, Françoise Boudreau, is associate dean at Glendon College, York University, and is a renowned scholar in the field of mental health. We have written scholarly works together, in both English and French, in the fields of mental health, Asian philosophy, ethics, and martial arts.

"My book *Samurai Spirit: Ancient Wisdom for Modern Life* recounts the great samurai stories, legends, and ethics. Not only are these stories both profound and fascinating, full of action and intrigue, they are a vivid portrait of Asian wisdom and illustrate how people can take control of their lives and become the men and women they truly wish to be. These stories have inspired me all my life. I have seen them inspire new generations of boys and girls and men and women as they have come into my *dojo*. I am happy that they have also inspired my children to become the great young women they are. I also believe that many years ago, when I first knew Françoise, they helped inspire her to take a chance and marry me."

BIOGRAPHICAL AND CRITICAL SOURCES:

PERIODICALS

Canadian Materials, September, 1994, review of *Noguchi the Samurai,* p. 132.

Gazette (Montreal, Quebec, Canada), May 22, 2000, Donna Nebenzahl, review of *Girl Power: Self-Defence for Teens.*

Journal of Asian Martial Arts, Volume 10, number 3, 2001, Elisa Hendrey, review of *Girl Power,* pp. 103-104.

Quill and Quire, April, 1994, review of *Noguchi the Samurai,* p. 36.

Resource Links, February, 2003, Lori Lavallee, review of *Samurai Spirit: Ancient Wisdom for Modern Life,* pp. 40-42.

School Library Journal, June, 2003, Vicki Reutter, review of *Samurai Spirit,* p. 144.

Toronto Star, November 6, 1994, Margot Griffin, review of *Noguchi the Samurai;* April 27, 2003, Margot Griffin, review of *Samurai Spirit.*

ONLINE

Toronto Academy of Karate, Fitness, and Health Web site, http://www.torontoacademy.com/ (March 11, 2004).

*   *   *

KRASKE, Robert

PERSONAL: Born in Detroit, MI.

ADDRESSES: Agent—c/o Author Mail, Orchard Books, 557 Broadway, New York, NY 10012.

CAREER: Author of children's books; editor.

WRITINGS:

Crystals of Life: The Story of Salt, Doubleday (New York, NY), 1968.

Silent Sentinels: The Story of Locks, Vaults, and Burglar Alarms, Doubleday (Garden City, NY), 1969.

The Treason of Benedict Arnold, 1780: An American General Becomes His Country's First Traitor, Watts (New York, NY), 1970.

The Statue of Liberty Comes to America, illustrated by Victor Mays, Garrad Publishing Company (Champaign, IL), 1972.

America the Beautiful: Stories of Patriotic Songs, Garrad Publishing Company (Champaign, IL), 1972.

Harry Houdini, Master of Magic, Garrad Publishing Company (Champaign, IL), 1973.

The Story of the Dictionary, Harcourt Brace Jovanovich (New York, NY), 1975.

Is There Life in Outer Space?, Harcourt Brace Jovanovich (New York, NY), 1976.

The Sea Robbers, Harcourt Brace Jovanovich (New York, NY), 1977.

The Twelve Million Dollar Note: Strange but True Tales of Messages Found in Seagoing Bottles, T. Nelson (Nashville, TN), 1977.

Daredevils Do Amazing Things, illustrated by Ivan Powell, Random House (New York, NY), 1978.

Magicians Do Amazing Things, illustrated by Richard Bennett, Random House (New York, NY), 1979.

Riddles of the Stars: White Dwarfs, Red Giants, and Black Holes, Harcourt Brace Jovanovich (New York, NY), 1979.

(And illustrator) *Asteroids: Invaders from Space,* Atheneum (New York, NY), 1995.

The Voyager's Stone: The Adventures of a Message-Carrying Bottle Adrift on the Ocean Sea, illustrated by Brian Floca, Orchard Books (New York, NY), 1995.

SIDELIGHTS: Robert Kraske began his career as an editor of a children's magazine, but started writing books for children in 1964. He has written both fiction and nonfiction books that cover a wide range of topics, from history to science.

Three of Kraske's titles confront themes of intrigue. *Silent Sentinels: The Story of Locks, Vaults, and Burglar Alarms* explains the workings of these anti-theft devices, from ancient times to the present, while *Harry Houdini, Master of Magic* provides an account of the man who achieved fame and fortune by defying such devices. A third book, *Magicians Do Amazing Things,* further explores the techniques by which magicians elicit seemingly impossible effects.

American history has also provided Kraske with material for several books, including *The Treason of Benedict Arnold, 1780: An American General Becomes His Country's First Traitor, America the Beautiful: Stories of Patriotic Songs,* and *The Statue of Liberty Comes to America. The Story of the Dictionary* explains the history of the dictionary and describes the process by which dictionaries are made.

Kraske's titles relating to the sciences have earned particular praise. In two different books, he describes what happens when people put messages into bottles that they then throw into the sea. *The Twelve Million Dollar Note: Strange but True Tales of Messages Found in Seagoing Bottles* presents a collection of true stories about these messages and how they were found. A later title, *The Voyager's Stone: The Adventures of a Message-Carrying Bottle Adrift on the Ocean Sea* explains the science of ocean currents and discusses coastal ecosystems where bottles with messages have washed ashore. According to Mary Harris Veeder in *Booklist,* Kraske's approach in this book is exceptionally engaging. Among Kraske's books on space are *Is There Life in Outer Space?, Riddles of the Stars: White Dwarfs, Red Giants, and Black Holes,* and *Asteroids: Invaders from Space. Booklist* reviewer Julie Yates Walton praised *Asteroids* for its readable style and rich descriptions, concluding that the book "makes the mind-boggling accessible."

Kraske has also written a novel for young readers, *The Sea Robbers,* which features pirates, a kidnapping, and a subsequent rescue attempt in colonial Massachusetts.

BIOGRAPHICAL AND CRITICAL SOURCES:

PERIODICALS

Booklist, March 1, 1995, Mary Harris Veeder, review of *The Voyager's Stone: The Adventures of a Message-Carrying Bottle Adrift on the Ocean Sea,* p. 1237; July, 1995, Julie Yates Walton, review of *Asteroids: Invaders from Space,* p. 1875.
School Library Journal, March, 1980, Helen Gregory, review of *Magicians Do Amazing Things,* p. 122; March, 1995, Steven Engelfried, review of *The Voyager's Stone,* p. 214; September, 1995, Margaret M. Hagel, review of *Asteroids,,* p. 210.*

*   *   *

KRUGER, Ehren 1972-

PERSONAL: Born October 5, 1972. *Education:* Graduated from New York University.

ADDRESSES: Home—San Francisco, CA. *Agent*—c/o DreamWorks, 1000 Flower St., Glendale, CA 91201.

CAREER: Screenwriter. Worked as an executive assistant at the Fox Broadcasting Company (Fox) and a script assistant for Sandollar Productions.

AWARDS, HONORS: Nicholl fellowship, Academy of Motion Picture Arts and Sciences, 1996, for *Arlington Road.*

WRITINGS:

SCREENPLAYS, EXCEPT AS INDICATED

Killers in the House (teleplay), USA Network, 1998.
Arlington Road, Screen Gems, 1999.
Scream 3, Dimension Films, 2000.
Reindeer Games, Dimension Films, 2000.
Texas Rangers, Miramax, 2001.
Impostor, Dimension Films, 2002.
The Ring, DreamWorks, 2002.

Also author of *New World Disorder,* 1999.

WORK IN PROGRESS: Screenplays for numerous upcoming films, including *The Brothers Grimm, Skeleton Key, Blood and Chocolate, The Talisman,* and *The Ring 2.*

SIDELIGHTS: Screenwriter Ehren Kruger has written a number of high-profile, high-grossing movies in Hollywood, but he still "enjoys being a reclusive screenwriter" who is generally "unknown to San Francisco's cognoscenti," reported Ruthe Stein in an interview with Kruger in the *San Francisco Chronicle.* Though he lives in San Francisco and loves "the diversity and openness here," he told Stein, he still prefers to remain as anonymous as possible. "Kruger wouldn't send a photo to run in the paper because he really doesn't want to be recognized," Stein commented.

Kruger, a graduate of New York University's Tisch School of the Arts, received the 1996 Nicholl fellowship from the Academy of Motion Picture Arts and Sciences for his then-unproduced screenplay, *Arlington Road.* In 1999, Kruger attained veteran status when *Arlington Road* appeared as a full-length motion picture starring Jeff Bridges, Tim Robbins, and Joan Cusack. The movie is "a topical thriller predicated on the sturdy dramatic notion that the guy next door to you—the one you think is a dangerous weirdo—really is a dangerous weirdo," remarked Lisa Schwarzbaum in *Entertainment Weekly.* As the film opens, Michael Faraday (Bridges) finds a badly injured young boy wandering a suburban street. Faraday rushes him to the hospital, much to the appreciation of the boy's parents, Oliver (Robbins) and Cheryl (Cusack) Lang, who are Faraday's new neighbors.

Faraday, a history professor who teaches about terrorism, still grieves for his wife, an FBI agent killed several years prior in a botched terrorist attack. At first he welcomes the new friendship with the Langs and their son, who is close to his own son's age. As he gets better acquainted with the family, however, they seem odd, and details of their behavior and lives become inconsistent. Suspicious, Faraday begins looking into the Langs' background and uncovers sinister possibilities and militia groups looking to blow up a prominent government building.

"*Arlington Road* is an intelligent, insidiously plotted Hitchcockian thriller directed in souped-up, modern expressionistic style," wrote Todd McCarthy in *Variety.* McCarthy called the movie an "absorbing and surprising political melodrama [that] sometimes tries too hard for its own good," but further commented that "in an era when most suspensers are hopelessly contrived, derivative, and one-dimensional, this one has some real weight" and credible main characters. The movie is "obviously inspired by the Oklahoma City bombing of the Federal Building," noted James Greenberg in *Los Angeles* magazine, adding that "writer Ehren Kruger and director Mark Pellington have fashioned a plausible what-if tale."

Stepping away from the world of the political thriller and squarely into the horror-comedy hybrid genre, Kruger provided the screenplay for *Scream 3,* released in 2000. Kruger came in to write the screenplay after Kevin Williamson, the writer of the first two *Scream* movies, was unable to write the third due to scheduling problems. In this self-referential conclusion of the *Scream* trilogy, the survivors of the carnage of the previous episodes gather in Hollywood, where a film is being made about the murders that occurred in the first two movies. Eventually, the masked killer makes his appearance, and the "victims, real and potential, of the slasher in the ironic mask—they are many— continue to put up game, liberated fights for their

lives," commented Richard Schickel in *Time.* Schickel called Kruger's work on the film "more competent than inspired—not that one imagines that affecting the grosses."

Although *Scream 3* is founded on horror elements, Kruger said in a *In Focus* Web site interview that he approached the movie "as working on a comedy, not so much a horror picture. It's kind of funny to me when they file the *Scream* movies in the 'horror' genre. I'm not sure it's on the proper shelf."

Kruger's most prominent film project is probably *The Ring,* an atmospheric horror movie from 2002. Based on a popular Japanese movie, *Ringu, The Ring* involves a mysterious videotape and its fatal effects— anyone who watches it and its surrealistic imagery immediately receives a phone call telling them they will die in seven days. So far, no one has been able to escape the chilling seven-day deadline. When two teenage girls watch the tape, both die. Rachel, the aunt of one of the girls, puts her investigative journalism skills to work to find out what happened. She watches the video and receives the expected call, and the clock starts ticking for Rachel to solve the mystery. Adding to the urgency: Rachel realizes that others have also recently viewed the tape, including her son, Aidan.

The Ring is "more driven by character and atmosphere," Kruger remarked on the *In Focus* Web site. "But it's really about dread and doom, and that sense permeates every scene. It's about what that sense—of believing there's a deadline on your life and possibly your loved ones—does to those relationships."

The Ring contains a definite "element of formula," of reuse of familiar creepy movie elements, observed C. W. Nevius in *San Francisco Chronicle.* "All your favorites are here: the creepy, big-eyed kid who whispers freaky predictions, the phone call that makes you jump, the dripping ghost, and the farmhouse with a secret. But this is better than that," Nevius remarked. "In fact, *The Ring* is so good it's scary." Critic Andrew Sarris, writing in the *New York Observer,* found the movie lacked consistency and coherence, stating that Kruger and director Gore Verbinski "seem to make up new rules as they go along, with the result that at the final fade-out we are left hanging, able to figure out neither what else is about to happen, nor exactly what has already happened and who is responsible for it."

Angus Wolfe Murray, writing in *Evening News* (Edinburgh, Scotland), commented that "the adaptation by Ehren Kruger is intelligent." Generally, "Hollywood remakes of foreign hit movies are famous for being flops," Murray stated. "This won't be one of them."

BIOGRAPHICAL AND CRITICAL SOURCES:

PERIODICALS

Chicago Sun-Times, February 25, 2000, Roger Ebert, "No Fun in 'Games,' Yapping Will Result in Napping," p. 31.
Courier-Mail (Brisbane, Australia), August 14, 1999, Des Partridge, "Flaws in the Flash," review of *Arlington Road,* p. 12.
Daily Herald (Arlington Heights, IL), October 18, 2002, Dann Gire, "Hollow 'Ring': Japanese-Inspired Horror Film Long on Scary Images, Short on Suspense," p. 42.
Daily Variety, October 23, 2002, "'Key' Unlocks Kruger Deal," p. 4; December 10, 2002, Marc Graser, "D'Works Springs for Sequel to 'Ring,'" p. 4.
Entertainment Weekly, July 16, 1999, Lisa Schwarzbaum, "Grim Neighbors: In the Chilling Arlington Road, Paranoia Comes a-Knockin' When Jeff Bridges Discovers That the Folks across the Way Keep Explosive Secrets," p. 45; February 11, 2000, Owen Gleiberman, "Hack Work: The Postmodern Slasher Series Comes to a Choppy Close in *Scream 3,* a Scare-Fest with a Shockingly Dull Edge," p. 48; March 31, 2000, "The Write Stuff: The Emergence of the Script-Driven Movie Is Not Only Shaking Up the Industry, It's Turning a Generation of Screenwriters into Pricey Stars," p. 18.
Evening News (Edinburgh, Scotland), February 20, 2003, Angus Wolfe Murray, "The Ring: The Japanese Do It Best," p. 6.
Los Angeles, June, 1999, James Greenberg, "Film High Anxiety," review of *Arlington Road,* p. 36.
Los Angeles Times, July 4, 1999, Joe Leydon, "So Much for Keeping Secrets: The Makers of 'Arlington Road' Wanted to Remain Completely Tight-lipped about Its Plot. But the Marketers Had Other Ideas," p. 6; February 24, 2000, Gene Seymour,

"The Time Has Come: Up-and-Comer Charlize Theron May Make It to the Next Level with Her Two Latest Film Roles," p. 14.
New Yorker, July 19, 1999, Anthony Lane, review of *Arlington Road,* pp. 98-99.
New York Observer, October 28, 2002, Andrew Sarris, "The Ring Is Incoherent, Chilling—and Naomi Watts Looks Great," p. 23.
Plain Dealer (Cleveland, OH), January 4, 2002, Julie E. Washington, "Boring 'Impostor' Masquerading as a Real Sci-fi Movie," review of *Impostor,* p. 10; October 18, 2002, Joanna Connors, "A Ring around Another Stupid Horror Movie," p. 46.
San Francisco Chronicle, October 25, 2002, Ruthe Stein, "'Ring' Writer Happily Goes Unnoticed in San Francisco," J4; March 7, 2003, C. W. Nevius, "Watch This Video at Your Own Expense: 'The Ring' Thrills with Killer Images," D14.
Sight and Sound, April, 1999, Ken Hollings, review of *Arlington Road,* pp. 36-37; May, 2000, Kim Newman, review of *Scream 3,* pp. 59-60.
Time, February 14, 2000, Richard Schickel, "Scream-ish: Terror Seems Squarer in This Sequel and Finale," p. 78.
Variety, August 31-September 6, 1996, Steve Chagollan, "Ten Writers to Watch," pp. 66-70; March 22, 1999, Todd McCarthy, review of *Arlington Road,* p. 35.
Washington Times, February 25, 2000, Gary Arnold, "'Reindeer' Delivers Wit and Drama," p. 7.

ONLINE

Cinemas Online Web site, http://www.cinemas-online.co.uk/ (July 15, 2004), "The Ring: About the Filmmakers."
In Focus Web site, http://www.infocusmag.com/ (October, 2002), interview with Ehren Kruger.
Lycos Entertainment Web site, http://entertainment.lycos.com/ (June 30, 2004), profile of Ehren Kruger.
Scream3 Fan Web site, http://www.angelfire.com/co/erocscream/s3ehren.html (July 15, 2004) "Ehren Kruger, Writer."
Still Screaming Web site, http://www.stillscreaming.com/ (July 15, 2004), "Crew of the Scream Trilogy."*

L

LANE, Nick

PERSONAL: Male; married, wife's name, Ana. *Education:* Imperial College, University of London, B.Sc. (honors), 1988; Royal Free Hospital Medical School, University of London, Ph.D., 1995. *Hobbies and other interests:* Opera, folk music, classical music, fiddle, rock climbing, fossil hunting, mountaineering, literature, history, traveling, photography, cooking, wines, exploring Romanesque churches.

ADDRESSES: Home—London, England. *Agent*—Caroline Dawnay, PFD, Drury House, 34-43 Russell St., London WC2B 5HA, England. *E-mail*—n.lane@ rfc.ucl.ac.uk.

CAREER: Science writer, biochemist, freelance communications consultant, musician, and researcher. MRC Clinical Research Centre, scientific officer, 1988-91; Oxford Clinical Communications, medical writer, 1995-96; Medi Cine International, London, England, senior writer/producer, 1996-99; Adelphi Medi Cine, London, strategic director, 1999-2002. University College, University of London, honorary senior research fellow, 1997—. Fiddle player with the London-based Celtic band Probably Not.

AWARDS, HONORS: Isaac Holden Scholarship, Imperial College, University of London, 1985-88; Young Science Writer of the Year Award, *Daily Telegraph,* 1993; prize winner, New Scientist Millennial Science Essay Competition, 1994; Gold and Silver Awards, Prix Leonardo International Film Festival; Silver "Hugo," Intercom Chicago International Film Festival.

WRITINGS:

Oxygen: The Molecule That Made the World, Oxford University Press (New York, NY), 2002.
(Editor, with Erica E. Benson and Barry J. Fuller) *Life in the Frozen State,* CRC Press (Boca Raton, FL), 2004.

Contributor to publications such as *Scientific American, New Scientist, Lancet,* and *British Medical Journal.*

WORK IN PROGRESS: Power, Sex, and Suicide: Mitochondria and the Making of Man, for Oxford University Press.

SIDELIGHTS: Without oxygen, humans would perish within minutes—but over a lifetime, oxygen metabolism drives the slow and ultimately deadly effects of aging. In *Oxygen: The Molecule That Made the World,* biochemist and science writer Nick Lane presents "a piece of radical scientific polemic, nothing less than a total rethink of how life evolved between about 3.5 billion and 543 million years ago, and how that relates to the diseases we suffer from today," remarked Jerome Burne in *Financial Times.*

Only a small amount of oxygen existed in the primordial atmosphere of Earth some four billion years ago. When levels of oxygen began to rise sharply as the result of photosynthesis in cyanobacteria, other life forms adapted, using oxygen in respiration and spurring further evolutionary advances. Higher levels of atmospheric oxygen may account for the stunning diversity of life in the Cambrian period, and might have allowed creatures such as the Meganeura dragonfly, with its two-foot wingspan, to attain great size. Laurence A. Marschall, writing in *Natural History,* noted that Lane also suggests that "such high oxygen levels may have been lowered by a worldwide firestorm that ended the age of the dinosaurs sixty-five million years ago."

Oxygen has profound effects on the health and longevity of modern humans. Respiration and oxygen metabolism create free radicals, "reactive forms of the oxygen molecule that damage the proteins in our cells," explained Sanjida O'Connell in the London *Times.* Most free radicals are neutralized by natural antioxidants, "but a few slip through the net because our defenses are not perfect," O'Connell commented. The accumulated damage manifests in the familiar effects of aging. Lane, who conducted doctoral research on oxygen free radicals and metabolic function in organ transplants, examines the use of antioxidants such as vitamin C. Michael Peel, writing in *Times Literary Supplement,* stated that Lane's advice is simply "eat well and stay active rather than to seek solace in supposed chemical panaceas."

"Apart from the first chapter, which is cast in a style approaching the juvenile, the book is very well written and easy to read," commented Bernard M. Babior in the *New England Journal of Medicine.* Tim Radford, writing in the Manchester *Guardian,* commented that "Lane's chapters are dispatches from the frontiers of research into Earth and life history, but they contain nothing that will lose the patient reader, and much that will reward." A *Kirkus Reviews* critic commented that *Oxygen: The Molecule That Made the World* is "provocative and complexly argued."

BIOGRAPHICAL AND CRITICAL SOURCES:

PERIODICALS

American Scientist, July-August, 2003, Christian de Duve, review of *Oxygen: The Molecule That Made the World,* pp. 364-365.
Financial Times, November 16, 2002, Jerome Burne, "Luca Gets a Breath of Fresh Air; Jerome Burne Is Impressed by a Highly Ambitious Piece of Scientific Polemic on the Life-and-Death Powers of Oxygen," p. 4.

Guardian (Manchester, England), November 23, 2002, Tim Radford, review of *Oxygen,* p. 12.
Kirkus Reviews, February 15, 2003, review of *Oxygen,* p. 287.
Natural History, July-August, 2003, Laurence A. Marschall, review of *Oxygen,* pp. 58-62.
Nature, October 24, 2002, Thomas B. L. Kirkwood, "The Breath of Life and Death," p. 785.
New England Journal of Medicine, September 11, 2003, Bernard M. Babior, review of *Oxygen,* p. 1099.
Times (London, England), October 5, 2002, Sanjida O'Connell, review of *Oxygen,* p. 14.
Times Literary Supplement, January 31, 2003, Michael Peel, review of *Oxygen,* p. 33.
Wisconsin State Journal, April 13, 2003, review of *Oxygen,* G5.

ONLINE

Nick Lane Home Page, http://pages.britishlibrary.net/ (June 30, 2004).*

*   *   *

LANGLEY, Liz

PERSONAL: Female.

ADDRESSES: Home—Orlando, FL.

CAREER: Orlando Weekly, Orlando, FL, columnist.

WRITINGS:

Pop Tart: A Fresh, Frosted Sugar Rush through Our Pre-Packaged Culture, Octavo Books (Altamonte Springs, FL), 1999.

Author of "The Juice," a popular culture column for the *Orlando Weekly.*

BIOGRAPHICAL AND CRITICAL SOURCES:

PERIODICALS

Library Journal, February 1, 2000, Kimberly L. Clarke, review of *Pop Tart: A Fresh, Frosted Sugar Rush through Our Pre-Packaged Culture,* p. 107.
Publishers Weekly, February 14, 2000, review of *Pop Tart,* p. 191.*

LATHAM, Alison

PERSONAL: Female.

ADDRESSES: Agent—c/o Author Mail, Oxford University Press, 198 Madison Ave., New York, NY 10016.

CAREER: Writer, editor, and music scholar. Previously publications editor at the Royal Opera House, Covent Garden, London, England.

WRITINGS:

(Editor, with Stanley Sadie) *Stanley Sadie's Brief Guide to Music,* Prentice-Hall (Englewood Cliffs, NJ), 1986.

(Assistant editor, with Stanley Sadie) *The Norton/Grove Concise Encyclopedia of Music,* Norton (New York, NY), 1988.

(Editor, with Roger Parker) *Verdi in Performance,* Oxford University Press (New York, NY), 2001.

(Editor, with Stanley Sadie) *The Cambridge Music Guide,* Cambridge University Press (New York, NY), 2001.

(Editor) *The Oxford Companion to Music,* Oxford University Press (New York, NY), 2002.

(Editor) *Sing, Ariel: Essays and Thoughts for Alexander Goehr's Seventieth Birthday,* Ashgate (Burlington, VT), 2003.

(Editor) *The Oxford Dictionary of Musical Works,* Oxford University Press (New York, NY), 2004.

SIDELIGHTS: The Norton/Grove Concise Encyclopedia of Music, coedited by music scholar Alison Latham and Stanley Sadie, provides a single-volume reference covering a wide variety of musical genres, styles, and time periods. Condensed from the twenty-volume *New Grove Dictionary of Music and Musicians,* the book includes drawings, diagrams, musical examples, and tables. The core of the book offers listings and brief biographical information on performers, composers, publishers, and other professionals. Listings include brief descriptions of instruments and instrument makers, plus more than one thousand titles and nicknames of musical works. Coverage is given to both Western and non-Western forms of music. Geraldine Ostrove, writing in *Notes,* found a British bias in the encyclopedia, which is ostensibly aimed at an American market.

However, the book "stands alone as a reliable, up-to-date-one-volume desk encyclopedia of music in English," Ostrove remarked. For students, writers, and browsers "needing a handy book in order to look up something about music quickly without keeping an entire library on the shelves, *The Norton/Grove Concise Encyclopedia of Music* will take care of the situation," observed Harold C. Schonberg in the *New York Times Book Review.*

Verdi in Performance, edited by Latham and Roger Parker, originated in a 1995 conference, Performing Verdi, held at the Royal Opera House in Covent Garden. *"Verdi in Performance* summarizes the current state of research in the fertile, yet surprisingly underdeveloped field of Verdi performance," commented Nicole Baker in *Notes.* The first section of the book covers staging in Verdi performances, addressing issues of whether modern performances should try to recreate Verdi's contemporary performance conditions or if they should be staged in today's fashion. Part two explores vocal and instrumental performance in Verdi's works, while part three delves into issues of dance and ballet. Part four provides detailed discussion of editions of Verdi's work and the fundamental differences between a static, printed edition and a dynamic, unique, one-time performance that cannot be duplicated.

"The editors and participants are to be commended for seeing their ideas into print, for even though many of the issues discussed are specific to performing Verdi, much of the material is clearly applicable to modern performance of a wide range of music," stated Stephen A. Willier in *Opera Quarterly.* "The overall result of the collection is a fascinating, stimulating collection of reference materials, research, opinions, and arguments about four critical areas of Verdi scholarship," Baker wrote.

Latham and Sadie also edited *The Cambridge Music Guide,* an illustrated reference work on Western classical music. The guide offers definitions and discussion of topics such as musical structure, history, instruments, elements, and more. Brief biographies discuss individual composers, their works, and their musical eras. Also included are "listening notes" with detailed information on musical compositions. Lists and tables allow quick reference to common musical information, terms, and definitions. "I'd recommend this attractive and colorfully illustrated book as a first choice to anyone looking for a concise, scholarly, but not intimidating guide to classical music," stated Philip Haldeman in *American Record Guide.*

Latham is the sole editor of *The Oxford Companion to Music,* an exhaustive one-volume reference to Western classical music traditions throughout the world. First published in 1938 as *The Oxford Companion to Music, Self-Indexed and with a Pronouncing Glossary,* by Percy A. Sholes, and last updated in 1983 as *The New Oxford Companion to Music,* edited by Denis Arnold, Latham's book owes much to the volumes that came before it but is a distinct work from its predecessors. More than 150 scholars and writers contributed to the more than 8,000 entries in the volume. More than seventy percent of the book is new material since the 1983 volume and includes information on jazz, popular music, dance music, and other genres. Entries cover topics such as composers, theorists, some performers, instruments, forms, political influences on music, music from individual countries, musical terms, and more.

Tim Wadham, writing in *School Library Journal,* called *The Oxford Companion to Music* "a definitive work useful for both browsing and research," and "an accessible, authoritative resource." A *Publishers Weekly* reviewer noted that "the compendium is solidly researched, with useful biographical information and lists of suggested reading." Rick Jones, writing in *Evening Standard* (London, England), remarked that "Latham's Companion is certainly useful—you can never have too many reference books—but as a work it lacks a strong personality" and is "bereft of humour." But *Strings* reviewer Heather K. Scott called it "a rich reference for anyone interested in music history, theory, study, and/or application." And Tim Homfray, writing in *Times Educational Supplement,* concluded that "this is probably the best one-volume music reference book going."

BIOGRAPHICAL AND CRITICAL SOURCES:

PERIODICALS

American Record Guide, May-June, 2001, Philip Haldeman, review of *The Cambridge Music Guide,* pp. 259-260.

Booklist, November 15, 2002, review of *The Oxford Companion to Music,* pp. 621-622.

CHOICE: Current Reviews for Academic Libraries, October, 2002, J. Tsou, review of *The Oxford Companion to Music,* p. 257.

Evening Standard (London, England), March 11, 2002, Rick Jones, "Not Such a Good Companion," review of *The Oxford Companion to Music,* p. 51.

Instrumentalist, September, 2002, James Sellers, review of *The Oxford Companion to Music,* pp. 4-8.

Lancet, August 31, 2002, Thomas Sherwood, review of *The Oxford Companion to Music,* p. 257.

Library Journal, June 15, 2002, Bonnie Jo Dopp, review of *The Oxford Companion to Music,* p. 58.

Musical Times, spring, 2004, Arnold Whittal, review of *Sing, Ariel: Essays and Thoughts for Alexander Goehr's Seventieth Birthday,* pp. 97-101.

Music Educators Journal, January, 2003, review of *The Oxford Companion to Music,* p. 76.

New York Times Book Review, October 8, 1989, Harold C. Schonberg, review of *The Norton/Grove Concise Encyclopedia of Music,* p. 10.

Notes, March, 1991, Geraldine Ostrove, review of *The Norton/Grove Concise Encyclopedia of Music,* pp. 796-797; December, 2002, Nicole Baker, review of *Verdi in Performance,* pp. 348-350.

Opera, March, 2002, Richard Law, review of *Verdi in Performance,* pp. 362-363.

Opera Quarterly, autumn, 2002, Stephen A. Willier, review of *Verdi in Performance,* pp. 592-601.

Publishers Weekly, July 31, 2000, review of *The Cambridge Music Guide,* p. 88; May 13, 2002, review of *The Oxford Companion to Music,* p. 60.

School Library Journal, November, 2002, Tim Wadham, review of *The Oxford Companion to Music,* p. 102.

State (Columbia, SC), June 12, 2002, William W. Starr, review of *The Oxford Companion to Music.*

Strings, October, 2002, Heather K. Scott, review of *The Oxford Companion to Music,* pp. 89-90.

Sunday Times (London, England), March 10, 2002, Hugh Canning, "Who's In, Who's Out in the Fickle World of Classical Music," review of *The Oxford Companion to Music,* p. 39.

Times Educational Supplement, April 19, 2002, Tim Homfray, "Critics' Choice," review of *The Oxford Companion to Music,* p. 8.

Times Literary Supplement, February 1, 2002, Peter Porter, "Lost in the Byways," review of *Verdi in Performance,* p. 19; January 17, 2003, David Schiff, "Maddening Multitudes," review of *The Oxford Companion to Music,* p. 18.*

LATYNIN, Leonid (Aleksandrovich) 1938-

PERSONAL: Born 1938, in Privolzhsk, Union of Soviet Socialist Republics (now Russia). *Education:* Studied philology at Moscow University, 1960-64.

ADDRESSES: Home—Moscow, Russia. *Agent*—c/o Russian Press Service, 1805 Crain St., Evanston, IL 60202. *E-mail*—mail@latynin.ru or perova@glas.msk. su.

CAREER: Khudozhestvennaya Literatura Publishing House, radio commentator, *Youth* magazine, poetry division, 1962-74. Researcher of icons and local crafts in northern Russia, 1970s; translator of Central Asian poetry, 1980s.

WRITINGS:

V chuzhom gorode: "Grimer i Muza" (novel), Sov. Pisatel (Moscow, Russia), 1988.
Obriad: Stikhotvoreniia, 1965-1991, Glas (Moscow, Russia), 1993.
Spiashchii vo vremia zhatvy (novel), Glas (Moscow, Russia), 1993, translation by Andrew Bromfield published as *Sleeper at Harvest Time,* Zephyr Press (Boston, MA), 1994.
The Face-Maker and the Muse, translated by Andrew Bromfield, Glas (Moscow, Russia), 1999.
Foneticheskii shum. Evgenii Vitkovskii: Dialogi, Vodolei Publishers (Tomsk, Russia), 2002.
Russkaya Pravda, Vodolei Publishers (Tomsk, Russia), 2003.

Also author of *Stavr and Sarah* and *The Den,* both from Glas, and *Patriarshie prudy,* 1977.

WORK IN PROGRESS: Two more novels to complete a trilogy begun with *Sleeper at Harvest Time.*

SIDELIGHTS: Hailed as a post-realist Russian writer, Leonid Latynin was trained as a philologist and has become an expert in pre-Christian Russian culture and in Russian icons. Both of these interests are apparent in his fiction, including two novels translated into English: *Sleeper at Harvest Time* and *The Face-Maker and the Muse.* Though published later, *The Face-Maker* is actually the earlier novel; it was written in

the 1960s and distributed in 1977 in the underground samizdat of the day. "Readers of samizdat were engrossed in the anti-utopia—Orwell, Zamyatin, Huxley, Kafka—and my novel was inevitably perceived in terms of that familiar, standard code," Latynin noted on his Internet home page. In fact, Latynin further explained, he had no such intention with his novel. Instead, *The Face-Maker and the Muse* "is basically a novel about the fate for an artist and a prophet, about his rise and his downfall, about his responsibility for the metamorphoses undergone by his own ideas. The novel is, if you wish, a metaphor for the fate of the artist in the world."

In Latynin's fable, inhabitants of a nameless city have no names unless they are part of the privileged class. Everyone else is assigned numbers instead of names, and their numerical ranking depends on how similar they look to the prescribed features of the model face that was designed and sculpted by the Great Face-Maker. A contributor for *Publishers Weekly* described the novel as "dense and challenging." Isobel Montgomery, writing in the Manchester *Guardian,* found the novel an "over-determined allegory," but she also had praise for it, noting that it "resonates with beguiling ideas."

Sleeper at Harvest Time pursues Latynin's style farther, employing some of the structures of magic realism in a fable-like story about a young boy born to a sorceress and fathered by a bear. Described as "part history, part imaginary chronicle, part incantation and part biblical narrative" by Michael Scammell in the *New York Times Book Review,* the novel chronicles the life and times of Emelya, a wanderer in both time and place. Born in the tenth century on the very spot where modern Moscow would later be built, he faints at seeing his mother burned to death after she is accused of bringing the plague to their village. Awaking in twenty-first-century Moscow, Emelya is caught between worlds. Latynin's narrative switches back and forth between this modern totalitarian Russia and various historical epochs, ending with Emelya's ultimate execution by stoning in the modern world. In this dystopic future, Russian blood determines all; when it is discovered that Emelya has a strange ethnic blood in his veins, his fate is sealed.

Scammell felt that Latynin's novel represents an "interesting new direction in which to take the post-Communist search for Russia's roots." Though Scammell felt that Latynin's "reach exceeds his grasp," creating a book with a "paper-thin" plot and "sketchy" characterization, he also noted that the work "is not without interest." But for V. D. Barooshian, writing in *Choice,* Latynin "evinces a rich lore of Russian religious history." And Jerzy R. Krzyanowski, reviewing *Sleeper at Harvest Time* in *World Literature Today,* thought that the book was written in a "highly ornamental, rich style" and stated that it "makes fascinating reading." *Sleeper at Harvest Time* is the first novel of a projected trilogy.

BIOGRAPHICAL AND CRITICAL SOURCES:

PERIODICALS

Choice, June, 1995, V. D. Barooshian, review of *Sleeper at Harvest Time,* p. 1600.
Guardian (Manchester, England), May 13, 2000, Isobel Montgomery, review of *The Face-Maker and the Muse,* p. 11.
New York Times Book Review, December 25, 1994, Michael Scammell, review of *Sleeper at Harvest Time,* p. 9.
Publishers Weekly, February 28, 2000, review of *The Face-Maker and the Muse,* p. 62.
World Literature Today, autumn, 1995, Jerzy R. Krzyanowski, review of *Sleeper at Harvest Time,* p. 824.

ONLINE

Leonid Latynin Home Page, http://www.latynin.ru/ (January 22, 2004).
Russian Press Service Web site, http://www.russianpress.com/ (January 22, 2004).

*   *   *

LEE, Helene 1947(?)-

PERSONAL: Born c. 1947.

ADDRESSES: Office—Libération, 11, rue Béranger, 75154 Paris Cedex 03. *E-mail*—helene.lee@free.fr.

CAREER: Libération, Paris, France, music journalist.

WRITINGS:

Rockers d'Afrique, Albin Michel (Paris, France), 1988.
The First Rasta: Leonard Howell and the Rise of Rastafarianism, translated by Lily Davis and Helene Lee, edited an with an introduction by Stephen Davis, Lawrence Hill Books (Chicago, IL), 2003.

Lee's writings on music have appeared in international magazines and journals.

SIDELIGHTS: French music journalist Helene Lee undertook a study of the man considered the founder and father of the Rastafarian movement in her biography of Leonard Howell, translated into English and published in the United States in 2003 as *The First Rasta: Leonard Howell and the Rise of Rastafarianism.* Inevitably, Lee's book also deals in part with reggae music whose practitioners, such as Bob Marley, are much better known to the world than Howell. Her biography was in part intended to redress that imbalance. Lee in fact first encountered the work of Howell in the late 1970s when visiting Jamaica to write about reggae. "'The music turned lousy and I chose to go beyond that and research the roots of rasta,'" Lee told Howard Campbell on *IPS.*

Lee managed, through "impeccable research and dogged sleuthing," as a contributor for *Publishers Weekly* commented, to produce an "extraordinarily useful book." She did extensive research in Jamaica, visiting the ruins of the commune, Pinnacle, which Howell founded and governed for fifteen years. Born in Jamaica, Howell moved to the United States in 1914, and was influenced by black nationalist leaders such as Marcus Garvey. He was deported in 1932 and began the roots of his movement, focusing on the return of God in the form of the Ethiopian King Ras Tafari, from whom the Rastafarian movement takes its name. Borrowing from Hinduism and from Ethiopian religions, he structured a new religion, gathered followers, and formed a commune. He found himself at odds with the Jamaican government for his religion's reverence of Ras Tafari rather than the English George V, as well as for its cultivation of marijuana as a cash crop. Things came to a head when the police raided Howell's commune in 1954; after that, the founder of Rastafarianism was lost in obscurity. The *Publishers Weekly* critic further called Lee's work a "passionate biography." *Library Journal*'s L. Kris similarly found *The First Rasta* an "engaging account," while a writer for *Kirkus Reviews* commented that "the loose threads of Rasta history [are] impressively woven into a flag of green, red, and gold by French music journalist Lee." Vanessa Bush, writing in *Booklist,* noted that Lee "draws on extensive knowledge about the Rastafarian movement." Speaking with Campbell on the *Jamaica Observer Online,* Lee said, "'[Howell] has always been depicted as a crazy guy and a violent person which he was not. . . . With this book I'm trying to do him justice.'"

BIOGRAPHICAL AND CRITICAL SOURCES:

PERIODICALS

Booklist, July, 2003, Vanessa Bush, review of *The First Rasta: Leonard Howell and the Rise of Rastafarianism,* p. 1849.
Kirkus Reviews, May 15, 2003, review of *The First Rasta,* pp. 732-733.
Library Journal, June 1, 2003, L. Kris, review of *The First Rasta,* p. 129.
Publishers Weekly, June 23, 2003, review of *The First Rasta,* p. 60.

ONLINE

IPS, http://www.hartford-hwp.com/ (March 17, 1998), Howard Campbell, "Book on Founding Father of Rastafarians."
Jamaica Observer Online, http://jamaicaobserver.com/ (May 5, 2002), Howard Campbell, "Preserving the First Rasta."*

* * *

LEE, Mark 1950-

PERSONAL: Born 1950, in MN; married; children: two. *Education:* Yale University, B.A., 1973.

ADDRESSES: Home—Los Angeles, CA. *Agent*—c/o Author Mail, Algonquin Books, P.O. Box 225, Chapel Hill, NC 27515.

CAREER: Writer, journalist, and poet.

MEMBER: PEN (vice president).

WRITINGS:

The Lost Tribe, Picador (New York, NY), 1998.
The Canal House, Algonquin Books (Chapel Hill, NC), 2003.

Contributor to periodicals including *Atlantic Monthly, Los Angeles Times,* and the *Times Literary Supplement* (London, England).

SIDELIGHTS: Mark Lee's first novel, *The Lost Tribe,* features Ben Chase, a Reuters reporter who is stationed in Africa. Lee was a Reuters reporter, and in the early 1980s he was living in Uganda during a civil war and was eventually expelled from the country for writing about military acts committed during the conflict. *The Lost Tribe* has Chase digging his own grave after he reports on a story dealing with the kidnapping and rape of schoolgirls by soliders. A reviewer for *Publishers Weekly* noted, "Lee succeeds in capturing the chaotic, terrifying nature of African life during times of upheaval," but the reviewer went on to say that "the inner lives of his characters don't get as full a treatment." And in a review for *Library Journal,* Bettie Alston Shea claimed that the novel "never quite lives up to the reader's expectations."

Lee's second novel, *The Canal House,* again features a journalist in Africa. This time it is Daniel McFarland, a war correspondent who has teamed up with photojournalist Nicky Bettencourt. "Lee is a foreign correspondent who creates a powerful aura of realism that will forever alter your perception of the news," wrote Elsa Gaztambide in a review for *Booklist.* Daniel begins an affair with Dr. Julia Cadell, a relief worker in the war zones. *The Canal House* title refers to a house that the two share in London in-between stints in the dangerous war-torn areas. A reviewer for *Publishers Weekly* claimed that "there's no denying the eloquence and terror of Lee's vistas of contemporary war."

BIOGRAPHICAL AND CRITICAL SOURCES:

PERIODICALS

Booklist, March 15, 2003, Elsa Gaztambide, review of *The Canal House,* p. 1275.

Kirkus Reviews, May 9, 2003, review of *The Canal House,* p. 168.

Library Journal, June 1, 1998, Bettie Alston Shea, review of *The Lost Tribe,* pp. 152-153; February 15, 2003, Marc Kloszewski, review of *The Canal House,* p. 169.

Publishers Weekly, April 13, 1998, review of *The Lost Tribe,* p. 48; February 10, 2003, review of *The Canal House,* p. 160.*

*   *   *

LEESE, Peter (Jeremy)

PERSONAL: Male. *Education:* University of Hertfordshire, B.A. (humanities; with honors), 1983; University of Warwick, M.A. (European cultural history), 1984; Open University, Ph.D. (history), 1989.

ADDRESSES: *Office*—English Department, Jagiellonian University, Al. Mickiewicza 9, 31-120 Krakow, Poland.

CAREER: Educator and author. Jagiellonian University, Krakow, Poland, assistant professor of English.

MEMBER: British Council (Poland) Inter-University Seminar on Intercultural Studies (project coordinator), Oral History Society.

AWARDS, HONORS: Ph.D. grant award, ESRC, 1986-89; curriculum development grants, HESP/Civic Education Project, 1992-95; curriculum development grants, British Council, 1996-98; travel research grant, DAAD, for visiting archives and libraries in Germany, 1998; development grant, British Council "Link," 1998-2001; publication grant, British Council, 2002.

WRITINGS:

(With C. Cook) *St. Martin's Guide to Sources in Contemporary British History,* Palgrave Macmillan (New York, NY), 1994, published as *The Longman Guide to Sources in Contemporary British History,* Longman (London, England), 1994.

(Translator, with Elżbieta Wójcik-Leese) Włodzimierz Szturc, *A Short History of Polish Literature,* Polish Academy of Sciences (Krakow, Poland), 1998.

Shell Shock: Traumatic Neurosis and the British Soldiers of the First World War, Palgrave (New York, NY), 2002.

(Editor, with B. Piatek and I. Curyllo-Klag) *The British Migrant Experience, 1700-2000: An Anthology,* Palgrave Macmillan (New York, NY), 2002.

(Editor, with W. Witalisz, and contributor) *PASE Papers in Cultural Literature: Proceedings of the Tenth International Conference of PASE, 2001,* IFA/Jagiellonian University (Krakow, Poland), 2003.

Contributor of papers and articles to publications including *British Journal of Psychology, Historical Journal, Pears Cyclopedia, Yes,* and *Times Higher Education Supplement.*

SIDELIGHTS: Peter Leese's book *Shell Shock: Traumatic Neurosis and the British Soldiers of the First World War* is an in-depth account of the experiences of British soldiers during World War I and their psychological response to the trauma of combat that came to be known in early 1915 as "shell shock." Maureen T. Moore, a contributor to *Journal of Military History,* noted that the study is "well founded on an impressive body of primary documents . . . [and] a wide array of periodical literature, memoirs, medical journals and histories, and solid secondary sources on England's war experience, military medicine, war literature, and cultural contexts."

Leese organized his book into three sections titled "Discoveries," "Wartime," and "Legacies." He traces the origins of the awareness of shell shock to discussions relating to "traumatic neurasthenia," an adverse psychological reaction that often appeared in people who, in the latter part of the nineteenth century, had experienced train accidents. Similar adverse reactions were noted in soldiers, who thus became psychological casualties of war. Part two examines the wartime diagnosis and treatment of the neurosis, describes the diverse methods and varying quality of care received by officers and men from the ranks, and compares British home-front and frontline treatments with those given by French and Germans. The third section addresses the enduring effects of shell shock on veterans and civilians alike.

Leese wrote that "shell-shock cannot be understood without an awareness of those socio-cultural forces which shaped its definition and reception by the wider society," a point of departure that J. A. A. Black, who reviewed the book for *Albion,* observed was "well made and sustained consistently throughout the main part of the book." Black commented that the book is clearly written and accessible and "a worthy contribution to the existing literature." Moore noted that the book is "densely packed with information" that sometimes causes the chronology of events to get lost, but commented that "those willing to pay attention, however, will be rewarded by this first full-length treatment of Britain's 'shell shock' experience."

When Daniel Crewe reviewed *The British Migrant Experience, 1700-2000: An Anthology,* for the *Times Literary Supplement,* he noted that Leese and his coeditors intended to create a "cubist depiction of Britain's migrant past rather than an ultimate reproduction," and that they succeeded in doing so. The anthology covers 300 years of immigration to Britain and is divided into three sections: the eighteenth, nineteenth, and twentieth centuries. The book includes personal recollections and commentaries from more than 250 sources and depicts experiences of immigrants from around the world, including Irish, Jewish, Arab, Lithuanian, and Moroccan peoples. Crewe commented that "these tales add up to a striking view of Britain, including immigrants' responses to snow (more than once), railway carriages and the [National Health Service], and through the reactions of Britons, which varied from the welcoming to disturbing talk of lynchings."

BIOGRAPHICAL AND CRITICAL SOURCES:

BOOKS

Leese, Peter, *Shell Shock: Traumatic Neurosis and the British Soldiers of the First World War,* Palgrave (New York, NY), 2002.

PERIODICALS

Albion, winter, 2004, J. A. A. Black, review of *Shell Shock: Traumatic Neurosis and the British Soldiers of the First World War,* p. 699.

Journal of Military History, April, 2003, Maureen T. Moore, review of *Shell Shock,* pp. 588-589.
Times Literary Supplement, January 31, 2003, Daniel Crewe, review of *The British Migrant Experience, 1700-2000: An Anthology,* p. 30.

ONLINE

Life Stories Project Web site, http://www.lifestories project.org/peter.html (July 8, 2004), "Dr. Peter Leese."*

* * *

LEGGETT, Richard G. 1953-

PERSONAL: Born April 27, 1953, in South Ruislip, Middlesex, England; son of Richard D. (a drafter and graphic artist) and Thelma Jane (an early childhood educator; maiden name, Broom) Leggett; married Paula Lee Porter (an Anglican priest), July 6, 1984; children: David Michael, Anna Frances, Owen Thomas. *Ethnicity:* "Anglo-Celt." *Education:* University of Denver, B.A. (magna cum laude), 1975; Nashotah House Theological Seminary, M.Div. (cum laude), 1981; University of North Dame, M.A., 1987, Ph.D., 1993.

ADDRESSES: Home—7249 Cypress St., Vancouver, British Columbia V6P 5M2, Canada. *Office*—Vancouver School of Theology, 6000 Iona Dr., Vancouver, British Columbia V6T 1L4, Canada. *E-mail*—rleggett@vst.edu.

CAREER: Anglican priest in Denver, CO, 1981-84, and South Bend, IN, 1984-87; Vancouver School of Theology, Vancouver, British Columbia, Canada, professor, 1987—.

MEMBER: North American Academy of Liturgy, Societas Liturgica, Associated Parishes for Liturgy and Mission.

AWARDS, HONORS: Eugene Stetson fellow, Episcopal Church Foundation, 1985.

WRITINGS:

A Companion to the Waterloo Declaration, Anglican Book Centre, 2000.

Contributor of articles and reviews to periodicals, including *Liturgy Canada, Open, Liturgical Ministry, Liturgy 90, Sewanee Journal of Theology,* and *Anglican Theological Review.*

WORK IN PROGRESS: A historical, theological, and pastoral study of the liturgical rites of Holy Week in the Anglican and Lutheran churches in North America; a historical study of Anglican liturgical revision in Canada.

*   *   *

LERNER, Henry M.

PERSONAL: Male. *Education:* Harvard Medical School, M.D., 1975.

ADDRESSES: Home—Newton, MA. *Agent*—c/o Author Mail, Perseus Books Group, 387 Park Ave. S., New York, NY 10016.

CAREER: Physician and author. Newton-Wellesley Hospital, Newton, MA, private practice in obstetrics and gynecology; Women's Urinary Continence Center, Newton, director. Member of board of directors, Pro-Mutual Insurance Company.

WRITINGS:

Miscarriage: Why It Happens and How Best to Reduce Your Risks, Perseus Publishing (New York, NY), 2003.

Contributor to *New York Times.*

SIDELIGHTS: Henry M. Lerner is an obstetrician/gynecologist with more than twenty years of experience in his field. Lerner's 2003 work, *Miscarriage: Why It Happens and How Best to Reduce Your Risks,* addresses an emotional issue by fielding "questions about the nature and causes of miscarriage as well as presenting available treatments and supports following it," wrote Sheila K. Vernick on the *Massachusetts Psychologist* Web site. According to *Library Journal*

critic Linda M. G. Katz, Lerner's work "offers clear and detailed explanations to questions concerning the etiology, diagnosis, prevention, and treatment of miscarriage."

BIOGRAPHICAL AND CRITICAL SOURCES:

PERIODICALS

Daily News Tribune (Waltham, MA), March 31, 2004, Sasha Brown, "How to Mend a Broken Heart."
Library Journal, March 15, 2003, Linda M. G. Katz, *Miscarriage: Why It Happens and How Best to Reduce Your Risks,* pp. 106-107.

ONLINE

Massachusetts Psychologist Web site, http://www.masspsy.com/ (October, 2003), Sheila K. Vernick, "Miscarriage: Its Aspects Explored."
OBGYN.net, http://www.obgyn.net/ (April 17, 2004), "A Conversation with Dr. Henry Lerner."
StorkNet.com, http://www.storknet.com/ (April 17, 2004), "StorkNet's Guest Room."*

*   *   *

LEVINE, Noah 1971(?)-

PERSONAL: Born c. 1971; son of Stephen (a writer) and Patricia Levine. *Education:* Attended California Institute of Integral Studies.

ADDRESSES: Home—San Francisco, CA. *Agent*—c/o Author Mail, HarperCollins, 10 East 53rd St., 7th Fl., New York, NY 10012.

CAREER: Spirit Rock Meditation Center, Woodacre, CA, teacher-in-training. Mind Body Awareness Project, cofounder and director.

WRITINGS:

Dharma Punx: A Memoir, HarperSanFrancisco (San Francisco, CA), 2003.

SIDELIGHTS: Noah Levine tells the story of his life in *Dharma Punx: A Memoir*, tracing his journey from drug addict and street thief to practicing Buddhist. According to Kerri Hikida, writing in the *Whole Life Times* online, in his memoir Levine seeks to "integrate the punk ethic with spiritual practice."

The son of Stephen Levine, a writer on New Age spiritual topics, Noah had a troubled childhood which included suicide attempts, drug addiction, vandalism, and crime. When his parents divorced, Levine lived with his mother and stepfather, a situation he fought against. Part of Noah's rebellion against his family was a turn to punk rock, embracing the violent style of the scene. By the age of seventeen Noah had been arrested so often that a final arrest found him sentenced to three months in the Santa Cruz Country Juvenile Hall. At this time his father approached him with the suggestion that he try meditation, a suggestion that set Noah on the path to kick his drug habit, finish school, and study Buddhism. "I turned my attention inwards and started to see I wanted to decrease the anger, fear, envy and greed I had within myself. . . . I began to see that a lot of [punk] music was actually encouraging hatred, encouraging grief—not necessarily the influences I wanted to have," Levine explained to Hikida.

An homage to twentieth-century Beat writer Jack Kerouac's book *Dharma Bums*, Levine's *Dharma Punx* was derived from several essays he wrote for school. These papers were "on things I had done and learned in life that I hadn't received school credit for," Levine explained to Jessica Rae Patton of the *Buddhist News Network* Web site. "My topics were recovery, Buddhist pilgrimage, community health. My teachers were impressed, and I realized I'd had a pretty interesting life." The resulting book "is dramatic," a critic for *Kirkus Reviews* admitted in reviewing *Dharma Punx*. Making his home in San Francisco, Levine teaches Buddhist meditation techniques and counsels young prisoners.

BIOGRAPHICAL AND CRITICAL SOURCES:

PERIODICALS

Kirkus Reviews, April 15, 2003, review of *Dharma Punx: A Memoir*, p. 588.

ONLINE

Buddhist News Network, http://www.buddhistnews.tv/ (August 7, 2003), Jessica Rae Patton, "Punk Monk."

Noah Levine's Home Page, http://www.dharmapunx. com/ (October 6, 2003).

Salon.com, http://www.salon.com/ (November 19, 2002), Sean Elder, "From Street Thug to Dharma Punk."

Whole Life Times Online, http://www.wholelifetimes. com/ (November 24, 2003), Kerri Hikida, "Dharma Punk Noah Levine: Buddhism's Next Generation."*

*   *   *

LEVY, Alan 1932-2004

OBITUARY NOTICE—See index for *CA* sketch: Born February 10, 1932, in New York, NY; died of cancer, April 2, 2004, in Prague, Czech Republic. Journalist, editor, and author. Although American by birth, Levy spent most of his career in Prague and Vienna and was acclaimed for his work as writer and editor for the *Prague Post*. Graduating from Brown University in 1952, he earned a master's degree the next year from Columbia University. His career as a journalist began at the *Louisville Courier-Journal*, where he was a reporter until 1960. For the next seven years, Levy worked as a freelance writer in New York City, and for one year he was an investigator for the Carnegie Commission on Educational Television. In 1967, he moved to Prague in what was then still Czechoslovakia. There he worked as a freelance writer and correspondent, reporting on such events as the 1968 Prague Spring and the Warsaw Pact invasion. Expelled from Czechoslovakia in 1971 by the government, he settled in Vienna and wrote for various international publications. He was able to return to his beloved city of Prague in 1990, and the next year was made the editor in chief of the *Prague Post*, a position he maintained until his death. Levy was also a prolific author, writing various biographical and political books, including *The Elizabeth Taylor Story* (1961), *Rowboat to Prague* (1972; second edition published in 1980 as *So Many Heroes*), *Forever, Sophia* (1979), *Ezra Pound: A Jewish View* (1987), *The Wiesenthal File* (1993), and *An American Jew in Vienna* (2000).

OBITUARIES AND OTHER SOURCES:

PERIODICALS

Los Angeles Times, April 5, 2004, p. B9.
New York Times, April 7, 2004, p. A19; April 9, 2004, p. A2.
Washington Post, April 7, 2004, p. B6.

*   *   *

LIM, Johnson T. K. 1952-

PERSONAL: Born September 5, 1952, in Singapore; son of Kerry (a supervisor) and Jenny (a homemaker) Lim. *Ethnicity:* "Chinese." *Education:* Trinity Evangelical Divinity School, M.A., 1987; University of Edinburgh, M.Phil., 1997; University of Queensland, Ph.D., 2001. *Religion:* Christian. *Hobbies and other interests:* Reading.

ADDRESSES: Home—Block 86, Whampoa Dr. 15-925, Singapore. *Office*—W.I.N., Singapore. *E-mail*—sonrise@singnet.com.sg.

CAREER: W.I.N., Singapore, director, 1998—.

WRITINGS:

This One Thing I Know, (Singapore), 1995.
The Sin of Moses, Van Gorcum, 1997.
A Different Gospel, Publish the Word, 2002.
Grace in the Midst of Judgement, Walter de Gruyter, 2002.
Power in Preaching, University Press of America (Lanham, MD), 2002.

Contributor to periodicals, including *Asia Journal of Theology, Jewish Bible Quarterly, Church and Society, Stoulos Theological Journal,* and *Church and State.*

WORK IN PROGRESS: Research for *A Time to Laugh; Holy Scripture, Human Script; Oasis of God's Grace; A Practical Guide to Preaching; Fitly Spoken Words Are Like . . .;* and *Tomorrow the Sun Will Rise Again.*

SIDELIGHTS: Johnson T. K. Lim told *CA:* "My primary motivation for writing is to bless the readers and to share what I believe is important. My work is influenced by my faith in God."

*   *   *

LINDSAY-POLAND, John 1960-

PERSONAL: Born April 7, 1960, in New York, NY; son of Robert (a university professor) and Helen (an activist) Lindsay; partner of James Groleau. *Ethnicity:* "European-American." *Education:* Attended Harvard College, 1980-82; New College of California, B.A. (U.S. history), 2003. *Politics:* Independent. *Religion:* Humanist.

ADDRESSES: Office—Fellowship of Reconciliation, 2017 Mission St., No. 305, San Francisco, CA 94110.

CAREER: Fellowship of Reconciliation, San Francisco, CA, director of task force on Latin America and the Caribbean. *Panama Update,* editor and staff writer.

AWARDS, HONORS: United Nations Association Human Rights Award.

WRITINGS:

(With Tom Barry, Marco Gandásequi, and Peter Simonson) *Inside Panama: The Essential Guide to Its Politics, Economy, Society, and Environment,* Resource Center Press (Albuquerque, NM), 1995.
Emperors in the Jungle: The Hidden History of the U.S. in Panama, Duke University Press (Durham, NC), 2003.

Contributor to periodicals, including *San Francisco Chronicle, NACLA Report on the Americas, Progressive, Covert Action Quarterly,* and *Fellowship.*

SIDELIGHTS: John Lindsay-Poland is a journalist and human rights activist who published *Emperors in the Jungle: The Hidden History of the U.S. in Panama* in 2003. In his book Lindsay-Poland "discloses decades of hidden history, clandestine environmental activities, and covert chemical weapons tests," observed *Library Journal* critic Sylvia D. Hall-Ellis. Reviewing *Emperors in the Jungle* for *Perspectives on Political Science*, Margaret E. Scranton remarked that Lindsay-Poland "sheds new light on such familiar topics as military intervention and brings to light some relatively esoteric ones." Scranton added, "The book is a well-researched and documented survey of U.S. policy on these issues, interpreted in terms of key events and socioeconomic forces in both countries: the psychological images of Panama held by U.S. policymakers and officials and the broader pattern of hemispheric relations." A *Kirkus Reviews* critic found *Emperors in the Jungle* to be an "eye-opening history of the tangled, racially freighted dealings of the American government with its sometime client state of Panama over a hundred years," while *Panama News* contributor Eric Jackson stated that the work "adds a new dimension to the study of U.S.-Panamanian relations."

Lindsay-Poland told *CA:* "I am most drawn to research that serves some purpose besides the increase of knowledge for its own sake, but that helps us to understand how to act, to respond to history and what is before us. As a pacifist descending from both American warriors and pacifists, I am interested in understanding how U.S. military forces have affected us and others, and in the people's movements that have envisioned and practiced unarmed means for resolving conflicts and for resisting illegitimate power."

BIOGRAPHICAL AND CRITICAL SOURCES:

PERIODICALS

Kirkus Reviews, February 1, 2003, review of *Emperors in the Jungle: The Hidden History of the U.S. in Panama,* pp. 210-211.
Library Journal, April 1, 2003, Sylvia D. Hall-Ellis, review of *Emperors in the Jungle,* pp. 113-114.
Panana News, February 9-22, 2003, Eric Jackson, "Glances Back at an Old Relationship."
Perspectives on Political Science, summer, 2003, Margaret E. Scranton, review of *Emperors in the Jungle,* p. 173.

ONLINE

Duke University Press Web site, http://www.dukeu press.edu/ (April 18, 2004), "John Lindsay-Poland."
Fellowship of Reconciliation Web site, http://www. forusa.org/ (April 18, 2004).*

LOEVINGER, Lee 1913-2004

OBITUARY NOTICE—See index for *CA* sketch: Born April 24, 1913, in St. Paul, MN; died of complications from heart disease, April 26, 2004, in Washington, DC. Attorney and author. Loevinger was best known for his work as an antitrust attorney and as a former commissioner of the Federal Communications Commission. A Minnesota native, he attended the University of Minnesota for both his undergraduate work and for his law studies, completing his J.D. in 1936. After working briefly for a Kansas City law firm, he joined the National Labor Relations Board in Washington, DC, as a trial and regional attorney in 1937. Enlisting in the U.S. Naval Reserve in 1942, Loevinger spent time in Europe and became a lieutenant commander at the same time he worked in the Department of Justice's Antitrust Division. After the war, he became a partner at a Minneapolis law firm until he was elected to the Minnesota Supreme Court in 1960. The next year, he left the bench for the U.S. Department of Justice, where he was an assistant attorney general in charge of the Antitrust Division, and, from 1963 to 1968, the FCC commissioner. One of his most significant career accomplishments came in 1963, when he successfully argued against the merger of two banks in Philadelphia because the business deal would harm competition in violation of the Clayton act; it was the first trial of its kind before the U.S. Supreme Court. It was also while at the FCC that Loevinger played a key role in establishing the 911 emergency telephone service. After leaving government service in 1968, Loevinger became a partner at Hogan & Hartson, entering semi-retirement in 1985 and serving as counsel to the firm for the remainder of his life. He was also vice president and director of Craig-Hallum Corp. in Minneapolis from 1968 to 1973. Loevinger was the author of several books concerning legal issues, including *The Law of Free Enterprise: How to Recognize and Maintain the American Economic System* (1949), *Jurimetrics: The Methodology of Legal Inquiry, Law, and Contemporary Problems* (1963), and *American Jurisprudence Trials,* Volume 24: *Defending Antitrust Lawsuits* (1977). The founder of the journal *Jurimetrics,* Loevinger became fascinated with science later in his life, founding the section on science and technology of the American Bar Association, contributing to science journals, and publishing *Science as Evidence* (1995).

OBITUARIES AND OTHER SOURCES:

PERIODICALS

Chicago Tribune, May 7, 2004, Section 3, p. 9.
Los Angeles Times, May 12, 2004, p. B11.
New York Times, April 8, 2004, p. A27.
Washington Post, May 5, 2004, p. B6.

*   *   *

LOGAN, Chuck 1942-

PERSONAL: Born 1942; married; children: one daughter.

ADDRESSES: Home—Stillwater, MN. *Agent*—c/o Author Mail, HarperCollins, 10 East 53rd St., 7th Fl., New York, NY 10012.

CAREER: Writer. Formerly worked in automobile factories; St. Paul Pioneer Press, St. Paul, MN, former member of staff. *Military service:* U.S. Army, served in Vietnam; became paratrooper.

WRITINGS:

Hunter's Moon, HarperCollins (New York, NY), 1996.
The Price of Blood, HarperCollins (New York, NY), 1997.
The Big Law, HarperCollins (New York, NY), 1998.
Absolute Zero, HarperCollins (New York, NY), 2002.
Vapor Trail, HarperCollins (New York, NY), 2003.

SIDELIGHTS: Chuck Logan has written several thrillers featuring fictional protagonist Phil Broker, a Vietnam veteran and ex-cop who lives in Minnesota. A critic for *Publishers Weekly* called Logan "an awesome storyteller with a unique voice and a flawless sense of place and mood."

Hunter's Moon, Logan's first novel, is based in part on the author's own experiences. In this tale, Vietnam vet Harry Griffin goes hunting in northern Minnesota with old friend Bud Maston. Both men are recovering alcoholics, but Bud has fallen off the wagon for a reason Harry cannot discover. It may be because of the rough crowd Bud is seeing. Or perhaps Bud is having troubles with his seductively attractive wife. During the hunting trip Harry is forced to kill another man to save Bud's life. Before the trip is over, he must also untangle the dark mysteries surrounding his friend. A critic for *Publishers Weekly* claimed that Logan "knows how to grab the souls of his characters and hold them up, squirming, to the light," while Mark Terry in *Armchair Detective* praised Logan's prose as "visceral, vibrant, filled with haunting to-the-heart imagery." A. J. Wright, reviewing *Hunter's Moon* for the *Library Journal,* found that "this suspense novel moves at a brisk pace and has well-drawn characters and landscapes," while *Booklist* critic Joe Collins dubbed the novel "a rousing, edgy first novel."

According to Logan in a statement posted at the *HarperCollins* Web site, *Hunter's Moon* "was a rehash of many of the dark themes from my earlier life." Logan is himself a veteran of the Vietnam War, where he served as a paratrooper, and has been a recovering alcoholic for some twenty-five years. His father left the family when Logan was still an infant; his mother died in a car accident when he was eight. After working in auto factories in Detroit, Michigan, Logan joined the U.S. Army. A job at a St. Paul, Minnesota newspaper following his military discharge led to Logan trying his hand at writing.

After the success of *Hunter's Moon,* Logan developed the character of Phil Broker and has followed Broker's exploits through several novels. In *The Price of Blood* Vietnam veteran Broker is now working as a Minnesota law officer. Twenty years ago, as Vietnam fell to the communists, some ten tons of gold disappeared from the National Bank of Hue at the same time Broker's unit was in the area. To help clear the name of an old army friend whose memory was stained by a courts martial that implicated him in allegedly stealing the gold, Broker returns to Southeast Asia in search of the lost fortune. "Logan cranks up the voltage with some impressive plot twists," Chris Petrakos wrote in Chicago's *Tribune Books.* "Logan's novel offers genuine suspense, stomach-turning violence, a devilishly twisted plot, and larger-than-life characters," maintained Emily Melton in *Booklist,* while *The Price of Blood* was deemed "An admirably flinty, adroitly plotted, and worthy successor to Logan's first hardboiled thriller" by a *Kirkus Reviews* contributor.

The Big Law finds Broker at the heart of a tangled plot involving a crooked cop, a greedy newspaper reporter, and a frame-up for murder. Newspaperman Tom James gets a tip that cop Keith Angland is taking money from the mob, while Angland's wife Caren wants to turn state's evidence in exchange for inclusion in the witness protection program and the chance at a new life. She also wants to turn over the two million dollars in dirty money her husband has stashed away. But Caren is also Broker's ex-wife, and she wants him to use his police skills to help protect her from her violent husband. When she turns up dead, Broker must discover who killed her and where the money is. The story, a critic for *Kirkus Reviews* explained, is "replete with intrigue, chases, secret agendas, and bloody murder. . . . Logan can plot. And write. And what he serves up here is a satisfying throwback to the kind of suspense novel where complex people matter more than high-tech machines." "Virtually seamless, the prose mesmerizes," a *Publishers Weekly* reviewer added, concluding that "The ingenious plot and cast of well-fleshed-out characters" in *The Big Law* "continue to mark Logan as a standout in the genre."

Broker works as a wilderness guide for his uncle in *Absolute Zero,* but the first group he takes into the forest during midwinter runs into trouble as a raging river capsizes their boat and nearly kills them. When Broker's friend Hank Sommer is rushed to the hospital and goes into a coma on the operating table, the coma seems too convenient to Broker, who suspects someone is trying to kill his friend. The most likely suspect is Sommer's young wife, a woman with a notorious past, but she was no where near the hospital when her husband was stricken. "The first fifty stormy pages alone are worth the price of admission," Carrie Bissey claimed in *Booklist,* "and the shifting loyalties and shifting narrative perspectives that follow make the rest just as hard to put down." Logan's characters, according to Phillip Tomasso, III, in an online review for *Curled Up with a Good Book,* "are so real you can actually see them. . . . They are deep and well-defined, and the story is gripping, compelling and flawlessly plotted."

Vapor Trail finds Broker called in to help track down a serial killer known as the "Saint." The killer specializes in a particular kind of victim: those accused of being child molesters. Because the local community, and even the police department, sympathizes with his motive, the only way the Saint can be found is if an outsider like Broker is called in. "Drawing on the

theme that justice sometimes fails," Jo Ann Vicarel wrote in the *Library Journal,* "Logan clearly shows what the consequences are for the victims, the law enforcement officers, and the prosecutors." A critic for *Publishers Weekly* concluded: "With rich characters, a voice of unhesitating assurance and a plot refreshingly free of gimmickry, Logan once again delivers good old-fashioned storytelling."

BIOGRAPHICAL AND CRITICAL SOURCES:

PERIODICALS

Armchair Detective, spring, 1997, Mark Terry, review of *Hunter's Moon,* p. 226.
Booklist, December 15, 1995, Joe Collins, review of *Hunter's Moon,* p. 686; March 15, 1997, Emily Melton, review of *The Price of Blood,* p. 1226; November 15, 1998, Budd Arthur, review of *The Big Law,* p. 572; January 1, 2002, Carrie Bissey, review of *Absolute Zero,* p. 819; March 1, 2003, Carrie Bissey, review of *Vapor Trail,* p. 1149.
Entertainment Weekly, December 4, 1998, Charles Winecoff, review of *The Big Law,* p. 98; March 8, 2002, Daniel Fierman, review of *Absolute Zero,* p. 68.
Kirkus Reviews, January 15, 1997, review of *The Price of Blood,* p. 84; October 1, 1998, review of *The Big Law,* p. 1403; December 1, 2001, review of *Absolute Zero,* p. 1635; February 15, 2003, review of *Vapor Trail,* p. 260.
Library Journal, December, 1995, A. J. Wright, review of *Hunter's Moon,* p. 156; February 1, 2002, Jeff Ayers, review of *Absolute Zero,* p. 131; March 15, 2003, Jo Ann Vicarel, review of *Vapor Trail,* p. 115.
Minneapolis Star-Tribune, April 6, 2003, Ken Wisneski, review of *Vapor Trail.*
Publishers Weekly, October 23, 1995, review of *Hunter's Moon,* p. 58; February 17, 1997, review of *The Price of Blood,* p. 212; October 5, 1998, review of *The Big Law,* p. 79; February 4, 2002, review of *Absolute Zero,* p. 53; March 31, 2003, review of *Vapor Trail,* p. 42.
Tribune Books (Chicago, IL), March 16, 1997, Chris Petrakos, review of *The Price of Blood,* p. 6.

ONLINE

Books 'n' Bytes, http://www.booksnbytes.com/ (October 6, 2003), Carl Brookins, review of *The Big*

Law; (October 31, 2003) Carl Brookins, review of *The Price of Blood,* and Harriet Klausner, review of *Absolute Zero* and *Vapor Trail.*

Curled Up with a Good Book, http://www.curledup. com/ (October 6, 2003), Phillip Tomasso, III, review of *Absolute Zero.*

HarperCollins Web site, http://www.harpercollins.com/ (October 6, 2003), "Chuck Logan."*

                    *   *   *

LORAINE, Philip
     See ESTRIDGE, Robin

                    *   *   *

LORD, James 1922-

PERSONAL: Born November 27, 1922, in Englewood, NJ; son of Albert (a Wall Street broker) and Louise (Bennett) Lord. *Education:* Attended Wesleyan University.

ADDRESSES: Home—France. *Agent*—c/o Author Mail, Farrar, Straus & Giroux, 19 Union Square W., New York, NY 10001.

CAREER: Author. *Military service:* United States Military Intelligence Service during World War II, served in France.

WRITINGS:

No Traveler Returns (novel), Weidenfeld and Nicholson (London, England), 1955, J. Day (New York, NY), 1956.

The Joys of Success (novel), J. Day (New York, NY), 1958.

A Giacometti Portrait, Doubleday (Garden City, NY), 1965, revised edition, Farrar, Straus, & Giroux (New York, NY), 1980.

Alberto Giacometti Drawings, New York Graphic Society (Greenwich, CT), 1971.

Giacometti: A Biography, Farrar, Straus, & Giroux (New York, NY), 1985.

Sam Szafran: Recent Works, April 23-May 18, 1987, Claude Bernard Gallery (New York, NY), 1987.

Picasso and Dora: A Personal Memoir, Farrar, Straus, & Giroux (New York, NY), 1993.

Six Exceptional Women: Further Memoirs, Farrar, Straus, & Giroux (New York, NY), 1994.

Some Remarkable Men: Further Memoirs, Farrar, Straus, & Giroux (New York, NY), 1996.

A Gift for Admiration: Further Memoirs, Farrar, Straus & Giroux (New York, NY), 1998.

Plausible Portraits of James Lord: With Commentary by the Model, Farrar, Straus & Giroux (New York, NY), 2003.

Mythic Giacometti, Farrar, Straus & Giroux (New York, NY), 2004.

Also contributor of text to catalogues for art exhibitions.

SIDELIGHTS: American expatriate James Lord has had the good fortune to know many of the most famous artists of the twentieth century. His introduction into the Paris artistic community came during World War II, when, as an American soldier stationed in France, Lord tracked down renowned painter and sculptor Pablo Picasso and knocked on his door. Deciding to remain in France following the war, Lord eventually published his memories of Picasso, Picasso's mistress Dora Maar, sculptor Alberto Giacometti, and many other famous men and women in his numerous, highly praised books of memoir and biography.

Lord did not originally intend to become a memoirist, but throughout his life he kept meticulous journals, recording conversations that he had shortly after they occurred. When he began his memoirs, with *Picasso and Dora: A Personal Memoir,* these journals provided an invaluable aid to his memory. However, once he uses a journal to write a volume of memoirs, he destroys it, he told *New York Times Book Review* interviewer Sarah Boxer. "An autobiographer is doing something for himself he doesn't want done by someone else," he explained. "There's a lot of material in my journals I wouldn't want others perusing."

Lord's second volume of memoirs, *Six Exceptional Women: Further Memoirs,* tells of his relationships with women both famous, including writer Gertrude Stein, her companion Alice B. Toklas, and the French actress Arletty; and unknown, including Lord's Greek friend Errieta Perdikidi and his own mother, Louise Bennett Lord. Lord's use of language in this volume was particularly praised. *Booklist*'s Donna Seaman wrote that Lord has "an eloquence that gives full expression to his refined and generous sensibility," while *New York Times Book Review* contributor Florence King thought that Lord's "English [is] so pure and polished that the sentences almost ring like tapped crystal."

Lord gives his male friends a similar treatment in *Some Remarkable Men: Further Memoirs,* in which he "lifts the biographical portrait to the level of daring, soul-searching, adventurous art form," wrote a *Publishers Weekly* critic. The book discusses Lord's friendships with English novelist Harold Acton, dramatist and filmmaker Jean Cocteau, painter Balthus, and sculptor Alberto Giacometti. Lord tells humorous anecdotes about the men, but "underneath Lord's witty, dilettantish style, his recollections have a serious core about living the artistic life, with its hidden costs and uncertain legacies," commented a *Kirkus Reviews* contributor.

Giacometti, who appears in *Some Remarkable Men,* is one of Lord's most frequent subjects. Lord was friends with the Swiss surrealist artist from 1952 until Giacometti died in 1966, and his first book about the man was published in 1965. That book, *A Giacometti Portrait,* recounts conversations that Lord had with Giacometti while sitting as a model for one painting, which took eighteen sittings to complete. As such, it provides a fascinating glimpse inside the mind of an artist at work. "If there is a more endearing study of the artist as maniac, as child, as intelligence, as driven haunted slave, or selfless master, as who knows which of the nine orders of angels, I have not encountered it," William Maxwell declared in *New Republic.*

Lord gives a fuller account of Giacometti's life in *Giacometti: A Biography,* begun in 1970 and finally published in 1985. The book, which talks candidly of Giacometti's sadistic tendencies and mental torment, drew protests from more than forty of the sculptor's friends, who signed a public letter of protest against it. However, *Giacometti: A Biography* was praised by some critics. A *Kirkus Reviews* contributor, who declared the book "a definitive biography," commented that "one gets the impression upon reading this biography that [Lord] ... got a rare glimpse into the soul of a genius." Lord "has written a painstaking, powerful biography ... about a man he obviously loved without letting that love get between Giacometti and the truth," thought *Washington Post Book World* critic Seymour Krim. *Giacometti: A Biography* "is a very tender book," Krim concluded, "made strong by the rigors of close detail."

Over his years of friendship with various artists, many of them created portraits of Lord. Some of these works of art, which include sketches, photographs, paintings, and even sculptures, are collected in *Plausible Portraits of James Lord: With Commentary by the Model.* Covering twenty-four artists, including Picasso, Giacometti, and Balthus, *Plausible Portraits of James Lord* is "highly personal in content and tone yet self-reflective, detached, and perceptive," Cheryl Ann Lajos wrote in *Library Journal.* Lord places each work in context by explaining how he came to sit for each portrait and how he felt about it. As with his earlier books, Lord's use of language was praised by critics, including *Booklist*'s Donna Seaman, who called Lord's "syntax ... gloriously complex, sensibility exquisite, tone arch, and candor bracing."

BIOGRAPHICAL AND CRITICAL SOURCES:

PERIODICALS

American Spectator, January, 1994, M. D. Carnegie, review of *Picasso and Dora: A Personal Memoir,* pp. 62-64.

Art in America, November, 1994, Jill Johnston, review of *Picasso and Dora,* pp. 33-34.

ARTnews, January 1994, Jack Flam, review of *Picasso and Dora,* p. 107.

Belles Lettres, summer, 1994, review of *Six Exceptional Women: Further Memoirs,* p. 4.

Booklist, April 1, 1994, Donna Seaman, review of *Six Exceptional Women,* p. 1420; April 15, 1998, Ted Leventhal, review of *A Gift for Admiration: Further Memoirs,* p. 1410; April 15, 2003, Seaman, review of *Plausible Portraits of James Lord: With Commentary by the Model,* p. 1439; June 1, 2004, Seaman, review of *Mythic Giacometti,* pp. 1693-1694.

Kirkus Reviews, May 15, 1980, review of *A Giacometti Portrait,* p. 692; August 1, 1985, review of *Giacometti: A Biography,* p. 778; August 15, 1996, review of *Some Remarkable Men: Further Memoirs,* pp. 1213-1214.

Library Journal, January 1, 1972, Andrew Robison, review of *Alberto Giacometti Drawings,* pp. 65-66; September 1, 1996, David Keymer, review of *Some Remarkable Men,* p. 188; March 15, 1998, Richard K. Burns, review of *A Gift for Admiration,* p. 61; May 1, 2003, Cheryl Ann Lajos, review of *Plausible Portraits of James Lord,* p. 111; May 1, 2004, Douglas F. Smith, review of *Mythic Giacometti,* pp. 104-105.

London Review of Books, March 19, 1987, David Sylvester, review of *Giacometti,* pp. 8-9.

Los Angeles Times Book Review, October 27, 1996, Bret Israel, review of *Some Remarkable Men,* pp. 6, 9.

Nation, October 28, 1996, Vivian Gornick, review of *Some Remarkable Men,* pp. 48-49.

New Republic, July 19, 1980, William Maxwell, review of *A Giacometti Portrait,* pp. 27-29.

New York Review of Books, April 25, 2002, Marilyn McCully, review of *Picasso and Dora,* pp. 25-28.

New York Times Book Review, July 18, 1993, Sarah Boxer, "Geniuses Don't Doubt Themselves" (interview with Lord), p. 21; May 1, 1994, Florence King, review of *Six Exceptional Women,* p. 12; June 7, 1998, Ted Loos, review of *A Gift for Admiration,* p. 23; July 13, 2003, Roxana M. Popescu, review of *Plausible Portraits of James Lord,* p. 24.

Observer (London, England), June 29, 1986, Tim Hilton, review of *Giacometti,* p. 23.

Publishers Weekly, August 16, 1985, review of *Giacometti,* p. 56; February 28, 1994, review of *Six Exceptional Women,* p. 64; July 29, 1996, review of *Some Remarkable Men,* p. 76; March 9, 1998, review of *A Gift for Admiration,* p. 53; April 7, 2003, review of *Plausible Portraits of James Lord,* p. 61.

Southern Review, July, 1987, Harry Goldgar, review of *Giacometti,* pp. 719-727.

Spectator, April 25, 1981, John McEwan, review of *A Giacometti Portrait,* pp. 22-23.

Times Literary Supplement, August 21, 1981, Peter Greenham, review of *A Giacometti Portrait,* p. 960.

Town and Country, April, 1998, James Villas, "The Man Who Knew Everyone" (profile of Lord), pp. 65-68.

Virginia Quarterly Review, autumn, 1993, review of *Picasso and Dora,* p. 127.

Vogue, April, 1994, Jed Perl, reviews of *Six Exceptional Women* and *Picasso and Dora,* pp. 214-215.

Washington Post Book World, September 15, 1985, Seymour Krim, review of *Giacometti,* pp. 1, 4.

WWD, June 16, 1994, Lorna Koski, interview with Lord, p. 16.*

*   *   *

LUKKEN, Miriam 1960-

PERSONAL: Born December 22, 1960, in Marietta, GA; daughter of Charles, Sr. (an engineer) and Ruth (a homemaker; maiden name, Randolph) Willingham; married Peter John Lukken, October 6, 1984; children: Elizabeth, Catherine. *Ethnicity:* "White." *Education:* LaGrange College, B.A., 1982, M.Ed., 1985; attended Mercer University, 1983. *Politics:* Republican. *Religion:* Roman Catholic.

ADDRESSES: Agent—Joann Davis, Redbridge, Inc., 700 Washington St., New York, NY 10014. *E-mail*—mimilukken@charter.net.

CAREER: Worked as a schoolteacher, 1983-92; writer, 1992—. Troup County Humane Society, past president; LaGrange Junior Service League, member.

MEMBER: Authors Guild, Authors League of America, LaGrange Junior Woman's Club (past president).

AWARDS, HONORS: Named member of the year, LaGrange Junior League, 1994, for *Southern Born and Bread.*

WRITINGS:

Read This Book before Your Child Starts School, C. C Thomas, 1994.

(Editor) *Southern Born and Bread* (cookbook), Wimmer Co., 1996.

Mrs. Dunwoody's Excellent Instructions for Homekeeping, Warner Books (New York, NY), 2003.

WORK IN PROGRESS: "Further instruction from Mrs. Dunwoody is expected soon."

SIDELIGHTS: Miriam Lukken told *CA:* "I am a Southern writer, a lover of traditions and old-fashioned ways. Wit and wisdom has been handed down for generations in my family. I try to bring those elements into everything I write, regardless of the genre."

LUX, Maureen K. 1956-

PERSONAL: Born September 8, 1956, in Saskatoon, Saskatchewan, Canada. *Ethnicity:* "Canadian." *Education:* University of Saskatchewan, B.A., 1982, M.A., 1989; Simon Fraser University, Ph.D., 1996.

ADDRESSES: Office—Department of History, University of Saskatchewan, Campus Dr., Saskatoon, Saskatchewan, Canada. *E-mail*—mlux@sympatico.ca.

CAREER: Federation of Saskatchewan Indian Nations, historical consultant, 1999-2002; University of Saskatchewan, Saskatoon, Saskatchewan, Canada, assistant professor of history, 2002—.

AWARDS, HONORS: Postdoctoral fellow of Hannah Institute for the History of Medicine, 1999; Hannah Medal, Royal Society of Canada, and Clio Award for Regional History, Canadian Historical Association, both 2002, for *Medicine That Walks: Disease, Medicine, and Canadian Plains Native People, 1880-1930.*

WRITINGS:

Medicine That Walks: Disease, Medicine, and Canadian Plains Native People, 1880-1940, University of Toronto Press (Toronto, Ontario, Canada), 2001.

Contributor to *Canadian Bulletin for the History of Medicine.*

WORK IN PROGRESS: Research on "so-called Indian hospitals in Canada."

BIOGRAPHICAL AND CRITICAL SOURCES:

PERIODICALS

History: Review of New Books, fall, 2001, Dan Malleck, review of *Medicine That Walks: Disease, Medicine, and Canadian Plains Native People, 1880-1940,* p. 9.
Journal of Social History, winter, 2002, Nancy Shoemaker, review of *Medicine That Walks,* p. 483.
Manitoba History, spring-summer, 2002, Paul Hackett, review of *Medicine That Walks,* p. 35.

M

MACFARLANE, Malcolm R. 1942-

PERSONAL: Born December 27, 1942, in Birmingham, Warwickshire, England; son of George (an accountant) and Joan Browne (a district housing officer; maiden name, Jones) Macfarlane; married Patricia Brown (a secretary), October 2, 1965; children: Julia, Kathy, Alison. *Ethnicity:* "Anglo-Saxon." *Education:* Attended private boys' secondary school in Birmingham, England. *Hobbies and other interests:* Golf, genealogy.

ADDRESSES: Home—3 Osborne Close, Wilmslow, Cheshire SK9 2EE, England. *E-mail*—macwilmslo@ aol.com.

CAREER: Birmingham Corp., Birmingham, England, junior clerk, 1959-60; Lloyds Bank, Manchester, England, senior manager, 1960-99; writer, 1999—.

MEMBER: Chartered Institute of Bankers (fellow).

AWARDS, HONORS: Banking World Award, 1988, for an essay.

WRITINGS:

Bing Crosby: Day by Day (biography), Scarecrow Press (Lanham, MD), 2001.

Contributor to periodicals, including *Banking World.*

MACFARLANE, Robert 1976-

PERSONAL: Born 1976. *Education:* Attended Emmanuel College, Cambridge.

ADDRESSES: Agent—c/o Author Mail, Granta Books, 2/3 Hanover Yard, Noel Road, London N1 8BE, England.

CAREER: Writer. Emmanuel College, Cambridge, Cambridge, England, fellow.

AWARDS, HONORS: Guardian First Book Award, 2003, for *Mountains of the Mind.*

WRITINGS:

Mountains of the Mind, Pantheon Books (New York, NY), 2003.

Contributor to the London *Observer, Times Literary Supplement,* and the *London Review of Books.*

SIDELIGHTS: With *Mountains of the Mind,* writer and mountaineer Robert Macfarlane studies the roots of the current glorification of mountains and mountain climbing as a sport. While some have attributed this twentieth-century cultural evolution to artistic movements that have glorified the natural beauty of mountains, Macfarlane contends that the trend is actually an outgrowth of a changing view of the Earth as early geologists and biologists began to realize that mountains were not immovable objects but vestiges of an Earth moved by glaciers rather than static "warts" on a planted shaped by God. Romanticized by writers such as Voltaire, Thoreau, and Keats, they gained a spiritual quality as an earthly formation that brought men closer to the universal, the impenetrable, and the unbound.

With thorough research and first-hand knowledge of the mountain-climbing sport, Macfarlane delves into the rich history surrounding mountains and their cultural acceptance and evolution, creating what a *Kirkus Reviews* writer praised as a "crisp historical study of the sensations and emotions people have brought to (and taken from) mountains, laced with the author's own experiences scrambling among the peaks." During the seventeenth century and before, mountains were regarded in disdain and contempt, as something to avoid as an obstacle. While noting that "Much of Macfarlane's terrain is . . . previously traveled" by authors such as U.S. historian Simon Schama, London *Observer* contributor Ed Douglas added that the author, "a mountain lover and climber, has a more visceral appreciation of mountains than Schama. He is also a more engaging writer, his commentary, always crisp and relevant, leavened by personal experience beautifully related." A reviewer for *Publishers Weekly* called *Mountains of the Mind* "rather like some idiosyncratic, hand-drawn map of terra incognita. But for romantic mountain-struck readers, Macfarlane's rich thoughts may make snow clouds clear, revealing new peaks and new wonders." Roy Herbert, in *New Scientist*, called Macfarlane's debut a "magnificent book" and "a tumult of delights all the way," while *New York Times Book Review* contributor John Rothchild quipped that while "There's fascinating stuff here, and a clever premise," *Mountains of the Mind* "may cause recovering climbaholics to trace their addiction to their early homework assignments and file class-action lawsuits against their poetry teachers."

BIOGRAPHICAL AND CRITICAL SOURCES:

PERIODICALS

Kirkus Reviews, April 15, 2003, review of *Mountains of the Mind,* p. 590.
New Scientist, May 10, 2003, Roy Herbert, review of *Mountains of the Mind,* p. 52.
New York Times Book Review, July 13, 2003, John Rothchild, "Fatal Attraction."
Observer (London, England), May 11, 2003, Ed Douglas, "Peak Practice."
Publishers Weekly, May 5, 2003, review of *Mountains of the Mind,* p. 213.*

* * *

MAECHLER, Stefan 1957-

PERSONAL: Born May 30, 1957, in Baden, Switzerland; son of Karl (a farmer) and Agnes (Bruehlmeier) Maechler. *Ethnicity:* "Caucasian." *Education:* Lehrerseminar of Wettingen, B.A., 1977; University of Zurich, M.A., 1993.

ADDRESSES: Agent—Eva Koralnik, Liepman AG, Maienburgweg 23, Zurich, Switzerland CH-8044.

CAREER: Department of Education, Canton of Aargau, Switzerland, teacher, 1977-82; Foundation ECAP, Baden, Switzerland, teacher of German, 1985-88; Asylkoordination Zurich, Zurich, Switzerland, assistant manager, 1987-89; Department of Education, Canton of Zurich, teacher, 1990-95, project coordinator for educational reform, 1995-2003.

WRITINGS:

(With Kaspar Kasics) *Closed Country* (documentary film screenplay), Extra Film, 1999.
The Wilkomirski Affair: A Study in Biographical Truth, Schocken (New York, NY), 2001.
(With Franz Daengeli) *Wahre Szenen* (documentary film screenplay), Extra Film, 2003.

Contributor to books, including *Das Wilkomirski-Syndrom. Eingebildete Erinnerungen oder Von der Sehnsucht, Opfer zu sein,* Pendo (Zurich, Switzerland), 2002. Contributor to periodicals, including *History and Memory.*

WORK IN PROGRESS: The Federation of Jewish Communities in Switzerland and the Nazi Persecution of the Jews (working title).

SIDELIGHTS: Stefan Maechler's book *The Wilkomirski Affair: A Study in Biographical Truth* is an examination of a strange case of fraud involving a Swiss man named Bruno Doessekker who alleged that he was a Holocaust survivor. The man, claiming his true name was Binjamin Wilkomirski, was born Bruno Grosjean in Switzerland in 1941. His mother was an unmarried factory worker who was forced by the authorities to give away her child. Bruno ended up with a doctor's family in Zurich by the name of Doessekker, who much later adopted him. As an adult, he began to imagine a new identity for himself. Following visits to camps in Poland and discussions with actual survivors, he came to believe that he too was really a Jewish survivor of the Holocaust. Work with a therapist strengthened his belief in these memories and led him to write them down. In 1995, this text was published under the title *Bruchstücke (Fragments)* by the renowned Suhrkamp Publishers. The book was subsequently translated into nine languages, won a number of literary prizes, and received critical acclaim for its authentic description of traumatic memories. Wilkomirski traveled on an extensive book tour that included a warm welcome from the American Holocaust Museum in Washington, D.C., and a meeting with supposed cousins now living in New York. The memoir, Paul Maliszewski wrote in the *Wilson Quarterly,* made Wilkomirski "a prominent, revered figure in the survivor community." But by 1998, a Swiss journalist uncovered evidence that Wilkomirski's story was a fraud. The American television program *60 Minutes* followed with yet more evidence.

Wilkomirski denied these accusations, and, as the facts were still unclear, his agent approached Maechler to undertake a full investigation of the case. She gave Maechler access to all the relevant documents, including her correspondence with Wilkomirski. Maechler also dug into the archives of four countries, interviewed witnesses, and examined historical photographs to find the historical truth. His research proved beyond a doubt that Wilkomirski's claim that he had been in a concentration camp was absolutely false. Following this, the book was withdrawn from the market. How, then, had Wilkomirski come to promote such a story, and how had something so untrue become disseminated worldwide as an actual memoir? Maechler argues that Wilkomirski probably deluded himself into believing he was a Holocaust survivor. As an adopted child, he was unable to tell a coherent story of his origins. The metaphor of a Holocaust victim seem to express best the painful experiences of his childhood.

Why was the story believed by so many who should have known better? In a later article for *History and Memory,* Maechler argues that the Shoah has become "the most powerful, culturally sanctioned metaphor of suffering." Doessekker, equipped with its power of legitimization and rhetoric, could not be gainsaid. "Maechler's conclusions are clearly presented and thoroughly documented," Lawrence Birken noted in a review of *The Wilkomirski Affair* for *Shofar.* Robert Alter concluded in the *New Republic* that "Maechler's work reads as compellingly as a detective story."

Maechler told *CA:* "As a historian, I have always been interested in the relationship between form and content. My early encounters with the writings of Paul Ricoeur and Hayden White confirmed my rather intuitive belief that historiography cannot exist without narrative—a conviction which was not prevalent when I was at the university. In those days, a narrow structural approach held sway. I was convinced that narrative was a basic element of the discipline and in no way only a secondary aspect of it which merely transfers an independently existing context, or, even worse, a misleading illusion that hinders us in our analysis of historical events. On one hand, I was interested in the heuristic potential of the writing itself, namely in the discoveries made as a result of stringing together sentence after sentence. On the other hand, I was interested in the implications that the rhetoric of a text has for its reception.

"Closely related to these interests is my fascination with how people perceive and interpret their reality and come to terms with it, and how they transform the amorphous and contradictory variety of life into a meaningful, coherent story. I had the feeling that perhaps Wilkomirski's supposed autobiography had much in common with these concerns: indeed, I discovered a man who possessed no biography of his own, a man with an unportrayable past—a void out of which his existential trouble grew. Instead of bearing them, he invented a life story that both seemingly conserved and transcended the unspeakable. In order to do this, he used elements from the collective memory of humanity which have become the master narrative for a story of unspeakable victimization: the remembrance of the Shoah. A clever and cunning choice, we might say—if that didn't suggest an intentional process had taken place, which presumably was never the case with Wilkomirski."

BIOGRAPHICAL AND CRITICAL SOURCES:

PERIODICALS

Die Welt, June 22, 2000, Rolf Schneider, review of *The Wilkomirski Affair: A Study in Biographical Truth.*

Die Woche, June 30, 2000, Sylke Tempel, review of *The Wilkomirski Affair.*

Forward, June 8, 2001, Susan Rubin Suleiman, review of *The Wilkomirski Affair.*

History and Memory, fall-winter, 2001, Stefan Maechler, "Wilkomirski the Victim," p. 90.

Holocaust and Genocide Studies, Volume 17, number 1, 2003, David Scrase, review of *The Wilkomirski Affair,* pp. 161-163.

Jerusalem Report, May 21, 2001, Samuel Apple, review of *The Wilkomirski Affair.*

New Republic, April 30, 2001, Robert Alter, review of *The Wilkomirski Affair,* p. 35.

Shofar, summer, 2001, review of *The Wilkomirski Affair,* p. 175; fall, 2002, Lawrence Birken, review of *The Wilkomirski Affair,* p. 174.

Washington Post, April 15, 2001, Steven J. Zipperstein, review of *The Wilkomirski Affair.*

Wilson Quarterly, summer, 2002, Paul Maliszewski, review of *The Wilkomirski Affair,* p. 109.

*   *   *

MAGUIRE, Gregory (Peter) 1954-

PERSONAL: Born June 9, 1954, in Albany, NY; son of John (a journalist) and Helen (Gregory) Maguire; companion of Andy Newman (a painter); children: Luke, Alex, Helen. *Education:* State University of New York—Albany, B.A., 1976; Simmons College, M.A., 1978; Tufts University, Ph.D., 1990. *Politics:* Democrat. *Religion:* Roman Catholic. *Hobbies and other interests:* Painting in oils or watercolors, song writing, traveling.

ADDRESSES: Agent—William Reiss, John Hawkins and Associates, 71 West 23rd St., Ste. 1600, New York, NY 10010.

CAREER: Freelance writer, 1977—. Vincentian Grade School, Albany, NY, teacher of English, 1976-77; Simmons College Center for the Study of Children's Literature, Boston, MA, faculty member and associate director, 1979-87; Children's Literature New England, Cambridge, MA, codirector and consultant, 1987—. Residencies at Blue Mountain Center, 1986-90 and 1995-2001; artist-in-residence, Isabella Stewart Gardner Museum, 1994, Hambidge Center, 1998, and the Virginia Center for the Creative Arts, 1999.

AWARDS, HONORS: Fellow at Bread Loaf Writers' Conference, 1978; One Hundred Best Books of the Year citation, New York Public Library, 1980, for *The Daughter of the Moon;* Children's Books of the Year citation, Child Study Children's Books Committee, 1983, and Teachers' Choice Award, National Council of Teachers of English, 1984, both for *The Dream Stealer;* Best Book for Young Adults citation, American Library Association (ALA), and Choices award, Cooperative Children's Book Center, 1989, both for *I Feel like the Morning Star;* Parents' Choice Award, and Children's Books of the Year citation, Child Study Committee, both 1994, both for *Missing Sisters;* Notable Children's Book citation, ALA, 1994, for *Seven Spiders Spinning;* Books for the Teen Age selection, New York Public Library, 1996, for *Oasis;* One Hundred Best Books citation, Young Book Trust (England), and Reading Association of Ireland Book Award finalist, both 1997, and Notable Social Studies Trade Book, National Council for the Social Studies/Children's Book Council, all for *The Good Liar.*

WRITINGS:

FOR CHILDREN AND YOUNG ADULTS

The Lightning Time, Farrar, Straus (New York, NY), 1978.

The Daughter of the Moon, Farrar, Straus (New York, NY), 1980.

Lights on the Lake, Farrar, Straus (New York, NY), 1981.

The Dream Stealer, Harper (New York, NY), 1983, Clarion Books (New York, NY), 2002.

The Peace and Quiet Diner (picture book), illustrated by David Perry, Parents' Magazine Press (New York, NY), 1988.

I Feel like the Morning Star, Harper (New York, NY), 1989.

Lucas Fishbone (picture book), illustrated by Frank Gargiulo, Harper (New York, NY), 1990.

Missing Sisters, Margaret K. McElderry Books (New York, NY), 1994.

The Good Liar, O'Brien Press (Dublin, Ireland), 1995, Clarion Books (New York, NY), 1999.

Oasis, Clarion Books (New York, NY), 1996.

Crabby Cratchitt, illustrated by Andrew Glass, Clarion Books (New York, NY), 2000.

Leaping Beauty: And Other Animal Fairy Tales, illustrated by Chris Demarest, HarperCollins (New York, NY), 2004.

"HAMLET CHRONICLES"

Seven Spiders Spinning, Clarion (New York, NY), 1994.

Six Haunted Hairdos, illustrated by Elaine Clayton, Clarion Books (New York, NY), 1997.

Five Alien Elves, illustrated by Elaine Clayton, Clarion Books (New York, NY), 1998.

Four Stupid Cupids, illustrated by Elaine Clayton, Clarion Books (New York, NY), 2000.

Three Rotten Eggs, illustrated by Elaine Clayton, Clarion Books (New York, NY), 2002.

A Couple of April Fools, illustrated by Elaine Clayton, Clarion Books (New York, NY), 2004.

FOR ADULTS

Wicked: The Life and Times of the Wicked Witch of the West, Regan Books (New York, NY), 1995.

Confessions of an Ugly Stepsister, Regan Books (New York, NY), 1999.

Lost: A Novel, Regan Books (New York, NY), 2001.

Mirror Mirror, Regan Books (New York, NY), 2003.

OTHER

(Editor, with Barbara Harrison) *Innocence and Experience: Essays and Conversations on Children's Literature,* Lothrop (Boston, MA), 1987.

(Editor, with Barbara Harrison) *Origins of Story: On Writing for Children,* Margaret K. McElderry Books (New York, NY), 1999.

Reviewer for *Horn Book, School Library Journal,* and *Christian Science Monitor;* contributor of story "The Honorary Shepherds" to collection *Am I Blue,* 1994.

ADAPTATIONS: Confessions of an Ugly Stepsister was filmed as a two-hour segment of ABC's *Disney* program, airing in March of 2002; *Wicked* was adapted as a Broadway musical by writer Winnie Holzman and composer Stephen L. Schwartz and opened in 2003.

SIDELIGHTS: Gregory Maguire writes about people on the edge of crisis who manage to survive their ordeal and become stronger because of it. In forms as various as science fiction and fantasy, realistic problem novels, and rhyming picture books, Maguire explores the themes of loss, freedom, spirituality, the power of love, memory, and desire. Not one to shy away from complex plot development in his young-adult titles, Maguire also has a lighter side: his production might best be demonstrated by two 1994 titles: *Missing Sisters* and *Seven Spiders Spinning.* The former is a realistic portrait of growing up Catholic and handicapped; the latter is a broad farce about seven Ice Age spiders that have some fun in a small Vermont town.

"Maguire's talents now look unpredictable," Jill Paton Walsh wrote in *Twentieth-Century Children's Writers* in 1989, and characterized such talents as "formidable and still developing." Paton Walsh was a prescient critic: since the early 1990s Maguire has authored several more children's books as well as adult fiction and has edited writings on children's literature. While fantasy was his first inspiration, he has since expanded his genres to include realism and humor. However, through many of his stories, both light and serious, one motif recurs: the loss of a mother.

In fact, Maguire's own mother was lost; she passed away while giving birth to him. With his writer father sick at the time of his birth, Maguire and his three older siblings were sent to stay with relatives for a time, although Maguire ended up in an orphanage until he was reunited with his newly remarried father. Three more children were born to his father and his stepmother, and Maguire finished his childhood years in a family of seven children, supported by his father's work as a humor columnist at the Albany *Times-Union* and science writer for the New York Health Department.

Maguire grew up in a family that cared deeply about words. In addition to writing professionally, Maguire's father was also well known around Albany, New York, as a great storyteller, while his stepmother wrote poetry. Maguire wrote his first story at age five and continued writing them—some as long as a hundred pages—throughout high school and into college. In fact, he was only a junior in college when he wrote what would be his first published book, *The Lightning Time*. He had not intended the novel to be a children's novel. As Maguire explained to a reviewer for *Publishers Weekly,* "The publisher said, 'This protagonist is twelve years old. I'm sending you down to the juvenile department.' They were right."

The Lightning Time tells the story of young Daniel Rider, whose mother is away from home and in the hospital. The boy is staying with his grandmother in the Adirondacks. He meets a mysterious female cousin and together the two struggle to keep Saltbrook Mountain free from development. There is magic lightning that allows animals to talk, a villainous developer, and plenty of eerie effects. A contributor to *Publishers Weekly* thought that Maguire handled this first novel "with professional aplomb," and Ethel L. Heins concluded in *Horn Book* that Maguire "creates tension successfully, and writes with conviction and style."

Maguire followed up the success of his first fantasy with a related title, *The Daughter of the Moon,* which featured another cousin of Daniel Rider's, twelve-year-old Erikka. Again the missing-mother theme is explored, this time because Erikka's birth mother is dead and Erikka is being raised by a stepmother in Chicago. Searching for more refinement in her life, Erikka is drawn to a local bookshop as well as to a painting that an aunt has left with her. The painting is magic and Erikka can actually escape into the scene painted there, ultimately retrieving a long-lost lover of the Chicago bookshop owner. There are further sub-plots, resulting in a complexity that at least one critic found bogged down the novel. *Horn Book* critic Mary M. Burns, while noting that some elements of the ambitious novel did not work, nevertheless concluded that Maguire "has created a fascinatingly complex heroine and a rich collection of adult and child characters."

As the third of Maguire's early fantasy novels, *Lights on the Lake* was meant to form a trilogy of sorts. Again the protagonist is Daniel Rider, and he is once again in upstate New York, at Canaan Lake. This is Maguire country; a love for New York state's Lakes region developed during the author's youth. After the one

friend Daniel makes, an Episcopalian priest, leaves on a vacation, the young man suddenly finds himself living in two different dimensions, influenced by the strange mists on the lake. A poet devastated by the death of a friend soon occupies Daniel's attention, and he sees a way to help the grieving man by bridging space and time and linking the living with the dead. "The provocative theme incorporates philosophical and spiritual concepts," noted Mary M. Burns in *Horn Book*. Although a reviewer for *Bulletin of the Center for Children's Books* thought that the elements of fantasy and realism did not work together, the reviewer did concede that Maguire "has a strong potential for polished and substantive writing."

Maguire's next book, *The Dream Stealer,* was the first book where Maguire felt he had created his own form. Set in Russia, the tale incorporates several age-old motifs from Russian folktales: the Firebird, Vasilissa the Beautiful, and Baba Yaga. The story of how two children set out to save their village from the terrible wolf, the Blood Prince, *The Dream Stealer* blends magic and realism to create a "fantasy full of tension and narrative strength," according to Ethel L. Heins of *Horn Book*. "A first rate fantasy with blood chilling villainy countered with high humor and heroism," concluded Helen Gregory, reviewing the book in *School Library Journal*. And Paton Walsh, writing in *Twentieth-Century Children's Writers,* called *The Dream Stealer* the work of "a writer finding his voice, and putting not a foot wrong."

Meanwhile, Maguire had taken a position at Simmons College in their fledgling program in children's literature and was earning his doctorate in American and English literature. Busy with studies and teaching as well as with the compilation of a book of essays in children's literature, Maguire did not publish his next fiction title for five years. *I Feel like the Morning Star* was a bit of a departure in that the fantasy element was played down. Set in a post-atomic underworld, the book has a science-fiction form, but is at heart an adventure novel about three rebellious teenagers who want to break out of their prison-like underworld colony. Roger Sutton, reviewing the novel in *Bulletin of the Center for Children's Books,* called attention to Maguire's penchant for figurative language and detail as a quality that "mired" an otherwise suspenseful escape novel. Other reviewers, such as Jane Beasley in *Voice of Youth Advocates,* thought the work compelling, with Beasley noting that the "suspense builds to a 'can't-put-it-down' threshold." And Pam Spencer, writing in *School Library Journal,* called the book a "top choice for young adults."

A picture book, *The Peace and Quiet Diner,* followed, and then came *Lucas Fishbone,* an attempt at a sophisticated picture book for young adults. "Actually," Maguire once explained, "the writing in *Lucas* is some that I'm the most proud of. The story is a poetic meditation on death and the cycle of life, but somehow it never found its audience." Some critics were less than pleased, such as *School Library Journal* contributor Heide Piehler, who found the work "overwhelming and confusing," and a *Publishers Weekly* contributor who dubbed *Lucas Fishbone* "overwritten."

After the lukewarm reception accorded *Lucas Fishbone,* there followed another hiatus in Maguire's publishing career, although he continued to write his usual five pages a day. While living in London he did the writing on what would become *Missing Sisters.* While on a speaking tour in the United States, "I saw something on television" Maguire explained. "It was the story of how two brothers who were separated at birth later re-discovered each other, and the story made a real impression on me." Maguire took that germ of an idea with him when he returned to England. Shorter than his other books, *Missing Sisters* is also Maguire's first realistic story, employing none of the fantasy and science fiction elements of his earlier books. It is set in the 1960s and tells the story of a hearing-and-speech-impaired girl who loses the one person close to her—a Catholic nun—but also finds her own missing sister. "The storytelling is sure and steady," wrote Roger Sutton of *Bulletin of the Center for Children's Books,* while a *Horn Book* contributor found it "An unusual and compelling picture of life in a Catholic home."

Maguire's next title was inspired by reactions of the kids to his speaking engagements. "Over the years," Maguire explained, "I've developed a very funny presentation. The kids usually howl at my speech, but when they learn that I don't have any humorous books, they're disappointed." Maguire set out to cure that disappointment with *Seven Spiders Spinning,* which has been characterized as something on the order of Roald Dahl meets Mother Goose. Seven spiders from Siberia escape en route to a lab for study and make their way to Vermont, where they discover seven girls

whom they focus on as their mothers. The problem is, the spiders literally have the kiss of death, and the girls dispatch several of them. There are humorous subplots galore in this "high-camp fantasy-mystery," according to a *Publishers Weekly* critic. Hazel Rochman, writing in *Booklist,* commended Maguire on the "comic brew" and noted that the book would be "the stuff of many a grade-school skit." "A lighthearted fantasy," concluded a *Kirkus Reviews* critic, "that, while easily read, is as intricately structured as a spider's web."

The Good Liar, first published in Ireland, was another stylistic departure for Maguire. Set in occupied France in 1942 and written in epistolary style, it tells the story of three brothers who have a fibbing contest that ultimately becomes a matter of life and death. "At once poignant and thoughtful, laced with humor," according to a reviewer for *Horn Book, The Good Liar* "offers readers an unusual perspective on history." Carolyn Phelan of *Booklist* commented that the novel "carries the conviction of memoir rather than invention."

Oasis, another young adult title, explores the effects of the loss of his father on thirteen-year-old boy Hand. When his father dies of a heart attack, Hand's mother returns from the West Coast (where she had moved three years earlier). He resents that she abandoned him and suspects that his Uncle Wolfgang may have had something to do with his father's death. But when he is able to help two immigrants the way his father would have if he had been alive, and when he discovers that his uncle is dying of AIDS, Hand begins to come to terms with his grief. According to a reviewer for *Publishers Weekly,* "Maguire steers clear of the earnest tones that often characterize YA bereavement stories." Debbie Carton, writing for *Booklist,* noted, "Complex, believable characterizations are Maguire's forte."

Maguire's largest shift in writing was the leap he made into adult fiction with *Wicked: The Life and Times of the Wicked Witch of the West.* He first began considering writing for adults in the early nineties, when he was living in England. "I wanted to write . . . about an evil character," Maguire explained to an interviewer for *Publishers Weekly.* In thinking of who he wanted to focus on, he stumbed onto the Wicked Witch of the West. "If to each person in life comes one moment of brainstorming genius, I just had mine, because everyone knows who she is," Maguire continued. "I wrote *Wicked* in five months." Robin J. Schwartz, in her review of *Wicked* for *Entertainment Weekly,* posited that Maguire had begun to wonder how the Wicked Witch of the West became so wicked. "Since no one had the answer," Schwartz wrote, "he did what any inventive, self-respecting writer would do—he created his own malicious character."

The Witch in Maguire's story "is not wicked; nor is she a formally schooled witch. Instead, she's an insecure, unfortunately green Munchkinlander who's willing to take radical steps to unseat the tyrannical Wizard of Oz," according to a *Publishers Weekly* reviewer. But *Wicked* was not just a retelling. An early reviewer for *Publishers Weekly* called the novel a "fantastical meditation on good and evil, God and free will." Though *Wicked*'s early public success was slow, the book became a "cult hit," according to a writer for *Entertainment Weekly,* and in 2003 an adaptation by Steven Schwartz and Winnie Holzman was launched on Broadway. The musical was an instant hit, received three Tony awards, and played to sold-out audiences for months.

Maguire continued focusing on an adult readership with *Confessions of an Ugly Stepsister,* a combination of mystery, fairy tale, and fantasy set in seventeenth-century Holland. The story begins at a time when the country is engulfed in tulip trade, with thousands on the verge of losing fortunes invested in tulip bulbs. Among these are Margarethe and her two daughters, Iris and Ruth. Margarethe is a native of England, and following the murder of her husband, she is bringing her daughters back home to begin life in the English village of Haarlem. Shunned by the locals, who believe she is a witch, Margarethe eventually finds work with an artist named Schoonmaker who lives on the outskirts of town. The family eventually moves to live with the van den Meers, a business family that has made its fortunes by luring people into making tulip investments. Iris, who is charged to serve as companion to Clara van den Meer, the daughter of the household, soon realizes that there is something amiss in the household and soon all their lives are in even greater turmoil as the three women learn to deal with this latest challenge. Reviewing *Confessions of an Ugly Stepsister* for the *Tribune News Service,* Brenda Cronin praised this "arresting" novel, in particular for its "precise and inventive use of language." Cronin was especially impressed with Maguire's ability to "conjure

familiar scenes with new descriptions" and his perceptive observations about human beings. Similarly, a reviewer for *Publishers Weekly* noted that Maguire is able to present "an astute balance of the ideal and sordid sides of human nature in a vision that fantasy lovers will find hard to resist."

Maguire merged his interest in children's fairy tales and adult fantasy fiction in his next publication, *Lost.* A "deftly written, compulsively readable modern-day ghost story," said a reviewer for *Publishers Weekly, Lost* traces the adventures of American writer Winifred Rudge, as she visits London to research a novel about Jack the Ripper. Planning to stay with her cousin, John, in a family-owned house that once belonged to Ozias Rudge, who supposedly served as a model for Charles Dickens's Ebenezer Scrooge, she arrives only to find that John has gone missing and no one seems to know where he has gone. As she attempts to solve the mystery, she realizes that strange, supernatural occurances are transpiring, and an angry poltergeist begins to influence her investigation. "Though *Lost* reads with the pace and urgency of a thriller, it gradually becomes apparent that we are also getting a sophisticated study of a woman whose past is pushing her beyond her limits," explained Robert Plunket in *Advocate.* Margee Smith, writing in *Library Journal,* proclaimed that Maguire "makes the supernatural chillingly real."

With *Mirror Mirror,* Maguire drew inspiration from the Brothers Grimm tale of "Snow White" to create a "dark and vivid" retelling, according to Susan H. Woodcock in *School Library Journal.* Maguire sets the familiar tale in seventeenth-century Italy, under the rule of the eerie Borgias, known historically for their tendency to poison their opponents. Snow White, here named Bianca de Nevada, is taken in by the family, but when Cesare (brother/lover of Lucrezia) begins to look too closely at the young maiden, jealous Lucrezia condemns her to death. When Bianca is rescued by dwarves, they are not the familiar fairy-tale characters, but are instead a type of hybrid creature of flesh and stone, wakened only by Bianca's presence. "Readers will be intrigued by the new story and yet curious as to how the familiar elements are brought in," commented Woodcock. A critic for *Kirkus Reviews* procliamed *Mirror Mirror* "every bit as good as *Wicked*: wicked good, in fact."

Though Maguire's adult novels earned him both critical and popular success in the adult market, he continues to write children's novels. His "Hamlet Chronicles," set in the town of Hamlet, Vermont, reached the sixth book in the series in 2004. The stories, which feature the fifth-grade class of Miss Earth and her warring factions the Tattletales (the girls) and the Copycats (the boys), have covered territory including mutant chickens, ghosts, rampant cupids, and mysterious disappearances. A critic for *Kirkus Reviews* called the formula for the titles a "relentlessly edgy and smart one, and as such, a breath of fresh air." Ten-year-old reviewer Mark DiBona of *Storyworks* commented that *Six Haunted Hairdos* "is perfect for you if you like ghosts," and continued that Maguire is "really funny!" *Commonweal* reviewer Daria Donnelly noted that her son adores the series, and quoted him as saying "This is a writer who knows how to make a kid laugh."

Beyond the "Hamlet Chronicles," Maguire also authored a collection of fractured fairy tales called *Leaping Beauty: And Other Animal Fairy Tales.* Not the same kind of retelling as his adult novels, Maguire still puts a spin on well known classics such as "Goldilocks and the Three Bears," casting "Goldifox" as the hero; and the title story, a play on the familiar "Sleeping Beauty," features a cursed tadpole. A critic for *Booklist* called the book "a delightful collection, sure to be popular with sophisticated readers."

Of his future plans as a writer, Maguire explained to a reviewer for *Publishers Weekly,* "I don't ever want to be a slave to my success, if you know what I mean. I don't want to write 'Rapunzel in Duluth' just because *Mirror Mirror* is in Tuscany." But critics will not be surprised if Maguire continues on in all his venues, creating more adult novels as well as continuing on with his works for children.

AUTOBIOGRAPHICAL ESSAY:

Gregory Maguire contributed the following autobiographical essay to *CA:*

One winter, when I was about twenty-two, I was vacationing with a college friend at his family home in Little Falls, New York. At 11:30 P.M. on New Year's Eve, we looked at each other and said, "We have just a half an hour left in this year—what can we do in the next half hour that we will never forget?" With his

Gregory Maguire

sister and another friend, we raced into the garage, hunting for some Flexible Flyer sleds. We dragged them across the street to the city park. There we spent the last thirty minutes of the old year sledding. We shrieked, we laughed, we tumbled into drifts together, we threw nets of snow over each other. We caught ourselves in memory.

It is New Year's Eve in 1995 as I write these opening paragraphs. I remember a number of other New Year's Eves. Curling up in a sleeping bag on a park bench in Geneva, Switzerland, because all the hotels were booked. Watching some Kikuyu dancers dressed only in swimsuits and fur anklets doing the hustle at the Bora Bora Club north of Mombasa, in Kenya. Playing record albums of music from the thirties and forties at my childhood home in Albany, New York. All New Year's Eves are a time of accounting of one's life: What have I done? What will I do? What need I change? What am I grateful for? It seems a good time to plunge into an autobiographical essay, to see what else the nets of memory can catch.

*

Every family has its own particular culture. Even little kids who visit the households of friends know this: Somehow the feeling in *your* house is different from the feeling in *our* house. Family culture is spun from ethnic origins, the personalities of parents, and family history. Made of good strong stuff, our family culture—such as I know it from my earliest memories in the late 1950s—was strict, respectful of books and learning, warm in some ways and less warm in others, and suffused with a sense that the world was both wonderful and dangerous.

My father, John (Jack) Maguire, had been born in Brooklyn, New York, in 1917, of Catholic stock originating in the north of Ireland. He was a gifted raconteur and had an encyclopedic memory for funny stories to deliver in his social and professional circles, but at home he maintained a grim Calvinist suspicion about enjoying life. Jack Maguire was in the army during World War II; afterward he resumed his career as a writer. He settled for a time in Albany, New York, where he met Helen Gregory, the second daughter of a Greek immigrant family.

Helen's family had had its own difficulties. Newly immigrated from northern Greece, Helen's mother had died in a hospital fire in the 1920s, leaving a husband who spoke only Greek, as well as seven children, the youngest of whom was still a baby. Helen and two of her sisters took turns staying home from school on a rotating basis, so that there would always be one sister at home to care for the little ones.

By all accounts Helen Gregory was a vivacious woman, full of fun and strong feeling. For a time she worked at her father's Greek diner, called the Famous Restaurant. When she got her pay envelope once a week, though it was the depression and times were hard, she always gave some money to the unemployed men who would come around looking for work or something to eat. And maybe they came to look at her, too: Helen was a beauty. She and my father were married in 1944, and lived in New York City, Washington, D.C., and, eventually, back in Albany. Helen bore four

children. She died of complications resulting from childbirth a week after her fourth child was born. That was in 1954, and I was the baby.

For all that he made his living as a freelance writer, my father wasn't an expressive man. His sorrow and panic must have been immense, but it was tamped down by an Irish habit of stoic acceptance. In the aftermath of the disaster, Helen's sisters offered to care for the children until Jack could pull his life together again. I went to stay with my Aunt Sophia until she realized she was going to find it difficult giving me back to my father. (She told me that my father would come and mind me now and then, so she could go shopping or have some time alone; when she returned, she'd say, "But Jack, you didn't change his diapers!" "He never cried," my father answered, "he didn't fuss, how was I to know?") Though they already had two children, Aunt Sophia asked if she and her husband could adopt me. My father, hoping he might salvage something of family life for his children, didn't want to let me go. Instead, he put me in the Saint Catherine's Infant Home in Albany. The nuns and nurses there called me "Gregory the Executive" because I smiled so seldom. I didn't scowl, I wasn't bad-tempered or fussy: I simply kept my feelings to myself—had I inherited the Irish gene for stoicism? Or maybe did my silence just allow me to observe?

In time my father decided to remarry. The family lore has it that he asked Marie McAuliff of North Albany, "What would you say if I asked you to marry me?" and that she answered, "You'll have to try me and see." He asked, and she agreed. Marie had been a close childhood friend of Helen and all her siblings, and my brothers and sisters knew her already—in fact, she was my godmother, too. So the second marriage started out with some real advantages. The children of the diaspora were brought back together under one roof, and by the time I was six there were three more Maguire children, born of Jack and Marie. We rattled our family list off in nighttime prayers, at breakneck speeds, racing each other to see who could be fastest:

> God bless Daddy, God bless Mommy,
> God bless John, God bless Rachel, God bless Michael, God bless Gregory,
> God bless Matthew, God bless Annie, God bless Joseph.

Seven seemed a good number of kids to have in a family. We didn't feel like an especially large family—in Albany, with its substantial Irish Catholic population, there were plenty of families with eight, ten, twelve, even fourteen children. Seven seemed just about right to us.

We never forgot Helen, our first mother; even I never forgot her, though I hadn't known her. One of my earliest memories takes place at dusk on a cold winter Sunday afternoon, in our turn-of-the-century house on Lancaster Street, in the Pine Hills neighborhood of Albany. I was leaning up against the metal wall of the stove, soaking up the heat; Marie was taking something out of the oven. Had we been chatting about the arrival of a new baby in the family—Annie, perhaps? At any rate, with all the happy egoism of a four-year-old, I probably made some remark about when *I* was in Mommy's stomach. Marie replied, "You know, of course, that you were never in my stomach. You remember that I'm your second mother, and Helen was your first mother." I said, "I *know*, Mommy," in aggrieved and somewhat insulted tones. Maybe the moment is captured in my memory, however, because I had never before really stopped to think about that mysterious bit of family dogma.

Our first mother was part of our growing up. Helen's sisters were warmly welcomed in our home. Marie and Jack both told stories of Helen so that we would come to know her. In the Catholic pantheon of saints and angels we could picture so well, Helen hovered in a category all of her own—not angel, not saint, but some sort of mysterious Greek goddess of warmth, recovery, and love.

Helen watched us from heaven. Jack grumbled at us through his cigar smoke. But it was Marie who taught us to read.

*

We were not well-to-do. When we whined to find out our socioeconomic status, we received the noncommittal reply, "Comfortable. We're comfortable." And comfortable we were—more or less. Teenagers during the Great Depression, both Marie and Jack had formed lifelong habits of frugality. We children wore hand-me-downs from cousins and from each other. We drank gallons of Carnation instant milk, hoping not to get the inevitable lump of undissolved milk powder at the bottom of the pitcher. Marie bought a barber's home

haircut set and gave crew cuts to all five boys as we lined up in our underwear in the basement. Five napes one after the other, five crowns, five right temples, five left temples, and drifts of brown curly hair all over the laundry floor, hiding our chilly ankles.

We didn't see these indignities as economies. We saw them as the campaign of our inventive parents to regularize and oppress us. "Our parents are so mean," we'd say to our friends. If ever some friend would make a claim for equally strict parents, we'd drag out our big guns. "Well, *our* parents won't let us ride two-wheeler bicycles until we're sixteen and we pass the New York State driver's license exam!" Which was true, and usually shut up any stunned competition.

But what we lacked in material luxury—bicycles, horseback-riding lessons, our own individual televisions or stereos, or even new clothes to show off—we made up in our reading lives. Our parents shared a love of reading and the written and spoken word, and the ceremony of a young Maguire getting his or her first library card was treated with as much solemn joy as a First Communion or a birthday.

I'm told that I was read to often as a small boy, but I don't remember it at all. I learned my letters well before kindergarten and was reading simple stories to myself and to my younger brothers and sister with panache and invention if not with accuracy. In the late 1950s, we moved to North Pearl Street in North Albany, to help care for Marie's mother, whose health was failing. In North Albany, the library was too far away for us children to walk to. So Marie went weekly, with a huge carton in which our family groceries had been delivered, and she took out forty or fifty children's books at a go. (She later learned that for years the librarians had assumed that she was the principal of a grade school.)

When I was nine, we moved back to the bigger house on Lancaster Street, and the old Pine Hills Library on Madison Avenue became the destination of most of my outings. The library was housed in a huge, bloated, late Victorian extravaganza of a private home, with a wrap-around porch, stained-glass windows, and ornate polished woodwork, balustrades, and screens. A grand staircase in the front hall twisted up and around to the children's room. There, behind the hugest desk I'd ever seen, the good women of the Albany Public Library oversaw the borrowing of thousands of books a day.

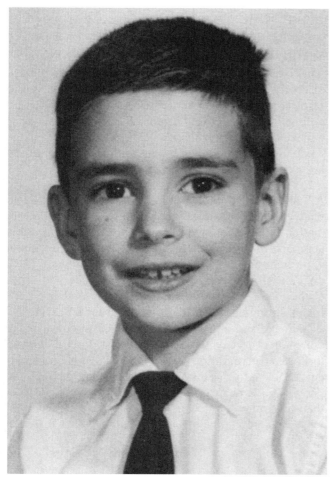

The author, about 1960

I read like a fiend. This will not surprise any reader of this essay; it would be the rare writer who *hadn't* found the love of books while he or she was a child. Once I decided to read through the entire children's collection and brazened my way through all those thick Louisa May Alcott books on the top shelf. But I was derailed when I got to James Barrie's *Peter Pan,* for I took home all the different editions the library had. On finishing the first and turning to the second, I was disappointed to find that different covers and different artists didn't mean a different text—all four editions had the same story in it. I then decided to read just what I wanted. I loved the smell of books, the feel of their covers, even the patterns of library paste spilled on the endpapers. I loved the pictures.

My parents invented a few strategies to help us love to read. We talked about books constantly, for one, and on occasion my parents would post a book chart. For limited periods of time we could write down every title we read and earn five cents for each one. But more important than this was the attitude toward the television. The TV occupied a central place in our family living room, but it was not allowed to cut into reading time. Access to the TV was limited, and access to books was not. We complained—of course we complained! Capably, volubly, constantly. But our accusation that we were being deprived went blithely ignored.

I sometimes tell this to children when I visit them in schools. (I do a lot of work as a writer-in-residence.) I point out that four of the seven Maguire siblings are professional writers, and that *reading makes the difference.* In every class there is some child with a glimmer in the eye, who nods, who knows already.

What a time to be reading, though! I was ten in 1964. My favorite book was Jane Langton's *The Diamond in the Window,* which with its blend of domestic warmth and transcendental fantasy showed me for the first time how books can expand your ideas about the world you live in. When I was done reading any Langton book, I felt I knew something crucial that I hadn't known before. Is this where a new writer really begins to hatch, at the moment of understanding the life-changing power of the written word?

I was primarily a lover of fantasy, and my favorite books in childhood are the obvious ones. The Narnia books. *A Wrinkle in Time. Peter Pan* and *The Wizard of Oz* (more because I knew the stories through the films and TV adaptations). The Edward Eager books delighted me. *Alice in Wonderland* scared me, but it captivated me too. *Charlotte's Web*—no surprise—and *Mary Poppins* and *Homer Price.* The Borrowers tales by Mary Norton, the books about Miss Bianca by Margery Sharp. A lesser known book called *Loretta Mason Potts* by Mary Ellen Chase. Eventually, books like *The Hobbit* and *The Once and Future King.* If I loved a book, I read and reread it, and eventually, with my allowance, bought the books I loved.

But next to Jane Langton's books about the Hall children in Concord, Massachusetts, the books that most caught my imagination were Lucy Boston's stories of Green Knowe. In fact, *The Children of Green Knowe* had been the first full-length chapter book I ever read. I wandered into the kitchen once again with the book in my hand. "Mommy, this is a strange book," I said.

"Is it scary?" said Marie. "You don't have to finish it if it's scary."

"I think it's a ghost story," I said, "but it's not scary. It's sort of sad. I don't know what it is. But there's something neat in it."

I remember this passage from when I was seven. The child goes to stay with a grandmother who lives in an ancient manor house in the lowlands of Cambridgeshire, England.

> The entrance hall was a strange place. As they stepped in, a similar door opened at the far end of the house and another man and boy entered there. Then Toseland saw that it was only themselves in a big mirror. The walls round him were partly rough stone and partly plaster, but hung all over with mirrors and pictures and china. There were three big old mirrors all reflecting each other so that at first Toseland was puzzled to find what was real, and which door one could go through straight, the way one wanted to, not sideways somewhere else. He almost wondered which was really himself.

What was in *The Children of Green Knowe*—though I had no words for it—was atmosphere. Literary atmosphere. *The Children of Green Knowe* taught me many things, including that the optimum growing condition for magic is the sense of mystery you develop by observing things closely.

I believed in magic. It was not hard to do, being a good Catholic boy.

*

It may seem scandalous, even heretical, to talk about magic and religion together. The type of Roman Catholicism I was raised in was rich in narrative. We read about the lives of saints and dreamed about the chance to be put to death in some wonderfully bloody way for refusing, let's say, to spit on the Blessed Sacrament. We listened to the Gospels and to the stories of the travels and adventures of Paul. The Christmas story and the Easter tragedy and triumph gave shape and meaning to our lives—not simply theologically, but in a personal way, too. Since we carried the death of Helen in an interior pocket in our hearts, we were well inclined by personal need to accept the doctrine of everlasting life. Anyway, children don't analyze what they believe, but they do believe fervently. I believed in saints and angels. I believed in Jesus in a way that has become more metaphoric and political as I have gotten older, but no less strong. I believed in the archangel with his fiery sword at the garden of Eden, and Moses in the bulrushes, and talking animals at the manger at Bethlehem.

As an adult I find it difficult not to be a skeptic in matters of faith, at least intellectually—but I am aware that an intellectual perspective is not the only possible approach to take. Like most people, I can be impatient with hierarchy and with arcane points of dogma. But I do cherish the religious teaching I received from Catholic schools for its emphasis on moral integrity, for its strong narrative traditions, and for its giving me a language and a grammar with which to consider the crises of everyday life. When all else fails, I rely on the prayerful traditions of my parents, my grandparents, back into the dim ages further than anyone can know. The Roman Catholic tradition may be no truer than any other—but it is *my* tradition. It is a part of what I called earlier my family culture. And it is rich in mystery.

*

I had two best friends all throughout grade school. For different reasons I am not in touch with them now—one died of AIDS a few years ago, and the other, sadly, has been estranged from me for some years. Both of these good, dear friends helped me understand the pleasure of making things. The story of growing up to be an artist of one sort or the other always involves the meeting of soul mates, the sudden, life-enhancing realization that you are not alone.

After I had read the Narnia stories and shared them with these valuable grade-school friends, I wanted more than anything else to find a magic land of my own. Doorways to magic lands are not easy to come across in Albany, New York. I would have preferred looking in Europe, or in the Adirondack Mountains where we vacationed for a week every summer. But if faith could grow in unlikely soil, so must magic. I poked around in improbable places looking for a bit of proof. I wanted to see some tiny hint of magic, some clue—it didn't need to be much!

One winter afternoon I walked my younger sister, Annie, to her ballet lesson on Colvin Avenue in Albany. I was with one of the friends mentioned above. We decided to explore a no man's land between the commercial strip and the Little League playing fields a half-mile beyond. Just over a pile of soil and construction debris, probably mounded there by bulldozers, we came upon a small, frozen pond. It was hidden from sight of the well-traveled street, and overgrown on three sides by stands of some sort of feathery-headed weed or marsh grass.

With something like Balboa's delight, we slid down the slope onto the ice. From the sunken level of the pond, the street and its noise disappeared; the buildings were hidden by the high grass. All that could be seen were the gray, wind-scrubbed skies, and the grass whistling around us. "It's a magic place!" I whispered. I was partly pretending, but I was also partly responding to the otherworldly atmosphere. How come this secret place suddenly revealed itself to us, who had marched up and down that sidewalk dozens of times earlier? "We were never *meant* to find this place before now," we decided. "It has called us here!"

I hope I'm not betraying the confidences of my deceased friend or of our younger sisters—his sister Sue, my sister Annie—to publish the name of our private magic land. It was Fliaan—pronounced Fly-ann. We made a map of Fliaan and its environs, naming sections like "The Witch's Brambles" and "The Cliffs at the Edge of the World." Our adventures there weren't much to report—we generally had run-fling and sliding competitions across the ice, or sometimes played hide-and-seek in the overgrown reeds. When spring came and the ice melted, the place lost a good deal of its sense of mystery, but the following winter the eerie atmosphere returned, and we celebrated. We wrote a national anthem of Fliaan (mercifully, I've suppressed the memory of it). On our departure from our private paradise each week, we sang the anthem and then we said the "Our Father"—just to prove to any attendant nosy-parker saints that we weren't constructing false idols, that we knew what side our immortal souls were buttered on, so to speak.

The story of Fliaan would have no point in this autobiography except that, stirred by hope and longing, I began to write a novelistic history of Fliaan. I had written many stories before this, starting at the age of about seven. But they had been more or less

realistic adventure stories, derivatives of *The Man from U.N.C.L.E.* and Disney Sunday night movies such as *The Moonspinners*. My first invented characters had all been adults; they could drive; they were fabulously rich and adventurous; they were independent and competent and popular—all things I doubted I'd ever achieve for myself. But the characters in my stories about Fliaan were comfortably, familiarly fantastic— witches, saints, dragons, gods, dwarves, the whole gamut from fantasy's central casting. The two childhood friends mentioned above helped with the text and with illustrations. I completed four or five volumes of "The Chronicles of Fliaan." They're not very good. But they were my first attempt at fantasy. They were also my first attempt to integrate into a story some atmosphere, some mood that I had experienced firsthand.

*

It wasn't all that surprising that the Maguire kids turned to writing. John Maguire was well established as a journalist for the *Albany Times-Union;* by the mid-1960s he was writing a humorous column four times a week that was second only to "Dear Abby" in reader popularity. Through most of our childhood, he also maintained another full-time job as a speech writer for the New York State Health Commissioner. Marie was a poet whose work had been published in the *New York Herald Tribune* and reprinted in the *Congressional Record.* Even Helen had been known to scribble lines of doggerel from time to time. When we wanted to play at being our parents, we organized piles of scrap paper and stapled them together and produced newspapers, stories, plays, and cycles of poems.

With the assistance of the Gaffneys, our good friends from around the corner, we mounted theatrical productions on Sunday evenings after dinner. One extravaganza concluded with the San Francisco earthquake, which we simulated by tossing into the air every sofa cushion and pillow we could gather up. My brother Joe played a small child who was killed in the disaster. The ketchup we used for blood was effective, and the stains came out of the carpet with water and a little Tide.

When I was in fourth grade, I wrote a class play by invitation of Sister Mary Salvator. It was called "The First Thanksgiving," and it involved two Pilgrim kids,

"Young writers": (back to front) Michael, Gregory, John, and Rachel Maguire, about 1957

Billy and Suzy, who get lost one day late in November. A friendly Indian named Squanto finds them and brings them home, and since all the Pilgrims are so grateful, they decide to have a big dinner to celebrate. Squanto shows them how to make creamed onions, and olives with little red pimentos stuck in them, and turkey, and crouton stuffing. "It's the first Thanksgiving!" they all decide happily. The play draws to a dramatic close when the priest arrives and the Pilgrims genuflect and cross themselves and follow him off to mass. This play was mounted in fourth grade to great critical success. No one ever told me that the Pilgrims weren't Roman Catholics; I'm not sure that Sister Mary Salvator, who hailed from County Kerry, knew much about the Pilgrims to begin with. But eight years later, when I returned to that grade school to take up my first teaching job, I found that the fourth graders were still mounting annual productions of "The First Thanksgiving," though my byline had long since disappeared from the script.

One year, because Marie was taking a course in the history of movies at the local state university, I cor-

ralled some siblings and Gaffneys to help make a Christmas present that was meant to simulate an old film. This was before the days of camcorders, nor did our family even have a Super-8 camera. So I wrote and blocked out the story ahead of time—it was called "Passion, Pride, and a Place to Pray"—and we marched on the local Woolworth's in Westgate Shopping Center. We were armed with props, costumes, and backdrops. We installed ourselves in a booth where, back in those days, you could get a strip of four photos for twenty-five cents. We thought it would make a great present, with the photos stapled down on the left of each page and a running synopsis of the action written, frame by frame, on the right.

Then we acted out the melodrama, which included a wonderful scene where the villain attempts to force the hand in marriage of a poor widow lady by threatening to foreclose her mortgage. The widow lady, played with élan by my sister Annie, shrieked her best line, "You can take my baby, but not me!" and flung her child at the villain, played with equal zest by the irrepressible John Gaffney. Luckily we used a plastic baby doll, for in Annie's zeal the infant went soaring out of the booth and over the heads of six Woolworth's cashiers. We were cordially invited never to come to Woolworth's again.

By the time I graduated from eighth grade, I had finished fifty or sixty stories, ranging in length from four pages to several hundred, many of them co-written with John Gaffney. Each story was handwritten, usually in a spiral-bound notebook. I never revised my work when I was young—when I admit this to schoolchildren, teachers at the back of classrooms blanche, and frown, and purse their lips, and shake their heads. But since I was a fluent writer as a child, who at an early age had mastered the art of keeping myself interested in what I was doing, I didn't belabor finished work. In fact I scarcely looked at it again. I just went on to the next project.

I have talked earlier about the fantasies I read. In adult life I have gone on to have an appreciation for a wider range of writing. But there was another keynote event in my childhood reading, and this was the groundbreaking book of the middle sixties—for me and for many other young readers—*Harriet the Spy.*

Harriet M. Welsch maintained a spy route and wrote down what she discovered about life in her spy notebook. I had no sooner finished reading Louise Fitzhugh's masterpiece than I decided I needed to keep a spy notebook if I, like Harriet, wanted to be a writer. I still have the first dozen spy notebooks I filled up, mostly from when I was eleven and twelve. They immediately dispel any notion of my having been a child prodigy. But they also do what journals are supposed to do. They provide two pictures: a picture of the world as seen by the writer, and a self-portrait of the writer that he may not know he's constructing. I include a few sample entries, verbatim. All proper nouns refer to my brothers and sisters unless otherwise noted.

> Rachel's nice. She nearly saved someone's life. Yesterday when she was in the Church she grabbed someone's sleeve out of the flames.

> Joe just said I'd be a nice father to him, and he'd like it.

My mother's sipping coffee and reading the paper on the kitchen table. Rachel's eating, and Matthew's playing ball in the bathroom hall. Daddy and Joe are watching somebody make a vase on Captain Kangaroo.

Seduced—what does that mean?

Lying right here on my bed, I think I'll write all the sounds I hear:

The water draining out of the bathtub.

Billions of cars on Pine Avenue.

Joe saying his prayers.

My pen scratching.

Me sneezing.

Matt arguing with Joe.

My bed creaking.

A slight ringing in my ears.

A distant siren.

The side doorbell.

Rachel coming in.

Daddy talking to Rachel.

The Tijuana Brass Tijuana-ing away.

The nailbrush being plunked in the bathtub water.

My mother's sewing machine.

On the TV: "The day you become a woman, your system needs more iron."

Also: "Lady, take your summer kitchen on a date with Reynolds."

Joe's playing with a slinky which he says is his dog Money.

Matthew is in a terrible mood tonight. He said to my mother, "I pity you." I think he said that because we were in a fight. Anyway he got a great big spanking.

All alone! How wonderful it feels, stretched out on Michael's bed, with the wind rustling the leaves of the tree outside his window. I could be in a treehouse, or a balloon, or in a raft, I'm SO alone!

The tree has stopped rustling. I can see it, perfectly still. Oh blessed wind! A picture into reality. How beautiful to find your daydreams ARE reality.

[Neighborhood kids] Richie and Charlotte just walked past. Richie is turning into a pain in the neck.

We went to 5:30 mass. It was a riot. We walked in the front doors, the priest was pleading for somebody to come up and be the lector. But nobody would. (Including me.) Finally he induced this one fair, oversized youth of about twelve to read. He, the boy, had to be the worst one that the priest could possibly have chosen. He stammered, stuttered, mispronounced about every other word, and skipped lines. Whenever he stuttered or paused over a word, members of the congregation would help him out. They all must have sounded like bleating sheep. Then at another time I noticed this stout old lady occupying the pew in front of us. She wore a plaid purple dress that looked like an Indian blanket. She always was unable to find the pages from which the responses were being recited, and she kept on looking over her husband's shoulder to read from his booklet. He was more than a little annoyed at this. And then during the Kiss of Peace, about twenty seconds after the rest of the congregation had finished giving the appropriate congenial handshake, she turned and beamed at Matthew and said, "Peace be with you." After this I could see her slyly looking at her husband to see what he thought of this openness on her part. (He was indifferent.)

Tonight when we were going to swim, Annie said, "Aaahh! There's a spider in my goggles."

Joe said, "Drown it! Throw it in the lake!"

Annie said, "No, don't drown it!"

I said, "Annie, since when have you cared about the welfare of a measly spider?"

She said, "It's not that. I just don't want any drowned spiders in any lake that *I* intend to swim in."

I don't make any claims for this journal except that it was yet another way I cemented the habit of writing on a regular basis. When I was in high school, I began another journal, this time in earnest, one that has—at this writing—accompanied my whole adult life. In a few months I will buy a new spiral-bound notebook and begin volume number 48 of my adult journal—I've been keeping it since about 1970. Harriet the Spy in midcareer, just as compulsive as ever.

*

At the Vincentian Institute, my high school, I felt like a nerd—though we didn't use that word at the time. I wore glasses with thick black plastic frames and began to grow my hair long. I hung around with the kids who played the guitar at daily mass in the chapel. I was a good student, but not a great one. I spent more time writing stories, painting, composing songs, or writing letters than I did studying. High school was not the disaster it can sometimes be, especially for an oddball, because the atmosphere of the times—the early 1970s—encouraged self-expression. I began to sing in a folk quintet with some good friends and discovered that all those years of belting out the hymns at church had helped me develop a serviceable tenor. In the world beyond me—a world I was only beginning to notice—the campaign against the war in Vietnam was building, and my friends wore black armbands to draw attention to the shooting of student protesters at Kent State by National Guardsmen.

High school is a time when making friends is of paramount importance, and I was lucky to have a wide circle of interesting pals to hang around with. I'm still in touch with most of them—Annie Franze, Eileen Reedy, Mike Savage, Jayne O'Hare, MaryEllen Harmon. For a year or so in high school my habit of journal writing caught on among my friends. We all were scribbling down our thoughts and opinions and anxieties—mostly worrying about our friends, and whether or not our friendships were true and robust! Then, for a time, we started to pass our journals around for comments, and we would scrawl warm remarks in the margins of one another's notebooks, or append notes of devotion on the first blank page to follow. But too much revelation can be risky.

One afternoon I was invited to attend a music rehearsal of a rock band being organized by three guys in my circle of friends. The rehearsal was in the basement of the home of the lead guitarist. Though I preferred acoustic music to amplified, I still enjoyed hanging around with these guys. At a break, we headed upstairs to get some hot chocolate—it was the dead of winter—and we settled in the living room. The guitarist closed the sliding doors to the hall and the dining room, and said, "Greg, we have something we want to say to you."

This was not good, I could feel it. "What?"

"We've been talking about it, and we think that we guys should stop writing in journals. You, too."

"Why?" I said, but I knew what was coming.

"We think it's a pretty girlish thing to do, actually. We're not going to do it any more and we recommend that you stop, too."

I don't remember what I said. I'm not much of a fighter so I probably thanked them for the hot chocolate and got my coat and left. I do remember walking home through the snow, feeling rejected right down into the deepest private part of my self. But though I usually avoided conflict in favor of negotiation and reconciliation, I didn't for a minute stop to consider their proposal seriously. Those guys were just wrong. Writing had nothing to do with gender stereotypes. My *dad* was a writer, my *brothers* were writers. And even if those friends were right—even if I was getting a reputation for being odd—there was no way I was going to change my habits for them. Writing was too much a part of me by then.

The English novelist Jill Paton Walsh said once, "You know that you're a writer when you find it impossible *not* to write." By that definition I think I realized, that

grim and lonely afternoon, that I was a writer. Perhaps I wouldn't make my living at it; there were other things I also wanted to do. But how could I *not* write?

*

I didn't have a lot of choice in what college to attend, as there was no family money to spare for dorm fees or tuition. With the help of a New York State Regents' Scholarship, I enrolled at the State University of New York (SUNY) at Albany, whose cold, unwelcoming modern campus sprawled about three miles west of our family home. I was a diligent and uninspired college student, increasingly shy in a class that numbered, I think, three thousand. I rode the commuter bus back and forth, did my work, and took no part in the social life on campus.

But my life wasn't as dismal as all *that*. To pay for textbooks and fees, I accepted a weekend job at the Church of Saint Vincent de Paul, my home parish. I was to form and direct a contemporary music group—musicians and singers. It would consist of those high-school friends still, like me, living in Albany during their college years, as well as college students living at the university and other nearby colleges. My pastor was Father Leo O'Brien, who had said the daily mass at the high school, and who had become a good friend, as had his associate, Sister Joan Byrne. My more immediate colleague in the music effort, however, was a newly ordained young priest named Father John Turner.

Almost twenty-five years later, it is hard to describe the sense of awakening that accompanied my friendship with Jack Turner. Jack was an intense man, prayerful, private, poetic. We met once a week to discuss the liturgical readings and search for appropriate music, drawing both from sacred and secular traditions. My family had taught me to respect the power of words, for which I am grateful, but Jack—more than any of my undergraduate professors—taught me to honor the power of ideas. He was only eight years older than I, but I felt like a novice sitting at the foot of an Old Testament patriarch or prophet in the making. Among many other gifts he gave me, he taught me that asking questions was more challenging than answering them. After a conversation that ranged widely over literature, art, music, theology, personal experience (mine), existential reflection (his), I would

Father John Turner, 1975

leave the parish house and walk home under the bleaching light of streetlamps. I felt more intimately connected with limitless celestial time and with the workings of my heart than all those childhood years of reading had prepared me for. I no longer hungered for a magic land.

Once I wrote a song in his honor, that said, in part,

> He always got mad when I called him my
>   teacher.
> The lessons are there in the sky, he'd say.
> Don't assign me a part that I don't want to play
> Oh Merlin, oh poet, oh friend of mine, where
>   are you now?
> Oceans away, I know it . . .
> Attending some marvel of God
> And ascending some ladder to God
> And leaving me watching you leaving me.

He laughed at it and was embarrassed at the starry-eyed hero worship of the song. He asked me to sing it once more, and then he said, "You never need to sing it to me again, for now it exists in the world and in my memory; you should go on and write something new."

Jack left the parish in Albany and moved to the North Country, to a retreat center called Barry House on Brant Lake, New York. At his encouragement, I applied for a summer job at an amusement park on the west shore of Lake George, which was only fifteen or twenty miles away. On weekends and long summer evenings we were able to continue our friendship uninterrupted—singing, swimming, reading poetry, wandering in to Lake George Village to poke around the bookstore. During the day I worked at Time Town. Occasionally, for reasons that now escape me, I had to dress up as a rooster with a twelve-foot comb and strut about, terrifying the toddlers. However, I also ran the park's small theater, and while I was waiting for the films to rewind, I sat on the steps of the projection booth and worked on a novel set in the Adirondacks. I was twenty years old.

At the end of the summer, Jack drove me to the Amtrak stop at Ticonderoga—there was so little traffic that you had to flag the train down if you wanted it to stop—and I caught the train to Montreal. There I took my first overseas flight to Dublin, Ireland, to spend part of my junior year abroad, studying for a semester and then traveling for three months.

Incredibly naive and thunderstruck with excitement and loneliness, I wandered from Ireland to northern Greece. Opposite stony corners of Europe, and the twin homes of my bloodlines. In 1974, my brother John joined me in Athens, and together we traveled to Thessalonika to look for the younger sister of my Greek grandmother—the grandmother who had died in the hospital fire. Our communication with the Greek branch of the family had been lost following the deaths of those in my mother's generation who still spoke Greek. We were the first members of the family to return to Greece since our maternal grandparents had left fifty-some years earlier. In a tiny house behind a blue iron gate, we found her. My great-aunt was a short, stout woman, who, though not expecting us, knew at once from our familiar faces who we must be. She screamed, "Amerikani!" and barreled into us with arms outstretched. Tears, and hugs, and glasses of ouzo. In my great-aunt's simple house, we found her walls hung with black-and-white photos of the American nephews and nieces she'd never met, including Helen's wedding portrait from 1944.

I went back to the States to finish my degree at SUNY and to take up my music leader's job at church again. I saw Jack Turner a few times, but we no longer lived near each other. I never sang his song to him again, for three years after we met, Jack was killed in a car accident in the Adirondacks. I went to his funeral and sat at the back, thinking, "No one knows how important he is to me!" But the kind of person Jack Turner was meant that dozens, even hundreds of people in that church were feeling the same thing. He was only twenty-nine when he died.

The last year of my undergraduate education was spent in private grief. I was grateful for my musician friends—Roger Mock and Francisco Pabalan, particularly, and later Debbie Kirsch and Margaret O'Brien—but I felt adrift without Jack there. I felt I had lost some vital, irreplaceable key to unlocking significance in daily events. I was sad with a sadness I could hardly name, nor even much share with my family or friends.

*

I didn't stop writing, though. I graduated from the university and took a job as a teacher in what would now be called a middle school. I taught seventh-and eighth-grade English literature and grammar. What I lacked in teacher training I made up for in enthusiasm for the subjects and for the kids themselves. Toward the end of the academic year I organized a field trip to New York City to go to the Museum of Modern Art and to see a Broadway musical matinee. Somehow I managed to get separated from the fourteen students—during rush hour in Times Square—and I had to drive back to Albany with my pal Roger, who was serving as a chaperone. Neither of us knew where the students were or whether the sole remaining adult was even still with them. The kids all did make it home safely—thanks to Mike Savage, the responsible chaperone among us. Because I was well liked as a teacher, none of the students ever told their parents what had happened. But the mishap made me consider whether I should be teaching, especially when I realized that my year of full-time teaching was the only year I could remember being too tired to write any fiction at all.

I had decided, on my return from Europe, to look at the novel I'd written over the previous summer. It had seemed no worse than some of the children's books I still enjoyed reading, so with great labor I typed up the manuscript and began to mail it to publishers who had brought out my favorite books. I sent it to Harper, to Dutton, to Little, Brown. Each submission usually

took three to four months, after which the manuscript was returned with a polite note saying that the book "doesn't suit our needs at this time." I wasn't much daunted. I told myself: It took you a whole year to write this book and type it, the least you can do is take a year to submit it. Don't be discouraged. The point is *determination.* If a publisher rejects it, just send it out to the next house on your list, whether you feel like it or not.

So I did. I sent the book to the fourth publisher, Farrar, Straus, and Giroux, and when five months had elapsed, I suddenly thought: *I never made a carbon copy of the finished draft.* (It didn't even occur to me to photocopy it, as this was before the days of photocopy stores; it was also years before everyone had a personal computer.) What if the U.S. Postal Service had lost the only copy of my first real book? So I wrote to Farrar, Straus again, explaining my bad case of nerves.

They answered that they *had* read the manuscript, apologies for the delay, and they would like to talk to me about it.

A week or two later I took a day off of teaching and went to Manhattan with my friends Roger and Margy. Farrar, Straus was—and still is—a small and prestigious firm located in Union Square. I walked in to meet Sandra Jordan, the children's book editor, with my new three-piece banker's suit so crisply pressed that it could give surface cuts to anyone who brushed against it. I had a fountain pen and a hand-tooled leather notebook in which to make notes of our conversation. I was twenty-three, and still very shy. Meeting a publisher in New York seemed more terrifying to me than hiking with a backpack and sleeping roll through central Europe. Sandra Jordan wore a black hat and a cape, and she smoked thin, aromatic cigars. She was good-natured and ironic, with that brusque, New York City edge that Catholic boys from upstate find hard to read. I never knew exactly what she meant; I had perfected *sincerity* as a posture and a policy. But Sandra found a way to talk to me so I understood her. She guided me through margin notes and Post-it observations tagged onto nearly every one of the 220 pages of the manuscript. When we had finished—several hours of talking—she handed me back the pile of typescript and said, "Well, that's how *we* think it might be changed. Mull it over and if you want to revise it and submit it again, we'd be happy to look at it. Otherwise, good luck, and it was nice meeting you."

I was devastated. I was sure I had just been made a fool of. Sandra Jordan, by her own admission, was newly hired to be the head of children's books at Farrar, Straus. Probably she was just trying to fill up her workday and look busy. Why wasn't there a contract, an offer to publish? Roger and Margy and I drove back to Albany that afternoon; those good friends tried to cheer me up. However dejected I felt, though, I was determined to try, and I revised the book and sent it back to Farrar, Straus.

That same spring I had received a letter from Jane Langton, to whom I had written a fan letter, finally, and with whom a firm friendship had developed. Jane told me about a new master's degree program in children's literature that was being established at Simmons College in Boston. I left my teaching job and moved to Cambridge, Massachusetts, in the early summer of 1977, having the good fortune to find lodging with an elderly doyenne named Sarah Reginald Seabury Parker. Sarah Parker lived in Harvard Square, in a fine old federal-style home dating from the 1840s. The house was like something out of Masterpiece Theater. Standing on a table in the front hall was a coat of ceremonial brass armor from the Spanish occupation of the Philippines. A Dutch cuckoo clock dating back three centuries hung near the dining-room door. Above my bed in the back room was an original Winslow Homer watercolor. And Sarah Parker herself, frail, soft-spoken, liberal, well educated, was a wonderful new friend. The difference in our ages was only sixty-eight years or so, hardly enough to worry about. I changed light bulbs and collected the trash, and before long I also was doing modest cooking for her. Sarah paid the bills and accepted no rent from me, for, as she said, "Dear boy, if I charged you for your room then I'd have to see that everything was perfect, and if I don't charge then I don't have a care in the world, do I?"

I was happy to be studying at Simmons College. My professors there included Paul and Ethel Heins, who have both been editors of the influential *Horn Book* magazine; Betty Levin, the novelist and sheep farmer; and Jane Langton. Barbara Harrison, the founder and first director of the Center for the Study of Children's Literature, was zealous at raising public awareness about the value of literature in the lives of children. I found new friends among the students, especially Maggie Stern (now Maggie Stern Terris) and Patricia McMahon, both of whom have gone on to their own writ-

ing careers. Even more thrilling than the chance to live in Harvard Square and study the history and criticism of children's books in Boston, however, was the news that arrived a month into my first semester as a graduate student: Sandra Jordan approved of my revisions and accepted my first children's novel for publication by Farrar, Straus, and Giroux.

The book was called, eventually, *The Lightning Time.* It has the excesses and enthusiasms of a first novel; it is derivative of my favorite writers, but not brilliantly so. I look back at the story of twelve-year-old Daniel Rider and his attempt to help save his grandmother's mountain home from unscrupulous developers, and I see mostly an encoding in fantasy of some of the things that Jack Turner and I talked about. Jack is a character in the story—thinly disguised as Father August Petrakis, an Anglican minister. As a character he is too wise, too lovable, too impenetrably good to get much of a handle on. I hadn't yet learned that readers best love characters who reveal their contradictions and complications, too—but then I had hardly learned to accept the complications in myself or in my own friends. I saw people as WONDERFUL or HORRIBLE, with few exceptions. In my early books I wrote them as such, too.

The publication of *The Lightning Time* in 1978 coincided with my receiving a master of arts degree in children's literature. My old friends in Albany and my new friends in Boston and Cambridge helped me celebrate my first publication. The book earned me a fellowship to the Bread Loaf Writers' Conference in Middlebury, Vermont, and that the reviews were mixed didn't bother me much. At least some wise critics saw my work as "lively" and "imaginative," and I had no place to go but up, didn't I? Still, in retrospect, I wonder what only those who published young can have the temerity to ponder: Had *The Lightning Time* and its two sequels, *The Daughter of the Moon* and *Lights on the Lake,* been turned down, perhaps I would have tried *harder* to write something more original. Perhaps I would have learned the craft of revision earlier. As it was, my earliest books were published to generally good reviews but modest sales. Alas, I had started writing fantasy at just a moment when the interest in fantasy for children, for the time being anyway, had started to wane.

For another year I lived with Sarah Parker. One evening, awaking from uneasy dreams, I had a sense of foreboding, and for the first time ever I went to check on Sarah. She was awake, but had suffered a heart attack. I called the ambulance, and while we were waiting I tried to console her. She consoled me instead. "Dearie," she said, "it has meant more to me than I can say to have you here in the house with me these two years. You mustn't get yourself stirred up for I have been very happy to know you. The gloves downstairs on the sofa belong to Mabel Colgate and should be returned to her; she left them here at tea on Saturday last."

I visited her in the hospital every day for several weeks. When she began to complain about the food I suspected she would pull through. She was well enough to spend the summer at the seashore. The last time I saw her, I took the commuter train for a day visit, bringing with me a thermos of Manhattans, because Rockport is a dry town. We sat in the gardens and looked at the sea. She died about ten days later. At her funeral, in the blistering heat of late August, the minister declared, "Mrs. Parker requested that, irrespective of the liturgical season, her service begin with the congregation singing Joy to the World." I love to sing, but it was hard to sing. Hard, and necessary.

*

In the autumn of 1979 I found myself a small apartment in Porter Square in Cambridge. My dear friend Maggie Stern had a place just up the street, and other friends lived nearby, including Mark Miller, a young research assistant at Howard Gardner's Project Zero at Harvard University. I had not attended Harvard, and for the first couple of years living near Harvard Square I hardly had the courage even to walk through Harvard Yard on my way to the Cambridge Public Library. The university seemed like a huge furnace, a dragon in bricks and slate, dangerously seething with intellectual pomp and superiority. Becoming friends with Mark helped break down that fear somewhat, for Mark was warm and open-minded, a breath of fresh air in my life, even if he had gone to Harvard.

I was increasingly devoted to my friends, but the lives we played at, rich and strange and at times daring, in the exploratory spirit of the times and of youth, weren't anything like the lives of adults in children's books. They were even less like the lives of neighbors in my solid, respectable Irish Catholic neighborhood back home. Growing up in part is realizing that you can invent for yourself the kind of adult you want to be.

One thing I knew is that I loved to travel, so whenever I had the chance I accepted any invitation to visit anyone—anywhere. In 1981 I flew off to the Philippines for a month with my college chum Francisco Pabalan, who was just graduating from medical school. In 1983 I went to Kenya with Rafique Keshavjee, a Harvard graduate student I'd met several years earlier at the card catalog in Widener Library. My writing began to show signs of greater experimentation, maybe as a result of traveling. *The Dream Stealer,* published by Harper and Row in 1983, was a fantasy like my earlier books, but it was set in a mythical Russia at the turn of the century. It featured as a central character the famous witch from the folktales named Baba Yaga. Depending on the fairy tale she appears in, Baba Yaga can be either fairy godmother or treacherous villainess. In trying to accommodate both sides of her reputation, I learned the pleasure of writing a fully rounded character. Perhaps I also was remembering the fun of the fantastic writing I had tried to do about our own childhood mythical country of Fliaan.

In the mid-1980s I continued to live in Cambridge, sharing a luxurious prewar flat with my friend Rafique. I worked full time at Simmons College as an assistant professor and associate director of the Center for the Study of Children's Literature. My former professors became my colleagues and, even more precious to me, my friends. Furthermore, due to the rigors of college teaching, I was mastering some of my shyness and trying to develop some confidence in my own thoughts. However, Rafique—who had graduated with a doctorate in anthropology and Middle Eastern studies from Harvard—took exception to my self-deprecating remarks about how weak my sense of logic was, how pedestrian my opinions. "I couldn't even get accepted into a doctoral program," I once declared, which provided Rafique with the opening he took. He said, "I don't believe you. I dare you to apply somewhere. Furthermore, I'll pay the application fee, I'm that convinced you'd be an ideal candidate."

Once dared, I had to commit: I applied to the doctoral program in English at Tufts University. I was accepted in 1986. I had thought the dare was done, and Rafique had proved his point. But the letter from Tufts announced their willingness to waive my tuition fees entirely, and a conversation with the head of the English department revealed that Tufts would also overlook the normal requirement of graduate students to teach there. I felt I had no real reason *not* to enroll. By this time I had been teaching at Simmons College for long enough that coming up for tenure was likely within a couple of years, and I wanted to give myself at least a fighting chance at that exercise.

In the middle of my doctoral studies, problems began to emerge at the Simmons College Center for the Study of Children's Literature. The master-of-arts-degree program, founded in 1977 by Barbara Harrison, had rooted itself securely and had weaned itself off the so-called "soft money" that the National Endowment of the Humanities had provided initially. But following a 1984 federal report decrying the state of teacher education in the United States, the Simmons College education department, like education departments all over the country, suffered a drop in enrollments. The president and dean of graduate studies decided to move the Center for the Study of Children's Literature into the education department to bolster enrollments. To a person, the faculty of the Center protested. We felt that the Simmons College management was betraying the original intention of the program—to be a humanities discipline—by taking away its autonomy and placing it under the aegis of education, a service discipline.

We negotiated for more than a year, to no avail. Thus, with early announcement so that our currently enrolled students might finish their degrees with the existing faculty while there was time, in 1986 the faculty of the Center resigned in protest at the administration's decision. There was some hoopla over this, both in Boston and nationally.

Soon thereafter, I helped cofound—with Barbara Harrison, Ethel and Paul Heins, Betty Levin, Jill Paton Walsh, and John Rowe Townsend—a small educational charity called Children's Literature New England (CLNE). As I write this, CLNE prepares to celebrate its tenth anniversary as an independent organization dedicated to the same ideals that the Center at Simmons College was set up to foster. I don't know for how long CLNE will continue; every organization, like every relationship, has a natural life span. For ten years, however, CLNE has gathered to its annual summer conferences a stellar company of writers and illustrators for children. Many of them have become

friends as well as colleagues: Ashley Bryan, Eleanor Cameron, Susan Cooper, Virginia Hamilton, John Langstaff, Ursula K. Le Guin, Madeleine L'Engle, Katherine Paterson, Maurice Sendak—more, really, than I can name here. I've made good friends from all over the United States, as well as abroad—Japan, Ireland, England, Australia, New Zealand, South Africa. Among them, Martha Walke is one of the most treasured to me.

Every summer we meet in the new community of friends and colleagues, holding in common a belief that early exposure to literature is essential to the survival of a humane and literate society. Doesn't that last line sound like a grant proposal? But everything in my childhood prepared me to feel a missionary zeal about children and their reading. Though I was sorry to resign from Simmons after eight years of teaching fine students there, CLNE satisfied my compulsion to continue advocacy work. This time, free of the authoritarian dictates of jittery-stomached college overseers.

*

My love affair with the Adirondacks had begun in childhood. Ever since the late 1950s, our parents had bundled us seven children into one car and driven to a camp on the east side of Lake George—what was then the undeveloped side—for a week of hiking, swimming, and living in the shadows of the mountains in summer. As an adult I have been to Nicaragua, Egypt, Kenya, Turkey, Romania, the Philippines, and all over western and Mediterranean Europe. I learned the pleasure of travel by going away to the mountains when young. But thanks to the invitation of another good friend and fellow intrepid traveler, Maureen Vecchione, I went to stay in the Adirondacks for the first time in ten years—I hadn't been there since the death of Jack Turner. We rented an A-frame chalet outside of Indian Lake, New York. A day's excursion in a hired speedboat took Maureen and me from Blue Mountain Lake into Eagle Lake. The taciturn local guide pointed to a rustic mansion on a secluded stretch of lakefront property and grumbled, "Oh, that's where all the pinko feminists and faggots and artsy types go to write and paint."

I was just about to start my doctoral work, but I was curious. When I got back to Cambridge, I sent a postcard addressed to the postmistress at Blue

"The founding board members of Children's Literature New England": (from left) John Rowe Townsend, Jill Paton Walsh, Gregory Maguire, Barbara Harrison, Ethel Heins, Betty Levin, and Paul Heins, Oxford, England, 1992

Mountain Lake. If there was an arts colony nearby, would she forward this request for information to them? She did, and they replied, and so I came to know about Blue Mountain Center, New York.

Set up by Adam Hochschild, who is well known as a writer and as a cofounder of *Mother Jones* magazine, Blue Mountain Center was intended to provide a nurturing atmosphere for creative work for artists, especially those who work for social change. I hardly thought of myself as being an agitator for social change; indeed, I hardly knew whether to call myself liberal or conservative. But in my application packet I included an editorial I had written that had been printed in the *Christian Science Monitor*—an essay on the 1982 march in New York City to protest the proliferation of nuclear weapons. And I've always had a sympathy for those who fight hard battles. Hadn't I just fought the one at Simmons College myself, and in resigning hadn't I given up my chance for a tenured

position? Though my children's fantasies were not what I would consider provocative, at least on a sociological level, I was accepted for a late summer residency in 1986.

Due to a car problem, I arrived at the session late, when new residents had already had a week to begin to form a community. I let myself in the kitchen door, stumbling in the dark, not really sure I had the nerve or the right to be there. But I was willing to put up with anything to spend a month by an Adirondack lake. No doubt a children's book writer was considered only marginally an artist, so I would just keep my mouth shut and drink in the aromatic smell of pines.

The sixteen or so residents that summer worked in areas of poverty and urban renewal, of nuclear disarmament, of AIDS activism, of ecology, of civil liberties. I hardly thought my single editorial in the

Monitor made me an expert on anything, so I kept my mouth shut. I nearly scuttled my chances at making any friends.

But one noontime I volunteered to take the rowboat across the lake to accompany the swimmers, a precaution against disaster because of cramp or speedboats. Though I had been shy about arguing political points, I didn't mind opening my mouth and singing to entertain my fellow residents. Hymns, folk songs, Broadway show tunes, anything. As we neared the shore on our return trip, I glanced over my shoulder to navigate. The spirited and indefatigable director, Harriet Barlow, stood on the end of the dock with a look of contentment. She loved the sound of singing over water. Politics is important, but so is singing. I had arrived.

That summer session came at a perfect time in my private life. Earlier that year, my father had died of a brain tumor; also, a devastating schism had developed with one of my oldest, dearest friends. I needed a place to recuperate, and Blue Mountain Center was it—not a holiday, but a haven; not just a haven, but a home.

In the ten years since, I have been back at Blue Mountain a number of times. For a while the Center had winter sessions. Once I resigned from Simmons, my schedule was my own; I could afford to take four to six weeks off every winter in order to write. The friends I have made there—John Copoulos, Jill Medvedow, L-R Berger, Cassandra Medley, Dorothy Semenow, Christopher Sindt, Jessica Dunne, to name only a few—connect me to fields of the arts I would otherwise have no access to. More to the point, though, Blue Mountain reminded me for the first time in years that I *could* continue to gather new friends in. I had begun to behave—without realizing it—as if, blessed with good friends as I was, my dance card was filled.

As a resident last summer, I was walking back through the woods beyond Utowana Lake, and I came across an animal lumbering up the trail toward me. I thought at first it was a dog, and I called out, "Hello!" in a bright, I'm-okay-you're-okay voice. Then I saw that it was a black bear on all fours. It sniffed the air—good thing I wasn't carrying any food, Harriet said later—and it waited. I looked off to the lake, to be submissive, and again said, "Hello," in the same voice, think-

ing that the bear might identify this as my friendly, untroubled chirp. I looked for trees to climb—or should I rush into the lake? I, the lousy swimmer? The bear didn't move forward or backward—not until I said "Hello" again, same tone of voice. Then it backed up a few feet. Every time I said "Hello," it backed away some more, until finally it lumbered off the path and up the slope. When it was out of sight, I heard it crashing in the woods for eight or ten seconds. The noise would stop—I'd say in a carrying voice, "Hello!"—and the bear would start moving off again.

There have been times, out walking past the deer in the overgrown fairway behind the firs, that I have felt a shiver of connection with the whole world—its natural and its metaphoric aspects—such as I have not much felt since Jack Turner died. I am less and less inclined to put such notions into words, not even in my journal. It is enough that, now and then, one feels at home in one's place on the planet. Hello, indeed.

*

In 1987 Lothrop issued a book published for teachers and librarians called *Innocence and Experience: Essays and Conversations on Children's Literature*. I coedited it with my then-Simmons and now-CLNE colleague, Barbara Harrison; it is a massive compendium of talks on children's books and related subjects, given while Barbara was director and I was associate or acting director of the Center at Simmons College. I have done some teaching at Lesley College and Emmanuel College, and worked with teacher training through the Foundation for Children's Books, which I helped found—but my energies are always at their strongest when I get back to writing.

As a novelist I was feeling bolder and experimented more. Partly as a result of my growing interest in nuclear disarmament, I tried my hand at a science-fiction novel for teenagers called *I Feel Like the Morning Star*. This was published by Harper in 1989. *I Feel Like the Morning Star* concerns a colony of post-nuclear-holocaust survivors trapped in their underground city. During my initial residency at Blue Mountain Center, I set for myself the task of writing a sequel, which I wanted to call *The Guy at the Top of the World*. It represented my first return to the Adirondacks as a locale since 1981's *Lights on the Lake*, and I had high hopes for it.

Alas, it never came to find its way into print; several New York editors found it too bleak a story, too dark a moral. I consoled myself by deducing that the Reagan tag phrase "It's morning in America" had made books about political corruption and moral ambiguity unpopular. In the Reagan years, whatever else you might think about them, Right was Right and Wrong was Somebody Else, not Us.

However, while working on *The Guy at the Top of the World,* I found myself one evening unable to sleep. After tossing and turning, I got up and scribbled down at one sitting the text for a picture book called *Lucas Fishbone* (Harper). I had never written a picture book before, and to date have only managed one other (*The Peace-and-Quiet Diner,* Parents Magazine Press), but *Lucas Fishbone* was a gift outright. I had jotted down the odd name in my journal several years earlier, but hadn't been able to make anything of it until this insomniacal midnight. By asking myself the question at the top of the page: "Who is Lucas Fishbone?"—I finally prompted the internal muse to answer. I'm not all that happy with the production of *Lucas Fishbone* as a book (nor were the critics, by and large). Though I admire the artwork of Frank Gargiulo, in the end I'm not sure it's right for the story. The text was poetic and open; the pictures ought to have been concrete and specific. As it is, there's not enough to hang onto.

The book is a meditation on time and change, following the relationship of a grandchild and a grandmother through the last year of the grandmother's life. Children ask me, sometimes with glee and sometimes with irritation: "But who *is* Lucas Fishbone?" I don't want to say outright, for, outright, I don't know. Lucas Fishbone appears to be a lion, though, who derives partly from an image of Walt Whitman with his wonderful shaggy beard and glowing, loving eyes, and partly—perhaps—from the warmer of the images of Asian in the Narnia books.

But Lucas Fishbone is also our guardian angel, our dead parent, our long-lost lover, our estranged best friend: come back, reunited at last.

*

Once in 1988—we still lived in Cambridge—Rafique showed up at Logan Airport at 11:30 P.M., to pick me up from a ten-day speaking trip in L.A. I was instantly

suspicious; we had a habit of making our own ways home, on the T or in a taxi. Door-to-door delivery service, given Boston's lousy traffic, was beyond any call of duty. "What's up?" I said. I knew I was getting this first-class escort service for something.

It seemed we had some household guests. They were immigrants from Iran, and because Rafique had known their parents when he did his doctoral research in the late 1970s in a mountain village, the little family of three had shown up on our doorstep one spring evening. "For how long?" I said.

"They're very good people," he answered. "You'll like them."

I met them the next morning when I bustled into the kitchen to make my coffee. Abbas and Parvin Mirshahi were the young parents, dark-haired, solemn, brewing tea. The little one, Razi, was six: a small perky bundle with permanently arching eyebrows and a worried look. "We made you tea," he said. His English was better than his parents'.

"I like coffee," I said.

"I like our home," he answered. "I like you. Do you want to see where we sleep? I can say our phone number: 864-6094. Let's watch TV."

"We have a rule in this house, Razi," I shot out, the stillborn parent in me emerging instinctively. "No TV during mealtimes."

He caught himself in midlunge and twirled—yes, like a dervish, arms outstretched—and said, "Okay, Uncle Gregory."

My jaw dropped, and I was hooked. In one moment, Razi installed himself as a new nephew, joining the ranks that also include Stephen, Peter, and Anne-Marie MacDonell, and numerous Maguire nephews and nieces named Daniel, Justin, Matthew, Rob, Patrick, and Elizabeth. I *love* all my nephews and nieces. I didn't feel the need for an honorary nephew. But Razi didn't know that. As the son of immigrant parents, he had spent most of his young life on the go, moving from Iran to Germany to Texas to Boston. He was

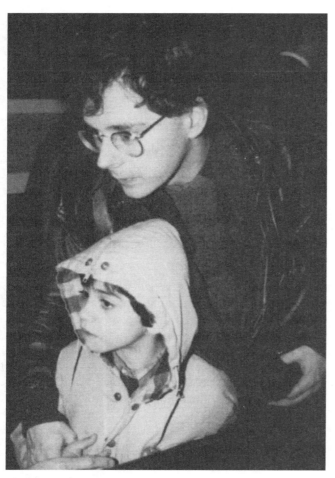

With Razi Mirshahi, Cambridge, Massachusetts, 1989

gifted at making instant family of the closest friendly adult. He did not stint with his affection, and suddenly there was room for Razi and his parents in my life—and I couldn't believe that I had managed *without* knowing them for so long.

Now Razi has a younger sister, a feisty, adorable little thing named Matin. Readers of my novel called *Oasis* (Clarion) will see a portrait of the young Razi in the figure of Vuffy Ziba.

*

Another New Year's memory occurs to me as I think of Razi and Matin—but it's a memory of New Year's Day, not New Year's Eve.

Rafique and I were flying to Florida to visit his niece. The plane had several stops to make, and in Philadelphia we picked up a grumpy-looking family who

plopped themselves into seats across the aisle and a few rows ahead of us. Maybe the parents were suffering from too much New Year's Eve celebrating, or maybe they were sick—or maybe they just weren't good parents. The mother kept her head turned to the window and held an infant loosely, almost dismissively. The father carried on his lap a whining, restless daughter of about two, who squirmed and complained and wouldn't settle down. I watched for a while. The father set the girl down between his knees, where she wailed; then he picked her up and stood her on his lap, where she wailed. He went through this again and again, and the girl only fussed louder. "He's not paying attention to what she needs," I muttered to Rafique, who couldn't see as well as I, and anyway was deep in his book. The girl's head twisted around several times. She was panicking for something that she wasn't getting. Her eye caught mine, and though by now she was screaming, and annoying all the passengers, I smiled at her and waved. She kept flinging herself about, tantrum-struck, but when her head swiveled and she happened to look my way again, again I smiled and waved, as if I found her entrancing despite her noisy behavior.

She immediately raised her hands up over her head, the universal signal of toddlers that they want to be picked up. Before I could stop myself, I was out of my seat and saying to the father, "Shall I take her for a little walk? Give you a rest?" and reaching down to get her. The father was shocked at my boldness, and so was I, but in midair I obviously wasn't about to kidnap his child, and he was too bleary with annoyance to resist. The little girl clasped onto my sweater like a barnacle and sobbed. I began to stroll up and down the aisle, rubbing her back and singing to her, and her screams stopped within ninety seconds. In another couple of minutes she was asleep, but she was a fretful child. She kept waking up with a start and an urge to wail, and only settled down again when I rubbed her back and sang.

What is this story for? When we landed in Gainesville and I handed the girl back to her parents, the other passengers on the flight thanked me. Someone joked that they should pass the hat for me. The girl began to scream again in the arms of her father, who was probably not such a bad guy—just inattentive, maybe exhausted, maybe unsympathetic to babies. I tried to keep out of her sight, but at the luggage carousel the girl saw me again, and reached out for me, this time wailing for me to come get her. I said to Rafique as we left the airport, "If that father had said, 'Look, here, take this girl, we don't want her,' I would have happily bundled her under my arm and given her a home."

The folksinger named Bob Franke has a song that talks about "the hole in the middle of the prettiest life." My life is pretty good, but sometimes there is a hole in it about the size of a child. That hole gets filled by a bunch of wonderful kids, the children of many of the friends I've mentioned here—my own nephews and nieces, Razi and Matin, the Pabalan kids, the Mock kids, the Miller-Downey kids, the Terris kids, Conor Clarke McCarthy. I'm surrounded by a tribe of great masterpieces of childhood in their prime. But when my toothsome young friends are absent, the hole is there. I notice it at some times more than others. I think that's one of the reasons I spend so many weeks every year traveling around to classrooms as a visiting author or as a teacher of creative writing. Kids are a natural resource; I need them as I need light and air and laughter.

*

For a brief time Rafique and I lived in Jamaica Plain in Boston, where we had bought a turn-of-the-century house with skylights, exposed brick, and a bad problem of dog smell from the neighbor's yard next door. But in 1990 Rafique was offered a good job in London, and with the blessings of my colleagues at CLNE, I decided to spend the larger part of every year in London too. We rented out the Jamaica Plain house, grateful that our dear friend Betty Levin invited me to stay at her farm whenever I needed to return to Boston for speaking, teaching, or CLNE work. With the disappointing response to *Lucas Fishbone,* my career felt stalled; I wrote several novels in a row that I couldn't interest any of my regular editors in. Having just graduated with my doctorate—and having no inclination at the time to go back to college teaching—I put my library in storage and took a deep breath, and left the United States.

Renting—and then purchasing—a flat in central London was an education in fiscal management, and I found myself learning to live without a car, without constant phone conversation with old friends and family. I missed the geography of New York and New England; I missed the informal, unplanned exchanges with friends and family. I missed the chance to help Razi become a better reader. On the other hand, I felt as if I did need a shake-up in my life. By the time I moved to London, I had been writing children's books for twelve years. The critical response had been warm, except for *Lucas Fishbone,* but I had the sense of treading water. Living abroad, it seemed, might teach me more about what it meant to be an American, or maybe about being an adult.

Though I have always loved to travel, living abroad could have been a dismal undertaking. Rafique was busy at his job, and as a freelance writer I had no professional circle to speak of. However, my time was made richer by the warmth and friendship of the English novelists John Rowe Townsend and Jill Paton Walsh. I had known John and Jill through Simmons, and we all served together on the Board of Directors of CLNE. Up until the time I moved to England, however, I had only considered John and Jill as colleagues and august eminences in the field. John's ground-breaking work *Written for Children,* a history of children's literature, was my constant companion through all my graduate work, while Jill's brilliant novels, like *Unleaving* and *A Chance Child,* had joined that small group of titles that, in an alternative universe, I would most like to be able to claim as having written myself.

From the start John and Jill welcomed us into their social circle in Cambridge and in London. They served up a real American Thanksgiving, with turkey and homemade pumpkin pie and all the trimmings. With Rafique joining us when he could, John and Jill and I made several motoring trips across England. (I confess to the affectation of calling them motoring trips instead of car journeys, but with erudite and irrepressible polymaths like John Rowe Townsend and Jill Paton Walsh, the term car journey just doesn't carry enough literary *oomph.*) We spent weekends in Devon with Tony and Barbara Watkins; we traipsed around the Lake District in weather both foul and fair. John and Jill set for me a new standard of hospitality.

Rafique and I lived on the edge of Hampstead, which for its tree-lined streets and brick homes—and for the famous Heath—attracted other expat Americans. Though we had English friends as well, we were delighted when a social group began to coalesce in our neighborhood. With Ann and Sid Seamans, Bob

Piller and Beatrice von Mach, and Susan Mashkes, we came to feel we had rooted ourselves pretty successfully. We all laughed at *Absolutely Fabulous* long before it made it to the Comedy Channel in America. We wrangled over the relative merits of the *Independent* and the *Times,* of BBC One and Channel Four. We argued incessantly about the royal family. We found transplanted elements of American culture appealing, too, things we wouldn't have spent the time on if we'd been back in Boston—like *Twin Peaks;* and the presidential debates featuring Bush, Clinton, and Perot; and the Olympic figure-skating soap opera starring Tonya Harding and Nancy Kerrigan. We craved Reese's peanut-butter cups and American cheeseburgers, and pigged out instead on fish and chips and full-cream teas.

And then, as Rafique had predicted, many of our friends and family visited us, too. Debbie Kirsch and I zipped around Wales, playing Merlin and Guinevere in a rented Austin mini. With Mark Miller, in whose warm family circle I am so pleased to be welcomed, I trudged in the great stone circle at Avebury, lugging the great stone weight of baby Maeve or toddler Kate. I got to the Continent, too. Maureen Vecchione and I zipped over to spend a Thanksgiving in Paris, sipping pumpkin soup at Charles De Gaulle International Airport. Margy O'Brien and I met for lunch in the shadow of Notre Dame, and then strolled up and down the Champs-Elysées, singing snatches of the Joni Mitchell song about just such a carefree afternoon.

Living in England, there were inevitable reminders of my childhood reading, since England has produced so many of the great fantasists. When Roger Mock visited, we had lunch at the Eagle and Child pub in Oxford, the place where C. S. Lewis and J. R. R. Tolkien and the other Inklings had met and shared their fantastic writing. Even more thrilling, in one of my inaugural trips, John Townsend and Jill Paton Walsh brought me to visit their good friend, the elderly novelist Lucy Boston, who had written *The Children of Green Knowe* that I quoted from earlier. I had spent so many days in childhood looking for magic places, and here I was entering the building in England that the author had used as the inspiration for Green Knowe—the Manor House at Hemingford Grey, Cambridgeshire. I walked into that very hall, wondering which was myself—the young man visiting a venerable writer whose work he had loved—or the seven-year-old novice reader walking through the text into the hallway

described in the book—or maybe I was Tolly, the child protagonist, all over again? The three mirrors hung in the hall just as in the description I'd read as a child, twenty-five years earlier.

*

During the Gulf War crisis, Rafique and I were in Kenya visiting his parents. To show how my journal writing has changed from when I was twelve years old, here's an entry from February, 1991. It refers to an overnight train journey from Mombasa to Nairobi.

> Perhaps 2:30 . . . I hear the sounds in my sleep of people running and screaming, thudding and banging along the corridor—it is a narrow gauge railway—but I don't wake up until I hear from Cabin E next door the unmistakable calm, insistent tones of a mother waking her children from their sleep because something is terribly wrong. And so I wake up, fully, and say, "Rafique, Rafique, get up, something's wrong." There is more shouting and running outside. I think first of sabotage: a bomb, explosives, a terrorist attack—but on a train. There are British soldiers on the train too, coming back from exercises on the coast—we saw all those laughing young men leaning out the windows when we came down the platform to find our reserved compartment. But Kenya is just as much Muslim as it is Christian. A Gulf War incident? I am scrambling into my shorts. I think: fire—the car is on fire. Rafique says, "Don't open the door—" Is the corridor filled with smoke and flames? We are still rollicking along the rails. Rafique says, "Quick, climb up on the top bunk, quick." I don't yet think to feel the metal door to see if it's hot. From the top bunk I can push the screen down—can we jump safely from the top half of a broad sashed window? Can we roll away from the train? Are we passing through game park, will we be safe? The children in the next compartment are chattering excitedly, and the mother is still being calm and steely; it is all in German or Dutch but there is no mistaking the presence of danger. It is dawning on me that the sound of men's voices are raised in anger, not fear. I remember the scene from the end of *The Jewel in the Crown,* where a train is ambushed and

The Maguire family: Gregory in front, with (from left) John, Matthew, Rachel Maguire MacDonell, Anne, Marie McAuliff Maguire, Michael, and Joseph, Albany, New York, 1995

the male passengers executed. Rafique [who was raised in Kenya] later tells me he is envisioning a band of brigands systematically breaking into each compartment; he has thought to drag the ladder onto the top bunk with us, so we could fight if we had to from there. But the noise lulls suddenly, and I think it will be easier to jump from the doorway at the end of the car than the window; you can spring with your legs away more easily. By now we have grabbed shirts as well, and sandals. Rafique unbolts the door and slides it open, looks out, right, left, moves out. I grab our satchels with money, documents, and my journal and writing, and follow him. There is a crowd of men at the end of the car, including several stocky Germans in jockey shorts. Are they jumping? Footsteps pound behind us; two uniformed attendants running. To allow them passage we step into the open

doorway of another compartment. A woman in her thirties is there, in underpants and a T-shirt, weeping. Rafique pushes ahead again and rounds the corner toward the door at the end of the car, looks out and down, then pushes back. "Go back," he says, "go back," and I don't see. But once in the compartment, our door closed and bolted again, he says, "It was a thief. They were beating him."

My journal entry continues in another direction, but I recall that once Rafique had informed me of the circumstances, we agreed he should return to the end of the car and try to convince the irate travelers—some of whom were drunk—to leave law enforcement to the railway officials. Rafique can speak English, Swahili, and a smattering of German, and he is a man of moral conviction, possessed of a persuasive voice. I lay in my bunk, reviewing the drama. I sang to myself to still the pounding of my chest: "Be brave, my heart; my heart, be bold."

It wasn't the first time I have sung to summon courage, and it won't be the last. A few years earlier I had gone to Nicaragua with my friend Maureen Casey, as a member of a Witness for Peace delegation. Our itinerary took us into the mountain village of Quilalí, in a zone that Sandinistas and contras were both working to control. We were told that the road might be mined; indeed, the day we arrived from Miami, for the first time in the civil war, a peace delegate from another country had been shot. Seeing signs of hardship and terrorism all around, we sang—"Hello, Dolly?" and "Dona Nobis Pacem" were our favorite numbers.

One night, when the power was cut, we were warned to expect an attack by the contras. There was no protection, no way out. The children of my host came under my arms like chicks, and I sang "Old Mac-Donald" to them, translating into Spanish as best I could. Not knowing what was coming, and only "Old MacDonald" to hold us steady in the dark. In a way, I was more terrified than ever before in my life, yet since I did not approve of the Reagan administration's policies in Central America, I was glad to be there. Singing is important—but so is politics.

*

In the years in which we lived in London, the economy was suffering the severe depression of the early nineties. My British agent, Gina Pollinger, worked hard on my behalf, but I seemed incapable of landing a contract with a British publisher for my children's books. I had turned my hand to realistic fiction for children and young adults—emboldened, perhaps, by the success of *I Feel Like the Morning Star*—and after several years of slogging I placed a children's novel with an American publisher. *Missing Sisters* (Margaret K. McElderry) is about a pair of twins who, though separated at birth, find each other halfway through the novel and struggle to resolve the dilemma that one is adopted and the other is still in an orphanage.

Missing Sisters is, in many ways, my favorite of my children's novels. For the first time I was eschewing any fantasy overtone and relying on my memories of growing up Irish Catholic in the Albany area in the 1960s. Alice Colossus, the main character, is well meaning, a bit dense, intends to be as holy as she can, but at the same time yearns to make connections with people in her world: her beloved friend, Sister Vincent de Paul, her newly found twin, Miami Shaw, and a pair of prospective parents who just might adopt her. In a sense, I managed to capture one of the great mysteries of life—to me—in two sentences toward the end of the book. Alice is getting ready to leave the orphanage, and in response to what she thinks is a platitudinous remark by the Mother Superior—that the sisters love her and always will—Alice comments, "'How can you love all of us? There's so many.' 'It's a miracle,' said Sister John Bosco. 'The heart has infinite room inside it.'"

That's as good a summary as any of what my childhood experiences and these twenty years of adult life have taught me so far. You think you have gone as far as you can go; sometimes you feel exhausted at the work of living, perceiving, connecting, being responsible, being reliable, being resilient. But there is always room for another person, especially one who needs you. It is one of the central miracles. I keep learning it again and again.

*

When I finished *The Guy at the Top of the World*—that book I couldn't sell—I dedicated it to Rafique with this quote freely paraphrased from the Persian poet Hafiz: "My head has no protection than your portal, my body no rest but at your threshold." The story of Alice Colossus looking for a home—a portal, a threshold, a context—has echoes of my looking for a family from the Saint Catherine Infant Home. One definition of home is the place you can be most yourself, and so for some years my home has been with Rafique.

Late in 1994, we returned to Massachusetts. We bought a house in Concord, from which I write this memoir. We live only a mile or two from 40 Walden Street, memorialized in Jane Langton's books and known among aficionados as the Diamond in the Window house—as inspiring a literary site to me as Louisa May Alcott's Orchard House or the Old Manse of Hawthorne. Private lives can still be festooned with loops of significance—hinges of fate, as Winston

The author with Rafique Keshavjee and Marie

Churchill called them. I didn't imagine as a child that I'd live in Concord one day. I have come to trust in the circularity of experience, the building up of references, echoes, reverberations of the past in the present. Of the future, who can say: the pathways ahead from now are no clearer than they've ever been. But we get more used to that as we get older.

My narrative has almost reached the present day. Not all significant events can be narrated as stories—but here are a few notable moments of the past year or two.

In 1994 I was an artist-in-residence at the Isabella Stewart Gardner Museum in Boston, a mock-Venetian palazzo built in the Boston fens and stuffed to the ceiling with early Italian paintings, plants, music, statuary, and artifacts—a frothy overload of high culture all crammed into one setting, part surrealist dream, part art warehouse. Talk about magic places! For a month I slept in a flat over the greenhouses and had dreams art-directed by the Renaissance.

Recently I have also embarked on a series of comic novels for children—broad farces, you might call them. *Seven Spiders Spinning* (Clarion) is the inaugural volume. In a small town called Hamlet, Vermont, seven Siberian snow spiders defrost out of a glacier and imprint themselves most amorously on seven schoolgirls in an after-school club. The girls don't know they are being stalked by the lovesick arachnids until a spider manages to take a big luscious bite out of the neck of their teacher—and then pandemonium breaks loose. The book is to be followed by a ghost story tentatively named *Six Haunted Hairdos*. There are others in the series—I call them the Hamlet Chronicles—waiting to be written.

Though to date it has found no American publisher, a book set in France during World War II, *The Good Liar,* was published in Ireland by O'Brien Press. I like to think that my dad would have been pleased about my having an Irish publisher. I was tickled that both German and French prospective publishers found the novel realistic enough to ask probing questions about where I was during the war, was I from a German or French family, how did I know what I knew? *Careful research* was the only answer I could give, since the war in Europe ended ten years before I was born.

On another front, and following a stint doing volunteer work at an AIDS ward, I was asked to contribute a story to the groundbreaking anthology called *Am I Blue? Coming Out from the Silence*—original fiction about children growing up gay and lesbian. The critical success of the book showed that there is a gap that needs to be filled, more work that needs to be done. All children need a climate of tolerance and security in order to thrive. I credit a good deal of my adult happiness to growing up in such a climate—a climate largely created by my parents, but maintained by my loving brothers and sisters, too.

In the year before Rafique and I returned from London, I threw myself into a new endeavor. After eight months of feverish composition, I finished a draft of my first novel for adults, called *Wicked: The Life and Times of the Wicked Witch of the West*. Once the book was signed up with a new HarperCollins imprint—Reganbooks, directed by Judith Regan—I set about revising *Wicked,* relying on the careful reading and good advice of friends like Betty Levin and Rafique. *Wicked* can sound like a campy send-up of the lovable MGM film—and it is partly meant to be just that—but *Wicked* is also a serious fantasy in the tradition, I hope, of T. H. White and J. R. R. Tolkien. Living in England gave me a new distance from my American youth, and a different culture with which to understand and assess my own culture—and Oz's. My characterization of Elphaba as the Wicked Witch of the West owes a little bit to my earlier depiction of Baba Yaga, but this time the heroine is writ large and human. She is morally ambiguous, she is brave and foolish, she is crippled, and yet she defies being labeled as merely "the green anomaly" or even "the wicked witch." Coming back to the United States with *Wicked* sold, and a national promotional tour to embark on, I found myself coming full circle once again. Throughout the United States, friends from folk music days at Saint Vincent's, from Simmons days, or from CLNE, or from Blue Mountain sessions all showed up at the readings—as did my loyal and warmhearted family. It was a chance for me to have a national reunion with most of the beloved people in my life.

There are many inside jokes that readers of *Wicked* will enjoy; I'll divulge only one here. If you look at the map printed on the end papers, you'll see an arrow pointing off the top left margin of the page, indicating that travelers heading in that direction would eventually reach Fliaan—the magic country my friends and sister Annie discovered and invented in Westland Hills, Albany, New York.

*

I have been asked to write this autobiographical essay when I am forty-one, which I hope is too early for a definitive picture of my personal history and accomplishments. It is a couple of days after the New Year as I come to the end of this writing exercise, and though I'm not superstitious, I don't want to draw any conclusions about my life. I made my New Year's resolutions; that seems enough thinking about the future for one week.

The snow comes down tonight, fifteen inches they say. Rafique is working on an animation project at the computer in his study. I'm going to put on my big boots and go out in the dark, and shovel the walk, and knock some icicles from the eaves. I'll think about what I've put in here, and how I've said it, and what I've left out, and why. Maybe I'll get another chance, another time, to augment what I've said, or to update the installment. Let's just call this a chapter break, not FINIS. It is, after all, the start of a new year.

POSTSCRIPT

Gregory Maguire contributed the following update to *CA* in 2004:

Some years ago, I concluded the preceding essay by admitting a lack of clairvoyance about the future. I could feel the girders of my domestic situation straining; I could hear mutterings on the horizon, suggesting for the world a stormy patch ahead.

It has been almost ten years since my essay was published, and much has happened in those years. In our global world, the signal catastrophe of the events of September 11, 2001, and the effects on our society and globally, were both unexpected and unsavory. Who can fathom the seismic power of historic moments as they happen? As every year passes, the world seems in more precarious health, politically and ecologically, and yet still more dear. And more dear.

The author with Andy Newman and their children (left to right) Alex, three, Helen, two, and Luke, six, Christmas Day, 2003

I write on a glum afternoon in late May, when the unrelenting clouds of this rainy spring threaten yet more outburst. I live in the same house outside of Boston that I did ten years ago. There are many changes, though.

The house itself is changed—a second floor added, a neat purpose-built study, a library. Extra bedrooms . . . for now there are three children living here. Luke, Alex, and Helen Maguire Newman—ages six, four, and two, at this writing.

The children's other father is the painter Andy Newman. I met Andy at the Blue Mountain Center in New York in September of 1997. A representational painter of landscapes and figures, he exhibits in a dozen galleries in the United States, Canada, and Europe. Neither of us were looking to be attached to someone new, but the fates had another idea. Andy moved permanently to Massachusetts in the spring of 1999, and twenty-eight days later we flew to Phnom Penh to collect our oldest child, Luke, then fifteen months old.

I returned from Cambodia in late 2000 with baby Alex, then eight-and-a-half-months old, and in the spring of 2002, Andy collected Helen from Guatemala. Our family is complete—so far as we know today—but we have learned to expect the unexpected.

The possibility of a family arose in part from the continuing success of my adult novels. Always a decent seller, my novel *Wicked* has become something of a cult favorite. My estimable agent, William Reiss at John Hawkins and Associates, had predicted something of the sort ten years ago. "It won't hit the bestseller lists, not in a way that shows on the radar screens," he had said, "but it's likely to be a steady seller through the years." So it has done, at least in its first decade.

Wicked was optioned by a production company headed by Demi Moore and Suzanne Todd, working in collaboration with Universal Studios. The excitement was significant, but after three or four serious drafts, Universal decided they didn't have a script strong enough to spend one hundred million dollars to film (a literal hundred million, not a figurative "lots"). In Hollywood, even five years ago, there were few if any female stars who could "open" a film with so massive a budget—and *Wicked*'s male roles are secondary ones. The glass ceiling still obtains, or did five years ago.

But other possibilities for *Wicked* were cropping up. The folksinger Holly Near had read the novel and recommended it to her friend, composer/lyricist Stephen Schwartz, whose Broadway work had included *Pippin* and *Godspell,* and whose stint in Hollywood had brought him onto the creative teams for *Pocahontas, The Prince of Egypt,* and *The Hunchback of Notre Dame,* among other films. Stephen Schwartz's lawyers hunted about to find out whether the rights were available for a Broadway musical version. They weren't—then. But Marc Platt, a producer at Universal who had been taken with the story of *Wicked,* saw the dramatic possibilities when Stephen Schwartz mentioned it to him. Therefore, when Universal finally decided not to buy the story outright and the rights reverted to me, I was able to authorize a Broadway musical version as well as, eventually, an ABC television movie or miniseries version, as yet unwritten.

In the summer of 2003, ten years to the day that I began to write *Wicked,* the first paying audiences made their way into San Francisco's Curran Theater for the initial preview. *Wicked*'s music and lyrics are by Stephen Schwartz, its book by Winnie Holzman (author of *My So-Called Life,* among other television scripts), and it is directed by the Tony-Award winning Joe Mantello.

It was, for me, a moment of glee and solemn glory, too. When the dazzling Kristin Chenoweth descended from the flies in an industrially bolted steel bubble, the audience was charmed to see Glinda again and to applaud the more famous of the play's two stars. Kristen glistened and used most of her four octaves in the demanding numbers written expressly for her. However, a few moments later a door at the back of the stage opened, and in stamped Idina Menzel, done up in green makeup as the Wicked Witch of the West, a young woman on her way to college. The roar that greeted her, I thought then, had only something to do with Ms. Menzel as a star from *Rent* and *The Wild Party.* It had as much to do with the audience's appreciation for the witch in my story. The audience had

already signed on to the notion of the Witch as being an acceptable heroine—mostly because of my novel. I can't imagine a writer enjoying a more public approval—all the better because it wasn't I standing on the stage, receiving an award or cashing a royalty check, nor I opening my mouth and singing "The Wizard and I." It was the Witch. They were on her side.

In October, 2003, the play opened to mixed reviews—genuinely mixed. Some were raves, and some were hesitant, dismissive of this part or that, but there was no review that trashed the whole enterprise.

It hardly mattered. The audience took *Wicked* to its heart, and as of this writing—a few days after this year's Tony awards, during which *Wicked* won three, including Idina Menzel's award for best actress in a musical—the production has played to sold out houses for seven months. Like a book, a play will have a life of its own, and now I just sit back and laugh, admiringly and, I admit, incredulously.

Other adult novels have followed. *Confessions of an Ugly Stepsister* inspired an ABC television film starring Stockard Channing and Jonathan Pryce. *Lost,* a contemporary ghost story set in London, catches strands of my life from the early 1990s and entwines them into a story about love, loss, and the hope for children.

The most recent published book is called *Mirror Mirror.* I traveled several times to Tuscany to research the background on a story set in the High Renaissance, featuring Lucrezia Borgia as the poisoning stepmother of my docile heroine, Bianca de Nevada.

My work in Children's Literature New England has continued, and CLNE with the Cambridge Public Library was honored to present the artist Maurice Sendak giving the annual Arbuthnot Lecture. Children's books have also kept coming: I have now concluded the Hamlet Chronicles; *The Final Firecracker* (working title) is being edited this week. Furthermore, I am proud to have several forthcoming children's books: a collection of comic short stories called *Leaping Beauty and Other Animal Fairy Tales* and, down the road a piece, a work-in-progress tentatively titled *Gangster Teeth.*

Gregory Maguire

I would write more, but the boys need to be collected from preschool. The gardeners are sinking delphiniums and impatiens into the soil, to prepare for the wedding that will take place here. Thanks to the so-called activist judges of this great, funny commonwealth of ours, Andy and I will be married at home next month. Many of the people mentioned in the previous essay will be on hand to cheer us on, to hope for the future, to remember the past.

Our children will give us away, and then take us back in time for supper.

BIOGRAPHICAL AND CRITICAL SOURCES:

BOOKS

Twentieth-Century Children's Writers, 3rd edition, St. James Press (New York, NY), 1989.

PERIODICALS

Advocate, October 17, 1995, Peter Galvin, review of *Wicked: The Life and Times of the Wicked Witch of the West,* p. 56; December 25, 2001, Robert Plunket, review of *Lost,* p. 67.

Booklist, March 15, 1994, p. 1342; June 1, 1994, p. 1798; September 15, 1994, Hazel Rochman, review of *Seven Spiders Spinning,* p. 136; September 15, 1996, Debbie Carton, review of *Oasis,* p. 232; April 15, 1999, Carolyn Phelan, review of *The Good Liar,* p. 1530; January 1, 2000, review of *The Good Liar,* p. 822; December 1, 2000, GraceAnne A. DeCandido, review of *Four Stupid Cupids,* p. 706; October 15, 2001, Kristine Huntley, review of *Lost,* p. 383; April 1, 2002, Kay Weisman, review of *Three Rotten Eggs,* p. 1328; September 1, 2003, Hazel Rochman, review of *Mirror Mirror,* p. 57; June 1, 2004, Kay Weisman, review of *Leaping Beauty: and Other Animal Fairy Tales,* p. 1726.

Bulletin of the Center for Children's Literature, July-August, 1980, p. 219; February, 1982, review of *Lights on the Lake;* May, 1989, Roger Sutton, review of *I Feel like the Morning Star,* p. 230; June, 1994, Roger Sutton, review of *Missing Sisters,* pp. 327-328.

Commonweal, April 19, 2002, Daria Donnelly, "Illuminated Manuscripts," p. 22.

Entertainment Weekly, November 17, 1995, Robin J. Schwartz, review of *Wicked,* p. 73; October 24, 2003, Jennifer Reese, "Grimm Reaper," p. 109.

Horn Book, October, 1978, Ethel L. Heins, review of *The Lightning Time,* pp. 517-518; June, 1980, Mary M. Burns, review of *The Daughter of the Moon;* April, 1982, Mary M. Burns, review of *Lights on the Lake,* pp. 167-168; October, 1983, Ethel L. Heins, review of *The Dream Stealer,* pp. 576-577; July-August, 1994, review of *Missing Sisters,* pp. 454-455; July, 1999, review of *The Good Liar,* p. 471; January, 2000, review of *Origins of Story: On Writing for Children,* p. 105.

Kirkus Reviews, July 15, 1978, p. 750; May 1, 1980, p. 585; February 1, 1982, p. 136; March 1, 1989, p. 380; February 15, 1994, p. 229; July 15, 1994, review of *Seven Spiders Spinning,* p. 989; August, 15, 2001, review of *Lost,* p. 1154; March 1, 2002, review of *Three Rotten Eggs,* p. 339; September 5, 2003, review of *Mirror Mirror,* p. 1147; April 1, 2004, review of *A Couple of April Fools,* p. 333.

Library Journal, September 1, 1999, Francisca Goldsmith, review of *Confessions of an Ugly Stepsister,* p. 234; October 1, 2001, Margee Smith, review of *Lost,* p. 141.

Los Angeles Times Book Review, October 29, 1995, p. 4.

New York Times, October 24, 1995, Michiko Kakutani, review of *Wicked,* p. C17.

New York Times Book Review, November 26, 1995, review of *Wicked,* p. 19; December 12, 1999, Gardner McFall, review of *Confessions of an Ugly*

Stepsister, p. 28; December 26, 1999, Malachi Duffy, review of *Wicked,* p. 19.

People Weekly, November 3, 2003, Jason Lynch, "Every Witch Way," p. 133.

Publishers Weekly, June 5, 1978, review of *The Lightning Time,* p. 89; September, 1978, Pam Spencer, review of *I Feel like the Morning Star,* p. 143; September 28, 1990, review of *Lucas Fishbone,* pp. 101-102; August, 1994, review of *Seven Spiders Spinning* p. 80; August 21, 1995, review of *Wicked,* p. 45; October 28, 1996, review of *Oasis,* p. 82; March 22, 1999, review of *The Good Liar,* p. 93; August 16, 1999, review of *Confessions of an Ugly Stepsister,* p. 58; September 10, 2001, review of *Lost,* p. 60; September 15, 2003, review of *Mirror Mirror,* and Ben P. Indick, interview with Gregory Maguire, p. 42; December 1, 2003, review of *Wicked* (audiobook), p. 20.

School Library Journal, September, 1978, p. 143; May, 1980, Marjorie Lewis, review of *The Daughter of the Moon,* p. 69; February, 1984, Helen Gregory, review of *The Dream Stealer,* p. 75; May, 1989, Pam Spencer, review of *I Feel Like the Morning Star,* p. 127; December, 1990, Heide Piehler, review of *Lucas Fishbone,* p. 84; May, 1996, Judy Sokoll, review of *Wicked,* p. 148; November, 1996, Renee Steinberg, review of *Oasis,* p. 108; May, 1999, Linda Greengrass, review of *The Good Liar,* p. 128; October, 2000, Eva Mitnick, review of *Four Stupid Cupids,* p. 164; March, 2002, Connie Tyrrell Burns, review of *Three Rotten Eggs,* p. 234; March, 2004, Susan H. Woodcock, review of *Mirror Mirror,* p. 249.

Storyworks, February-March, 2004, Mark DiBona, review of *Six Haunted Hairdos,* p. 7.

Tribune News Service, December 22, 1999, Brenda Cronin, review of *Confessions of an Ugly Stepsister,* p. K2155.

Voice of Youth Advocates, June, 1989, Jane Beasley, review of *I Feel like the Morning Star,* p. 117; December, 1994, pp. 277-278; April, 1995, p. 24; February, 1997, p. 330.

Wilson Library Bulletin, December, 1989, p. 113; September, 1990, p. 12.

* * *

MANFREDI, Nino 1921-2004

PERSONAL: Full name, Saturnino Manfredi; born March 22, 1921, in Castro del Volsci, Italy; died June 4, 2004; married Erminia Ferrari, 1955; children: two daughters and one son.

CAREER: Actor, director, and screenwriter. Actor in films, including *Monastero de Santa Chiara* (also known as *Napoli ha fatto un sogno*), 1949; (as Francisco) *Torna a Napoli* (also known as *Simme e' Napule, paisà*), 1949; (as Enrico) *Anema e core,* 1951; (as Tonino's friend) *Viva il cinema,* 1952; *Ho scelto l'amore* (also known as *I Chose Love*), 1952; (as Stornello) *La prigionera della torre di fuoco,* 1953; *Canzoni, canzoni, canzoni* (also known as *Carnival of Song*), 1953; (as Lello) *La domenica della buona gente* (also known as *Good Folk's Sunday*), 1953; *C'era una volta Angelo Mosco,* 1953; (as Carla's future brother-in-law) *Lo scapolo* (also known as *Alberto il conquistadore* and *The Bachelor*), 1955; (as Mario Giorgi) *Revelación* (also known as *Prigionieri del male* and *Revelation*), 1955; (as Otello) *Gli innamorati* (also known as *Wild Love*), 1955; (as Gianni's friend) *Toto, Peppino, e . . . la malafemmina* (also known as *Toto, Pepinno, and the Hussy*), 1956; (as Carletto) *Tempo di villeggiatura* (also known as *Time of Vacation*), 1956; (as Paolo) *Guardia, guardia scelta, brigadiere e maresciallo,* 1956; *Susanna tutta panna,* 1957; *Femmine tre volte* (also known as *Female Three Times*), 1957; (as Nino) *Camping,* 1957; *Il bacio del sol,* 1958; (as pilot) *Pezzo, capopezzo e capitano* (also known as *Always Victorious, Cannon Serenade,* and *Il Capitano*), 1958; (as Toni) *Venezia, la luna, e tu* (also known as *Venice, the Moon, and You*), 1958; (as Otello Cucchiaroni) *Guardia, ladro e camera* (also known as *Maid, Thief, and Guard*), 1958; (as Toto Improta) *Carmela è una bambola,* 1958; (as Enea Serafino) *Caporale di giornata,* 1958; (as Mario) *Adorabili e bugiarde* (also known as *Adorable and a Liar*), 1958; *I ragazzi dei parioli* (also known as *Boys of the Parioli*), 1959; (as Nando) *L'impiegato,* 1959; (as Ugo Nardi) *Audace colpo dei soliti ignoti* (also known as *Fiasco in Milan*), 1959, released in the United States by Avion-Trans-Universe/Jerand, 1963; (as voice) *Totò, Fabrizi e i giovani d'oggi,* 1960; (as Dr. Nino Pasqui) *Le Pillole d'ercole* (also known as *Hercules' Pills*), 1960; (as Quirino) *Crimen* (also known as *. . . And Suddenly It's Murder!, Criminals,* and *Killing in Monte Carlo*), 1960, released in the United States by Royal, 1964; (as waiter) *Il giudizio universale* (also known as *The Last Judgement*), 1961; (as Giacinto Rossi) *A cavallo della tigre* (also known as *Jail Break* and *On the Tiger's Back*), 1961; (as Franco Bartolucci) *Il carabiniere a cavallo,* 1961; (as Tomagra) *L'amore difficile* (also known as *Of Wayward Love* and *Sex Can Be Difficult*), 1962, released in the United States by Pathe, 1964; (as Nino Borsetti) *I motorizzati,* 1962; (as Omero Battifiori) *Anni ruggenti* (also known as *Roaring Years*), 1962; (as José Luis Rodriguez) *El Verdugo* (also known as *Not on Your Life*), 1963, released in the United States by Pathe Contemporary, 1965; (as Nino) *La Parmigiana* (also known as *The Girl from Parma*), 1963; (as Quirino) *I cuori infranti*, 1963; (as Stefano Liberati) *Il gaucho* (also known as *The Gaucho*), 1964; (as Francesco) *Alta infedeltà* (also known as *High Infidelity*), 1964, released in the United States by Magna, 1965; (as Andrea and Spadini) *Controsesso* (also known as *Countersex*), 1964; (as Quirino Raganelli) *I complessi* (also known as *Complexes*), 1965; (as Giorgio) *Le bambole* (also known as *The Dolls* and *Four Kinds of Love*), Columbia, 1965; (as Nanni Galassi) *Thrilling*, 1965; (as the industrialist) *Questa volta parliamo di uomini* (also known as *Let's Talk about Men, Now Let's Talk about Men,* and *This Time Let's Talk about Men,* 1965; (as sleeping car attendant) *Io, io, io . . . e gli altri* (also known as *I, I, I . . . and the Others* and *Me, Me, Me . . . and the Others,*) 1965; (as Atilio Lamborecchia) *Made in Italy,* 1965, released in the United States by Royal, 1967; (as Cianfanna) *Io, la conoscevo bene* (also known as *I Knew Her Well*), 1966; (as Franco Finali) *Adulterio all'italiana* (also known as *Adultery Italian Style*), 1966; (as Armandino Girasole) *Operazione San Gennaro* (also known as *Operation San Gennaro* and *Treasure of San Gennaro*), 1966, released in the United States by Paramount, 1968; (as the doctor) *Una rosa per tutti* (also known as *A Rose for Everyone* and *Everyman's Woman*), 1967; (as Marino Balestrini) *Straziami, ma di baci saziami* (also known as *Kill Me with Kisses* and *Torture Me but Kill Me with Kisses*), 1968; (as Marco) *Il padre de famiglia,* Paramount, 1968, released as *The Head of the Family,* Allied Artists, 1970; (as Oresti Sabatini) *Riusciranno i nostri eroi a ritrovare l'amico misteriosamente scomparso in Africa?* (also known as *Will Our Friends Succeed in Finding Their Friend Who Disappeared in Africa?* and *Will Our Heroes Be Able to Find Their Friend Who Has Mysteriously Disappeared in Africa?*), 1968; (as Natalino Tartufato) *Italian Secret Service,* Cineriz, 1968; (as Capopardo) *Vedo nudo,* 1969; (as Benedetto Parisi) *Per grazia ricevuta* (also known as *Between Miracles* and *The Cross-Eyed Saint*), Cineriz, 1970; (as Cornacchia/Pasquino) *Nell'anno del Signore* (also known as *The Conspirators*), 1970; (as Rosolino Paternò) *Rosolinò Paterno—Soldato* (also known as *Operation Sanfu; Situation Normal, All Fouled Up;* and *Situation Normal: A.F.U.*), 1970; (as Beretta) *Contestazione general* (also known as *Let's Have a Riot*), 1970; (as Quintilio Tartamella) *Roma bene,* 1971; (as Carmelo Mazzullo) *Trastevere,* Produzione Europee Associates, 1971; (as Nale) *La betia—ovvero in amore per ogni gaudienzia ci vuole sofferenza* (also known as

In Love, Every Pleasure Has Its Pain), Titanus Distribuzione, 1971; (as Gino Girolimoni) *Girolimoni, il mostro di Roma* (also known as *The Assassin of Rome*), Columbia, 1972; (as Paolo Antonazzi) *Lo chiameremo Andrea* (also known as *We'll Call Him Andrew*), Cinema International/Verona Produzione, 1972; (as Nino Garofalo) *Pane e cioccolata* (also known as *Bread and Chocolate*), CIC/World Northal, 1973; (as Antonio) *C'eravamo tanto amanti* (also known as *We All Loved Each Other So Much*), Almi/Cinema V, 1974; (as Marcello Ferrari) *Attenti al buffone!* (also known as *Eye of the Cat*), Medusa Distribuzione, 1975; *Un sorriso, uno schiaffo, un baccio in bocca,* 1975; *Carosello per la campagna referendaria sul divorzio,* 1975; (as Enzo Lucarelli and Paolo Gallizzi) *Basta che no si sappia in giro!,* 1976; (as Giacinto Mazzatella) *Brutti, sprochi, e cattivi,* (also known as *Down and Dirty* and *Ugly, Dirty, and Bad*), Gold Film, 1976; (as Antonio Pecorari) *Quelle strane occasioni* (also known as *Strange Events* and *Strange Occasion*), Cineriz, 1976; (as Cardinal Caprettari) *Signore e signori, buonanotte* (also know as *Goodnight, Ladies and Gentlemen*), Titanus Distribuzione, 1977; (as Monsignor Colombo) *In nome del papa re* (also known as *In the Name of the Pope King*), Rizzoli, 1977; *Il conte di Monte Cristo,* 1977; *I nuovi mostri* (also known as *The New Monsters* and *Viva Italia!*), Filmverlag der Autoren/Cinema V, 1977; (as Sasà Iovine) *La mazzetta* (also known as *The Payoff*), United Artists, 1978; (as Vittorio Barletta) *Il giocattolo,* 1979; *Il viaggiatori della sera,* 1979; *Insieme,* 1979; (as Michele) *Café Express,* Vides International, 1980; (as Parisi) *Gros câlin* (also known as *Cocco mio*), 1980; (as Sandro) *Nudo di donna* (also known as *Portrait of a Nude Woman* and *Portrait of a Woman, Nude*), Cineriz, 1981; (as Bedouin) *Testa o croce* (also known as *Heads I Win, Tails You Lose* and *Heads or Tails*), CIDIF/SACIS, 1982; (as Domenico) *Spaghetti House,* Titanus Distribuzione, 1982; (as Sandro) *Questo a quello* (also known as *This and That*), CIDIF, 1983; (as Marco Salvietti) *Grandi magazzini* (also known as *Department Store*), Columbia Pictures Italia, 1986; (as Colonel Vinci) *Il tenente dei carabinieri* (also known as *The Lieutenant Carabineer* and *The Police Lieutenant*), Columbia, 1986; (as Stella's father) *Helsinki Napoli All Night Long* (also known as *Helsinki-Naples All Night Long,* 1987; (as beggar) *I picari* (also known as *The Picaros* and *The Rogues*), Warner Bros., 1987; (as Pontius Pilate) *Secondo Ponzio Pilato* (also known as *According to Pontius Pilate*), United International, 1987; (as Alberto's father) *Alberto Express,* 1990; (as Angelo Brunetti detto Ciceruacchio) *In nome del popolo sovrano* (also known as *In the Name of the*

Sovereign People), 1990; (as Grandpa) *Mima,* 1991; (as Campanelli) *De Vliegende Hollander* (also known as *The Flying Dutchman*), 1995; (as Salvatore) *Colpo di luna* (also known as *Moon Shadow*), 1995; (as Pietro) *Grazie di tutto,* Instituto Luce, 1998; *Al ristorante della Sora Lella,* 1999; (as Cardinale) *La carbonara,* 2000; *Una Milanese a Roma,* 2001; and (as Galapago) *La luz prodigiosa* (also known as *Marvelous Light*), 2003.

Director of films, including *L'amore difficile* (also known as *Erotica, Of Wayward Love,* and *Sex Can Be Difficult*), 1962, released in the United States by Pathe, 1964; (and producer; also vocalist and composer) *Per grazia ricevuta* (also known as *Between Miracles* and *The Cross-Eyed Saint*), 1971; and *Nudo di donna* (also known as *Portrait of a Nude Woman* and *Portrait of a Woman, Nude*), Cineriz, 1981. Also provided vocals for the film *A cavallo della tigre* (also known as *Jail Break* and *On the Tiger's Back*), 1961.

Actor in television miniseries, including (as Gepetto) *Le avventure di Pinocchio* (also known as *Pinocchio*), 1972; and (as Cardinal Fonseca) *Dio ci ha creato gratis,* 1998. Played Nino Fogliani in the series *Linda e il brigadiere,* 1997. Actor in made-for-television movies, including (as Endre the Second) *Julianus barát, Julianus barát II,* and *Julianus barát 3,* all 1991; *Specchio d'acqua,* 1992; (as Michele) *Una storia qualunque,* 2000; (as Antonio) *Mieux vaut tard que jamais* (also known as *Meglio tardi che mai*), 2001; (as Francesco Gammarota) *Un difetto di famiglia,* 2002; (as Sor Peppe) *Chiaroscuro,* 2003; (as Pasquino) *La notte di Pasquino,* 2003; and (as Padre Roberto) *Un posto tranquillo,* 2003.

WRITINGS:

SCREENPLAYS

(With others) *Le pillole d'ercole* (also known as *Hercules' Pills*), Dino de Laurentiis, 1960.
(With Dino Risi, Adriano Caracco, and Ennio De Concini) *Operazione San Gennaro* (also known as *Operation San Gennaro* and *Treasure of San Gennaro*), 1966, released in the United States by Paramount, 1968.
(With Eduardo Borras, Ennio De Concini, and Franco Rossi) *Una rosa per tutti* (also known as *Everyman's Woman* and *A Rose for Everyone*), Royal, 1967.

(With Leonardo Benvenuti and Piero de Bernardi) *Per grazia ricevuta* (also known as *Between Miracles* and *The Cross-Eyed Saint*), Cineriz, 1970.
(With others) *La betia—Ovvero in amore per ogni gaudienzia ci vuole sofferenza* (also known as *In Love, Every Pleasure Has Its Pain*), Titanus Distribuzione, 1971.
(With Franco Brusati and Iaia Fiastri) *Pane e cioccolata* (also known as *Bread and Chcolate*), CIC/World Northal, 1973.
(With others) *Attenti al buffone!* (also known as *Eye of the Cat*), Medusa Distribuzione, 1975.
(With Nanni Loy and Elvio Porta) *Cafe Express,* Vides International, 1980.
(With Agenore Incrocci, Ruggero Maccari, and Furio Scarpelli) *Nudo di donna* (also known as *Portrait of a Nude Woman* and *Portrait of a Woman, Nude*), Cineriz, 1981.
(With Nanni Loy, Franco Ferrini, Enrico Oldoini, and Renato Pozzetto) *Testa or croce* (also known as *Heads or Tails* and *Heads I Win, Tails You Lose*), CIDIFSACIS, 1982.
(With Agenore Incrocci, Furio Scarpelli, Peter Barnes, and Giulio Paradisi) *Spaghetti House,* Titanus Distribuzione, 1982.
(With Bernardino Zapponi and others) *Quest e quello* (also known as *This and That*), CIDIF, 1983.

Also author of (with others) *Camping,* 1957, *L'impiegato,* 1959, (with others) *I cuori infranti,* 1963, and *Il giocattolo,* 1979. Author, with Fabio Carpi, Giuseppe Orlandini, and Ettore Scola, of the episode "L'avventura di un soldato," from the film *L'amore difficile* (also known as *Erotica, Of Wayward Love,* and *Sex Can Be Difficult*), 1962, released in the United States by Pathe, 1964.

OTHER

(With Aldo Bernardini) *Nino Manfredi,* introduction by Oreste Del Buono, Gremese (Rome, Italy), 1979.
(Editor) *Proverbi e altre cose romanesche,* Musumeci (Quart, Aosta, Italy), 1983.
La vera alimentazione mediterranea, Musumeci (Quart, Aosta, Italy), 1985.
Viva gli sposi: appunti di vita coniugale, Biblioteca universale Rizzoli (Milan, Italy), 1986.
(With Antonio Cocchia) *Nudo d'attore* (autobiography), Mondadori (Milan, Italy), 1993.

BIOGRAPHICAL AND CRITICAL SOURCES:

BOOKS

Bernardini, Aldo, and Nino Manfredi, *Nino Manfredi,* introduction by Oreste Del Buono, Gremese (Rome, Italy), 1979.

Contemporary Theatre, Film and Television, Volume 35, Gale (Detroit, MI), 2001.

Katz, Ephraim, *The Film Encyclopedia,* Crowell (New York, NY), 1979.

Smith, John M., and Tim Cawkwell, *The World Encyclopedia of Film,* A. & W. Visual Library (New York, NY), 1972.

Stewart, John, *Italian Film,* McFarland (Jefferson, NC), 1994.

PERIODICALS

American Film, April, 1983, review of *Portrait of a Woman, Nude,* p. 78.

Library Journal, June 15, 1989, Randy Pitman, review of *Down and Dirty,* p. 92.

New Republic, May 30, 1981, Stanley Kauffmann, review of *Cafe Express,* p. 22; July 4, 1981, Stanley Kauffmann, review of *Cafe Express,* p. 26.

New York, May 11, 1981, David Denby, review of *Cafe Express,* p. 67.

New York Times, May 13, 1983, Chris Chase, "Nino Manfredi Objects to Pants for Michelangelo," pp. 20, C10; July 8, 1983, Sheila Benson, review of *Nudo di donna,* p. 11; May 16, 1986, Nina Darnton, review of *In nome del Papa Re,* pp. 16, C5; May 13, 1989, Janet Maslin, review of *Nudo di donna,* p. 20; December 1, 2000, A. O. Scott, review of *Moon Shadow,* pp. B24, E25.

People, May 30, 1983, review of *Portrait of a Woman, Nude,* p. 13.

San Francisco Chronicle, June 9, 2000, Peter Stack, review of *Moon Shadow,* p. C3.

Star-Ledger (Newark, NJ), December 1, 2000, Stephen Whitty, review of *Moon Shadow,* p. 39.

Variety, September 10, 1980, review of *Cafe Express,* p. 32; April 29, 1981, review of *Cafe Express,* p. 32; November 25, 1981, review of *Nudo di donna,* p. 22; December 2, 1981, review of *Spaghetti House,* pp. 14-15; March 6, 2000, Deborah Young, review of *La carbonara,* p. 25.

ONLINE

Internet Movie Database, http://www.imdb.com/ (April 16, 2003), "Nino Manfredi."*

*   *   *

MANZONI, Jean-François

PERSONAL: Male. First name also cited as Jean-Francois. *Education:* McGill University, M.B.A.; Harvard University, D.B.A.

ADDRESSES: Office—INSEAD, Blvd. de Constance, 77305 Fontainebleau, France. *E-mail*—jean-francois. manzoni@insead.edu.

CAREER: Ernst & Young, worked as auditor and consultant; École des Hautes Études Commerciales de Montréal, Montreal, Quebec, Canada, former faculty member; INSEAD (also known as European Institute of Business Administration), Fontainebleau, France, began as visiting professor, became associate professor of management and director of Research Initiative on High Performance Organizations.

AWARDS, HONORS: Case of the Year Awards, change management and public sector management categories, European Foundation for Management Development, 1998.

WRITINGS:

(With Soumitra Dutta) *Process Re-engineering, Organizational Change, and Performance Improvement,* McGraw-Hill (New York, NY), 1999.

(Editor, with Marc J. Epstein) *Performance Measurement and Management Control: A Compendium of Research,* JAI Press (London, England), 2002.

(With Jean-Louis Barsoux) *The Set-up-to Fail Syndrome: How Good Managers Cause Great People to Fail,* Harvard Business School Press (Boston, MA), 2002.

Contributor to periodicals, including *Harvard Business Review.*

BIOGRAPHICAL AND CRITICAL SOURCES:

PERIODICALS

HR, October, 2002, Mike Frost, review of *The Set-up-to Fail Syndrome: How Good Managers Cause Great People to Fail,* p. 137.

Pay for Performance Report, November, 2002, "Make Performance Feedback Easier to Give—and to Take," p. 1.

Publishers Weekly, July 29, 2002, review of *The Set-up-to-Fail Syndrome,* pp. 62-63.

ONLINE

Business 2.0, http://www.business2.com/ (November, 2002), Ian Mount, review of *The Set-up-to Fail Syndrome: How Good Managers Cause Great People to Fail.*

INSEAD Web site, http://www.insead.edu/ (December 5, 2002), "Faculty Profile: Jean-François Manzoni."

Workopolis.com, http://www.workopolis.com/ (September 19, 2002), interview by David Creelman.*

*　　*　　*

MAOR, Eli 1937-

PERSONAL: Born October 4, 1937. *Education:* Israel Institute of Technology, Ph.D. (mathematics), 1969.

ADDRESSES: E-mail—emaor@math.luc.edu.

CAREER: Has taught mathematics at Ben Gurion University, Israel, at the University of Wisconsin—Eau Claire, and at Oakland University in Michigan; Oakton Community College, Des Plaines, IL, adjunct professor, 1990—; Loyola University of Chicago, Chicago, IL, professor of mathematics, 1995—.

AWARDS, HONORS: National Council of Teachers of Mathematics Award, 1980, for article "What Is There So Mathematical about Music?"

WRITINGS:

To Infinity and Beyond: A Cultural History of the Infinite, Birkhäuser (Boston, MA), 1987.

e: The Story of a Number, Princeton University Press (Princeton, NJ), 1994.

Trigonometric Delights, Princeton University Press (Princeton, NJ), 1998.

June 8, 2004: Venus in Transit, Princeton University Press (Princeton, NJ), 2000, expanded edition published as *Venus in Transit,* 2004.

The Facts on File Calculus Handbook, Facts on File (New York, NY), 2003.

Consulting editor and contributor, *Encyclopedia Britannica.* Contributor of articles to *Orion* and *Sky & Telescope.*

SIDELIGHTS: A longtime mathematician, Eli Maor has taught college mathematics in Israel and the United States and has done much to bring the complexities of higher mathematics to a popular audience through his writings. By incorporating the history of mathematics into his lectures and books, Maor conveys the revolutionary impact of mathematical discoveries that otherwise might seem commonplace or dull to non-mathematicians. As Melissa Houck put it in the *Mathematical Intelligencer,* "Maor is one of a small handful of mathematical authors who create a satisfying blend of historical anecdote and mathematical information that appeals to amateur and expert alike."

In 1987 he published *To Infinity and Beyond: A Cultural History of the Infinite,* which traces this curious concept from the ancient Greeks up through present speculations. As an example of the way infinity upends normal mathematical concepts, Maor retells Zeno's paradox, which showed that since a rock falling to ground must always fall half the distance, and then half of half the distance, and then half of *that* distance, and so on, it would theoretically never reach the ground. As Michael Guillen explained in *Sciences,* Maor sees this paradox as "a reflection of the Greeks' 'horror infiniti,' their deeply rooted suspicion of the infinite.' He then recounts Western man's long struggle to grasp the infinite, from the classical era through the Renaissance and up to selected mathematical breakthroughs of the past two centuries—breakthroughs that, according to Maor, 'finally demystified infinity and put it on a firm basis.'" While noting Maor's wide range in exploring infinity's impact on science, philosophy, and art, Guillen and some other reviewers faulted him for what they felt was a lack of coherence. *New York Times* reviewer B. G. Yovovich, for one, found that "the book provides little more than a series of standard presentations of mathematical ideas and fails to integrate those ideas into the cultural history promised in the subtitle."

Maor turned to another mathematical oddity in *e: The Story of a Number*. Long eclipsed by pi in the world of abstract numbers, e is a number that actually represents a vital part of calculus, and its importance crops up in such practical areas as compound interest, as Maor reveals. As usual, his goal is to move beyond the cloisters of higher mathematics. "In the number e, Maor has found a unifying theme for some of the most exciting history of calculus," commented *Times* reviewer Ulrike Tillmann. "Yet his book should be accessible to anyone with a basic knowledge of mathematics." As usual for Maor, there is a good deal of history and personality in the book, including the story of eccentric Scottish mathematician John Napier's near miss in discovering e, and the bitter priority dispute between Leibniz and Isaac Newton over who really invented calculus. A *Kirkus Reviews* contributor commented, "Adults with open minds and students just beginning to make their way through algebra and trigonometry will find much that is easily digestible and even palatable in this lively presentation."

Those trigonometry students could also benefit from Maor's next book, *Trigonometric Delights*. Again, Maor "brings the subjects to life in a compelling blend of mathematics, history, and biography," according to a *Science News* contributor. Starting with the building of the Egyptian Pyramids, Maor brings out the curious interplay of trigonometry with geometry, astronomy, architecture, and cartography. He also provides a number of biographical sketches, including one on early female mathematician Maria Agnessi. "Students of trigonometry and their teachers will enjoy finding the core syllabus so refreshingly opened up," wrote mathematician Jeremy Gray in a review for *Nature* magazine. "If they find the accounts, especially towards the end of the book, to be tantalizingly short, this is all the more reason to emulate the author and find out more for themselves, and Maor gives advice on how this can be done."

The history of mathematics is intimately associated with the history of astronomy, and in *June 8, 2004:* *Venus in Transit*, which was later revised as simply *Venus in Transit*, Maor brings these strands together while also providing a surprisingly dramatic adventure story. The orbital patterns of Earth and Venus are somewhat in synch, so that a curious pattern develops. As Johannes Kepler predicted, Venus passed exactly between the Earth and the Sun in 1631, but he did not realize that the same thing would happen eight years later, and then not again until 1761, to be repeated in 1769, and then not until 1874 in a recurring eight-year/122-year pattern. By the eighteenth century, astronomers not only understood the pattern, but they believed that by figuring out the exact moment when Venus entered and left the Sun's disk they could calculate the size of the solar system. As 1761 approached, astronomers were eagerly seeking out the best vantage points, but just as in the space race of the 1950s and 1960s, national rivalries came into play. One French astronomer was unable to reach an ideal spot in Pondicherry because of the English-French struggle over India. Eight years later, a sudden fog dashed his hopes. Englishmen Charles Mason and Jeremiah Dixon—of Mason-Dixon line fame—had to dodge French gunfire to get to their spot in the Cape of Good Hope. As *Booklist* reviewer Michael Spinella observed, "Maor brings science history vividly alive in a manner reminiscent of Eco, with tales of eccentric astronomers, political corruption, and conspiracy." Similarly, *Astronomy* contributor William Schomaker commented, "This book will please the history aficionado and the most ardent astronomer."

BIOGRAPHICAL AND CRITICAL SOURCES:

PERIODICALS

American Scientist, November-December, 1998, William Thompson, review of *Trigonometric Delights,* p. 584.

Astronomy, October, 2000, William Schomaker, review of *June 8, 2004: Venus in Transit,* p. 110.

Booklist, February 15, 1994, Bryce Christensen, "The Story of a Number," p. 1044; March 1, 2000, Michael Spinella, review of *June 8, 2004,* p. 1182.

Dr. Dobb's Journal, July, 1999, Michael Swaine, "Another Kind of E-Book."

Isis, September, 2001, James Evans, review of *June 8, 2004,* p. 585.

Journal of the History of Science, June, 1995, Erik Sageng, review of *e: The Story of a Number,* p. 308.

Kirkus Reviews, April 1, 1994, review of *e,* pp. 462-463; February 15, 2000, p. 230.

Library Journal, February 1, 1994, Harold D. Shane, review of *e,* p. 108; April 1, 1998, Harold D. Shane, review of *Trigonometric Delights,* p. 119.

Mathematical Intelligencer, winter, 2001, Melissa Houck, review of *e,* pp. 74-75.

National Forum, winter, 1995, William L. Deaton, review of *e,* p. 47.

Nature, July 23, 1998, Jeremy Gray, "The Joy of Secants," p. 333; August 10, 2000, Don Fernie, "Venusian Visitation," p. 562.

New York Times, September 27, 1987, B. G. Yovovich, review of *To Infinity and Beyond,* p. 36.

New York Times Book Review, September 27, 1987, "Science and Technology; In Short," p. 36.

Science, June, 1994, Peter Borwein, review of *e,* p. 1952.

Science News, April 13, 2002, review of *Trigonometric Delights,* p. 240.

Sciences, September-October, 1987, Michael Guillen, review of *To Infinity and Beyond: A Cultural History of the Infinite,* p. 55; May, 2000, Laurence A. Marschall, review of *June 8, 2004,* p. 45.

Times (London, England), January 2, 1995, Ulrike Tillmann, review of *e,* p. 1.

Times Literary Supplement, August 11, 2000, Owen Gingerich, "There She Blows."

Whole Earth, summer, 1998, Michael Stone, review of *e,* p. 111.*

*   *   *

MARKEN, Bill
See MARKEN, William Riley

*   *   *

MARKEN, William Riley 1942-
(Bill Marken)

PERSONAL: Born September 2, 1942, in San Jose, CA; son of Harry L. and Emma Catherine (Kraus) Marken; married Marilyn Tonascia, August 30, 1964; children: Catherine, Elizabeth, Michael, Paul. *Education:* Attended Occidental College; University of California—Berkeley, B.A., 1964. *Hobbies and other interests:* Tennis, skiing, basketball.

ADDRESSES: Agent—c/o Author Mail, IDG Books Worldwide, 919 E. Hillsdale Blvd., Suite 400, Foster City, CA 94404.

CAREER: Sunset, Menlo Park, CA, editor-in-chief, 1981-96; eHow.com, editor-in-chief, 1999; garden.com, former columnist; *Garden Escape,* former editor; *Rebecca's Garden,* former editor; *Taste,* former consultant; *Garden Design,* Orlando, FL, editor-in-chief.

AWARDS, HONORS: Horticultural Communication Award, American Horticultural Society.

WRITINGS:

AS BILL MARKEN

(With National Gardening Association editors) *Container Gardening for Dummies,* IDG Books Worldwide (Foster City, CA), 1998.

(With National Gardening Association editors) *Annuals for Dummies,* IDG Books Worldwide (Foster City, CA), 1998.

(With Michael MacCaskey and National Gardening Association editors) *Gardening for Dummies,* IDG Books Worldwide (Foster City, CA), 1999.

How to Fix (Just about) Everything, Free Press (New York, NY), 2002.

SIDELIGHTS: Bill Marken has had positions with gardening and how-to magazines and Web sites for most of his professional career. He is former editor-in-chief of *Sunset,* a magazine that provides information on home improvement, cooking, and gardening, and is also former editor of *Rebecca's Garden,* a magazine that provides tips and ideas on gardening.

In *Container Gardening for Dummies,* Marken and the National Gardening Association editors provide ideas and steps for planting and growing flowers, herbs, berries, vegetables, and even trees in containers, such as terra-cotta pots or hanging baskets. A *GardenBed* contributor noted, "Guaranteed to show you everything you need to know to create a container garden."

In *Annuals for Dummies,* Marken and the National Gardening Association editors provide new gardeners with instructions on how to choose annual flowers, and plant and maintain an annual garden. In *Gardening for Dummies,* Marken and his coeditors broaden the subject matter and provide instructions and tips on how to plant and maintain various types of gardens, including ones of flowers, vegetables, and shrubs.

In *How to Fix (Just about) Everything,* Marken provides steps for fixing things such as a broken toilet, a wobbly table, a ring stuck on a finger, a hangover, a broken zipper, bad breath, and even bad credit. Included in the book are illustrations, tips, and warnings. *Library Journal* contributor Bonnie Poquette claimed, "This book's focus on problem-solving, enumerated instructions, and clear layout make it worthwhile." *Booklist* contributor Barbara Jacobs concluded, "To cherish—and to chuckle at."

BIOGRAPHICAL AND CRITICAL SOURCES:

PERIODICALS

Advocate, January 27, 2003, Greg Langley, "Do-it-Yourselfers in a Fix Can Get Help from Fix-It Guide."

Booklist, October 15, 2002, Barbara Jacobs, review of *How to Fix (Just about) Everything,* p. 370.

Library Journal, December, 2000, Phillip Oliver, review of *Annuals for Dummies,* p. 87; October 1, 2002, Bonnie Poquette, review of *How to Fix (Just about) Everything,* p. 84.

Orlando Business Journal (Orlando, FL), November 2, 2001, Bob Mervine, "Green Genes?," p. 17.

Publishers Weekly, October 21, 2002, review of *How to Fix (Just about) Everything,* p. 69.

Seattle Times (Seattle, WA), December 1, 2002, Darrell Hay, "Books to Improve Just about Anything; Well, Most Will, Anyway."

ONLINE

GardenBed, http://gardenbed.com/ (January 27, 2003), review of *Container Gardening for Dummies.**

*   *   *

MARLES, Robin J(ames) 1955-

PERSONAL: Born September 5, 1955, in Victoria, British Columbia, Canada; son of J. Watson (an antique and book dealer) and Poppy (a homemaker) Marles; married Jung Hee Lee, January 4, 1986; children: Thomas, James. *Ethnicity:* "Euro-Canadian."

Education: University of Victoria, B.Sc., 1977; University of Saskatchewan, M.Sc., 1984; University of Illinois—Chicago Circle, Ph.D., 1988. *Hobbies and other interests:* Hiking, camping, fishing, reading, photography.

ADDRESSES: Home—2319 Princess Ave., Brandon, Manitoba R7B 0J1, Canada. *Office*—Department of Botany, Brandon University, Brandon, Manitoba R7A 6A9, Canada; fax: 204-728-7346. *E-mail*—marles@ brandonu.ca.

CAREER: University of Ottawa, Ottawa, Ontario, Canada, postdoctoral fellow in biology, 1988-92; Brandon University, Brandon, Manitoba, Canada, assistant professor, 1992-95, associate professor of botany, 1995—, department chair, 1999-02. University of Saskatchewan, adjunct professor, 1994—; University of London, King's College, visiting scientist, 1999; University of Manitoba, adjunct professor and member of academic committee for Natural Resources Institute, 2001—; public speaker; guest on media programs. Volunteer nature interpreter at parks in Saanich, British Columbia, Canada, summers, 1970-73; British Columbia Fish and Wildlife Service, wildlife assistant in Nanaimo, British Columbia, Canada, summer, 1974; Canadian Forestry Association, forestry assistant in Victoria, British Columbia, Canada, summers, 1985-86, nature interpreter at John McInnis Environmental Education Centre, summer, 1978, forestry technician at Pacific Forest Research Centre, 1979; MacMillan-Bloedel Co., wildlife biologist with Land Use Planning Advisory Team, summer, 1979; conducted field research in subarctic, boreal, temperate, and tropical habitats. Wheat Belt Community Futures Development Corp., member of Alternate Crops Committee, 1992-99; Canadian College of Naturopathic Medicine, member of professional advisory board, 1997-99; Species Survival Commission of the International Union for the Conservation of Nature and World Conservation Union, member of Medicinal Plant Specialist Group, 2001—; consultant to Canadian Institutes of Health Research, New England Technology Group, Fundy Model Forest, Vita Health Co., and Virtual Learning, Inc. B. J. Hales Museum of Natural History, chair of board of trustees, 1994-98, member of board of trustees, 1999—; judge of science fairs.

MEMBER: International Society for Ethnopharmacology, Phytochemical Society of North America, Canadian Herb Society, Society of Ethnobotanists (fellow), Society for the Advancement of Native Studies (member of board of directors, 1993—), Society for Economic Botany, Society for Ethnobiology, American Society of Pharmacognosy, American Botanical Council, American Herb Association, Medicinal and Aromatic Plants Association of Manitoba (member of board of directors, 1997—), Manitoba Association of Plant Biologists, Native Plant Society of Saskatchewan.

AWARDS, HONORS: Fellow, Natural Sciences and Engineering Research Council, 1988-90; travel grants from Canadian Ethnology Society and American Society of Pharmacognosy, 1988, and Phytochemical Society of North America, 1990; fellow, Health and Welfare Canada, 1990-92; major grants from Canadian Forest Service, University of Illinois—Chicago Circle, Manitoba Agriculture and Food, Manitoba Industry, Trade, and Tourism, and National Museums of Canada.

WRITINGS:

(Editor, with Christina Clavelle, Leslie Monteleone, and others, and contributor) *Aboriginal Plant Use in Canada's North-West Boreal Forest,* University of British Columbia Press (Vancouver, British Columbia, Canada), 2000.

Contributor to books, including *Economic and Medicinal Plant Research,* edited by H. Wagner and N. R. Farnsworth, Academic Press (London, England), 1994; and *Voice of the Drum: Indigenous Education and Culture,* edited by Roger Neil, Kingfisher Publications (Brandon, Manitoba, Canada), 2000. Contributor of articles and reviews to scientific journals, including *Phytomedicine, Photochemistry and Photobiology, Journal of Natural Products, Pesticide Biochemistry and Physiology, Sachets, Pharmacist News,* and *Pharmacology and Toxicology.* Associate editor, *Pharmaceutical Biology,* 1992-2001; member of editorial board, *Archives of Pharmacal Research,* 1997-99.

WORK IN PROGRESS: Research on ethnobotany and the production of high-quality herbal medicines.

SIDELIGHTS: Robin J. Marles told *CA:* "Having been interested in nature from my earliest memories of childhood, it was only natural that I should become a scientist studying nature for my career. In addition to the love and support of my parents, sibling, wife, and children, credit for my motivation and success as a researcher and writer must be given for the mentoring of Mr. Freeman Foard King, 'Skipper' to hundreds of children. Mr. King was a park nature interpreter, scout leader, and journalist who led people of all ages and backgrounds on hikes through the parks of southern Vancouver Island, and who wrote about nature rambles in the newspaper (later these were compiled into a book). He was able to explain the complex relationships between plants and animals in terms simple enough for all to understand, despite having no academic training in science.

"Many of the children Skipper taught went on to become biologists and ecologists, including Dr. Nancy Turner of the University of Victoria, who introduced me to the field of ethnobotany, the study of the dynamic relationships between people of a particular culture and their botanical environment. For more than twenty years now, I have had the privilege of learning about traditional uses of plants from native elders belonging to cultures of northern Canada's forests and the Amazonian jungle of eastern Ecuador. By hiring, training, and working alongside native researchers, we have been documenting through interviews and participant research those aspects of traditional knowledge that the elders want preserved and shared with other people. Native communities have asked us to do this work in order to preserve the botanical aspects of their traditional knowledge, prepare teaching materials that are culturally, geographically, and ecologically relevant so that this knowledge can be passed on to their children and grandchildren by incorporation into school curricula, and to identify plant products such as traditional foods, medicine, or handicrafts which they might be able to develop economically to provide local employment and income. We only publish what the elders have given us permission to share, in order to protect their sacred knowledge from inappropriate use and abuse.

"Many of the novel uses for plants provided by the native elders stimulate the curiosity of scientists like myself, so in addition to trying to understand the cultural basis for the plant's use, we like to investigate the plant's physical, chemical, and pharmacological properties, to try to understand the scientific basis for how it works as a health-maintaining food or healing herb. This research often provides completely new insights into how plants and animals function and interact among themselves and with their physical environment, driving the amazing adaptations that they have evolved to survive and succeed.

"Through my scientific writings, I try to share some of the wonder and fascination that I experience as I begin to see how different fields of science and human culture can be brought together to describe the natural world around us."

*   *   *

MARSHALL, Christopher D(avid) 1953-

PERSONAL: Born March 21, 1953, in Wellington, New Zealand; son of Thomas (a teacher) and Jenny (a clerk) Marshall; married Margaret Hart, February 16, 1974; children: Peter, Andrew. *Ethnicity:* "European." *Education:* Victoria University of Wellington, B.A. (with honors), 1976; Melbourne College of Divinity, B.D., 1980; King's College, University of London, Ph. D., 1986; Associated Mennonite Biblical Seminary, Elkhart, IN, M.A., 1996. *Religion:* Protestant.

ADDRESSES: Home—24 Poinsettia Pl., Henderson, Auckland 1008, New Zealand. *Office*—Bible College of New Zealand, 221 Lincoln Rd., Henderson, Auckland 1231, New Zealand. *E-mail*—c.marshall@xtra.co. nz.

CAREER: Teacher at secondary schools in New Zealand, 1977-78; Mennonite Centre, London, England, tutor, 1985; Bible College of New Zealand, Henderson, Auckland, New Zealand, lecturer, 1986-99, reader in New Testament at Tyndale Graduate School of Theology, 1999—. Massey University, member of advisory board of Centre for Peace and Justice Development, 2001—.

MEMBER: Anabaptist Association of Australia and New Zealand (member of executive committee, 1995—; vice president), Aotearoa-New Zealand Association for Biblical Studies, Catholic Biblical Association, Society for Biblical Literature, Society for the Study of Christian Ethics, Anabaptist-Mennonite Scholars Network, Tyndale Fellowship for Biblical Research (past member), Tear Fund New Zealand (board member, 1989-90).

AWARDS, HONORS: Grant from E. M. Blaiklock Memorial Fund, 1986-87.

WRITINGS:

Faith as a Theme in Mark's Narrative, Cambridge University Press (Cambridge, England), 1989.
Kingdom Come: The Kingdom of God in the Teaching of Jesus, Impetus Publications (Auckland, New Zealand), 1993.
Beyond Retribution: A New Testament Vision for Justice, Crime, and Punishment, William B. Eerdmans Publishing (Grand Rapids, MI), 2001.
Crowned with Glory and Honor: Human Rights in the Biblical Tradition, Pandora Press (Telford, PA), 2001.

Contributor to books, including *Human Rights and the Common Good: Christian Perspectives,* edited by B. Atkin and K. Evans, Victoria University Press (Wellington, New Zealand), 1999; *Living in the Lamb Light: Christianity and Contemporary Challenges to the Gospel,* edited by Hans Boersma, Regent College Publishing (Vancouver, British Columbia, Canada), 2001; *Engaging Anabaptism: Conversations with a Radical Tradition,* edited by J. D. Roth, Herald Press (Scottdale, PA), 2001; *Overcoming Violence in New Zealand,* edited by J. Roberts, Philip Garside Publishers (Wellington, New Zealand), 2002; and *Faith and Freedom: Christian Ethics in a Pluralist Culture,* edited by D. Neville, Australian Theological Forum (Sydney, Australia), 2003. Contributor to periodicals, including *Mennonite Quarterly Review, On the Road, Reality, Stimulus, Evangelical Review of Theology, Challenge Weekly, Shaker,* and *Reaper.* Member of editorial committee, *Themelios: International Journal for Theological and Religious Studies Students,* 1982-85; editorial associate, *Today's Christian,* 1988-93; associate editor, *Faith and Freedom: Journal of Christian Ethics,* 1994-99.

SIDELIGHTS: Christopher D. Marshall told *CA:* "I write partly because that is what the academic vocation is all about and partly because I believe in the things I write about. I am committed to developing the ethical implications of Christian faith—especially in terms of peace and justice. To ground a justice commitment in one's understanding of God and transcendence is of profound worth. Religion can be a great force for peace as well as a deep source of violence. I want to see God's name associated with humanization, not with jihad."

BIOGRAPHICAL AND CRITICAL SOURCES:

PERIODICALS

America, March 11, 2002, Daniel J. Harrington, review of *Beyond Retribution: A New Testament Vision for Justice, Crime, and Punishment,* p. 24.

Booklist, February 15, 2002, Steven Schroeder, review of *Crowned with Glory and Honor: Human Rights in the Biblical Tradition,* p. 974.

First Things: Monthly Journal of Religion and Public Life, August, 2001, review of *Beyond Retribution,* p. 76.

*   *   *

MARTELL, Christopher R. 1956-

PERSONAL: Born December 11, 1956, in Burlington, VT; son of Francis O. (a farmer) and Rita B. (a homemaker; maiden name, Gelineau) Martell. *Ethnicity:* "Caucasian." *Education:* St. Michael's College, B.A. (magna cum laude), 1983; Hofstra University, M.A., Ph.D., 1988.

ADDRESSES: Home—2628 Fourth Ave. N., No. 305, Seattle, WA 98109. *Office*—Associates in Behavioral Health, 818 12th Ave., Seattle, WA 98122. *E-mail*—c.martell@attbi.com.

CAREER: Associates in Behavioral Health, Seattle, WA, clinical psychologist in private practice, 1989—. University of Washington, Seattle, clinical assistant professor, 1996—.

MEMBER: American Psychological Association (member of Committee on Lesbian, Gay, and Bisexual Concerns), Association for the Advancement of Behavior Therapy, Washington State Psychological Association (president, 2000-01), Delta Epsilon Sigma (Alpha Nu chapter).

AWARDS, HONORS: Distinguished Service Award, Washington State Psychological Association, 1997.

WRITINGS:

(With Michael E. Addis and Neil S. Jacobson) *Depression in Context: Strategies for Guided Action,* Norton (New York, NY), 2001.

(With Steven A. Safren and Stacey E. Prince) *Cognitive-Behavioral Therapies with Lesbian, Gay, and Bisexual Clients,* Guilford Press (New York, NY), 2004.

Contributor to books, including *Comprehensive Textbook of Psychotherapy,* Volume 2: *Cognitive-Behavioral Approaches,* Wiley (New York, NY), 2002; and *Clinical Handbook of Couple Therapy,* 2nd edition, edited by Neil S. Jacobson and A. Gurman, Guilford Press (New York, NY), 2002. Contributor to periodicals, including *Behavior Therapist* and *Clinical Psychology: Science and Practice.*

SIDELIGHTS: Christopher R. Martell told *CA:* "It would be nice to say that writing was in my blood, but that would not be true. Realistically, dreaming was in my blood. I've dreamed of writing since I was very young. The process of getting to a point where I had something to say took longer than I had initially imagined. Actually I'd put aside the idea of writing when I entered graduate school in a doctoral program that heavily emphasized professional psychology and applied science. It was clear that holding a doctorate, however, meant being a scholar, even in an applied field. I wanted to be true to my original dream, as well as to my degree. The opportunities as a professional psychologist were limited by the number of hours that I spent providing psychotherapy services or volunteering in professional organizations.

"This all changed when I began working as a research therapist with Dr. Robert Kolhenberg and the late Dr. Neil Jacobson. Both academicians, these two men were very interested in sharing ideas with the clinicians who worked with them. I found myself in both the scientist and practitioner arena when Jacobson eventually asked me to coauthor a book with him. I was afforded the opportunity to continue writing on subjects that I found meaningful, drawing on the theories of B. F. Skinner, Aaron T. Beck, and writers who have provided innovative approaches to their original ideas to inform my thinking as I write. I have applied my years of practical experience to my work as well, and have written chapters and books that have primarily been of interest to other mental health clinicians."

*   *   *

MARTIN, Michael T. 1947-

PERSONAL: Born September 13, 1947, in New York, NY; son of Alida (Comellini) Martin; children: Pilar. *Ethnicity:* "African American." *Education:* City College of the City University of New York, B.A., 1970; Columbia University, M.A., 1971, Ed.M., 1972; University of Massachusetts—Amherst, Ph.D., 1979.

ADDRESSES: Office—Department of Ethnic Studies, Bowling Green State University, Bowling Green, OH 43403.

CAREER: California State University—Los Angeles, Los Angeles, CA, professor and department chair, 1981-84; Princeton University, Princeton, NJ, adjunct professor of African-American studies and director of Third World Center, 1984-90; Wayne State University, Detroit, MI, professor and department chair, 1990-97; Bowling Green State University, Bowling Green, OH, professor of ethnic studies and department chair, 1997—. Consultant to National African American Museum Project of the Smithsonian Institution and International Student Identity Scholarship Fund of the U.S. Department of Education.

MEMBER: Latin American Studies Association, Society for Cinema Studies.

AWARDS, HONORS: Award of merit, film category, Latin American Studies Association, 1989; Mellon Foundation grant, 1990.

WRITINGS:

(Editor, with Terry Kendal, and contributor) *Studies of Development and Change in the Modern World,* Oxford University Press (New York, NY), 1989.

(Editor and contributor) *Cinemas of the Black Diaspora: Diversity, Dependence, and Oppositionality,* Wayne State University Press (Detroit, MI), 1995.

(Editor and contributor) *New Latin American Cinema,* Volume 1: *Theory, Practices, and Transcontinental Articulations,* Volume 2: *Studies of National Cinemas,* Wayne State University Press (Detroit, MI), 1997.

The Cinema of Gillo Pontecorvo (monograph), Wayne State University Press (Detroit, MI), in press.

Contributor to books, including *Perspectives in International Development,* edited by Mekki Mtewa, Allied Publishers (New Delhi, India), 1986. Contributor to periodicals, including *Latin American Perspectives, Transafrica Forum, Transition, Phylon, Quarterly Review of Film and Video, Film Quarterly, Third World Quarterly, Political Psychology, Western Journal of Black Studies,* and *Research in African Literatures.* Guest coeditor, *California Sociologist,* 1985.

BIOGRAPHICAL AND CRITICAL SOURCES:

PERIODICALS

Cineaste, fall, 1996, Cliff Thompson, review of *Cinemas of the Black Diaspora: Diversity, Dependence, and Oppositionality,* p. 66.

Contemporary Sociology, January, 1991, Robert Fiala, review of *Studies of Development and Change in the Modern World,* p. 31.

Film Criticism, winter, 1996, Wheeler Winston Dixon, review of *Cinemas of the Black Diaspora,* p. 62.

Historical Journal of Film, Radio, and Television, March, 1997, Onookome Okome, review of *Cinemas of the Black Diaspora,* p. 163; August, 1998, Luis Elbert, review of *New Latin American Cinema,* Volume 1: *Theory, Practices, and Transcontinental Articulations,* p. 467.

Journal of Economic History, December, 1989, David Felix, review of *Studies of Development and Change in the Modern World,* p. 1084.

Journal of Popular Film and Television, fall, 2000, Barbara F. Weissberger, review of *New Latin American Cinema,* p. 142.

Research in African Literatures, winter, 1998, Kenneth W. Harrow, review of *Cinemas of the Black Diaspora,* p. 192.

MARTINO, Rick 1947-

PERSONAL: Born June 10, 1947, in Silver Spring, MD; son of Patrick (a realtor) and Betty (an analysis manager; maiden name, Conant) Martino; married, 1970; wife's name, Gail (divorced); children: Tim, Wendy. *Education:* University of Maryland, B.S., 1970.

ADDRESSES: Home—5883 Southeast Riverboat Dr., Stuart, FL 34997. *Office*—Professional Golfers Association, 100 Avenue of the Champions, Palm Beach Gardens, FL 33410. *E-mail*—rmartino@pgahq.com.

CAREER: Professional Golfers Association, Palm Beach Gardens, FL, director of instruction, 1998—. Turner Network Television (TNT), golf commentator.

MEMBER: Professional Golfers Association (master professional).

AWARDS, HONORS: Named National Teacher of the Year, Professional Golfers Association, 1997.

WRITINGS:

(With Don Wade) *The PGA Manual of Golf,* Warner Books (New York, NY), 2002.

Contributor to magazines, including *Golf, Golf Digest, Golf Illustrated,* and *Journal of Human Movement Studies.*

BIOGRAPHICAL AND CRITICAL SOURCES:

PERIODICALS

Desert Sun (Palm Springs, CA), September 26, 2002, review of *The PGA Manual of Golf,* p. D2.

*   *   *

MASON, Linda 1954-

PERSONAL: Born 1954, in United States; daughter of a homemaker (mother) and an internist (father); married Roger Brown (a business consultant); children: three. *Education:* Cornell University, B.A.; studied piano at Sorbonne, University of Paris; Yale School of Management, M.B.A.

ADDRESSES: Home—Boston, MA. *Office*—Bright Horizons Family Solutions, 200 Talcott Avenue S., Watertown, MA 02472. *E-mail*—welcome@brighthorizons.com.

CAREER: Booz-Allen, New York, NY, consultant, 1984; Save the Children Federation's emergency program in Sudan, codirector, 1985; Bright Horizons Family Solutions, cofounder and president, 1986-98, and chairman, 1998—; author. Also cofounder of Horizons Initiative, a nonprofit serving homeless mothers and their children in the Boston area. Prior to joining Booz-Allen, directed large-scale food program for refugee children in Cambodia. Serves on the boards of the Horizons Initiative, *Boston Globe,* Mercy Corps International, and Yale School of Management Advisory Board. Yale University, trustee.

AWARDS, HONORS: Ernst & Young/*USA Today,* Entrepreneur of the Year Award, 1996; *Redbook,* Mothers and Shakers Award honoree, 1998; *Working Mother* magazine, Twenty-five Most Influential Mothers in America Award; *Fortune* selected Bright Horizons as one of the "One Hundred Best Companies to Work for in America."

WRITINGS:

(With husband, Roger Brown) *Rice, Rivalry, and Politics: Managing Cambodian Relief,* University of Notre Dame Press (Notre Dame, IN), 1983.
The Working Mother's Guide to Life: Strategies, Secrets, and Solutions, Three Rivers Press (New York, NY), 2002.

SIDELIGHTS: Linda Mason combined her management skills with her passion for making a difference in the world to become cofounder of Bright Horizons Family Solutions child care and early education centers. In 1986, in an era when mothers were entering the workforce in huge numbers, Mason and her husband, Roger Brown, saw a dire need for quality child care. They launched their entrepreneurial venture, which ultimately became the world's largest employer-based, work-site, child-care provider. Mason's and Brown's prior experience managing feeding programs for refugee children in Cambodia and the Sudan, along with their consulting experience for large U.S. firms, prepared them well for their venture. Their experience in Cambodia led to their coauthored book, *Rice, Rivalry, and Politics: Managing Cambodian Relief.* Mason's second book, *The Working Mother's Guide to Life: Strategies, Secrets, and Solutions,* evolved from her personal and professional involvement with day care and as a working mother.

Mason's passion was piano. However, while studying under a professor at the Sorbonne in Paris, France, she realized that she probably would not be among the elite few pianists to attain top concert career status. While in France she began volunteer work with North African refugees and discovered an entirely new passion. She returned to the United States, entered Yale School of Management to get an M.B.A., believing it would help with her international pursuits. During her second year at Yale, she met her future husband and his friend, Neil Keny, who that summer would volunteer in Cambodian refugee camps in the aftermath of the killing fields of 1979-80. Mason became inspired and decided to join them. Mason and Brown stayed much longer than planned, but eventually returned to take up consulting work—Mason with Booz-Allen in New York and Brown with Bain Consulting in Boston. A year later Mason moved to Boston where her consulting work allowed her time to travel to the Ivory Coast and Nigeria.

Mason and her husband-to-be were less than enthralled with their consulting careers. "I was so uninspired that winter," Mason was quoted by Mark S. Albion in *Making a Life, Making a Living* e-newsletter. "I felt trapped on a treadmill." The couple decided they must make a change and, when the opportunity arose, they were ready. After becoming reacquainted with Keny, now head of African operations with Save the Children Federation, he introduced them to David Guyer, also with Save the Children and who had recently returned from the Sudan and Ethiopia, distressed with the extent of suffering there. He said he had two million dollars in funding to begin a relief organization and would Mason and Brown commit? He needed an answer the next day. Mason and Brown knew their answer within two minutes, and three weeks later they were in the Sudan directing an emergency fund providing relief to 400,000 victims of war and famine. The success of their operation was so great that, after US AID spent six months monitoring their operations, they were commended for having the most superior health and nutrition program in the country. Their model became the new standard for all other efforts in the Sudan. Al-

bion wrote: "Little did they know that their success in the Sudan would lead to the 1986 launch of their 350 million dollar public company, Bright Horizons Family Solutions, the industry leader in on-site corporate child care."

After a good harvest in the Sudan, Mason and Brown returned to the United States and established new goals. Neither wanted to return to consulting, and their career decisions would be based on something personally satisfying and fulfilling. They acknowledged four principles that would be the foundation for their future: they would work together, they would begin something of their own, they would use their business and social services skills, and they had a deep passion for children. Researching their options, they discovered a need for quality child care in corporate facilities because so many mothers were entering the workforce. Backed financially by Mitt Romney of the venture capital firm Bain Capital, Bright Horizons Family Solution was established and began operations in two corporations—Prudential Real Estate and the Athenaeum Group.

In spite of their success, no other corporation followed suit. Educating employers about the benefits of such a program was the next step. However, the recession of the mid-1980s hit and the future looked dim. With one child of their own to think of, and extremely stressed, the couple took one of their long evening walks to discuss the situation. "We said that the worst that could happen is the company would collapse, we'd sell the house, go back to Africa, and return to relief work with children," Mason told Albion. "The more we thought about it, the more we both felt that the worst looked pretty good." Reinspired, the couple set out to raise funds for their business and, after a slow summer, were remarkably successful. In 1997 they took the company public, merged the following year with the number two provider in the nation, and even expanded into primary education.

While researching her book about working women, Mason told Albion: "I am one and our business is in response to working women. I've got lots of ideas on how to do it." Mary Frances Wilkens, in *Booklist,* described the resulting *The Working Mother's Guide to Life* as an "all-encompassing manual" that will help working mothers to attain a balance in their lives. A *Publishers Weekly* reviewer commented of Mason's book: "In some instances, however, her utopian ideas conflict with reality." The reviewer felt that—although she included poor working mothers in her book—Mason's advice is more easily attainable by women with greater financial resources. Kay Brodie commented in *Library Journal* that Mason's tips and strategies take into account a myriad of beliefs and personalities, and concluded: "Without a doubt, Mason's book belongs in every library and many homes."

BIOGRAPHICAL AND CRITICAL SOURCES:

PERIODICALS

Booklist, October 15, 2002, Mary Frances Wilkens, review of *The Working Mother's Guide to Life: Strategies, Secrets, and Solutions,* p. 270.
Everett Business Journal, May, 2004, Brendan Shriane, "Life after baby: moms talk about the trade-offs of working or staying at home," p. A12.
Fortune, February 1, 1988, Susan Caminiti, "On the Rise," p. 98.
Library Journal, November 1, 2002, Kay Brodie, review of *The Working Mother's Guide to Life,* p. 116.
Publishers Weekly, November 4, 2002, review of *The Working Mother's Guide to Life,* p. 82.

ONLINE

Making a Life, Making a Living, http://www.makingalife.com/ (March 25, 1999), e-newsletter, Mark S. Albion, "Linda Mason: An Inventive Live; A Life Alive; A Bright Horizon."

* * *

McCANN, Maria 1956-

PERSONAL: Born 1956, in Liverpool, England. *Education:* University of Durham (England); University of Glamorgan (Wales), M.A. (writing). *Hobbies and other interests:* Attending plays, reading fiction, country walks.

ADDRESSES: Agent—Annette Green Authors' Agency, 1 East Cliff Rd., Tunbridge Wells, Kent TN4 9AD, England.

CAREER: Author and educator. Strode College, Somerset, England, lecturer in English, 1988—. Worked a series of jobs, including artist's model and English as a foreign language (EFL) teacher.

WRITINGS:

As Meat Loves Salt, Flamingo Press (London, England), 2001, Harcourt (San Diego, CA), 2002.

SIDELIGHTS: Maria McCann gained widespread acclaim in Great Britain with her first novel, titled *As Meat Loves Salt.* Born in Liverpool, England, McCann was a voracious reader as a child. After her undergraduate studies, she held a series of jobs before getting her master's degree in English and becoming a lecturer at Strode College in England. McCann had written haphazardly for years but without any serious ambition. The premature death of a close friend led her to sign up for a five-day course in writing, which gave her the confidence to tackle a novel.

As Meat Loves Salt is set in seventeenth-century England and tells the story of narrator Jacob Cullen, an antihero who is selfish and has a violent temper. Cullen is also a homosexual who has rashly murdered a young boy. When he flees with his wife and brother, who ultimately desert him, he ends up becoming a mercenary in Cromwell's army, and he forms a friendship with another soldier, Christopher Ferris. The two eventually become lovers and set out to form a type of farming commune.

"It's hard to believe that this accomplished and potent historical tale is a first novel—a sentiment repeatedly echoed by the rapturous review that greeted its initial publication in England," wrote a contributor to *Kirkus Reviews.* Several reviewers found the first half of the novel to move rather slowly as McCann builds up the historical narrative and atmosphere. Writing in *Times Literary Supplement,* Alexandra Walsham thought that "McCann seeks to weave too many historical threads into her narrative and, at times, the results can seem slightly contrived." Nevertheless, Walsham also noted, "This is a novel which creeps up on the reader from behind, gathering an emotional momentum and intensity which is eventually compelling."

Another reviewer questioned whether McCann should have used such a flawed character as Cullen to serve as the novel's narrator. In *Washington Post,* Bruce

Cook asked if was necessary to "like the narrator of a novel" and concluded that it wasn't. "The sole obligation of the author to the reader is to make a book's characters interesting, and the leading character should be most interesting of all," wrote Cook. "Jacob Cullen is likely to be of interest only to those who eagerly lap up tales of serial killers and child murderers in the tabloids."

Many other reviewers, however, were enthralled, both with the self-destructive character of Cullen and with McCann's talent. According to Karen T. Bilton in *Library Journal,* "McCann's brilliant debut is an eloquent narrative that is historically rich and enthralling." David Bahr, writing in *Advocate,* called the book "astonishing in its psychological insights." A contributor to *Publishers Weekly* said the book is a "brilliant, ambitious epic." The reviewer went on to note, "The scope of the narrative, the unusual conceit, and the resonant writing combine to make this a powerful, unusual debut."

McCann told *CA* that she is currently working on a book set in the 1920s and 1930s but has to balance her writing with other commitments. She does not see herself primarily as a historical writer and hopes to explore other kinds of fiction. It is likely, however, that her work will continue to rehearse the themes of power and self-knowledge (or lack of it). As she told *CA:* "I'm fascinated by what people are willing to put up with and to inflict on others—pretending all the time that it isn't happening. My aim isn't to celebrate these power games, though I do try to convey the intoxication they induce. What I hope to do is dissect and demystify them."

BIOGRAPHICAL AND CRITICAL SOURCES:

PERIODICALS

Advocate, February 4, 2003, David Bahr, review of *As Meat Loves Salt.*

Booklist, November 15, 2002, Margaret Flanagan, review of *As Meat Loves Salt,* p. 573.

Kirkus Reviews, November 1, 2002, review of *As Meat Loves Salt,* p. 1559.

Library Journal, November 1, 2002, Karen T. Bilton, review of *As Meat Loves Salt,* p. 129.

Publishers Weekly, October 28, 2002, review of *As Meat Loves Salt,* p. 46.

Times Literary Supplement, March 23, 2001, Alexandra Walsham, review of *As Meat Loves Salt,* p. 10.

Washington Post, January 12, 2003, Bruce Cook, review of *As Meat Loves Salt,* p. T5.

*   *   *

McCULLOUGH, Kate 1961-

PERSONAL: Born 1961. *Education:* Brown University, B.A. (magna cum laude), 1983; National University of Ireland, University College (Dublin, Ireland), M.A. (with honors), 1984; University of California—Berkeley, Ph.D., 1992.

ADDRESSES: Office—Department of English, Bachelor Hall, Miami University, Oxford, OH 45056. *E-mail*—mccullmk@muohio.edu.

CAREER: University of California, Santa Cruz, temporary lecturer in women's studies, 1991; Miami University, Oxford, OH, teacher of English and women's studies, 1992—. Guest speaker at colleges and universities, including Salisbury State University, University of Notre Dame, Ohio State University, and University of Kentucky.

MEMBER: Modern Language Association of America, Pacific and Ancient Modern Language Association, Phi Beta Kappa.

WRITINGS:

Regions of Identity: The Construction of America in Women's Fiction, 1885-1914, Stanford University Press (Stanford, CA), 1999.

Contributor to *The Unruly Voice: Rediscovering Pauline Elizabeth Hopkins,* edited by John Gruesser, University of Illinois Press (Champaign, IL), 1996, and *The New Nineteenth Century: Feminist Readings of Underread Victorian Texts,* edited by Susan Meyer and Barbara Herman, Garland Publishing (New York,

NY), 1996. Contributor of articles and reviews to periodicals, including *Pacific Coast Philology* and *American Literature.*

BIOGRAPHICAL AND CRITICAL SOURCES:

PERIODICALS

Choice, November, 1999, D. D. Knight, review of *Regions of Identity: The Construction of America in Women's Fiction, 1885-1914,* p. 538.*

*   *   *

McLAREN, Joseph 1948-

PERSONAL: Born February 14, 1948, in New York, NY; son of Joseph and Edna Louise (Stuart) McLaren; children: Natasha, Anikah. *Education:* Queens College of the City University of New York, B.A., 1970; City College of the City University of New York, M.A., 1974; Brown University, A.M., 1977, Ph.D., 1980. *Hobbies and other interests:* Jazz improvisation, jogging, photography, travel.

ADDRESSES: Office—Department of English, 312C Calkins Hall, Hofstra University, Hempstead, NY 11549. *E-mail*—engjzm@hofstra.edu.

CAREER: Mercy College, Dobbs Ferry, NY, professor of English, 1976-90; Hofstra University, Hempstead, NY, associate professor of English, 1990—.

MEMBER: African Literature Association, African Studies Association, Popular Culture Association, Duke Ellington Society.

AWARDS, HONORS: Duke Ellington Legacy Award, Black American Heritage Foundation, 1994; grant from National Endowment for the Humanities, 1994.

WRITINGS:

Langston Hughes: Folk Dramatist in the Protest Tradition, 1921-1943, Greenwood Press (Westport, CT), 1997.

Contributor to books, including *Harlem Renaissance: Revaluations.*

BIOGRAPHICAL AND CRITICAL SOURCES:

PERIODICALS

Modern Drama, Volume XLI, number 4, 1998, Lisa M. Anderson, review of *Langston Hughes: Folk Dramatist in the Protest Tradition, 1921-1943,* pp. 664-665.*

*   *   *

MEDEARIS, John 1963-

PERSONAL: Born September 12, 1963, in Baltimore, MD; son of Donald Norman, Jr. (a physician) and Mary Ellen (Marble) Medearis; married Jessica M. Goodheart (a researcher), 1993; children: Max Goodheart. *Education:* Harvard University, A.B., 1985; University of California—Los Angeles, Ph.D., 1998.

ADDRESSES: Office—Department of Political Science, University of California—Riverside, Riverside, CA 92521-0102. *E-mail*—medearis@citrus.ecr.edu.

CAREER: California State University—Northridge, Northridge, CA, assistant professor of political science, 1999-2001; University of California—Riverside, Riverside, CA, assistant professor of political science, 2001—.

AWARDS, HONORS: Thomas J. Wilson Prize, Harvard University Press, c. 2001, for *Joseph Schumpeter's Two Theories of Democracy.*

WRITINGS:

Joseph Schumpeter's Two Theories of Democracy, Harvard University Press (Cambridge, MA), 2001.

Contributor to academic journals, including *American Political Science Review* and *British Journal of Political Science.*

WORK IN PROGRESS: Democracy Where It's Difficult.

BIOGRAPHICAL AND CRITICAL SOURCES:

PERIODICALS

Perspectives on Political Science, summer, 2002, James L. Danielson, review of *Joseph Schumpeter's Two Theories of Democracy,* p. 185.

*   *   *

MELOY, Ellen (Ditzler)

PERSONAL: Married; husband, a river ranger.

ADDRESSES: Home—Bluff, UT. *Agent*—c/o Author Mail, Pantheon, Random House, 201 East 50th St., New York, NY 10022.

CAREER: Writer, illustrator, and naturalist. Conducts workshops in natural history and in nature writing for Canyonlands Field Institute. Commentator for Utah Public Radio.

AWARDS, HONORS: Spur Award, Western Writers of America, 1995, for *Raven's Exile: A Season on the Green River;* Whiting Foundation Writer's Award, 1997; Pulitzer Prize for nonfiction finalist, 2002, and *Los Angeles Times* Book of the Year Award, and Utah Book Award, both 2003, all for *The Anthropology of Turquoise: Meditations on Landscape, Art, and Spirit.*

WRITINGS:

Raven's Exile: A Season on the Green River, Holt (New York, NY), 1994.
The Last Cheater's Waltz: Beauty and Violence in the Desert Southwest, Holt (New York, NY), 1999.
The Anthropology of Turquoise: Meditations on Landscape, Art, and Spirit, Pantheon (New York, NY), 2002.

Contributor of essays to anthologies, including *Shadow Cat,* Sasquatch Press; *Water, Earth, and Sky,* University of Utah Press; *The Place Within: Portraits of the American Landscape,* Norton; and *Testimony,* Milkweed Press. Contributor to *Northern Lights, Utne Reader, Orion,* and other periodicals.

ILLUSTRATOR

Sandra Chisholm Robinson, *Expedition Yellowstone: A Mountain Adventure,* Roberts Rinehart (Boulder, CO), 1986.
Chris Hunter, *Better Trout Habitat: A Guide to Stream Restoration,* Island Press (Washington, DC), 1991.

SIDELIGHTS: Naturalist, artist, and writer Ellen Meloy communicates her love of the American Southwest in several volumes of collected essays, among them the Pulitzer Prize-nominated *The Anthropology of Turquoise: Meditations on Landscape, Art, and Spirit.* Connected by a loose history of the regional turquoise stone, as well as traditions regarding the color turquoise as a symbol of yearning, she "contemplates the mysteries of life and death, visits the backcountry of the Navajo nation . . . considers what it means to be attached to one particular place, and takes a few potshots at . . . urban civilization," explained a *Kirkus Reviews* critic. Citing Meloy for her "kaleidoscopic writing bursting with intensely felt colors," *School Library Journal* contributor Sheila Shoup praised the author's profound comments, expressed in a "narrative that is both captivating and informative." Along with the colors of the desert, she reflects on her need for solitude and the visual beauty found in nature. "Knowledgeable and lyrical, Meloy's meditations should resonate with those who find sustenance in the natural world," noted a *Publishers Weekly* contributor.

Meloy's first award-winning volume of essays, 1994's *Raven's Exile: A Season on the Green River,* recounts her experiences during one season—late March through early October—patrolling the 730-mile-long river that stretches across Utah, Colorado, and Wyoming. Traveling with her husband, a ranger with the U.S. Bureau of Land Management, she traverses such areas as the Desolation Canyon gorge, a true wilderness area where "bears and cougars still prowl, peregrine falcons soar, the extreme rare humpback chub swims, and ghosts of Anasazi Indians roam," according to *Kliatt* contributor Randy M. Brough. Praising *Raven's Exile* as a "scintillating account" of Meloy's river trip, a *Publishers Weekly* contributor cited her use of "rich and sensuous language," in bringing to the mind's eye the stark, spare beauty of the region. Noting the author's arch humor, *Booklist* reviewer Donna Seaman also described Meloy as "as prickly as a cactus, as observant and teasing as a raven, as sensual as a cat," her sensitive insights transformed to "scathing analysis" of Western politics as the journey's end finds her in Las Vegas. Brough called *Raven's Exile* "an eloquent testament, a wry polemic, a spirited adventure."

In *The Last Cheater's Waltz: Beauty and Violence in the Desert Southwest* Meloy examines the intersection between wilderness and technology as she describes the impact upon a New Mexico desert used as the Trinity site of U.S. Army nuclear testing in 1945. Described by *New York Times Book Review* contributor as a "sad irony," the sparse desert region that was unable to sustain large-scale agriculture proved to fit the needs of the U.S. government during World War II and after; while appearing lifeless, the Jornada del Muerto desert actually was home to many species of indigenous life. During her travels of over 200 miles of desert on the Colorado plateau, Meloy argues that the effects of such tests, as well as the government's uranium mining in the region, are yet unknown; her "sadness and anger over human predations on the landscape are heartfelt and moving," added a *Publishers Weekly* reviewer, while Bryce Christensen noted in *Booklist* that Meloy's "intense regional attachment" resonates with significant "global implications."

BIOGRAPHICAL AND CRITICAL SOURCES:

PERIODICALS

Alternatives Journal, fall, 2002, Pamela Banting, "Nuclear Landscape," p. 53.
Booklist, June 1, 1994, Donna Seaman, review of *Raven's Exile: A Season on the Green River,* p. 1763; January 1, 1999, Bryce Christensen, review of *The Last Cheater's Waltz: Beauty and Violence in the Desert Southwest,* p. 821; July, 2002, Donna Seaman, review of *The Anthropology of Turquoise: Meditations on Landscape, Art, and Spirit,* p. 791
Kirkus Reviews, April 15, 2002, review of *The Anthropology of Turquoise,* p. 584.
Kliatt, November, 1995, Randy M. Brough, review of *Raven's Exile,* p. 38.

Library Journal, June 15, 1994, Nancy Moeckel, review of *Raven's Exile,* p. 90; February 15, 1999, Dale Ebersole, Jr., review of *The Last Cheater's Waltz,* p. 179; June 15, 2002, Maureen J. Delaney-Lehman, review of *The Anthropology of Turquoise,* p. 91.
New York Times Book Review, April 11, 1999, Bill Sharp, review of *The Last Cheater's Waltz,* p. 25.
Publishers Weekly, May 23, 1994, review of *Raven's Exile,* p. 72; January 25, 1999, review of *The Last Cheater's Waltz,* p. 79; June 17, 2002, review of *The Anthropology of Turquoise,* p. 55.
School Library Journal, February, 2003, Sheila Shoup, review of *The Anthropology of Turquoise,* p. 174.
Washington Post Book World, August 7, 1994, review of *Raven's Exile,* p. 13.*

*   *   *

MERLE, Robert (Jean Georges) 1908-2004

OBITUARY NOTICE—See index for *CA* sketch: Born August 29, 1908, in Tebessa, Algeria; died March 27, 2004, in Monfort L'Amaury, France. Educator and author. Merle was a literature professor in France who also won awards and critical recognition for his novels and was most familiar in the United States for writing the book that became *The Day of the Dolphin.* Born in Algeria, he was educated at the Sorbonne, where he earned a doctorate degree. He taught high school literature classes during the 1930s, and with the onset of World War II served in the French Army and was captured in 1940. After the war, he returned to academia, teaching English and American literature at various institutions, including the University of Rennes, the University of Toulouse, the University of Caen, the University of Rouen, and the University of Paris X in Nanterre; he also taught at the University of Algiers during the mid-1960s. When he was not teaching, Merle proved himself a talented writer, winning the prestigious Prix Goncourt in 1949 for his military novel *Weekend à Zuydcoote,* as well as the Prix de la Fraternité in 1962 for *L'Ile* and the Prix Franz Hellens in 1974 for the science fiction novel *Les hommes protégés.* Occasionally, he would venture into speculative science fiction, as with *Un animal doué de raison* (1967), which was adapted as the 1973 George C. Scott film, *The Day of the Dolphin,* and the post-holocaust story *Malevil* (1972). He was also a serious student of history, penning an ambitious, thirteen-volume fictional work set in France during the sixteenth and seventeenth centuries, collectively titled *Fortune de France.* Other books of note by Merle include *La Mort est mon métier* (1952) and *Derrièr la vitre* (1970). Also working as a translator of books by writers ranging from Jonathan Swift to Erskine Caldwell, he continued publishing into the twenty-first century, with his last novel, *Complots et cabalas,* being released in 2001.

OBITUARIES AND OTHER SOURCES:

BOOKS

Reginald, Robert, *Science Fiction & Fantasy Literature, 1975-1991,* Gale (Detroit, MI), 1992.

PERIODICALS

Los Angeles Times, April 1, 2004, p. B11.
New York Times, April 3, 2004, p. A25.
Times (London, England), May 21, 2004, p. 40.
Washington Post, April 2, 2004, p. B9.

*   *   *

MILLER, Alan 1954-

PERSONAL: Born March 5, 1954. *Education:* Wesleyan University, B.A., 1976; University of Hawaii, M.A., 1978.

ADDRESSES: Office—c/o Los Angeles Times, 202 West First St., Los Angeles, CA 90012.

CAREER: Journalist. *Times Union,* Albany, NY, political reporter and state investigative reporter, 1978-81; *Record,* Hackensack, NJ, county political reporter and state political reporter, 1982-87; *Los Angeles Times,* Los Angeles, CA, staff writer, 1989-94, investigative reporter in Washington bureau, 1994—.

MEMBER: Committee of Concerned Journalists.

AWARDS, HONORS: George Polk Award, 1996; Goldsmith Prize for investigative reporting, 1996; Investigative Reporters and Editors Medal, 1996; National Headliners Award, 1996; Pulitzer Prize for national reporting, 2003.

WRITINGS:

Numerous articles for the *Los Angeles Times.*

SIDELIGHTS: Journalist Alan Miller, on the reporting staff of the *Los Angeles Times,* won the 2003 Pulitzer Prize for national reporting along with colleague Kevin Sack for their "The Vertical Vision," a series on the U.S. Marines Corps vertical-lift Harrier jet aircraft. Linked to the death of forty-five pilots and nicknamed the "Widow Maker," the Harrier aircraft ultimately became the subject of panel discussion in the U.S. House of Representatives, which agreed to hold hearings to discuss military aviation safety following Miller and Sack's investigations. Hoping to advance its aviation capabilities beyond those of the U.S. Navy and Air Force, the Marine Corps instead advanced the death toll of its recruits through the Harrier, along with the Osprey part of its developmental all-vertical fleet.

The journalists' four-part series began as a human-interest story about the surviving families in Marine Corps crashes. Using the Freedom of Information Act, Miller and Sack scoured the National Archives, press clippings, and other databases to discover the names of the pilots killed in Harrier-related accidents, and interviewed these men's families. They also gained maintenance and combat records on Harrier jets directly from Marine Corps officials. Together with photographs depicting the pilots how lost their lives, "The Vertical Vision" series profiled the accident record of the aircraft through the loss to the military of these dedicated pilots; as Sack told Joseph Eaton and Makeba Scott Hunter in an article posted on the *Investigative Reporters and Editors* Web site, "I think it was an accurate portrayal. We let the chips fall where they might."

BIOGRAPHICAL AND CRITICAL SOURCES:

ONLINE

Associated Press Managing Editors Web site, http://www.apme/com/ (May 17, 2004).
Investigative Reporters and Editors Web site, http://www.ire.umd.edu/ (June 6, 2002), "Pulitzer-Winning Defense Story Combined Facts with Faces."
Pulitzer Board Web site, http://www.pulitzer.org/ (May 15, 2003).*

MOCKRIDGE, Norton 1915-2004

OBITUARY NOTICE—See index for *CA* sketch: Born September 29, 1915, in New York, NY; died of pneumonia, April 18, 2004, in San Antonio, TX. Journalist and author. Mockridge was an award-winning journalist who was also a noted humor columnist. He went into his profession right out of high school, working variously for the *Mt. Kisco Recorder, White Plains Daily Reporter,* and *New York World-Telegram and Sun* during the 1930s and early 1940s. World War II saw him enlisting in the U.S. Army, where he rose to the rank of first lieutenant. After the war, he returned to the *World-Telegram and Sun,* where he became city editor in 1956, a humor columnist from 1963 to 1966, and entered into syndication from 1966 until 1980. While working as the city editor, Mockridge and his staff received a Pulitzer Prize in 1963 for local reporting. In 1978, he filed an age-discrimination lawsuit against Scripps-Howard Newspapers, saying he was being forced into an early retirement; the suit was settled out of court in Mockridge's favor. He kept busy in the 1980s as a foreign correspondent for United Features Syndicate and as president of Valnor Productions. Mockridge, who also hosted radio shows for CBS during the 1960s, was the author of several books, ranging from nonfiction, such as *This Is Costello* (1951), written with Robert H. Prall, to humorous pieces such as *Fractured English* (1965). Among his other writings are *Mockridge, You're Slipping!* (1967) and *Eye on the Odds* (1976).

OBITUARIES AND OTHER SOURCES:

PERIODICALS

New York Times, April 24, 2004, p. A13.

* * *

MOONEY, Robert

PERSONAL: Born in Rochester, NY; married; wife's name, Maureen; children: two. *Education:* Boston College, B.A., 1977; Binghamton University, M.A., 1983; Ph.D., 1996.

ADDRESSES: Office—Department of English, Washington College, 300 Washington Ave., Chestertown, MD 21620. *E-mail*—rmooney2@washcoll.edu.

CAREER: Educator and novelist. Washington College, Chestertown, MD, assistant professor of English and creative writing; director of O'Neill Literary House.

WRITINGS:

Father of the Man, Pantheon (New York, NY), 2002.

Contributor of short fiction to periodicals.

SIDELIGHTS: In his debut novel, set in the early 1980s, Robert Mooney weaves a story about the love between a father and son against the backdrop of a United States still bitter about the Vietnam War and unsupportive of those whose families were fractured by that war. Readers of *Father of the Man* meet middle-aged bus driver Dutch Potter as the World War II veteran is reaching a crisis point in his life; he ultimately snaps and hijacks his bus and passengers. As local police give way for F.B.I. agents in the standoff that follows, Potter demands to be reunited with his son, a young man who was declared Missing in Action somewhere in southeast Asia more than a decade before and whose whereabouts have obsessed Potter ever since. When a retired Marine colonel who specialized in tracking down MIAs is called to the scene, the clues to Potter's son's disappearance begin to multiply, and Potter starts to come to terms not only with his relationship with his son but also with his family and his memories of his own wartime experiences.

In the *Philadelphia Inquirer,* contributor Phaedra Trethan called Mooney's 2002 novel debut "touching without being sentimental," citing as effective the author's use of a "reportorial style not unlike a dispatch from a combat zone." While a *Kirkus Reviews* critic dubbed the book "rather stiff," a contributor to *Publishers Weekly* was more appreciative, praising *Father of the Man* as a "solid effort" and noting that by adding "an unusual twist to the usual hostage standoff plot" Mooney "establishes him[self] as a promising newcomer."

BIOGRAPHICAL AND CRITICAL SOURCES:

PERIODICALS

Kirkus Reviews, August 15, 2002, review of *Father of the Man,* p. 1167.

Philadelphia Inquirer, January 2, 2003, Phaedra Trethan, review of *Father of the Man.*
Publishers Weekly, September 2, 2002, review of *Father of the Man,* p. 53.*

*   *   *

MRAZEK, Robert J. 1945-

PERSONAL: Born November 6, 1945, in Newport,
RI; son of Harold Richard and Blanche Rose Mrazek;
married Catherine Susan Gurick, March 31, 1971;
children: Susannah Rose, James Nicholas. *Education:*
Cornell University, B.A. (government), 1967.

ADDRESSES: Home—RR 2, Box 195, Broadway, VA
22815. *Agent*—c/o Author Mail, St. Martin's Press,
175 Fifth Ave., New York, NY 10010.

CAREER: Congressman, writer. Special assistant to
U.S. Senator Vance Hartke, Washington, DC, 1969-71;
Town of Huntington, NY, special projects coordinator,
1971; member of New York state legislature for Suffolk County, Hauppauge, NY, 1975-82, minority
leader, 1979-82; member of the U.S. House of
Representatives, Third District, New York, five terms,
1983-93. Youth Development Association, Huntington
Village, NY, board of directors, 1971-76, president,
1972-74. *Military service:* U.S. Navy, 1967-68.

WRITINGS:

Stonewall's Gold: A Novel, maps by Martie Holmer,
St. Martin's Press (New York, NY), 1999.
Unholy Fire: A Novel of the Civil War, Thomas Dunne
Books (New York, NY), 2003.

ADAPTATIONS: Stonewall's Gold was adapted for
audio (six cassettes), read by Jeff Woodman, Recorded
Books, 1999.

SIDELIGHTS: Robert J. Mrazek's books have been
published in the years after his time spent in the U.S.
House of Representatives, where he served five terms,
representing his constituents on Long Island, in New
York's Third District. Mrazek was scrutinized on a
number of occasions, once, as *Forbes* contributor

Edward Giltenan wrote, because he was "identified as
the incumbent who overdrew his House bank account
the most times, with almost 1,000 overdrafts over
twenty-three months." Questions also arose over the
purchase of St. Pierres Island in the Bahamas, which
Mrazek acquired in partnership with a number of other
Democratic congressmen.

Mrazek was coauthor of a bill to prevent the Manassas
Civil War Battlefield from being turned over to
developers, and his interest in, and knowledge of, the
Civil War period is reflected in his writing. His first
book, *Stonewall's Gold: A Novel,* is presented as a
manuscript discovered in a Harrisonburg, Virginia,
courthouse, and "irresistibly combines the classic
motifs of Civil War, buried treasure and romantic heroism," noted a *Publishers Weekly* contributor. The setting is Shenandoah Valley during the final winter of
the war. Fifteen-year-old Jamie Lockhart's father has
gone to fight, and his mother takes in a boarder to
earn the money they need to survive. When the man
attempts to rape her, Jamie kills him, after which they
find a map of a treasure site called "the Mouth of the
Devil" among the dead man's possessions.

The treasure is several crates of gold that was seized
by the Union from the Confederates in 1861, then
stolen back by a group of Confederate officers who
kept it hidden, hoping that by the time the war ended,
it would have been forgotten. Jamie, now the only one
with a map to the gold, is pursued by the last remaining member of this group, along with his band of
cutthroats. Another group that wants the gold intends
to use it for the betterment of newly emancipated
slaves. Jamie, who wants to deliver the gold to General
Robert E. Lee to help the rebel cause, is joined by
Katherine Dandridge, whose father has been killed by
the Confederate deserters who are pursuing Jamie.

The *Publishers Weekly* writer concluded by saying
that Mrazek's tale "possesses a compelling narrative
drive. His sense of landscape is expert, and his cast of
heroes and villains is complete." A *Kirkus Reviews*
critic called *Stonewall's Gold* "a deft and fast-paced
historical adventure" and "a gripping, well-researched,
and vivid debut."

Unholy Fire: A Novel of the Civil War is about Union
officer John "Kit" McKittredge, a Harvard senior who
enlists and is commissioned as a lieutenant. When Kit

receives what seems to be a mortal stomach wound, the doctors decide to ease his pain during his last days with laudanum. Astonishingly, Kit survives but with a serious drug addiction. He is reassigned to investigate corruption and crime in Washington, D.C., but when he delves into his first case, involving companies who sold defective ammunition to the army, he is warned by a stranger, then a congressman, not to pursue the case. He ignores them and continues, but is soon involved with the murder of a prostitute with ties to members of government and who was last seen with Union General Joseph Hooker. Kit is buying opium on the black market to feed his addiction but is saved from self-destruction by Colonel Valentine Burdette, who believes in him and joins him in investigating crooked military officers and politicians. Central to the plot is Kit's love for a friend of the dead woman, also a prostitute.

Booklist's Margaret Flanagan wrote that Mrazek's story "underscores the brutal nature of both the physical and psychological casualties associated with war." A *Kirkus Reviews* writer called *Unholy Fire* "tautly gripping, with vividly malevolent characters and some excellent historical color." A *Publishers Weekly* contributor wrote that "Mrazek's portrayal of Civil War battle is stark, graphic, bloody and exciting, and is only exceeded by his memorable description of Washington, D.C., as a Gomorrah on the Potomac."

BIOGRAPHICAL AND CRITICAL SOURCES:

PERIODICALS

Booklist, December 15, 1998, Gilbert Taylor, review of *Stonewall's Gold: A Novel,* p. 1481; March 1, 2003, Margaret Flanagan, review of *Unholy Fire: A Novel of the Civil War,* p. 1147.

Forbes, April 1, 1991, James R. Norman, "Shrewd Timing?," p. 46; April 13, 1992, Edward Giltenan, "Mrazek's Folly," p. 14.

Kirkus Reviews, November 15, 1998, review of *Stonewall's Gold,* p. 1627; February 1, 2003, review of *Unholy Fire,* p. 171.

Publishers Weekly, November 9, 1998, review of *Stonewall's Gold,* p. 57; March 17, 2003, review of *Unholy Fire,* p. 51.

School Library Journal, April, 1999, Molly Connally, review of *Stonewall's Gold,* p. 161.*

MURPHY, Gregory L(eo)

PERSONAL: Male. *Education:* Johns Hopkins University, B.A., 1978, M.A., 1978; Stanford University, Ph.D., 1982.

ADDRESSES: Office—Dept. of Psychology, New York University, 6 Washington Pl., New York, NY 10003. *E-mail*—gregory.murphy@nyu.edu.

CAREER: Brown University, Providence, RI, began as assistant professor, became associate professor, 1982-91; University of Illinois, Champaign-Urbana, began as associate professor, became professor, 1991-2001; New York University, New York, professor of psychology, 2001—.

WRITINGS:

The Big Book of Concepts, MIT Press (Cambridge, MA), 2002.

Writings included in books by others, including *Discourse Ability and Brain Damage: Theoretical and Empirical Perspectives,* edited by Y. Joanette and H. H. Brownell, Springer-Verlag (New York, NY), 1990; *Discourse Representation and Text Processing,* edited by J. Oakhill and A. Garnham, Erlbaum (Hillsdale, NJ), 1993; *Explanation and Cognition,* edited by R. A. Wilson and F. C. Keil, MIT Press (Cambridge, MA), 2000; *Lexicology: An International Handbook on the Nature and Structure of Words and Vocabularies,* edited by D. A. Cruse and others, Walter de Gruyter (Berlin, Germany), 2002; and *The Psychology of Learning and Motivation,* Volume 43, edited by B. H. Ross, Academic Press (San Diego, CA), 2003. Contributor to periodicals and journals, including *Child Development, Journal of Memory and Language, Journal of Experimental Psychology, Psychonomic Bulletin and Review, Memory & Cognition,* and *Psychological Science.*

SIDELIGHTS: Gregory L. Murphy is a professor of psychology whose research interests focus on concepts. *The Big Book of Concepts* opens with the statement that concepts "are the glue that holds our mental world together." Because humans grasp concepts—especially the idea that generalizations can be made from specific examples—there is no need to relearn that one can sit in a chair, whether it be a traditional chair, or an object that is very different, like a beanbag chair, but which serves as a place to sit. Paul Bloom noted in *Nature* that Murphy's book "is so big because it reviews experimental research from several research areas . . . such as the sorts of concepts formed by babies and young children, the comprehension of new conceptual combinations, and the effects of expertise on categorization."

Choice reviewer D. S. Dunn pointed out that Murphy "writes with clarity and wit about what many psychologists consider a technical (if not dry) topic." Jerry Fodor suggested in *Times Literary Supplement* that the book "summarizes, and comments on, an impressive variety of the key experimental findings, and it is a reliable guide to the standard interpretations of these data. Murphy has provided a really invaluable resource for students and researchers, and the merely curious will benefit from skimming. At a minimum, the nearly forty pages of references are a godsend for those of us who are bibliographically challenged."

Bloom called Murphy "one of the leading scholars in this area. . . . This is going to be the classic text in the field for a very long time. It is one of those rare cases in which the standard back-of-the-book blurb is actually true. Anyone interested in concepts and categorization . . . must read this book."

BIOGRAPHICAL AND CRITICAL SOURCES:

PERIODICALS

Choice, April, 2003, D. S. Dunn, review of *The Big Book of Concepts,* p. 1447.
Nature, January 16, 2003, Paul Bloom, review of *The Big Book of Concepts,* pp. 212-213.
Times Literary Supplement, January 17, 2003, Jerry Fodor, review of *The Big Book of Concepts,* pp. 3-4.

ONLINE

Gregory L. Murphy Home Page, http://www.psych. nyu.edu/murphy (June 9, 2004).

N

NAIM, Asher 1929-

PERSONAL: Born December 28, 1929, in Tripoli, Libya; immigrated to Israel, 1944; son of Baruch and Emilia (Vature) Naim; married Hilda Glick, August 23, 1956; children: Ronit, Ari, Gideon. *Education:* Hebrew University, Master of Jurisprudence, 1956.

ADDRESSES: Office—6, Nayot, Jerusalem 93704, Israel. *Agent*—c/o Author Mail, Ballantine Publishing Group, Random House, 1745 Broadway, New York, NY 10019. *E-mail*—anaim@mofet.macam98.ac.il.

CAREER: Diplomat. Government of Israel, cultural and press attaché, Tokyo, Japan, 1956-60, embassy staff, Kenya and Uganda, 1961-64, chief operating officer of the assistance program for developing nations, Jerusalem, 1964-68, attaché, Israeli embassy, Washington, DC, 1968-73, consul-general, 1976-88, ambassador to Finland, 1988-90, Ethiopia, 1990-91, the United Nations, 1991, and South Korea, 1992-95. Cofounder of Keren Hanan Aynor Foundation, a scholarship fund for Ethiopian Jews.

MEMBER: Israel-Korea Friendship Association (chair).

AWARDS, HONORS: Distinguished Israel Civil Servant, 1991; Hanyan University (Seoul, Korea), honorary doctorate.

WRITINGS:

(With Dr. Shang Hee Rhee) *I.Q. 100 and Smart, I.Q. 150 Unexplored,* Chuson Ilbo Publishing (Seoul, Korea), 1996.

(With Dr. Shang Hee Rhee) *Natural Growth Skill for the Gifted,* Yollu-Sah Publishing (Seoul, Korea), 1998.

(With Dr. Won-Sol Lee) *Jerusalem in Human Destiny,* Korean Christian Press (Seoul, Korea), 1998.

The Jewish People's Inner Strength for Survival, Sanyo Shuppan Publishing (Tokyo, Japan), 1999.

Let the Child Develop His Utmost, Mytos Publishing (Tokyo, Japan), 2000.

Saving the Lost Tribe: The Rescue and Redemption of the Ethiopian Jews, Ballantine Books (New York, NY), 2003.

Contributor of articles on Jewish history, Korea-Israel relations, and child education to publications.

SIDELIGHTS: Israeli career diplomat Asher Naim was born in Libya and moved with his family to Israel after his bar mitzvah. He served his country in many positions, among them as ambassador to Ethiopia, beginning in 1990. Naim arrived in Addis Ababa amidst a brutal civil war and quickly recognized that the Falashas, or black Jews of Ethiopia, were in peril. In his memoir, *Saving the Lost Tribe: The Rescue and Redemption of the Ethiopian Jews,* Naim documents how he arranged and executed the airlift that was named "Operation Solomon" and that would save more than 14,000 people. This is the first book on the subject written in English, although several others have been published in Hebrew.

The Falashas, who refer to themselves as Beta Israel, can trace their beginnings back 3,000 years to King Solomon and the Queen of Sheba. Their existence was unknown until Christian missionaries encountered their society in the nineteenth century. Naim, who had previously secured the release of Soviet Jews through Finland, negotiated with Ethiopian dictator Mengistu Haile Meriam (referred to by some historians as "the Butcher of Addis"), coordinated logistics with the Israeli military, and set about raising thirty-five million dollars, much of it from donors in America. It took nine months to bring the plan together, and when the time was right, Naim called for the Israeli planes that landed at the Addis airport and collected the Falashas under protection of armed Israeli commandos. They were all transported over a period of twenty-five hours, taking with them nothing but the clothes on their backs and a few religious items.

Other players in the operation included Uri Lubrani, an official in the Ministry of Defense who also took part in the negotiations on behalf of the Israeli government. *Jewish Week Online* contributor Sandee Brawarsky wrote that "some of the events seem like they're right out of the script of a thriller, although at one point after an extraordinary request, Lubrani reminds Kasa Kabede, Mengistu's close advisor, 'This isn't a James Bond film, Kasa.'"

As the Falashas attempted to integrate into Israeli society, they were met with hostility by the conservative wing and were feared as being carriers of AIDS and tuberculosis, causing many, particular the elders, to express the wish to return to Ethiopia. Naim argued before the United Nations that Operation Solomon should "erase the hideous UN resolution equating Zionism with racism."

A *Kirkus Reviews* contributor noted that in spite of all the problems, Naim "still views Operation Solomon as a success. Effectively argued, though the reader may pause to wonder how the Falashas are doing today." The immigrants had difficulty with such everyday activities as modern farming, because centuries had passed them by.

Naim is a cofounder of the Keren Hanan Aynor Foundation, which raises funds to help with the education of Ethiopian Jews. It benefits not only those who came through Operation Solomon, but also families from Operation Moses, an earlier migration that took place in 1984, and those who traveled on their own from Ethiopia to Israel.

BIOGRAPHICAL AND CRITICAL SOURCES:

BOOKS

Naim, Asher, *Saving the Lost Tribe: The Rescue and Redemption of the Ethiopian Jews* (memoir), Ballantine Books (New York, NY), 2003.

PERIODICALS

Booklist, December 15, 2002, Jay Freeman, review of *Saving the Lost Tribe: The Rescue and Redemption of the Ethiopian Jews,* p. 712.
Kirkus Reviews, December 1, 2002, review of *Saving the Lost Tribe,* p. 1754.
Publishers Weekly, December 23, 2002, review of *Saving the Lost Tribe,* p. 59.

ONLINE

Jewish Week Online, http://www.thejewishweek.com/ (March 21, 2003), Sandee Brawarsky, review of *Saving the Lost Tribe.*
Keren Hanan Aynor Foundation Online, http://www.kerenaynor.co.il (November 18, 2003).

*   *   *

NASDIJJ, 1950-

PERSONAL: Born 1950; children: Tommy Nothing Fancy (deceased), Crow Dog, Awee (deceased), (adopted sons).

ADDRESSES: Agent—c/o Author Mail, Random House, 1745 Broadway, New York, NY 10019.

CAREER: Writer. Worked variously as a journalist and teacher.

WRITINGS:

The Blood Runs Like a River Through My Dreams: A Memoir, Houghton Mifflin (Boston, MA), 2000.
The Boy and the Dog Are Sleeping (memoir) Ballantine Books (New York, NY), 2003.
Geronimo's Bones: A Memoir of My Brother and Me, Ballantine Books (New York, NY), 2004.

SIDELIGHTS: The first of Nasdijj's autobiographical works is *The Blood Runs Like a River Through My Dreams.* He explains on the dust jacket that Nasdijj is "Athabaskan for 'to become again.'" He uses the single name from the linguistic group that includes Apache and Navajo because he does not want to write about tribal culture under his real name. The book is several things. It is the memoir of a very hard childhood, of one man's determination to become a writer, and a tribute to a young son who never lived beyond childhood.

The son of migrant workers, Nasdijj was physically and sexually abused by his white cowboy father, who also sold his mother to other men for a few dollars. Because she was a heavy drinker during her pregnancy with Nasdijj, he was born with Fetal Alcohol Syndrome (F.A.S.), which significantly affected his health and left him with very poor vision, learning disabilities, and a constant battle with depression.

Nasdijj wrote as a child, hiding in barns and farm machinery in the migrant camps. He wrote dozens of journals and eventually as many novels, none of which he was able to publish. His early work was destroyed when found, and he was forced back into the fields.

High school friends, including Bad Nell and Frankie, are introduced in the book, and then reintroduced as adults. Nasdijj lived on a cultural edge; although he looks white, he identifies with the Navajo heritage his mother claimed. Much of his life was spent on reservations, where his whiteness was often a cause for suspicion. He married, and he and his wife adopted a Navajo boy, Tommy Nothing Fancy, who they soon realized also suffered from F.A.S. Nasdijj loved and dedicated himself to Tommy, whose health deteriorated rapidly, and while they were on a fishing trip, the boy suffered a seizure and died. He was six years old. The title chapter of the book, about Tommy, was published in *Esquire* to considerable acclaim. It is the most painful section of the book and one that the author finally refused to read at literary events.

In reviewing the book in the *New York Times Book Review,* Ted Conover wrote that "this is an outsider's book; Nasdijj has sympathy for the downtrodden and anger toward the world that marginalizes them. In these pages we meet Native Americans and others who, like the author, don't fit stereotypes: A Navajo

bull rider with AIDS, a pair of young Sioux heroin addicts, male prostitutes in the Tenderloin district of San Francisco, a delinquent Indian teenager he mentors, the author's deaf cousin whose depth, not his debility, is insisted upon." Conover noted that the author doesn't provide the names of his wives, nor does he talk about any living relatives. Conover said that "while Nasdijj exposes a pain so deep in the Tommy chapters that he breaks your heart, he is stingy with other self-revelation. . . . Yet this is a fascinating book, unlike anything you are likely to have read. . . . his book reminds us that brave and engaging writers lurk in the most forgotten corners of society."

Salon.com's Maria Russo observed that the "singular language" of the memoir "blends Native American mythological rhythms and imagery, stirring Whitmanesque catalogs and unadorned observations about life on and around the reservation. Nasdijj's terse, elemental sentences don't so much follow one another as nestle on top of the next, like a desert rock formation. His anger at the 'white people world' just about reaches off the page and shoves you, and yet there's a disciplined quality to his fury. For all its descriptions of drunken violence and crushing poverty, the book has a gentleness at its core."

A cowboy dying of AIDS had a last chance to view horses in the desert when Nasdijj rented a wheelchair and took him there. When Nasdijj was living, homeless, at a campground, he befriended a desperate woman, took her daughters to the library, and bought them new dolls when he received an unexpected check. Nasdijj's homelessness led to his asthma and brushes with death. His feet became permanently damaged from frostbite, and he lost the feeling in his fingers and tongue. Nasdijj recalls his four-hundred-mile walk across New Mexico to the Bosque Redondo, recreating the forced march by the U.S. military of the defeated Navajo, which resulted in deaths from starvation and illness, and death by bullet of those too weak or old to continue on.

Christopher D. Ringwald wrote in *Washington Post Book World* that "much as a drumming circle or meditative chanting may bring participants to an altered state, Nasdijj's repetitious, episodic style taps a deeper conscious." *Kliatt*'s Edna M. Boardman found that Nasdijj, "who once had a novel about Indians returned torn into small pieces by an editor, does indeed touch the heart. He may be one of America's great writers today."

The Boy and the Dog Are Sleeping is also autobiographical and a remembrance of an adopted son named Awee, who died of AIDS. He and Nasdijj shared similar pasts. Both had been raised by drunken parents, beaten, and raped. Martin Naparsteck wrote for the *Salt Lake Tribune Online* that "some pages . . . will shred your heart. Some will boil your blood. Seldom has one book contained so much pain and anger and so thoroughly drawn the reader into its emotional sandstorm. This memoir of an angry, defiant father waiting for his adopted son to die from AIDS is extraordinarily difficult to read. It is a book that required great courage to write."

Nasdijj had adopted his son Crow Dog, who also suffered from F.A.S., when he was approached by a Navajo couple who had heard of his kindness. They were both near death from AIDS, and they begged him to take their eleven-year-old son, Awee. Nasdijj took the boy and raised him, but on his own terms. He did not force him to go to school, and although he brought him to the hospital for medical care, he regretted that he subjected Awee to the needle sticks and poking and being tied to the bed so that he would not pull out his catheter. As with Tommy, the lack of adequate medical care on the reservations negatively impacted the condition of the boy.

Nasdijj took him on a tour of the Southwest on a motorcycle, which he eventually sold to pay medical bills. He arranged to have him experience sex with a gentle young man and gave him marijuana, then heroin to ease his pain. He cleaned up his messes and watched bravely as Awee fought the disease that was wasting his body. At the same time, Awee reached out to Nasdijj, becoming parent to the suicidal man who was agonized by his inability to halt the disease's progress.

Michael Robertson reviewed the book for the *Austin Chronicle Online,* noting that this is not your usual AIDS memoir book. "Nasdijj rough-hews the English language until it takes stunning forms. He dismisses narrative linearity because memory is 'the exploded junk from hand grenades' and words become the most elemental stuff, crushed rock and flowers to sift through his fingers with a disciplined intensity."

L. W. Milam, who reviewed *The Boy and the Dog Are Sleeping* for the *Review of Arts, Literature, Philosophy, and the Humanities* online, wrote that he closed the book on page 318, choosing not to finish it, not "to read the words of this sad writer of his great love that tears us up more than it should." "To hell with dying and the sadness of it all," commented Milam, who added, "Let someone else read the last pages, because if I go to the very end, the author will have taken something from me, and I am not so sure that he should be allowed to do this to me, to the boy with 'black desert eyes,' to take him from us in such a fashion so that we are pissed at the disease and the world that lets this disease go on and the world that won't take the time nor the money to stop this death of children." Milam concluded by saying that "because we all have something better to do, what we think are more pressing things to do—speculate in real estate, declare wars, go on a cruise, get drunk—we do these things because we have decided that the fate of a young man and the world and his disease are not worth the candle, are not worth our effort at all, at all."

BIOGRAPHICAL AND CRITICAL SOURCES:

BOOKS

Nasdijj, *The Blood Runs Like a River Through My Dreams: A Memoir,* Houghton Mifflin (Boston, MA), 2000.
Nasdijj, *The Boy and the Dog Are Sleeping* (memoir) Ballantine Books (New York, NY), 2003.

PERIODICALS

Book, September, 2000, Ann Collette, review of *The Blood Runs Like a River Through My Dreams: A Memoir,* p. 83; January, 2003, Beth Kephart, review of *The Boy and the Dog Are Sleeping,* p. 75.
Booklist, August, 2000, Grace Fill, review of *The Blood Runs Like a River Through My Dreams,* p. 2106; January 1, 2003, Kristine Huntley, review of *The Boy and the Dog Are Sleeping,* p. 841; March 15, 2004, Kristine Huntley, review of *Geronimo's Bones: A Memoir of My Brother and Me,* p. 1259.
Kirkus Reviews, December 1, 2002, review of *The Boy and the Dog Are Sleeping,* p. 1754; January 15, 2004, review of *Geronimo's Bones,* p. 73.
Kliatt, January, 2002, Edna M. Boardman, review of *The Blood Runs Like a River Through My Dreams,* p. 26.

Library Journal, November 1, 2000, Kay L. Brodie, review of *The Blood Runs Like a River Through My Dreams,* p. 90; January, 2003, Kay Brodie, review of *The Boy and the Dog Are Sleeping,* p. 126; February 15, 2004, Kay Brodie, review of *Geronimo's Bones,* p. 134.

New York Times Book Review, October 15, 2000, Ted Conover, review of *The Blood Runs Like a River Through My Dreams,* p. 12; February 16, 2003, Nell Casey, review of *The Boy and the Dog Are Sleeping,* p. 20.

Publishers Weekly, October 2, 2000, review of *The Blood Runs Like a River Through My Dreams,* p. 68; December 2, 2002, review of *The Boy and the Dog Are Sleeping,* p. 42; February 2, 2004, review of *Geronimo's Bones,* p. 66.

Washington Post Book World, September 17, 2000, Christopher D. Ringwald, review of *The Blood Runs Like a River Through My Dreams,* p. 6.

World and I, April, 2001, Elizabeth Blair, review of *The Blood Runs Like a River Through My Dreams,* p. 244.

ONLINE

Austin Chronicle Online, http://www.austinchronicle.com/ (February 14, 2003), Michael Robertson, review of *The Boy and the Dog Are Sleeping.*

FAS Community Resource Center Online, http://come-over.to/FASCRC/ (November 18, 2003), Teresa Kellerman, interview with Nasdijj.

Rebecca Reads, http://www.rebeccasreads.com/ (November 5, 2000), Rebecca Brown, review of *The Blood Runs Like a River Through My Dreams,* interview with Nasdijj; (March 23, 2003), Rebecca Brown, review of *The Boy and the Dog Are Sleeping.*

Review of Arts, Literature, Philosophy, and the Humanities, http://www.ralphmag.org/ (November 18, 2003), L. W. Milam, review of *The Boy and the Dog Are Sleeping.*

Salon.com, http://www.salon.com/ (October 26, 2000), Maria Russo, review of *The Blood Runs Like a River Through My Dreams.*

Salt Lake Tribune Online, http://www.sltrib.com/ (May 18, 2003), Martin Naparsteck, review of *The Boy and the Dog Are Sleeping.*

USAToday.com http://www.usatoday.com/ (November 18, 2003), Virginia Holman, review of *The Boy and the Dog Are Sleeping.**

NEIMAN, Susan 1955-

PERSONAL: Born March 27, 1955, in Atlanta, GA; children: Benjamin, Shirah, Leila. *Education:* Harvard University, A.B., 1977, A.M., 1980; Ph.D., 1986; attended Freie Universitat-Berlin, 1982-88.

ADDRESSES: Office—Einstein Forum, Am Neuem Market 7, 14467 Potsdam, Germany. *E-mail*—susan.neiman@einsteinforum.de.

CAREER: Yale University, associate professor, 1989-96; Tel Aviv University, associate professor, 1996-2000; Einstein Forum, director, 2000—; author.

MEMBER: Berlin-Brandenburg Academy of Sciences, Phi Beta Kappa.

AWARDS, HONORS: Deutscher Akademischer Austauschdienst fellowship, 1980; Bowen Prize, Harvard University, 1980; Sheldon fellowship, 1982; Fulbright fellowship, 1982-83; Henrich Heine fellowship, 1984; Carrier Dissertation Prize, 1987; Ribicoff Prize for teaching excellence in the humanities, 1991; PEN Award, 1993, for *Slow Fire;* American Council of Learned Societies fellowship, 1999-2000; Rockefeller Foundation Study Center fellowship, 2000; Association of American Publishers Award for best scholarly work on philosophy, 2002, for *Evil in Modern Thought: An Alternative History of Philosophy;* American Academy of Religion Award for Excellence, 2003.

WRITINGS:

Slow Fire, Schocken Books (New York, NY), 1992.
Unity of Reason, Oxford University Press (New York, NY), 1994.
Evil in Modern Thought: An Alternative History of Philosophy, Princeton University Press (Princeton, NJ), 2002.

Also the author of numerous articles and chapters for scholarly publications.

SIDELIGHTS: After completing her education in philosophy at Harvard University, Susan Neiman taught philosophy at Yale University for many years before traveling to Israel, where she taught at the University of Tel Aviv. More recently, she has taken on the directorship of the Einstein Forum in Germany. Her specialty is moral and political philosophy and the history of modern philosophy, subjects that are reflected in her books. So far, she has written three books and won numerous awards.

Neiman's first book, *Slow Fire,* began her career as a book author and won a prestigious award granted by PEN, an international group of writers. In this book, Neiman recounts six years of living in Berlin, from 1982 to 1988, while she was enrolled in graduate studies at the Freie Universitat (Free University). *Library Journal*'s Ian Wallace found *Slow Fire* to be an "entertaining memoir, strongly colored by the author's inquiring mind, bohemian inclinations, and Jewish background."

Neiman studies the efforts of many German people, after the fall of the Berlin Wall, to either come to terms with, or to ignore, their political past, in particular their history of Nazism. The book is written through what a *Kirkus Reviews* writer called "lively vignettes, verbatim barroom conversations, a journal kept with intellect and sympathy." While living in Berlin, Neiman discovers that anti-Semitism is not yet dead. She encounters people who are still frightened about revealing their Jewish ancestry. She also comes across a neo-Nazi computer game and an exhibit called "Synagogues in Berlin: Destroyed Architecture," which upset her. Her German friends, Neiman soon discovers, have great difficulties in talking about the Holocaust. This is, wrote *Booklist*'s George Cohen, "a frightening and thought-provoking book." A reviewer from *Publishers Weekly* also found the book to be upsetting in many ways. Neiman's book, the reviewer wrote "provides a harrowing portrait" of Berlin and its inability "to cope with its past."

Neiman's next book, *The Unity of Reason: Rereading Kant,* is an extended essay and, as Richard Velkley for the *Review of Metaphysics* described it, "a very important general account of Kant's critical philosophy." In this book, Neiman claims that previous interpretations of Kant's work have led to misunderstandings. According to Neiman, Kant set out to demonstrate that the true function of reason was not purely to gain knowledge but rather to serve as a guide. In other words, at the core of Kant's work, the philosopher attempted to separate reason from

cognition. *Ethics* contributor Pablo De Greiff highly praised Neiman's reinterpretation of Kant's philosophy, calling her study "the most careful analysis of this difficult area of Kant's work." *The Unity of Reason* is a re-working of Neiman's doctoral dissertation for which she won the Carrier Dissertation Prize while at Harvard.

For *Evil in Modern Thought: An Alternative History of Philosophy,* Neiman won the 2002 Association of American Publishers Award for the best scholarly work on philosophy. In this study, Neiman takes an historic view of evil, from the Inquisition through the Holocaust to contemporary terrorism. Through her examination she asks: What has humanity become in the three hundred years since the era of Enlightenment? How can there be meaning in life when innocent people suffer at the hands of evil? How does a concept of a god coexist in a world that also produces evil? In her attempts to answer these questions, Neiman reviews the philosophical stances of two distinctive groups of philosophers. From a period that included the thoughts of Rousseau to Arendt, she found that the conclusion these philosophers came to was that morality insists that evil be understood. However, in the group that runs from Voltaire to Adorno, she found a consensus among the philosophers that stated that morality demands no such thing.

In 1755, in Lisbon, Portugal, the people of this city were celebrating All Saints' Day when an earthquake completely shattered not only their lives but also the philosophical stance of the world. Lisbon's churches were demolished and over 60,000 people were incinerated in fires that lasted six days. Many philosophers asked: Was their god evil to have destroyed their city? Or was this an act of nature that could neither be judged as good nor evil? What then is the definition of evil? Can evil be produced only by people? Is there, for instance, a distinction to be made between the horror experienced by the citizens of Lisbon and the terror experienced in Hiroshima or Auschwitz? There is, wrote Jonathan Ree for the *Times Literary Supplement,* in his review of *Evil in Modern Thought,* "and the question leads to the center of Neiman's argument. The demand for a clear separation between accidental suffering and malicious evil, she argues, is a peculiarly modern obsession." Neiman believes that the understanding of evil is central to philosophy, central to living intelligible lives. "Philosophy is driven by the need to make sense of a world riddled with natural and moral evil," wrote Leslie Armour in her *Library Journal* review of Neiman's book. In order to better understand evil, Neiman separates it from acts of crime. Crime can be defined and understood by the experience of the individual prior to the commitment of the act. Evil, on the other hand, is not easily categorized or understood. Walter Sundberg, for *First Things,* wrote that Neiman uses Descartes' definition of evil as something that "shatters our trust in the world." It threatens, Neiman believes, humanity's ability "to act in the world and to understand it." Sundberg concluded his review by stating that Neiman's book was meant "for mature people who do not expect pat answers, who are willing to be disturbed by arguments instead of having their prejudices satisfied."

BIOGRAPHICAL AND CRITICAL SOURCES:

BOOKS

Neiman, Susan, *Slow Fire,* Schocken Books (New York, NY), 1992.
Neiman, Susan, *Evil in Modern Thought: An Alternative History of Philosophy,* Princeton University Press (Princeton, NJ), 2002.

PERIODICALS

Booklist, February 15, 1992, George Cohen, review of *Slow Fire,* p. 1085.
Books and Culture, March-April, 2003, Alan Wolfe, "Desperately Wicked: Reckoning with Evil," review of *Evil in Modern Thought: An Alternative History of Philosophy,* pp. 26-28.
Choice, November, 1994, review of *The Unity of Reason,* p. 469; June, 2003, review of *Evil in Modern Thought.*
Common Knowledge, April, 2003, review of *Evil in Modern Thought.*
Ethics, January, 1996, Pablo De Greiff, review of *The Unity of Reason,* pp. 500-501.
First Things: A Monthly Journal of Religion and Public Life, January, 2002, Walter Sundberg, "The Conundrum of Evil," review of *Evil in Modern Thought,* pp. 53-58.
Kirkus Reviews, January 15, 1992, review of *Slow Fire,* p. 99.
Library Journal, March 15, 1992, Ian Wallace, review of *Slow Fire,* p. 108; August, 2002, Leslie Armour, review of *Evil in Modern Thought,* p. 100.

New Republic, April 7, 2003, Erin Leib, "Earthquakes," review of *Evil in Modern Thought,* p. 35.
New York Review of Books, June 12, 2003, review of *Evil in Modern Thought.*
New York Times, October 5-6, 2002, review of *Evil in Modern Thought.*
Philosophical Review, April, 1997, Paul Guyer, review of *The Unity of Reason,* pp. 291-295.
Publishers Weekly, January 20, 1992, review of *Slow Fire,* p. 55; July 1, 2002, "Blessed Order for Rage," review of *Evil in Modern Thought,* p. 71.
Review of Metaphysics, March, 1996, review of *The Unity of Reason,* pp. 668-70.
Times Literary Supplement, October 18, 2002, Jonathan Ree, "A Mean and Rootless Fungus," review of *Evil in Modern Thought,* p. 10.
Wall Street Journal, September 3, 2003, review of *Evil in Modern Thought.*

ONLINE

Susan Neiman Home Page, http://www.susan-neiman.de (October 31, 2003).

*   *   *

NESBITT, Marc

PERSONAL: Male. Education: University of Wisconsin, B.A., 1993; University of Michigan, M.A.

ADDRESSES: Home—Brooklyn, NY. *Agent*—c/o Author Mail, Grove Press, Grove-Atlantic, 841 Broadway, 4th Fl., New York, NY 10003.

CAREER: Video game producer and fiction writer.

AWARDS, HONORS: New Yorker Debut Fiction Writer Honor, 2001.

WRITINGS:

Gigantic: Stories, Grove Press (New York, NY), 2002.

Contributor to periodicals, including the *New Yorker* and *Harper's.*

SIDELIGHTS: Marc Nesbitt's debut collection of short fiction, *Gigantic: Stories,* is an offbeat collection of ten tales, each narrated by a young black male and all focusing on sometimes boring, sometimes amusing, but always out of control lives. Bearing such titles as "Man in Towel with Gun" and "Quality Fuel for Electric Living," Nesbitt's tales veer into a landscape of hopelessness, and "suggest a wild, violent reality, moving freely between slapstick and tragedy, calm and calamity," according to *Book* reviewer Kevin Greenberg. Regarding his fictionalized world view, Nesbitt told Heather Lee Schroeder in the *Capital Times Online:* "For the most part, people aren't who they say they are, and the more you deal with people, the more you see it. It never ceases to amaze me how badly people treat each other."

Widely praised when his stories first appeared in the pages of the *New Yorker* and *Harper's,* some critics were disappointed with *Gigantic.* Marc Kloszewski, writing in *Library Journal,* even went so far as to comment that "the average reader will probably be better off reading Nesbitt in those small doses." Kloszewski's reason, he explained, is the "sense of aimlessness, apathy, and confusion, exhibited by Nesbitt's young African American characters." Noting that "all ten narrators sound identical," a *Kirkus Reviews* critic added: "They usually drink too much, but they seem to do this not out of need but because their author couldn't contrive anything else for them to do." Because of the lack of character development, the critic continued, reader attention "shifts to the style. Nesbitt's style, though often bold and winning, can't carry the whole load" in *Gigantic.*

Despite such caveats, other critics were highly enthusiastic about Nesbitt's debut. A *Publishers Weekly* contributor called *Gigantic* a "clever, raucous debut collection," full of stories that "explore a hard, racially charged world, bitterness and compassion vying for top billing." The reviewer also praised the author for his "idiosyncratic voice, his sharp-tongued observations and his convincing, colloquial dialogue," tools with which he effectively communicates "a unique and arresting worldview." Margaret Wappler, writing in *In These Times Online,* stated that, "Breaking noses and bruising hearts, this debut short-story collection is as heady as a Charles Bukowski poem and as rowdy as that poet's many barroom brawls, but the stories are never clumsy or banal—just clamorous and passionate. Like the best of jazz improvisers, Nesbitt is almost spazzy in his enthusiasm for the potential of language." And Sam Sifton, writing in the *New York Times Book Review,* concluded that, "At his best . . . Nesbitt is smart, dark and funny, like a young Elmore Leonard with a drinking problem."

BIOGRAPHICAL AND CRITICAL SOURCES:

PERIODICALS

American Book Review, March-April, 2003, J. D. Smith, review of *Gigantic: Stories,* pp. 38-39.

Book, March-April, 2002, Kevin Greenberg, review of *Gigantic,* p. 75.

Kirkus Reviews, December 15, 2001, review of *Gigantic,* p. 1710.

Library Journal, February 15, 2002, Marc Kloszewski, review of *Gigantic,* p. 180.

New York Times Book Review, March 31, 2002, Sam Sifton, review of *Gigantic,* p. 21.

Publishers Weekly, August 21, 2000, John F. Baker, review of *Gigantic,* p. 20; November 19, 2001, review of *Gigantic,* p. 45.

Southern Review, summer, 2002, Eric Miles Williamson, review of *Gigantic,* p. 666.

ONLINE

Capital Times Online, http://www.madison.com/captimes/ (April 5, 2002), Heather Lee Schroeder, review of *Gigantic.*

In These Times Online, http://www.inthesetimes.com/ (December 2, 2003), Margaret Wappler, review of *Gigantic.**

*   *   *

NEWSOME, David Hay 1929-2004

OBITUARY NOTICE—See index for *CA* sketch: Born June 15, 1929, in Leamington Spa, England; died April 28, 2004. Historian, educator, and author. Newsome was a scholar of Victorian England and former master of Wellington College. A graduate of Emmanuel College, Cambridge, where he earned a B.A. and M.A. with first class honors in 1954, his first post was as history master at a private boys school in Wellington, where he later also headed the department for three years. In 1959, he joined the faculty at Cambridge University as a fellow of Emmanuel College. He served in a variety of tutor and lecturing posts there until becoming headmaster of Christ's Hospital in 1970. A conflict with the school in 1979 concerning coeducation policies led Newsome to resign, but he was quickly appointed master of Wellington College, which he headed until his 1989 retirement. Always conservative in his ideas about education, which often stressed the Christian history of the institutions for which he worked, Newsome was respected by his colleagues even when they tended to adhere to the more liberal theories of education that began to spring up in the 1960s and 1970s. His history books reflected his concerns, including *A History of Wellington College, 1859-1959* (1959), *Godliness and Good Learning: Four Studies in a Victorian Ideal* (1961), and *The Victorian World Picture: Perceptions and Introspections in an Age of Change* (1997). Newsome, who was a fellow of the Royal Historical Society and member of the Royal Society of Literature, also earned a Whitbread Book of the Year Award in 1980 for editing *On the Edge of Paradise: A. C. Benson, the Diarist* (1979).

OBITUARIES AND OTHER SOURCES:

PERIODICALS

Times (London, England), April 30, 2004, p. 39.

*   *   *

NICIEZA, Fabian 1961-

PERSONAL: Born December 31, 1961, in Buenos Aires, Argentina; immigrated to United States, 1965; children: two daughters. *Education:* Rutgers University, B.A. (advertising and public relations), 1983.

ADDRESSES: Agent—c/o Author Mail, Dark Horse Comics, 10956 South East Main St., Milwaukie, OR 97222.

CAREER: Writer, comics creator. Berkley Publishing, New York, NY, became managing editor; Marvel Comics, New York, 1985-1996, began as manufacturing as-

sistant, became advertising manager and writer; Acclaim Comics, Glen Cove, NY, 1996-98, began as editor-in-chief and writer, became president; Marvel Comics, writer, 1998—; freelancer.

WRITINGS:

NFL Superpro: Fourth and Goal to Go, Marvel (New York, NY), 1991.

(Editor, with others) *Hook: The Official Movie Adaptation* (*Hook,* numbers 1-4), Marvel (New York, NY), 1991.

Bill and Ted's Bogus Journey, Marvel (New York, NY), 1991.

(With others) *The New Warriors: Beginnings,* Marvel (New York, NY), 1992.

(With Rob Liefeld and Todd McFarlane) *Stan Lee Presents X-Force and Spider-Man in Sabotage* (*X-Force,* numbers 3, 4, and *Spider-Man,* number 16), Marvel (New York, NY), 1992.

(With Tom DeFalco) *The New Warriors: Beginnings* (*The New Warriors,* numbers 1, 2, 3, and 4, and *Thor,* numbers 411 and 412), Marvel (New York, NY), 1992.

Gambit and the X-Ternals, illustrated by Salvatore Larroca and Al Milgrom, Marvel (New York, NY), 1995.

The Amazing X-Men, Marvel (New York, NY), 1995.

X-Men: Fatal Attractions, Marvel (New York, NY), 1995.

(With others) *Justice League: Midsummer's Nightmare* (*Justice League: A Midsummer's Nightmare,* numbers 1-3), DC Comics (New York, NY), 1996.

Deadpool: The Circle Chase, illustrated by Joe Madureira, Marvel (New York, NY), 1997.

The Blackburne Covenant, illustrated by Stefano Rafeale, Dark Horse Comics (Milwaukie, OR), 2004.

Cable/Deadpool: If Looks Could Kill, edited by Jeff Youngquist, illustrated by Mark Brooks, Marvel (New York, NY), 2004.

Writer of and contributor to comic books, including *Psi-Force, New Warriors, X-Men, Spider-Man, Nomad, Captain America, Gambit, Hawkeye,* and *Thunderbolts,* all Marvel; *Troublemakers, Turok,* and *Classics Illustrated Study Guides,* all Acclaim Comics; *The Blackburne Covenant, Buffy the Vampire Slayer,* and *Hellboy,* all Dark Horse Comics; *Justice League,* DC Comics.

SIDELIGHTS: Comic book writer Fabian Nicieza was born in Buenos Aires, Argentina, and moved with his parents to the United States when he was four. He grew up in New Jersey and graduated from Rutgers University with a degree in advertising and public relations and was hired by Marvel for a position in manufacturing, but he soon became the advertising manager. Nicieza's true calling, however, was writing comics, and he created his first, *Psi-Force,* in 1987. He followed with *New Warriors, Nomad,* and the "X" series, *X-Force* with Scott Lobdell, *Uncanny X-Men,* and *X-Men.*

Nicieza left Marvel in 1996 to join Acclaim Comics, where he developed the character of Turok and created the new series. As he told Roger Ash of *Westfield Comics* online, "The current Turok is a concept more than a person. Turok means 'son of stone' in the fictional Native American Saquin language. The eldest-born male in the Fireseed family is responsible for assuming the responsibilities of Turok and guarding Earth from a race of evolved dinosaurs and from attacks which emanate from an other-dimensional 'sewer of the universe' known as the Lost Land."

The responsibility has now fallen to Josh Fireseed, a star college baseball player who is neither prepared nor interested in carrying out the task. Fortunately, he has a brainy roommate in Barry Hackowitz, who helps him accomplish his missions.

Nicieza's *Troublemakers* for Acclaim features four kids who are the children of scientists working for a pharmaceutical company. They were genetically bred to be perfect human beings and live below the complex where their abilities are developed and tracked.

Nicieza returned to Marvel in 1998 to write the new *Gambit* series and then *Thunderbolts. Sequential Tart* interviewer Keri Wilson said *Gambit* "touched lightly into central themes in Southern literature with a liberal dose of a science-fiction fantasy blended with adventure/suspense stories. [Nicieza] showed an unusual sensitivity and accuracy in capturing the [Southern, Cajun] culture."

When Nicieza again left Marvel he concentrated on his new project, *The Blackburne Covenant,* the book and the series, for Dark Horse Comics. It is about Richard Kaine, a man with no prospects who writes a blockbuster novel. The plot revolves around the question of where his sudden talent came from. A *Dark Horse Comics Online* writer said in an interview with Nicieza that "Kaine's search for the source of his ideas forms the backbone of the book. What Kaine believed was fiction as he wrote it turns out to be factual, and he begins to uncover the world's secret history . . . and the organization that has been steering it. But to reveal more would be unfair."

Wilson asked Nicieza what advice he would give his daughters if one or both of them decided to follow in his footsteps, and whether he would advise them to work for a publisher or write independently. Nicieza replied that "having worked a staff job at Marvel for so long, I wouldn't trade those years for anything ever. They were some of the happiest of my life. And on a creative end as a writer, it was both a boon and a burden. The thrill of getting my first freelance job, of knowing that my work was generating some buzz within the editorial offices, that was unparalleled. Growing slowly, sometimes frustratingly so, getting better and better assignments, all of that was incredibly fulfilling."

He went on to say that if his daughters were creatively driven, he would "encourage they go the independent route. Ultimately, on that road, I think the potential for creative and financial reward is commensurate to the quality and enjoyment of the work. If they were driven towards staff-oriented careers, like editorial or advertising, then a job at any of the companies is worthwhile. Hell, making comics still beats just about any other job I can imagine in terms of day-to-day satisfaction. What would someone rather be doing to earn a living?"

BIOGRAPHICAL AND CRITICAL SOURCES:

ONLINE

Dark Horse Comics Online, http://www.darkhorse. com/ (January 23, 2003), interview with Nicieza.

Rational Magic, http://www.rationalmagic.com/ (August 15, 2003), review of *The New Warriors: Beginnings.*

Sequential Tart, http://www.sequentialtart.com/ (November, 2001), Keri Wilson, interview with Nicieza.

Westfield Comics, http://westfieldcomics.com/ (January, 1998), Roger Ash, interview with Nicieza.*

NOONE, John 1936-

PERSONAL: Born February 7, 1936, in Darlington, England. *Education:* King's College, University of Durham.

ADDRESSES: Agent—c/o Author Mail, St. Martin's Press, 175 Fifth Ave., New York, NY 10010.

CAREER: Author and educator. *Military service:* Durham Light Infantry, 1954-56.

AWARDS, HONORS: Geoffrey Faber Memorial Prize for fiction, for *The Man with the Chocolate Egg;* Arts Council Award, for *The Night of Accomplishment.*

WRITINGS:

The Man with the Chocolate Egg, Hamish Hamilton (London, England), 1966.
The Night of Accomplishment, Hamish Hamilton (London, England), 1974.
The Man Behind the Iron Mask, St. Martin's Press (New York, NY), 1988.

SIDELIGHTS: John Noone taught English for several years at universities in North Africa and Japan before writing his first novel, *The Man with the Chocolate Egg.* This book, which brought Noone considerable acclaim, tells the story of a young British soldier who attempts, unsuccessfully, to deliver a stolen hand grenade (the chocolate egg of the title) to his terrorist brother. Critics compared the book, which juxtaposes vividly realistic segments against boldly surrealistic ones, with the work of film directors Ingmar Bergman, Alfred Hitchcock, Federico Fellini, and Michelangelo Antonioni. As a contributor for *Dictionary of Literary Biography* wrote, the novel "has the tension, suspense, and air of foreboding of a first-rate psychological thriller." The imagery, as the critic noted, emphasizes the grotesque and the violent, including images of crucifixion, blood, and violent death. A writer for *Sunday Times* observed that the novel "depicts the heavy coldness of horror so accurately it is a relief to be able to close it and look around." *The Man with the Chocolate Egg* won the Geoffrey Faber Memorial Prize for fiction.

Noone's second novel, *The Night of Accomplishment,* a mix of autobiography, fiction, and myth, centers on Luke, who is described as the author of *The Man with the Chocolate Egg.* Luke—who, like Noone, is a lecturer in Kyoto—is now trying to write another book titled *Proteus.* But things are going badly for Luke; he cannot concentrate on his art; physical problems leave him immobilized; and an illicit love affair threatens his marriage. "Noone writes with intensity and intelligence about the complex interrelationships between an artist's life and his work and about the need to destroy in order to create," wrote the *Dictionary of Literary Biography* contributor. *The Night of Accomplishment* received an Arts Council Award.

In his third book, Noone departed from fiction to explore the history of the anonymous prisoner who, during the reign of Louis XIV, was ordered to wear an iron mask to hide his identity. Made famous by Alexandre Dumas's novel *The Man in the Iron Mask,* this prisoner has been the subject of much historical speculation, yet his identity has never been definitively established. Noone's book *The Man Behind the Iron Mask* examines the mystery and offers a fresh interpretation of the evidence. As Noone explained to Eden Ross Lipson in *New York Times Book Review,* he had originally set out to write another novel, which he had begun years earlier while teaching in Japan. Noone had moved to Cannes to complete the manuscript. From his apartment he could see the famous prison on the island of Sainte-Marguerite where the Man in the Iron Mask was believed to have been incarcerated. He began to think about this prisoner so much that he eventually abandoned the novel, which was going to be about "double identity or identical appearance— two people with the same face or one face with two personalities" and set about researching and writing *The Man Behind the Iron Mask.* Critics admired the book's treatment of its intriguing subject. A reviewer in *Trenton Times* described the book as "an engrossing non-fiction tale of mystery, money, greed, intrigue, cover-up and myth." In *New York Times Book Review,* Joan DeJean noted that Noone "is excellent at setting scenes and providing the historical information necessary to understand the sometimes complicated plots he unravels." The critic added that "In all his incarnations, the man behind the iron mask is the stuff of high (melo)drama, and Mr. Noone makes the most of this sometimes outrageous material. In addition, he never fails to highlight those aspects of the story that show the power of rumor to reduce someone to anonymity while appearing to be driven by the desire to identify."

BIOGRAPHICAL AND CRITICAL SOURCES:

BOOKS

Dictionary of Literary Biography, Volume 14: *British Novelists Since 1960,* Gale (Detroit, MI),1983.

PERIODICALS

New Statesman, October 25, 1974.
New York Times Book Review, December 25, 1988, Eden Ross Lipson, "Identity Crisis," p. 2, Joan DeJean, "The Rumor That Will Not Die," p. 2.
Observer, October 20, 1974.*

*   *   *

NORTON, (William) Elliot 1903-2003

PERSONAL: Born May 17, 1903, in Boston, MA; died, July 20, 2003, in Fort Lauderdale, FL; son of William Laurence and Mary Elizabeth (Fitzgerald) Norton; married Florence E. Stelmach; children: David A., Elizabeth N., and Jane Norton Hardy. *Education:* Harvard College, A.B., 1926. *Hobbies and other interests:* Gardening.

CAREER: Drama critic. Theater critic for *Boston Post,* 1934-56; *Boston Record American,* 1956-62; and *Boston Herald American* (now *Boston Herald*), 1973-82; host of public television series "Elliot Norton Reviews," 1958-82. Lecturer and part time faculty member at numerous colleges, including Emerson College, Boston College, and Boston University.

AWARDS, HONORS: Boston College Citation of Merit, 1947; Connor Memorial Award of Phi Alpha Tau, 1956; George Foster Peabody Award, 1962, for "Elliot Norton Reviews"; Rodgers and Hammerstein College Presidents' Award, 1962; George Jean Nathan Award 1963-64; Antoinette Perry Award, 1971; Humanities Award of the National Council of Teachers of English, 1971; New England Theatre Conference Award, 1974; designated a Grand Bostonian, 1978; voted into Theater Hall of Fame by the American Theater Critics Association, 1988; nine honorary degrees.

WRITINGS:

Broadway Down East: An Informal Account of the Plays, Players, and Playhouses of Boston from Puritan Times to the Present, Trustees of the Public Library of the City of Boston (Boston, MA), 1978.

SIDELIGHTS: Considered one of the great figures of twentieth-century drama criticism, Elliot Norton reviewed more than 6,000 plays during his forty-eight-year career with Boston newspapers. His style of writing, as *Boston Globe* contributor Ed Siegel explained in Norton's obituary, was known as "play doctoring." Producers would often bring their Broadway-bound plays to Boston first to test critical response. In many cases, reviewers pointed toward adjustments that, once implemented, improved the plays. Norton was considered one of the major figures among Boston's "play doctoring" critics. Directors as diverse as Neil Simon, Joshua Logan, and Robert Brustein credited him with sound judgment and helpful criticism in the service of the theater, which he obviously loved. Siegel noted in his obituary that producer Alexander Cohen called Norton "the most valuable critic in America," while Brustein noted that "his incisive, understanding, and encouraging reviews of our work [at Theatre on the Green at Wellesley] marked him as a man with a true devotion to the stage. . . . He was the exemplary critic, never an adversary, always a friend."

According to Norton's colleague Kevin Kelly, who served as *Boston Globe* theater critic from 1962 to 1994 and was quoted in Siegel's obituary, Norton "has always written from a strict moral point of view, sometimes dismissing ugly, if true-to-life, plays for their lack of edification, or uplift, which is based on [the poet and playwright John] Dryden's assumption that art must entertain and instruct. . . . He is sometimes unsettled by 'unpleasant' themes. But all this is not posture, nor attitude. It is the genuine man whose opinions are informed and intelligent, and the measure of his being."

OBITUARIES:

PERIODICALS

American Theatre, September, 2003, p. 20.
Boston Globe, July 21, 2003, Ed Siegel, "Elliot Norton, One Hundred, legendary critic of American theater," p. C12.

Daily Variety, July 22, 2003, p. 9.

Los Angeles Times, July 23, 2003, "Elliot Norton, One Hundred, Boston Theater Critic Wrote 6,000 Reviews," p. B11.

New York Times, July 23, 2003, "Elliot Norton, One Hundred, a Critic in Boston Read on Broadway," p. A17.*

*   *   *

NUTTGENS, Patrick 1930-2004

OBITUARY NOTICE—See index for *CA* sketch: Born March 2, 1930, in Whiteleaf, Buckinghamshire, England; died March 15, 2004, in York, England. Architect, educator, and author. Nuttgens was best known as the former architecture professor and director of the Institute of Advanced Architectural Studies at York University, as well as the director of Leeds Polytechnic. His diploma in architecture was from the Edinburgh College of Art; he then became the first graduate in architecture at the University of Edinburgh, where he earned a master's in 1954 and a Ph.D. in 1959. Nuttgens remained in Edinburgh to lecture in architecture until 1962, when he joined the York University faculty as a reader and director of the Institute of Advanced Architectural Studies, later becoming a professor of architecture in 1968. Under his leadership, the institute became famous for its hands-on approach to learning in which students were first thrown into work to solve real-life architectural problems and only after this experience taught the basic principals involved. Nuttgens called this his "learning by doing" approach. In 1969, he left York for Leeds Polytechnic, where he served as director until 1986. After retiring, Nuttgens spent the rest of his days back at York University as an honorary professor. In addition to his work as a teacher, Nuttgens became a familiar face on British television sets as the host of various BBC programs about historic and modern architecture, such as *Spirit of the Age* (1975), *Edwin Lutyens: Last Architect of the Age of Humanism* (1981), and *The Home Front: Housing the People, 1840-1990* (1989), which was adapted as a book of the same title in 1989. Named a Commander of the Order of the British Empire in 1982, he was the author of several other books, including *The Story of Architecture* (1983) and *Understanding Modern Architecture* (1988).

OBITUARIES AND OTHER SOURCES:

PERIODICALS

Daily Telegraph (London, England), April 5, 2004.
Guardian (Manchester, England), March 17, 2004, p. 25.
Independent (London, England), April 10, 2004, p. 44.
Times (London, England), March 29, 2004, p. 27.

*   *   *

NWANKWO, Victor 1944-2002

PERSONAL: Born December 12, 1944, in Ajalla, Nigeria; died of gunshot wounds, August 29, 2002, in Enugu, Nigeria; son of Emmanual O. and Janet (Ikejiani) Nwankwo; married Theodora Ndigwe, 1979; children: Uzoma, Oby, Ogo, Ral. *Education:* Attended Yaba College of Technology; University of Nigeria, graduated, 1971.

CAREER: Author; Federal Ministry of Works, assistant technical officer, 1962-63; Ove Arup and Partners, design engineer, 1971-74; Brunelli Construction Company, design engineer; Maiduguri Airport, assistant project manager; Cubitts Nigeria, head of design, 1975-76; Joart United Construction and Engineering Ltd, director of production, 1976-78; Fourth Dimension Publishing Company, founder/managing director, 1984-2002. *Military service:* Biafran Army, Engineers Squadron, combat officer.

MEMBER: African Books Collective, African Publishers Network (chairman), Nigerian Publishers Association, African Book Publishing Record, African Books Collection (member of council of management), Nigerian Book Foundation (board of trustees), Book Aid International (trustee), Nigerian Society of Engineers.

WRITINGS:

Der Weg Nach Udina, translated into German by Ruth Bowert, Afrika-Presse Dienst (Bonn, Germany), 1969, published as *The Road to Udima,* Fourth Dimension Publishers (Enugu, Nigeria), 1985.

(Contributor and coeditor, with Chinua Achebe) *The Insider: Stores of War and Peace from Nigeria,* Fourth Dimension Publishers (Enugu, Nigeria), 1971.

Also wrote a daily newspaper column.

SIDELIGHTS: Although Victor Nwankwo was an author of a book of fiction and frequent contributor to a daily newspaper, he was best known around the world as a promoter of books, especially books written in Africa. As described by Hans M. Zell in the on-line publication, the *Bellagio Publishing Network Newsletter,* Nwankwo was a "bookish person and an avid reader," who adapted to the world of books with ease. Although he had been the editor of his school's magazine, Nwankwo had studied to be an engineer. In the early part of his career, he worked as an engineer, but his passion for books seemed to overtake him. In 1977, he and his brothers pooled their money and started a publishing house called Fourth Dimension Publishers. Nwankwo worked at the publishing house only on a part-time basis, at first, because he was enjoying a successful career in engineering. But seven years later, Nwankwo found himself running the family publishing business practically by himself and was soon to be hailed by an international community of peers as one of Africa's leading publishers.

Nwankwo was born in Ajalla, Nigeria, and educated at the University of Nigeria. His education was interrupted by war in 1967 when the Igbo people of eastern Nigeria proclaimed independence from the rest of Nigeria. The war raged for many years as the Igbo people attempted to set up a nation they called Biafra. During this time, Nwankwo joined the Biafran army as a writer for the army's publication called *Biafra.* Later, he served on the frontline as a combat officer in the Engineers Squadron. In 1970, the civil war ended, and after hiding for several months in fear of reprisals against him by the Nigerian troops, Nwankwo returned home and completed his degree in engineering.

After college, Nwankwo took on several jobs in his trade, working for various construction companies. Then when his brothers, Aruther and Ejiofor, began discussing a publishing house, Nwankwo took an interest in the enterprise and helped them set up the Fourth Dimension Publishing Company. The name of their company came from insights the brothers had learning

during the war. As Nwankwo told Katherine Salahi, also writing for the *Ballagio Publishing Network Newsletter,* "the experience of war taught us there were more than the three physical dimensions of life. The fourth coordinate is the human spirit that's needed to make change in the life of a nation."

Nwankwo's life began to change rather dramatically in 1983, when the political climate in Nigeria worsened, and, in consequence, the economy suffered, lessening the number of construction and engineering projects available. In the meantime, Nwankwo's brothers had both become involved in politics and had little time to tend to the publishing house. So that was when Nwankwo stepped in, applying, as he told Salahi, his "engineering mind into the organisation."

Books were nothing new to Nwankwo, who was used to reading a novel a day. He had also written poetry, a daily newspaper column on life in Nigeria, and a novel. But the publishing end of the business was relatively new to him, and as he told Salahi, "I was largely trained by my staff." It did not take long, however, for publishing to become his passion. He had learned early the power of words. Through his publishing house, he allowed many other Nigerian voices to be heard. "I've discovered you can contribute more by writing than through political activity," Nwankwo told Salahi. He planned to return to his writing upon retiring from the publishing business. Nwankwo was only fifty-seven when he was shot down in front of his home, in what many have called a political assassination.

In the late 1960s, Nwankwo wrote a book he called *The Road to Udima.* In it he recalled his experiences during the Biafran war. In his obituary in the London *Times,* Nwankwo's book is referred to as "unusual in its portrayal of the corruption and propaganda of the Biafran Army." The original manuscript of this book was taken to Germany by a journalist who liked what he had read. The book was first published in German, although it had been written in English. The original manuscript was then lost. But in 1985, Fourth Dimension had the German edition translated back into English and published their own version of Nwankwo's novel, which Zell described as a book that "captures the fears and emotions of Biafran society during the civil war and tackles corruption and other issues not normally mentioned by the Biafran propaganda machine." Before his death, Nwankwo also coedited a collection of short stories about the war and subsequent peace. He also contributed a story of his own to this collection, called "The End of the Road."

Nwankwo died on August 29, 2002, of gunshot wounds.

BIOGRAPHICAL AND CRITICAL SOURCES:

ONLINE

Bellagio Publishing Network Newsletter, http://www.bellagiopublishingnetwork.org/ (October, 1998), Katherine Salahi, "Talking Books, Chief Victor Nwankwo in Conversation with Katherine Salahi"; (November, 2002), Hans M. Zell, "In Memoriam: Chief Victor Nwankwo."

OBITUARIES:

PERIODICALS

Bookseller, October 11, 2002, Tim Rix, Gary Pulsifer, "Obituaries," p. 11.
Publishers Weekly, September 30, 2002, Sally Taylor, "Nigerian Murder Draws Concern," p. 18.
Times (London, England), October 25, 2002, "Obituaries."*

O

OBERMAN, Sheldon 1949-2004

OBITUARY NOTICE—See index for *CA* sketch: Born May 20, 1949, in Winnipeg, Manitoba, Canada; died of cancer, March 26, 2004, in Winnipeg, Manitoba, Canada. Educator, artist, and author. Oberman, a diverse talent whose interests included creating found-art objects and song writing, composed books for all ages but was best known for his award-winning children's books, a number of which drew on his experiences growing up in a Jewish family. After studying literature at the University of Winnipeg, where he earned a B.A. in 1972, and at the University of Jerusalem, he completed a B.Ed. at the University of Manitoba and started a career as a high school English and drama teacher at Joseph Wolinsky Collegiate in Winnipeg. His routine of telling bedtime stories to his children evolved into an interest in writing his own stories, which include award-winning works such as *The Lion in the Lake/Le Lion dans le Lac* (1988), *This Business with Elijah* (1993), and *The Always Prayer Shawl* (1994). Oberman enjoyed performing these stories live in front of young audiences, and to keep his acting talents honed, he took on small movie roles; he also wrote screenplays and directed short films. In addition, he wrote lyrics for the popular Canadian children's entertainer Fred Penner, and five of the albums released by Penner featuring Oberman's songs received Juno nominations. More recently, Oberman gained critical acclaim for his 1999 title, *The Shaman's Nephew: A Life in the Far North,* written with Simon Tookoome, which was shortlisted for the Governor General's Award and won the Norma Fleck Award, and 2000's *The Wisdom Bird: A Tale of Solomon and Sheba.* Though he developed inoperable cancer in his throat, Oberman continued working in his last months, publishing *Island of the Minotaur* in 2003 and completing a two-volume set of Jewish folk tales, which will be published posthumously. Other honors earned by Oberman include the National Jewish Book Award and the Sydney Taylor Book Award from the Association of Jewish Libraries; after his death, the Manitoba Writers' Guild named their writing program for emerging authors after Oberman.

OBITUARIES AND OTHER SOURCES:

PERIODICALS

Globe & Mail (Toronto, Ontario, Canada), May 25, 2004.
Winnipeg Free Press (Winnipeg, Manitoba, Canada), June 10, 2004.

* * *

O'CONNOR, Rebecca K. 1971-

PERSONAL: Born February 2, 1971, in Riverside, CA. *Ethnicity:* "Caucasian." *Education:* Attended University of California—Davis, 1989-92; University of California—Riverside, B.A., 1994.

ADDRESSES: Agent—c/o Author Mail, Avalon Books, 160 Madison Ave., 5th Floor, New York, NY 10016. *E-mail*—palisade@gate.net.

CAREER: Grace's Attorney Services, Riverside, CA, owner, 1993-98; Natural Encounters, Lake Wales, FL, bird trainer and supervisor, 1998-2001; Living Desert, Palm Desert, CA, animal trainer and development associate, 2001—.

MEMBER: Romance Writers of America (Orange County chapter).

WRITINGS:

Falcon's Return (romance fiction), Avalon Books (New York, NY), 2002.
Endangered Animals and Habitats (young adult nonfiction), Lucent Books (San Diego, CA), 2002.

*   *   *

OLSON, Steve E. 1956-

PERSONAL: Born September 5, 1956, in San Diego, CA; son of Frank (an accountant) and Diane (a day care administrator; maiden name, Taylor) Olson; married Lynn Richman (an education writer), June 8, 1980; children: Eric, Sarah. *Ethnicity:* "Mixed." *Education:* Yale University, B.A., 1978. *Politics:* Independent. *Religion:* Unitarian-Universalist. *Hobbies and other interests:* Swimming.

ADDRESSES: Agent—Rafe Sagalyn, 7201 Wisconsin Ave., Suite 675, Bethesda, MD 20814. *E-mail*—solson@his.com.

CAREER: Freelance writer, 1978-88; White House Science Office, Washington, DC, writer, 1988-91; freelance writer, 1991—.

AWARDS, HONORS: Nomination for National Book Award, nonfiction category, National Book Foundation, 2002, for *Mapping Human History: Discovering the Past through Our Genes.*

WRITINGS:

Biotechnology: An Industry Comes of Age, National Academy Press (Washington, DC), 1986.
Shaping the Future: Biology and Human Values, National Academy Press (Washington, DC), 1989.
Mapping Human History: Discovering the Past through Our Genes, Houghton Mifflin (Boston, MA), 2002.

Contributor to magazines, including *Atlantic Monthly, Science, Washingtonian, Teacher, Washington Monthly, Astronomy,* and *Discovery Channel Online.*

WORK IN PROGRESS: A narrative account of the Forty-second International Mathematical Olympiad, publication expected in 2004; research on genetics and behavior.

SIDELIGHTS: Steve E. Olson told *CA:* "I grew up in a small cattle-ranching, wheat-growing town in eastern Washington State, came east to college, and have lived in Washington, DC, ever since. Maybe my small-town roots account for my fascination with going to new places and learning new things. I've always been interested in math and science, partly because of the new worlds they opened up to me when I was a child. I can remember reading about famous mathematicians as a kid and marveling at those long-ago men and the ideas they left behind.

"I entered college thinking vaguely about becoming a scientist or mathematician, but my ambitions soon changed. At college I had a wonderful series of professors and teachers who revealed to me parts of life that had nothing to do with math or science but were just as exciting. I took history courses, literature courses, language courses, music courses. And I began to read again, something I hadn't done much since elementary school. I began writing essays, stories, and articles, both for my classes and for various campus publications. I met other writers and realized that a person could make a living at this exasperating, exhilarating activity, even if the path ahead was far from clear.

"I never lost my interest in science, and I graduated with a science degree. For most of the twenty-five years since then I've been a freelance writer, specializing in math, science, and science education (I'm married to an education writer). I did have one job during that time. I worked for three years as a writer in the White House Science Office. It was a wonderful experience, but I came to realize that it was a digression for me, and I left the White House resolved to return to freelancing for good.

"My ideas for articles and books tend to ferment for a long time. I've wanted to write about anthropological genetics, which was the subject of *Mapping Human*

History: Discovering the Past through Our Genes, since I read about mitochondrial Eve in the late 1980s. My next book will be a narrative account of the Forty-second International Mathematical Olympiad, which is an annual mathematics competition that I've followed for many years. I'm not sure what I'll do after that, but something will turn up—it always has.'"

BIOGRAPHICAL AND CRITICAL SOURCES:

PERIODICALS

American Journal of Human Genetics, December, 2002, Lynn Jorde, review of *Mapping Human History: Discovering the Past through Our Genes,* p. 1484.

Futurist, November-December, 1990, review of *Shaping the Future: Biology and Human Values,* p. 39.

Kirkus Reviews, April 1, 2002, review of *Mapping Human History,* p. 474.

Publishers Weekly, April 29, 2002, review of *Mapping Human History,* p. 52.

Science News, June 15, 2002, review of *Mapping Human History,* p. 383.

*   *   *

OPPENHEIMER, Michael 1924-

PERSONAL: Born May 27, 1924, in Los Angeles, CA; son of Michael and Caroline Magdalen (Harvey) Oppenheimer; married Helen Lucas-Tooth (a theologian), July 12, 1947; children: Henrietta Oppenheimer Scott, Matilda Oppenheimer King, Xanthe Oppenheimer Mosley. *Ethnicity:* "European." *Education:* Christ Church, Oxford, M.A., 1947, B.Litt., 1953. *Religion:* Anglican.

ADDRESSES: Home—L'Aiguillon, Grouville, Jersey, Channel Islands.

CAREER: Oxford University, Oxford, England, lecturer in history at Lincoln College, 1955-68, lecturer in history at Magdalen College, 1966-68. *Military service:* South African Army, 1942-45; served in Egypt and Italy; became lieutenant.

WRITINGS:

The Monuments of Italy: A Regional Survey of Art, Architecture, and Archaeology from Classical to Modern Times, six volumes, I. B. Tauris and Co. (London, England), 2002.

WORK IN PROGRESS: Continuing historical research.

SIDELIGHTS: Michael Oppenheimer told *CA:* "My interest in history began when I was about ten years old; and it was after school, the wartime army, and the university that I became a university lecturer at Oxford. I taught European and English history, English constitutional history, and historical geography. It was during my war service in Italy that I became enthralled with Italian architecture and art, and from about 1950 my wife and I were able to visit Italy regularly. I used to write notes about places we planned to visit, and as these grew it occurred to me that they might be useful to others. This was the genesis of *The Monuments of Italy: A Regional Survey of Art, Architecture, and Archaeology from Classical to Modern Times.* In 1955 I began working on it seriously. It entailed visits to every archaeological site, every museum, and every building of even marginal interest, selecting what should be in the book, making notes, and taking photographs. Through the years all but very minor objects were visited twice, and important ones several times.

"The book is long, about a million words in six volumes. It is organized in such a way that information can be found easily when it is wanted. Five volumes cover the various regions of Italy. The sixth has a biographical index of architects and artists and a large glossary. This includes virtually all other people mentioned; numerous subjects such as Greek pottery, Roman painting, or architectural styles; all technical terms; and a number of necessary translations of Italian words.

"The book is a work of scholarship, but except for the close observation of the objects described, it is not a work of original research. It is a teaching book, written for anyone of reasonable education in any subject, who wishes to visit Italy but knows little or nothing about the pleasures in store."

BIOGRAPHICAL AND CRITICAL SOURCES:

PERIODICALS

Library Journal, September 1, 2002, Anna Youssefi, review of *The Monuments of Italy: A Regional*

Survey of Art, Architecture, and Archaeology from Classical to Modern Times, p. 170.

Spectator, May 25, 2002, David Ekserdjian, review of *The Monuments of Italy,* p. 48.

* * *

ORIZIO, Riccardo 1961-

PERSONAL: Born 1961, in Italy; married Pia-Sophie (a pediatrician).

ADDRESSES: Home—Saruni Camp, Nairobi, Kenya. *Agent*—Shirley Stewart, 21 Denmark St., London WC2H 8NA England. *E-mail*—info@riccardoorizio. com.

CAREER: Journalist and foreign correspondent. Worked as a correspondent for CNN, *Corriere della Sera,* and *La Repubblica.*

AWARDS, HONORS: Thomas Cook Travel Book Award shortlist, for *Lost White Tribes: Journeys among the Forgotten.*

WRITINGS:

Lost White Tribes: Journeys among the Forgotten, Secker & Warburg (London, England), 2000, published as *Lost White Tribes: The End of Privilege and the Last Colonials in Sri Lanka, Jamaica, Brazil, Haiti, Namibia, and Guadeloupe,* translated by Avril Bardoni, Free Press (New York, NY), 2001.

Talk of the Devil: Encounters with Seven Dictators, translated by Avril Bardoni, Walker (New York, NY), 2003.

Works have been translated into Dutch, Turkish, and English.

SIDELIGHTS: Italian journalist Riccardo Orizio has had two lives, according to a biographer on the *Riccardo Orizio* Web site. In his "first life," Orizio has been an international correspondent for CNN and prominent Italian newspapers, with dispatches from more than eighty countries. He covered the wars in the Balkans, the tentative periods of peace, and the lives of those affected by the wars. He has resided in Milan, Brussels, Atlanta, and London. Orizio lives his "second life" in Nairobi, Kenya, among the Maasai warriors and tribespeople at Saruni, a safari camp in Kenya's Masai Mara.

In his 2000 book, *Lost White Tribes: Journeys among the Forgotten* (published in 2001 as *Lost White Tribes: The End of Privilege and the Last Colonials in Sri Lanka, Jamaica, Brazil, Haiti, Namibia, and Guadeloupe*), Orizio carefully examines six groups of people comprising the remaining populations of colonial settlers who "went semi-native; adopting many of the customs and attitudes of the people whose lands they colonized, yet clinging all the while to customs and attitudes of the countries they left behind," wrote Jonathan Yardley in *Washington Post Book World.* Orizio recounts how he met his first "white tribe" when he encountered in Sri Lanka "a young white waiter who doesn't look local but actually is," Yardley noted. The waiter was a member of a group of Dutch Burghers living in decaying eighteenth-century mansions with no heat, running water, or electricity. In other places, Orizio finds similar anachronisms. In Haiti, the Blancs Matignon, descendants of Poles who fought in Napoleonic war-era regiments, have congregated on a single mountaintop in the area and live in African huts without a single modern convenience. Though dark-skinned, their features and blond hair make their ancestry clear. A group of French colonists founded a Utopian retreat in the remote interior of the island of Guadeloupe, but found themselves "isolated and despised by both blacks and the elite whites of the island," wrote Charles Sprawson in the *Times Literary Supplement.* The group evinces a great deal of malnutrition and debilitation "as a result of generations of incestuous marriages," noted Sprawson.

Orizio also located a group derived from the American Civil War, "the outpost of descendants of Confederate diehards who fled to Brazil at the end of the Civil War," Yardley commented. Many still cling to Civil War-era ideas, decorating their houses with Confederate flags and pictures of Robert E. Lee. Traditional music from banjos and trumpets can still be heard in their homes and during their parties. The group holds annual celebrations of their history where boys don gray uniforms and girls dress up like southern belles, and where a faux Miss Arkansas competes in a beauty pageant with a similarly displaced Miss Tennessee. In all of the countries he visits, Orizio finds "small communities of whites who have been bypassed by history," commented a *Publishers Weekly* reviewer.

"Orizio's is a perceptive and often amusing, well-translated study, of the tragic remnants of a lost world," remarked Sprawson. Orizio "is a connoisseur of languor and decay—plantation houses, lattice-work verandas and seventeenth-century balconies, that now stand empty, 'reduced to crumbling shells shrouded in detritus,' and people too weary to move," with little or nothing to do to occupy their time, Sprawson commented. "Orizio is a keen observer and a fine writer," wrote L. D. Meagher on the *CNN* Web site. "His descriptions of the landscapes and the people who inhabit them immerse readers in distant and exotic places, where they are not always welcome."

Talk of the Devil: Encounters with Seven Dictators presents interviews Orizio conducted with seven overthrown, fallen, deposed, or otherwise out-of-power dictators—or their strong-willed wives. "I deliberately chose those who had fallen from power in disgrace, because those who fall on their feet tend not to examine their own conscience," Orizio explained in the book. Interview subjects include Idi Amin, Ugandan dictator and alleged cannibal; Central Africa's self-proclaimed emperor, Jean-Bedel Bokassa; Poland's Wojciech Jaruzelski; Haiti's Jean-Claude "Baby Doc" Duvalier; Albania's Enver and Nexhmije Hoxha; Ethiopia's Mengistu Haile-Mariam; and Yugoslavia's Slobodan Milosevic and his wife, Mira Markovic. A letter from Panamanian strongman Manuel Noriega rounds out the contents. Some of the interviews were hurried and short; others were conducted under dangerous circumstances; still others were done in prisons. In all cases, Orizio lets the fallen dictators, emperors, and power-players speak for themselves, telling their own stories in their own words. If the book's interview subjects "come off as villains, they are hung by their own words, by their own distorted views and their places in it," commented David Pitt in a review for *Booklist*.

"None of the fallen tyrants is notably well off now, even though, with the possible exception of Jaruzelski, they had looted or squandered their national treasuries with a rapacity breathtaking to behold," commented Roger K. Miller on the *Pittsburgh Tribune-Review* Web site. "They live in a world of denial, stoutly proclaiming the rightness of their actions and expressing not a scintilla of regret or apology for the misery they visited upon their countries." Amin, for example, is found shopping in a local grocery store while in exile in Saudi Arabia. Bokassa lives in relative comfort in France but claims himself to be the thirteenth apostle of the Catholic church. Duvalier protests "that he never wanted the luxuries of rule but took over out of a sense of duty to his nation," commented Jad Adams on the *Guardian Unlimited* Web site. Albania's Nexhmije Hoxha declared that "The ethnic conflicts seen in Yugoslavia were averted in Albania" because of "the destruction of mosques and churches and the abolition of religion," Adams wrote. "Dictators are like movie stars, the rich and the famous: we can vicariously identify with their power and glory when they're riding high, and more righteously, enjoy their fall," observed Adam Hochschild in a review for the *Times Literary Supplement*. Steven Menashi, writing in *National Review*, commented that "Successful tyrants might at least have some experience of living in actual reality on which to reflect; Orizio's disgraced, fallen dictators have nothing but their own illusions."

Menashi called *Talk of the Devil* "compelling reading," and a *Publishers Weekly* reviewer noted that "some of the interviews are stunning" in what they reveal about the interviewee. "Readers will take deserved pleasure in these tyrants' falls, and in Orizio's sharp, literate prose," commented a *Kirkus Reviews* critic.

BIOGRAPHICAL AND CRITICAL SOURCES:

PERIODICALS

Booklist, April 15, 2003, David Pitt, review of *Talk of the Devil: Encounters with Seven Dictators,* p. 1432.

Kirkus Reviews, March 15, 2003, review of *Talk of the Devil,* p. 447.

National Review, September 1, 2003, Steven Menashi, "Focus on Evil," review of *Talk of the Devil.*

Observer (London, England), March 18, 2001, review of *Lost White Tribes: Journeys among the Forgotten,* p. 18.

Publishers Weekly, June 4, 2001, review of *Lost White Tribes: The End of Privilege and the Last Colonials in Sri Lanka, Jamaica, Brazil, Haiti, Namibia, and Guadeloupe,* p. 70; May 12, 2003, review of *Talk of the Devil,* p. 60.

Spectator, May 6, 2000, Simon Courauld, review of *Lost White Tribes: The End of Privilege and the Last Colonials in Sri Lanka, Jamaica, Brazil, Haiti, Namibia, and Guadeloupe,* pp. 34-35.

Times Literary Supplement, May 12, 2000, Charles Sprawson, "Dragged Down for Ever," review of *Lost White Tribes: Journeys among the Forgotten,* p. 28; February 28, 2003, Adam Hochschild, "Lovely Chaps," review of *Talk of the Devil,* p. 36.

Washington Post Book World, July 22-28, 2001, Jonathan Yardley, review of *Lost White Tribes: The End of Privilege and the Last Colonials in Sri Lanka, Jamaica, Brazil, Haiti, Namibia, and Guadeloupe,* p. 2.

OTHER

CNN Web site, http://www.cnn.com/ (November 7, 2001), L. D. Meagher, review of *Lost White Tribes: The End of Privilege and the Last Colonials in Sri Lanka, Jamaica, Brazil, Haiti, Namibia, and Guadeloupe;* (July 24, 2003), "Review: Heroes and Villains," review of *Talk of the Devil: Encounters with Seven Dictators.*

Complete Review Web site, http://www.complete-review.com/ (March 12, 2004), review of *Talk of the Devil.*

Guardian Unlimited Web site, http://books.guardian.co.uk/ (January 18, 2003), Jad Adams, "Forked Tongues," review of *Talk of the Devil.*

Pittsburgh Tribune-Review, http://www.pittsburghlive.com/ (May 4, 2003), Roger K. Miller, "'Talk of the Devil' Pulls Together Stories of Dictators," review of *Talk of the Devil.*

Riccardo Orizio Home Page, http://www.riccardoorizio.com (March 12, 2004).

Walker & Company Web site, http://www.walkerbooks.com (March 12, 2004).*

* * *

OTOMO, Katsuhiro 1954-

PERSONAL: Born April 14, 1954, in Sannuma, Miyagi, Japan.

ADDRESSES: Agent—c/o Author Mail, Dark Horse Comics, 10956 South East Main St., Milwaukie, OR 97222.

CAREER: Writer, graphic artist, comic book creator, film animator. Creator of commercial print and television advertising for clients that include Honda and Canon.

AWARDS, HONORS: Science Fiction grand prize, Japan, 1983, for *Dohmu;* the Dark Horse Comics black and white edition of *Akira* was the winner of two Eisner Awards, for best archival collection/project, and for best U.S. edition of foreign material, both 2002.

WRITINGS:

WRITER; EXCEPT AS NOTED

Domu, [Japan], c. 1981, published as *Domu: A Child's Dream,* Dark Horse Comics (Milwaukie, OR), 1996, 2nd edition, 2001.

Akira (colorized version), Epic Comics, 1988—, (black and white version), Volumes 1-6, Dark Horse Comics (Milwaukie, OR), 2000-02.

(And director) *Akira* (film), Streamline (Japan), 1988.

Legend of Mother Sarah: Tunnel Town (collection), Dark Horse Comics (Milwaukie, OR), 1996.

(Animator) *Spriggan* (animated film), ADV Films, 1998.

Osamu Tezuka's Metropolis (animated film), TriStar Pictures, c. 2001.

Creator of series, including *Jyu-sei* (title means "Gun Report") *Fireball, Katsuhiro Otomo's Memories, Katsuhiro Otomo's Farewell to Weapons, Akira, Domu: A Child's Dream, The Legend of Mother Sarah, The Legend of Mother Sarah: City of the Children,* and *The Legend of Mother Sarah: City of the Angels.*

ADAPTATIONS: Akira was adapted for film in Japan, 1988, in DVD format, Pioneer, 1988, and again in 2001.

SIDELIGHTS: Writer and graphic artist Katsuhiro Otomo is best known for his *manga,* or Japanese comic, *Akira,* which was originally serialized in Japan between 1981 and 1993 and reprinted in the United States in the 1990s by Dark Horse Comics. Dark Horse later published the epic, in the original black and white, in six volumes from 2000 to 2002.

Otomo, who was born near Tokyo, had a love of American films and often traveled for hours to the nearest theater to see seventies films like *Bonnie and Clyde* and *Easy Rider*. He moved to Tokyo after graduating high school to become a comics artist. His first work, *Jyu-sei,* was published in 1973. It is an adaptation of Prosper Merimee's *Mateo Falcone. Fireball,* published in 1979 and a precursor to Otomo's later successes, is the story of humans against a supercomputer. *Domu,* was serialized from 1980 to 1982, and in 1983, the collected edition was awarded the Science Fiction grand prize, the first time the literary prize was awarded to a comic book, and this honor established Otomo as a master artist and comics writer.

The futuristic story, which was completed at more than 2,000 pages, was a monumental achievement, first as a serial in Japan, and then as a film and a multi-volume graphic novel. A *Publishers Weekly* contributor who reviewed the first volume wrote that it "is all action, nonstop car chases and gun fights strung together with exaggerated speed lines and lots of gigantic machinery."

Akira was released as a film in Japan in 1988 and on CAV laser disc, an early form of DVD. The film that runs more than two hours became a cult hit, both in Japan and the United States, where it continued to be a popular late-night feature on the movie circuit. The story begins in 1988 and flashes forward to 2019, when Tokyo, destroyed in World War III, has been rebuilt, but the city is now corrupt, immoral, and overrun with gangs.

Time's Jay Cocks wrote that "Tokyo is imagined down to the last noodle shop and intersection, a place of deep night and lurid neon that looks like *Blade Runner* on spoiled mushrooms. . . . Berserk graphic imagery and a tempering idealism make for a real sci-fi skull buster."

Akira was rereleased on two discs in 2001. The first disc contains the digitally restored images along with new sound, and both the original Japanese-language film, with subtitles, and an English dub. A "capsule option" feature is offered with the Japanese-language version, which appears as a floating graphic that points to translations of road signs and other words that are not part of the translated dialogue. The second disc contains a documentary on the film's production and restoration, storyboards, trailers, a glossary, and an interview with Otomo. An *Entertainment Weekly* writer who reviewed the DVD version wrote that "parts of *Akira* are as well-directed as anything you'll ever see."

Steven Aoun reviewed the DVD version for *Metro,* commenting that "the digital restoration and transfer bears witness to its original cinematic achievements. That's just a polite way of saying, of course, that *Akira* doesn't let credible characters or a focused storyline get in the way of the spectacular action and elaborate set pieces. . . . Themes and characters visually coalesce in a hallucinogenic revelatory encounter."

Otomo also wrote the series *The Legend of Mother Sara,* the first eight issues of which Dark Horse collected as *The Legend of Mother Sara: Tunnel Town.* The story is less violent and more of a girl's story than his previous comics. Survivors of a nuclear holocaust on earth have established colonies in space. Two factions, Epoch and Mother Earth, are at odds over a proposal to use a bomb to alter the earth's axis so that the changed climate would cover over the irradiated northern hemisphere. Sarah is separated from her children during the ensuing conflict and seeks them for years on earth, leading her to Tunnel Town, where a corrupt military has taken prisoners and uses them as slaves.

Katharine Kan reviewed *The Legend of Mother Sarah* in *Voice of Youth Advocates,* saying that "while the story contains violence, it is more upbeat with a strong heroine commitment to justice and to helping others even as she [Sarah] continues her own quest."

In *Spriggan,* Noah's Ark is a powerful, hi-tech alien machine that has the potential for controlling life on earth. The protagonist is Yu Ominae, a teenager who hides the fact that he is a Spriggan, a powerful cyborg who works for ARCAM, an organization that preserves and protects historical artifacts, and who in an apocalyptic showdown on Mount Ararat, confronts the leader of the rogue U.S. Machine Corps.

Otomo wrote, and Rintaro directed, *Osamu Tezuka's Metropolis,* based on the 1940s comic that *Hollywood Reporter*'s David Hunter commented is "in some ways reminiscent of Fritz Lang's brilliant silent film of the same name." The main character is Tina, a robotic girl who lives in a world of futuristic modes of travel, superweapons, evil scientists, and a Japanese detective. Hunter called the film "both beautiful and distant," and "a bleak, sometimes overly familiar cautionary tale of technology run amok."

BIOGRAPHICAL AND CRITICAL SOURCES:

PERIODICALS

Entertainment Weekly, July 27, 2001, review of *Akira* (DVD), p. 51.

Hollywood Reporter, January 29, 2002, David Hunter, review of *Osamu Tezuka's Metropolis,* p. 20.

Metro (Australia), winter, 2003, Steven Aoun, review of *Akira* (DVD), p. 266.

Publishers Weekly, May 7, 2001, review of *Akira: Book One,* p. 227.

Time, February 1, 1993, Jay Cocks, review of *Akira* (DVD), p. 66.

Voice of Youth Advocates, February, 1997, Katherine Kan, review of *The Legend of Mother Sarah: Tunnel Town,* p. 324.*

P

PARENTE, Stephen L. 1961-

PERSONAL: Born December 17, 1961, in Boston, MA; son of Lawrence (a civil engineer) and Ann (a homemaker; maiden name, Amoriggi) Parente; married E. Cathrine Berg (a professor of applied linguistics), July 3, 1999; children: Magnus. *Ethnicity:* "Italian." *Education:* College of the Holy Cross, B.A., 1984; University of Minnesota, Ph.D., 1990. *Religion:* Roman Catholic.

ADDRESSES: Office—University of Illinois—Urbana-Champaign, 1206 South Sixth St., Champaign, IL 61820. *E-mail*—parente@uiuc.edu.

CAREER: U.S. Department of Justice, Washington, DC, economist, 1989-91; Northeastern University, Boston, MA, assistant professor of economics, 1991-96; University of Pennsylvania, Philadelphia, visiting lecturer in economics, 1996-99; University of Illinois—Urbana-Champaign, Champaign, associate professor of economics, 1999—. University of Lausanne, Walras-Pareto lecturer.

MEMBER: American Economic Association, Society for Economic Dynamics.

WRITINGS:

(With Edward C. Prescott) *Barriers to Riches,* MIT Press (Cambridge, MA), 2000.

Contributor to periodicals, including *Journal of Political Economy, American Economic Review,* and *Journal of Economic Theory.*

SIDELIGHTS: Stephen L. Parente told *CA:* "My book attempts to explain why some countries are so poor relative to others. In my opinion, this is the single most important question. The book is based on a series of articles written with Edward C. Prescott, dating back to 1991. When we initiated this research agenda, we had no idea that it would lead to a book. Quite frankly, we would not have started the endeavor were it not for the request from the School of Advanced Commercial Studies at the University of Lausanne in Switzerland, following an invitation to give the Walras-Pareto Lecture there. The writing of the book was more difficult than we anticipated. It proved to be a very valuable experience, because it forced us to really develop a coherent thesis for the evolution of international income levels."

*   *   *

PASSERINI, Luisa 1941-

PERSONAL: Born 1941. *Education:* University of Turin, Italy, degree in philosophy and history (magna cum laude), 1965.

ADDRESSES: Office—Dipartimento di Storia, Universita' di Torino, Via Sant'Ottavio 20, 10123 Torino, Italy. *E-mail*—luisa.passerini@kwi-nrw.de.

CAREER: Teacher in high schools in Turin, Italy, 1969-73; University of Turin, assistant professor of contemporary history, 1974-84, associate professor of methodology of history, 1984-93; European University

Institute, Florence, Italy, professor of history; fellow at Kulturwissenschaftliches Institut, Essen, Germany, 1991, and Wissenschaftskolleg, Berlin, Germany, 1992-93. Visiting professor at University of Western Australia, Perth, 1989, New School for Social Research, New York, NY, 1990, and New York University, 1993, 1998; director of studies at Maison des Sciences de l'Homme, Paris, France, 1990; visiting professor at University of California—Berkeley, 2001; coordinator of Advanced Oral History Summer Institute at University of California—Berkeley, 2002; resident fellow at the Kulturwissenchaftliches Institut, Essen; external professor at the Department of History, European University Institute (EUI), Florence; director of the Gender Studies Programme, Robert Schuman Centre, EUI; full professor of Cultural History at the University of Turin, Italy, 2004—. Member of the Centro Interdisciplinare Ricerche e Studi delle Donne at Torino University and of the Fondazione "Lelio Basso" in Rome, Italy.

MEMBER: Società Italiana delle Storiche, Società Italiana per lo Studio della Storia Contemporanea.

AWARDS, HONORS: Has received grants from Consiglio Nazionale delle Ricerche, 1965-66, Municipality of Turin, 1976-77, Ministry of Education, Italy, 1977-82, and other grants; "Clio" Prize for History, Accademia Internazionale delle Muse (Firenze, Italy), 1999; Pierro Martinetti prize, for Ph.D. dissertation; awarded the Research Prize of the Land of Nordrhein-Westphalen, 2002-04.

WRITINGS:

(Editor and author of introduction) *Colonialismo portoghese e lotta di liberazione nel Mozambico,* Einaudi (Turin, Italy), 1970.

(Editor and author of introduction) *Storia orale: Vita quotidiana e cultura materiale delle classi subalterne,* Rosenberg & Sellier (Turin, Italy), 1978.

Torino operaia e fascismo: Una storia orale, Laterza (Rome, Italy), 1984, translation by Robert Lumley and Jude Bloomfield published as *Fascism in Popular Memory: The Cultural Experience of the Turin Working Class,* Cambridge University Press (New York, NY), 1987.

Storia e soggettività Le fonti orali, le memoria, La Nuova Italia (Firenze, Italy), 1988.

Autoritratto di gruppo, Giunti Gruppo Editoriale, 1988, translation by Lisa Erdberg published as *Autobiography of a Generation: Italy, 1968,* University Press of New England (Hanover, NH), 1996.

Mussolini immaginario: Storia di una biografia, 1915-1939, Laterza (Rome, Italy), 1991.

(Editor, with Aldo Agosti and Nicola Tranfaglia, and contributor) *La cultura e i luoghi del '68,* F. Angeli (Milan, Italy), 1991.

Storie di donne e femminste, Rosenberg & Sellier (Torino, Italy), 1991.

(Editor) *International Yearbook of Oral History and Life Stories,* Volume 1: *Memory and Totalitarianism,* Volume 4, with Selma Leydesdorff and Paul Thompson, *Gender and Memory,* Oxford University Press (New York, NY), 1992.

(Editor) *Identità culturale europea: Idee, sentimenti, relazioni,* La Nuova Italia (Firenze, Italy), 1998.

L'Europa e l'amore, Il Saggiatore (Milan, Italy), 1999, translation published as *Europe in Love, Love in Europe: Imagination and Politics between the Wars,* New York University Press (Washington Square, NY), 1999.

(Editor) *Across the Atlantic: Cultural Exchanges between Europe and the United States,* Bruxelles (New York, NY), 2000.

Il mito d'Europa: Radici antiche per nuovi simboli, Giunti (Firenze, Italy), 2002.

(Editor and contributor) *Images and Myths of Europe,* Bruxelles (New York, NY), 2003.

Memoria e utopia: Il primato dell'Intersoggettività, Bollati Boringhieri (Turin, Italy), 2003.

Contributor to numerous books and periodicals.

SIDELIGHTS: Cultural historian Luisa Passerini has attempted to convey the ways readers remember and misremember such dramatic events as the African liberation movement and the 1968 student upheavals, as well as such experiences as living under totalitarianism. In *Torino operaia e fascismo: Una storia orale,* translated as *Fascism in Popular Memory: The Cultural Experience of the Turin Working Class,* for example, she combines oral history with close analysis of the different "narrative modes" that men and women, Catholics and Communists, and various types of workers fall into. More recently, she has delved deeply into the European heritage of emotions, drawing connections between the cultural legacy of courtly love and the hopes for European unifications, and exploring the complexities of the cultural relationship between Europe and the United States.

Fascism in Popular Memory, explained reviewer Joe Foweraker in the *British Journal of Sociology,* is an "ambitious and inventive book [that] uses oral histories to reconstruct a particular cultural universe. The boundaries of this universe are buttressed by references to general social theory . . . so allowing the author to concentrate not so much on what is said, but on the way it is told." For Passerini, the ways of telling are as interesting as the stories themselves, and she finds a number of patterns, such as the fact, in historical context, that men habitually spoke of themselves as capable workers while women tended to be more self-deprecating about their jobs. On the other hand, she finds more "born" rebels and socialists among the women than the men. Passerini also investigates the use of jokes, parodies, and graffiti as instances of rebellion, making clear that this is not a simple tale of passive, oppressed workers. "For me, part 3 . . . is the most interesting," wrote *American Historical Review* contributor Charles F. Delzell. "Here the author explores, in turn, the degree to which workers expressed some social acceptance of Fascism, their widespread resistance to the regime's efforts to increase the birthrate . . . and their cold reception for Mussolini when he visited." Noting that most of Passerini's subjects "took no part in active politics," *International Affairs* contributor Richard Knowles observed that her "study shows how the fascist regime decisively shifted the boundary between private life and politics at the expense of the former. . . . Fascism itself made such minor acts of opposition to the regime as joke-telling, graffiti and legal abortion into political actions."

In *Autoritratto di gruppo,* translated as *Autobiography of a Generation: Italy, 1968,* Passerini tells the story of her own contemporaries, whose memories of Mussolini are dim at best. According to *Rethinking History* contributor Perry Wilson, the "author's primary purpose is not to write an orthodox history in any sense but rather to draw upon the insights raided by her own experience of psychoanalysis to continue exploring the thread which links much of her published work—how we remember and make sense of the past." Inevitably, much of this is autobiographical, as the title implies, and Passerini freely discusses her sex life, her abortion, and her experiences with psychoanalysis. At the same time, she "weaves the oral history testimony of forty-seven other participants in the 1968 student movement in Italy among her own reflections on her past and her day-to-day life now," reported Valerie Raleigh Yow in the *Oral History Review.* Not all reviewers were entirely pleased with the proportion between her voice and that of other participants. For example, *Village Voice* contributor James Marcus maintained, "Sure, Luisa Passerini may well have set out to write a panoramic portrait of what the Italians call the *sessantottini*—the generation that went to the barricades in 1968. . . . What she's ended up with, however, is something quite different: an autobiography of, well, herself, with the rest of her generation relegated to the role of a muffled Greek chorus." Nevertheless, Marcus found the book "oddly endearing."

Passerini takes another penetrating look at a previous generation in *L'Europa e l'amore,* published in America as *Europe in Love, Love in Europe: Imagination and Politics between the Wars,* which looks at the role of courtly love in shaping Europeans' self-perceptions and the attempt to unify Europe. This "well-written and erudite work of cultural and intellectual history deals with questions of European identity, unity, and the emotional basis of the idea of a unified Europe as it was expressed mainly between the world wars," explained *Canadian Journal of History* reviewer Rosemarie Schade. An ambitious project, it is "the product of formidable research, and few academic fields lie outside her scope. Novels, poems, political tracts, mythology and wartime love letters . . . feature among her sources," observed *Political Quarterly* reviewer Mark Garnett. Although political figures such as Winston Churchill do enter the scene, the focus is on cultural figures, from religious writers like C. S. Lewis and historian Christopher Dawson, to Sigmund Freud and Carl Jung, novelists and poets, and a surprising number of esoteric figures, such as the Yugoslavian mystic Dmitrije Mitrinovic. The result is "guaranteed to renew one's interest in the passions, loves, hopes, dreams, and emotional worlds of the men and women reconstructed in this book," concluded Schade in her review.

BIOGRAPHICAL AND CRITICAL SOURCES:

PERIODICALS

American Historical Review, October, 1988, Charles F. Delzell, review of *Fascism in Popular Memory:*

The Cultural Experience of the Turin Working Class, p. 1082.

Asian Folklore Studies, October, 1995, James R. Dow, review of *Memory and Totalitarianism,* p. 326.

British Journal of Sociology, March, 1989, Joe Foweraker, review of *Fascism in Popular Memory,* p. 167.

Canadian Journal of History, April, 2001, Rosemarie Schade, review of *Europe in Love, Love in Europe: Imagination and Politics between the Wars,* p. 147.

Contemporary Sociology, September, 1988, Richard Bellamy, review of *Fascism in Everyday Life,* pp. 626-627.

History Today, June, 1993, Martin Evans, review of *Memory and Totalitarianism,* p. 55.

International Affairs, spring, 1988, Richard Knowles, review of *Fascism in Popular Memory,* pp. 291-292.

Journal of Modern History, December, 1989, review of *Fascism in Popular Memory,* p. 823.

Journal of Women in Culture & Society, spring, 1999, Ernestina Pellegrini, "Book Reviews," pp. 798-802.

Modern Language Review, April, 1998, Derek Duncan, "Corporeal Histories: The Autobiographical Bodies of Luisa Passerini," p. 370.

Oral History Review, summer-fall, 1999, Valerie Raleigh Yow, review of *Autobiography of a Generation: Italy, 1968,* p. 167.

Political Quarterly, July-September, 1999, Mark Garnett, review of *Europe in Love, Love in Europe.*

Publishers Weekly, August 26, 1996, review of *Autobiography of a Generation,* p. 84.

Rethinking History, spring, 1998, Perry Wilson, review of *Autobiography of a Generation,* pp. 107-109.

Village Voice, January 21, 1997, James Marcus, review of *Autobiography of a Generation,* p. 53.

*   *   *

PASTI, Umberto

PERSONAL: Born in Milan, Italy. *Hobbies and other interests:* Islamic ceramics, botany.

ADDRESSES: Home—Milan, Italy; Tangiers, Morocco. *Agent*—c/o Author Mail, Pushkin Press, 123 Biddulph Mansions, Elgin Ave., London W9 IHU, England.

CAREER: Writer.

AWARDS, HONORS: Premio Viareggio shortlist, 2000, for *L'età fiorita.*

WRITINGS:

(Translator) *Marcel Proust: Letters to His Mother,* Tartaruga, 1986.

L'età fiorita, Saggiatore (Milan, Italy), 2000, translation by Alastair McEwen published as *The Age of Flowers,* Pushkin Press (London, England), 2003.

Contributor to periodicals, including *Il Giornale, La Voce, Vogue, Elle, House and Garden,* and *World of Interiors.*

SIDELIGHTS: Italian writer Umberto Pasti published *L'età fiorita* in 2000. The work was translated by Alastair McEwen and published in 2003 as *The Age of Flowers.* The novel concerns Irene and Luca, an expatriate European couple living in Tangiers, Morocco. Irene and Luca are part of a decadent community of artists and aristocrats who choose to ignore Tangiers' growing Islamic fundamentalist movement. When Irene is diagnosed with breast cancer, Luca retreats into his garden, shutting himself off not only from Irene's pain but from the world around him as well. According to *Library Journal* critic Philip Santo, "this excellent translation should go some way toward building Pasti the kind reputation in America that he enjoys in Europe."

BIOGRAPHICAL AND CRITICAL SOURCES:

PERIODICALS

Library Journal, Philip Santo, review of *The Age of Flowers,* April 1, 2003, p. 130.*

*   *   *

PAYNE, Larry

PERSONAL: Male. *Education:* California State University—Long Beach, B.A., 1969; Pacific Western University, M.A., 1985, Ph.D., 1987; additional study in physical therapy at California State University; studied yoga in India, France, and Denmark.

ADDRESSES: *Home*—Los Angeles, CA. *Office*—Samata Yoga Center, 4150 Tivoli Ave., Los Angeles, CA 90066. *E-mail*—samatayoga@earthlink.net.

CAREER: Advertising executive prior to 1979; Samata Yoga Center, Los Angeles, CA, founder/director, 1981—. Cofounder and director, Yoga Therapy Clinic, International Sports Medicine Institute, 1984-86; cofounder and chairman, International Association of Yoga Therapists, 1989—; president, Healthy Back/ Healthy Mind Institute, Marina Del Rey, CA, 1990—; cofounder and instructor, yoga program at University of California—Los Angeles School of Medicine, 1998—. Leader of seminars on yoga; lecturer.

AWARDS, HONORS: Has received outstanding achievement awards in the United States and Europe for yoga instruction; Golden Lotus Award (South America), for yoga instruction.

WRITINGS:

(With Georg Feuerstein) *Yoga for Dummies,* IDG Publishing, 1999.
(With Richard Ustantine) *Yoga Rx: A Step by Step Program to Promote Health, Wellness, and Healing for Common Ailments,* Broadway Books (New York, NY), 2002.

Creator of video, *Healthy Back Exercises for High Stress Professionals,* Samata International Multi-Media (Los Angeles, CA), 1986.

SIDELIGHTS: Larry Payne began practicing yoga in the late 1970s to relieve his own back pain and stress. He found the discipline so healing that he devoted years to studying it in the United States, Europe, and India, and then founded a yoga center of his own in Los Angeles, California. Through his Samata Yoga Center and Healthy Back/Healthy Mind Institute, Payne has served the needs of athletes, film stars, and corporate executives who have sought help with chronic pain and stress reduction. Payne has also furthered the connection between yoga and healing by cofounding a yoga program at the University of California—Los Angeles School of Medicine.

Payne's first book, *Yoga for Dummies,* is part of the popular "For Dummies" series. Cowritten with Georg Feuerstein, the book is a primer of basic yoga

techniques and suggestions for wellness and healing. *Yoga Rx: A Step by Step Program to Promote Health, Wellness, and Healing for Common Ailments,* coauthored with Dr. Richard Ustantine, explores the use of yoga to control a wide variety of conditions, from joint pain to insomnia, arthritis, and even the common cold. *Booklist* contributor Jane Tuma recommended *Yoga Rx* for its "simple healing yoga therapy routines."

BIOGRAPHICAL AND CRITICAL SOURCES:

PERIODICALS

Booklist, October 1, 2002, Jane Tuma, review of *Yoga Rx: A Step-by-Step Program to Promote Health, Wellness, and Healing,* p. 293.

ONLINE

Samata Yoga Center, http://www.samata.com/ (May 6, 2003), information on Payne, his books, and his lectures.*

*   *   *

PENCE, Gregory E. 1948-

PERSONAL: Born January 17, 1948, in Washington, DC. *Education:* College of William and Mary, M.A., 1970; New York University, Ph.D., 1974.

ADDRESSES: *Office*—Philosophy, UAB, 900 13th Street S., Birmingham, AL 35294-1260. *E-mail*—pence@uab.edu.

CAREER: University of Alabama, Birmingham, professor of philosophy, 1976—, professor of medical ethics, 1977—. Has appeared on television programs, including *Talk Back Live, The Point, The Early Show with Bryant Gumbel,* and *Wolf Blitzer's Washington.* Has spoken at dozens of universities and has appeared on National Public Radio (NPR) and CNN.

AWARDS, HONORS: Ingalls Award for Best Teaching, University of Alabama, 1994.

WRITINGS:

Ethical Options in Medicine, Medical Economics Co. (Oradell, NJ), 1980.

Classic Cases in Medical Ethics: Accounts of Cases That Have Shaped Medical Ethics, with Philosophical, Legal, and Historical Backgrounds, McGraw-Hill (Boston, MA), 1990, 4th edition, 2003.

(With Lynn Stephens) *Seven Dilemmas in World Religion,* Paragon House (New York, NY), 1994.

(Editor) *Classic Works in Medical Ethics: Core Philosophical Readings,* McGraw-Hill (Boston, MA), 1998.

(Editor) *Flesh of My Flesh: The Ethics of Cloning Humans: A Reader,* Rowman & Littlefield (Lanham, MD), 1998.

Who's Afraid of Human Cloning?, Rowman & Littlefield (Lanham, MD), 1998.

A Dictionary of Common Philosophical Terms, McGraw-Hill (Boston, MA), 2000.

Re-creating Medicine: Ethical Issues at the Frontiers of Medicine, Rowman & Littlefield (Lanham, MD), 2000.

(Editor) *The Ethics of Food: A Reader for the Twenty-First Century,* Rowman & Littlefield (Lanham, MD), 2002.

Brave New Bioethics, Rowman & Littlefield (Lanham, MD), 2002.

Designer Food: Mutant Harvest or Breadbasket of the World?, Rowman & Littlefield (Lanham, MD), 2002.

Cloning after Dolly: Who's Still Afraid of Human Cloning?, Rowman & Littlefield (Lanham, MD), 2004.

Contributor to periodicals, including *Newsweek, New York Times,* and *Wall Street Journal.*

SIDELIGHTS: For nearly thirty years, ethicist Gregory E. Pence has been guiding readers through the minefields of modern medicine, covering deeply controversial issues such as mandatory AIDS testing, animal testing, and euthanasia. Drawing on science, philosophy, religion, and the law, Pence has provided guidelines for thinking through some of the thorniest issues in medical treatment. He has also come down in favor of both bioengineered food and human cloning, putting him at the forefront of these emotionally charged controversies. In 2001, Pence testified before the Subcommittee on Oversight and Investigation in Congress, "Should attempts to clone humans be a federal crime?"

Ethical Options in Medicine takes a case-by-case approach, providing the details of a medical dilemma and then a series of philosophical approaches that address the issues, followed by a discussion of which of these approaches Pence accepts and which he rejects. Pence also provides an ideal medical code that he hopes will prove useful to physicians. "This book is highly recommended for doctors, who should find the time to read it," concluded *Science Books and Films* reviewer John Hathaway.

Some ten years later, Pence followed up with *Classic Cases in Medical Ethics: Accounts of Cases That Have Shaped Medical Ethics, with Philosophical, Legal, and Historical Backgrounds.* Through such examples as the Quinlan case, the case of Nancy Cruzan, and the arrest of Jack Kevorkian, Pence again provides help in sorting out the issues in euthanasia, as well in-vitro fertilization and fetal tissue research. Jonathan D. Moreno, reviewing the book in the *Hastings Center Report,* found that "In at least one respect this volume is a tour de force, for Pence has assembled and mastered a wealth of detail. In spite of all the specifics I found rather few interpretations to quibble about. When he does falter . . . it is rare indeed and not grave enough to detract from the main point." The book, which has become a standard text in medical ethics, went into a fourth edition in 2003, with a fifth edition planned.

Pence has also collected a number of authoritative texts for physicians in *Classic Works in Medical Ethics: Core Philosophical Readings.* In addition to an introductory history of Western morality, Pence provides writings from notable authorities, such as James Rachels, Judith Jarvis Thomson, and Peter Singer, in twelve overarching areas, including abortion, suicide, and animal rights. While noting some problems in the book's organizational structure, Martin Harvey concluded in an American Philosophical Association newsletter, "It provides a thorough philosophical and readily accessible introduction to the primary ethical issues which have confronted physicians, as well as the public at large, over the past forty years."

Pence has often drawn on religious teachings to elucidate his ethical position. In *Seven Dilemmas in World Religion,* coauthored with Lynn Stephens, he approaches the question of what makes the major world religions differ by focusing on a central dilemma that each religion confronts. For Judaism, it is the dilemma of a universalistic religion with an exclusivist idea of a chosen people. For Christianity, it is the mystery of Jesus' combined humanity and divinity. And for Islam, it is the contrast between human freedom and the absolute sovereignty of Allah. Other dilemmas confront Hinduism, Buddhism, and Confucianism. Charles W. Swain, in the *Journal of Ecumenical Studies* wrote, "Perhaps inevitably, the values of 'tolerance' and 'curiosity,' so central to comparative study of religion, create an attitude of disengagement that may be off-putting to those for whom these are existential, life-and-death issues."

Despite this diversion into comparative religion, Pence has been primarily a medical ethicist, and in two highly charged areas, human cloning and bioengineered food, Pence has become a leading voice. In *Flesh of My Flesh: The Ethics of Human Cloning,* Pence brings together writings from Stephen Jay Gould, James D. Watson, and others in "a smorgasbord of hearty food for thought," according to a *Publishers Weekly* reviewer. In *Who's Afraid of Human Cloning?* Pence provides his own arguments in favor of cloning, in the face of nearly universal opposition to the very idea. Pence is particularly critical of the role of the National Bioethics Advisory Commission, which has come out strongly against the idea, arguing that the Commission succumbed to hysteria rather than provide a reasoned forum for debate or any true leadership on the issue. For Pence, fears of assembly-line clones identical to their parents neglected some basic facts, such as the impact of environment, the role of autonomous women, and the unfounded fears that once surrounded in-vitro fertilization. "Pence offers a rational, well-tempered voice in a discussion that too often is driven by emotion and fears fueled by science fiction. . . . Those strongly opposed to human cloning are, unfortunately, unlikely to be persuaded by Pence's arguments in favor of its permissibility and regulation. Nevertheless, even those opposed on religious grounds, as well as those who wish to engage religious arguments on the topic (and on assisted reproduction generally), may benefit from Pence's discussion of classic religious positions on God's will and reproduction without sex," commented Lisa S. Parker in the *Journal of the American Medical Association (JAMA)*. One such unconvinced critic was *First Things* contributor Jorge Garcia, who found the book "filled with arguments that are shallow, unfair,

and foolish" as well as "showing contempt for Catholic and Protestant alike" and doing "little to seriously engage the major objections to human cloning." In contrast, *Skeptical Inquirer* contributor Terence Hines claimed the book "is the best thing I've seen written about cloning since the birth of Dolly the cloned sheep in 1997. The vast majority of post-Dolly writing on cloning, especially in the nonscientific press, has been near-hysterical, fear-mongering drivel. . . . Gregory Pence . . . destroys such arguments against human cloning."

Pence has also taken on the issue of genetic manipulation of food. In *Designer Food: Mutant Harvest or Breadbasket of the World?*, "Pence attempts to cut through the propaganda to determine whether there are real and valid reasons to avoid consuming genetically altered foods," explained *Booklist* reviewer Mark Knoblauch. For proponents, these disease-resistant, insect-repellent foods are vital to feeding a still-growing world population. For critics, consumers are being used as guinea pigs in an experiment that even the food designers do not really understand. "Although Pence agrees that more research and sound policy is important, he has little patience for the motives of environmentalists, antitechnology activists, and proponents of organic farming," noted *Library Journal* contributor Irwin Weintraub. For *Choice* reviewer M. Kroger, "To sort facts from hype, debaters need to be informed, and this book is the best to date for that purpose."

BIOGRAPHICAL AND CRITICAL SOURCES:

PERIODICALS

Booklist, March 15, 2002, Mark Knobloch, review of *Designer Food: Mutant Harvest or Breadbasket of the World?,* p. 1194.

Choice, July-August, 2002, M. Kroger, review of *Designer Food,* p. 1985.

First Things, March, 1999, Jorge Garcia, review of *Who's Afraid of Human Cloning?,* p. 54.

Hastings Center Report, September-October, 1991, Jonathan D. Moreno, review of *Classic Cases in Medical Ethics: Accounts of Cases That Have Shaped Medical Ethics, with Philosophical, Legal, and Historical Backgrounds,* p. 42.

Journal of Ecumenical Studies, spring, 1996, Charles W. Swain, review of *Seven Dilemmas in World Religion,* pp. 282-283.

Journal of the American Medical Association (JAMA), November 25, 1998, Lisa Parker, review of *Who's Afraid of Human Cloning?,* p. 1798.

Library Journal, October 1, 1994, Henry Carrigan, review of *Seven Dilemmas in World Religion,* p. 86; May 1, 2002, Irwin Weintraub, review of *Designer Food,* p. 129.

Nursing Ethics, 2001, Brian D. Mohr, review of *Classic Cases in Medical Ethics,* p. 291.

Publishers Weekly, June 29, 1998, review of *Flesh of My Flesh,* p. 48.

Religious Studies Review, April, 1992, Joel Jay Finer, review of *Classic Cases in Medical Ethics,* p. 135.

Science Books and Films, September, 1981, John Hathaway, review of *Ethical Options in Medicine,* p. 4.

Skeptical Inquirer, November, 1999, Terence Hines, "Clear Thinking about Human Cloning," p. 57.

ONLINE

American Philosophical Association, http://www.apa.udel.edu/ (July 10, 2003), Martin Harvey, review of *Classic Works in Medical Ethics.*

Human Cloning Foundation, http://www.humancloning.org/ (June 2, 2004), discussion of Pence's work, as well as reviews of his books.

*   *   *

PENDREIGH, Brian 1957-

PERSONAL: Born 1957.

ADDRESSES: *Agent*—c/o Author Mail, Mainstream Publishing, 7 Albany St., Edinburgh EH1 3UG, Scotland.

CAREER: *Scotsman,* cinema writer and editor, 1987-97; freelance writer, beginning 1997.

WRITINGS:

On Location: The Film Fan's Guide to Britain and Ireland, Mainstream (Edinburgh, Scotland), 1995.

Mel Gibson and His Movies, Bloomsbury (London, England), 1997.

Ewan McGregor, Thunder's Mouth Press (New York, NY), 1998.

The Scot Pack: The Further Adventures of the Trainspotters and Their Fellow Travellers, Mainstream (Edinburgh, Scotland), 2000.

The Legend of "The Planet of the Apes": Or How Hollywood Turned Darwin Upside Down, Boxtree (London, England), 2001.

The Pocket Scottish Movie Book, Mainstream (Edinburgh, Scotland), 2002.

Contributor to several periodicals, including the *Guardian,* the Sunday *Times,* and the *Herald.*

SIDELIGHTS: For much of his publishing career, cinema writer Brian Pendreigh has kept an eye on his nearby surroundings. His first work, *On Location: The Film Fan's Guide to Britain and Ireland,* examines the on-location sites of over 200 films shot in the British Isles since the 1930s. Designed as part fun travel guide and part film history, the book includes information on the movies and their shooting locations, anecdotes from the sets, and photos of the surroundings. Carol J. Binkowski, in the *Library Journal,* called the guide "educational and well-researched," but in *People Weekly,* Mark Lasswell felt the "black-and-white—often muddy-gray—publicity stills" diminished *On Location*'s visual impact.

In the late 1990s, Pendreigh wrote celebrity biographies of fellow Scotsman Ewan McGregor and non-Brit Mel Gibson. A *Sight and Sound* critic enjoyed the McGregor bio, declaring it a "wittily written and absorbing account of McGregor's life . . . [that] captures the actor's significance to current British cinema without trying [too] hard."

Writing about McGregor seemed to have laid the groundwork for Pendreigh's next major work, *The Scot Pack: The Further Adventures of the Trainspotters and Their Fellow Travellers,* a collective profile of major Scottish actors, directors, and films of the past and present. In addition to examining such Scottish film icons as Sean Connery, the book looks at how McGregor's breakthrough role in the 1996 film *Trainspotting* raised the international profile of the Scottish film industry.

BIOGRAPHICAL AND CRITICAL SOURCES:

PERIODICALS

Library Journal, March 15, 1996, Carol J. Binkowski, review of *On Location: The Film Fan's Guide to*

Britain and Ireland, p. 73; February 1, 2001, Kim Holston, review of *The Scot Pack: The Further Adventures of the Trainspotters and Their Fellow Travellers,* p. 98.

People Weekly, March 25, 1996, Mark Lasswell, review of *On Location,* p. 36.

Sight and Sound, February, 1999, review of *Ewan McGregor,* p. 32.*

*　　*　　*

PEREZ, George 1954-

PERSONAL: Born June 9, 1954, in Bronx, NY; married Carol Flynn.

ADDRESSES: Office—CrossGen Entertainment, Inc., 4023 Tampa Road., Suite 2400, Oldsmar, FL 34677.

CAREER: Graphic artist, 1970s—; CrossGen Entertainment, Inc., Oldsmar, FL, senior artist.

WRITINGS:

COLLECTIONS

(With others) *The Project Pegasus Saga Starring the Thing,* Marvel Comics (New York, NY), 1988.

(With Peter David) *The Incredible Hulk: Future Imperfect,* Marvel Comics (New York, NY), 1994.

(With Marv Wolfman) *New Teen Titans Archives,* DC Comics (New York, NY), 1999—.

Penciler or inker for comics, including *Man-Wolf, Deathlok the Demolisher, Fantastic Four, The Avengers, The Inhumans, Justice League of America* (JLA), *X-Men, Spider-Man, The New Teen Titans, JLA/Avengers, CrossGen Chronicles, The Incredible Hulk,* and *Wonder Woman.*

ADAPTATIONS: The New Teen Titans was adapted for television as *Teen Titans* by the Cartoon Network.

SIDELIGHTS: George Perez has been creating comic book art since the 1970s and has been a penciler or inker for all the major publishers. Born in the South Bronx, the self-taught artist is probably best known for his work on *The New Teen Titans,* which was adapted for television and which DC Comics published as collections. *Library Journal*'s Steve Raiteri reviewed one of these, *The New Teen Titans: The Terror of Trigon,* which reprints the first five issues of the second series from 1984 to 1985. Raiteri noted that the popular series, like Marvel's *X-Men,* featured strong female heroes. Raiteri wrote that "Perez's work from this period set a new standard for superhero comics with its meticulous attention to realistic detail."

Marvel and DC comics had planned a collaboration of their *New Justice League of America* (*Superman, Batman, Wonder Woman*) and *Avengers* (*Captain America, Iron Man, Thor*) superheroes in the 1980s, both of which Perez had contributed to, but the project never reached fruition. In 2003, that dream became a reality with *JLA/Avengers. Entertainment Weekly*'s Tom Russo wrote that "Perez supplies the art, and his fantastically detailed old-school line work has only grown finer over time."

Most recently, Perez became senior artist for Cross-Gen where he works on the *CrossGen Chronicles* alongside a new generation of young artists.

BIOGRAPHICAL AND CRITICAL SOURCES:

PERIODICALS

Entertainment Weekly, September 5, 2003, Tom Russo, review of *JLA/Avengers,* p. L2T20.

Library Journal, November 1, 2003, Steve Raiteri, review of *The New Teen Titans: The Terror of Trigon,* p. 63.

ONLINE

George Perez Home Page, http://www.george-perez.com (May 3, 2004).*

*　　*　　*

PÉREZ-PETIT, Manuel 1967-

PERSONAL: Born January 20, 1967, in Seville, Spain. Surname also cited as Perez-Petit. *Religion:* Roman Catholic.

ADDRESSES: Home—Doctor Esquerdo 124, No. 3G, 28007 Madrid, Spain. *E-mail*—macpoet@terra.es.

CAREER: Writer.

AWARDS, HONORS: Certamen poético anual, University of Navarre, 1989, for *Otros perfiles;* Ruta de la Plata, García-Plata de Osma, 1991, for *El arco de la voz;* Amantes de Teruel, Ayuntamiento de Teruel, 1995, for *El desierto.*

WRITINGS:

(With others) *Actas del I Congreso de Cultura Europea,* Ed. Aranzadi, 1991.

Other writings include *Diario ovaciones, Diario ABC de Sevilla, Diario las pronivincias, Otros perfiles, El arco de la voz,* and *El desierto.* Editor, with Grupo Liceo Navarro, of *Primera claridad* (poetry), 1990. Contributor to periodicals, including *Revista Época* and *Revista de Humanidades Liceus.*

*   *   *

PESIC, Peter (Dragan) 1948-

PERSONAL: Born May 11, 1948, in San Francisco, CA; son of Paul Sviatoslavonic and Milena Ljubomirovna (Boyonic) Pesic; married Ssu Isabel Weng, June 2, 1984; children: Andrei Petrovic, Alexie Petrovic. *Education:* Harvard University, A.B., 1969; Stanford University, M.S., 1970, Ph.D. (physics), 1985. *Politics:* Democrat. *Religion:* Russian Orthodox.

ADDRESSES: Office—St. John's College, 1160 Camino Cruz Blanca, Santa Fe, NM 87505-4599. *E-mail*—ppesic@mail.sjcsf.edu.

CAREER: Educator, writer, musician, and editor. Stanford Linear Accelerator Center, Stanford, CA, research assistant and associate, 1976-80; St. John's College, Santa Fe, NM, tutor, 1980—, musician-in-residence, beginning 1984. Concert pianist, performing throughout the United States. Presenter of papers.

AWARDS, HONORS: Danforth Foundation graduate fellow, 1969-75; *Choice* Outstanding Academic Book designation, 2003, for *Seeing Double.*

WRITINGS:

(Editor and author of introduction and notes) Max Planck, *Lectures in Theoretical Physics,* Dover (Mineola, NY), 1998.

Labyrinth: A Search for the Hidden Meaning of Science, MIT Press (Cambridge, MA), 2000.

(Editor and author of introduction and notes) James Clerk Maxwell, *Theory of Heat* (revision of ninth edition, published in 1888), Dover Publications (Mineola, NY), 2001.

Seeing Double: Shared Identities in Physics, Philosophy, and Literature, MIT Press (Cambridge, MA), 2002.

Abel's Proof: An Essay on the Sources and Meaning of Mathematical Unsolvability, MIT Press (Cambridge, MA), 2003.

Contributor to periodicals, including *American Journal of Physics, Crpyographia, Daedalus, European Journal of Physics, Historia Mathematica, Isis, Literature and Theology, Mathematical Intelligencer, Nineteenth-Century Music, Physical Review,* and *Studies in Philology.*

Pesic's works have been translated into Japanese and German.

SIDELIGHTS: In addition to being an educator and a concert pianist, Peter Pesic has written widely on the interplay among science, philosophy, and the arts in modern society. His books include *Seeing Double: Shared Identities in Physics, Philosophy, and Literature, Labyrinth: A Search for the Hidden Meaning of Science,* and *Abel's Proof: An Essay on the Sources and Meaning of Mathematical Unsolvability,* the last the story of nineteenth-century Norwegian mathematician Niels Henrik Abel, whose proof involving an abstract algebraic equation advanced human intellectual thought.

In *Labyrinth* Pesic follows the scientific quest to unlock the "secrets" of nature, and its effect upon both individual men and the development of mathematics as a symbolic language. Basing his study on the life and innovations of early seventeenth-century scientist William Gilbert, mathematician François Viète, and Francis Bacon, he takes what a *Kirkus Reviews* contributor described as a "romantic" perspective. In his timeless view, according to the critic, three factors are at play in the advancement of science, each represented in turn by Gilbert, Bacon, and Viète: "First is the scientist's labyrinthine struggle to understand nature; second is the ardent desire . . . that inspires the scientist's pursuit; and third is the role that symbolic mathematics plays in facilitating the pursuit." The *Kirkus Reviews* contributor went on to call *Labyrinth* a "distinct contribution" to science writing, while in *American Scientist* S. S. Schweber commented that the author "brilliantly conveys the meaning and motivation for the attempts of Gilbert, Kepler, Newton, and the other [scientific] virtuosi to read the Book of Nature and to decipher her secrets." Although maintaining that Pesic's focus is slightly different from what his book's subtitle might suggest—*Labyrinth* "really discusses the meaning of the hidden in science, not the hidden meaning of science"—*Eighteenth-Century Studies* reviewer Helmut Müller-Sievers praised the work as "elegantly written and . . . quite well documented."

Pesic makes the argument that quantum theory, which holds that basic particles are not unique, creates the need to re-define what is meant by individuality in his 2003 book *Seeing Double*. In literature ranging from Homer to Kafka, and philosophers ranging from Leibniz to Kant, he ponders the significance of what he calls "indenticality" as well as what is really meant by "identity": being an exact duplicate of something else or being different from it? Reviewing Pesic's deeply researched work, Ray Olson noted in *Booklist* that the writer "suavely creates a masterpiece by saying much in little space." Although a *Publishers Weekly* reviewer found the book to be "suggestive but almost terse" in its study of the concept of individuality in light of modern science, *Isis* contributor Jonathan Bain called *Seeing Double* an "entertaining" work that "seamlessly combines an accurate and well-referenced history of atomic theories of matter with literary and philosophical accounts of identity."

BIOGRAPHICAL AND CRITICAL SOURCES:

PERIODICALS

American Scientist, November, 2000, S. S. Schweber, review of *Labyrinth: A Search for the Hidden Meaning of Science,* p. 553.

Booklist, March 1, 2002, Ray Olson, review of *Seeing Double: Shared Identities in Physics, Philosophy, and Literature,* p. 1067; January 1, 2003, review of *Seeing Double,* p. 791.

Choice, October, 2000, F. Potter, review of *Labyrinth,* p. 352; October, 2002, J. P. McKinney, review of *Seeing Double,* p. 361.

Chronicle of Higher Education, August 4, 2000, p. 22.

Eighteenth-Century Studies, spring, 2001, Helmut Müller-Sievers, review of *Labyrinth,* pp. 478-481.

English Historical Review, February, 2001, R. G. A. Dolby, review of *Labyrinth,* p. 207.

Isis, December, 2002, Jonathan Bain, review of *Seeing Double,* p. 670.

Kirkus Reviews, May 15, 2000, review of *Labyrinth,* p. 702.

Publishers Weekly, January 21, 2002, review of *Seeing Double,* p. 75.

Renaissance Quarterly, winter, 2002, Pamela O. Long, review of *Labyrinth,* p. 1323.

ONLINE

MIT Press Web site, http://mitpress.mit.edu/ (October 7, 2003).*

* * *

PILBEAM, Pamela M.

PERSONAL: Born in England; daughter of Sidney (a welder) and Alice May (a worker in a pot factory) Cartlidge; married Stephen Pilbeam (a life guard trainer), 1967; children: Natalya, Rhys, Llewellyn. *Ethnicity:* "British." *Education:* University College, University of London, Ph.D., 1966. *Religion:* "Pagan." *Hobbies and other interests:* Swimming, cycling.

ADDRESSES: Office—Royal Holloway College, University of London, Egham, Surrey TW20 0EX, England. *E-mail*—p.pilbeam@rhul.ac.uk.

CAREER: University of London, Royal Holloway College, Egham, Surrey, England, professor of French history.

MEMBER: Royal Historical Society (fellow).

AWARDS, HONORS: Fulbright fellow; awards from French government.

WRITINGS:

The Middle Classes in Europe, 1789-1914: France, Germany, Italy, and Russia, Lyceum Books (Chicago, IL), 1990.
The French Revolution of 1830, St. Martin's Press (New York, NY), 1991.
Republicanism in Nineteenth-Century France, 1814-1871, St. Martin's Press (New York, NY), 1995.
(Editor) *Themes in Modern European History, 1780-1830,* Routledge (New York, NY), 1995.
The Constitutional Monarchy in France, 1814-1848, Longman (New York, NY), 1999.
French Socialists before Marx: Workers, Women, and the Social Question in France, McGill-Queen's University Press (Montreal, Quebec, Canada), 2000.
Madame Tussaud and the History of Waxworks, Hambledon & London (New York, NY), 2003.

WORK IN PROGRESS: Research on "cross-Channel perceptions."

BIOGRAPHICAL AND CRITICAL SOURCES:

PERIODICALS

Contemporary Review, July, 2001, review of *The Constitutional Monarchy in France, 1814-1848,* p. 62.
Labour/Le Travail, spring, 2002, David Gregory, review of *French Socialists before Marx: Workers, Women, and the Social Question in France,* p. 331.
Nineteenth-Century French Studies, fall, 2002, Claudia Moscovici, review of *French Socialists before Marx,* p. 153.
Utopian Studies, spring, 2001, Leslie Jean Roberts, review of *French Socialists before Marx,* p. 357.

*   *   *

PIMLOTT, Ben(jamin John) 1945-2004

OBITUARY NOTICE—See index for *CA* sketch: Born July 4, 1945, in London, England; died of leukemia, April 10, 2004, in London, England. Historian, educator, journalist, and author. Pimlott was an award-winning biographer and most recently served as

warden of Goldsmiths College at the University of London. Educated at Worcester College, Oxford, he earned a B.A. there in 1967 and a B.Phil. in 1969; his doctorate was completed at the University of Newcastle-upon-Tyne in 1978, which was also where he began his academic career as a lecturer in politics in 1970. Ignoring the chance to make tenure at Newcastle, in 1979 he took up a research post at the London School of Economics, where he studied the papers of Hugh Dalton, the chancellor of the exchequer in Britain after World War II. This research resulted in his biography *Hugh Dalton* (1985), which earned the author the Whitbread Book of the Year award; he also edited Dalton's diaries, which were published as *The Second World War Diary of Hugh Dalton, 1940-45* (1986) and *The Political Diary of Hugh Dalton, 1918-40, 1945-60* (1987). In 1981, Pimlott accepted a post as lecturer in politics at the University of London's Birkbeck College, and in 1987 he was made a full professor of politics and contemporary history. Besides history, politics was Pimlott's other main interest; he even ran, unsuccessfully, for office under the Labour Party ticket in 1979. Although Pimlott's ideals were commensurate with the Labour Party's, he was disappointed by the political group's ineffectiveness, and when he became an active journalist in the 1980s, he often wrote about his frustrations with Labour. Despite failing to hold office, Pimlott was active in political committees, chairing the Economic and Social Research Council Cabinet Office Whitehall project's steering committee from 1993 to 1994. Contributing to such periodicals as the *Guardian, Independent, Times,* and *New Statesman,* Pimlott actually preferred writing for the popular press over contributing to scholarly journals. His biographies also received popularity among the general public, with *Harold Wilson* (1992) and *The Queen: A Biography of Elizabeth II* (1996) becoming bestsellers in England. Pimlott left Birkbeck College in 1998 to become warden of Goldsmiths College, where he served two terms in office for an institution well known for its creative and performing arts departments. Also distinguished for his book *Labour and the Left in the 1930s* (1977) and *Frustrate Their Knavish Tricks: Writings on Biography, History, and Politics* (1994), Pimlott completed one more book before his death, *Governing London,* written with Nirmala Rao, in 2002.

OBITUARIES AND OTHER SOURCES:

PERIODICALS

Daily Telegraph (London, England), April 13, 2004, p. 1.

Financial Times, April 13, 2004, p. 3.
Guardian (Manchester, England), April 12, 2004, p. 19.
Herald (Glasgow, Scotland), April 13, 2004, p. 18.
New York Times, April 17, 2004, p. A13.
Times (London, England), April 13, 2004, p. 24.
Washington Post, April 19, 2004, p. B7.

*   *   *

PRESCOTT, Peter S(herwin) 1935-2004

OBITUARY NOTICE—See index for *CA* sketch: Born July 15, 1935, in New York, NY; died of liver disease, complicated by diabetes, April 23, 2004, in New York, NY. Editor and author. Prescott was best known as a book critic for periodicals such as *Look* and *Newsweek.* He was a graduate of Harvard University, where he earned a bachelor's in 1957, and also studied at the Sorbonne for a year. From 1958 to 1967, Prescott was senior editor for the publisher E. P. Dutton; he then took up a career as a book editor for various magazines, including *Women's Wear Daily* and *Look.* His longest stint was with *Newsweek,* where he was senior writer from 1978 to 1991. Later in his career, Prescott taught journalism at Columbia University as an adjunct professor from 1979 to 1986. A winner of the George Polk Award for criticism in 1978, he considered himself to be somewhere between a literary critic and a book reviewer, the former having a much more academic bent, while the latter merely discussed the content of the book at hand; Prescott, in comparison, wrote about the content of the book but also tried to analyze more deeply why a literary venture did or did not work. In addition to his criticism, he was also the author of the biographical *A World of Our Own: Notes on Life and Learning in a Boys' Preparatory School* (1970), the essay collection *A Darkening Green: Notes from the Silent Generation* (1974), and *The Child Savers: Juvenile Justice Observed* (1981), which won the Robert F. Kennedy Book Award.

OBITUARIES AND OTHER SOURCES:

PERIODICALS

Los Angeles Times, April 26, 2004, p. B11.
New York Times, April 24, 2004, p. A13.
Washington Post, April 26, 2004, p. B7.

Q-R

QUESADA, Roberto 1962-

PERSONAL: Born 1962, in Olanchito, Honduras.

ADDRESSES: Home—New York, NY. *Agent*—c/o Arte Público Press, University of Houston, 452 Cullen Performance Hall, Houston, TX 77204-2004.

CAREER: Author and journalist. *SobreVuelo* (literary magazine), founder and former director. Delegate for the Honduras Embassy to the United States.

AWARDS, HONORS: Latin American Institute of Writers in the United States Award, for *El humano y la diosa.*

WRITINGS:

El desertor, G. Fiallos Paz (Honduras), 1985.

Los barcos (novel), Baktun Editorial (Tegucigalpa, Honduras), 1988, translation by Hardie St. Martin published as *The Ships,* Four Walls Eight Windows (New York, NY), 1992.

El humano y la diosa (novel; title means "The Human and the Goddess") Cocolo Editorial (Santo Domingo, Dominican Republic), 1996.

When the Road Is Long, Even Slippers Feel Tight: A Collection of Latin American Proverbs, Andrews McMeel Publishing (Kansas City, MO), 1998.

The Big Banana (novel), translation by Walter Krochmal, Arte Público Press (Houston, TX), 1999.

Nunca entres por Miami (novel), Mondadori (Mexico City, Mexico), 2002, translation by Patricia J. Duncan published as *Never through Miami,* Arte Público Press (Houston, TX), 2002.

Contributor of articles to *El Tiempo.*

SIDELIGHTS: Award-winning author Roberto Quesada was born and raised in Honduras but has lived in New York City since 1989. His first novel to be translated into English, *Los barcos*—published as *The Ships* in 1992—deals with the travails of his troubled homeland. In the early twentieth century, the American-owned United Fruit Company, with the help of corrupt Honduran officials, essentially confiscated Honduran land for its fruit operations and forced indigenous people to work the plantations.

The title of *The Ships* implies reference to the three small caravels that made the voyage of discovery to the Americas under Christopher Columbus. In Quesada's story, however, they are the white ships of the North American Standard Fruit Company. To the poor plantation workers—among them protagonist Guillermo Lopez, a pineapple picker aspiring to be a writer—the arriving ships mean more work and a pittance more pay. Writing in *Bloomsbury Review,* David Unger noted: "In a neat example of how symbols change meaning, the ships—emblems of exploitation and slavery in the thirties, forties, and fifties—are now fondly awaited for the work, money, and entertainment they bring to the coastal regions." By the 1980s, however, the ships are U.S. naval vessels carrying military supplies for a civil war in neighboring Nicaragua, with the local population caught in the crossfire between the warring factions.

Quesada tells the story through conversations and comments exchanged by fruit pickers to amuse themselves during their long, tedious days. Jack Shreve commented in *Library Journal,* "It is this communication that gives the novel its special flavor." Unger had one criticism for the novel, noting that "in Quesada's desire to tell a complex story simply, he has understated, and to a certain degree, soft-pedalled, another tragic chapter in Honduran history." But Unger's overall assessment was positive, as he termed *The Ships* "a tiny gem of a novel."

In 1999's *The Big Banana,* Quesada brings aspiring actor Eduardo Lin from Honduras to the Bronx, where he is given his nickname because he hails from a "banana republic." Eduardo finds work in construction, charms all those he meets, womanizes prolifically, and develops friendships with a diverse array of fellow Latinos. "The group's basic modus vivendi is to uncork a gallon of cheap wine, put on some music and argue over which of their Latin American countries is most miserable," wrote Sandra Tsing Loh in the *New York Times.* Lawrence Olszewski commented in *Library Journal,* "Quesada is at his inventive peak when re-creating the bohemian Latino colony." Eventually, Eduardo gets an audition with film director Steven Spielberg and becomes Honduras's most famous actor. Loh commented that while the book "has very little real plot . . . there is a breezy literary self-confidence here that dares one to find fault."

In *Never through Miami,* published in Spanish as *Nunca entres por Miami,* Latin American sculptor Elias Sandoval arrives at Miami International Airport with a one-way ticket, sixty dollars, dreams of becoming famous, and no visa. There, he is confronted by grim immigration officials in a scene that Sheila Shoup, in *School Library Journal,* called "hilarious." Elias finally gains admission, and in New York he finds work waiting tables. He promised his girlfriend Helena in Honduras that, once settled, he would bring her and her mother to the United States. But Elias becomes attracted to a fellow worker, and his calls home become progressively more sporadic. By the time Helena and her mother reach the United States, Helena has lost faith in Elias and vanishes in Miami. Shoup commented, "Quesada shines with his gently satirical insight on relationships, the art world, and life as an immigrant." A *Publishers Weekly* reviewer called the book an "amusing story bolstered by its knowledgeable meditations on the Central American immigration experience."

BIOGRAPHICAL AND CRITICAL SOURCES:

PERIODICALS

Bloomsbury Review, March-April, 1993, David Unger, review of *The Ships,* p. 7.
Library Journal, August, 1992, Jack Shreve, review of *The Ships,* p. 151; February 15, 1999, Lawrence Olszewski, review of *The Big Banana,* p. 185.
New York Times, September 12, 1999, Sandra Tsing Loh, review of *The Big Banana.*
Publishers Weekly, July 27, 1992, review of *The Ships,* p. 50; February 1, 1999, review of *The Big Banana,* p. 77; February 25, 2002, review of *Never through Miami,* p. 43.
School Library Journal, December, 2000, Sheila Shoup, review of *Never through Miami,* p. 174.*

*   *   *

QUINTON, Ann 1934-
(Margaret Dewar)

PERSONAL: Born October 27, 1934, in Ipswich, England; daughter of Charles Francis (an engineer) and Mary (a homemaker; maiden name, Dewar) Cole; married Geoffrey Naylor Quinton (a research chemist), November 3, 1961; children: Stuart Naylor, Neill Naylor, Kathryn Naylor. *Ethnicity:* "British." *Education:* Attended Royal College of Music. *Religion:* Church of England. *Hobbies and other interests:* Music, art, gardening, swimming, travel, wildlife.

ADDRESSES: Home—Chelford, 31 Rectory Lane, Kirton, Ipswich, Suffolk IP10 0PY, England.

CAREER: East Suffolk County Library, library assistant, 1952-57; Fisons Research Station, research library assistant, 1957-62; freelance pianist for primary schools, dancing schools, and play groups, 1975-89; writer, 1989—. Freelance artist, with work exhibited throughout the east of England.

MEMBER: Crime Writers Association, Royal Society for the Protection of Birds, British Trust for Ornithology, Suffolk Wildlife Association, Suffolk Wildlife Trust, Felixstowe Art Group, Garden Bird Watch.

WRITINGS:

CRIME NOVELS

To Mourn a Mischief, Piatkus Books (London, England), 1989.

Death of a Dear Friend, Piatkus Books (London, England), 1990.

A Fatal End, Pitakus Books (London, England), 1992.

A Little Grave, Severn House Publishers (New York, NY), 1994.

The Sleeping and the Dead, Severn House Publishers (New York, NY), 1994.

Some Foul Play, Severn House Publishers (New York, NY), 1996.

This Mortal Coil, Severn House Publishers (New York, NY), 1998.

Put Out the Light, Severn House Publishers (New York, NY), 2000.

Bought with Blood, Severn House Publishers (New York, NY), 2002.

OTHER

Philippa (historical novel), Robert Hale (London, England), 1982.

The Rosslyn Heir (historical novel), Robert Hale (London, England), 1982.

The Loyalty Game (historical novel), Robert Hale (London, England), 1984.

Storm Islands (romantic suspense novel), Piatkus Books (London, England), 1985.

The Ragusa Theme (romantic suspense novel), Piatkus Books (London, England), 1986.

Author of historical novels published under the pseudonym Margaret Dewar in the 1980s.

WORK IN PROGRESS: Research for another crime novel.

SIDELIGHTS: Ann Quinton told *CA:* "I have been a compulsive reader all my life, devouring the works of Conan Doyle (Sherlock Holmes) at the tender age of nine, which surely influenced my present writing genre of crime and detection fiction. My early career was spent in the library service (both public and research), and while working with books I always wanted to be on the other side of the fence; that is, to write them myself rather than deal with other people's work.

"While starting out on my writing career I was working as a freelance pianist and accompanist. All my life I have also been a painter, and I am now a recognized artist in East Anglia, painting mostly landscapes in pastels. I juggle this occupation with my writing.

"My writing is initially done in longhand before being transposed into a word processor/computer, and much of it is done in my gypsy caravan, which my husband and I restored and keep in my shed down the garden.

"I start off with a basic plot for my crime novels, but I am never sure exactly how it is going to develop. All sorts of things happen along the way! I am deeply influenced by my love of the English countryside and nature, and I particularly enjoy developing the relationships and interplay between my characters, for which the crime genre is an excellent vehicle.

"I suppose the two writers who have most influenced me are Dorothy Dunnett and Mary Stewart."

BIOGRAPHICAL AND CRITICAL SOURCES:

PERIODICALS

Booklist, December 15, 1996, Ilene Cooper, review of *Some Foul Play,* p. 713; October 1, 1998, John Rowen, review of *This Mortal Coil,* p. 311; May 1, 2000, Ilene Cooper, review of *Put Out the Light,* p. 1624; March 1, 2002, John Rowen, review of *Bought with Blood,* p. 1097.

Publishers Weekly, October 28, 1996, review of *Some Foul Play,* p. 60.

*   *   *

RAHIMI, Atiq 1962-

PERSONAL: Born 1962, in Kabul, Afghanistan; immigrated to France, 1984; father, a provincial governor; mother, a teacher; married. *Education:* Attended University of Kabul; University of Paris, Sorbonne, Ph.D. (audio-visual communications).

ADDRESSES: Home—Paris, France. *Agent*—c/o Author Mail, Harcourt Trade Publishers, 15 East 26th St., New York, NY 10010.

CAREER: Novelist and documentary filmmaker. Worked as a film critic in Afghanistan. Organizer of writing center in Kabul, Afghanistan, with Bernard-Henri Lévy.

WRITINGS:

Khākistar va khvāb, translated into French by Sabrina Nouri, Éditions Khavaran (France), 1999, translated by Erdağ M. Göknar as *Earth and Ashes,* Harcourt (New York, NY), 2002.

Also author of a second novel.

WORK IN PROGRESS: Adapting *Earth and Ashes* for film.

SIDELIGHTS: Atiq Rahimi left his native Afghanistan five years after the Union of Soviet Socialist Republics invaded that country in 1979, and since age twenty-two has claimed France as his second home, graduating from the University of Paris and embarking on a career as a documentary filmmaker. He has sensitively woven the memories he retains of his home and family into a compelling, moving, and oddly optimistic first novel, published in English as *Earth and Ashes.* Praising the novel in *Booklist* as a "richly nuanced and broadly illuminating tale of one father's grief," Donna Seaman added that Rahimi provides readers with a timely look into "the hearts of innocent people who bear the brunt of terrorism."

Rahimi was raised in a literate home: his mother was a teacher, and his father was a provincial governor under King Zahir Shah. After a military coup dethroned Shah in 1973, Rahimi's father was imprisoned for three years, after which he and Rahimi fled to India. After the Soviets ousted the military government, the two returned, and Rahimi attended the University of Kabul and studied literature. His family connections eventually threatened his safety, however, and in 1984 he joined twenty others in fleeing Afghanistan and seeking asylum at the French Embassy in neighboring Pakistan. Rahimi, who wrote his novel in the Afghan dialect called Dari as a way of coming to terms with his own experiences fleeing on foot through the mountains into Pakistan as a college student, tells his story in the second person, narrated by an elderly man overcome by the loss of his family.

In Rahimi's novel, five-year-old Yassin and his grandfather, Dastaguir, are on a journey inspired by a vision the old man had. The village these two inhabit lies in ruins, smoke still rising from the bombing it received at the hands of Soviet troops. The pair are the only local survivors of their family. Yassin, deaf as a result of the attack, now depends on the heartsick Dastaguir, who is determined to make the difficult trip to the remote coal mine where his son, Murad, works, telling him of the tragedy and of the death of Murad's wife, Yassin's mother.

As the old man and his grandson wait at a post on the Afghan border in search of a truck willing to take them to the mine, the old man chews tobacco, tosses stones, talks with those around him, but is detached from his surroundings. Dastaguir's "strained" narration is poignant, "both inviting the reader to share his experiences and insisting on his own detachment from them," according to *Guardian* reviewer Rachel Aspden. "The cumulative effect is one of shocked numbness."

A brief book at just over fifty pages, *Earth and Ashes* reads more like a short story, a short story that "remains unfinished," in the opinion of *Times Literary Supplement* contributor Tim Glencross. References to Afghan history and Persian epic poems are threaded subtly through Rahimi's text, but, as Aspden pointed out in her *Guardian* review, "if these go unnoticed, most of [the novel's] . . . resonance is lost." Glencross noted that "the fate of the boy and his grandfather [remains] still hanging in the air" by the story's end. "With this brevity," Glencross continued, "Rahimi seems to be suggesting that grief and loss cannot be filled out with language, that the writer must attempt to conjure a void." Calling *Earth and Ashes* "a parable of familial dysfunction," *Independent* writer Gerry Feehily thought that its author "has compressed ten years of Soviet occupation into less than sixty devastating pages." Interviewing Rahimi, Feehily gained a sense of the author's purpose: to give a voice to the many children whose lives were devastated when the Soviet troops entered Afghanistan and destroyed their families in 1979. Many of these same children grew up to join organizations such as the Taliban, gaining a new family within the terrorist network and also gaining an outlet for the violence that marked their lives. "Many Taliban were war orphans," Rahimi explained to Feehily. "Having never had a mother, having never had relationships with women, knowing only the Koran and the fear of hell, they were psychically crippled. Although I set *Earth and Ashes* during the Soviet occupation, I was really trying to find a way to explain to myself the roots of [the Taliban's] . . . ascendancy."

BIOGRAPHICAL AND CRITICAL SOURCES:

PERIODICALS

Booklist, October 15, 2002, Donna Seaman, review of *Earth and Ashes,* p. 389.
Guardian (Manchester, England), December 14, 2002, Rachel Aspden, "Short and Bitter."
Independent, December 7, 2002, Gerry Feehily, interview with Rahimi.
Kirkus Reviews, August 1, 2002, review of *Earth and Ashes,* p. 1069.
Publishers Weekly, November 25, 2002, review of *Earth and Ashes,* p. 44.
Times Literary Supplement, October 18, 2002, Tim Glencross, "A Road in Afghanistan," p. 25.
World Literature Today, April-June, 2003, Ali Nema-tollahy, review of *Les mille maisons du reve et de la terreur,* p. 91.*

*   *   *

RANDLE, Kevin D. 1949-

PERSONAL: Born 1949, in Cheyenne, WY. *Education:* Attended Humboldt State University.

ADDRESSES: Agent—c/o Author Mail, St. Martin's Press, 175 Fifth Ave., New York, NY 10010.

CAREER: Science fiction writer. UFOlogist. *Military service:* U.S. Army, assault helicopter companies, 1968-69; Iowa National Guard, helicopter pilot, 1971-73; Air Force ROTC, University of Iowa, 1973-75; Air Force, intelligence officer, 1975-91, became captain.

WRITINGS:

"SEEDS OF WAR" SERIES; WITH ROBERT CORNETT

Seeds of War, Ace Books (New York, NY), 1988.
Aldebaran Campaign, Ace Books (New York, NY), 1988.
The Aquarian Attack, Ace Books (New York, NY), 1989.

"REMEMBER!" SERIES; WITH ROBERT CORNETT

Remember the Alamo!, Diamond Books (New York, NY), 1986.
Remember Gettysburg!, Diamond Books (New York, NY), 1988.
Remember Little Big Horn!, Diamond Books (New York, NY), 1990.

"JEFFERSON'S WAR" SERIES

The Galactic Silver Star, Ace Books (New York, NY), 1990.
The Price of Command, Ace Books (New York, NY), 1990.
The January Platoon, Ace Books (New York, NY), 1991.
Death of a Regiment, Ace Books (New York, NY), 1991.
Chain of Command, Ace Books (New York, NY), 1992.

OTHER FICTION

(With Richard J. Randisi) *Once Upon a Murder,* Bantam (New York, NY), 1987.
Spanish Gold, M. Evans (New York, NY), 1990.
Dawn of Conflict, Bantam (New York, NY), 1991.
(With Richard Driscoll) *Star Precinct,* Ace (New York, NY), 1992.
(With Richard Driscoll) *Star Precinct 2: Mind Slayer,* Ace (New York, NY), 1992.
(With Richard Driscoll) *Star Precinct: Inside Job,* Ace (New York, NY), 1993.
Galactic MI, Ace Books (New York, NY), 1993.
Galactic MI #2: The Rat Trap, Ace Books (New York, NY), 1993.

Operation Roswell, Tor (New York, NY), 2002.

Signals, Ace Books (New York, NY), 2003.

Starship, Ace Books (New York, NY), 2003.

NONFICTION

The October Scenario: UFO Abductions, Theories about Them, and a Prediction of When They Will Return, Middle Coast Publishing (Iowa City, IA), 1988.

UFO Casebook, Warner (New York, NY), 1989.

(With Donald R. Schmitt) *UFO Crash at Roswell,* Avon (New York, NY), 1991.

(With Donald R. Schmitt) *The Truth about the UFO Crash at Roswell,* M. Evans (New York, NY), 1994.

Lost Gold and Buried Treasure: A Treasure Hunter's Guide to One Hundred Fortunes Waiting to Be Found, M. Evans (New York, NY), 1995.

A History of UFO Crashes, Avon (New York, NY), 1995.

Roswell UFO Crash Update: Exposing the Military Cover-up of the Century, Global Communications (New Brunswick, NJ), 1995.

Project Blue Book Exposed, Marlowe & Company (New York, NY), 1997.

Conspiracy of Silence, Avon (New York, NY), 1997.

(With Russ Estes) *Faces of the Visitors: An Illustrated Reference to Alien Contact,* Fireside (New York, NY), 1997.

The Randle Report: UFOs in the '90s, M. Evans (New York, NY), 1997.

Project Moon Dust: Beyond Roswell—Exposing the Government's Continuing Covert UFO Investigation in Cover-Ups, Avon (New York, NY), 1998.

(With Russ Estes and William P. Cone) *The Abduction Enigma: An Investigation of the Alien Abduction Phenomenon,* Forge (New York, NY), 1999.

Scientific UFOlogy: How the Application of Scientific Methodology Can Analyze, Illuminate, and Prove the Reality of UFOs, Avon (New York, NY), 1999.

(With Russ Estes) *Spaceships of the Visitors: An Illustrated Guide to Alien Spacecraft,* Simon & Schuster (New York, NY), 2000.

The Roswell Encyclopedia, HarperCollins (New York, NY), 2000.

Case MJ-12: The True Story behind the Government's UFO Conspiracies, HarperCollins (New York, NY), 2002.

SIDELIGHTS: After nearly twenty years in the armed services, Kevin D. Randle began writing science fiction series in the late 1980s. His "Seeds of War" series, coauthored with Robert Cornett, drew heavily on his own extensive military service—as a helicopter pilot during the Vietnam War and an Air Force intelligence officer—to create solid and believable military sci-fi. In *Seeds of War,* which launched the series, a punitive expedition is sent to a planet in the Tau Centi system after a peaceful probe from Earth is destroyed. *Fantasy Review* contributor Glenn Reed found it a "competently written novel for those who enjoy war adventure." About the same time, Randle and Cornett also produced the "Remember!" series, a trio of time-travel books in which modern soldiers travel to famous battles to prevent a corporation's attempted alterations in history. "Well worth your time," wrote a *Science Fiction Chronicle* reviewer of *Remember the Alamo!,* the first of the series.

Randle returned to straightforward military sci-fi with *The Galactic Silver Star,* first of the "Jefferson's War" series, which chronicles the adventures of the United States Space Infantry, and particularly Colonel Jefferson. In a review of *The Price of Command,* *Booklist* contributor Roland Green noted Randles's "keen insight into the internal politics of the military" as one of the series' highlights. Randle followed this up with the "Star Precinct" series, a trio of sci-fi stories about an intergalactic police force, coauthored with Richard Driscoll, and two "Galactic MI" books, which tell of an undercover team that travels to alien worlds before official contact is made. In addition, Randle produced a mystery, *Once Upon a Murder,* and a Western adventure, *Spanish Gold.*

While establishing a solid reputation in genre fiction, Randle also emerged as a prominent figure in the study of UFOs and related fields, particularly the Roswell crash and the alien abduction phenomenon. In the 1970s he investigated animal mutilations as a field investigator for the Aerial Phenomena Research Organization. In the 1980s, he became especially interested in the question of the alien crash that many claim happened in 1947 in Roswell, New Mexico, interviewing hundreds of participants connected to that mystery. In 1991, he and fellow-investigator Donald Schmitt produced *UFO Crash at Roswell,* which set forth in meticulous detail the evidence for the crash, including a great deal of testimony from witnesses. Writing in *Voice of Youth Advocates,* John

Lord wrote, "the first thing that this reviewer notes is the authors' attention to facts. . . . And this is where the book begins to fall short, mainly because there are too many details repeated too many times." Still, Lord admitted, the book "has no glaring problems" and thought readers would find it "interesting and even exciting." In 1994, Randle and Schmitt followed up with *The Truth about the UFO Crash at Roswell,* "the most thorough and objective account currently available," according to *Library Journal* contributor Gary Barber, a SUNY professor. This update included new witnesses, adding a number who claimed to have been threatened by the military, and a revised event chronology. In 1997, Randle went on to produce *The Randle Report: UFOs in the '90s,* a comprehensive and rigorous examination of various UFO sightings and contact, debunking some famous examples but leaving room for accepting some of the lesser-known claims. A *Publishers Weekly* reviewer praised Randle as one of the few UFO researchers "willing to weigh the evidence for what it's genuinely worth."

In addition to Roswell, Randle has taken a strong interest in the alien abduction claims that have proliferated in recent decades. In *Faces of the Visitors: An Illustrated Reference to Alien Contact,* he and coauthor Russ Estes sort through the various sightings and compile sketches and descriptions of over one hundred different types of aliens that supposedly have visited Earth. In addition, they attempt to rate the credibility of the sightings. *New Scientist* contributor David Barrett found the book "a complete waste of a good tree."

In 1999, Randall and Estes teamed up with psychotherapist William P. Cone to take a more critical look at the wide-ranging field of abduction claims. Together, they published *The Abduction Enigma: An Investigation of the Alien Abduction Phenomenon,* "A well-written anti-abduction perspective on alien encounters that systematically examines and refutes each argument used by abduction proponents," according to a *Kirkus Reviews* contributor. The book sets forth a short history of alien abductions, the role of folklore, popular culture, and false memory syndrome in creating the present-day image of alien visitations, and examines the alleged physical proofs, such as implants and scars. In addition, they analyze the more well-known abduction investigators, combing through numerous transcripts and uncovering numerous examples of leading questions, pseudoscientific analysis, and possible fraud. The book "should

convince even the most dedicated believer in aliens and alien abductions that he not only has been badly misinformed over the past five decades but also been sorely misled by the popular press, the abduction researchers, and even by the abductees themselves," wrote Robert Baker in the *Skeptical Inquirer.*

Randle would probably not go that far. Although a skeptic when it comes to abductions, he remains a key figure in the study of UFO claims and a firm believer in the military cover-up of the events at Roswell. He has even produced a thinly-veiled fictionalization of what may have happened, titled *Operation Roswell.* He writes and lectures widely on UFOs and remains one of the most visible, and most respected, figures in that controversial field.

BIOGRAPHICAL AND CRITICAL SOURCES:

PERIODICALS

Booklist, December 1, 1990, Roland Green, review of *The Price of Command,* p. 720; May 15, 1994, George Eberhart, review of *The Truth about the UFO Crash at Roswell,* p. 1646; September 15, 2002, Roland Green, review of *Operation Roswell,* p. 212; March 15, 2003, Roland Green, review of *Signals,* p. 1286; January 1, 2004, Roland Green, review of *Starship,* p. 840.

Fantasy Review, December, 1996, Glenn Reed, review of *Seeds of War,* p. 37.

Kirkus Reviews, May 1, 1999, review of *The Abduction Enigma: An Investigation of the Alien Abduction Phenomenon,* p. 705; August 15, 2002, review of *Operation Roswell,* p. 1184.

Library Journal, June 1, 1994, Gary Barber, review of *The Truth about the UFO Crash at Roswell,* p. 152; September 15, 2002, Jackie Cassada, review of *Operation Roswell,* p. 97.

New Scientist, January 24, 1998, David Barrett, review of *Faces of the Visitors: An Illustrated Reference to Alien Contact,* p. 45.

New Yorker, January 10, 2000, C. Niemann, review of *The Abduction Enigma,* p. 14.

Publishers Weekly, April 14, 1997, review of *The Randle Report: UFOs in the '90s,* p. 68; September 16, 2002, review of *Operation Roswell,* p. 55.

Science Fiction Chronicle, December, 1986, review of *Remember the Alamo!,* p. 48; April, 1992, review of *Star Precinct,* p. 30.

Skeptical Inquirer, January, 2000, Robert Baker, review of *The Abduction Enigma,* p. 49.

Voice of Youth Advocates, December, 1991, John Lord, review of *UFO Crash at Roswell,* p. 340.

Washington Post Book World, January 4, 1988, Elaine Showalter, review of *Faces of the Visitors,* p. 1.

ONLINE

SF Site, http://www.sfsite.com (May 11, 2004), Thomas Myer, review of *Conspiracy of Silence.**

*   *   *

RAPPAPORT, Doreen

PERSONAL: Born in New York, NY; married to a painter and sculptor. *Education:* Brandeis University, B.A.

ADDRESSES: Home—New York, NY; Copake Falls, NY. *Agent*—c/o Author Mail, HarperCollins, 10 East 53rd St., 7th Fl., New York, NY 10022. *E-mail*—rapabook@aol.com.

CAREER: Teacher of music and reading in schools in New York and New Rochelle, NY, 1961-1968; teacher at a freedom school, McComb, MS, 1965; writer.

AWARDS, HONORS: Gradiva Award Honor, National Association for the Advancement of Psychoanalysis and the World Association of Psychoanalysis, Best Book on Africa for Young Readers citation, African Studies Association, One Hundred Titles for Reading and Sharing selection, New York Public Library, and Notable Trade Book in the Field of Social Studies citation, National Council for the Social Studies (NCSS), all for *The New King;* Carter G. Woodson Honor Book, and Notable Trade Book in the Field of Social Studies, NCSS, both for *The Flight of Red Bird: The Life of Zitkala-Sa;* Coretta Scott King Honor Book, American Library Association (ALA), and Notable Book selection, ALA, for *Freedom River;* Jane Addams Children's Book Award (picture book category), 2002, Children's Choice selection, International Reading Association, Orbis Pictus Honor Book, National Council of Teachers of English, Caldecott

Honor Book, ALA, Coretta Scott King Honor Book, ALA, and Notable Book selection, ALA, all for *Martin's Big Words: The Life of Dr. Martin Luther King, Jr.,* illustrated by Bryan Collier; Flora Stieglitz Straus Award, Bank Street College of Education, Notable Trade Book in the Field of Social Studies citation, NCSS, One Hundred Books to Read and Share selection, New York Public Library, Fanfare citation, *Horn Book,* Gold Award, *Parents* magazine, and Best Book of the Year citation, *Child* magazine, all for *No More! Stories and Songs of Slave Resistance;* Notable Trade Book in the Field of Social Studies citations, NCSS, for *Escape from Slavery: Five Journeys to Freedom* and *We Are the Many: A Picture Book of American Indians.*

WRITINGS:

NONFICTION

(With Susan Kempler and Michele Spirn) *A Man Can Be . . .,* photographs by Russell Dian, Human Sciences Press (New York, NY), 1981.

(Editor) *American Women: Their Lives in Their Words,* Harper & Row (New York, NY), 1990.

Escape from Slavery: Five Journeys to Freedom, illustrated by Charles Lilly, Harper & Row (New York, NY), 1991.

Living Dangerously: American Women Who Risked Their Lives for Adventure, Harper & Row (New York, NY), 1991.

The Flight of Red Bird: The Life of Zitkala-Sa, Dial Books for Young Readers (New York, NY), 1997.

Freedom River, illustrated by Bryan Collier, Jump at the Sun (New York, NY), 2000.

Martin's Big Words: The Life of Dr. Martin Luther King, Jr., illustrated by Bryan Collier, Jump at the Sun (New York, NY), 2001.

We Are the Many: A Picture Book of American Indians, illustrated by Cornelius Van Wright and Ying-Hwa Hu, HarperCollins (New York, NY), 2002.

No More! Stories and Songs of Slave Resistance, illustrated by Shane W. Evans, Candlewick Press (Cambridge, MA), 2002.

(With Joan Verniero) *Victory or Death! Stories of the American Revolution,* illustrated by Greg Call, HarperCollins (New York, NY), 2003.

Free at Last! Stories and Songs of Emancipation, illustrated by Shane W. Evans, Candlewick Press (Cambridge, MA), 2004.

John's Secret Dreams: The Life of John Lennon, illustrated by Bryan Collier, Hyperion (New York, NY), 2004.

The School Is Not White! A True Story of the Civil Rights Movement, illustrated by Curtis James, Jump at the Sun (New York, NY), 2004.

In the Promised Land: Lives of Jewish Americans, illustrated by Cornelius Van Wright and Ying-Hwa Hu, HarperCollins (New York, NY), 2005.

Also creator of *Freedom River,* an animated video about the Underground Railroad, for Disney Educational Productions.

"BE THE JUDGE/BE THE JURY" SERIES; NONFICTION

The Lizzie Borden Trial, HarperCollins (New York, NY), 1992.

The Sacco-Vanzetti Trial, HarperCollins (New York, NY), 1992.

The Alger Hiss Trial, HarperCollins (New York, NY), 1993.

Tinker vs. Des Moines: Student Rights on Trial, HarperCollins (New York, NY), 1993.

FICTION

"But She's Still My Grandma!," illustrated by Bernadette Simmons, Human Sciences Press (New York, NY), 1982.

Trouble at the Mines, illustrated by Joan Sandin, Crowell (New York, NY), 1987.

The Boston Coffee Party, Harper & Row (New York, NY), 1988.

(Reteller) *The Journey of Meng: A Chinese Legend,* illustrated by Yang Ming-Yi, Dial Books for Young Readers (New York, NY), 1991.

(Reteller) *The Long-Haired Girl: A Chinese Legend,* illustrated by Yang Ming-Yi, Dial Books for Young Readers (New York, NY), 1995.

The New King, illustrated by E. B. Lewis, Dial Books for Young Readers (New York, NY), 1995.

(With Lyndall Callan) *Dirt on Their Skirts: The Story of the Young Women Who Won the World Championship,* illustrated by E. B. Lewis, Dial Books for Young Readers (New York, NY), 2000.

The Secret Seder, illustrated by Emily Arnold McCully, Hyperion (New York, NY), in press.

ADAPTATIONS: Martin's Big Words was adapted as a video by Weston Woods (Norwalk, CT); *Freedom River* was adapted as a video by Disney Educational Productions.

WORK IN PROGRESS: With Joan Verniero, *United No More! Stories of the Civil War,* for HarperCollins (New York, NY); *Freedom Ship,* illustrated by Curtis James, for Jump at the Sun; *The "Keep Quiet" Girl: The Life of Eleanor Roosevelt,* for Hyperion Books for Children; *Nobody Gonna' Turn Me 'Round,* illustrated by Shane Evans, for Candlewick Press; *Lady Liberty: An Autobiography,* for Candlewick Press.

SIDELIGHTS: Doreen Rappaport is the author of numerous nonfiction and historical fiction books for children which attempt to convey American and world history to children ages four to seventeen. As a young woman, Rappaport was a music and reading teacher, first in the ethnically diverse New York City and New Rochelle public schools, and later in a Southern "freedom school" for African-American students. Teaching in the freedom school in McComb, Mississippi, was what first inspired Rappaport to write about history. The African Americans she met in Mississippi "were heroic" in their struggle to secure their rights, Rappaport wrote on her Web site. "I knew there had to be many more 'unknown heroes,' people who helped change history. I set out to recover and write about this 'lost' history."

Many of Rappaport's books draw heavily on primary sources and integrate historical figures' own words into the text. Rappaport and illustrator Shane W. Evans collaborated on one such trilogy, about the black experience in America from the kidnappings in Africa to the civil rights movement. In the first book of the trilogy, *No More! Stories and Songs of Slave Resistance,* Rappaport uses this technique to tell the stories of Underground Railroad conductor Harriet Tubman, slave rebellion leader Nat Turner, and other African Americans. In a few vignettes, Rappaport sticks less closely to history, creating composite characters and fictionalized accounts. "But the research is documented," Hazel Rochman noted in *Booklist,* so students who need factual information for reports can draw on Rappaport's bibliography. In addition to the narratives, Rappaport also uses folktales and songs which were told and sung by African Americans. The collection of actual and fictional narratives, stories, and songs forms "an excellent account of the many ways in which slaves participated in bringing down the greatest evil in our nation's history," thought a *Kirkus Reviews* contributor.

In the second book, *Free at Last! Stories and Songs of Emancipation,* Rappaport and illustrator Shane W. Evans "reprise the passion and power that informed" *No More!,* wrote a *Kirkus Reviews* contributor. *Free at Last!* covers African-American culture from 1863 to 1954. Again, Rappaport tells the stories of famous African Americans (such as intellectual Booker T. Washington and baseball player Jackie Robinson) and some less-famous ones, interspersed with writings by African Americans (including gospel songs and Langston Hughes's famous poem "I, Too, Sing America"). As with *No More!,* the book includes an extensive bibliography and further reading list for children who are researching reports.

Moving to an earlier period of U.S. history, in *Victory or Death! Stories of the American Revolution* Rappaport and coauthor Joan Verniero tell the stories of eight famous and not-yet celebrated participants in the Revolutionary War. Although they cover such well-known figures as General George Washington and future first lady Abigail Adams, Rappaport and Verniero also write about multicultural figures on both sides, including Francis Salvador, a Jew from South Carolina who risked his life to rally his neighbors to the Patriot cause, and Grace Growden Galloway, a Philadelphia loyalist who attempted to defend her family's property from the rebellious Colonists. "Each chapter is very short and relies on vivid characterization," noted *Booklist*'s GraceAnne A. DeCandido, making it a good introduction to Revolutionary history for younger children. The narratives are arranged chronologically and "each story is set in its historical context," a critic commented in *Kirkus Reviews,* so "readers will learn a good deal of history and gain a sense of the ebb and flow of the war."

Martin's Big Words: The Life of Dr. Martin Luther King, Jr. is an atypical biography right from the start. Instead of the title and author information, the cover features nothing but a close-up portrait of civil rights leader Dr. Martin Luther King, Jr. As in her other books, "the text is a mix of Rappaport's finely honed biographical narrative and appropriate quotes from King himself," explained *Horn Book*'s Mary M. Burns. Although the text is designed for early readers, with

short, simple sentences, it still covers all of the major events in King's life, from his childhood as the son of a preacher in segregated Atlanta to his assassination. The title refers to the young King's determination to speak with big words just like his father did, but could also refer to the large-type font in which King's quotations are printed, noted reviewers. *Martin's Big Words* is "a stunning, reverent tribute" to Dr. King, concluded *School Library Journal* contributor Catherine Threadgill.

Based on a historical event but told through a fictional story, *Dirt on Their Skirts: The Story of the Young Women Who Won the World Championship* offers readers an account of the 1946 championship game of the All-American Girls Professional Baseball League. Formed in 1942, the league provided much-needed entertainment on the home front during and after World War II. In *Dirt on Their Skirts,* coauthored with Lyndall Callan, a young girl named Margaret watches the game from the stands with her mother, her brother, and her father, recently returned from the war. Finding Racine Belles second basewoman Sophie Kurys a favorite, Margaret is thrilled when Kurys steals second base and eventually slides into home to win the game, a tough play, as Margaret's mother comments, if you are wearing a skirt. "With its economy of language and telling period details, this book provides an exciting slice of sports history and an appealing bit of Americana," Luann Toth wrote in *School Library Journal.* A *Publishers Weekly* critic commended Rappaport for "judiciously using end matter to relate a historical overview of the league," information which is useful for children to understand the importance of the story. By relegating the historical facts to the afterword, the *Publishers Weekly* reviewer continued, Rappaport and Callan can "serve up a fan's view of the game."

BIOGRAPHICAL AND CRITICAL SOURCES:

PERIODICALS

Black Issues Book Review, January-February, 2002, Clarence V. Reynolds, review of *Martin's Big Words: The Life of Dr. Martin Luther King, Jr.,* p. 80.
Booklist, September 1, 1992, Hazel Rochman, review of *The Lizzie Borden Trial,* pp. 45-46; August, 1993, Janice Del Negro, review of *Tinker vs. Des*

Moines: Student Rights on Trial, p. 2048; January 1, 1994, Hazel Rochman, review of *The Alger Hiss Trial,* p. 815; January 15, 1995, Hazel Rochman, review of *The Long-Haired Girl: A Chinese Legend,* p. 933; May 1, 1995, Hazel Rochman, review of *The New King,* pp. 1577-1578; July, 1997, Karen Hutt, review of *The Flight of Red Bird: The Life of Zitkala-Sa,* p. 1810; January 1, 2000, Todd Morning, review of *Dirt on Their Skirts: The Story of the Young Women Who Won the World Championship,* p. 936; October 1, 2000, Hazel Rochman, review of *Freedom River,* p. 341; October 1, 2001, Hazel Rochman, review of *Martin's Big Words,* p. 338; February 15, 2002, Hazel Rochman, review of *No More! Stories and Songs of Slave Resistance,* p. 1033; October 15, 2002, Hazel Rochman, review of *We Are the Many: A Picture Book of American Indians,* pp. 408-409; June 1, 2003, GraceAnne A. DeCandido, review of *Victory or Death! Stories of the American Revolution,* p. 1770; February 14, 2004, Hazel Rochman, review of *Free at Last! Stories and Songs of Emancipation,* p. 1076.

Book Report, January-February, 1994, Edna Boardman, review of *Tinker vs. Des Moines,* pp. 61-62.

Childhood Education, fall, 2002, Nancy S. Maldonado, review of *Freedom River,* pp. 63-64.

Horn Book, March-April, 1987, Hanna B. Zeiger, review of *Trouble at the Mines,* p. 212; September-October, 1988, Mary M. Burns, review of *The Boston Coffee Party,* pp. 623-624; March-April, 1991, Ellen Fader, review of *American Women: Their Lives in Their Words,* p. 219; November-December, 1991, Margaret A. Bush, review of *The Journey of Meng: A Chinese Legend,* pp. 748-749; January-February, 2002, Mary M. Burns, review of *Martin's Big Words,* pp. 105-106; March-April, 2002, Joanna Rudge Long, review of *No More!,* pp. 231-232.

Instructor, March, 1994, Judy Freeman, review of *Living Dangerously: American Women Who Risked Their Lives for Adventure,* p. 79.

Kirkus Reviews, August 15, 2001, review of *Martin's Big Words,* p. 1120; January 1, 2002, review of *No More!,* p. 49; August 15, 2002, review of *We Are the Many,* p. 1233; April 1, 2003, review of *Victory or Death!,* p. 539; December 15, 2003, review of *Free at Last!,* p. 1454.

Language Arts, May, 2002, Mingshui Cai and Junko Yokata, review of *No More!,* p. 433; September, 2002, review of *Martin's Big Words,* p. 72.

New Yorker, November 26, 1990, Faith McNulty, review of *American Women,* p. 144.

New York Times Book Review, May 17, 1987, Lee Smith, review of *Trouble at the Mines,* p. 33; April 10, 1988, Elisabeth Griffith, review of *The Boston Coffee Party,* p. 39; January 13, 1991, Elizabeth Gleick, review of *American Women,* p. 21; November 18, 2001, James McMullan, review of *Martin's Big Words,* p. 47.

Publishers Weekly, April 10, 1987, review of *Trouble at the Mines,* p. 96; March 22, 1991, review of *Escape from Slavery: Five Journeys to Freedom,* p. 81; August 30, 1991, review of *The Journey of Meng,* pp. 82-83; October 11, 1991, review of *Living Dangerously,* p. 64; February 27, 1995, review of *The Long-Haired Girl,* p. 103; June 12, 1995, review of *The New King,* pp. 60-61; March 27, 2000, review of *Dirt on Their Skirts,* p. 79; October 8, 2001, review of *Martin's Big Words,* p. 64; December 17, 2001, review of *No More!,* p. 91.

Reading Teacher, November, 2002, review of *Martin's Big Words,* p. 259.

Reading Today, February-March, 2002, Lynne T. Burke, review of *Martin's Big Words,* p. 32.

School Library Journal, April, 1987, Mary Beth Burgoyne, review of *Trouble at the Mines,* p. 102; May, 1988, Sylvia S. Marantz, review of *The Boston Coffee Party,* p. 87; February, 1991, Ruth K. MacDonald, review of *American Women,* p. 100; May, 1991, Elizabeth M. Reardon, review of *Escape from Slavery,* pp. 105-106; December, 1991, April L. Judge, review of *Living Dangerously,* p. 127, and John Philbrook, review of *The Journey of Meng,* pp. 126-127; January, 1993, Sylvia V. Meisner, review of *The Lizzie Borden Trial,* p. 120; March, 1993, Beth Tegart, review of *The Sacco-Vanzetti Trial,* p. 216; January, 1994, Doris A. Fong, review of *Tinker vs. Des Moines,* p. 128; February, 1994, Todd Morning, review of *The Alger Hiss Trial,* p. 128; March, 1995, Margaret A. Chang, review of *The Long-Haired Girl,* pp. 199-200; July, 1995, Donna L. Scanlon, review of *The New King,* p. 74; July, 1997, Lisa Mitten, review of *The Flight of the Red Bird,* p. 111; March, 2000, Luann Toth, review of *Dirt on Their Skirts,* p. 212; October, 2000, Cynde Marcengill, review of *Freedom River,* p. 152; October, 2001, Catherine Threadgill, review of *Martin's Big Words,* p. 146; February, 2002, Ginny Gustin, review of *No More!,* p. 150; September, 2002, Anne Chapman Callaghan, review of *We Are the Many,* p. 217; June, 2003, Jean Gaffney, review of *Victory or Death!,* p. 168; February, 2004, Tracy Bell, review of *Free at Last!,* p. 168.

ONLINE

BookPage, http://www.bookpage.com/ (February, 2004), Heidi Henneman, interview with Rappaport.

Doreen Rappaport Web Site, http://www.doreen rappaport.com/ (January 14, 2002).*

* * *

RAYNER, Hugh
(Shoo Rayner)

PERSONAL: Born in Kingston upon Thames, England; son of a British Army officer; married; children: two. *Education:* Attended Cambridge Art School.

ADDRESSES: Home—Forest of Dean, Gloucestershire, England. *Agent*—c/o Author Mail, Hodder and Stoughton, 338 Euston Rd., London NW1 3BH, England. *E-mail*—fromwebsite@shoo-rayner.co.uk.

CAREER: Author and illustrator; previous jobs include painting signs and silk screening, and working as a mapmaker for the Land Registry, Peterborough, England.

WRITINGS:

SELF-ILLUSTRATED PICTURE BOOKS; AS SHOO RAYNER

Lamb Drover Jim: The Champion Sheepdog, Bedrick/Blackie (New York, NY), 1988.

Victoria: The Wednesday Market Bus, Bedrick/Blackie (New York, NY), 1988.

Gruesome Games, Blackie (London, England), 1988.

The Hardacres of Hardacre Farm, Blackie (London, England), 1989.

Harvest at Hardacre Farm, Blackie (London, England), 1989.

Santa's Diary, Puffin (London, England), 1990.

Games from the Twenty-First Century, Blackie (London, England), 1990.

Noah's ABC, Viking (London, England), 1992.

Cat in a Flap, Blackie (London, England), 1992.

Hey Diddle Diddle and Other Mother Goose Rhymes (sequel to *Cat in a Flap*), Dutton (London, England), 1995.

Super Dad the Super Hero, Macdonald Young Books (Hove, England), 1999.

Super Dad, Macdonald Young Books (Hove, England), 1999.

Rock-a-Doodle-Do! ("Orchard Crunchies" series), Orchard (London, England), 2000.

Treacle, Treacle, Little Tart ("Orchard Crunchies" series), Orchard (London, England), 2001.

Craig M'Nure, Barrington Stoke (Edinburgh, Scotland), 2002.

Cash Crazy! ("Millie and Bombassa" series), Scholastic (London, England), 2002.

Dizzy DIY! ("Millie and Bombassa" series), Scholastic (London, England), 2002.

SELF-ILLUSTRATED JOKE BOOKS; AS SHOO RAYNER

The Christmas Stocking Joke Book, Puffin (London, England), 1989.

My First Picture Joke Book, Viking (New York, NY), 1989.

Ready Teddy Go!, Puffin (London, England), 1991.

The Fairy-Tale Joke Book, Puffin (London, England), 1992.

The Midnight Feast Joke Book, Puffin (London, England), 1993.

The Little Book of New Year's Resolutions, Puffin (London, England), 1993.

Shaggy Ghost Stories, Hodder and Stoughton (London, England), 1997.

The Little Book of Millennium Resolutions, Puffin (London, England), 1999.

The Pirate's Secret Joke Book, Puffin (London, England), 1999.

"LYDIA" SERIES; SELF-ILLUSTRATED; AS SHOO RAYNER

Lydia and Her Cat, Oxford University Press (Oxford, England), 1988.

Lydia at Home, Oxford University Press (Oxford, England), 1988.

Lydia Out and About, Oxford University Press (Oxford, England), 1988.

Lydia and Her Garden, Oxford University Press (Oxford, England), 1994.

Lydia at the Shops, Oxford University Press (Oxford, England), 1994.

Lydia and the Present, Oxford University Press (Oxford, England), 1994.

Lydia and the Letters, Oxford University Press (Oxford, England), 1994.

Lydia and the Ducks, Oxford University Press (Oxford, England), 1994.

"VICTOR" SERIES; SELF-ILLUSTRATED; AS SHOO RAYNER

Victor and the Sail-Kart, Oxford University Press (Oxford, England), 1989.

Victor and the Kite, Oxford University Press (Oxford, England), 1989.

Victor the Hero, Oxford University Press (Oxford, England), 1989.

Victor and the Martian, Oxford University Press (Oxford, England), 1989.

Victor and the Computer Cat, Oxford University Press (Oxford, England), 1989.

Victor the Champion, Oxford University Press (Oxford, England), 1989.

"CYRIL'S CAT" SERIES; SELF-ILLUSTRATED; AS SHOO RAYNER

Cyril's Cat, Puffin (London, England), 1993.

Charlie's Night Out, Puffin (London, England), 1993.

Cyril's Cat and the Big Surprise, Puffin (London, England), 1993.

Mouse Practice, Puffin (London, England), 1996.

"JETS" SERIES; SELF-ILLUSTRATED; AS SHOO RAYNER

Grandad's Concrete Garden, A & C Black (London, England), 1994.

We Won the Lottery, A & C Black (London, England), 1996.

Aunt Jinksie's Miracle Seeds, A & C Black (London, England), 1996.

Boys Are Us, A & C Black (London, England), 1998.

"GINGER NINJA" SERIES; SELF-ILLUSTRATED; AS SHOO RAYNER

The Ginger Ninja, Hodder and Stoughton (London, England), 1995.

Return of Tiddles, Hodder and Stoughton (London, England), 1995.

Tiddle Strikes Back, Hodder and Stoughton (London, England), 1995.

Dance of the Apple Dumplings, Hodder and Stoughton (London, England), 1996.

St. Felix for the Cup!, Hodder and Stoughton (London, England), 1996.

World Cup Winners, Hodder and Stoughton (London, England), 1997.

Three's a Crowd, Hodder and Stoughton (London, England), 1997.

"REX FILES" SERIES; SELF-ILLUSTRATED; AS SHOO RAYNER

The Life-Snatcher, Hodder and Stoughton (London, England), 1999.

The Phantom Bantam, Hodder and Stoughton (London, England), 1999.

The Bermuda Triangle, Hodder and Stoughton (London, England), 1999.

The Shredder, Hodder and Stoughton (London, England), 1999.

The Frightened Forest, Hodder and Stoughton (London, England), 1999.

The Baa-Baa Club, Hodder and Stoughton (London, England), 1999.

"ORCHARD CRUNCHIES: LITTLE HORRORS" SERIES; SELF-ILLUSTRATED; AS SHOO RAYNER

The Pumpkin Man, Orchard (London, England), 2001.

The Swamp Man, Orchard (London, England), 2001.

The Spider Man, Orchard (London, England), 2002.

The Sand Man, Orchard (London, England), 2002.

The Shadow Man, Orchard (London, England), 2003.

The Snow Man, Orchard (London, England), 2003.

The Bone Man, Orchard (London, England), 2003.

"DARK CLAW" SERIES; SELF-ILLUSTRATED; AS SHOO RAYNER

Tunnel Mazers, Hodder and Stoughton (London, England), 2002.

Road Rage, Hodder and Stoughton (London, England), 2002.

Rat Trap, Hodder and Stoughton (London, England), 2002.

Breakout!, Hodder and Stoughton (London, England), 2002.

The Guiding Paw, Hodder and Stoughton (London, England), 2002.

The Black Hole, Hodder and Stoughton (London, England), 2002.

ILLUSTRATOR; AS SHOO RAYNER

Terry Deary, *The Ghosts of Batwing Castle,* A & C Black (London, England), 1988.

Sheila Greenwald, *All the Way to Wits' End,* Puffin (London, England), 1988.

Helen Cresswell, *Whatever Happened in Winklesea?,* Lutterworth (Cambridge, England), 1989.

Sonia Devons, *Shut the Gate!,* Bedrick/Blackie (New York, NY), 1991.

Eric Emmet, *The Christmas Stocking Book of Brainteasers,* Puffin (London, England), 1994.

Michael Rosen, editor, *Pilly Soems,* A & C Black (London, England), 1994.

Michael Rosen, *You Wait Till I'm Older Than You!,* Viking (London, England), 1996.

ILLUSTRATOR; WRITTEN BY MICHAEL MORPURGO; AS SHOO RAYNER

Mossop's Last Chance (see also below), A & C Black (London, England), 1988.

Albertine, Goose Queen (see also below), A & C Black (London, England), 1989.

Jigger's Day Off (see also below), A & C Black (London, England), 1990.

And Pigs Might Fly!, A & C Black (London, England), 1992.

Martians at Mudpuddle Farm, A & C Black (London, England), 1992.

Stories from Mudpuddle Farm (contains *Mossop's Last Chance; Albertine, Goose Queen;* and *Jigger's Day Off*), A & C Black (London, England), 1994.

Mum's the Word, A & Black (London, England), 1995.

ILLUSTRATOR; "ANIMAL CRACKERS" SERIES; WRITTEN BY ROSE IMPEY; AS SHOO RAYNER

Too Many Babies: The Largest Litter in the World, Orchard (London, England), 1993.

Tiny Tim: The Longest Jumping Frog in the World, Orchard (London, England), 1993.

A Birthday for Bluebell: The Oldest Cow in the World, Orchard (London, England), 1993.

Hot Dog Harris: The Smallest Dog in the World, Orchard (London, England), 1993.

Precious Potter: The Heaviest Cat in the World, Orchard (London, England), 1994.

Phew, Sidney!: The Sweetest-Smelling Skunk in the World, Orchard (London, England), 1994.

A Fortune for Yo-Yo: The Richest Dog in the World, Orchard (London, England), 1994.

Sleepy Sammy: The Sleepiest Sloth in the World, Orchard (London, England), 1994.

Rhode Island Roy: The Roughest Rooster in the World, Orchard (London, England), 1995.

Welcome Home, Barney: The Loneliest Bat in the World, Orchard (London, England), 1995.

Pipe Down, Prudie!, Orchard (London, England), 1995.

We Want William: The Wisest Worm in the World, Orchard (London, England), 1995.

Long Live Roberto: The Most Royal Rabbit in the World, Orchard (London, England), 1997.

A Medal for Poppy: The Pluckiest Pig in the World, Orchard (London, England), 1998.

Stella's Staying Put: The Most Stubborn Swan in the World, Orchard (London, England), 1999.

The Animal Crackers Joke Book, Orchard (London, England), 2001.

Open Wide, Wilbur: The Most Welcoming Whale in the World, Orchard (London, England), 2003.

OTHER

Also author of *The Bear That Wouldn't Growl, The Elephant That Forgot, The Snake That Couldn't Hiss,* and *The Shark with No Teeth,* available as a pack of four from Heinemann (Oxford, England). Contributor of stories to anthologies, including "Victoria at the County Show" in *The Martian and the Supermarket;* and "The Trifle Tower" in *Stories for Six-Year-Olds* (book and tape set). Works have been translated into Welsh and Gaelic.

SIDELIGHTS: Prolific British author and illustrator Hugh Rayner, who writes under the first name of Shoo, has had a hand in several popular series for early readers. He is the illustrator for Rose Impey's long-running "Animal Crackers" books, and as both author and illustrator, he created the "Dark Claw," "Rex Files," and "Ginger Ninja" series. These series have very different themes—the "Dark Claw" books are a spoof of *Star Wars* and other such science-fiction stories, starring cats and rodents; the "Rex Files" (a take-off on the television series *The X-Files*) feature a duo of canine sleuths named Rex and Franky who investigate various terrifying paranormal happenings; and the "Ginger Ninja" books are about a pawball-mad kitten named Ginger who faces typical elementary-school problems such as bullies. Rayner has said that *The Ginger Ninja* is his favorite book, both because the Ginger Ninja is the character most like him (Rayner himself had bright red hair as a child) and "because that was the book where I looked deepest into the darkesty regions of my character and managed to come up almost sane at the end," he said in an interview with *Word Pool*.

Despite their different subject matter, all of Rayner's books were designed to be both easy to comprehend and entertaining for children who are just learning to read on their own. They feature short sentences, short chapters, and almost comic-book-like illustrations. Explaining what he finds most rewarding about his work, Rayner said in the *Word Pool* interview, "My readers are at the most important stage of reading development, where they can be put off or enthused for life." While he admits that the early-reader genre is often overlooked by critics, "children find it for themselves and read my books by the bucket load. That's my reward."

BIOGRAPHICAL AND CRITICAL SOURCES:

PERIODICALS

Guardian (Manchester, England), September 10, 2002, review of *The Dark Claw Saga*, p. 65; February 25, 2003, Lindsey Fraser, review of *A Medal for Poppy: The Pluckiest Pig in the World*, p. 61.
Herald (Glasgow, Scotland), March 3, 2001, Michael Thorn, review of *Shoo Rayner Web site*, p. 19.
School Library Journal, March, 1991, JoAnn Rees, review of *Shut the Gate!*, p. 170, and Jeanne Mary Clancy, review of *My First Picture Joke Book*, pp. 189-190.

ONLINE

Buckinghamshire County Council, http://www.buckscc. gov.uk/ (January 14, 2004), "Author of the Month: December: Shoo Rayner."

Penguin Putnam Web site, http://www.penguinputnam. com/ (April 13, 2004), "Shoo Rayner."
Shoo Rayner Web site, http://www.shoo-rayner.co.uk/ (March 31, 2004).
Word Pool, http://www.wordpool.co.uk/ (January 14, 2004), "Author Profile of Shoo Rayner."*

*   *   *

RAYNER, Shoo
See RAYNER, Hugh

*   *   *

REES, Frank D. 1950-

PERSONAL: Born March 1, 1950, in Yallourn, Victoria, Australia; son of Charles (a plant attendant) and Muriel (a homemaker; maiden name, Maguire) Rees; married August 17, 1974; wife's name, Merilyn (an anesthetist); children: Lachlan, Nick, Felicity. *Education:* University of Melbourne, B.A. (with honors), 1971, M.A., 1973; Melbourne College of Divinity, B.D. (with honors), 1975, M.Theol., 1980; University of Manchester, Ph.D., 1983.

ADDRESSES: Office—Whitley College, University of Melbourne, 50 the Avenue, Parkville, Victoria 3052, Australia. *E-mail*—frees@whitley.unimelb.edu.au.

CAREER: Baptist minister in Melbourne, Victoria, Australia, 1973-80, and Hobart, Tasmania, Australia, 1983-90; University of Melbourne, Whitley College, Parkville, Victoria, Australia, professor of theology, 1991—.

WRITINGS:

(Editor) *Fair Dinkum Ministry: Stories of Authentic Australian Spirituality and Struggle*, Spectrum Publications (Richmond, Victoria, Australia), 1999.
Wrestling with Doubt: Theological Reflections on the Journey of Faith, Liturgical Press (Collegeville, MN), 2002.

Contributor to books, including *Gentle Darkness*, edited by Rowland Croucher, Albatross (Sutherland, New South Wales, Australia), 1994; and *Prophecy and*

Passion: Essays in Honour of Athol Gill, edited by David Neville, Australian Theological Forum (Adelaide, Australia), 2002. Contributor to periodicals, including *Pacifica, Evangelical Quarterly,* and *Colloquium.*

WORK IN PROGRESS: A Conversational Church (tentative title).

SIDELIGHTS: Frank D. Rees told *CA:* "I am presently engaged in teaching theology with several hundred people who find the institutional forms of religion and church a turn-off. My theological writing draws upon the people-based insights of the 'free church' traditions—which those groups have almost completely lost! I also draw upon my own experiences as a pastor and as a frustrated person of little faith but much hope. Like most academics, writing is something that is squeezed into the very little time available, but it is a passion that keeps working on me, even when I am unable to work on it!

"I am motivated by a passion for people-based and 'conversational' community. This is the topic of my next book, based on the radical theology of the book *Wrestling with Doubt: Theological Reflections on the Journey of Faith.* I am also strongly committed to what is called 'contextual theology.' As an academic I have supervised many students from third-world and liberationist perspectives in their quests for local or contextual theologies to relate to their peoples. My own work is part of the quest for an Australia contextual theology.

"I write within and for a community setting: the quest of many people to find a more meaningful expression of faith. My theological work is part of that quest, in my own life and my pastoral involvement with such dissident or searching people. I am especially convinced that story theology and the metaphor of conversation are the most valuable images and models for the contemporary context. I am also quite passionate about the contribution of Australian writers to the wider world community, if only we could get a voice (*so* hard to get published!) and if only we believed in that voice, without needing to mimic other cultures—especially the juggernaut of American culture, everywhere."

BIOGRAPHICAL AND CRITICAL SOURCES:

PERIODICALS

Theological Studies, September, 2002, Joseph S. Pagano, review of *Wrestling with Doubt: Theological Reflections on the Journey of Faith,* p. 648.

*   *   *

REID, Cindy 1964(?)-

PERSONAL: Born c. 1964. *Education:* Arizona State University, B.A., 1985.

ADDRESSES: Office—Director of Instruction, TPC at Sawgrass, 110 TPC Blvd., Ponte Vedra Beach, FL 32082. *E-mail*—cindy@cindyreidgolf.com.

CAREER: Professional golfer and golf instructor. Tournament Players Club at Sawgrass, Ponte Vedra Beach, FL, director of instruction.

MEMBER: Class A member of the PGA of America; Class A member LPGA teaching division.

AWARDS, HONORS: Top Fifty U.S. Women Instructors, *Golf for Women,* 2003; nominated three times as Top One Hundred Teachers by *Golf Magazine.*

WRITINGS:

Cindy Reid's Ultimate Guide to Golf for Women, Atria Books (New York, NY), 2003.

Contributor to periodicals, including *Golf for Women* and *PGA Tour Partners.*

SIDELIGHTS: Cindy Reid did not enter the world of professional golf until she was in her twenties. Since then she has become a leading member of the golf community, teaching professional althetes and celebrities. *Cindy Reid's Ultimate Guide to Golf for Women* is a comprehensive guide which covers all of the basics for women. Kathy Ruffle, a reviewer for

Library Journal, commented that Reid's "tips on buying clubs, how to practice, and drills to improve practice are practical and sensible."

BIOGRAPHICAL AND CRITICAL SOURCES:

PERIODICALS

Library Journal, May 1, 2003, Kathy Ruffle, review of *Cindy Reid's Ultimate Guide to Golf for Women,* pp. 124-125.

ONLINE

Cindy Reid Golf, http://www.cindyreid.com (March 15, 2004).*

* * *

REID, Elwood

PERSONAL: Born in Cleveland, OH; children: one daughter. *Education:* Attended the University of Michigan.

ADDRESSES: Agent—c/o Author Mail, Random House, Inc., 1745 Broadway, New York, NY 10019; c/o Midnight Mind Magazine, P.O. Box 146912, Chicago, IL 60614.

CAREER: Novelist, short story writer, and screenwriter. Has worked as a carpenter.

WRITINGS:

If I Don't Six (novel), Doubleday (New York, NY), 1998.
What Salmon Know (short stories), Doubleday (New York, NY), 1999.
Midnight Sun (novel), Doubleday (New York, NY), 2000.
The Pennsylvania Miners' Story, (television movie screenplay), American Broadcasting Companies, Inc. (ABC), 2000.
DB (novel), Doubleday (New York, NY), 2004.

Contributor of short stories to periodicals, including *GQ.*

WORK IN PROGRESS: A screenplay for *If I Don't Six.*

SIDELIGHTS: Author Elwood Reid grew up in a working-class area of Cleveland, Ohio, where he developed a taste for literature and skills at football. "His only hope of escape was a football scholarship to the University of Michigan," wrote Ronald Sklar on the *Pop Entertainment* Web site. "But here's the catch: Reid loved books and writing more than the game," Sklar remarked. "In fact, while on the field, he longed for the moment when he could go back to his dorm room, crawl into bed and get back to reading a book." Unusual behavior for a football player, perhaps, but Reid persisted, eventually selling his short story "What Salmon Know" to *GQ,* directly out of the slush pile. While that story would serve as the centerpiece of a later collection, Reid also parlayed his gridiron experience and his love of the written word into his first novel, *If I Don't Six.*

In the book, Elwood Riley arrives on the University of Michigan campus, a recipient of a football scholarship that will allow him to attend the expensive school and escape the factory-work drudgery that claimed his father. The world of the collegiate football player, however, has its own dark side. Riley finds he is no longer an individual, but part of a system larger than himself, designed only to win. He endures vicious, screaming coaches urging him and his teammates to greater acts of violence; he suffers through the pain of injury and physical overwork; he learns to interact with teammates he does not like, to accept grades that he did not really earn, and to bed women who are little more than groupies. The players live in perpetual fear that they will "six," which means becoming ineligible to play because of a failed class or an injury. Sixing would be a disaster for Riley because he would lose his scholarship and the chance at a genuine education. As his distaste for the world of college football grows, so does his desire to enrich himself through academics rather than athletics.

The book is partly a coming-of-age novel and partly an autobiography. Riley serves as a stand-in for Reid himself, who also played football at Michigan until he was sidelined by a neck injury. Reid offers "a harrowing (if sometimes exhaustingly detailed) description of the politics and logistics of daylong football practices and parties at which fights and rapes are commonplace," noted a *Publishers Weekly* reviewer. The author "has a sure hand for immersing the reader in the workings of the football machine, where young men are treated like animals to be trained to perform feats of gridiron glory for the huddled and howling fans and alumni," observed Ira Berkow in the *New York Times Book Review.*

Reid's short story collection, *What Salmon Know,* explores the "depressing, destructive, and self-destructive sides of American masculinity" in ten bleak, sometimes violent stories, commented a reviewer in *Publishers Weekly.* In "Overtime" a factory foreman deals with the consequences of forcing a worker to stay late when the worker's daughter is kidnapped and murdered; consequently, the foreman slides ever deeper into despair and ruin. In "No Strings Attached" a rough-and-tumble man's man falls in love with a quiet, gentle woman who is his opposite, and learns to deal with her tragic, complicated emotional background. The title story finds two drunken salmon poachers in a vicious fight with two soldiers over a mutilated fish, but neither side has a moral advantage. "While Reid's prose is always crisp and clear, his images striking and memorable, it can be hard to feel for his characters; many come across simply as obnoxious drunks," the *Publishers Weekly* critic remarked. "Hard-edged and violent, these are characters struggling to survive in difficult economic and social situations," commented Lawrence Rungren in *Library Journal.*

Reid's next novel, *Midnight Sun,* takes place in the remote, dangerous Alaskan wilderness, where charismatic leader Nunn has established a small, cult-like camp for the disillusioned, washed out, and disgusted. Jack and Burke, two rugged construction workers, agree to retrieve a friend's daughter from the shadowy Nunn's equally mysterious encampment. But the wilderness is unforgiving, and along the way they discover how dangerous the river they travel and the untamed areas they cross can be. Equally dangerous but with deliberate motives, a gold hunter attacks the pair before they arrive at Nunn's compound and is killed by Burke. Nunn and his acolytes prove to be a tough target, too. Seemingly peaceful, the camp does not look like a place of evil, and when Jack and Burke arrive, they are told the woman does not want to leave. Burke is attacked and beaten so badly he cannot continue his mission with Jack. Then Jack begins to unravel the unsavory secrets behind the camp and the physically and mentally scarred Nunn.

The novel is "a more or less explicit homage" to Joseph Conrad's *Heart of Darkness,* noted Jonathan Miles in the *New York Times Book Review.* "In taut, well-sculpted prose, Reid expertly evokes end-of-the-road Fairbanks, his characters' physical and spiritual rootlessness, and the magnificent, dangerous country they travel through," commented a *Publishers Weekly* reviewer.

BIOGRAPHICAL AND CRITICAL SOURCES:

PERIODICALS

Booklist, September 1, 2000, Ted Leventhal, review of *Midnight Sun,* p. 67.
Hollywood Reporter, November 22, 2002, Barry Garron, review of *The Pennsylvania Miners' Story,* p. 41.
Library Journal, June 1, 1998, Marylaine Block, review of *If I Don't Six,* p. 158; July, 1999, Lawrence Rungren, review of *What Salmon Know,* p. 139; May 15, 2000, Dan Bogey, review of *What Salmon Know,* p. 152; August, 2000, Lawrence Rungren, review of *Midnight Sun,* p. 161.
New York Times Book Review, August 2, 1998, Ira Berkow, "Tackling Dummies," p. 19; October 15, 2000, Jonathan Miles, review of *Midnight Sun,* p. 23.
Publishers Weekly, June 29, 1998, review of *If I Don't Six,* p. 35; July 12, 1999, review of *What Salmon Know,* p. 72; August 7, 2000, review of *Midnight Sun,* p. 71.

ONLINE

Anchorage Press, http://www.anchoragepress.com/ (September 27, 2001), Alyson Williams, "Off the Shelf."
Michigan Daily, http://www.pub.umich.edu/daily/ (October 6, 1998), Corinne Schneider, "Former 'U' Football Player Relates Story."
Midnight Mind, http://www.midnightmind.com/ (April 2, 2004), profile of Elwood Reid.
Pop Entertainment, http://www.popentertainment.com/ (April 2, 2004), Ronald Sklar, "Elwood Reid."
Random House, http://www.randomhouse.com/ (April 2, 2004), profile of Elwood Reid.*

*   *   *

REIDEL, James

PERSONAL: Born in Cincinnati, OH. *Education:* Columbia University, M.F.A; Rutgers University, M.A.

ADDRESSES: Home—3195 North Farmcrest Dr., Cincinnati, OH 45213-1111. *E-mail*—jreidel@cinci.rr. com.

CAREER: Poet, editor, translator, biographer, and independent scholar. Has worked variously in a nursery and as a truck driver

WRITINGS:

(Selector) Weldon Kees, *Limericks to Friends,* Jordan Davies (Brooklyn, NY), 1985.
(Editor) Weldon Kees, *Reviews and Essays, 1936-55,* University of Michigan Press (Ann Arbor, MI), 1988.
(Editor) Weldon Kees, *Fall Quarter,* Story Line Press (Ashland, OR), 1990.
Vanished Act: The Life and Art of Weldon Kees, University of Nebraska Press (Lincoln, NE), 2003.

Translator of verse by German writers Ingeborg Bachmann, Thomas Bernhard, and Franz Werfel. Contributor to periodicals, including *New Yorker, Conjunctions, Paris Review, Ploughshares, TriQuarterly, Ironwood, Verse,* and *New Criterion.*

SIDELIGHTS: Cincinnati native James Reidel is a poet, translator, independent scholar, and the editor of several books by poet Weldon Kees, among them *Fall Quarter* and *Limericks to Friends.* In addition, he shares his knowledge of Kees' short life in the biography *Vanished Act: The Life and Art of Weldon Kees.*

Written in 1941, *Fall Quarter,* is the only surviving novel by Kees, who mysteriously disappeared at age forty-one in 1955. Rejected for publication because its subject matter was considered inappropriate during World War II, *Fall Quarter* introduces twenty-five-year-old William Clay, a recent graduate who accepts a post teaching English at a Midwestern college. Clay's naiveté quickly becomes apparent as his unrealistic dreams are soon shattered in Kees screwball commentary. The plot focuses on Clay's attempts to bed and wed the woman of his desires while his efforts are interrupted by the often-eccentric characters he encounters on campus. Glenn O. Carey, writing in the *Library Journal,* commented that while "Kees

seemingly was successful in his other occupations," *Fall Quarterly* is a "hybrid novel" that is "deficient as either humor or satire, with Clay's preposterous innocence further weakening the story." Also less than enthusiastic about Kee's fiction, Beatrice Tauss called the novel "merciless" and "labored," and added in her *New York Times Book Review* appraisal that *Fall Quarter* "surrealistically evokes the nightmare of disappointed lives. It could have been written yesterday, alas."

Reidel's own work has been much more enthusiastically received by critics. In *Vanished Act: The Life and Art of Weldon Kees,* Reidel chronicles the poet's life and studies Kees's many artistic endeavors. Kees has been characterized by some scholars as the "nearly" man of the twentieth-century, due to his dabbling in everything from expressionist painting, filmmaking, and traditional jazz to writing. While Kees was accomplished in many areas—his works appeared in many of the best literary journals of the twentieth-century—he never attained the same level of recognition as peers such as Robert Lowell and Elizabeth Bishop. While his primary aspiration was to become a successful writer, bad luck seemed to play a part in keeping Kees in the background: *Fall Quarter,* for instance, was submitted for publication the day after Pearl Harbor, a clear case of bad timing. In recent years, Kees has attainted minor cult status, helped by "enthusiastic champions like his biographer [who] have determined to alter that river's course," according to a *Kirkus Reviews* contributor. Michael Hofmann, writing in the *New York Times Book Review,* stated that "Until I read the poet James Reidel's biography *Vanished Act,* I had not realized how 'nearly' Kees was, and how far he came, in so many fields of artistic endeavor." In closing, Hofmann praised Reidel's biography a "really good, well-written and thoughtful" appraisal of an underappreciated author.

Writing in *Ploughshares,* Reidel stated "I have this thing about apprenticeship and performing my service to the muse. So I have conducted my career from a monklike angle, perhaps more than is necessary." "But these are benighted times," the author/editor added, "and I may have left the discovery of my work to others as others have left theirs to me."

BIOGRAPHICAL AND CRITICAL SOURCES:

PERIODICALS

Kirkus Reviews, April 15, 2003, review of *Vanished Act: The Life and Art of Weldon Kees,* p. 593.

Library Journal, September 15, 1990, Glenn O. Carey, review of *Fall Quarter,* p. 102.

New York Times Book Review, November 25, 1990, Beatrice Tauss, review of *Fall Quarter,* p. 18; August 17, 2003, Michael Hofmann, review of *Vanished Act,* p. 12.

ONLINE

Adirondack Review Online, http://www.adirondackreview.homestead.com/ (October 10, 2003), interview with Reidel.

Ploughshares, http://www.pshares.org/ (July 4, 2003), "James Reidel."*

*   *   *

REINER, Thomas 1959-

PERSONAL: Born August 12, 1959, in Bad Homburg, West Germany (now Germany); son of Oskar and Ursula (Fleischer) Reiner; married August 13, 1999; wife's name, Lindsey; children: Celeste. *Education:* La Trobe University, B.A., 1983; studied musical composition at Kölner Hochschule für Musik, 1984-86; University of Melbourne, M.Mus., 1989, Ph.D., 1996.

ADDRESSES: Office—School of Music, Monash University, Clayton, Victoria 3800, Australia. *E-mail*—thomas.reiner@arts.monash.edu.au.

CAREER: Monash University, Clayton, Victoria, Australia, senior lecturer and coordinator of music composition, 1993—. "Re-sound" (contemporary music ensemble), artistic director; performer with Tasmanian Symphony Orchestra at National Orchestral Composers' School, 1990.

MEMBER: Australian Music Center, German Performing Rights Association, Melbourne Composers' League.

AWARDS, HONORS: Dorian Le Gallienne Composition Award, Dorian Le Gallienne Award Trust, 1994; Albert H. Maggs Composition Award, University of Melbourne, 1996.

WRITINGS:

Semiotics of Musical Time, Peter Lang Publishing (New York, NY), 2000.

Musical compositions include "Paraphrase, Surge, and Repose" (orchestral work), "Two Movements for Orchestra," 1990, "Bali Suite" (chamber work), "Three Sketches" (for cello), "Septet" (chamber work), "Oblique" (flute solo), "Contemplation" (guitar piece), and "mechanics in time" (chamber work); some compositions have been included in recorded albums by other performers, including *Hard Chamber,* released by Move Records, 2003. Contributor to books, including *Sound Ideas,* edited by Brenton Broadstock, Australian Music Centre (Sydney, Australia), 1995. Contributor to periodicals, including *Context, Revista Muzica,* and *Pauta.*

WORK IN PROGRESS: Research on musical composition, the investigation of musical time, and popular electronic music.

*   *   *

RENNELL, Tony

PERSONAL: Male.

ADDRESSES: Home—London, England. *Agent*—c/o Author Mail, Viking, 345 Hudson St., New York, NY 10014.

CAREER: Freelance journalist and writer. Former associate editor of the *Sunday Times* and *Mail on Sunday.*

WRITINGS:

When Daddy Came Home: How Family Life Changed, Pimlico (London, England), 1996.

Last Days of Glory: The Death of Queen Victoria, Viking (New York, NY), 2000.

(With John Nichol) *The Last Escape: The Untold Story of Allied Prisoners of War in Europe, 1944-1945,* Viking (New York, NY), 2003.

SIDELIGHTS: Tony Rennell writes historical nonfiction, touching on subjects such as World War II and the death of Queen Victoria. In the *Last Days of Glory: The Death of Queen Victoria,* Rennell explores the last days in the life of Queen Victoria, the funeral following, and the reaction of the British people to her death. A reviewer for *Publishers Weekly* noted, "While the last days of a monarch's life may seem a slight subject for a book, this is ultimately a lively and detailed slice of social history, which captures the mood and mindset of turn-of-the-century England." Rennell sets out to capture how the Queen's death marked the end of an era. A reviewer for *Kirkus Reviews* called the book, "An admirable success at generating the sense of impending change that surrounded the death of Queen Victoria."

Rennell paired up with Gulf War POW John Nichol to write *The Last Escape: The Untold Story of Allied Prisoner's of War in Europe, 1944-1945.* The book is composed from historical accounts and interviews with surviving veterans and POWs of World War II. In *Contemporary Review,* James Munson stated that "it was a story that needed to be told . . . this book not only tells these men's stories but gives readers an insight into the fear and horror that POWs faced." By 1944 there were hundreds of thousands of American and British prisoners of war held by the Germans. During the final months these men were forced to march deeper into Germany—the POWs refer to it as "the death march." A reviewer for *Kirkus Reviews* called *The Last Escape,* "A fine tale of great and not-so-great escapes, along with the ordinary business of surviving confinement in Hitler's stalags in the final months of WWII."

BIOGRAPHICAL AND CRITICAL SOURCES:

PERIODICALS

Contemporary Review, May, 2003, James Munson, review of *The Last Escape: The Untold Story of Allied Prisoners of War in Europe, 1944-1945,* p. 310.
History Today, November, 2001, Anne Pointer, review of *Last Days of Glory: The Death of Queen Victoria.*
Kirkus Reviews, July 15, 2001, review of *The Last Days of Glory,* p. 1009; May 1, 2003, review of *The Last Escape,* p. 663.

Library Journal, August, 2001, Isabel Coates, review of *Last Days of Glory,* p. 132; May 15, 2003, Edwin B. Burgess, review of *The Last Escape,* p. 103.
Publishers Weekly, June 16, 2001, review of *Last Days of Glory,* p. 173; June 16, 2003, review of *The Last Escape,* pp. 124-125.

ONLINE

Post-Gazette.com, http://www.post-gazette.com/books/reviews/ (November 4, 20003), Gerard A. Patterson, review of *The Last Escape.**

*   *   *

REYNOLDS, Bessie
    See AITKEN, Rosemary

*   *   *

RICHARDSON, Paul 1963-

PERSONAL: Born 1963.

ADDRESSES: Agent—c/o Author Mail, Little, Brown and Company, Brettenham House, Lancaster Place, London WC2E 7EN, England.

CAREER: Food and travel writer.

WRITINGS:

Not Part of the Package: A Year in Ibiza, Macmillan (London, England), 1993.
Our Lady of the Sewers: And Other Adventures in Deep Spain, Abacus (London, England), 1999.
Cornucopia: A Gastronomic Tour of Britain, Little, Brown (London, England), 2000.
Indulgence: Around the World in Search of Chocolate, Little, Brown (London, England), 2003.

Contributor to periodicals, including *Harper's Bazaar* and *Attitude.*

SIDELIGHTS: Paul Richardson's first book, *Not Part of the Package: A Year in Ibiza,* is a guided tour of the tiny island off the coast of Spain that was compared by *Times Literary Supplement*'s Robert Carver to Marin County, California: "all Tarot readings and ageing hippies." Richardson writes of the drug culture, the gay beaches, and the discos, and food is a central theme. Carver felt that in spite of the tourism, "there is still a magic to the island which has clearly touched Richardson." Carver described the book as "likeable, well-written and good-humoured."

In reviewing *Our Lady of the Sewers: And Other Adventures in Deep Spain,* Carver said that Richardson writes in the vein of "the posh British gay male who chooses to live madly, truly, deeply, even flamboyantly, by the Med[iterranean]." Richardson describes his Spanish explorations in the Moorish section of Granada, his meeting of modern Spanish Muslims in the Alpujarra mountains, and his taking part in sheepherding and in a pig killing, and provides a tongue-in-cheek account of a sighting of the Virgin Mary. He includes some short stories of a sexual nature and describes the renovation of a home shared by him and his lover. Carver noted that Richardson's writing becomes more tender when he writes about this last topic, suggesting that Richardson "can be puckish, witty, casually erudite, and when he wants to, delivers acute and sharply observed portraits of both people and places."

A London *Observer* contributor called Richardson's *Cornucopia: A Gastronomic Tour of Britain* "Sunday-supplement food writing made flesh: hedonistic, leisurely fodder for foodies." Richardson writes of hearty food, from leg of lamb to wild mushrooms and farm cheeses. Paul Levy remarked in *Times Literary Supplement* that the book is an "account of a belly-stretching solo tour of English, Irish, and Scottish producers of specialty foods, entailing endless beds-and-breakfasts and far too many grisly meals in greasy spoons of various ethnic cuisines." Levy commented on Richardson's lack of acknowledgment of previously published books similar to the author's own as well as Richardson's failure to address the specifics of "intensive farming and the diet of the underclass that he constantly moans about." Levy also commented on the fact that many low-income people in Britain cannot cook, and consequently spend more than is necessary for "added value" and convenience factors. Levy suggested that "food writers have an important job to do, to cajole the well-off to spend more money on food, and to educate and persuade the less well-off to swap their expensive microwaved food for less expensive and better food that they cook themselves."

Richardson begins *Indulgence: Around the World in Search of Chocolate* by describing a gift he received as a child from his grandmother in the late 1960s. The box of Lindt Chocolate Animals contained sculpted animals, each in its own compartment, that his grandmother urged him to eat slowly to make them last. In the book Richardson studies the history of chocolate and how cocoa was discovered in the New World by conquering Europeans, who found it unappetizing. Settlers who followed, particularly of religious orders, took to it readily, even incorporating it into their feast days, but in the seventeenth century, the Catholic Church deemed the food that had first been used by Native Americans decadent and dangerous, filled with "malignity and the ferment of revolt." This was a self-fulfilling prophecy in that a few years later, the Society of Jesus realized that rather than give up their chocolate, many of its members were leaving the order.

Chocolate soon reached Europe, where Catholics enjoyed it and where Quakers who had difficulty finding work in already established trades took up chocolate making, particularly concentrating on producing cocoa. They set up cocoa rooms, which were acceptable alternatives to pubs. "What's more," noted Kathryn Hughes in the *Times Literary Supplement,* "as if to show that God approved, chocolate turned a tidy profit for its masters." Richardson comments on the Quaker companies, including Cadbury, Fry, and Rowntree, and American chocolate producers Hershey and Mars. Hughes noted that Richardson has an easy time describing the chocolate-making process, while putting into words the smells and tastes of various types of chocolate is more difficult. "It is here that Richardson pushes up against the limits of language, trying to find a way of talking about chocolate that moves beyond simile to reach the essence of the thing." Hughes felt that a great triumph of the book is that Richardson makes readers "feel—and taste—those Lindt Chocolate Animals as if for the very first time."

BIOGRAPHICAL AND CRITICAL SOURCES:

BOOKS

Richardson, Paul, *Indulgence: Around the World in Search of Chocolate,* Little, Brown (London, England), 2003.

PERIODICALS

Observer (London, England), September 19, 1993, Jonathan Keates, review of *Not Part of the Package: A Year in Ibiza,* p. 56; February 11, 2001, review of *Cornucopia: A Gastronomic Tour of Britain,* p. 18.

Spectator, February 8, 2003, Henry Hobhouse, review of *Indulgence: Around the World in Search of Chocolate,* p. 33.

Times Literary Supplement, June 4, 1993, Robert Carver, review of *Not Part of the Package,* p. 31; April 24, 1998, Robert Carver, review of *Our Lady of the Sewers: And Other Adventures in Deep Spain,* p. 30; July 28, 2000, Paul Levy, review of *Cornucopia,* p. 8; February 14, 2003, Kathryn Hughes, review of *Indulgence,* p. 24.*

*   *   *

RIMSTEAD, Roxanne L. 1953-

PERSONAL: Born July 24, 1953, in Bracebridge, Ontario, Canada; daughter of Paul (a worker) and Rose-Marie (a homemaker; maiden name, Ranger) Rimstead; married Fernando Guerrero (a youth worker). *Education:* York University, B.A., 1975; Université de Montréal, M.A., 1988, Ph.D., 1995.

ADDRESSES: Office—Faculté des sciences humaines, Université de Sherbrooke, Sherbrooke, Quebec J1K 2R1, Canada. *E-mail*—rrimstead@sympatico.ca.

CAREER: McGill University, Montreal, Quebec, Canada, assistant professor, 1995-98; Université de Sherbrooke, Sherbrooke, Quebec, Canada, assistant professor, 1999-2002, associate professor, 2002—.

MEMBER: Association of Canadian and Quebec Literatures (president, 2002-03).

AWARDS, HONORS: Don D. Walker Award, Western Literature Association, 1992, for the article "Klee Wyck: Redefining Region through Marginal Realities"; Gabriel Roy Prize, Association of Canadian and Quebec Literatures, 2001, for *Remnants of Nation: On Poverty Narratives by Women.*

WRITINGS:

Remnants of Nation: On Poverty Narratives by Women, University of Toronto Press (Toronto, Ontario, Canada), 2001.

Contributor to books, including *What We Hold in Common: Introduction to Working-Class Studies,* edited by Janet Zandy, Feminist Press (New York, NY), 1995; and *The Language and Politics of Exclusion: Others in Discourse,* edited by Steven Riggins, Sage Publications (Thousand Oaks, CA), 1997. Contributor to periodicals, including *Race, Gender, and Class: Interdisciplinary Multicultural Journal, Women's Studies Quarterly, Michigan Feminist Studies Journal, Canadian Forum,* and *Canadian Literature.* Guest editor, *Essays on Canadian Writing,* 2003.

WORK IN PROGRESS: Remembering the Unemployed: The Making of Memories; research on the importance of cultural memory to counter-cultural identity.

SIDELIGHTS: Roxanne L. Rimstead told *CA:* "I write about disenfranchised people, poor women in particular, in order to discover the secret behind their resilience and their resistance. I write out of anger for injustices and inequality. And I write out of my past, growing up on welfare with many sisters and brothers and two disabled parents in small-town northern Ontario. The British school of cultural studies has influenced my cultural criticism, along with writers like Paulo Freire and Franz Fanon. My current research is on cultural memory, dissent, and the way we represent the social identity of domestics, prostitutes, workers, the unemployed, welfare recipients, and school dropouts."

BIOGRAPHICAL AND CRITICAL SOURCES:

PERIODICALS

Essays on Canadian Writing, fall, 2002, Sally Chivers, "Resisting Poverty," pp. 50-56.

Resources for Feminist Research, fall, 2002, Jennifer J. Nelson, review of *Remnants of Nation: On Poverty Narratives by Women,* p. 263.

ROACH, Catherine M.

PERSONAL: Born in Ottawa, Quebec, Canada; married Ted Trost; children: Nathaniel, Benjamin. *Education:* University of Ottawa, B.A., 1987, M.A., 1989; Harvard University, A.M., 1991, Ph.D., 1998.

ADDRESSES: Office—Department of Religious Studies, University of Alabama, P.O. Box 870264, Tuscaloosa, AL 35487-0264. *E-mail*—croach@nc.ua.edu.

CAREER: University of Alabama, Tuscaloosa, assistant professor of religious studies.

WRITINGS:

Mother/Nature: Popular Culture and Environmental Ethics, Indiana University Press (Bloomington, IN), 2002.

Contributor to *Just Fish: Ethics and Canadian Marine Fisheries,* ISER Books (St. John, Newfoundland, Canada), 2000, and *Encyclopedia of Religion and Nature,* Continuum (London, England), 2003.

SIDELIGHTS: Catherine M. Roach's *Mother/Nature: Popular Culture and Environmental Ethics* is an examination of the feminine portrayal of nature in the popular culture of the West. Combining religious, feminist, and environmental approaches to the subject, Roach exposes what she argues is a widespread use of problematic imagery and language that is detrimental to both the environment and to women. Carolyn M. Craft in *Library Journal* called the scholarly study a "deeply thoughtful book."

BIOGRAPHICAL AND CRITICAL SOURCES:

PERIODICALS

Library Journal, March 15, 2003, Carolyn M. Craft, review of *Mother/Nature: Popular Culture and Environmental Ethics,* p. 89.*

*   *   *

ROBEY, David

PERSONAL: Male.

ADDRESSES: Office—Dept. of Italian Studies, School of Modern Languages, University of Reading, Whiteknights, Reading RG6 6AA, England. *E-mail*—d.j.b.robey@reading.ac.uk.

CAREER: Educator, Italian scholar, writer, editor. University of Manchester, Manchester, England, professor of Italian; Wolfson College, Oxford, England, emeritus fellow; University of Reading, Reading, England, professor of Italian, head of the School of Modern Languages, director of ICT in Arts and Humanities Research Program, and member of Arts and Humanities Research Board.

WRITINGS:

(Editor) *Structuralism: An Introduction to Wolfson College Lectures, 1972,* Clarendon Press (Oxford, England), 1973.
(Editor, with Ann Jefferson) *Modern Literary Theory: A Comparative Introduction,* Barnes & Noble Books (Totowa, NJ), 1982, revised edition, 1986.
Sound and Structure in the Divine Comedy, Oxford University Press (New York, NY), 2000.
(Editor, with Peter Hainsworth) *The Oxford Companion to Italian Literature,* Oxford University Press (New York, NY), 2002.

Contributor of introduction to *The Open Work,* by Umberto Eco, Harvard University Press (Cambridge, MA), 1989.

SIDELIGHTS: David Robey's specialty is Italian literature, and he has taught in several colleges in England. Robey is editor of *Structuralism: An Introduction,* a collection of seven lectures given at Wolfson College, Oxford, in 1972. Contributors John Lyons, Edmund Leach, Jonathan Culler, Umberto Eco, John Mepham, Robin Gandy, and Tzvetan Todorov examine structuralist theory within a number of disciplines, as well as its linguistic roots, its use in social anthropology and semiology, and its relation to mathematics and philosophy. A structural analysis of American novelist Henry James's tales is provided by Todorov, which a *Times Literary Supplement* reviewer felt "is better to read than it perhaps was to listen to." Peter Caws wrote in *Comparative Literature* that "the virtue of David Robey's collection . . . is that it does not pretend to be a unified account, but calls on representatives of some of these diverse fields to interpret structuralism as it has made theoretical contributions to each."

Robey is also editor, with Ann Jefferson, of *Modern Literary Theory: A Comparative Introduction,* which in its first edition contains six chapters that focus on

Russian formalism, modern linguistics, Anglo-American New Criticism, structuralism and post structuralism, modern psychoanalytic criticism, and Marxist theories. The second edition adds chapters on reading/interpretation and feminist theory, as well as expands upon previously covered areas.

Robey's *Sound and Structure in the Divine Comedy* is a computer-based analysis of the famous philosophico-political poem by Italian poet Dante Alighieri, and was called a "fine book" by Pietro G. Beltrami in *Modern Language Review*. Robey wrote a paper titled "Sound and Structure in Dante's Divine Comedy" while he was with the Department of Italian Studies of the University of Manchester. It was presented in 1998 at the Joint International Conference ALLC/ACH (Association for Literary and Linguistic Computing and Association for Computers and the Humanities), and posted on the Web site of the *Center for Applied Linguistics Online*. In the paper, Robey explains that the project "produces (1) an electronic test of the *Divine Comedy* and Dante's lyric poetry marked up in terms of syllable count and accent; (2) on the basis of this, a systematic structural description of Dante's rhythmical practice, in the sense of the distribution of accentual structures and the application of syllable divisions . . .; (3) a much more powerful account of assonance and alliteration in the *Comedy*, since I am now able to link these features (as I could not do in my earlier studies) to accentual structure."

The book analyzes the sounds and distribution of sounds within Dante's text, compares them to occurrences in related texts, and comes to the conclusion that the work contains unusually high occurrences of specific features. It is, therefore, a further examination of the poem and an example and study of how technology can be used for scholarly research.

In addition, Robey is editor, with Peter Hainsworth, of *The Oxford Companion to Italian Literature,* a collection of 2,400 entries arranged alphabetically, by Italian scholars, primarily academics in Great Britain and Ireland, with a number from the United States. Very well-known works appear under their English titles, while lesser-known works are titled in Italian. The volume covers writers over nine centuries, as well as some general entries, in categories that include genres and types, literary movements, themes and issues, humor and irony, cultural contexts and institutions, language, social and political context, non-Italian writ-

ing and influences, other arts, and sources for further reference. Notable Italian filmmakers are covered as well as lesser-known figures from the 1930s, such as Mario Camerini and Alessandro Blasetti.

Times Literary Supplement reviewer Masolino D'Amico noted that "the turn-of-the-century trinity, Giosuè Carducci, Giovanni Pascoli, and Gabriele D'Annunzio, viewed with undiluted admiration and awe in their day but now almost completely absent from anthologies, are discussed with wisdom and balance."

Historians, critics, and philosophers are included, as are Italians who worked abroad, and playwrights. There is an entry for Carlo Collodi, author of the children's story *Pinocchio. Booklist* reviewers Susan Awe and Barbara Bibel called *The Oxford Companion to Italian Literature* "the most comprehensive reference tool for Italian literature in English."

BIOGRAPHICAL AND CRITICAL SOURCES:

PERIODICALS

Booklist, September 15, 2003, Susan Awe and Barbara Bibel, review of *The Oxford Companion to Italian Literature,* p. 268.
Choice, January, 1974, review of *Structuralism: An Introduction,* p. 1732.
Comparative Literature, fall, 1977, Peter Caws, review of *Structuralism,* pp. 351-353.
Modern Language Review, April, 2002, Pietro G. Beltrami, review of *Sound and Structure in the Divine Comedy,* pp. 449-450.
Style, spring, 1990, James R. Bennett, review of *Modern Literary Theory: A Comparative Introduction* (second edition), pp. 126-132.
Times Literary Supplement, August 3, 1973, review of *Structuralism,* p. 913; January 31, 2003, Masolino D'Amico, review of *The Oxford Companion to Italian Literature,* pp. 10-11.

ONLINE

Center for Applied Linguistics Online, http://lingua. arts.klte.hu/allcach98/abst/abs40.htm (June 10, 2004), David Robey, "Sound and Structure in Dante's *Divine Comedy*" (conference paper).*

ROBINSON, Alex
   See ROBINSON, Wayne Alexander

*   *   *

ROBINSON, Wayne Alexander 1969-
   (Alex Robinson)

PERSONAL: Born August 8, 1969, in Bronx, NY; son of Wayne Robinson and Irene Phillips; romantically involved with Kristen Siebecker since October, 1994. *Education:* Attended State University of New York— Brockport, 1988-89; graduated from School of Visual Arts, 1994.

ADDRESSES: Home and office—208 W. 23rd St., Dept. 1616, New York, NY 10011. *E-mail*— ComicBookAlex@aol.com.

CAREER: Independent cartoonist and graphic novelist, 1994—.

AWARDS, HONORS: Will Eisner Comic Industry Award, Talent Deserving of Wider Recognition, 2001; nominated for Ignatz Award, Best Reprint or Collection, 2001, for *Box Office Poison;* nominated for Harvey Award, Best Graphic Album of Previously Published Work, 2002; nominated for Firecracker Award, Best Graphic Novel, 2002; nominated for Eisner Award, Best Graphic Album-Reprint, 2002.

WRITINGS:

Box Office Poison (graphic novel; originally published in twenty-one installments, Antarctic Press, 1996-2000), Top Shelf Productions (Marietta, GA), 2001.

BOP! (graphic short stories; sequel to *Box Office Poison*), Top Shelf Productions (Marietta, GA), 2003.

Created "Bloppo the Clown" mini-comics and others; contributed short story to David Hahn's *Private Beach,* number 4.

WORK IN PROGRESS: A second graphic novel, *Sophomore Slump* (working title).

SIDELIGHTS: American graphic novelist Wayne Alexander Robinson, who often writes under the name Alex Robinson, grew up reading comics and began drawing his own comics as a child. He studied art at New York's School of Visual Arts, where the comics legend Will Eisner (creator of *The Spirit*) was one of his teachers. Robinson began drawing mini-comics when he graduated from art school in 1994 and soon published "Bohemian Girl," the first installment in what became his 600-page graphic novel, *Box Office Poison.* A coming-of-age story whose main characters are two underachieving college graduates living in New York City in the 1990s, the story has been praised by critics and was nominated for several comics awards.

Box Office Poison is the story of frustrated novelist Sherman Davies, who has an English degree but still works at a bookstore for college-days wages, and his best friend Ed Velasquez, who graduated with a business degree at his parents' insistence, although he wants to draw comics. Ed works at his family's hardware store and lives at home. The two interact with Jane and Stephen, an older couple from whom Sherman rents a room; Dorothy Lestrade, a magazine editor with whom Sherman falls in love; and the Golden Age comics artist Irving Flavor, with whom Ed finally finds work as an assistant, even though his most desperate quest is to find romance. Ed encourages the aging Flavor to try and gain the rights to cartoon characters he created in his younger days. Other characters come and go, and reviewers have called this graphic novel as good as the best novels, television programs, and movies, of its genre.

Julio Diaz, in a review for *Ink 19,* lauded Robinson's "fully realized, complex characters," saying he "breathes life into his characters rarely seen in any medium." A character-enhancing technique Robinson uses is one-page panels in which he asks the characters an important life question, such as "Where will you be in ten years?" and lets their answers reveal depth perhaps not found in the current story line. A plot twist that many reviewers noted was that by the end of the graphic novel, the main protagonist turns out to be just the opposite of the one they thought would have this designation. Diaz observed, "It's so realistic and honest, it's almost heartbreaking. . . . It's by turns hilarious, tense, sad, shocking, and thoroughly gripping." Diaz concluded, "*Box Office Poison* is one of the most engrossing and rewarding pieces of literature—graphic or otherwise—that I've had the privilege to read."

Matthew Craig, in a review for *RobotFist,* compared it to "the world's best pineapple upside-down cake: layers upon layers of rich dramatic goodness." Craig thought the book would have made a better television show than most existing shows in its genre and that in the future it would be regarded "as the acme of comic book drama, and will almost certainly be a strong influence on the current generation of creators." A *Publishers Weekly* reviewer noted that *Box Office Poison* "supplies both visual wit and dramatic honesty" and called it "a convincing, absorbing and satisfying fictional portrait."

Alex Dueben, in a review for *Ninth Art,* observed, "Robinson has a very acute feeling for the way people talk and movement of conversations, the way they drift and sway, and often end up accidentally revealing more about themselves than they intend." Although Dueben felt Robinson's art was not as strong as his writing, he said the art does a good job of conveying emotion throughout the book. He thought the story of Irving Flavor was not as strong as it could have been and found most of Robinson's characters in the comic book office more like stereotypes of people in the industry. However, he liked the fact that Robinson does not make Dorothy into the story's villain, as easy as that might have been. Dueben described *Box Office Poison* as "ragged on the edges and unfinished in places," but he said, "a lot of the sheer power and emotion comes from this rawness. It's not slick, polished and glossy. It feels real. Realism is just a genre, it's not the be-all and end-all of art, but it's hard to get right." Dueben concluded that the book "is a more than respectable debut, and it demonstrates that Robinson is clearly poised to be one of the industry's breakout talents in the next decade."

In an interview with Steve Conley of *iComics,* Robinson said *Box Office Poison* has very little autobiography, although he did once work in a bookstore like Sherman does. However, said Robinson, he does base other characters on friends and acquaintances. For example, Ed is based on a cartoonist friend, Tony Consiglio. Some of the cartoons that Ed creates are those Robinson drew as an adolescent.

Christian A. Dumais interviewed Robinson for *Legion Studios,* and the author said he thinks of himself as a writer who draws, rather than an artist who writes. He said the single biggest influence on his work was Dave Sim's *Cerebus,* but that he was also inspired by Har-

vey Pekar's *American Splendor,* the *Archie* comics, and *Mad* magazine. He described *Box Office Poison* as "like *Archie* but with cursing and nudity!" He also noted that loyalty vs. betrayal is a major theme of the novel. Robinson said he works with a loose idea of plot and lets the characters take the story where it will go. A master at dialogue, Robinson commented that readers "jokingly say I must be following them around taking notes. It's a great compliment." Robinson remarked that he enjoys picking up a character from a previous story and adding them into a new one. The character Caprice from the end of *Box Office Poison,* for example, will appear in his new graphic novel, tentatively titled *Sophomore Slump.*

BIOGRAPHICAL AND CRITICAL SOURCES:

PERIODICALS

Booklist, March 1, 2004, Ray Olson, review of *BOP!,* p. 1148.

Library Journal, May 1, 2004, Steve Raiteri, review of *BOP!,* p. 94.

Publishers Weekly, November 19, 2001, review of *Box Office Poison,* p. 38; October 22, 2001, review of *Box Office Poison,* p. 56.

ONLINE

Artbomb, http://www.artbomb.net/ (August 19, 2003), Kelly Sue DeConnick, review of *Box Office Poison.*

iComics, http://www.icomics.com/ (April 1, 1998), Steve Conley, "Box Office Success: An iComics Interview with Alex Robinson."

Ink 19, http://www.ink19.com/ (July, 2001), Julio Diaz, review of *Box Office Poison.*

Lambiek, http://www.lambiek.net/ (August 12, 2003), "Alex Robinson."

Legion Studios Web site, http://www.legion-studios. com/ (August 19, 2003), Christian A. Dumais, "Legion Interviews Alex Robinson, Creator of *Box Office Poison.*"

Ninth Art, http://www.ninthart.com/ (August 16, 2002), Alex Dueben, review of *Box Office Poison.*

RobotFist, http://www.robotfist.com/ (September 18, 2002), Matthew Craig, review of *Box Office Poison.**

RONAN, Charles E. 1914-2004

OBITUARY NOTICE—See index for *CA* sketch: Born June 1, 1914, in Chicago, IL; died of respiratory failure, April 8, 2004, in Chicago, IL. Priest, educator, and author. Ronan was a Jesuit priest and professor emeritus at Loyola University. Educated at Loyola, where he earned an M.A. in 1955, he had been ordained a priest in 1945 and went on to earn a Ph.D. from the University of Texas in 1958; he also attended West Baden College in New Jersey. A historian as well as a priest, Ronan pursued a career in teaching. He began as an English and Latin teacher at Loyola Academy in 1941, and, in the 1950s and early 1960s, taught history at such institutions as the University of Detroit and Xavier University. He joined the Loyola University faculty in 1964, where he remained until his 1984 retirement as professor of history emeritus. As an author, Ronan wrote and edited histories concerning Latin America and the Jesuits, including *Francisco Javier Clavigero, S.J. (1731-1787): Figure of the Mexican Enlightenment; His Life and Works* (1977) and *Juan Ignacio Molina: The World's Window on Chile* (2002).

OBITUARIES AND OTHER SOURCES:

PERIODICALS

Chicago Tribune, April 15, 2004, Section 3, p. 9.

* * *

ROTHENBERG, Laura 1981-2003

PERSONAL: Born 1981, in New York, NY; died of complications from a lung transplant, 2003, in New York, NY; daughter of Jon Rothenberg (a doctor) and Mary Rothenberg. *Education:* Attended Brown University.

CAREER: Student and writer.

AWARDS, HONORS: Bronze Award, Third Coast Audio Festival, 2002, for "My So-Called Lungs" on National Public Radio's (NPR) *All Things Considered.*

WRITINGS:

Breathing for a Living, Hyperion (New York, NY), 2003.

Also author of "My So-Called Lungs" (audio diary), edited and produced by Joe Richman, appearing on "Radio Diaries," part of NPR's *All Things Considered,* 2002.

SIDELIGHTS: Laura Rothenberg was born in New York City in 1981. She was diagnosed with cystic fibrosis, a genetic disease which causes a mucus build-up in the victims' lungs and other organs, leading to serious respiratory and digestive problems and eventually death. She underwent surgery at three days old, and had countless other operations and hospital visits throughout her life. She tried to live as normal a life as possible, attending Brown University and living in the dorms, where she was exposed to possible illness. At nineteen she made the difficult decision to receive a double lung transplant to help deter the progression of the disease. In July 2002 she underwent the twelve hour operation and began the difficult recovery. Unfortunately her body ultimately rejected the organs, and Rothenberg suffered from bowel obstructions, pneumonia, and lymphoma. She died on March 22, 2003 at the age of twenty-two, due to chronic rejection of her lung transplant, complicated by infection.

Rothenberg's story was featured on National Public Radio's "Radio Diaries," a part of *All Things Considered.* She recorded over forty hours of tape for the audio diary which was then edited by producer Joe Richman into a twenty-two minute piece called "My So-Called Lungs." The "Radio Diaries" series started by Richman is intended to allow teenagers to document their own lives, often revealing more than they would in conversation with a reporter. Rothenberg's broadcast on August 5, 2002, generated unprecedented listener response and received more e-mail than producers could recall ever seeing.

Rothenberg was reluctant to record her thoughts and feelings when Richman first approached her about the project. She recorded material off and on for two years, including trips to the hospital, conversations with parents and friends, and her personal late-night thoughts. In November of 2002, "My So-Called Lungs" received the bronze award at the Third Coast International Audio Festival in Chicago. Mathew Flamm of *Entertainment Weekly* praised Rothenberg's "haunting, sometimes humorous voice."

After the reception of her audio diary, Hyperion approached Rothenberg about turning her experiences into a book. Rothenberg was an avid writer of poetry and agreed to the project, which chronicled her decision to receive a lung transplant and her consequential deterioration in health. What resulted is *Breathing for a Living,* the memoir of a young woman constantly aware of her own mortality. A contributor for *Kirkus Reviews* wrote, "This finely wrought chronicle about choosing to live to the full in the face of death admirably balances the author's fears and hopes." Emily Mead of *Entertainment Weekly* called the book "a remarkably clear-eyed (if jargon-ridden) account," but found it "fails to capture the intimacy and immediacy of her recorded voice." A reviewer for *Publishers Weekly* praised the memoir, commenting that in her "refus[al] to indulge in even a wisp of false hope or consolation, Rothenberg reminds us that there is a power in us that is greater than even the greatest suffering."

BIOGRAPHICAL AND CRITICAL SOURCES:

PERIODICALS

Entertainment Weekly, September 6, 2002, Mathew Flamm, "Between the Lines: The Inside Scoop on the Book World," p. 77; July 25, 2003, Emily Mead, review of *Breathing for a Living,* p. 76.
Home Care, September 1, 2002, "Listen and Learn."
Kirkus Reviews, May 15, 2003, review of *Breathing for a Living,* p. 738.
Publishers Weekly, May 12, 2003, Tracy Cochran, "A Far From Typical Life: Talks with Laura Rothenberg," p. 53; review of *Breathing for a Living,* p. 51.
U.S. News and World Report, August 5, 2002, Dan Gilgoff, "On the Radio: A Well-Examined Life Lived Unwell," p. 40.

ONLINE

Brown Daily Herald Online, http://www.browndaily herald.com/ (November 4, 2003), Lisa Mandle, "Laura Rothenberg, a Student Remembered."

George Street Journal, http://www.brown.edu/ (November 4, 2003), Kristen Cole, "Student's Memoir, *Breathing for a Living,* Set for Summer Publication."
National Public Radio, http://www.npr.org/ (November 4, 2003), Joe Richman, "Laura Rothenberg Remembered."

OBITUARIES:

PERIODICALS

Los Angeles Times, March 23, 2003, p. B16.*

*   *   *

ROWE, Rosemary
    See AITKEN, Rosemary

*   *   *

RUBIN, Gretchen (Craft) 1966(?)-

PERSONAL: Born c. 1966, in Kansas City, MO; daughter of Jack Craft (an attorney); married Jamie Rubin (an investment banker); children: Eliza. *Education:* Yale University, B.A. (English), J.D., 1994.

ADDRESSES: Home—New York, NY. *Agent*—c/o Author Mail, Ballantine, Random House, 201 East 50th St., New York, NY 10022. *E-mail*—grubin@ gretchen.rubin.com.

CAREER: Educator and writer. Clerk for U.S. Supreme Court Justice Sandra Day O'Connor; chief advisor to Federal Communications Commissions chairman Reed Hundt; former summer associate at law firms Skadden, Arps, Slate, Meagher & Flom and Davis Polk & Wardwell. Yale University, New Haven, CT, instructor at Yale Law School and Yale School of Management.

WRITINGS:

Power, Money, Fame, Sex: A User's Guide, Pocket Books (New York, NY), 2000.
Forty Ways to Look at Winston Churchill: A Brief Account of a Long Life, Ballantine Books (New York, NY), 2003.

SIDELIGHTS: Gretchen Rubin is the author of two nonfiction titles that on first glance seem to have very little in common, either with each other or with their author, a Yale Law School graduate. Her first book, *Power, Money, Fame, Sex: A User's Guide,* serves as both a guide for social climbers—or as *Booklist* contributor David Rouse described, "people who use people"—and a self-help book wrapped into one. The guide seeks to offer ambitious individuals succinct strategic advice on how to make their way in the world. In contrast, *Forty Ways to Look at Winston Churchill: A Brief Account of a Long Life* is a serious examination of the life of the late British Prime Minister that was given praise by several critics.

Among Rubin's pointers in *Power, Money, Fame, Sex* are things like "Never give anonymously" and "Those who marry for money earn every penny," and the author finds a perfect medium, noted critics, between seriousness and tongue-in-cheek humor as she cites as examples such people as Bill Gates, Madonna, and Lyndon B. Johnson. A reviewer for *Publishers Weekly* called *Power, Money, Fame, Sex* a "delicious hybrid of two popular genres: self-help and lifestyles-of-the-rich-and-famous," that abounds with "wisdom and fun." "Mining sources that range from classical literature to *People* and *Vanity Fair. . . .* Rubin never comes up short in her effort to illustrate where her strategies can lead," Rouse added. While one might question an advice book that some critics noted puts a Machiavellian spin on modern social practices and might make readers question the author's own ethical code, as Rubin noted on her Web site, "It seemed to me that an examination of power, money, fame, and sex should include all the methods that people actually use—not just the methods that people ought to use. So I include techniques that I'd never endorse. The guide is supposed to help you understand all the methods that work—so that you understand what your boss or neighbor is doing, even if you'd never do it yourself. If you're determined to use sex to get money, a paternity suit against a basketball player is a successful approach."

In *Forty Ways to Look at Winston Churchill,* Rubin offers readers an examination of the character of a man noted for both his wisdom and his talent for self-promotion. While many historians have criticized Churchill for his actions following World War II, Rubin takes an alternative route and dissects this criticism. While a *Kirkus Reviews* contributor argued that Rubin is perhaps too "breezy" in her handling of such an important historical figure, Alan Prince wrote in an online review for *Bookpage* that her work serves general readers as "an accessible study of one of history's most fascinating figures." Explaining why she chose to write in such an unconventional format—*Forty Ways to Look at Winston Churchill* approaches its subject from a number of different perspectives, with contrasting and often conflicting results—Rubin noted: "Rather than detail the facts of Churchill's life, as most biographies do—which can make them so long and dense that a reader loses the big picture—*Forty Ways* answers essential questions. . . . What was Churchill's decisive moment? What was his greatest strength? Was he an alcoholic, did he suffer from depression, did he have a happy marriage?"

In addition to writing nonfiction, Rubin is an adjunct instructor at Yale University's Law School and the Yale School of Management. A Yale alumni herself, Rubin currently resides in New York City with her husband, Jamie Rubin, and daughter, Eliza. After obtaining her law degree from Yale, Rubin went on to clerk for U.S. Supreme Court Justice Sandra Day O'Connor, and also worked as an adviser to Federal Communications Commissions chairman Reed Hundt.

BIOGRAPHICAL AND CRITICAL SOURCES:

PERIODICALS

American Lawyer, November, 2000, John Anderson, "Almost Famous," p. 128.
Booklist, September 1, 2000, David Rouse, review of *Power, Money, Fame, Sex: A User's Guide,* p. 33.
Kirkus Reviews, April 15, 2003, review of *Forty Ways to Look at Winston Churchill: A Brief Account of a Long Life,* p. 594.
New Yorker, September 11, 2000, Nick Baumgarten, review of *Power, Money, Fame, Sex,* p. 37.
Publishers Weekly, July 31, 2000, review of *Power, Money, Fame, Sex,* p. 82.

ONLINE

Bookpage Web site, http://www.bookpage.com/ (October 10, 2003), Alan Prince, review of *Forty Ways to Look at Winston Churchill.*
Gretchen Rubin Web site, http://www.gretchenrubin.com (May 6, 2004).
Rebecca's Reads Web site, http://rebeccasreads.com/ (October 10, 2003), Rebecca Brown, review of *Forty Ways to Look at Winston Churchill.**

RUCKER, Patrick Michael 1974-

PERSONAL: Born April 22, 1974, in Portland, OR; son of Donald Brian and Lucy Ann (East) Rucker. *Ethnicity:* "White; Irish American." *Education:* University of Richmond, B.A., 1996. *Religion:* Methodist.

ADDRESSES: Home—25 Livingston Dr., Howell, NJ 07731. *Agent*—Gail Ross, 1666 Connecticut Ave. N.W., Washington, DC 20009. *E-mail*—patrick_rucker@hotmail.com.

CAREER: Freelance journalist.

WRITINGS:

This Troubled Land: Voices from Northern Ireland on the Front Lines of Peace, Ballantine (New York, NY), 2002.

Contributor to periodicals.

SIDELIGHTS: Patrick Michael Rucker told *CA:* "I wrote about the Irish peace process and the fitful, often tragic way it was unfolding after a long personal interest in the region. No American journalist had explained events in the region to my satisfaction, and I felt compelled to write. I was fortunate enough to find an agent and publisher that got behind the project."

BIOGRAPHICAL AND CRITICAL SOURCES:

PERIODICALS

Kirkus Reviews: Voices from Northern Ireland on the Front Lines of Peace, November 15, 2001, review of *This Troubled Land,* p. 1601.
Library Journal, December, 2001, Robert Moore, review of *This Troubled Land,* p. 147.
Publishers Weekly, February 11, 2002, review of *This Troubled Land,* p. 178.

S

SANCHEZ, Alex 1957-

PERSONAL: Born April, 1957, in Mexico City, Mexico; immigrated to the United States, 1962. *Education:* Virginia Tech University, B.A., 1978; Old Dominion University, M.S. Ed., 1985.

ADDRESSES: Home—Rosslyn, VA. *Agent*—Miriam Altshuler, 53 Old Post Road N., Red Hook, New York, NY 12571. *E-mail*—Alex@AlexSanchez.com.

CAREER: Writer. Previously worked as a Web site manager, organizational development consultant, juvenile probation officer, family counselor, scuba instructor, program coordinator, admissions official, college recruiter, movie projectionist, agent trainee, movie production assistant, theater usher, stock clerk, and tour guide.

MEMBER: Authors Guild, National Writers Union, Society of Children's Book Writers and Illustrators.

AWARDS, HONORS: Best Book for Young Adults selection, American Library Association, Blue Ribbon Winner, *Bulletin of the Center for Children's Books,* Books for the Teen Age selection, New York Public Library, and finalist, Lambda Literary Award, all 2002, all for *Rainbow Boys.*

WRITINGS:

Rainbow Boys, Simon & Schuster (New York, NY), 2001.
Rainbow High, Simon & Schuster (New York, NY), 2003.
So Hard to Say, Simon & Schuster (New York, NY), 2004.

Contributor of short story "If You Kiss a Boy" to *13: Thirteen Stories That Capture the Agony and Ecstasy of Turning Thirteen,* edited by James Howe, Atheneum (New York, NY), 2003.

WORK IN PROGRESS: Rainbow Road, for Simon & Schuster (New York, NY), publication expected in 2005.

SIDELIGHTS: Alex Sanchez is one of several new voices in young adult literature that explore gay, lesbian, bisexual, transgender, and questioning (GLBTQ) themes in fiction. Sanchez's 2001 *Rainbow Boys* takes the familiar high school triangle plot and gives it a new twist, positing it in the form of gay romance and awakening. "I've been told my writing is fundamentally about relationships," Sanchez told interviewer J. Sydney Jones. "What brings people together and pulls them apart, particularly in terms of love, friendship, family, gender, culture and sexuality." As Sanchez further noted in his interview, young adult literature has undergone a "sea change" in the past ten years, allowing the exploration of subjects taboo only a decade ago. Speaking with Toby Emert of the *ALAN Review,* Sanchez reported to Jones that a decade earlier "the story lines and characters would've been very different." At that time, according to Sanchez, "only a handful of gays and lesbians came out as teenagers; the process was almost entirely limited to adults." The average age for coming out in the United States had fallen to fifteen by 2000, leaving many high school students to deal with this difficult transition on their own. "Unfortunately, the predominant experience for most GLBTQ youth is still one of isolation, harassment, persecution, and self-loathing," Sanchez remarked. The need, therefore, for books such as *Rainbow Boys* is great. "A book like it provides a vicarious emotional experience that can be tremendously valuable in helping teens navigate the transition to psychologically mature, healthy, integrated adults." It can also help to instill within straight students an understanding and empathy for gays and their difficulties. "I think the story of *Rainbow Boys* grew out of my own internal struggle between wanting to accept myself and being afraid to," Sanchez remarked to Emert.

Sanchez was born in Mexico City, Mexico, in 1957, to parents of Cuban and German heritage. When he was five, the family moved to the United States, "forever altering the course of my life," the author commented in his interview with Jones. "As I began school, I spoke no English. I watched people's lips move and had no idea what they were saying. I experienced growing up as an outsider. I got picked on for being different. It was my first experience with prejudice." One of his childhood icons was the cartoon character "Speedy Gonzalez," the "most positive Latino in a medium most familiar to me as a child—cartoons. Speedy broke stereotype by being smart, hardworking, the fastest mouse in all *Méjico*."

Sanchez attempted to assimilate rapidly into his new environment. "I learned English as fast as I could. When I told other children I was from Mexico, they told me: 'But you don't look Mexican.' I began to realize that even knowing the language, Mexicans and other darker-skinned people in the United States were looked down upon by both children and adults. The shame I felt caused me to stop speaking Spanish. When my parents took me shopping or to a restaurant, I didn't want other people to know we were from Mexico. I didn't want them to look down upon us. Because I was relatively light-skinned, I learned I could pass as white. I could hide who I was, so that others would like and accept me. By the time I reached middle school, I had buried a core part of myself—my Mexican heritage. I was no longer different. Or so I thought."

Sanchez found solace at home, encouraged into self-expression by his artist mother and his father, "who exemplified the ethic of hard work." Books also became a refuge, especially *The Story of Ferdinand* by Munro Leaf. That classic story of a Spanish bull that prefers sniffing flowers to fighting in the bull ring ap-

pealed to the young outsider, letting him know it was okay to be different and to be who you are.

Who he was, however, became more complicated when Sanchez reached adolescence. "I was thirteen when I first heard the word 'gay,'" Sanchez told Jones "Immediately, I knew that's what I was. And I hated myself for it. Like so many gay, lesbian, bisexual, transgender, or questioning teens, for the remainder of my school years I withdrew, depressed. Alone in my room after school, I would tell myself, 'I'm not going to feel this way. I refuse to let this happen.'"

As a teenager in the early 1970s, "there was no such thing as being 'out' in high school," Sanchez recalled. "I do remember one boy, who was labeled 'gay' and consequently got beat up every day. I watched and stood silent, afraid that if I said anything, I might be found out too. So instead, I looked on, feeling guilty. The way I coped was by becoming 'the best little boy in the world,' just as in Andrew Tobias's book of that title—a classic overachiever, being the best at everything, in order to mask the shame I felt. I hated high school, and raced through it, finishing a year and a half early. What young person wouldn't hate a setting that leads them to hate themselves? That's probably what led me to revisit the setting in a novel."

Sanchez went to college at Virginia Tech, graduating with honors in 1978. After college he went to Hollywood, hoping to break into the film industry. For several years he worked at a variety of minor jobs—theater usher, movie projectionist, TV production assistant, studio tour guide, and script reader—waiting for his big chance. In fact, such a chance came with his script-reading job, which convinced him that he could write better than most of the people submitting scripts. He tried his own hand at script writing with limited results, but the experience let him know that he had found his true calling.

Before that time, he had enjoyed writing, but had always shied away from expressing his true feelings or revealing his gay identity. "Like many writers, I loved to write since I was a child," Sanchez explained to Jones. "But as I grew up, I learned it wasn't safe to share who I was. In college I wrote a picture book for a children's lit class but it wasn't anything truly personal. Not until grad school did I finally summon the courage to write a story with a gay character. The instructor's homophobia caused him to lash out at it. After that I didn't write for years. But the dream of writing stayed with me. When I finally summoned the courage to try again, I reached out to several friends working on their own creative projects. We encouraged one another. In addition, I discovered the Fine Arts Work Center in Provincetown, which offers one-week workshops with many of America's finest writers."

Sanchez had meanwhile also completed a master's degree in guidance and counseling, and worked in family and youth counseling for many years. When he left that field and went into human resources, he decided it was time for him to put his thoughts down on paper. Little did he know at the time that he would be facing a five-year writing project for his first book. "I didn't write *Rainbow Boys* with a particular audience in mind," Sanchez told Jones. "As the novel took shape, however, it became apparent I was writing the book I desperately wanted and needed to read when I was a teenager—one that would have told me: 'You don't have to hate yourself for being gay. It's okay to be who you are.' My intention was to write an upbeat and affirming book that would inspire and encourage empathy."

The book ultimately gained the attention of a sympathetic agent. "An instructor who liked my work recommended me to her agent, a straight suburban mom," Sanchez explained, "who liked the manuscript because of its themes of acceptance and personal integrity. It's a book she hopes her kids will read when they're teenagers. She was a huge champion of the manuscript and had the contacts at Simon & Schuster."

Published in 2001, *Rainbow Boys* is the story of three high school seniors who confront their sexual identities and learn to deal with issues of self-worth and self-image. Kyle is smart and athletic, a serious student with a secret crush on Jason, a jock and one of the most popular boys in school. Jason, however, is seemingly very straight, going steady with an equally popular girl. Completing the triangle is Nelson, dubbed Nellie by his classmates, as he is a "flamboyant loner," according to a reviewer for *Book*. Nelson is outspokenly gay and helps to establish a Gay-Straight Alliance at his school. Because Nelson and Kyle are best friends, it is assumed that Kyle too is gay, even though he does not advertise it. Kyle, thus, is subject to the same harassment at school that Nelson is. To compli-

cate matters, Nelson hopes to turn his close friendship with Kyle into a romantic relationship. Jason, meanwhile, is confused about his own sexuality, not knowing if he is straight, bisexual, or gay. In an attempt to clarify these issues he attends a Rainbow Youth meeting where he is met by both Nelson and Kyle, who are surprised to see him in attendance. "This uncomfortable confrontation starts the ball rolling down a path of deception, denial, revelation, and acceptance," according to Betty S. Evans in a *School Library Journal* review. Such a difficult path involves not only the three boys themselves, but their friends and parents, as well.

Sanchez's gay coming-of-age novel was greeted with critical praise. Evans called it a "gutsy, in-your-face debut," that uses "real life" language to speak to gay issues at the high school level. The reviewer for *Book* similarly found that Sanchez "writes with clear, honest language about . . . first sexual experiences." Reviewing the novel in *Lambda Book Report*, Bob Witeck felt that Sanchez's "story telling is fluent, direct and authentic," exploring "the universal nature of romance." Witeck also thought that the novel would present more "truthful . . . flesh and blood" gay characters for a straight audience. Likewise, *Booklist* contributor Michael Cart commented that "Sanchez writes with passion and understanding," ultimately demonstrating that "coming out is really coming in—entering a circle of support." More praise came from a critic for *Kirkus Reviews* who noted, "this is a fine first effort, thought-provoking and informative for all young adults." Lynn Evarts, reviewing the novel in *Voice of Youth Advocates*, pointed to the "remarkable job" Sanchez does in portraying the "feelings and emotions of a gay teenager experiencing his first crush," and *Kliatt*'s Paula Rohrlick also felt that "YAs who are struggling with some of the same issues will appreciate this realistic, caring portrayal." And a contributor for *Publishers Weekly* similarly lauded Sanchez for creating "modern situations that speak to contemporary teens." Awarded a Best Book for Young Adults citation by the American Library Association, *Rainbow Boys* was an impressive debut for Sanchez.

A sequel, *Rainbow High*, explores the second half of the senior year of Sanchez's three protagonists. At first reluctant to jump back into the lives of his characters after living five years with them, Sanchez soon became immersed in the project. "The boys face new and different challenges," he explained to Emert. "The dramatic storylines explore more deeply issues about HIV, safer sex, and teen relationships told through characters that readers can care about and learn from." Writing in *Publishers Weekly,* a critic thought that the author "expertly mixes coming-out issues with the universal complications of first love," while *School Library Journal* contributor Robert Gray claimed that "mature YAs will identify with the problems and decisions these individuals must face."

"I'm an equal opportunity writer," Sanchez said to Jones, "not writing for any particular demographic. I write on the premise that a reader picks up a book in order to think and feel, to be entertained or inspired. The only 'audience' I have in mind when writing is the characters themselves. Am I capturing how they think, feel, and reveal themselves through actions? Am I being true to them? If they were to pick up the book would they say 'That's me!' I believe that meaningful, truly powerful writing springs from the heart, describes the conflict of the human heart, and reaches out to move the reader's heart. If I can come close to that, I've achieved my goal."

Describing his other goals in writing, Sanchez concluded to Jones, "Books can provide a moral compass, a system of values, a way to understand yourself. Usually you learn these things from peers, or at school, or from family. But what happens when all those avenues tell you that what you're feeling is bad and wrong? Books can hold a special place, providing hope for a world in which it's okay to be who you are. . . . To inspire, empower, and help change the world for the better—one heart and one mind at a time. That's my dream. That's my hope."

BIOGRAPHICAL AND CRITICAL SOURCES:

BOOKS

Sanchez, Alex, interview with J. Sydney Jones for *Authors and Artists for Young Adults,* Volume 51, Gale (Detroit, MI), 2003.

PERIODICALS

ALAN Review, fall, 2002, Toby Emert, "An Interview with Alex Sanchez, Author of *Rainbow Boys,*" pp. 12-14.

Book, September, 2001, review of *Rainbow Boys,* p. 91.
Booklist, November 15, 2001, Michael Cart, review of *Rainbow Boys,* p. 566.
Horn Book, January-February, 2004, Roger Sutton, review of *Rainbow High,* p. 83.
Kirkus Reviews, October 15, 2001, review of *Rainbow Boys,* p. 1492.
Kliatt, September, 2001, Paula Rohrlick, review of *Rainbow Boys.*
Lambda Book Report, October, 2001, Bob Witeck, "They're Only Mysteries Themselves," p. 21; April, 2002, Martin Wilson, "Listening to 'My Inner Teenager,'" p. 30.
Publishers Weekly, November 26, 2001, review of *Rainbow Boys,* p. 62; December 24, 2001, "Flying Starts," pp. 30-35; November 24, 2003, review of *Rainbow High,* p. 65.
School Library Journal, October, 2001, Betty S. Evans, review of *Rainbow Boys,* p. 169; November, 2003, Robert Gray, review of *Rainbow High,* p. 146.
USA Today, June 26, 2001, Deirdre Donahue, "Books Give Honest Portrayal of Growing Up Gay."
Voice of Youth Advocates, December, 2001, Lynn Evarts, review of *Rainbow Boys.*

OTHER

Alex Sanchez Home Page, http://www.alexsanchez. com (December 1, 2002).*

*   *   *

SANDFORD, Cedric Thomas 1924-2004

OBITUARY NOTICE—See index for *CA* sketch: Born November 21, 1924, in Basingstoke, Hampshire, England; died of cancer, March 5, 2004, in Bath, Somerset, England. Economist, educator, and author. Sandford was an economics professor who specialized in public finance and, especially, in the study of taxation laws and practices. After training as a fighter pilot with the Royal Air Force during World War II, he returned to England before seeing any action and attended Manchester University. He earned a B.A. in economics in 1948, followed by an M.A. the next year; he later also completed a B.A. in history from the University of London in 1955. Joining the Burnley

Municipal College faculty in 1949, he taught there through the 1950s, moving on to the Bristol College of Science and Technology in 1959, where he was head of the department of social studies from 1960 to 1965. While at Bristol, he helped with the founding of Bath University, where he was professor of political economy from 1965 to 1987 and head of the School of Humanities and Social Sciences intermittently during the 1960s and 1970s. At Bath University, Sandford was the founding director of the Centre for Fiscal Studies, which later led to his establishing Fiscal Publications with his second wife. As a tax expert, Sandford was concerned with tax-compliance laws, discovering through his research that the time and money it took for British citizens to comply with filing their taxes was more onerous than even the government's investment, and that laws were especially unfair to the lower classes in this regard. He wrote on this and other tax-related subjects in a number of books, including *Economics of Public Finance* (1969; third edition, 1984), *Hidden Costs of Taxation* (1973), *The Economic Structure* (1982), *Successful Tax Reform: Lessons from an Analysis of Tax Reform in Six Countries* (1993), and *Why Tax Systems Differ* (2000). Sandford retired as a professor emeritus in 1987, but continued to write, conduct research, and advise organizations such as the United Nations and the World Bank.

OBITUARIES AND OTHER SOURCES:

PERIODICALS

Financial Times March 19, 2004, p. 7.
Guardian (Manchester, England), April 16, 2004, p. 27.
Independent (London, England), March 18, 2004, p. 32.
Times (London, England), March 23, 2004, p. 30.

*   *   *

SANSOM, C. J.

PERSONAL: Male. *Education:* Earned Ph.D. (history); earned J.D.

ADDRESSES: Agent—c/o Author Mail, Viking, Penguin USA, 375 Hudson St., New York, NY 10014.

CAREER: Attorney and fiction writer.

WRITINGS:

Dissolution, Viking (New York, NY), 2003.

SIDELIGHTS: C. J. Sansom worked as a lawyer prior to becoming a professional writer. His debut novel, *Dissolution,* "provides readers with a vivid Tudor historical mystery," according to Harriet Klausner in an online review for *Books 'n' Bytes. Dissolution* takes place in England in 1537, as Thomas Cromwell, vicar-general to King Henry VIII, is aiding the king in his efforts to undermine the authority of the Roman Catholic Church within England. Cromwell eagerly accepts the challenge, although he is concerned about a possible uprising from those opposed to the Crown as well as by demoralized Catholics, or Papists. When an agent of the King turns up dead while on the King's business at the remote Monastery of St. Donatus the Ascendant in Scarnsea, Cromwell fears his worries have come to pass. He enlists the help of hunchbacked lawyer Matthew Shardlake and Shardlake's young, handsome assistant Mark Poer in investigating the death and finding the agent's killer. Shardlake gladly accepts the case; he has been an enemy of the Catholic Church since being refused the priesthood due to his deformity. The task proves to be anything but easy, however, as Shardlake and Poer find themselves outnumbered and despised for being outsiders at the remote monastery, where they are surrounded by corruption, uncooperative monks, and sexual depravity. When Shardlake discovers the remains of another victim in the monastery pond, he realizes that all is not what it seems, including Cromwell, who Shardlake realizes may hold a threat after he uncovers some disturbing and potentially damaging information about his respectable employer.

Michael Spinella, reviewing *Dissolution* for *Booklist,* stated that Sansom's debut fiction "will not disappoint fans of historical fiction," while Toronto *Globe and Mail Online* contributor Margaret Cannon noted that the author's "great talent" brings to life the intrigue of pre-Elizabethan England "in all its squalor and fright." Laurel Bliss, in the *Library Journal,* criticized the author's storyline, noting that although "Sansom clearly harbors a deep affection for and knowledge of this historical period. . . . his novel is unrelentingly grim in tone." In contrast, a reviewer for *Publishers Weekly* complimented the novel, stating that "Sansom paints a vivid picture of the corruption that plagued

England during the reign of Henry VIII, and the wry, rueful Shardlake is a memorable protagonist." Praising *Dissolution* as "cunningly plotted and darkly atmospheric," the contributor added that "Sansom proves himself to be a promising newcomer" in the historical fiction genre.

BIOGRAPHICAL AND CRITICAL SOURCES:

PERIODICALS

Booklist, April 1, 2003, Michael Spinella, review of *Dissolution,* p. 1382.
Kirkus Reviews, March 1, 2003, review of *Dissolution,* p. 342.
Library Journal, April 1, 2003, Laurel Bliss, review of *Dissolution,* p. 130.
Publishers Weekly, March 17, 2003, review of *Dissolution,* p. 51.

ONLINE

Books 'n' Bytes Web site, http://www.booksnbytes. com/ (October 12, 2003), Harriet Klausner, review of *Dissolution.*
Crime Time Web site, http://www.crimetime.co.uk/ (October 12, 2003), Ingrid Yornstrand, review of *Dissolution.*
Globe and Mail Online, http://www.globeandmail.com/ (August 30, 2003), Margaret Cannon, review of *Dissolution.**

*   *   *

SAULNIER, Beth 1969-

PERSONAL: Born September 23, 1969, in North Adams, MA; daughter of Wilfred (a history teacher) and Elizabeth (a paralegal) Saulnier; married David Andrew Bloom (in senior management), August 10, 2003. *Education:* Vassar College, B.A., 1990; attended graduate school at Cornell University.

ADDRESSES: Home—New York, NY. *Agent*—c/o Author Mail, Warner Books, 1271 Avenue of the Americas, New York, NY 10020.

CAREER: Cornell Magazine, former associate editor and staff writer; *Ithaca Journal,* former movie reviewer and columnist. Former cohost of *Take Two* (movie review show), Channel 13, Ithaca, NY; currently a freelance author. Has worked as a reporter and editor on newspapers in MA and NY.

MEMBER: Society for the Prevention of Cruelty to Animals (board of directors, Tompkins County, NY, chapter).

AWARDS, HONORS: Associated Press Award, for newspaper column "Saulnier on Cinema."

WRITINGS:

"ALEX BERNIER" MYSTERY SERIES

Reliable Sources, Warner Books (New York, NY), 1999.
Distemper, Warner Books (New York, NY), 2000.
The Fourth Wall, Warner Books (New York, NY), 2001.
Bad Seed, Warner Books (New York, NY), 2002.
Ecstasy, Mysterious Press/Warner Books (New York, NY), 2003.

Also author of column "Saulnier on Cinema," for *Ithaca Journal.*

WORK IN PROGRESS: A two-book contract with Warner Books/Mysterious Press, starting with *Give 'Em Hell, Isabelle,* a thriller novel, and *Run,* an "Alex Bernier" mystery novel.

SIDELIGHTS: Mystery writer Beth Saulnier spent more than twelve years in the "crunchy-intellectual town of Ithaca, New York," where she was a newspaper and television journalist, she commented on the *Beth Saulnier* Home Page. It was in Ithaca that she wrote more than five hundred of her "Saulnier on Cinema" movie review columns for *Ithaca Journal,* for which she won an Associated Press Award; she also hosted a weekly movie review program called "Take Two" on Ithaca's Channel 13. She gave up those jobs, as well as her position as associate editor and staff writer on

Cornell Magazine, when she got married in 2003 and moved to New York City to concentrate on her fiction and magazine-writing career.

Saulnier's popular "Alex Bernier" mystery series debuted with 1999's *Reliable Sources.* The heroine, Alex Bernier, a young reporter for the upstate Gabriel, New York, newspaper, *Gabriel Monitor,* is devastated to discover that her boyfriend, Adam Ellroy, has turned up at the bottom of North Creek Gorge; he is another in a string of apparent suicides linked to local Benson University. She is not convinced that Adam, a police reporter, would have leapt to his own death, and suspects someone angered by his controversial reporting. Her own investigation, aided by *Monitor* coworkers, uncovers a decades-old scandal on campus and sets her up to be the next "suicide" found at the bottom of the gorge. Saulnier "intersperses the witty dialogue and Gen-X narrative with *Monitor* staff articles, adding credibility and charm to Alex's" investigation, a *Publishers Weekly* reviewer commented.

The sequel, 2000's *Distemper,* picks up a year later and finds Alex pursuing her journalism career but still in mourning over Adam's death. Alex becomes embroiled in another mystery when naked female corpses with unexplained scrapes on their hands and knees are found one after the other in the local hills. The victims' dogs, however, cannot be located. At first, Alex investigates as a journalist, but when her roommate becomes a victim, too, she dives deeper into the case, becoming a target herself. Romance flares again when Alex falls for the lead police investigator. "Although the denouement falls just a touch flat, Saulnier's energetic prose provides such pleasure that readers aren't likely to mind," a *Publishers Weekly* critic commented. "If ever a mystery novel about serial mutilation could be called delightful, this one could," the reviewer concluded.

The third "Bernier" mystery, *The Fourth Wall,* involves Alex in the investigation of a body found bricked up in the basement of a historic theater, which has been at the center of a debate to save the building. The victim turns out to be a young actress who disappeared in 1926, and the suspects include "a duplicitous former child star, a cadre of Martha Stewart-esque academic wives with nasty secrets, and a vicious mob boss," noted a writer on the *Time Warner Bookmark* Web site.

Bad Seed, Alex's first appearance in hardcover, finds her covering protests at Benson University by kids in vegetable costumes, who are decrying genetically engineered food as a conference on that topic gets underway. When the agriculture building explodes, Alex barely escapes serious injury, and when the university's leading plant researcher is found beaten to death, the stakes increase. Meanwhile, fellow reporter Jake Madison seems to have tried to drink-and-drug himself to death after a failed romance. Alex finds connections between these events that suggest someone is going to great lengths to uphold their beliefs. "A funny, smart, refreshingly human heroine and a strong sense of place should make this one a hit," commented Carrie Bissey in *Booklist.* "Alex, a better dresser than Stephanie Plum and maybe a tad funnier, is delightful," remarked a *Kirkus Reviews* critic. And Rex Klett, writing in *Library Journal,* called the book "a memorable read."

Ecstasy, the fifth "Bernier" mystery, addresses issues related to the dangers of illicit drugs. After grudgingly agreeing to cover the Melting Rock Music Festival, an annual Woodstock-like event in upstate New York, Alex Bernier interviews a group of high school kids who are repeat attendees. A short time later, the boys of the group begin dying, victims of tainted LSD. Alex, along with her police detective boyfriend, penetrate the peace-and-love veneer of the festival to discover who would want to commit multiple murders and why. Bissey, in another *Booklist* review, called *Ecstasy* a "well-plotted, entertaining read." Saulnier "captures the filth, the crowds, the drug haze, the goofiness, and the rapture of a mini-Woodstock/ Monterrey," commented a *Kirkus Reviews* critic. Klett, writing in another *Library Journal* review, remarked favorably on the "super plotting, believable characterization, and seamless prose" in the book.

In a transcript of a chat session on the *Time Warner Bookmark* Web site, Saulnier said that the character of Alex Bernier "is based pretty tightly on myself. Alex is, basically, me, except that she is much, much braver, and with a much better sex life." Saulnier endured more than 150 rejections before getting the first Alex Bernier mystery published, she remarked on her home page. To aspiring writers, she said, "My advice would be to set aside vast blocks of time if you can, and just write." She added, "Don't agonize over it; just write!"

BIOGRAPHICAL AND CRITICAL SOURCES:

PERIODICALS

Booklist, January 1, 2002, Carrie Bissey, review of *Bad Seed,* p. 820; February 1, 2003, Carrie Bissey, review of *Ecstasy,* p. 975.

Kirkus Reviews, December 15, 2001, review of *Bad Seed,* p. 1726; January 1, 2003, review of *Ecstasy,* pp. 30-31.

Library Journal, January, 2002, Rex Klett, review of *Bad Seed,* p. 157; March 1, 2003, Rex Klett, review of *Ecstasy,* p. 122.

Publishers Weekly, October 11, 1999, review of *Reliable Sources,* p. 73; May 8, 2000, review of *Distemper,* p. 209; January 14, 2003, review of *Bad Seed,* p. 44; February 17, 2003, review of *Ecstasy,* p. 61.

ONLINE

Beth Saulnier Home Page, http://www.bethsaulnier.com/ (April 5, 2004), biography of Beth Saulnier.

MurderExpress, http://www.murderexpress.net/ (April 5, 2004), biography of Beth Saulnier.

Time Warner Bookmark, http://www.twbookmark.com/ (February 8, 2001), transcript of online chat with Beth Saulnier.*

*   *   *

SEDARIS, Amy 1961-

PERSONAL: Born March 29, 1961, in New York, NY; daughter of Lou (an employee at IBM) and Sharon (a homemaker; maiden name, Leonard) Sedaris.

ADDRESSES: Home—New York, NY. *Agent*—c/o Author Mail, Hyperion Books, 77 West Sixty-sixth St., Eleventh Floor, New York, NY 10023.

CAREER: Writer, playwright, and actress. Worked as a waitress, 1990s. Actress in films, including *Commandments,* 1997, *Bad Bosses Go to Hell,* 1997, *Six Days, Seven Nights,* 1998, *Jump Tomorrow,* 2001, *Maid in Manhattan,* 2002, and *My Baby's Daddy,* 2004; in television series, including *Just Shoot Me,* 2001, *Sex*

and the City, 2002-03, *Monk,* 2002-03, *Ed,* 2004, *Cracking Up,* 2004, and *Law and Order: Special Victims Unit,* 2004; and as a guest on television shows, including *Late Show with David Letterman,* 2001-04, and *Late Night with Conan O'Brien,* 2003. Appeared in *The Most Fabulous Story Ever Told,* by Paul Rudnick, produced in New York, NY, 1998, Douglas Carter Beane's *The Country Club,* produced 1999, and *Wonder of the World,* by David Lindsay-Abaire, produced 2001.

AWARDS, HONORS: Obie Award special citation (with David Sedaris), for *One Woman Shoe;* Drama Desk Award nomination, best featured actress, for *The Country Club.*

WRITINGS:

PLAYS; WITH BROTHER, DAVID SEDARIS; AND ACTRESS

Stitches, produced in New York, NY, 1994.

One Woman Shoe, produced in New York, NY, 1995.

Incident at Cobbler's Knob, produced in New York, NY, 1997.

The Book of Liz (produced in New York, NY, 2001), Dramatists Play Service (New York, NY), 2002.

Other plays include *The Little Frieda Mysteries,* produced 1999, *Jamboree,* and *Stump the Host.*

OTHER

(Cocreator and actress) *Exit 57* (television series), Comedy Central, 1995-97.

(With Paul Dinello and Stephen Colbert; and actress) *Strangers with Candy* (television series), Comedy Central, 1999-2000.

(With Paul Dinello and Stephen Colbert) *Wigfield: The Can-Do Town That Just May Not* (novel), photographs by Todd Oldham, Hyperion (New York, NY), 2003.

Reader of audio versions of work by brother, David Sedaris, including *Naked,* 1997, and *Barrel Fever and Other Stories,* 1998, both Time Warner AudioBooks (New York, NY).

ADAPTATIONS: Strangers with Candy went into production as a film by Silverstar Productions, 2003; *Wigfield: The Can-Do Town That Just May Not* was adapted for audio, HighBridge (Minneapolis, MN), 2003.

WORK IN PROGRESS: Writing a film version of *Strangers with Candy* with Paul Dinello and Stephen Colbert for Silverstar Productions.

SIDELIGHTS: Amy Sedaris is a multitalented writer and actress who has written a number of plays—all of which she has performed in—with her brother, David. They bill themselves as the Talent Family. She is well known to Comedy Central viewers, particularly for the series *Strangers with Candy,* which she cowrote and in which she played the main character.

Sedaris was born in New York City and raised in North Carolina with two brothers and three sisters, and the family wrote their own plays and performed them. Sedaris had an active imagination and was always on stage, performing, as though for an audience, while doing routine tasks like cooking. She did well in school and worked odd jobs after graduation, including at a Winn-Dixie grocery store, and in restaurants. She eventually acted on David's advice and moved to Chicago, Illinois, and in the early 1990s, Sedaris joined Second City, the comedy troupe that produced such outstanding comics as Dan Aykroyd, Gilda Radner, Bill Murray, and Jim Belushi. She dated fellow cast member Paul Dinello for eight years, and with him and Stephen Colbert, she created her early characters and skits.

In 1993 Sedaris and her brother began working together in New York City. They produced a number of plays, including their first, *Stitches,* in which Sedaris played an attractive high school girl who is involved in a boating accident, but goes on to become a television star, in spite of her disfigured face. This play and the next, *One Woman Shoe,* opened at the La MaMa Experimental Theater Club. *Back Stage* contributor David Sheward reviewed *One Woman Shoe,* writing that "the simple premise skewers both government bureaucracy and pretentious performance art." A group of women on welfare are required to put on shows in order to collect their benefits. Sedaris played both Barbara Sheriden, a fifty-eight-year-old former golf pro who has gone on welfare on a lark, as well as

a biker chick in her twenties. Sheward noted that Sedaris and her brother "take dozens of pop references . . . put them in a blender, and pour us a frothy and sharp commentary on our short-attention-span culture."

Incident at Cobbler's Knob is about a community of animals whose lives are interrupted by a coven of witches that move into their woods. Sedaris played the parts of a witch and a raunchy, smelly donkey. Other animals include a lonely worm, a squirrel who spouts family values, and a beaver who advocates gay rights. *Nation* reviewer Laurie Stone wrote that "the only creatures who survive are free of pretension and the impulse to coerce, like old witch Patty from Shatwell, who has a hefty appetite for killing but posts no platforms for how others should live. The sweet, yearning Worm squiggles through admitting it's his nature to scavenge in decay, and the Donkey, whose flanks are caked with dried feces, observes, matter-of-factly, that everyone's face has some kind of s——on it. That's the play's moral—cleanliness is a myth—and the Sedarises can't imagine why anyone would even want to avoid the warm goo of existence."

In *The Little Frieda Mysteries,* Sedaris played Aunt Frieda, a woman who collects dollhouse furniture on Long Island and takes on the care of her namesake niece, who is recuperating from a gymnastics accident. *Back Stage*'s Robert Simonson called Sedaris's performances "fearless. There is apparently no role so ugly, so unflattering, that she won't embrace it: She courts embarrassment. And she has an unfailing knack for playing middle-aged, middle-class busybodies like Aunt Frieda."

The central character of *The Book of Liz* is Sister Elizabeth Donderstock (Sedaris), who supports her Amish-type community with the sale of her cheese balls. When the group's leader, Reverend Tollhouse, hands her operation over to Brother Brightbee, Liz departs for the outside world, of which she knows almost nothing, and where she becomes friends with a Ukrainian immigrant with a Cockney accent who earns his living impersonating the Planter's peanut charcter. Sedaris sold her own cheese balls and cupcakes in the lobby during intermission. Her creations have been a sideline business for years. Sedaris has also appeared in plays written by others, including *The Most Fabulous Story Ever Told,* a satire about the Bible, and *The Country Club,* in which she played a suburban socialite named Froggy.

Sedaris began writing for Comedy Central, first with *Exit 57,* and then with *Strangers with Candy,* which she wrote with Dinello and in which she addresses her character's problems in an "After School Special" kind of way. Sedaris played Jerri Blank, a former addict and prostitute who returns to high school at age forty-six. *Salon.com*'s Rex Doane said that the show "tipped the scales with a warped wit rarely encountered on the small screen." It was a cult hit but lasted only three seasons when the management in charge of programming changed.

Sedaris had roles in a number of films and television series, including *Just Shoot Me* and *Sex and the City.* With Dinello and Colbert, she wrote *Wigfield: The Can-Do Town That Just May Not,* the photographs for which are provided by designer Todd Oldham. The story finds hack journalist Russell Hokes checking out an assigned story, the payment for which he has already spent. The town of Wigfield is his subject, threatened with extinction if the federal government destroys a nearby dam, and he hopes to capture its small-town essence through interviews with its residents, who, in fact, would like to profit from the government's action. *Book* reviewer Steve Wilson commented that "complete with outrageous photographs of derelict townies, this book is smart and often hysterical." A *Publishers Weekly* contributor wrote that the story "is one of those rare works of satire that combine creative form, uproariously funny text, and a painfully sharp underpinning of social criticism."

BIOGRAPHICAL AND CRITICAL SOURCES:

PERIODICALS

Back Stage, June 23, 1995, David Sheward, review of *One Woman Shoe,* p. 29; February 28, 1997, Robert Simonson, review of *The Little Frieda Mysteries,* p. 60; July 18, 1997, Robert Simonson, review of *Incident at Cobbler's Knob,* p. 40.

Book, May-June, 2003, Steve Wilson, review of *Wigfield: The Can-Do Town That Just May Not,* p. 76.

Booklist, April 15, 2003, Carol Haggas, review of *Wigfield,* p. 1451.

Entertainment Weekly, April 13, 2001, Melissa Rose Bernardo, review of *The Book of Liz,* p. 67.

Hollywood Reporter, June 6, 2003, Chris Gardner, "'Strangers' Principals Prep Movie," p. 1.

Nation, September 8, 1997, Laurie Stone, review of *Incident at Cobbler's Knob,* p. 32.

New York, June 12, 1995, Chris Smith, "The Lighter Side of Welfare: Amy Sedaris on Dependency, Performance Art, and Not-So-Old Ladies Who Live in a Shoe," p. 52; July 28, 1997, John Simon, review of *Incident at Cobbler's Knob,* p. 46; April 16, 2001, John Simon, review of *The Book of Liz,* p. 72.

New Yorker, April 9, 2001, John Lahr, review of *The Book of Liz,* p. 128.

Publishers Weekly, April 28, 2003, review of *Wigfield,* p. 46.

Rolling Stone, May 13, 1999, David Wild, review of *Strangers with Candy,* p. 101.

US Weekly, June 26, 2000, Tom Conroy, review of *Strangers with Candy,* p. 45.

Variety, October 4, 1999, Charles Isherwood, review of *The Country Club,* p. 96; April 2, 2001, Isherwood, review of *The Book of Liz,* p. 30.

ONLINE

Salon.com, http://www.salon.com/ (May 5, 2000), Rex Doane, "Amy Sedaris Digs Wigs and Baking" (interview).*

* * *

SELBY, Hubert, Jr. 1928-2004

OBITUARY NOTICE—See index for *CA* sketch: Born July 23, 1928, in New York, NY; died of chronic obstructive pulmonary disease, April 26, 2004, in Highland Park, CA. Educator and author. Selby, whose books were sometimes compared to those by such authors as Henry Miller and William S. Burroughs, was known for dark, controversial novels such as *Last Exit to Brooklyn.* Growing up in Brooklyn, he quit school when he was fifteen to work on the waterfront, and in 1944 he joined the Merchant Marine. When he contracted tuberculosis at eighteen, he spent the next several years in hospitals, having a lung and several ribs removed in the process. Illness plagued him throughout the rest of his life, including one asthma attack that almost killed him; drug and alcohol addictions also plagued him all his life. But these health problems only made Selby more determined to defy his doctors' grim prognoses and do something with his life. So he set out to write his first novel, and after six years of labor completed *Last Exit to Brooklyn* (1964), which was later adapted as a 1988 film. The story was so full of violence, illicit sex, and foul language, that censors often tried to ban it. His subsequent publishing struggles meant that many of Selby's later writings were often released by small presses; nevertheless, critics consistently praised his work as valuable literary contributions. Among these are *The Room* (1971), *Requiem for a Dream* (1979), and *The Willow Tree* (1998), as well as the short story collection *Song of the Silent Snow* (1986). To pay the bills, Selby taught writing at the University of Southern California for about twenty years as an adjunct professor, and he was known as a dedicated teacher, even in his final months when illness forced him to bring an oxygen tank to class. Also the author of screenplays, including *Day and Night* (1986), *Remember the Sabbath Day* (1974), *Love You Buddy Week* (1978), and *Fear the X* (2000), he adapted *Requiem for a Dream* as a 1998 screenplay. Selby's last book, published in 2002, was *Waiting Period.*

OBITUARIES AND OTHER SOURCES:

BOOKS

Contemporary Novelists, seventh edition, St. James (Detroit, MI), 2001.

PERIODICALS

Chicago Tribune, April 29, 2004, Section 3, p. 9.
Los Angeles Times, April 28, 2004, p. B12.
New York Times, April 27, 2004, p. C21.
Times (London, England), April 28, 2004, p. 26.
Washington Post, April 28, 2004, p. B6.

*   *   *

SENNETT, Frank (Ronald, Jr.) 1968-

PERSONAL: Born February 16, 1968, in Missoula, MT; son of Frank Ronald Sennett and Leslie Denise (Crowe) McClintock. *Education:* Northwestern University, B.S. (journalism), 1990; attended the University of Montana.

ADDRESSES: Office—324 West Sussex, Missoula, MT 59801. *Agent*—c/o Author Mail, Corwin Press, 2455 Teller Rd., Thousand Oaks, CA 91320. *E-mail*—frank@franksennett.com.

CAREER: Writer. Chicago Convention and Tourism Bureau, public relations consultant, 1988—; *Relax,* assistant editor and columnist, 1990-91; former editor of *Slipup.com, Newcity,* Chicago, IL, *NewCity.com,* and *Curriculum Review;* KPBX public radio, Spokane, WA, host of *The Alternative Source,* 2001—; University of California—Los Angeles Extension, Los Angeles, CA, humor writing instructor.

WRITINGS:

It Takes Two: Wise Words and Quotable Quips on the Attraction of Opposites, Contemporary Books (Chicago, IL), 2003.
Teacher of the Year: More than 400 Quotes of Insight, Inspiration, and Motivation from America's Greatest Teachers, Contemporary Books (Chicago, IL), 2003.
Nash, Rambler (novel), Five Star (Waterville, ME), 2003.
(Editor) *400 Quotable Quotes from the World's Leading Educators,* Corwin Press (Thousand Oaks, CA), 2004.
101 Stunts for Principals to Inspire Student Achievement, Corwin Press (Thousand Oaks, CA), 2004.
Nash, Metropolitan (novel; sequel to *Nash, Rambler*), Five Star (Waterville, ME), 2004.

Contributor to periodicals, including *Woman's World* and *Tradeshow Week.*

SIDELIGHTS: Frank Sennett has written and/or edited a number of volumes that collect quotes, as well as an ongoing series starring Nash Hansen, a Chicago student of journalism who interns at the *San Bernardino Ledger.* In the first installment, *Nash, Rambler,* Nash heads west, where he meets a Denny's waitress named Wendy and stumbles upon his first story. While they are at a drive-in movie in southern California, a bear trap set near the concession stand ensnares the foot of a teen patron, and Nash is soon drawn into a huge story of murder and corruption. Though he is fired by his editor, Nash investigates on his own, convinced that Evan Carr, a local businessman who renovates drive-ins and is connected to a group of right-wing survivalists, is somehow involved. Nash is aided in his investigation by Homer, a biker he picked up at the Evanston on-ramp and who made the trip to California with Nash.

Booklist reviewer John Green wrote that "witty dialogue and excellent pacing make for fun reading" and described Nash as "a protagonist readers will hope to see again." In the sequel, *Nash, Metropolitan,* Nash is back in Chicago, working for a newspaper and investigating the death of a homeless man. As the story unfolds, he becomes involved with the KGB (the Soviet secret police) and crooked politics.

Among Sennett's other publications is *101 Stunts for Principals to Inspire Student Achievement,* targeted at principals in kindergarten to grade eight settings.

BIOGRAPHICAL AND CRITICAL SOURCES:

PERIODICALS

Booklist, February 1, 2003, John Green, review of *Nash, Rambler,* p. 976.
Editor and Publisher, June 19, 2000, Greg Mitchell, "To Air Is Human," review of *Slipup.com,* p. 100.

ONLINE

Frank Sennett Home Page, http://www.franksennett. com (June 11, 2004).*

*   *   *

SHAY, Kathryn

PERSONAL: Female. Married; children: two. *Education:* Earned B.A. (English), and M.S. (education).

ADDRESSES: Home—New York. *Agent*—c/o Author Mail, Berkley Books, Penguin Putnam, 375 Hudson St., New York, NY 10014. *E-mail*—kshayweb@ rochester.rr.com.

CAREER: Writer. Teacher in New York, retired 2004.

AWARDS, HONORS: Five *RT Book Club* Reviewers Choice Awards, three Holt Medallions, two Desert Quill Awards, and a Gold Leaf Award.

WRITINGS:

"BAYVIEW HEIGHTS" SERIES

Cop of the Year, Harlequin (New York, NY), 1998.
Because It's Christmas, Harlequin (New York, NY), 1998.
Count on Me, Harlequin (New York, NY), 2001.

"AMERICA'S BRAVEST" SERIES

Feel the Heat, Harlequin (New York, NY), 1999.
The Man Who Loved Christmas, Harlequin (New York, NY), 1999.
Code of Honor, Harlequin (New York, NY), 2000.
The Fire Within, Harlequin (New York, NY), 2001.

"SERENITY HOUSE" TRILOGY SERIES

Practice Makes Perfect, Harlequin (New York, NY), 2002.
A Place to Belong, Harlequin (New York, NY), 2002.
Against the Odds, Harlequin (New York, NY), 2003.

OTHER

The Father Factor, Harlequin (New York, NY), 1995.
A Suitable Bodyguard, Harlequin (New York, NY), 1996.
Michael's Family, Harlequin (New York, NY), 1997.
Just One Night, Harlequin (New York, NY), 1997.
Finally a Family, Harlequin (New York, NY), 2000.
A Christmas Legacy ("Riverbend" series), Harlequin (New York, NY), 2000.
Caught Off Guard (novella; and online), Harlequin (New York, NY), 2002.
Promises to Keep, Berkley Books (New York, NY), 2002.
Trust in Me, Berkley Books (New York, NY), 2003.

Opposites Attract (novella; and online at www.eHarlequin.com), Harlequin (New York, NY), 2003.
After the Fire, Berkley Books (New York, NY), 2003.
The Unknown Twin, Harlequin (New York, NY), 2004.
On the Line, Berkley Books (New York, NY), 2004.

Contributor to *The Lipstick Chronicles: Book One* (anthology), Berkley Books (New York, NY), 2003, and *More Lipstick Chronicles: Book Two* (anthology), Berkley Books (New York, NY), 2003.

SIDELIGHTS: Kathryn Shay began her second career, as a writer, just ten years before retiring as a teacher in the New York state school system. Many of Shay's books are written as part of romance novel series, including one of her first, *Cop of the Year,* from her "Bayview Heights" series. In the novel Cassie Smith is a high school teacher of at-risk students in a small Long Island town, one of whom is picked up on suspicion of theft. The arresting officer, Mitch Lansing, becomes a volunteer in Cassie's classroom, but Cassie is uncomfortable with his presence because she experienced a difficult period during her own teen years. Mitch, a Vietnam veteran, has his own issues and does his job of showing the police as being kid-friendly, while not allowing himself to get close to any of them. A romance evolves, and *Romance Reader* reviewer Cathy Sova commented that although it is "satisfying, it's the secondary characters of the kids I remember most. . . . The teenage pregnancies, the gang involvement, the drug usage; all are a part of today's high school scene, but Shay makes this a story of hope, not despair."

The third story in the "Bayview Heights" series, *Count on Me,* is also about a caring woman, Zoe Caufield, who works with troubled teens. Kurt Lansing, a doctor who has returned to the town to set up a medical clinic for young people, is a kind man who is torn between his love for Zoe and his loyalty to his wife. Kurt's past behavior toward Zoe prevents her from trusting him completely with the students who have volunteered at the clinic. *Romance Reader*'s Irene Williams found the teen characters to be "fascinating" and Zoe's friends equally so. "Their change of feelings through the book—from thinking Kurt is a worm to urging Zoe to forgive him—makes Kurt's redemption more believable."

Feel the Heat is the first book in Shay's "America's Bravest" series, set in fictional Rockford, New York, and loosely based on the Rochester, New York, fire department. Francey Cordaro is a thirty-year-old fire-fighter from a family of firefighters who suffers a broken arm while carrying a man from a burning building. Wealthy Alex Templeton goes to the hospital to thank his rescuer, expecting to find a male firefighter. Finding Francey, instead, Alex becomes entranced by her, but she at first wants nothing to do with him because she has dedicated her life to her work and because his status marks him as an outsider. Sova, in *Romance Reader,* wrote that "the characterizations of Alex and Francey could be fairly described as exquisite. . . . Francey is that girlfriend of yours whose smarts and fierce independence have caused her to turn her back on the whole dating scene. Alex is perfect as the guy who's weary of the pointless women who see him as a good catch but know nothing of the man underneath the suit."

In the sequel to *Feel the Heat, The Man Who Loved Christmas,* Francey's wedding brings together her fire-fighter friend Dylan O'Rourke and emergency medical techniques instructor Beth Winters, who are included in the wedding party. Beth had instructed Dylan when he was a recruit, and she has never approved of what she considers his foolhardy approach to firefighting. He considers her aloof and abrasive, but he does not know about her past and how this impacts her feelings. Sue Klock, in *Romance Reader,* pointed out that "Shay's years of teaching illuminate *The Man Who Loved Christmas.* Her research into the world of professional firefighters shows clearly. The outstanding feature of this book is the insight gained into the heads and hearts of recruits in a grueling training program for firefighters."

The firefighting theme continues in the third and fourth books of the series—*Code of Honor* and *The Fire Within*—both of which were reviewed by *Romance Reader*'s Jean Mason. Mason called Shay "an immensely talented author who has succeeded in recreating the world of urban firefighters with impressive fidelity."

Another series is named for the group home for girls that provides the setting for the stories. In the first of the "Serenity House" trilogy series, *Practice Makes Perfect,* Paige Kendrick is a pediatrician who was one of the first residents of Serenity House and who gave up her baby for adoption. Ian Chandler is a doctor who has also experienced loss, and these two lonely people meet when he asks her to work at the inner city obstetrics and gynecology clinic he is establishing. Wendy Crutcher reviewed the novel for *Romance Reader,* writing that Shay "has literally created a whole town, full of interesting townspeople itching to have their own stories further explored. . . . The author has a real talent for writing about younger women from troubled circumstances, without succumbing to cliché."

Among Shay's stand-alone stories is *Finally a Family,* about a search-and-rescue helicopter unit. In *A Christmas Legacy*—a romance Shay wrote as part of the "Riverbend" series—a former resident of Riverbend returns to claim his inheritance and falls for Kate, the single mother of twin girls. In reviewing *A Christmas Legacy, Romance Reader* contributor Sova stated that "it takes a talented author to turn an arrogant jerk of a hero into someone not only likeable, but a man you'd root for."

In *Romance Reader,* Sova called Shay's first mainstream romantic suspense, *Promises to Keep,* "a gripping story that will haunt readers with its authenticity." The book offers two romances and a plot that pairs up high school principal Suzanna Quinn with Joe Stonehouse, who comes to the school as a counselor after a student's suicide, but who is, in reality, a Secret Service agent working undercover to investigate possible school shooters. His partner, twenty-six-year-old Luke, is a hothead who falls for his unsuspecting social studies teacher, and she for him, a romance that is complicated by the fact that he is passing for a nineteen-year-old senior. *Booklist* contributor Shelley Mosley wrote that "Shay does an admirable job with a difficult subject."

Trust in Me is about a group of troubled teens in 1983 Glen Oaks, New York, who call themselves "The Outlaws." Fast-forward twenty years to find that the leader, Linc Grayson, is a minister, still in love with his atheist high school sweetheart, Margo. Beth, another member, had married Danny, who later died in a NASCAR accident, and Tucker Quaid, who may have been responsible for the tragedy and who has gone on to become a star on the circuit, is asked to help revitalize the town. Other characters and interweaving storylines flesh out this novel. Mosley, in *Booklist,* concluded that "this powerful tale of redemption, friendship, trust, and forgiving shows once again that Shay knows how to pack an emotional wallop."

Shay told *CA:* "I was always a writer. In high school and college, I had planned to make it my career, but then I did my student teaching and fell in love with education. Still, I wrote during all those years. At forty, I decided to try my hand at writing a book. I love to read romance, so I chose that genre. Though it's been tough balancing two careers, this path has worked for me.

"Early on, my work was influenced greatly by Judith Guest, Judith McNaught, and LaVryl Spencer. They remain among my favorite authors.

"My writing process? Well, since I've had a full-time teaching job for my entire career as a writer, that's difficult to say. I would catch an hour, or even twenty minutes, where ever I could (including at swim meets, riding in the car, and during lunch hours) and do a scene. I used to outline everything, but now, even if I do, the characters seem to take over, and I veer greatly from the notes. Usually, I come up with an idea, then write a summary for the contract, then flesh it out scene by scene. Again, the book rarely stays true to the summary."

Reflecting on the most surprising thing that she has learned as a writer, Shay said, "That I don't often know what's going to happen next in a book. I'll be plugging along and all of a sudden, a character will do something unexpected, and I'll rant and rave about it. But I've learned to allow it to happen, because then the story is fresh, unpredictable, and more fun to read. It's scary, though, not knowing where you're going."

Shay concluded to *CA,* "Primarily, I hope my books entertain readers. Second, I hope they learn about the nature of men and women and kids, learn about how most people deserve second chances, and learn that life is not black and white."

BIOGRAPHICAL AND CRITICAL SOURCES:

PERIODICALS

Booklist, August, 2002, Shelley Mosley, review of *Promises to Keep,* p. 1935; February 1, 2003, Shelley Mosley, review of *Trust in Me,* p. 978; October 15, 2003, Shelley Mosley, review of *After the Fire,* p. 397.

ONLINE

Kathryn Shay Home Page, http://www.kathrynshay. com (June 12, 2004).

Romance Reader, http://www.theromancereader.com/ (January 24, 1998), Cathy Sova, review of *Cop of the Year;* (November 4, 1999), Cathy Sova, review of *Feel the Heat;* (December 6, 1999), Sue Klock, review of *The Man Who Loved Christmas;* (December 31, 1999), Jean Mason, review of *Code of Honor;* (April 21, 2000), Linda Mowery, review of *Finally a Family;* (December 10, 2000), Cathy Sova, review of *A Christmas Legacy;* (February 26, 2001), Irene Williams, review of *Count on Me;* (November 11, 2001), Jean Mason, review of *The Fire Within;* (June 28, 2002), Wendy Crutcher, review of *Practice Makes Perfect;* (July 27, 2002), Cathy Sova, review of *Promises to Keep;* (February 5, 2003), Jean Mason, review of *Trust in Me.*

*   *   *

SHEPHERD, Gordon
    See BROOK-SHEPHERD, (Frederick) Gordon

*   *   *

SIXEL, Friedrich W. 1934-

PERSONAL: Born July 1, 1934, in Wuppertal, Germany; married Margrit Meyer (a lecturer), May 17, 1958; children: Friederike Sixel-Döring, Caroline Sixel-Hueller, Katharina. *Education:* Attended University of Cologne, University of Marburg, and University of Bonn; earned D.Phil., 1963. *Religion:* Protestant. *Hobbies and other interests:* Sailing.

ADDRESSES: Home—4408 Bath Rd., Kingston, Ontario K7N 1A2, Canada. *E-mail*—fws@post.queensu. ca.

CAREER: University of Bonn, Bonn, West Germany (now Germany), research assistant in anthropology, 1963-69; Queen's University, Kingston, Ontario, Canada, associate professor of sociology, 1969-2000.

AWARDS, HONORS: Grants from Social Sciences and Humanities Research Council of Canada, 1975-76, 1985.

WRITINGS:

Crisis and Critique, E. J. Brill (Leiden, Netherlands), 1988.
Understanding Marx, University Press of America (Lanham, MD), 1995.
Nature in Our Culture, University Press of America (Lanham, MD), 2001.

Contributor to books. Contributor to sociology and anthropology journals.

WORK IN PROGRESS: Translating *Nature in Our Culture* into German, for Königshausen & Neumann; research on developments in German social structure and politics.

*   *   *

SMITH, Tim(othy R.) 1945-
    (Buck Wilder)

PERSONAL: Born 1945; children: three.

ADDRESSES: Agent—c/o Alexander & Smith Publishing, 4160 M 72 E., Williamsburg, MI 49690. *E-mail*—buck@buckwilder.com.

CAREER: Entrepreneur, speaker, and writer.

AWARDS, HONORS: Benjamin Franklin Award (sports/recreation category), Publishers Marketing Association, 1998, for *Buck Wilder's Small Twig Hiking and Camping Guide: The Complete Introduction to the World of Hiking and Camping for Small Twigs of All Ages.*

WRITINGS:

UNDER NAME BUCK WILDER

Buck Wilder's Small Fry Fishing Guide: A Complete Introduction to the World of Fishing for Small Fry of All Ages, illustrated by Mark Herrick, Alexander & Smith (Williamsburg, MI), 1995.

Buck Wilder's Small Twig Hiking and Camping Guide: The Complete Introduction to the World of Hiking and Camping for Small Twigs of All Ages, illustrated by Mark Herrick, Alexander & Smith (Traverse City, MI), 1997.

Buck Wilder's Little Skipper Boating Guide: A Complete Introduction to the World of Boating for Little Skippers of All Ages, illustrated by Thomas G. Mills, Alexander & Smith (Williamsburg, MI), 2001.

ADAPTATIONS: Smith's "Buck Wilder" character was incorporated into Michigan's Natural History Curriculum by the Michigan Department of Natural Resources, 1999-2003.

SIDELIGHTS: Tim Smith is the author behind the titles in the "Buck Wilder" series, which focuses on providing young readers with an introduction to a variety of natural resources and outdoor pursuits. Inspired by childhood camping and fishing trips he took with his uncle, Smith created the Buck Wilder character in order to help teach his audience how to enjoy the great outdoors in a safe and respectful way. *Buck Wilder's Small Fry Fishing Guide: A Complete Introduction to the World of Fishing for Small Fry of All Ages,* the first book in the series, covers the basics of the sport, including descriptions of lake fish and their habitat. In *Buck Wilder's Small Twig Hiking and Camping Guide: The Complete Introduction to the World of Hiking and Camping for Small Twigs of All Ages,* Smith includes regional overviews of different hiking and camping locations, a list of recommended gear, and information about the more practical aspects of camping, such as first aid and cooking. Kendal Rautzhan of the *Daily Item* praised Smith's "clear, concise text" and called the book "a sensational beginner's guide to the great outdoors."

Smith spends much of the school year speaking to elementary-aged children, giving presentations on his "Buck Wilder" outdoor guides. In his storytelling style, Smith is known to entertain as he educates his audience. During his presentations, he explains the value of hard work and persistence while also emphasizing to children the importance of imagination and creativity. Smith once commented: "Creating and publishing books was new for me. I made mistakes, kept on working at it even with major obstacles in my way, and did more than was expected to finish the

books." Smith also stresses the importance of believing in yourself and humorously shows kids how they can get creative.

BIOGRAPHICAL AND CRITICAL SOURCES:

PERIODICALS

Boating, December, 2001, review of *Buck Wilder's Little Skipper Boating Guide: A Complete Introduction to the World of Boating for Little Skippers of All Ages.*

Daily Item, August 13, 1997, Kendal Rautzhan, review of *Buck Wilder's Small Twig Hiking and Camping Guide: The Complete Introduction to the World of Hiking and Camping for Small Twigs of All Ages,* p. E3.

Detroit Free Press, June 28, 1995, Ellen Creager, review of *Buck Wilder's Small Fry Fishing Guide: A Complete Introduction to the World of Fishing for Small Fry of All Ages,* p. 3F; July 24, 2003, Janice Campbell, "Meet the Real Buck Wilder," p. 8F.

Detroit News, September 5, 1995, Fannie Weinstein, "A Prize Catch, Witty 'Buck Wilder' Fishing Guide Reels in Readers."

Family Life, March, 1999, review of *Buck Wilder's Small Twig Hiking and Camping Guide: The Complete Introduction to the World of Hiking and Camping for Small Twigs of All Ages,* p. 33.

ONLINE

Buck Wilder Adventures and Books, http://www.buckwilder.com (February 12, 2004).

*   *   *

SOBILOFF, Hy(man Jordan) 1912-1970

PERSONAL: Born December 16, 1912; died from a heart attack, August, 1970; son of Israel and Fannie Gollub Soboloff; married Adelaide Goldstein; children: Stephen. *Education:* Attended University of Arizona; Boston University, B.A.; attended New York University.

CAREER: Filmmaker, industrialist, philanthropist, and poet. Founder of Albert Einstein College of Medicine, New York, NY, Technion-Israel Institute of Technology, New York, NY, and Edward Adaskin Educational Foundation, Fall River, MA. Founder and trustee of the National Foundation for Research of Allergies. At the time of his death, he was chair of Larchfield Corporation in New York, NY, Marshall-Wells International in Nassau, Johnson Stores of Raleigh, NC, and Auto-Lec Stores of New Orleans, LA.

AWARDS, HONORS: Honorary chancellor, Florida Southern College, 1955; Doctor of Laws degree, Florida Southern College, 1956; Academy Award nomination, and First Boston International Film Festival citation for color photography, both for short film *Montauk.*

WRITINGS:

POETRY

When Children Played as Kings and Queens, privately printed, 1948.
Dinosaurs and Violins, foreword by Conrad Aiken, Farrar, Straws & Young (New York, NY), 1954.
In the Deepest Aquarium, introduction by Allen Tate, Dial (New York, NY), 1959.
Breathing of First Things, introduction by James Wright, Dial (New York, NY), 1963.
Hooting across the Silence, introduction by Edwin Honig, Horizon (New York, NY), 1971.

Also contributor to *Poetry* and numerous anthologies, including *The New Pocket Anthology of American Verse from Colonial Days to the Present,* edited by Oscar Williams, World (Cleveland, OH), 1955.

SHORT FILMS

Montauk, narrated by Ed Begley, Sobiloff, 1959.
Central Park, narrated by Jason Roberts, Jr., Sobiloff, 1960.
Speak to Me Child, narrated by David Wayne, Sobiloff, 1962.
Market to Market, Sobiloff, 1968.

SIDELIGHTS: According to Nicki Sahlin in the *Dictionary of Literary Biography,* "Despite Hy Sobiloff's demanding business career, and in spite of periods of great emotional uncertainty, the man had always been a poet. In the earliest poems, he had written well, and from a number of angles, about what it means to be a poet, and then he began to explore what it means to be a child. The last volume brings such themes to their fullest development, at a time when the poet's voice, refined but fresher than ever, was just getting around to addressing, for better or worse, exactly what it meant to be Hy Sobiloff."

Sahlin continued, "Sobiloff, whose poetry was respected by many of his better-known contemporaries for its fresh, honest, unpretentious qualities, was also widely known as a filmmaker, industrialist, and philanthropist. . . . [Hy] was constantly writing and associating with other poets. . . . Introductions to his books were written by highly regarded figures: Anatole Broyard, Conrad Aiken, Allen Tate, James Wright, and Edwin Honig. He contributed to *Poetry* and was represented in a number of anthologies, including Oscar Williams's *The New Pocket Anthology of American Verse from Colonial Days to the Present.*" "Among poets [Sobiloff] was a fellow poet, conscious of his limitations, humble about the status of his poetry, yet unafraid to make direct statements on occasion," contended Sahlin, specifying the recognition by Sobiloff's contemporaries of his "forthright behavior" and "the truthfulness of observation in [his] poetry." "While praising his work, both Aiken and Tate come close to representing the poet as a primitive, particularly by their use of words such as 'folk' or 'unaware,'" wrote Sahlin.

"If Sobiloff had not been a poet, his accomplishments as a businessman would have been impressive in themselves," asserted Sahlin, recognizing that "the ways in which he used the resources made available to him by his success in business suggest a great concern for others, a concern which becomes explicit in certain of his poems. . . . On a more personal level, Hy Sobiloff was known for his expansive gestures of good will, such as throwing large and lavish parties for friends on special occasions. His townhouse on 77th Street in New York City was visited by poets and other writers—including such members of the Beats as Jack Kerouac and Allen Ginsberg, celebrities from the film industry, and internationally known businessmen."

"Sobiloff's four highly successful short films illustrate his desire to enrich the lives of others through poetry," observed Sahlin, adding, "Commenting on these experimental films, Sobiloff expressed the conviction 'that an experiment should be made to develop poetry in three dimensions through the mass media of motion pictures and television. My aim was to add meanings to poetry by combining the visual and auditory appeal of film with the emotional appeal of words thereby bringing poetry to a wider audience.'" Sahlin commented on the films: "The first film, *Montauk* (1959) . . . concerns Montauk Point, Long Island, the setting for a number of Sobiloff's poems and the site of a house he owned. . . . [*Central Park* was] filmed in and around Central Park in New York City, it is closely related to Sobiloff's city poems and street vignettes. *Speak to Me Child* (1962) . . . presents some of the poet's most characteristic poems, those dealing with childhood and children. . . . *Market to Market* (1968) was filmed in the predawn hours at New York City's Washington Market shortly before it was demolished; the film now stands as a historical document."

Describing the poet and the focus of his work, Sahlin noted, "James Wright, in a lengthy introduction to *Breathing of First Things,* piece which does a great deal toward compensating for the lack of critical attention to Sobiloff's work, specifically denied that the poet is 'primitive' or 'anti-intellectual.' Instead, Wright argued convincingly, Sobiloff is exploring a central theme, 'the search for the child within the self,' which is more complex than it appears and which also manifests itself in 'the struggle to be true to one's own self.'" Sahlin maintained that "[i]t is not just the rediscovery of childhood innocence that Sobiloff undertook but also a quest that is both psychological and spiritual. Wright's valuable perceptions are based upon only one collection, Sobiloff's longest; yet they also apply to the entire body of his work."

Discussing Sobiloff's evolution as a poet, Sahlin stated, "Wright's observations on the quest motif suggest the possibility of viewing each new volume of poetry as one phase of a cycle, a cycle which perhaps ends in joy, which as Edwin Honig points out in his introduction to *Hooting across the Silence* (1971), is the most recurrent word in Sobiloff's poetry. The tone of each volume is refined and developed by a process of careful selection, rearrangement, minor revisions, and, frequently, a renewal of earlier poems by their placement in a fresh context."

In *When Children Played as Kings and Queens,* Sobiloff's first poetry collection, "there are poems which might be termed metaphysical, yet they do not stand out as such in context of that volume," identified Sahlin, judging, "There is a random quality to the volume, a lack of direction which Sobiloff seemed eager to correct, since he often asked fellow poets for advice on revision, urging them to be as harsh as the poems warranted and not to spare his feelings. . . . Early on Sobiloff was well aware of the complex nature of an outwardly playful poem. The technique that made the expression of such awareness possible still needed development, however, and some of the earliest poems possess an air of sophistication at odds with the poets relatively immature poetic technique."

"*Dinosaurs and Violins,* the first volume to be published commercially, draws heavily on the previous collection but is dominated by poems of personal experience, making the concern with personal identity clearer," assessed Sahlin, who noted a particular segment of one poem: "Sobiloff refers to other poets infrequently, so it is significant that here he invokes Walt Whitman, a poet to whom he would later be compared, most extensively by James Wright." Remarking on a different poetic segment in *Dinosaurs and Violins,* Sahlin generalized: "The appearance of outright naiveté, even confusion, combined with a complex concept, in this case the poet's proper attitude, is representative of a large proportion of Sobiloff's poetry. From this volume, however, no clear pattern emerges. There are some lively city poems, a few descriptive nature poems, and some poems about the poet's own past. . . . Several poems form a sort of psychological series. . . . As Sobiloff's poetry continued to develop, he apparently abandoned the explicitly psychological exploration in favor of poems that were directed at the simpler level of childlike perception."

"A delightful experience awaits the reader of *Dinosaurs and Violins*" lauded a *Saturday Review* critic. "Endings are sometimes a problem for Mr. Sobiloff for his special forte is the clearly outlined object of attention. At times, too, the tone is that flat melancholy, one so familiar in many younger poets, a desolate little chant," determined a reviewer for *US Quarterly Book Review,* continuing, "Often the speaking personality tends to be submerged in the pictures, and the verse line is unsure of its key. Yet there is strong promise here, for the vision is fresh, the strong feeling behind it urgent and there is no soft padding for its own sake." "The poems in *Dinosaurs and Violins* have great clarity," declared Sahlin, "but it is a clarity of the moment, of the object, or of the past, more than a clarity of poetic voice."

"Five years later, with the poems of *In the Deepest Aquarium,* there is the sense of the poet's artistic concerns being worked out in a deeper, more consistent way than before," contended Sahlin. "Here is the modern scene interpreted by an especially receptive mind," praised B. A. Ribie in a *Library Journal* review of *In the Deepest Aquarium.* In *New York Herald Tribune Book Review,* John Holmes complimented Sobiloff's perspective: "Sobiloff looks at what he looks at, as if it had never been seen before, and reports it that way. The poems are the reports of an eye and mind that size the object and tighten on it with words." Less positive were Kimon Friar's judgments of the collection, as presented in *Saturday Review:* "Sobiloff's poems are monolithic, his lines lack cadence, there is no melodic progression within a single stanza or between stanzas. Instead, we have staccato and precise descriptions of objects, but with little of the poetic realism of a William Carlos Williams or of the subtlety of Wallace Stevens."

Sahlin proposed: "Though Sobiloff was developing his own poetic voice through his first several volumes, there is no doubt that in his fourth volume, *Breathing of First Things,* he combined a fully developed voice with a sense of purpose stronger than ever before. The book is divided into four sections: 'Speak to Me Child,' 'Oddballs,' 'Love Poems,' and 'Nature Poems.' The first section informs the entire volume, its many perspectives on the natural wisdom of the child in turn expanding the sense of newness and freshness in the sections that follow. . . . Sobiloff does not disguise his poetic goal in associating with children." "[Sobiloff] may have found the child, but," judged Judson Jerome in *Saturday Review,* "he has not found the cadence of the shaggy master, the verve and explosion of his rhetoric, the vividness of his imagery, and the scope of his vision." "I would like very much to know what Sobiloff's roster of eminent admirers [Allen Tate, Conrad Aiken, Oscar Williams, and James Wright] find in his work that I miss," announced Jerome. John Woods, writing in *Poetry,* presented a more positive assessment of *Breathing of First Things:* "Although Mr. Sobiloff wishes to see as a child, he usually avoids one of the sentimental traps: he doesn't try an inspired baby talk. . . . This is suspended poetry. . . . The effect of such suspension is that it gives each line equal

weight, equal attention, although also, at times, a spurious excitement. But if Sobiloff has for the most part avoided one trap of sentimentalism, there is another he has not completely avoided. . . . [The child] can be seen as father of the worst of man as well as of the best."

According to Sahlin, "*Breathing of First Things* gained part of its strength from the grouping of the poems into categories, but in *Hooting across the Silence* his last volume, Sobiloff's new, stronger voice is evident without such grouping and labeling. There are more than a dozen animal poems, and a few explicitly about poetry. Most notably, there are poems about personal emotion which surpass any in previous volumes in terms of their directness of language and imagery."

BIOGRAPHICAL AND CRITICAL SOURCES:

BOOKS

Dictionary of Literary Biography, Volume 48: *American Poets 1880-1945,* Second Series, Gale (Detroit), 1986.

PERIODICALS

Library Journal, October 1, 1959; April 15, 1964.
New York Herald Tribune Book Review, July 3, 1960.
Poetry, August, 1955; May, 1964.
Saturday Review, March 12, 1955; February 6, 1960, July 6, 1963.
US Quarterly Book Review, June, 1955.*

*   *   *

SODEN, Dale E. 1951-

PERSONAL: Born May 4, 1951, in Spokane, WA; son of Dale A. (in sales) and Margaret (Priestley) Soden; married Margaret Kringen, December 29, 1974; children: Joel, Marta. *Ethnicity:* "White." *Education:* Pacific Lutheran University, B.A., 1973; University of Washington (Seattle, WA), M.A., 1976, Ph.D., 1980. *Religion:* Lutheran.

ADDRESSES: Home—1012 West 28th Ave., Spokane, WA 99203. *Office*—Department of History, Whitworth College, Spokane, WA 99251. *E-mail*—dsoden@whitworth.edu.

CAREER: Oklahoma Baptist University, Shawnee, OK, assistant professor of history, 1980-85; Whitworth College, Spokane, WA, began as associate professor, became professor of history, 1985—. Pacific Lutheran Theological Seminary, member of board of directors; Young Men's Christian Association, member of board of directors.

WRITINGS:

The Reverend Mark Matthews: An Activist in the Progressive Era, University of Washington Press (Seattle, WA), 2001.

Also author of *A Venture of Mind and Spirit: An Illustrated History of Whitworth College,* 1990.

BIOGRAPHICAL AND CRITICAL SOURCES:

PERIODICALS

Journal of Southern History, August, 2002, Jack P. Maddex, Jr., review of *The Reverend Mark Matthews: An Activist in the Progressive Era,* p. 734.
Oregon Historical Quarterly, winter, 2001, Philip D. Jordan, review of *The Reverend Mark Matthews,* p. 529.

*　　*　　*

SODEN, Garrett

PERSONAL: Born in California; married Kate Shein (a writer/performer).

ADDRESSES: Home—Pasadena, CA. *Agent*—c/o Author Mail, Norton, 500 Fifth Ave., New York, NY 10110-0017. *E-mail*—Garrett@GarrettSoden.com.

CAREER: Writer and graphic designer. Occidental College, Los Angeles, CA, graphic designer; works as corporate communications executive.

WRITINGS:

The One-Minute Maniac, Andrews, McMeel & Parker (Kansas City, MO), 1987.
I Went to College for This?: True Stuff about Life in the Business World—And How to Make Your Way through It, Peterson's (Princeton, NJ), 1994.
Looking Good on Paper: How to Create Eye-Catching Reports, Proposals, Memos, and Other Business Documents, American Management Association (New York, NY), 1995.
Hook Spin Buzz: How to Command Attention, Change Minds, and Influence People, Peterson's/Pacesetter Books (Princeton, NJ), 1996.
Falling: How Our Greatest Fear Became Our Greatest Thrill: A History, Norton (New York, NY), 2003.

SIDELIGHTS: Before becoming an author, Garrett Soden was a lead guitarist and songwriter for the California-based band Central. After leaving Central, Soden, a college dropout, launched a career in communications as a writer and graphic designer. However, his youthful career as a musician was not totally behind him: Soden's experiences with Central prompted his first book, *The One-Minute Maniac.* Published in 1987, *The One-Minute Maniac* was successful enough to inspire its author to tackle more writing projects, and *I Went to College for This?: True Stuff about Life in the Business World—And How to Make Your Way through It* and *Hook Spin Buzz: How to Command Attention, Change Minds, and Influence People* are among the results.

I Went to College for This? presents a humorous glimpse of the office-cubicle lifestyle and its target audience in recent college graduates who are contemplating a corporate career. Soden discusses the constant power struggles of corporate life and encourages readers to think hard about the costs of independence. *Hook Spin Buzz* presents Soden's three-pronged approach to becoming a more powerful communicator, the "hook" being the ability to attract an audience, the "spin," being presenting your idea, and the "buzz" being inspiring listeners to action. While all three together might not always be required, Soden argues that thinking in terms of these steps assures successful communications in business and elsewhere. While a *Publishers Weekly* reviewer felt that "more developed examples of both effective and less successful conversations would have made this practical guide even more useful," the critic praised *Hook Spin Buzz* as a book that "should help readers who struggle with effective office presentations."

In *Falling: How Our Greatest Fear Became Our Greatest Thrill—A History*, Soden explores the human fascination and phobia of falling as it has become an element in popular sports. Tracing the human fascination with scaling heights back through time, Soden acquaints readers with individuals who have made falling-related activities either their hobby or career. Particularly with the technological advances of the late twentieth century, sports involving heights have increased in popularity, as Soden can himself attest. He admits his own fascination with individuals who engage in death-defying sports or activities in total disregard for any potential financial gain, such as Sam Patch, who jumped from immense heights into water, and the athletes who engage in surfing, skateboarding, and parachute jumping. In preparing to write the book, Soden spent nearly a decade researching his topic: he attended the X-Games, visited science libraries, and conducted numerous interviews with individuals such as extreme sports stars Mat Hoffman and Andy Macdonald, stuntwomen Nancy Thurston and Jeannie Epper, and rock climber Mike Pont. Jonathan Yardley, reviewing *Falling* for the *Washington Post*, called Soden's book a "provocative, well-researched" read, while a contributor to *Kirkus Reviews* added that Soden successfully "takes readers into the strange world of the thrill gene and the chemistry of the urge."

BIOGRAPHICAL AND CRITICAL SOURCES:

PERIODICALS

Kirkus Reviews, April 15, 2003, review of *Falling: How Our Greatest Fear Became Our Greatest Thrill—A History*, p. 596.
Publishers Weekly, August 14, 1995, review of *Hook Spin Buzz: How to Command Attention, Change Minds, and Influence People*, p. 76.
Washington Post, June 19, 2003, Jonathan Yardley, review of *Falling*, p. C4.

ONLINE

Garrett Soden Web site, http://www.garrettsoden.com (May 15, 2004).*

SOLOMON, Nina 1961-

PERSONAL: Born September 8, 1961; children: Nathaniel. *Education:* Columbia University, M.A.

ADDRESSES: Home—Manhattan, NY. *Agent*—c/o Author Mail, Algonquin Books of Chapel Hill, P.O. Box 2225, Chapel Hill, NC 27515-2225. *E-mail*—dialogue@algonquin.com (put author's name in subject line).

CAREER: Writer.

WRITINGS:

Single Wife, Algonquin Books of Chapel Hill (Chapel Hill, NC), 2003.

SIDELIGHTS: Nina Solomon's debut novel, *Single Wife,* is one which *Library Journal* contributor Joanna M. Burkhardt claimed "captures the essence of the struggle for self." Manhattanite Grace Brookman is married to journalist Laz, who has disappeared in the past for short periods of time; but this time he does not come back for months. As his absence lengthens, Grace leads his life for him rather than admit to his absence. For the benefit of the housekeeper, she leaves the toilet seat up and rumples the sheets on Laz's side of the bed. She continues his ritual of leaving coffee for the doorman and plays his favorite music so that the neighbors can hear. Grace comes to realize that she had never been fully aware of Laz's life when friends mention that he has e-mailed them or when one says she saw him in a television interview. She continues her charade, however, fooling her parents and their friends as well, until the day Laz returns. By then, however, Grace has learned self-reliance, accepted her failed marriage for what it is, and returned to her own interests, which include sculpting.

A *Publishers Weekly* contributor wrote that the author "knows how to confound her readers' preconceptions even as she carries her captivating premise to a surprising denouement. Gripping and dreamy, this tale will please fans of Margaret Atwood and Alice Hoffman." *Rocky Mountain News* critic Justin Matott noted *Single Wife*'s "great examination of lives lived for others, fine character development, and lively, fresh writing." And a *Kirkus Reviews* writer concluded that *Single Wife* is "a strong debut" that is set apart by "its spirit of playful inventiveness."

BIOGRAPHICAL AND CRITICAL SOURCES:

PERIODICALS

Booklist, April 15, 2003, Joanne Wilkinson, review of *Single Wife,* p. 1451.
Kirkus Reviews, April 1, 2003, review of *Single Wife,* p. 504.
Library Journal, June 15, 2003, Joanna M. Burkhardt, review of *Single Wife,* p. 102.
Publishers Weekly, May 12, 2003, review of *Single Wife,* p. 42.
Rocky Mountain News, December 5, 2003, Justin Matott, review of *Single Wife,* p. D30.*

*   *   *

SPENCER, Stuart S. 1957-

PERSONAL: Born September 6, 1957, in Neenah, WI; son of Selden (in sales) and Geraldine (Kuehmsted) Spencer. *Ethnicity:* "Anglo/Scots/Alsatian." *Education:* Lawrence University, B.A., 1979. *Politics:* Independent. *Religion:* Episcopalian.

ADDRESSES: Agent—Ron Gwiazda, Rosenstone Wender, 38 East 29th St., 10th Floor, New York, NY 10016. *E-mail*—StuartSSpencer@aol.com.

CAREER: Sarah Lawrence College, Bronxville, NY, teacher of play writing, 1991—. Playwright; Ensemble Studio Theater, member.

MEMBER: Dramatists Guild.

WRITINGS:

(With Maureen McDuffee) "Arrayed for the Bridal" (one-act play), *Trifocal* (triple-bill), produced in New York, NY, at Samuel Beckett Theater, 1998.
Plays by Stuart Spencer, Broadway Play Publishing, 2000.
The Playwright's Guidebook, Faber & Faber, 2002.

Author of several other plays, including *Resident Alien.*

BIOGRAPHICAL AND CRITICAL SOURCES:

PERIODICALS

Back Stage, March 27, 1998, Jane Hogan, review of *Arrayed for the Bridal,* p. 39.
Library Journal, February 15, 2002, Lisa J. Cihlar, review of *The Playwright's Guidebook,* p. 156.

*   *   *

STALLMAN, Richard Matthew 1953-

PERSONAL: Born 1953, in New York, NY; son of Daniel (operator of a printing brokerage company) and Alice (a teacher; maiden name, Lippman) Stallman. *Ethnicity:* "Jewish." *Education:* Harvard University, B.A., 1974. *Politics:* "Liberal in the tradition of Franklin D. Roosevelt." *Religion:* "Scientific atheist and secular humanist."

ADDRESSES: Office—545 Tech Sq., Rm. 425, Cambridge, MA 02139. *E-mail*—rms@gnu.org.

CAREER: Computer scientist. Massachusetts Institute of Technology, Cambridge, MA, software developer, 1971-83; GNU Project, Boston, MA, founder, 1984—; Free Software Foundation, Boston, founder, president, 1985—.

AWARDS, HONORS: MacArthur Foundation fellowship, 1990; Grace Hopper Award, Association for Computing Machinery, 1991; Pioneer Award (with Linus Torvalds), Electronic Frontier Foundation, 1998; Yuri Rubinski Award, 1999; Takeda Award (with Linus Torvalds and Ken Sakamura), Takeda Foundation (Japan), 2001, for social/economic betterment; elected to the National Academy of Engineering, 2002. Honorary doctorates from the Royal Institute of Technology (Sweden), 1996, University of Glasgow (Scotland), 2001, and Vrij Universitet (Brussels, Belgium), 2003. Honorary professor, Universidad Naciobal de Ingeniería (Peru), 2003.

WRITINGS:

No Sir, No Monopoly!: Free Software: A Perspective, Prajasakti Book House (Hyderabad, India), 2002.
Free Software, Free Society: Selected Essays of Richard M. Stallman, edited by Joshua Gay, GNU Press (Boston, MA), 2002.

Author of software, including EMACS, 1975, GNU EMACS, 1984, GNU C Compiler, 1988, and software manuals. Author's works have been translated into Italian, and are due to be published in Spanish and Portuguese.

SIDELIGHTS: Richard Matthew Stallman is a revolutionary leader of the hacker movement, which promotes the unlimited freedom of information. Stallman maintains that once someone has a copy of a program, they should have the freedom to use them, improve them, and then share the results. By doing so, duplication of effort is avoided, freedom, community, and creativity is encouraged, and the most advanced programming is made available to everyone. Stallman is the creator of EMACS, the forerunner of modern word processing programs, and GNU ("GNU's Not Unix"), which, together with the kernel developed by Linus Torvalds, became GNU/Linux.

Stallman became hooked on programming when, at the age of twelve, he discovered a computer manual that belonged to a camp counselor. While he was in high school, Stallman wrote programs for IBM. He was a young undergraduate at Harvard University when he began working in the Artificial Intelligence (AI) lab of the Massachusetts Institute of Technology (MIT), studying by day and programming at night. The environment was open, the computer files unprotected, and the young hackers were loosely supervised by Marvin Minsky, known as the father of artificial intelligence. The AI lab developed its own computer, the LISP (List Processing) Machine, with its own operating system designed for AI applications. Then things began to change. Two separate groups left to set up companies, one called the Lisp Machine, Inc., and the other Symbolics. Both licensed the LISP Machine operating system from MIT and, according to their contracts, returned any improvements made. The industry benefited as cooperation continued.

In 1982, that changed when Symbolics found a loophole in their agreement that allowed that they did not have to give MIT the right to redistribute their improvements. Stallman took every improvement and rewrote it in a shareable form. But the mood had been set, and other hackers had already left, many to join the companies. Stallman left too, in 1984, but rather than fight the LISP fight, he developed an entirely new operating system, called GNU. He began at an old,

empty office at MIT, where in 1984 he developed GNU EMACS, a program that could be used to edit programs, write them, play games, and read e-mail. It could be used with UNIX, the program that had been purchased from AT&T and been vastly improved upon at Berkeley.

The following year, Stallman founded the Free Software Foundation, a nonprofit that is generously supported and which sells manuals and other support materials for the GNU programs. The organization became staffed and received gifts of computers from many companies. Stallman's second program, GNU C Compiler translates machine code into source code, and programmers around the world improved the program that could generate code for many types of microprocessors. Large corporations, like Hewlett-Packard, who were benefiting from Stallman's creations, gave generous grants to the Free Software Foundation.

Sam Williams, who first met Stallman in 1999, wrote a biography of the computing genius titled *Free as in Freedom.* Chris Bidmead, who reviewed the book in *MicroScope,* noted that "Stallman argues—or more accurately, because he hates argument, declares" that his intent, the open distribution of source code, "was hijacked" by Torvalds and Eric Raymond, a former associate of the GNU project, "in their 'New Testament' version that came to be called 'open source.' The book chronicles this rift, examining it with objectivity, but also some sympathy for Stallman's increasingly isolated position."

Bidmead noted that "like any true hero, Stallman's faults and virtues are almost inextricably intertwined. The near pathological meticulousness that can drive his peers to distraction was an essential ingredient in the GNU General Public License, the complex legal definition that Stallman drew up to ensure the freedom of the code even through subsequent mutations. The avid dogmatism that frightens away potential sympathizers powers the dogged effort that in a decade produced the EMACS editor, the GNU compiler, and the host of essential tools and utilities. Linux was able to turn GNU into a complete operating system."

Stallman maintains an extensive Web site for GNU, and a personal site where he posts not only his views on free software, but also on civil liberties, the use of medical marijuana, privacy, human rights, commercialism, the media, government foreign policy, and many other subjects. Links to sites and petitions are provided. Stallman reveals his personal history, likes and dislikes, and adds stories, jokes, and travel tales. A man who lives simply, he derives much of his income from speaking engagements.

Stallman's own book, *Free Software, Free Society: Selected Essays of Richard M. Stallman,* is a collection of reprinted and new essays that explain Stallman's philosophy regarding free software. In it, he sets forth his four freedoms for its use and comments on what he considers abuse of copyright law and patents. *Library Journal*'s Joe J. Accardi called the book an "important collection by a software visionary." Mikael Pawlo reviewed the volume for *GrepLaw,* noting that Stallman "could never be accused of being boring. The thoughts on computer programs are mind-boggling, and regardless of how Stallman will be looked upon in history, his thoughts have dominated the debate on regulation and ethics of computer programs . . . and most probably will affect current major strategy choices of companies like IBM, Apple, and Microsoft. Every IT policy maker and IT procurement officer should read this book. However, the book touches on subjects affecting a much larger audience, and everyone who ever thought of the architecture that regulates the Internet and our computers will have plenty of defining moments with *Free Software, Free Society.*"

BIOGRAPHICAL AND CRITICAL SOURCES:

BOOKS

Levy, Steven, *Hackers: Heroes of the Computer Revolution,* Anchor Press (Garden City, NY), 1984, with revised afterword, Penguin Books (New York, NY), 2001.
Williams, Sam, *Free as in Freedom: Richard Stallman's Crusade for Free Software,* Farnham/O'Reilly (Sabastopol, CA), 2002.

PERIODICALS

Economist, July 15, 1989, "The hacker's return," p. 81.
EDN, October 1, 1990, Jay Fraser, "Keeper of the faith: Richard Stallman is leading a crusade to preserve your programming freedom," p. 175.

Library Journal, October 1, 2002, Joe J. Accardi, review of *Free Software, Free Society: Selected Essays of Richard M. Stallman,* p. 120.
MicroScope, May 7, 2002, Chris Bidmead, "The man behind the project: in his book *Free as in Freedom,* Sam Williams takes the reader on a voyage of discovery into Richard Stallman's obsession with the GNU/Linux label," p. 24.
Network World, January 11, 1999, Robin Holman, "GNU's Not Linux" (interview).
Technology Review, February-March, 1991, Simson L. Garfinkel, "Programs to the people: computer whiz Richard Stallman is determined to make software free—even if he has to transform the industry single-handed," p. 52.

ONLINE

Byte.com, http://www.byte.com/ (March 13, 2001), Tom Henderson, "Free or Not Free" (interview).
GNU Project, http://www.gnu.org (July 8, 2003).
GrepLaw, http://www.grep.law.harvard.edu/ (September 13, 2004), Mikael Pawlo, review of *Free Software, Free Society: Selected Essays of Richard M. Stallman.*
Richard Stallman Home Page, http://www.stallman.org (September 13, 2004).

*   *   *

STAVRIANOS, Leften Stavros 1913-2004

OBITUARY NOTICE—See index for *CA* sketch: Born February 5, 1913, in Vancouver, British Columbia, Canada; died of respiratory failure, March 23, 2004, in La Jolla, CA. Historian, educator, and author. A professor of history, Stavrianos was considered one of the founders of the field of world history and was a noted expert on modern Greece and the Balkans. His undergraduate studies were completed at the University of British Columbia in 1933; he then received an M.A. from Clark University in 1934, followed three years later by a Ph.D. from the same institution. Stavrianos's academic career began at Queen's University in Kingston, Ontario, where he lectured for a year before moving on to Smith College in Massachusetts in 1939. From 1944 to 1945, he served with the Office of Strategic Services, returning to Smith College as an assistant professor of history. In 1946, he joined the

Northwestern University faculty as an associate professor, becoming a full professor of history in 1956 and retiring in 1973 as professor emeritus. Though retired, Stavrianos wished to maintain his connections with academia; therefore, he spent his remaining years as an adjunct professor at the University of California—San Diego, beginning in 1973. Left-leaning in his philosophy, Stavrianos believed that capitalism had a negative and exploitive impact on civilization because it can only survive by increasingly using up resources. As an educator and writer, he further felt that a complete understanding of history is not possible without being informed about current events as well. Among Stavrianos's published writings are *Greece: The War and Aftermath* (1945), *The Balkans, 1815-1914* (1963), *The World to 1500: A Global History* (1970; second edition, 1975; published as *A Global History: From Prehistory to the Twenty-first Century,* 1999), and *Lifelines from Our Past: A New World History* (1989).

OBITUARIES AND OTHER SOURCES:

ONLINE

Observer Online, http://www.northwestern.edu/observer/ (April 29, 2004).
SignOnSanDiego.com, http://signonsandiego.printthis.clickability.com/ (April 4, 2004).

*   *   *

STINE, Scott A(aron) 1968-
(Reginald Bloom)

PERSONAL: Born December 17, 1968, in Sacramento, CA; son of Gerald and Judy Stine. *Ethnicity:* "Caucasian." *Religion:* "Atheist." *Hobbies and other interests:* Archiving memorabilia, musician.

ADDRESSES: *Home*—P.O. Box 5273, Everett, WA 98206-5273. *E-mail*—Piltdown68@aol.com.

CAREER: Stigmata Press, publisher, 1992—.

MEMBER: Official Church of Satan.

WRITINGS:

The Gorehound's Guide to Splatter Films of the 1960s and 1970s, McFarland Publishing (Jefferson, NC), 2001.
(With Michael von Sacher-Masoch) *The Trashfiend's Guide to Collecting Videotapes,* Stigmata Press, 2002.
The Gorehound's Guide to Splatter Films of the 1980s, McFarland Publishing (Jefferson, NC), 2003.

Author of novels under pseudonym Reginald Bloom. Contributor to books, including *American Folklore: An Encyclopedia,* Garland Publishing (New York, NY), 1996. Contributor of articles to periodicals, including *Skeptical Inquirer;* contributor of short stories to periodicals, including *Raw Media Mags, Touchstone NW, Lethologica,* and *Lovecraft's Weird Mysteries,* all under pseudonym Reginald Bloom. Editor in chief, writer, and layout artist for *Painful Excursions,* 1988-96, *GICK! Journal of Horror, Splatter, and Exploitation Films,* 1998-2001, *Filthy Habits,* 2002—, and *Trashfiend,* 2002—.

*   *   *

STOCKLER, Bruce 1960(?)-

PERSONAL: Born c. 1960; married Roni Fischer (a corporate attorney); children: Asher; Hannah, Barak, Jared (triplets).

ADDRESSES: *Home*—Scarsdale, NY. *Agent*—c/o Author Mail, St. Martin's Press, 175 Fifth Ave., New York, NY 10010.

CAREER: Writer and humorist. Employed in public relations and marketing field; former editor-in-chief of a film trade magazine.

WRITINGS:

I Sleep at Red Lights: A True Story of Life after Triplets, St. Martin's Press (New York, NY), 2003.

Contributor to periodicals, including *New York Times, Los Angeles Times, Philadelphia Inquirer,* and *Christian Science Monitor;* author of column "Crazy Talk" for *Esquire.* Joke writer for Jay Leno.

SIDELIGHTS: In *I Sleep at Red Lights: A True Story of Life after Triplets,* writer and humorist Bruce Stockler recounts what happens to a fast-tracking Manhattan couple when triplets become part of life's plan. With a three-year-old son, Stockler and his corporate attorney wife, Roni, wanted another child, but joy turned to astonishment when Roni found she was not only pregnant but that three infants were in her future—along with three times the diapers, three times the feedings, and three times the sleepless nights. Calling *I Sleep at Red Lights* an "extremely funny, extremely perceptive memoir," *Booklist* reviewer David Pitt added that Stockler's tone ranges from "charming and tender" to "outright hilarity." A *Kirkus Reviews* critic also noted the humor, but added that "undercurrents of angst"—such as worries over money and employment—"make this a vivid status report on modern parenting."

BIOGRAPHICAL AND CRITICAL SOURCES:

PERIODICALS

Booklist, May 1, 2003, David Pitt, review of *I Sleep at Red Lights,* p. 1562.
Kirkus Reviews, April 15, 2003, review of *I Sleep at Red Lights,* p. 598.
Library Journal, May 5, 2003, p. 108.

ONLINE

Contemporary Literature Web site, http://www.contemporarylit.about/ (October 12, 2003), Mark Flanagan, review of *I Sleep at Red Lights.*
Mercury News Online, http://www.siliconvalley.com/mld/mercury/news/ (September 23, 2003), Nora Villagrán, "Triplets' Dad Takes a Shine to Parenting."*

                              *   *   *

SUN, Yifeng 1957-

PERSONAL: Born 1957, in Chongqing, China; son of Furu (a university professor) and Nairen (a university professor; maiden name, Fan) Sun; married Rong Yang, 1983; children: Stanley Mengjin. *Education:* Nanjing University, B.A., 1982; Cambridge University, M.Litt., 1993; University of Leiden, Ph.D., 1999.

ADDRESSES: Office—Department of Translation, Lingnan University, Tuen Mun, New Territories, Hong Kong.

CAREER: Lingnan University, Tuen Mun, New Territories, Hong Kong, associate professor of translation and head of Chinese Language Education and Assessment Centre. Guest professor at Chongqing University and Guangdong University of Foreign Studies; Sichuan International Studies University, guest professor and guest research fellow at Institute of Translation Studies; Beijing Language and Culture University, guest research fellow at Institute of Comparative Literature and Culture.

MEMBER: Royal Society of Arts (England; fellow), Translators Association of China, Hong Kong Translation Society (life member).

WRITINGS:

(Translator, with others) *Contemporary Chinese Women Writers VI: Four Novellas by Zhang Xin,* Panda Books (Beijing, China), 1998.
(Chief translator) *King of the Wizards: Selected Works by Lin Xi,* Chinese Literature Press (Beijing, China), 1998.
Fragments and Dramatic Moments: Zhang Tianyi and the Narrative Discourse of Upheaval in Modern China, Peter Lang Publishing (New York, NY), 2002.
Translation Terminology, Hong Kong Translation Society (Hong Kong), in press.

Contributor to books, including *The Construction of Translation Theory and Cultural Perspectives,* Shanghai Foreign Languages Education Press (Shanghai, China), 2000. Contributor of articles and translations to scholarly journals, including *Perspectives: Studies in Translatology, Literature and Thoughts, Tamkang Review, Chinese Culture, Classical Studies,* and *Research in Foreign Languages and Literature.* Executive editor, *Translation Quarterly;* member of editorial board, *Chinese Translators Journal, Abstracts of Translation Studies in China,* and *Journal of Sichuan International Studies University;* member of advisory board, *World of English.*

WORK IN PROGRESS: Perspective, Interpretation, and Utterance: Theory of Literary Translation, for Tsinghua University Press (Beijing, China); *Norms and Translation: Toury's Translation Theory,* Hennan renmin chubanshe (Zhengzhou, China); chief editor of *Translation Studies: Dialogue in the New Century;* research for *Crossing Barriers to Translation: Transcending Ideologies in China.*

SIDELIGHTS: Yifeng Sun told *CA:* "I am a translation scholar and literary critic and also a translator, mainly from Chinese into English. In its modern history, China has striven to learn from the West, and for this reason, its translation is principally from the West and dominantly from English. In this respect, Western Sinologists have done a good job, but in proportion to the rich Chinese cultural heritage, what has been made available in English is severely limited. My translation practice is somewhat dilettantish, but its profound connection to cross-cultural outreach is meaningful. My research work in literature is similarly related to the vital necessity to communicate with the West. Millions of Chinese are learning English, but since such enthusiasm is not reciprocated in the English-speaking world, Chinese scholars must write in English if they wish to enter cross-cultural discussions.

"In the Chinese context, whether in translation or literary studies, the term 'ideology' cannot be averted. I am fascinated by 'untranslatability' in both cultural and ideological terms. I am also acutely aware of the presence of ideology in modern Chinese literary history. My book *Fragmentation and Dramatic Moments: Zhang Tianyi and the Narrative Discourse of Upheaval in Modern China* is an attempt to argue that much modern Chinese writing is anathema to dominant ideologies. For many years, ideologically charged debates threatened to marginalize literature. But all this is changing; there is a great sense of excitement about China in practically all aspects of its development. Western prejudices aside, lack of knowledge and understanding of China contribute to misperceptions that are undoubtedly pernicious and thus need to be corrected or dispelled. My research, therefore, purports to examine how ideology and culture are indelibly intertwined, and to demonstrate that obstacles to cross-cultural communication are not insurmountable as long as a cross-cultural dialogue is promoted.

"My next research project is on ideology and translation in China. But ideological principles are increasingly flexible and to a considerable extent even

diminishing. Something positive must be done as an effective antidote to potential cultural, and worse still, ideological 'warfare.' Meanwhile, in my writings in Chinese, I intend to 'translate' Western ideas into Chinese discourse and to play the role of cultural ambassador to both West and East. Through my writing I hope to show that, although culturally insensitive incursions need to be reduced if not altogether avoided, different cultures will benefit one another through exchange and interaction while we appreciate and celebrate cultural diversity. The abandonment of antiquated ways of thinking makes it possible to transcend ideological and cultural barriers."

*   *   *

SUZUKI, Koji 1957-

PERSONAL: Born 1957, in Hamamatsu, Shizuoka Prefecture, Japan; married a teacher; children: two. *Education:* Graduated from Keio University. *Hobbies and other interests:* French and American literature, science.

ADDRESSES: Home—Tokyo, Japan. *Agent*—c/o Author Mail, Vertical, Inc., 257 Park Ave. S., 8th Fl., New York, NY 10010.

CAREER: Writer.

AWARDS, HONORS: Fantasy novel award (Japan), 1990, for *Rakuen;* Yoshikawa Eiji young writer award (Japan), 1996, for *Rasen.*

WRITINGS:

"RING" SERIES

Ring, Kadokawa (Tokyo, Japan), 1991, translation by Robert B. Rohmer and Glynne Walley, Vertical (New York, NY), 2002.
Rasen, Kadokawa (Tokyo, Japan), 1995, translation by Glynne Walley published as *Spiral,* Vertical (New York, NY), 2004.
Loop, Kadokawa (Tokyo, Japan), 1998.
Birthday, Kadokawa (Tokyo, Japan), 1999.

OTHER

Also author of *Rakuen* (title means "Paradise"), 1990, *Namida* (children's book; title means "Tears"), *Kami kami no Promenade* (title means "The Gods' Promenade"), and *Dark Water.* Author of nonfiction, including *Fusei no Tanjo, Kazoku no Kizuna,* and *Papa-ism.* Translator into Japanese of *The Little Sod Diaries* by Simon Brett.

ADAPTATIONS: *Ring* was adapted as the motion picture *Ringu,* Toho Pictures, 1998, as *The Ring,* Dreamworks, 2002, as a television mini-series in Japan, and as a motion picture in Korea; *Rasen* was adapted for film in Japan, 1998.

SIDELIGHTS: Koji Suzuki, dubbed the "Stephen King of Japan," is the author of the horror novel *Ring,* which was the basis for the Japanese film *Ringu* and its hugely popular American remake *The Ring.* Suzuki has written three other works in the "Ring" series: *Rasen* (translated as *Spiral*), *Loop,* and *Birthday.*

Ring launched a horror boom in Japan when it was first published in 1991, though Suzuki, who has also written extensively on the subject of child rearing, seems an unlikely candidate to have created such excitement. "While I've written *Ring* and a few other horror pieces, I'm really not a fan of horror," he told interviewer Norman England on the *Fangoria* Web site. Suzuki admitted that the impetus for *Ring* came to him unexpectedly. "At first, I didn't have the story; I didn't even have the idea," he told England. "I'd started out with four people who were going to share a strange experience, but I was just writing off the top of my head, not knowing where I was going. In my study, I had music playing and sunlight was streaming in from a window. An odd feeling came over me and, looking to the side of my desk, I saw a videotape. That's when it hit me. Why don't I have them watch a video together?"

In 2002 *Ring* was published in English translation by Vertical. In the work, four Japanese teenagers die under bizarre and mysterious circumstances, prompting an investigation by reporter Kazayuki Asakawa. Asakawa, whose niece was one of the victims, learns that the teens had watched a videotape that may be linked to their deaths. After Asakawa screens the video, which features a series of disturbing, surrealistic

images, he receives a chilling warning: whoever views the tape will die in exactly seven days. As Asakawa races to save his life, he unearths the tale of Sadako Yamamura, a missing child believed to possess incredible paranormal ability. "The source of [Sadako's] supernatural power, and its connection to the videotape, has resulted in an increasingly complex story that blends ancient legends and ghost stories with futuristic computer technology," observed John Paul Catton on *Metropolis Online.* According to *Library Journal* contributor Wilda Williams, *Ring* "will keep readers glued to its pages."

Despite the success of *Ring* and its sequels, Suzuki thinks of himself as much more than an author of horror fiction. As he told England, "I've written on other subjects, with much of my work pertaining to the ocean. I just happened to have written the horror stories successfully."

BIOGRAPHICAL AND CRITICAL SOURCES:

PERIODICALS

Booklist, May 15, 2003, David Pitt, review of *Ring,* p. 1649.
Kirkus Reviews, March 15, 2003, review of *Ring,* p. 427.
Library Journal, April 1, 2003, Wilda Williams, review of *Ring,* p. 132.

ONLINE

Fangoria Web site, http://www.fangoria.com/ (April 20, 2004), Norman England, "Fearful Feature: Ring Writer."
JapanReview Online, http://japanreview.net/ (April 20, 2004), Yuki Allyson Honjo, "Ringing."
Metropolis Online, http://metropolis.japantoday.com/ (April 20, 2004), John Paul Catton, "Big in Japan: Suzuki Koji."
Ringworld Web site, http://www.theringworld.com/ (April 20, 2004).
SciFi.com, http://www.scifi.com/ (April 20, 2004), John Clute, "Excessive Candour: Engine of Disquiet."
Vertical, Inc. Web site, http://www.vertical-inc.com/ (April 20, 2004).*

SWIFT, Sue 1955-

PERSONAL: Born 1955, in St. Louis, MS; father, a physician; mother, a homemaker; married Bruce Zweig (a dentist), 1995. *Education:* University of California—Davis, A.B., 1976, M.A., 1978; Hastings College of Law, J.D., 1981. *Hobbies and other interests:* Kenpo karate, ice hockey.

ADDRESSES: Home—Sacramento, CA. *Office*—P.O. Box 241, Citrus Heights, CA 95611-10241. *Agent*—Evan Fogelman, Fogelman Literary Agency, 7515 Greenville Ave., Suite 712, Dallas, TX 75231.

CAREER: Trial attorney in Sacramento, CA, 1981-2001; writer, 2001—.

MEMBER: Romance Writers of America, Mystery Writers of America, Novelists Inc.

AWARDS, HONORS: Beacon Award, Romance Writers of America, 2001, for *Hopelessly Compromised.*

WRITINGS:

Hopelessly Compromised (romance novel), Zebra Books (New York, NY), 2000.
His Baby, Her Heart (romance novel), Silhouette Books (Buffalo, NY), 2001.
In the Sheikh's Arms (romance novel), Silhouette Books (Buffalo, NY), 2001.
The Ranger and the Rescue (romance novel), Silhouette Books (Buffalo, NY), 2002.

Author of short stories. Note and comment editor, *Comm/Ent Law Journal,* 1981.

T

TAMARKIN, Jeff

PERSONAL: Married Caroline Leavitt (a novelist); children: Max.

ADDRESSES: Home—Hoboken, NJ. *Agent*—c/o Author Mail, Atria Books, Simon & Schuster, 1230 Avenue of the Americas, New York, NY 10020. *E-mail*—jeff@gotarevolution.com.

CAREER: Music historian, journalist, and author. *Goldmine* (magazine), editor for fifteen years; *Global Rhythm* magazine, editor.

WRITINGS:

Billy Joel: From Hicksville to Hitsville, Cherry Lane Books (Port Chester, NY), 1984.
David Schreiner, *Grateful Dead Comix,* Hyperion (New York, NY), 1992.
Got a Revolution! The Turbulent Flight of Jefferson Airplane, Atria Books (New York, NY), 2003.

Contributor to periodicals, including *Pulse, Mojo, Billboard,* and *Discoveries;* author of recording liner notes.

SIDELIGHTS: Jeff Tamarkin has been a professional music journalist for over twenty-five years. In addition to editing the magazine *Goldmine* for more than half his career, he has also contributed to many other music-related magazines, including *Billboard* and *Pulse.* In addition to his work as editor of *Grateful Dead Comix*—a combination of Grateful Dead song lyrics and underground comics—Tamarkin is the author of *Got a Revolution! The Turbulent Flight of Jefferson Airplane,* a project he undertook after penning over two dozen liner notes for the band's compact discs and becoming acquainted with Airplane musicians.

Got a Revolution!, based on five years of intense work, describes the band's monumental contribution to psychedelic rock during the 1960s and 1970s. The book was inspired by Tamarkin's love of rock and roll, and hearing the band's *Surrealistic Pillow* album for the very first time in the summer of 1967. Beginning with Jefferson Airplane's formation in San Francisco, California, in 1965, Tamarkin chronicles the band's early successes and the pitfalls caused by infighting and excessive drug use, to its eventual decline and demise. He draws from interviews with band members as well as their families, friends, crew members, and fellow musicians like Janis Joplin, the Grateful Dead, Paul McCartney, and the Rolling Stones. In addition, Tamarkin delves into the creative differences that made the early Airplane so innovative but ultimately contributed to its downfall. As a long-time fan, he weaves personal interpretations of songs within his chronological narrative, and includes a comprehensive discography as well as a look at what band members were doing at the time of the book's publication. He describes his inspiration for writing *Got a Revolution!* on *Gotarevolution.com,* noting that "Jefferson Airplane was one of the great rock bands of all time, hugely successful and influential, highly creative, beloved by millions—truly one of the major bands during rock's classic era. And yet their story has never really been told. There are hundreds of books on the Beatles, the Rolling Stones, Bob Dylan, the Grateful Dead, etc., but none on the Airplane. So I elected myself to tell their tale. Also, of course, because I love their music."

Reviewing *Got a Revolution!* for *Publishers Weekly,* a critic stated that "Although Tamarkin's hagiographic portrait of the band is hardly objective, his friendship with the complete access to the players in this story certainly makes his account the definitive one." Joe Hartlaub, writing in *Bookreporter.com,* criticized the author for occasional incorrect facts, but ultimately praised the book, noting that "A history of Jefferson Airplane was overdue; that the first one should also be the definitive one is a tribute to Tamarkin and his work." A *Kirkus Reviews* critic also lauded the book, noting that in *Got a Revolution!* Tamarkin presents fans with "a lively, detail-strewn history of the legendary band and how it took, with a vengeance, to the electricity of San Francisco in the mid-1960s."

BIOGRAPHICAL AND CRITICAL SOURCES:

PERIODICALS

Booklist, June 15, 1992, Gordon Flagg, review of *Grateful Dead Comix,* p. 1796.
Kirkus Reviews, April 15, 2003, review of *Got a Revolution! The Turbulent Flight of Jefferson Airplane,* p. 599.
Publishers Weekly, April 28, 2003, review of *Got a Revolution!,* p. 57.

ONLINE

BookReporter.com, http://www.bookreporter.com/ (October 12, 2003), Joe Hartlaub, review of *Got a Revolution!*
Gotarevolution.com, http://www.gotarevolution.com/ (October 12, 2003), "A Conversation with Jeff Tamarkin, Author of *Got a Revolution!*"
Pulse Web site, http://pulse.towerrecords.com/ (October 12, 2003), "Jeff Tamarkin."*

*   *   *

TATE, Greg

PERSONAL: Male.

ADDRESSES: Agent—Alison Loerke, ALIA Agency, 12258 12th Ave. NW, Seattle, WA 98177.

CAREER: Village Voice, New York, NY, staff writer. Cofounder of the Black Rock Coalition; musical director of Burnt Sugar.

WRITINGS:

Flyboy in the Buttermilk: Essays on Contemporary America, Simon & Schuster (New York, NY), 1992.
Brooklyn Kings: New York City's Black Bikers, Powerhouse Books (New York, NY), 2000.
(With Jessica Morgan and Rob Storr) *Ellen Gallagher,* Institute of Contemporary Art (Boston, MA), 2001.
Midnight Lighting: Jimi Hendrix and the Black Experience, Lawrence Hill Books (Chicago, IL), 2003.
(Editor) *Everything but the Burden: What White People Are Taking from Black Culture,* Broadway Books (New York, NY), 2003.

SIDELIGHTS: A *Village Voice* staff writer and cultural critic, founding member of the Black Rock Coalition, and musical director of the improvisational group Burnt Sugar, Greg Tate has a great deal of experience in the interplay of race, music, and the wider culture. "He also is an astute observer and chronicler of this post-everything and nouveau-whatever culture nobody has yet fit with a suitable moniker," according to Penny Mickelbury in *Africana.*

In *Flyboy in the Buttermilk: Essays on Contemporary America,* Tate brings together forty of his essays on music, art, and literature, an eclectic mixture of subjects from Miles Davis to George Clinton, Don DeLillo to Public Enemy. "Underlying nearly all Tate's work is, uh, you know, the color thing: structural racism in America, its permutations and fallout," observed *Nation* contributor Gene Santoro. Some essays deal directly with the color divide in such cases as the O. J. Simpson trial, the Central Park jogger rape, and Howard Beach. Others note the curious symmetries, as in Bill Clinton's, and even Lee Atwater's, embrace of black music for political effect. "The political pieces cut to the bone, sparing neither a white power structure that devalues black life nor blacks who cry racism to excuse sexism," noted a *Publishers Weekly* reviewer. Tate "writes with a laser. And his mixture of straight-up English, street-speak and scholarese can be quite dizzying. But the spin makes you think," wrote Tonya Bolden in *Black Enterprise.* Santoro further commented on "the fierce beauty, fanned by articulate rage and humor, that flames out from *Flyboy.* Miss it and you've missed something crucial about the world you are living in and will be."

After contributing essays for books on Ellen Gallagher, an African-American artist who uses stereotypes to undercut them, and the curious world of black bikers in *Brooklyn Kings,* Tate published *Midnight Lighting: Jimi Hendrix and the Black Experience,* "a jumpy, fast-talking take on Jimi Hendrix—the social meaning, the sexual mystery, and the music of a 'musician's musician,'" according to a *Kirkus Reviews* contributor. Tate's focus is not the "guitar god" of other Hendrix bios, but his unusual ability to cross the color line with seeming impunity, so much so that Tate conceived of his book as a "Jimi Hendrix primer for black folks" who may have forgotten his black roots. At the same time, "Tate shows how Hendrix's disregard for the race card put him decades ahead in society, as well as in music," explained *Library Journal* reviewer Eric Hahn. As usual, Tate mixes in academic theory with detailed research and the reminiscences of those who worked and played with Hendrix. "Oftentimes verbose, Tate unapologetically indulges in fits of hyperbolic, hyperanalytical fantasy," commented *Black Issues Book Review* contributor Malcolm Venable. "It's easy to pardon him, though, since his dead-on logic is intriguing and revealing. Plus, he's got a wicked imagination that he combines with a sense of high humor."

In his next book, *Everything but the Burden: What White People Are Taking from Black Culture,* Tate edited a collection by "a bunch of African-American writers, critics, scholars and other creative types to give their perspectives on white culture's 'sampling' of black culture," explained reviewer Craig Lindsey in the *Houston Chronicle.* The critic added, "From the way *Burden* tells it, black people, young and old, have been getting stole on by white folks for quite some time now." Poets, playwrights, musicians, and professors all weigh in on the elusive subjects of race as a social construct, race as a political reality, and race as a cultural given. A number of authors take Norman Mailer's essay, "The White Negro," as a starting point, some with approval, others with sharp dissent. Many focus on the hip-hop culture. Much is autobiographical. There is a great deal of ground to cover, and "the collection's stylistic diversity and idiosyncratic selection of topics create a provocative, if rather trying,

reading experience," according to *Library Journal* reviewer Janet Ingraham Dwyer. Together, the authors explore "the American attraction/repulsion, fascination, adoption, and obsession with the alternative" culture that African Americans have established, wrote Vernon Ford in *Booklist.* "And for those still wondering why the young people look like they do, *Burden* may not have the definitive answer, but it definitely will give you something else to think about," concluded Mickelbury in *Africana.*

BIOGRAPHICAL AND CRITICAL SOURCES:

PERIODICALS

Black Enterprise, December, 1992, Tonya Bolden, review of *Flyboy in the Buttermilk: Essays on Contemporary America,* p. 14.
Black Issues Book Review, May, 2001, Kira Lynn, review of *Brooklyn Kings: New York City's Black Bikers,* p. 48; September-October, 2003, Malcolm Venable, review of *Midnight Lighting: Jimi Hendrix and the Black Experience,* p. 49.
Booklist, January 1, 2003, Vernon Ford, review of *Everything but the Burden: What White People Are Taking from Black Culture,* p. 814.
Houston Chronicle, June 1, 2003, Craig Lindsey, review of *Everything but the Burden,* p. 18.
Kirkus Reviews, May 1, 2003, review of *Midnight Lighting,* p. 668.
Library Journal, December, 2002, Janet Ingraham Dwyer, review of *Everything but the Burden,* p. 157; June 1, 2003, Eric Hahn, review of *Midnight Lighting,* p. 124.
Nation, February 15, 1993, Gene Santaro, review of *Flyboy in the Buttermilk,* p. 206.
Publishers Weekly, April 6, 1992, review of *Flyboy in the Buttermilk,* p. 56.
Village Voice, July 30, 2003, Miles Marshall Lewis, "Deep Purple," p. 52.

ONLINE

Africana, http://www.africana.com/ (February 4, 2003), Penny Mickelbury, "Culture Vulture: Greg Tate Explains It All."*

TERRY, James L. 1949-

PERSONAL: Born 1949.

ADDRESSES: Home—Brooklyn, NY. *Agent*—c/o Author Mail, McFarland & Co., Box 611, Jefferson, NC 28640.

CAREER: New York University, New York, NY, social science librarian.

WRITINGS:

Long before the Dodgers: Baseball in Brooklyn, 1855-1884, McFarland (Jefferson, NC), 2002.

SIDELIGHTS: James L. Terry's interest in New York baseball history inspired his book *Long before the Dodgers: Baseball in Brooklyn, 1855-1884.* From baseball's roots in gentlemen's sporting clubs during the mid-nineteenth century, the book traces the history of the sport in Brooklyn and discusses the Dodgers' formation as a team, their decision to join the fledgling National League in 1876, and their rise to national prominence after 1884. Reviewing the book for *Choice,* P. L. de Rosa praised *Long before the Dodgers* as an extended history that "illuminates both urban and baseball history in the sport's formative period," while *Library Journal* contributor Paul Kaplan dubbed Terry's work "well-researched."

BIOGRAPHICAL AND CRITICAL SOURCES:

PERIODICALS

Choice, October, 2002, P. L. de Rosa, review of *Long before the Dodgers: Baseball in Brooklyn, 1855-1884,* p. 317.
Library Journal, February 1, 2002, Robert C. Cottrell, review of *Long before the Dodgers: Baseball in Brooklyn, 1855-1884,* p. 104.*

*   *   *

TESSARO, Kathleen 1965-

PERSONAL: Born 1965, in Pittsburgh, Pennsylvania. Married; husband's name, James (a pianist). *Education:* Studied drama at Carnegie Mellon University.

ADDRESSES: Home—London, England. *Agent*—c/o Author Mail, 7th Floor, HarperCollins Publishers, 10 East 53rd St., New York, NY 10022.

CAREER: Has worked as an movie, television, and theater actress, including several years with the English National Opera. Member of Wimpole Street Writers Workshop.

WRITINGS:

Elegance (novel), William Morrow (New York, NY), 2003.

SIDELIGHTS: After studying drama at Carnegie-Mellon University, Kathleen Tessaro moved to London to try her luck at a stage career. With a decade of modest success on stage and screen and television, Tessaro retired from performing to train as a drama and voice coach while working for the English National Opera. At the same time, she began to write short stories, joining a women's writing workshop to hone her skills.

Her first novel, *Elegance,* draws on her own experiences as an expatriate American and her encounter with a curious old book, also titled *Elegance,* a self-help guide written in the 1960s by a grand old lady of France to provide advice on everything from wearing the right scarf to choosing the right friends. In Tessaro's book, a frumpy, fortyish expatriate in a passionless marriage embraces the advice in the self-help guide, gradually discarding her shapeless dresses and Birkenstocks for a more elegant wardrobe. "Ironically, in her imitation of elegance, she somehow manages to find her true self," noted *Library Journal* reviewer Shelley Mosley. For with the new clothes comes a new self-confidence and a willingness to open herself to new experiences. "Through vivid descriptions, lively mishaps and devastating details, Tessaro serves up a witty, original, fast-moving debut. Louise's story lightheartedly reveals the frailties and possibilities in all of us," concluded a *USA Today* reviewer.

BIOGRAPHICAL AND CRITICAL SOURCES:

PERIODICALS

Booklist, June 1, 2003, Kathleen Hughes, review of *Elegance,* p. 1747.
Kirkus Reviews, May 1, 2003, review of *Elegance,* p. 640.

Library Journal, June 1, 2003, Shelley Mosley, review of *Elegance,* p. 170.

Publishers Weekly, July 7, 2003, review of *Elegance,* p. 53.

Times (London, England), May 26, 2003, Business section, p. 23.

USA Today, July 17, 2003, review of *Elegance,* Life section, p. 4.*

*   *   *

THOMAS, William J. 1946-

PERSONAL: Born October 18, 1946, in Welland, Ontario, Canada; son of Glyn (a gold miner) and Margaret (a homemaker; maiden name, McLean) Thomas. *Ethnicity:* "Irish/Welsh." *Education:* Waterloo Lutheran University (now Wilfrid Laurier University), B.A. *Politics:* "A cowering post-9/11 Liberal." *Religion:* "Failed Catholic." *Hobbies and other interests:* Reading, hiking, cooking.

ADDRESSES: Home and office—R.R.2, Port Colborne, Ontario L3K 5V4, Canada.

CAREER: Writer. *Alive and Well,* St. Catharine's, Ontario, Canada, editor and feature writer for two years; *What's Up Niagara?,* St. Catharine's, Ontario, Canada, editor for four years; Canadian Broadcasting Corporation, television writer for two years; teacher of humor writing classes for ten years, including courses at Chautauqua Institute in New York and at Stephen Leacock Museum, Orillia, Ontario, Canada; also works as a humorist speaker. Canadian Humane Societies, fund raiser.

MEMBER: Writers Union of Canada.

AWARDS, HONORS: Two Gemini Award nominations, Academy of Canadian Cinema and Television, for *Breaking All the Rules: The Story of Trivial Pursuit* and *Chasing the Dream;* Niagara Book Prize.

WRITINGS:

HUMOR

Malcolm and Me: Life in the Litter Box, Stoddart Publishing (Toronto, Ontario, Canada), 1993.

Margaret and Me: All Humour Needs a Victim and Your Mother Should Come First!, Stoddart Publishing (Toronto, Ontario, Canada), 1998.

The Dog Rules (Damn Near Everything!), Key Porter Books (Toronto, Ontario, Canada), 2001.

Never Hitchhike on the Road Less Travelled, Key Porter Books (Toronto, Ontario, Canada), 2002.

Other books include *Hey! Is That Guy Dead or Is He the Skip?* and *Guys: Not Real Bright and Damn Proud of It.* Television writings include *Breaking All the Rules: The Story of Trivial Pursuit* and *Chasing the Dream,* both for Canadian Broadcasting Corp. Author of "All the World's a Circus," a nationally syndicated newspaper column. Contributor to periodicals, including *Traveler* and *DreamScapes.*

WORK IN PROGRESS: The Un-authorized, Unnecessary, Un-conscionable Biography of Celine Dion; Why Elvis Is Dead but God Allows His Impersonators to Live.

BIOGRAPHICAL AND CRITICAL SOURCES:

OTHER

William J. Thomas, http://www.williamthomas.ca/ (February 28, 2003).

*   *   *

TIERNO, Michael

PERSONAL: Born in Brooklyn, NY; married Judy Quinn (a film producer). *Education:* College of Staten Island, City University of New York, degree in film.

ADDRESSES: Home—New York, NY. *Agent*—c/o Author Mail, Hyperion Books, 77 West 66th St., 11th Floor, New York, NY 10023. *E-mail*—moviepoetics@aol.com.

CAREER: Film editor, director, and writer. *Magazine and Bookseller,* former publisher; Miramax Films, New York, NY, story analyst in development office. Conducts seminars on writing for film.

AWARDS, HONORS: Best Feature Award, Bare Bones International Film Festival, and Flo Film Festival Award for best comedy, both for *Auditions.*

WRITINGS:

Aristotle's Poetics for Screenwriters: Storytelling Secrets from the Greatest Mind in Western Civilization, Hyperion (New York, NY), 2002.

Author and director of film *Auditions.*

SIDELIGHTS: Michael Tierno mines an ancient wisdom to guide a new art in his book *Aristotle's Poetics for Screenwriters: Storytelling Secrets from the Greatest Mind in Western Civilization.* While the great philosopher's *Poetics* might be required reading for most college-level philosophy classes, it is a book that rarely makes its way into the film school curriculum. This is an unfortunate reality in the opinion of Tierno, a film director and story editor at Miramax Films, who maintains that plot, rather than character development, is the key to screenwriting success.

His job as story analyst for Miramax Films has allowed Tierno to read some of the best and the worst that is being written for film by both professional and amateur film writers. As he explained in an interview with Kim Townsel for *Scriptsales.com,* "The amateur scripts . . . tend to make the same mistakes. . . . After forty, eighty [scripts], . . . you start seeing patterns." Realizing that some of the writers were obviously talented, Tierno became frustrated that he was not in a position to critique their work and offer some pointers. It was then that the idea for *Aristotle's Poetics for Screenwriters* was born.

Reviewing *Aristotle's Poetics for Screenwriters* in *Library Journal,* Nedra C. Evers commented that Tierno "successfully blends the ponderous with the popular" in his approach, "the whole idea [of which] is to evoke an emotional catharsis from the audience and thus create masterly drama." A reviewer for *Publishers Weekly* dubbed the book an "earnest how-to" that takes a tone with regard to Aristotle that is "respectful but informal." "Many of Aristotle's 'tips' are more than Post-It worthy," quipped *Variety* contributor Craig Teper, adding that in *Aristotle's Poetics for Screenwriters,*

Tierno has "created a slim, digestible and focused primer with some of the best advice on writing from one of the best treatises ever written on the subject."

Speaking as a writer himself, Tierno commented to Townsel: "We all write things that aren't so great. We do that to learn, to vent. Here's what I tell my students when I teach. When we begin, we often want to write what's in our heads, we purge. But what I got from *Poetics* is that in a screenplay you're supposed to be building an action that has a function. That function is to move an audience."

BIOGRAPHICAL AND CRITICAL SOURCES:

PERIODICALS

Library Journal, November 1, 2002, Nedra C. Evers, review of *Aristotle's Poetics for Screenwriters: Storytelling Secrets from the Greatest Mind in Western Civilization,* p. 101.
Publishers Weekly, June 24, 2002, review of *Aristotle's Poetics for Screenwriters,* p. 50.
Variety, August 5, 2002, Craig Teper, "My Big Fat Greek Guide Helps Scribes," p. 28.

ONLINE

Michael Tierno Web site, http://www.moviepoetics. com (September 9, 2002).
Scriptsales.com, http://www.scriptsales.com/ (January 29, 2003), Kim Townsel, interview with Michael Tierno.*

*   *   *

TJARDES, Tamara J. 1961-

PERSONAL: Born June 19, 1961.

ADDRESSES: Office—Museum of International Folk Art, P.O. Box 2087, Santa Fe, NM 87504-2087. *E-mail*—ttjardes@moifa.org.

CAREER: Museum of International Folk Art, Santa Fe, NM, former curator of Asian and Middle Eastern collections.

WRITINGS:

One Hundred Aspects of the Moon: Japanese Wood-
block Prints by Yoshitoshi, University of New
Mexico Press (Santa Fe, NM), 2003.

SIDELIGHTS: As a curator of Asian and Middle
Eastern art at the Museum of International Folk Art in
Santa Fe, New Mexico, Tamara J. Tjardes organized a
successful exhibition of nineteenth-century Japanese
artist Tsukioka Yoshitoshi's woodblock prints in 2001;
this inspired her to produce her first book, *One
Hundred Aspects of the Moon: Japanese Woodblock
Prints by Yoshitoshi.* Yoshitoshi specialized in a form
of art known as *ukiyo-e,* which, as Tjardes told *Santa
Fe New Mexican* writer Craig Smith, filled a niche in
Japanese publishing at the time that is comparable to
today's tabloids and comic books: "They were very
much used in social commentary in a cartoon type of
way, a way to comment on the aristocracy and the
samurai class. Satire. The current Japanese anime and
manga comic traditions owe a great deal to *ukiyo-e.*"
Although, Tjardes noted, "There are a couple of books
out there on Yoshitoshi, big ones, and you can get
reproductions," she "wanted something that was a little
more accessible in a smaller format and not inundated
with text." Her book, then, contains one hundred prints
of the artist's work. *Santa Fe New Mexican* contributor Lynn Cline called the book "a glorious celebration
of one of Japan's last great woodblock artists."

BIOGRAPHICAL AND CRITICAL SOURCES:

PERIODICALS

Deseret News (Salt Lake City, UT), March 16, 2003,
Dave Gagon, "'Moon' Is Stunning Tribute to
Yoshitoshi," p. E8.
Library Journal, May 1, 2003, Nadine Dalton Speidel,
review of *One Hundred Aspects of the Moon:
Japanese Woodblock Prints by Yoshitoshi,* p. 110.
Santa Fe New Mexican, June 2, 2000, Ellen Berko-
vitch, "Callooh! Callay!," p. 20; February 14,
2003, Craig Smith, "Faces of the Moon," p. 26;
December 26, 2003, Lynn Cline, "Fine Print Writ-
ten Word," p. 40.*

TOMKINS, Adam

PERSONAL: Male. *Education:* Earned master's
degree.

ADDRESSES: Office—St. Catherine's College, Manor
Rd., Oxford OX1 3UJ, England. *E-mail*—adam.
tomkins@stcatz.ox.ac.uk.

CAREER: Lawyer, legal scholar, educator. King's College, London, England, senior lecturer in law; St.
Catherine's College, Oxford, England, fellow and tutor
in law, 2000—.

WRITINGS:

(Editor, with Conor Gearty) *Understanding Human
Rights,* Mansell (New York, NY), 1996.
The Constitution after Scott: Government Unwrapped,
Oxford University Press (New York, NY), 1998.
(Editor, with Tom Campbell and K. D. Ewing) *Scepti-
cal Essays on Human Rights,* Oxford University
Press (New York, NY), 2001.
Public Law, Oxford University Press (New York, NY),
2003.

SIDELIGHTS: Adam Tomkins is a lawyer and educator whose research and teachings focus on public law,
constitutional law, administrative law, European Community law, and United States constitutional law. His
Understanding Human Rights, which he coedited with
Conor Gearty, is a collection of essays that resulted
from the 1994 W. G. Hart Legal Workshop held at the
Institute of Advanced Legal Studies in London,
England. The volume is divided into seven sections,
and a variety of rights are discussed by contributors
from the United Kingdom, the United States, Canada,
and South Africa. Among them are women's rights
and equality, homosexual rights, and human rights in
regard to the environment. In a section called "New
Frontiers," the perception of rights, as in the right to
life/freedom to choose debate, are considered, as well
as whether animals have rights. Human rights and
international law are discussed in the section titled
"Reappraising Orthodoxy."

New Law Journal contributor Ramnik Shah described
as "brilliant" an essay by Maleiha Malik, in which she
writes of the importance of communal or collective

rights around the world. G. E. Devenish contributed "Human Rights in a Divided Society" which studies post-apartheid South Africa and the structure of the new constitution.

Jonathan Herring wrote in the *Law Quarterly Review* that "the collection is well worth reading. By presenting a wide range of issues in which rights are relevant, this book demonstrates both the richness and limitations of human rights."

The Constitution after Scott: Government Unwrapped is Tompkins's study of Sir Richard Scott's "Report of the Inquiry into the Export of Defence Equipment and Dual-Use Goods to Iraq and Related Prosecutions." Scott, a Court of Appeals judge, was drafted to conduct an inquiry into the scandal surrounding allegations that ministers failed to inform either Parliament or the people about a 1988 loosening of a rather strict government policy that allowed the sale of weapons and military equipment to Iraq. In the 1990s, customs officials began prosecutions of firms for obtaining their export licenses under false pretenses. When the cases came to light, ministers were also accused of exploiting the law on public interest immunity to exclude this fact and their subsequent trades during criminal proceedings.

The report running nearly 2,000 pages is so complex that it was read by few. Ivan Hare commented in the *Cambridge Law Journal* that Scott's report "contains no summary of findings and includes elliptical language which many will find as impenetrable as Dickens's Chancery fog."

Tomkins studies and analyzes the report in language directed at a broader audience to include journalists, lawyers, and academics. Using quotes throughout, he first notes the constitutional significance of the report, then examines the relationships between the various entities involved, including the ministers, Parliament, the courts, intelligence and security, and the civil service. He even makes comparisons to the "Iraqgate" scandal in the United States. Scott's intention was not to force the resignation of the guilty—that was a matter for Parliament—but to document the facts. After the release of Scott's report, a number of changes were made. The civil service code was revised, new guidelines on immunity were issued, and Parliament passed a resolution on ministerial responsibility. Hare

noted that Tomkins "feels that these reforms are likely to prove more beneficial in strengthening the legislature's arm against the executive than the Constitution and Freedom of Information Act proved to be in the United States."

Choice reviewer H. Steck wrote that "this terrific book, its vigorous style, and the author's passion for the values he defends form a potent stimulant for thinking about British government." Steck noted that Tomkins' greater concern is constitutional government.

Jerry Waltman commented in the *Law and Politics Book Review* that "the chapter on ministers and parliament is the core of the book, but the remainder supplements it well. . . . This chapter is a thorough and admirable summary of what happened and why it had constitutional implications. The chapters on freedom of information and control of the intelligence services are similarly drawn. For American specialists, the chapter on public interest immunity may be the most interesting." Waltman continued, saying that in *The Constitution after Scott,* "we get a refreshing dose of the old-fashioned type of academic writing, in which the author is not hesitant to say 'this is good' or 'that is bad.' It has a position, but not a narrow partisan one; instead, his values are liberal constitutionalism and democratic accountability."

Tomkins is coeditor of *Sceptical Essays on Human Rights,* a collection published soon after the Human Rights Act of 1998 came into force in October 2000. The act incorporates into the laws of the United Kingdom certain freedoms and rights set out in the European Convention on Human Rights. The volume contains twenty essays by international scholars who, although they believe in the importance of human rights, question whether the responsibility for defining and enforcing laws that ensure these rights should be separated from the usual political processes of representative government. They also consider the constitutional impact of doing so and examine alternative ways of promoting and ensuring human rights.

London Review of Books contributor Stephen Sedley wrote that this volume "sits uncomfortably on the millennial cusp, looking back at a past which is now over and forward to a future which has barely begun. Even the sound pieces on Scotland, Northern Ireland, and Wales, all of which have somewhat richer recent experience than England, are rightly tentative."

BIOGRAPHICAL AND CRITICAL SOURCES:

PERIODICALS

Cambridge Law Journal, November, 1998, Ivan Hare, review of *The Constitution after Scott: Government Unwrapped,* pp. 624-625.
Choice, April, 1999, H. Steck, review of *The Constitution after Scott,* p. 1528.
International and Comparative Law Quarterly, July, 1997, Dominic McGoldrick, review of *Understanding Human Rights,* pp. 729-730.
Law and Politics Book Review, April, 1999, Jerry Waltman, review of *The Constitution after Scott,* pp. 173-176.
Law Quarterly Review, October, 2000, Jonathan Herring, review of *Understanding Human Rights,* pp. 696-697.
London Review of Books, September 19, 2002, Stephen Sedley, review of *Sceptical Essays on Human Rights,* pp. 17-18.
Modern Law Review, March, 1999, Ian Leigh, review of *The Constitution after Scott,* pp. 298-309.
New Law Journal, October 27, 2000, Ramnik Shah, review of *Understanding Human Rights,* p. 1576.
Parliamentary Affairs, April, 1999, Diana Woodhouse, review of *The Constitution after Scott,* pp. 342-353.
Times Higher Education Supplement, August 29, 2003, Laurence Lustgarten, review of *Sceptical Essays on Human Rights,* p. 25.*

* * *

TOTTEN, Mark D. 1962-

PERSONAL: Born November 27, 1962, in Ottawa, Ontario, Canada; son of Bill (in insurance sales) and Ann (an artist; maiden name, McLurg) Totten; married Sharon Dunn (a social worker), August 25, 1984; children: Daniel, Kaila, Leah. *Ethnicity:* "Caucasian." *Education:* Queen's University (Kingston, Ontario, Canada), B.A.H., 1985; Carleton University, M.S.W., 1986, Ph.D., 1997. *Hobbies and other interests:* Sea kayaking, running, biking.

ADDRESSES: Office—Youth Services Bureau of Ottawa, 1338 Wellington St., Ottawa, Ontario K1Y 3B7, Canada. *E-mail*—mtotten@ysb.on.ca.

CAREER: Self-employed therapist in Aylmer, Quebec, Canada, 1987—; Youth Services Bureau of Ottawa, Ottawa, Ontario, Canada, director of research, 1988—; certified social worker; certified "community justice forum and wraparound facilitator"; presenter and trainer on youth justice, child welfare, program evaluation, family violence, and youth violence, including classes at Carleton University. Social Sciences and Humanities Research Council of Canada, leader of Youth in Conflict with the Law Project; Justice Canada, past director of Community Reintegration Project. Also soccer, ringette, and running coach, 1990—.

MEMBER: Canadian Sociology and Anthropology Association, Ontario College of Certified Social Workers.

AWARDS, HONORS: Patricia Allen Memorial Fund scholarship, 1996; Frederic Milton Thrasher Award, National Gang Crime Research Center, 2001, for *Guys, Gangs, and Girlfriend Abuse.*

WRITINGS:

Guys, Gangs, and Girlfriend Abuse, Broadview Press (Peterborough, Ontario, Canada), 2001.
(With Katharine Kelly) *When Children Kill: A Social-Psychological Study of Youth Homicide,* Broadview Press (Peterborough, Ontario, Canada), 2002.
(With Katharine Kelly) *Restorative Justice: Working with Youth,* Broadview Press (Peterborough, Ontario, Canada), 2003.

Contributor of more than twenty articles to periodicals, including *Critical Criminology, Men and Masculinities, Social Worker, Health Canada,* and *Canadian Social Work Review.* Reviewing editor, *Journal of Gang Research,* 2001—.

SIDELIGHTS: Mark D. Totten told *CA:* "I am passionate about reducing the burden of suffering of far too many Canadian kids. My research and clinical work is motivated by a commitment to social justice. My other great passion in life is my three teenagers, my soul-mate Sharon, and my huge and goofy dogs—Shadow, a ninety-five-pound Newfoundland/border collie, and Sianna, a Great Pyranese mountain dog who, at the ripe age of seven months, weighs eighty-five pounds."

BIOGRAPHICAL AND CRITICAL SOURCES:

PERIODICALS

Canadian Review of Sociology and Anthropology, February, 2002, Gerry Coulter, review of *Guys, Gangs, and Girlfriend Abuse,* p. 119.

*   *   *

TRETHEWEY, Rachel 1967-

PERSONAL: Born October 12, 1967. *Education:* St. Edmund Hall, Oxford, B.A. (history), 1986.

ADDRESSES: Agent—c/o Author Mail, Hodder Headline, 338 Euston Rd., London NW1 3BH, England.

CAREER: Daily Express, features writer, 1989-92; *Daily Mail,* features writer, 1993-96; freelance journalist, 1996—. Health spokesperson for East Devon and Cornwall Liberal-Democrats chair, Torwood Branch Liberal-Democrats, Torbay.

WRITINGS:

Mistress of the Arts: The Passionate Life of Georgina, Duchess of Bedford (biography), Review (London, England), 2002.

SIDELIGHTS: British journalist and politician Rachel Trethewey is the author *Mistress of the Arts: The Passionate Life of Georgina, Duchess of Bedford,* a biography of Georgina Gordon, sixth Duchess of Bedford, who lived from 1781 to 1853. Gordon, a remarkable woman in her own right, was particularly known for her love affair with the famous artist Edwin Landseer. The relationship lasted some twenty years, during which time the duchess maintained a happy marriage to John Russell, the duke of Bedford, even though he knew of the affair. Gordon and Landseer, who was much younger than his lover and who painted many portraits of the duchess, shared a passion for art that matched a fiery relationship; at the same time, Gordon's husband offered her the stability she needed in her life. Amazingly, she was able to maintain a balance between the two and navigate a happy relationship with both throughout their lives. "It worked," Trethewey explains, "because of the characters of the two men. The Duke was very mellow and tolerant. He gave Georgina stability and position, Landseer gave her passion, excitement. She needed both aspects in her life. At times, I think neither man was entirely happy with the situation, but neither wanted to lose her because she was so life-enhancing." While *Spectator* writer Brian Masters merely described the biography as a "competent" effort, a *Kirkus Reviews* critic described *Mistress of the Arts* as "tactful yet open: much like Georgina's personality."

BIOGRAPHICAL AND CRITICAL SOURCES:

PERIODICALS

Australian, June 21, 2003, Diana Simmonds, "Portrait of Grand Lady as a Scamp," p. B11.
Guardian (Manchester, England), July 29, 1996, Roy Greenslade, "Commons Thread. Why Do Some Journalists Want to Swap Front Page Glory for Backbench Obscurity?," p. T14.
Kirkus Reviews, May 15, 2003, review of *Mistress of the Arts: The Passionate Life of Georgina, Duchess of Bedford,* p. 740.
Scotsman, July 20, 2002, Susan Mansfield, "Painted Lady of Passion."
Spectator, July 27, 2002, Brian Masters, "House Guests Rather than Friends," p. 38.*

*   *   *

TRIFKOVIC, Serge
(Srdja Trifkovic)

PERSONAL: Born in Belgrade, Yugoslavia (now Serbia). *Education:* Graduated from the University of Sussex; University of Southhampton, Ph.D.

ADDRESSES: Office—Chronicles, 928 N. Main St., Rockford, IL 61103.

CAREER: Journalist and historian. *Chronicles: A Magazine of American Culture,* foreign affairs editor, 1998—. Formerly broadcaster and producer, BBC

World Service, London, England, and Voice of America, Washington, DC; covered southeast Europe for *U.S. News & World Report* and the *Washington Times;* has appeared on BBC World Service, CNN International, and MSNBC, among other news outlets.

AWARDS, HONORS: Postdoctoral research grant at the Hoover Institution at Stanford, U.S. State Department.

WRITINGS:

(As Srdja Trifkovic) *Ustasa: Croatian Separatism and European Politics, 1929-1945,* The Lord Byron Foundation for Balkan Studies (London, England), 1998.

The Sword of the Prophet: Islam: History, Theology, Impact on the World, Regina Orthodox Press (Boston, MA), 2002.

Has also written commentary for the *Philadelphia Inquirer,* London *Times,* and *Cleveland Plain Dealer.*

SIDELIGHTS: Serge Trifkovic is the foreign editor of *Chronicles* magazine; he also holds a Ph.D. and has extensive experience as a broadcaster, producer, and political commentator. Trifkovic has published a book about the militant history of Islam, *The Sword of the Prophet: Islam: History, Theology, Impact on the World.* The book also calls itself "The Politically Incorrect Guide to Islam," which hints at the controversial nature of its subject. The book was published exactly one year after the September 11, 2001, terrorist attacks on the United States.

The author's object in *The Sword of the Prophet* is to show how, since the time of its founder Mohammed, Islam has sanctioned violence in the persecution of non-Muslims, victimized and debased women, and supported all methods of advancing the Muslim religion. Trifkovic warns that the West should defend itself against the aggression of "true" Muslims by limiting Muslim immigration and becoming less dependent on oil from Islamic countries. He asserts that while the majority of Muslims want peace, they do not represent the dangerous foundation of Islam and would lull others into not taking the threat of violence seriously.

The volatile nature of this argument was reflected by a review for *Media Monitors Network,* in which Habib Siddiqui called the author's perspective "repulsive" and remarked that he had a Serbian bias against Muslims. Writing for *Greco Report,* Michael M. Stenton supported the author's analysis but judged that "many Westerners will dismiss Trifkovic's account of Islam simply because they refuse to take religion seriously." Calling *Sword of the Prophet* more thorough and wide-ranging than similar books, *Booklist*'s Ray Olson commented that the author makes an "exceptionally fluid argument against militant Islam."

BIOGRAPHICAL AND CRITICAL SOURCES:

BOOKS

Trifkovic, Serge, *The Sword of the Prophet: Islam: History, Theology, Impact on the World,* Regina Orthodox Press (Boston, MA), 2002.

PERIODICALS

Booklist, October, 2002, Ray Olson, review of *The Sword of the Prophet,* p. 292.

ONLINE

Greco Report, http://www.grecoreport.com/ (May 7, 2003), Michael M. Stenton, "Islam: The Score."

Media Monitors Network, http://www.mediamonitors.com/ (July 31, 2003), Habib Siddiqui, "The Repulsive World of Serge Trifkovic."*

*   *   *

TRIFKOVIC, Srdja
See TRIFKOVIC, Serge

*   *   *

TROY, Tevi 1967-

PERSONAL: Born 1967. *Education:* University of Texas, Ph.D.

ADDRESSES: Agent—c/o Author Mail, Rowman & Littlefield Publishers, Inc., 4501 Forbes Rd, Lanham, MD 20706.

CAREER: Writer and U.S. government policymaker. White House Domestic Policy Council, special adviser. Worked at the Hudson Institute and American Enterprise Institute, as deputy assistant secretary for policy for the U.S. Department of Labor, and as policy director for former senator John Ashcroft.

WRITINGS:

Intellectuals and the American Presidency: Philosophers, Jesters, or Technicians?, Rowman & Littlefield Publishers, Inc., (Lanham, MD), 2002.

Contributor to periodicals, including *New Republic, Wall Street Journal,* and *Reason.*

SIDELIGHTS: The performance of the President of the United States is strongly influenced by the staff that surrounds him. With access to experts in areas such as economics, law, defense, and policy, the president's success depends largely on the accumulated wisdom, experience, and intellect of the staff that advises on the minutia of executive leadership. When the Executive Office of the President was created during Franklin D. Roosevelt's tenure, it was accompanied by the "unchallenged assertion" claiming that "the president needs help," wrote Roger Porter in *Times Literary Supplement.* In *Intellectuals and the American Presidency: Philosophers, Jesters, or Technicians?,* White House policy advisor Tevi Troy "examines the role intellectuals play in American political campaigns, what they do once a president is in office, and presidents' efforts to make connections between their staffs and the intellectual community," Porter wrote.

"Troy believes it is essential for presidential candidates to align themselves with highly visible academics," wrote Michael Genovese in *Library Journal.* Because of this association with the highly educated and with people of letters, the president's proposals and decisions gain credibility, bolstering the image of the president and his policies. "As the stories of the past eight administrations show, the interrelation of intellectuals and presidents has developed into a crucial factor determining presidential success," Troy wrote. *Intellectuals and the American Presidency* offers "a comprehensive account of how modern presidents have used public intellectuals as political and policy advisers," wrote Colleen Shogan on the *Institute for Human Studies* Web site. Troy explains that "intellectuals make a difference in the White House because they influence how presidents are perceived publicly, both in the near and distant future," Shogan observed. "Troy suggests," remarked Porter, "that intellectuals have often played a crucial role in persuading voters that a candidate has ideas, weight, and a coherent message."

Beginning with John F. Kennedy's 1960 campaign, Troy traces the evolution of intellectuals and their presence in presidential circles. The first true intellectual in the White House, Troy wrote, was historian Arthur M. Schlesinger, who served Kennedy's administration. "Troy uses Schlesinger to define what he means by an intellectual in the White House," wrote Matthew Robinson on the *Claremont Institution* Web site, which is "a person who has an independently established, well-respected reputation in the journalistic or scholarly community and who takes on the task of rallying intellectuals to the presidential standard."

To Troy, "the intellectual is not merely someone who combines in work and play the art of thinking," wrote Jackson Murphy on the *Enter Stage Right* Web site. "The intellectual is those things as well as someone harboring the characteristic of being in dire need of appreciation of his efforts." In that aspect, "Troy is less concerned with how intellectuals have fared in the White House than with how well or badly Presidents since 1960 have managed them," wrote James Nuechterlein in *Commentary.*

Some presidents made exceptionally astute use of intellectuals, Troy observed, noting that Bill Clinton made the most effective use of intellectuals since Kennedy. "Clinton courted the liberal intellectual establishment, and after twelve years of Republican administrations, they were hungry for attention," Shogan remarked. Clinton's influence with intellectuals was so strong that during the president's impeachment proceedings, "a group of 412 historians placed a full-page ad in the *New York Times* that defended Clinton and argued that the charges against him were not grounds for impeachment," Shogan wrote, unconcerned with any damage to their reputation or professional standing that such a stance might bring.

Other presidents, such as Jimmy Carter, Gerald Ford, and George Bush, Sr., were unable to connect with their intellectual aides and use their knowledge and skills to best advantage, largely due to lack of solid ideas, "political drift," or the "lack of ideological focus in an administration," Robinson observed. Ronald Reagan "had a clear and coherent set of beliefs," Nuechterlein commented, but "he had no interest in persuading liberal intellectuals of the rightness of his ideas, and conservative thinkers needed no persuasion."

In return for the aura of credibility intellectuals offered, they received validation for their positions, acclaim for their credentials, and sometimes simple ego-inflation. "The book pulls no punches and taps original sources to give readers a sense of how the egos are stroked and politics is conducted inside the White House," Robinson remarked. Kennedy's communications with Schlesinger included remarks such as: "I don't know if I mentioned to you before how impressed both Ted and I were with your memorandum on the future role of the Democratic Party. We are the wiser for reading it, and intend to use it further." Such compliments have consistently been paid to intellectuals in the White House. "From Troy's work it becomes clear such effusive language to critically minded intellectuals is common," Robinson continued. "And it works."

Troy himself is well aware of the treatment of intellectuals in American government. Possessing a Ph.D. in American civilization from the University of Texas, Troy has worked at such prominent think tanks as the American Enterprise Institute and the Hudson Institute. He has served as policy advisor to the U.S. Department of Labor and, most recently, to the White House Domestic Policy Council.

Frank J. Coppa, writing in *Perspectives on Political Science,* called *Intellectuals and the American Presidency* "an extraordinary work." Porter noted that the book could have been improved with "insights that could be gained by interviews with the participants themselves, most of whom are accessible and willing to explain nuances and to separate fact from speculation." Still, critics such as Robinson found it to be "a wonderfully written insight into politics today." The "readable and compelling account" makes it clear that "presidents cannot operate in a vacuum" in the White House, Murphy remarked. Intellectuals and academics "can be useful in shaping and articulating ideas, reflecting criticism, shoring up support on the political base, or partisan hackery," Murphy observed. "No

president is an island but intellectuals are no substitute for a president's personal political instinct."

BIOGRAPHICAL AND CRITICAL SOURCES:

BOOKS

Troy, Tevi, *Intellectuals and the American Presidency: Philosophers, Jesters, or Technicians?,* Rowman & Littlefield Publishers, Inc., (Lanham, MD), 2002.

PERIODICALS

Commentary, October, 2002, James Nuechterlein, "Brain Trust," review of *Intellectuals and the American Presidency: Philosophers, Jesters, or Technicians?,* pp. 81-83.
Library Journal, April 15, 2002, Michael Genovese, review of *Intellectuals and the American Presidency,* p. 111.
Perspectives on Political Science, fall, 2002, Frank J. Coppa, review of *Intellectuals and the American Presidency,* p. 250.
Public Interest, fall, 2003, Jason Bertsch, review of *Intellectuals and the American Presidency,* p. 120.
Reason, August, 2002, Sara Rimensnyder, "Potus and the Brain," interview with Tevi Troy, p. 17.
Times Literary Supplement, October 25, 2002, Roger Porter, "President's Professors," review of *Intellectuals and the American Presidency,* pp. 7-8.
Wall Street Journal, June 20, 2002, Lee Bockhorn, "Shallow Opinions, Misty Visions," review of *Intellectuals and the American Presidency,* p. D9.
Washington Post, May 2, 2002, Jonathan Yardley, "The Presidents' Brains," review of *Intellectuals and the American Presidency,* p. C02.
Wilson Quarterly, summer, 2002, Jeff Greenfield, review of *Intellectuals and the American Presidency,* pp. 122-124.

ONLINE

Claremont Institute Web site, http://www.claremont.org/ (October 5, 2002), Matthew Robinson, "Brains and Brawn in the White House," review of *Intellectuals and the American Presidency.*

Enter Stage Right, http://www.enterstageright.com/ (June 10, 2002), Jackson Murphy, review of *Intellectuals and the American Presidency.*

Institute for Human Studies, http://www.theihs.org/ (July 11, 2003), Colleen Shogan, review of *Intellectuals and the American Presidency.*

National Review Online, http://www.nationalreview. com/ (June 2, 2002) Kathryn Jean Lopez, "Eggheads in the White House," interview with Tevi Troy.*

*   *   *

TUCKER, Lisa

PERSONAL: Born in MO; married a jazz pianist; children: Miles. *Education:* University of Pennsylvania, M.A. (English and American literature), 1984; Villanova University, M.A. (mathematics); additional graduate studies at University of Pennsylvania.

ADDRESSES: Home—New Mexico. *Agent*—(Literary and film) Marly Rusoff, 811 Palmer Rd., Suite AA, Bronxville, NY 10708; (publicity) Megan Underwood or Lynn Goldberg, Goldberg/McDuffie Communications, 444 Madison Ave., Suite 3300, New York, NY 10022; Amy Pierpont, Simon & Schuster, 1230 Avenue of the Americas, New York, NY 10020.

CAREER: Has worked variously as a waitress, jazz musician, key-punch operator, office cleaner, writing instructor, and a math teacher at Bryn Mawr College.

WRITINGS:

The Song Reader (novel), Downtown Press (New York, NY), 2003.
Shout Down the Moon (novel), Downtown Press (New York, NY), 2004.

Contributor to books, including *Lit Riffs,* and to periodicals, including *Seventeen* and *Pages.*

SIDELIGHTS: The pages of Lisa Tucker's novels echo with music, with its ability to uplift as well as bring down, with its meaning, its performance, and its pervasive influence. Tucker's characters also know of life's struggles and how to use their talents and determination to rise above difficult odds. Leeann Norris narrates the story of herself and her sister in *The Song Reader,* Tucker's first novel. The sisters' absentee father walked out seven years before the time the novel begins, and their mother was killed in an automobile accident three years ago. Twenty-three-year-old Mary Beth serves as both sibling and parent to eleven-year-old Leeann, and to Mary Beth's adopted son, two-year-old Tommy, in a small Missouri town in the early 1980s. Mary Beth supports the family by working as a waitress, but her other "job" is her true passion: operating a small business as a song reader. Her clients experience a common phenomenon: sometimes a snippet of song will get stuck in their heads, repeating over and over. Other times, a fragment of lyric would seem suddenly significant, or a tune will trigger powerful emotions. As a song reader, Mary Beth interprets the meaning of the lyrics or music repeating themselves in her clients' heads. She finds the associations between songs and current and past emotional states; she knits together seemingly disparate connections between music and lyric and psychological condition.

At first well-accepted by the community, popular perception of Mary Beth's song-reading concern turns vicious when a client attempts suicide based on Mary Beth's counseling. The near-suicide also exposes a local scandal. Mary Beth's own psyche collapses as a result, and she is hospitalized. It then falls to Leeann to help Mary Beth recover, to locate their father, and to reconstruct the shattered family. "Tucker portrays characters with great depth who will tug at readers' heartstrings," commented Shelley A. Glantz in *Kliatt.* "Tucker's assured debut novel is an achingly tender narrative about grief, love, madness, and crippling family secrets," remarked a *Publishers Weekly* reviewer. And *Booklist* critic Carolyn Kubisz called the book an "engaging and bittersweet story of compassion, forgiveness, and the search for redemption," concluding that "this is a wonderful first novel."

"I think everybody senses that music has something to do with memory," Tucker said in an interview in *Publishers Weekly.* "When you're driving down the street and hear a song from a high school dance on the radio, you find yourself thinking about that dance." Songs often come back to people unbidden, whether triggered by a thought or something in the environment. "I couldn't help wondering: Why that particular song? Why Now?" Tucker remarked. "Could the song have entered your mind at this point in your life because it was telling you something you needed to know?"

Patty Taylor, the protagonist of Tucker's second novel, *Shout Down the Moon,* is also well-attuned to the rigors of struggle. A talented jazz singer, Patty is intent on making a career of music despite her creep of a manager and the band's disdain. She knows that music will make life better for her and her two-year-old son, Willie. After enduring repeated homelessness, the grinding drudgery of dead-end jobs, and devastating personal relationships, snide remarks or sleazy marketing campaigns are trivial obstacles to her career. When Rick, Willie's drug-dealer father, is released from prison, he tracks him and Patty down, and she finds herself faced with staying the course toward the dream she has found for herself or being drawn back into the violent, hopeless world that Rick represents and lives in. "Tucker's compulsively readable tale deftly moves over the literary landscape, avoiding genre classification; it succeeds as a subtle romance, an incisive character study, and compelling woman-in-peril noir fiction," observed a *Publishers Weekly* reviewer. "Tucker has stripped Patty's voice of all artifice," wrote Joanne Wilkinson in *Booklist,* "and her straight-from-the-heart narration is instantly gripping."

BIOGRAPHICAL AND CRITICAL SOURCES:

PERIODICALS

Booklist, April 1, 2003, Carolyn Kubisz, review of *The Song Reader,* pp. 1380-1381; February 15, 2004, Joanne Wilkinson, review of *Shout Down the Moon,* p. 1039.

Denver Post, May 4, 2003, Robin Vidimos, "Song Stuck in One's Head Holds Meaning," p. EE03.

Kirkus Reviews, February 15, 2003, review of *The Song Reader,* p. 267; February 1, 2004, review of *Shout Down the Moon,* p. 108.

Kliatt, September, 2003, Shelley A. Glantz, review of *The Song Reader,* p. 22.

Library Journal, April 15, 2003, Patricia Gulian, review of *The Song Reader,* p. 128.

Philadelphia Inquirer, September 24, 2003, "*Song Reader:* There's More to the Lyrics Than Just the Music."

Publishers Weekly, March 17, 2003, review of *The Song Reader,* p. 50; March 17, 2003, Kevin Howell, "Facing the Music," p. 51; December 22, 2003, review of *Shout Down the Moon,* p. 33.

Salt Lake Tribune, August 3, 2003, Christy Karras, "Music, Memory Harmonize in Tucker's *The Song Reader,*" p. D4.

School Library Journal, August, 2003, Susan H. Woodcock, review of *The Song Reader,* p. 188.

ONLINE

BookWeb, http://www.bookweb.org/ (May 13, 2003), "*The Song Reader*—Debut Novel Hits the Right Note."

Lisa Tucker Home Page, http://www.lisatucker.com (April 4, 2004).

University of Pennsylvania, http://www.upenn.edu/ (April 4, 2004), biography of Lisa Tucker.

*　　*　　*

TURNIPSEED, Erica Simone 1971-

PERSONAL: Born June 12, 1971; *Education:* Yale University, B.A. (anthropology), 1993; Columbia University, M.A. (anthropology), 1999.

ADDRESSES: Home—Brooklyn, NY. *Agent*—c/o Author Mail, HarperCollins Publishers, 10 East 53rd St., 7th Floor, New York, NY 10022. *E-mail*—erica@ ericasimoneturnipseed.com.

CAREER: Director of development at the Twenty-First Century Foundation. Member of board of directors of the Black Ivy League Alumni League; founder and cochair, Five Years for the House Initiative.

WRITINGS:

A Love Noire (novel), Amistad (New York, NY), 2003.

Contributor to *Children of the Dream: Our Own Stories of Growing Up Black in America,* compiled by Laurel Holliday, Washington Square Press (New York, NY), 2000.

SIDELIGHTS: In an autobiographical essay on her home page, Erica Simone Turnipseed describes herself as "an avid reader for as long as I could read." Teen novels by writers such as Judy Blume were supplemented with works by Harper Lee and Maya Angelou. In college, she delved into the works of literary greats such as James Baldwin, Toni Morrison, and Ralph Ellison, while searching out African writers and "keen women's voices," she remarked. "And through all those years," Turnipseed said, "I wrote." She "wrote poems and short stories about love and identity and displacement," she remarked on her home page. Despite the lifelong feast of reading and writing, "by my late twenties, I realized that I had read a lot and written a lot, but I still was looking for a story that explored an African diaspora that was neither long ago nor far away." She "longed to read that book but could never find it on library and bookstore shelves. So I wrote the book I wanted to read: *A Love Noire*."

In *A Love Noire* graduate student Noire Demain and investment banker Innocent Pokou have little in common when they meet at a book signing. She is a brilliant scholar pursuing a Ph.D. in comparative literature, idealistic, principled, a bit radical, and intellectually independent. He is a wealthy professional from the Ivory Coast, a handsome and well-educated man. Despite her own educational background, Noire is suspicious of privilege and dubious about the upwardly mobile black men she meets. Innocent, however, is different from his friends; he knows how to treat her with dignity and respect. Innocent also retains strong ties to his family and heritage in Africa, giving him a cultural richness and social consciousness that Noire finds irresistible. Noire and Innocent hesitantly embark on an energetic relationship that takes them throughout the world, to exotic locations where a variety of black cultures and expatriate viewpoints show "that everyone's experience is an authentic Black story," Turnipseed remarked in *Essence*.

A *Publishers Weekly* reviewer noted that "Turnipseed's take on star-crossed lovers breaks no molds, but her voice is strong and confident." In the book, "Turnipseed explores not only the much-hyped quest of Gen X brothers and sisters getting, and trying to stay, together amid a growing class divide and collapsing global boundaries," but love of all types, including "good, old-fashioned self-love," commented Angela Ards in *Village Voice*. Robert Fleming, writing in *Black Issues Book Review*, remarked favorably on Turnipseed's "splendid writing" and "the maturity and insight she shows on each page" of the novel. "Turnipseed's narrative is powerful, vital, and totally

entertaining," Fleming observed, concluding that "*A Love Noire* is a thoroughly engaging, provocative literary debut."

BIOGRAPHICAL AND CRITICAL SOURCES:

PERIODICALS

Black Issues Book Review, May-June, 2003, Robert Fleming, review of *A Love Noire,* p. 48.
Essence, June, 2003, review of *A Love Noire,* p. 136.
Kirkus Reviews, May 15, 2003, review of *A Love Noire,* p. 713.
Publishers Weekly, June 30, 2003, review of *A Love Noire,* p. 58.
Village Voice, July 2, 2003, Angela Ards, review of *A Love Noire,* p. 52.

ONLINE

Erica Simone Turnipseed Home Page, http://www.ericasimoneturnipseed.com/ (April 4, 2004), autobiography of Erica Simone Turnipseed.
HarperCollins, http://www.harpercollins.com/ (April 4, 2004), biography of Erica Simone Turnipseed; "A Conversation with Erica Simone Turnipseed."*

*   *   *

TYNAN, Ronan 1960-

PERSONAL: Born May 14, 1960, in Kilkenny, Ireland. *Education:* National College of Physical Education, graduated 1985; Trinity College, M.D., 1993; also attended College of Music (Dublin, Ireland). *Hobbies and other interests:* Horse breeding and riding, track and field.

ADDRESSES: Agent—c/o Author Mail, Simon & Schuster, 1230 Avenue of the Americas, New York, NY 10020. *E-mail*—contact@drronantynan.net.

CAREER: Physician in Kilkenny, Ireland; Irish Tenors, musician, 1998—. Has also worked as a salesman of prosthetic limbs. Performer on solo albums, including *My Life Belongs to You,* 2002, and *The Impossible*

TYNAN   *CONTEMPORARY AUTHORS • Volume 226*

Dream, 2002; has also performed with the Irish Tenors on albums *The Irish Tenors: McNamara, McDermott, Kearns, Tynan,* 1999, *Home for Christmas,* 1999, *Live in Belfast,* 2000, *Ellis Island,* 2001, *The Very Best of the Irish Tenors,* 2002, and *We Three Kings,* 2003.

AWARDS, HONORS: John McCormack Cup for Tenor Voice, 1991; "Go For It" talent show winner, British Broadcasting Corporation (BBC)/RTE, 1994; Best Male Voice, International Operatic Singing Festival (Marmande, France), 1996; eight Olympic gold medals and six world championship gold medals in track and field events for disabled athletes.

WRITINGS:

Halfway Home: My Life 'Til Now, Scribner (New York, NY), 2002.

SIDELIGHTS: One of the celebrated Irish Tenors, Ronan Tynan was thirty-three before he even undertook formal musical training. It all happened after a remarkable journey that has made him a poster boy for determination in the face of adversity. Born with a rare lower limb disability that forced him to wear leg supports, Ronan refused to accept any limitations. He became an avid soccer player and later an amateur jockey, winning show jumping medals. Then at age twenty, after breaking his leg in a motorbike accident, doctors told him they would have to amputate both his legs at the knee to prevent future health problems. It was a terrible blow, but already Tynan was suffering bouts of paralysis and even blindness from the pressure that standing up put on some of his nerve endings. So he told the doctors to go ahead.

For the first time, Tynan began to think seriously about academic credentials, seeing them as a means of maintaining his independence in the face of his disability. At the same time, he did not want to give up on athletics. So he applied to Ireland's National College of Physical Education, becoming the first disabled person accepted there. Using prosthetic limbs, he passed the school's mobility standards and even went on to win gold medals in Olympic competitions for the disabled. After graduation, he found a job as a salesman for a firm marketing prosthetic limbs, but Tynan still was not satisfied.

Musing one day about his dreams, Tynan decided he would love to become a doctor, and before long he was studying orthopedic sports injuries at Dublin's prestigious Trinity College. Despite the grueling schedule of studies and internships, Tynan decided to nurture another dream along the way. In his fifth year of medical school, he started taking voice lessons and soon was competing in regional contests and studying under Irish singer Veronica Dunne and Italian tenor Ugo Benelli. After graduating from medical school, he entered and won the British Broadcasting Corporation's talent show "Go For It." The doctors at the hospital where he was interning even took up a collection to send him to the Royal Conservatory of Music, and soon Tynan was winning international singing competitions. Then Tynan's body seemed to strike back again. This time, he suddenly lost his voice, and doctors discovered a blockage that had been damaging his vocal cords for years. They removed it, but it was unclear if his singing voice would ever return.

Tynan returned to his hometown of Kilkenny, Ireland, to set up a medical practice specializing in sports medicine and rehabilitation. He hesitated to sing in public, but in 1998 he sang at his father's funeral and discovered that his remarkable voice had returned. A short time later, he teamed up with Anthony Kearns and John McDermott and the Irish Tenors were born. Their first concert CD went platinum, as did Tynan's solo album *My Life Belongs to You.* Today, he shuttles between his practice in Kilkenny and filling concert halls on tour with the Irish Tenors, while continuing the competitive horse riding of his youth, this time on horses he raises himself. In *Halfway Home: My Life 'Til Now,* he recounts all these up and downs and triumphs. "In other hands, this litany of overachievement would have sounded like an exercise in self-congratulation, but Tynan treats his impressive—actually astounding—life matter-of-factly," concluded a *Kirkus Reviews* contributor. *Library Journal* reviewer Kate McCaffrey found that "Tynan's style is simple and direct, certainly not artful, but his physical and emotional bravery is so compelling that it doesn't matter."

BIOGRAPHICAL AND CRITICAL SOURCES:

PERIODICALS

Booklist, January 1, 2002, p. 791.

396

Kirkus Reviews, November 15, 2001, review of *Halfway Home: My Life 'Til Now,* p. 1604.

Library Journal, January, 2002, Kate McCaffrey, review of *Halfway Home,* p. 107.

People, March 11, 2002, Galina Espinoza and Debbie Seaman, "All of the Above."

Publishers Weekly, December 10, 2001, "Feel-Good Stories," p. 66.*

U-V

ULITSKAYA, Ludmila 1943-

PERSONAL: Born 1943, in Bashkiria, Siberia, Union of Soviet Socialist Republics. *Education:* Studied genetics at Moscow State University.

ADDRESSES: Home—Moscow, Russia. *Agent*—c/o Author Mail, Schocken Books, Random House, 1745 Broadway, New York, NY 10019.

CAREER: Biologist and writer of film scripts and prose works.

AWARDS, HONORS: Russian Booker Prize shortlist, Medici Prize for foreign fiction (France), 1995, and Penne Prize (Italy), 1998, all for *Sonechka;* Russian Booker Prize, 2001, for *Kazus Kukotskogo.*

WRITINGS:

Sonechka, Novy Mir, 1992, translation by Arch Tait published as *Sonechka and Other Stories,* Glas Publishers (Birmingham, England), 1998.
Bednye Rodstvenniki, Izd-vo Slovo (Moscow, Russia), 1994.
Medeia i Ee Deti: Povesti, Vagrius (Moscow, Russia), 1996, translation by Arch Tait published as *Medea and Her Children,* Schocken Books (New York, NY), 2002.
Veselye Pokhorony: Poest' i Rasskazy (stories), Vagrius (Moscow, Russia), 1998, translation by Cathy Porter published as *The Funeral Party,* Schocken Books (New York, NY), 2001.

Kazus Kukotskogo, EKSMO-Press (Moscow, Russia), 2000.
Pikovaia Dama i Drugie: Rasskazy (stories), Vagrius (Moscow, Russia), 2001.
Devochki, EKSMO-Press (Moscow, Russia), 2002.

Also author of *Skvoznava liniya* (short stories), and *Mily Shurik* (novel), 2004.

SIDELIGHTS: Acclaimed by some critics as Russia's best contemporary novelist, Ludmila Ulitskaya did not achieve literary recognition until she reached her fifties. Trained as a biologist, she lost her scientific accreditation from the Soviet state when she translated Leon Uris's novel *Exodus,* a banned book, into Russian. Ulitskaya later worked in a theater and began writing film scripts. Her own short stories and novellas, which she had been writing all her life, began to be published in Russia in the late 1980s. Critics have described her work as deeply humane, morally serious, and straightforward in technique—qualities that have earned the writer comparisons with Tolstoy. Unlike many leading Russian writers who emphasize absurdity and violence, Ulitskaya, according to *World Literature Today* contributor Bonnie C. Marshall, writes in the nineteenth-century tradition.

The novella *Sonechka,* which won the Medici Prize in France and the Penn Prize in Italy, follows the complex relationships within a family in mid-1900s Russia. The title character accepts her husband's infidelity and even assumes responsibility for his young mistress after he suddenly dies. Throughout it all, she considers herself blessed with immense happiness. Margaret Ziolkowski in *World Literature Today* found this strength of character, which is a common theme in Ulitskaya's fiction, "both credible and moving."

The Funeral Party, Ulitskaya's first novel to appear in English, was widely admired for its psychological depth and what *Review of Contemporary Fiction* contributor Michael Pinker called its "exquisite irony and tenderness." The novel is structured around the death in New York City of an exiled Russian artist, Alik. His wife, lovers, and friends gather at his bedside to say good-bye. What emerges, according to *New York Times Book Review* critic M. G. Lord, is a "deft, economical portrait of an engaging set of characters whose behavior, though occasionally screwball, is never one-dimensional. For Ulitskaya's book is also a meditation on Russian identity and the degree to which that identity can be sustained." Indeed, Alik never really left Russia because he "'built his Russia around him, a Russia which hadn't existed for a long time and perhaps never had.'"

Both Lord and Marshall pointed out the parallels between *The Funeral Party* and Tolstoy's novella "The Death of Ivan Ilyich." Marshall felt that Ulitskaya's "positive portrait of Alik is less convincing than Tolstoy's negative portrait of Ivan Ilyich" because Alik's considerable flaws cast doubt on the high esteem in which his friends hold him. Lord, on the other hand, suggested that Ulitskaya "seems to have set up deliberate parallels with [Tolstoy's] well-known work in order to make points about how the Soviet experience changed Russian life." Lord observed that Ulitskaya sets Alik's death against the televised backdrop of the 1991 attempted coup that ultimately drove Gorbachev from power, and that her characters, although they are "newly-minted Americans," cannot stop watching these events unfolding in their emotional homeland.

Critics also admired the humor and insight of *The Funeral Party.* A *Publishers Weekly* reviewer wrote that "Ulitskaya is adept at capturing the subtle nuances of thought and experience, expressing both human spirit and flaws without false sentimentality." A contributor to *Russian Life* hailed the novel as a "marvelous" and "delightful" work with "great emotional power." Lisa Rohrbaugh, in *Library Journal,* praised its "beautiful, lyrical prose," and Lord concluded by commending the "riotously funny" novel as a "quirky, tender story whose themes of love, loss, and identity soar over the boundaries of language and geography."

In *Medea and Her Children,* Ulitskaya presents a multi-generational family saga set in the Crimea, a peninsula in the Black Sea where Medea's Greek ancestors settled along with a diverse mix of Russians, Ukrainians, Jews, and Armenians. The novel is set during the summer of 1976, when Medea, a widow without children, awaits a visit from her scattered nieces and nephews. "The glow of nostalgia illuminates the novel's portrait of the détente decade," wrote *New York Times Book Review* contributor Ken Kalfus, who noted that the novel is "written with contagious affection for the peninsula's untamed landscape and easygoing people." As Medea welcomes her guests, Ulitskaya describes the eventful course of the family's history, going all the way back to the beginning of the century and tracing its many geographic moves, amorous adventures, heartbreaks, and triumphs.

Though Kalfus faulted the English translation for its literal adherence to literary Russian's elevated diction, he admired *Medea and Her Children* itself as an "evocative and intricate story." Reviewers for *Publishers Weekly* and *Booklist* expressed similar enthusiasm, praising the novel for its boisterous humor and lively writing. In *Kirkus Reviews,* however, a critic found the narrative "impossibly convoluted" and "as fascinating and tangled as an old woman's fireside reminiscences . . . striking, but badly out of focus." Mary Brennan in *Seattle Times* also noted the narrative's many complex strands, but considered these integral to a book that "offers rich rewards."

BIOGRAPHICAL AND CRITICAL SOURCES:

PERIODICALS

Booklist, January 1, 2001, Frank Caso, review of *The Funeral Party,* p. 919; November 15, 2002, Frank Caso, review of *Medea and Her Children,* p. 570.

Kirkus Reviews, September 15, 2002, review of *Medea and Her Children,* p. 1347.

Library Journal, January 1, 2001, Lisa Rohrbaugh, review of *The Funeral Party,* p. 158.

New York Times Book Review, February 11, 2001, M. G. Lord, review of *The Funeral Party,* p. 18; November 17, 2002, Ken Kalfus, review of *Medea and Her Children,* p. 15.

Publishers Weekly, December 18, 2000, review of *The Funeral Party,* p. 57; November 4, 2002, review of *Medea and Her Children,* p. 63.

Review of Contemporary Fiction, fall, 2001, Michael Pinker, review of *The Funeral Party,* pp. 213-214.

Russian Life, March, 2001, review of *The Funeral Party,* p. 60.

Seattle Times, January 5, 2003, Mary Brennan, review of *Medea and Her Children.*

Times Literary Supplement, March 12, 1999, Sarah A. Smith, review of *Sonechka and Other Stories,* p. 33.

World Literature Today, spring, 1999, Margaret Ziolkowski, review of *Sonechka and Other Stories,* p. 354; autumn, 2000, Bonnie C. Marshall, review of *The Funeral Party,* p. 882.*

*　　*　　*

ULLMAN, Ellen 1950(?)-

PERSONAL: Born c. 1950. *Education:* Cornell University, B.A. (English).

ADDRESSES: Home—San Francisco, CA. *Agent*—c/o Author Mail, Nan A. Talese, Doubleday Broadway Group, 1540 Broadway, New York, NY 10036.

CAREER: Software engineer and writer; worked as a computer programmer, beginning 1978; freelance consultant to software companies; guest commentator on National Public Radio.

WRITINGS:

Close to the Machine: Technophilia and Its Discontents: A Memoir, City Lights Books (San Francisco, CA), 1997.
The Bug, Doubleday (New York, NY), 2003.

Essays included in anthologies, including *Resisting the Virtual Light,* City Lights Books, 1994, and *Wired Women,* Seal Press, 1996. Contributor to periodicals, including *Harper's* and *Wired;* contributor to *Salon.com.*

SIDELIGHTS: Ellen Ullman marshals her twenty years of computer programming expertise in her 2003 novel *The Bug.* In *New Scientist,* Wendy M. Grossman noted that Ullman is a "rarity" among writers; her published work "explores the relationships between humans and computers in a way that is not open to anyone who hasn't been a programmer." In praise of Ullman's memoir *Close to the Machine: Technophilia and Its Discontents, New York Times Book Review* contributor J. D. Biersdorfer dubbed the book an "admirable" account of a middle-age woman "standing up to, and facing down, 'obsolescence' in two different, particularly unforgiving worlds—modern technology and modern society."

Taking place in 1984, shortly after the development of the first personal computer, Ullman's darkly humorous first novel *The Bug* introduces readers to Silicon Valley software tester Roberta Walton, a linguist with a Ph.D., no job prospects in her field, and an often-absent boyfriend, who discovers a bug in one of her company's programs. Walton shares her find with programmer Ethan Levin, who at first does not take her seriously because she is a) a woman; and b) not a programmer. When the bug proves to be a serious problem, Ethan attempts to track it down and find its genesis in his own program, but to no avail; the "Jester," as the bug is now known, only appears intermittently and always freezes the company's computer system at the worst time. As Roberta gains programming skills in an effort to forge an uneasy alliance with Ethan and help him at his task, the fate of Walton's company, Telligentsia, has dimmed to less than bright, and Ethan has become increasingly unhinged. Praising Ullman's characterization of the techie Ethan, a *Publishers Weekly* contributor noted that she "brings to the programmer mindset, in numerous finely wrought asides, a combination of poetic and philosophical sensibilities that plumb the abstruse depths of technological creation." Writing in *Library Journal,* Lawrence Rungren called *The Bug* a "deeply humanistic and surprisingly old-fashioned work that's certainly 'not for geeks only,'" while in *Kirkus Reviews,* an enthusiastic reviewer added that Ullman "sustains a haunting tone of revulsion mingled with nostalgia" in drawing readers into the "innermost circle of computerdom."

BIOGRAPHICAL AND CRITICAL SOURCES:

PERIODICALS

Booklist, May 1, 2003, Gavin Quinn, review of *The Bug,* p. 1582.
IEEE Software, May-June, 1998, interview with Ullman, pp. 42-45.

Kirkus Reviews, April 15, 2003, review of *The Bug,* p. 568.

Library Journal, May 1, 2003, Lawrence Rungren, review of *The Bug,* p. 157.

New Scientist, April 26, 2003, Wendy M. Grossman, review of *The Bug,* p. 53.

New York Times Book Review, November 30, 1997, J. D. Biersdorfer, review of *Close to the Machine: Technophilia and Its Discontents: A Memoir,* p. 21.

Publishers Weekly, April 28, 2003, review of *The Bug,* p. 46.

Women's Review of Books, February, 2001, interview with Ullman, p. 6; July, 2003, Martha Nichols, review of *The Bug,* pp. 26-28.

ONLINE

Nan A. Talese Web site, http://www.randomhouse.com/nanatalese/ (October 12, 2003).*

*   *   *

VANDERBES, Jennifer (Chase) 1974-

PERSONAL: Born 1974, in New York, NY. *Education:* Yale University, B.A. (English); Iowa Writers' Workshop, University of Iowa, M.F.A. (creative writing).

ADDRESSES: Office—Graduate Program in Creative Writing, University of Iowa, 102 Dey House, 507 North Clinton St., Iowa City, Iowa 52242-1000. *E-mail*—jennifer-vanderbes@uiowa.edu.

CAREER: Writer and educator. *Pittsburgh Post-Gazette,* Pittsburgh, PA, reporter; University of Wisconsin—Madison, James C. McCreight fiction fellow, 2000-01; Colgate University, Hamilton, NY, Olive B. O'Connor fellow in creative writing, 2001-02; Iowa Writers' Workshop, University of Iowa, Iowa City, visiting assistant professor, 2003-04.

AWARDS, HONORS: Truman Capote fellow.

WRITINGS:

The Applicant (one-act play), produced in New York, NY, 2000.
Easter Island (novel), Dial (New York, NY), 2003.

Contributor of short fiction to *Best New American Voices 2000,* edited by Tobias Wolff, Harcourt (San Diego, CA), 2000.

SIDELIGHTS: In 2003 Jennifer Vanderbes published her critically acclaimed debut novel *Easter Island.* In the work, Vanderbes interweaves the stories of two women, separated in age by sixty years, who discover the mysteries of Easter Island. In the Manchester *Guardian,* Rachel Hore called the work "part travel adventure, part absorbing scientific discovery, part love story."

Vanderbes was born and raised in New York City. Inspired by *The Diary of Anne Frank,* she began keeping a journal of her own at age twelve. Her interest in literature continued through high school and college, and while a student at Yale University, she enrolled in a class taught by Robert Stone that she credits as the turning point of her career. "He was not only devoted to his students and *available,*" Vanderbes told *Washington Post Book World* contributor Marie Arana of Stone, "he was willing to say the uncomfortable thing." "By the end of a semester with him," Vanderbes added, "I'd written one hundred pages of solid stuff." A few years later, while researching archeological expeditions, Vanderbes came upon the idea for *Easter Island.*

The novel follows Elsa Pendleton, a young Englishwoman, and Greer Faraday, an American botanist. Following the death of her father in 1912, Pendleton hastily marries the much-older Edward Beazley, a Royal Geographic Society anthropologist who is assigned to study Easter Island's giant *moai* statues. The recently widowed Faraday arrives on the island in 1973, still grieving the husband who plagiarized her work, thus damaging their marriage. A third narrative, involving the fate of World War I German Admiral Graf Von Spee, is intertwined with the women's stories. "The heart of the story . . . is the island's impenetrable mysteriousness, and Vanderbes extracts considerable drama and tension from questions not susceptible to final answers," according to a *Kirkus Reviews* critic. A *Publishers Weekly* reviewer stated that the author "knows how to craft suspense, and the narratives—while with vivid historical and scientific detail—move forward on the strength of her fully realized characters."

BIOGRAPHICAL AND CRITICAL SOURCES:

PERIODICALS

Book, July-August, 2003, Penelope Mesic, review of *Easter Island,* p. 81.

Booklist, May 15, 2003, Marta Segal Block, review of *Easter Island,* p. 1641.

Christian Science Monitor, May 29, 2003, Ron Charles, "Enigmas in Stone."

Guardian (Manchester, England), May 24, 2003, Rachel Hore, review of *Easter Island,* p. 28.

Independent Sunday (London, England), May 10, 2003, review of *Easter Island,* p. 19.

Kirkus Reviews, April 15, 2003, review of *Easter Island,* p. 569.

Library Journal, March 15, 2003, Barbara Hoffert, review of *Easter Island,* p. 118.

New York Times, June 15, 2003, Michael Upchurch, "Head Cases," p. 17.

Observer (London, England), May 18, 2003, Lisa Allardice, "Enigma Variation a la Mode," p. 17.

People, June 30, 2003, p. 41.

Publishers Weekly, May 19, 2003, review of *Easter Island,* p. 52.

San Francisco Chronicle, June 29, 2003, Megan Harlan, "Digging for Meaning on a Mysterious Island."

Times (London, England), May 10, 2003, Carola Longe, "Tendrils of Time," p. 19.

Vogue, March, 2003, Joanna Smith Rakoff, "Passionate Nomads," pp. 422-423.

Washington Post Book World, December 7, 2003, Maria Arana, "Jennifer Vanderbes: All in Her Head," p. 5.

ONLINE

Bookreporter.com, http://www.bookreporter.com/ (April 26, 2004), Bethanne Kelly Patrick, review of *Easter Island.*

Jennifer Vanderbes Easter Island Page, http://www.geocities.com/jvanderbes/ (April 26, 2004).*

*   *   *

Van METER, Jonathan W. 1963-

PERSONAL: Born May 5, 1963.

ADDRESSES: *Agent*—c/o Crown Publicity, 1745 Broadway, New York, NY 10019. *E-mail*—jvanmeter@ thelastgoodtime.com.

CAREER: Writer, editor, and journalist. *Vibe* magazine, creator and editor, 1992-94.

WRITINGS:

The Last Good Time: Skinny D'Amato, the Notorious 500 Club, and the Rise and Fall of Atlantic City, Crown Publishers (New York, NY), 2003.

Contributor to magazines and periodicals such as *Atlantic City, Spy, New York Times, Vanity Fair, Esquire, Tatler, Sunday Times,* and *Vogue.*

SIDELIGHTS: A prolific contributor to major American magazines, Jonathan W. Van Meter has written major profiles on celebrities such as Oprah Winfrey, Jodie Foster, and Liza Minnelli for magazines such as *Vanity Fair, Vogue,* and the *New York Times.* Van Meter was also the creator and first editor of the hip-hop magazine *Vibe.*

The chance sighting of a classified ad for an estate sale in 1986 introduced Van Meter to the world of Paul "Skinny" D'Amato, a prominent nightclub owner during Atlantic City's boom years in the 1950s and 1960s. His longtime fascination with the brash and colorful D'Amato led Van Meter to write *The Last Good Time: Skinny D'Amato, the Notorious 500 Club, and the Rise and Fall of Atlantic City,* the story of D'Amato's famed 500 Club, his connections to organized crime and the elite of 1950s celebrities, and his undeniable role in the development of Atlantic City. Mingled with D'Amato's story is the history of Atlantic City itself and how it became known as much for its essence of hipness as for the sins and temptations it offered its visitors.

D'Amato's fortunes rose along with those of the city he called home. A smooth talker and shrewd businessman, D'Amato "was a major figure on his home turf, beloved as a great host and Santa Claus-style tipper," commented Janet Maslin in the *New York Times Book Review.* Even while maintaining his own low profile, D'Amato set out to make his club the swankiest joint in the city. His 500 Club hosted some of the biggest names in entertainment, politics, and sports that the 1950s could offer. John F. Kennedy visited often. Dean Martin and Jerry Lewis debuted their act there in 1946 and continued to frequent the club. Frank Sinatra performed there regularly. Baseball legend Joe DiMaggio and Marilyn Monroe maintained a private booth. Meanwhile, the public, which came for the chance to see a star at the next table, kept the coffers filled.

The club also served as host to known members of the mob, though D'Amato was never implicated in any crimes. After a failed attempt by D'Amato and Sinatra to run a legal casino in Las Vegas, D'Amato's luck failed; his wife died, his son was convicted of a brutal murder, and the 500 Club burned down in 1973. The site of the 500 club is now a parking lot for one of Donald Trump's casinos.

Van Meter "succeeds fully in coalescing and elucidating the ins and outs, sins and faults, and value of the entertainment world," remarked William G. Kenz in *Library Journal.* David Pitt, writing in *Booklist,* concluded, "This is a fascinating tale of greed and corruption, and it enlightens as it entertains."

BIOGRAPHICAL AND CRITICAL SOURCES:

PERIODICALS

Advocate, November 3, 1992, Erik K. Washington, "The Big Dis," pp. 72-73.

American Heritage, October, 2003, review of *The Last Good Time: Skinny D'Amato, the Notorious 500 Club, and the Rise and Fall of Atlantic City,* p. 16.

Booklist, April 1, 2003, David Pitt, review of *The Last Good Time,* p. 1374.

Business Week, July 21, 2003, Robert McNatt, "An Ex-hoodlum with the Key to the City," p. 14.

Entertainment Weekly, June 27, 2003, Chris Nasawaty, review of *The Last Good Time,* p. 141.

Gay City News, November 13, 2003, Wickham Boyle, "Domestic Bliss."

Inside Media, May 11, 1994, John Motavalli, "Bad Vibes: Madonna Cover Sparks War," pp. 1-2.

Kirkus Reviews, May 1, 2003, review of *The Last Good Time,* p. 668.

Library Journal, July, 2003, William G. Kenz, review of *The Last Good Time,* p. 86.

New York Times Book Review, June 9, 2003, Janet Maslin, "For Gods of Night Life, The World's on a String," p. E7.

Publishers Weekly, June 12, 2000, John F. Baker, "The In Place in Atlantic City," p. 25; March 23, 2003, review of *The Last Good Time,* p. 69.

Rolling Stone, October 29, 1992, "*Vibe* Baptized by Fire."

Washington Post Book World, June 22, 2003, Wil Haygood, review of *The Last Good Time,* p. T03.

ONLINE

Bloomsbury, http://www.bloomsbury.com/ (April 6, 2004), biography of Jonathan Van Meter.

Last Good Time, http://www.thelastgoodtime.com/ (April 6, 2004).*

*   *   *

VAUGHAN, Brian K. 1976-(?)

PERSONAL: Born c. 1976, in Cleveland, OH. *Education:* Graduated from New York University Film School.

ADDRESSES: Home—San Diego, CA. *Agent*—c/o Author Mail, DC Comics, 1700 Broadway, New York, NY 10019.

CAREER: Writer.

WRITINGS:

"Y: LAST MAN" SERIES; GRAPHIC NOVELS

Y: The Last Man: Unmanned, illustrated by Pia Guerra, DC Comics (New York, NY), 2003.

Y: The Last Man: One Small Step, illustrated by Pia Guerra and Jose Marzan, DC Comics (New York, NY, 2004.

OTHER

(With others) *Green Lantern: Circle of Fire,* illustrated by Norm Breyfogle and others, DC Comics (New York, NY), 2002.

Also author of other comic book series, including *Ex Machina,* with artist Tony Harris; *Runaways; Mystique; The Hood;* and a prequel for the *X2* series. Author of issues for comic book series, including *Batman, Swamp Thing,* and *Chamber.* Also author of *For Art's Sake.*

SIDELIGHTS: Comic scriptwriter Brian K. Vaughan, author of the "Y: Last Man" series of graphic novels, became interested in writing for the comics genre when two editors from Marvel Comics came to visit New York University, where Vaughan was studying filmmaking. The editors met with students and taught them about comic book script writing, and Vaughan submitted some writing samples. In an interview with Nolan Reese on the *Movie Poop Shoot* Web site, Vaughan recalled, "[The editors] liked some of my samples, so they threw me little assignments, scripting gigs and whatnot. And I sort of crawled my way up the latter after that."

In *Y: The Last Man: Unmanned,* Vaughan presented the first of his ongoing novels about "Y," or Yorick Brown. In the novel, which is composed of the first five books of a comic series and illustrated by Pia Guerra, a mysterious plague has wiped out every male animal on Earth except Yorick and his pet monkey Ampersand. Although Yorick has survived, he is on the run from an Amazon-like tribe formed by women who want to make sure the last man on Earth is captured. As he tries to evade his pursuers, Yorick searches for a cloning researcher to find out why he survived and who can help him repopulate the world. In an interview in *Titan Magazine,* Vaughn noted, "Y was inspired by something I used to daydream about in third grade, that the pretty redheaded girl who sat across from me would fall madly in love with me . . . as soon as every other boy in the class dropped dead." Writing in *Booklist,* Gordon Flagg noted that the "yarn introduces a large number of intriguing characters and plotlines as it lays the groundwork for what promises to be a compelling series." *Library Journal* contributor Steve Raiteri said the book's "appeal is its fine story, well scripted with dryly humorous touches by Vaughan."

The next book in the series is titled *Y: The Last Man: One Small Step,* once again featuring Yorick and Ampersand. Yorick is still being hunted, this time by a group called the Culper Ring, whose aims are to study Yorick. As they track him across the country, they protect him from an Israeli strike team that wants Yorick for its own unsavory purposes and that is being aided in its hunt by the female president of the United States. In addition, a space station carrying two male astronauts is about to fall into a Kansas cornfield. The plot is further complicated when Yorick and his bodyguard from the Culper Ring appear to be falling in love. Writing in *Publishers Weekly,* a reviewer commented, "The stakes are high, and Vaughan masterfully interweaves story lines." The reviewer also noted, "This book is complete and utter comic gold."

BIOGRAPHICAL AND CRITICAL SOURCES:

PERIODICALS

Booklist, February 1, 2003, Gordon Flagg, review of *Y: The Last Man: Unmanned,* p. 970.
Entertainment Weekly, December 6, 2002, review of *Y: The Last Man: Unmanned,* p. 102.
Library Journal, May 1, 2003, Steve Raiteri, review of *Y: The Last Man: Unmanned,* p. 100.
Publishers Weekly, April 12, 2004, review of *Y: The Last Man: One Small Step,* p. 41.

ONLINE

Movie Poop Shoot Web site, http://www.moviepoopshoot.com/interviews/18.html (May 21, 2003), Nolan Reese, interview with Vaughan.
Suicide Girls Web site, http://suicidegirls.com/words/Brian+Vaughan/ (July 5, 2004), Daniel Robert Epstein, interview with Vaughan.
Titan Magazine Web site, http://www.titanmagazines.com/books_chat_brnkvghn0803.html (July 5, 2004), interview with Vaughan.*

*   *   *

VISCARDI, Henry, Jr. 1912-2004

OBITUARY NOTICE—See index for *CA* sketch: Born May 10, 1912, in New York, NY; died April 13, 2004, in Roslyn, NY. Activist and author. Viscardi was a renowned champion for the disabled, establishing numerous foundations, corporations, and training facilities for the disabled during a career that spanned five decades. Born with two stumps for legs, he developed a can-do attitude early in life despite this disadvantage. He worked to pay his own way through college, which included Fordham University and St. John's Law School. During the 1930s, he worked as a tax clerk for the Home Owners' Loan Corporation; when World War II began, he tried to enlist in each branch of the U.S. military but was rejected by all of them. However, the Red Cross employed him as a field service officer, and Viscardi proved that he had the right stuff when he successfully completed basic training at Fort Dix, becoming known, appropriately, as the "legless man from Fort Dix." During the war, he worked with amputees for the Office of the Surgeon General at Walter Reed Army Hospital in Washington, D.C. With the war over, Viscardi was hired by the Mutual Broadcasting System as assistant director of special events and sports, and in 1947 he became director of personnel at Burlington Mills Corporation. In 1949, Viscardi's career helping the handicapped took flight when he was asked to head Just One Break, a program that helped disabled people get jobs in the mainstream workplace. Up until that time, most people suffering from disabilities were grudgingly given menial tasks in places where they were separated from the rest of the work force. Viscardi, however, set out on a mission to prove that the handicapped had just as much to offer as everyone else and that they did not require charity to get by. He soon established a number of organizations to demonstrate his point, beginning with his 1952 founding of the nonprofit Abilities, Inc. That year, he also was made president and chair of the Human Resources Foundation. In the 1960s, he established the Human Resources Center, a think tank that studied the role of the disabled in the workplace, and he created a training center for children with disabilities that was renamed the National Center for Disability Services in 1991. From the administrations of Franklin Roosevelt through Jimmy Carter, Viscardi also served as a consultant to U.S. presidents. The author of several books on his favorite subject, including *Give Us the Tools* (1959), *Abilities Story* (1967), *But Not on Our Block* (1972), and *Matching Job and Worker Characteristics* (1973), Viscardi received numerous awards in recognition of his contributions to society, including the International Humanity Service Award, the Silver Medal from Paris, the Medal of Japan, the President's Award from the National Rehabilitation Association, and over two dozen honorary doctorates, among many others.

OBITUARIES AND OTHER SOURCES:

PERIODICALS

Los Angeles Times, April 16, 2004, p. B11.
New York Times, April 16, 2004, p. C10.

*   *   *

VISCUSI, Robert 1941-

PERSONAL: Born April 4, 1941; son of Joseph (an automobile mechanic) and Vera Di Rocco (a seamstress) Viscusi; married Ann Dolan, June 20, 1976; children: Robert Jr., Victoria. *Ethnicity:* "Italian American." *Education:* Fordham College, B.A. (English), 1962; Cornell University, M.A. (English), 1963; New York University, Ph.D. (English), 1979.

ADDRESSES: Home—Brooklyn, NY. *Office*—Wolfe Institute for the Humanities, Brooklyn College, Brooklyn, NY 11210; fax: 718-951-5249. *E-mail*—rviscusi@brooklyn.cuny.edu.

CAREER: Teaching fellow, New York University, 1964-68; Brooklyn College, City University of New York, New York, NY, adjunct lecturer, 1968-70, lecturer, 1973-74, adjunct lecturer, 1974-75, lecturer, 1979-80, instructor, 1980, assistant professor, 1981-83, associate professor, 1984-85, professor, 1986—, Claire and Leonard Tow Professor of English, 1999-2000, faculty associate of the Humanities Institute, 1981-82, director of the Humanities Institute, 1982-88, executive officer of the Humanities Institute, 1988-89, executive officer of the Ethyl R. Wolfe Institute for the Humanities, 1989—; Kean College of New Jersey, instructor, 1970-73, adjunct instructor, 1975-78; Saint Peter's College, adjunct instructor, 1975-78. Visiting assistant professor of Italian, New York University, 1980; visiting professor, University of Paris, 1986.

MEMBER: Italian American Writers Association (president), Golden Key Honor Society, Phi Beta Kappa, Pi Delta Phi (honorary member of Alpha Theta chapter).

AWARDS, HONORS: Named "Man of the Year," UNICO National, 1982; distinguished and outstanding service recognition, Italian Culture Club and Academic

Club Association, 1984; National Endowment for the Humanities fellowship, 1986-87; PSC-CUNY fellowship, 1988-89; faculty fellowship, John D. Calandra Italian American Institute, 1990-91; Distinguished Trustee Award, La Scuola New York, 1996; American Book Award, 1996, for *Astoria;* Outstanding Contribution to the Italian American Community, American Italian Cultural Roundtable, 1997; National Italian American Foundation grant, 1998-99; Professional Staff Congress of the City University of New York grant.

WRITINGS:

Max Beerbohm; or, The Dandy Dante: Rereading with Mirrors, Johns Hopkins University Press (Baltimore, MD), c. 1986.

(Editor) *Browning Institute Studies, 1988: Victorian Learning,* Armstrong Browning Library (Waco, TX), 1989.

An Oration upon the Most Recent Death of Christopher Columbus (poetry), Bordighera Publications (West Lafayette, IN), 1993, third edition, 1998.

Astoria (novel), Guernica Editions (Tonawanda, NY), 1995, second edition, 2002.

A New Geography of Time (poetry), Guernica Editions (Tonawanda, NY), 2003.

Contributor to books, including *Blood Brothers,* edited by Norman Kiell, International Universities Press (New York, NY), 1983; *Italian Americans in the Professions,* edited by Remigio Pane, American Italian Historical Association (New York, NY), 1983; *The Family and Community Life of Italian Americans,* edited by Richard N. Juliani, American Italian Historical Association (New York, NY), 1983; *The Writer's Mind: Writing as a Mode of Thinking,* edited by Janice Hayes and others, National Council of Teachers of English (Urbana, IL), 1984; *Il passato perpetuo/ fotografie di Ernesto Bazan; due saggi di Robert Viscusi e Jerre Mangione; presentazione di Giulio Andreotti,* by Ernesto Bazan, Novecento (Palermo, Italy), 1985; *The Italian-Americans through the Generations,* edited by Rocco Caporale, American Italian Historical Association (New York, NY), 1986; *Italian Ethics: Their Languages, Literature, and Lives,* edited by Dominic Candeloro, Fred L. Gardaphe, and Paolo A. Giordano, American Italian Historical Association (New York, NY), 1990; *American Declarations of Love,* edited by Ann Massa, Macmillan (London, Eng-

land), 1990; *From the Margin: Writings in Italian Americana,* edited by A. Tamburri, P. Giordano, and F. Gardaphé, Purdue University Press (Lafayette, IN), 1991; *British Writers,* Supplement 2, edited by George Stade, Scribner's (New York, NY), 1992; *Unsettling America: An Anthology of Contemporary Multicultural Poetry,* edited by Maria Mazziotti Gillan and Jennifer Gillan, Viking Penguin (New York, NY), 1994; *Social Pluralism and Literary History: The Literature of the Italian Emigration,* edited by Francesco Loriggio, Guernica (Toronto, Ontario, Canada), 1996; *Franco Accursio Gulino: Design and the Embalmer,* Sellerio editore (Palermo, Italy), 1997; *Beyond the Margin: Readings in Italian Americana,* by Paolo A. Giordano and Anthony Tamburri, Fairleigh Dickinson University Press (Madison, WI), 1998; *Adjusting Sites: New Essays in Italian American Studies,* edited by William Boelhower, Forum Italicum (Stony Brook, NY), 1999; *Il sogno italo-americano,* CUEN (Napoli, Italy), 1999; *The Italian American Heritage: A Companion to Literature and the Arts,* edited by Pellegrino D'Acierno, Garland (New York, NY), 1999.

Also author, with L. Ballerini, F. Weinapple, and J. Krase, of a proposed television series for Italian National Television titled *Oggetto Smarrito: The Cultural Dialectic of Italian America.* Contributor of essays to professional journals, including *English Literature in Transition: 1880-1920, Princeton University Library Chronicle, Spirales: Journal International de Culture, Studi emigrazione, Differentia: Review of Italian Thought, Italian Americana, Italian Journal,* and *Bridge Apulia/USA;* contributor of poems to *Brooklyn Review, Exquisite Corpse: A Journal of Letters and Life, Bridge Apulia/USA, Gradiva, Polytext, Footwork: Paterson Literary Review, Voices in Italian Americana, Italian Americana, Lines,* and *0 to 9.* Author of monthly column in *Italian American Writers Association Newsletter.* Associate editor, *Browning Institute Studies,* 1985-89; member of advisory board, *Italian Americana, Voices in Italian Americana: A Literary and Cultural Review, Differentia: Review of Italian Thought, VIA: Voices in Italian Americana,* and *Italian Journal.*

WORK IN PROGRESS: English as a Dialect of Italian, essays on Italian American Writing.

SIDELIGHTS: When many Americans think of Italian-American writers, the first images that typically springs to mind are Mafia stories by authors such as

Mario Puzo. As president of the Italian American Writers Association and author of the acclaimed novel *Astoria,* as well as the well-received poem *An Oration upon the Most Recent Death of Christopher Columbus* and numerous essays on Italian-American literature, Robert Viscusi has striven to amend this mindset; he strongly believes that writers such as Dana Giola, Anthony Valerio, and Carole Maso deserve a wider audience. As Felicia R. Lee explained Viscusi's position in a *New York Times* article, the author feels that "the struggle is not about feelings but about helping the larger culture understand Italian-Americans in a way that has 'nothing to do with a social club on Mott Street.'" In addition to promoting the work of other Italian Americans, Viscusi's own writings have gone a long way toward changing attitudes about this area of literature. His groundbreaking debut novel, *Astoria,* won an American Book Award in 1996, and his poetry reexamining the legacy of Christopher Columbus, a reaction against those who protested Columbus's legacy during the 500th anniversary of his voyage to the New World, has provided plenty of material for literary academics to ponder.

Before these works were published, however, Viscusi released his scholarly study *Max Beerbohm; or, The Dandy Dante,* a biography of nineteenth-century caricaturist and parodist Beerbohm. Beerbohm, who was friends with such luminaries as W. B. Yeats, Oscar Wilde, and Aubrey Beardsley, appeared on the surface to be a very modest person who, according to Kerry Powell in *Victorian Studies,* considered himself a "small" writer. As *Choice* reviewer R. T. Van Arsdel explained, however, it is Viscusi's position that Beerbohm's "preoccupation with smallness" was, in reality, "a screen for 'planning to establish himself as a "great,"' . . . an entirely original assessment." Viscusi bases this theory on two works: a story from the *Yellow Book* titled "The Happy Hypocrite," and, more substantially, the novel *Zuleika Dobson.* This novel, which has typically been regarded as an elaborate myth about unrequited love, attempts to portray Beerbohm as both a Dante and a dandy. Viscusi furthers this supposition by describing Beerbohm's imitation of Dante's rise from Hell to Heaven. A *Virginia Quarterly Review* critic noted that in his analysis Viscusi "blend[s] biography and criticism in order to delineate true 'dandyism.'" Powell concluded, "By his own admission, Viscusi has framed an unlikely argument, bold and allusive, at times both complicated and brilliant." The critic further noted that *Max Beerbohm* "will become for all those with a serious interest in 'the incomparable Max' a volume they cannot ignore."

Viscusi's first major work to address the identity of modern Italian Americans is his ambitious poem *An Oration upon the Most Recent Death of Christopher Columbus.* The work was written as a reaction to events in 1992 in which many Americans protested celebrations that were being held in honor of the 500th anniversary of Columbus's 1492 voyage. Columbus, who had for so long been regarded as a hero in American history books, was now being portrayed as a villain of sorts, a precursor of the European colonization of the Americas that many people were beginning to regard as a hostile invasion. Viscusi saw his poem "as a way to temper the debate with a better understanding of Italian-American reality," explained David Gonzalez in the *New York Times.* In the poem, which actually centers on Italian-American history and immigration, Columbus is seen as a symbol of Italian-American identity that is being threatened by revisionist historians. Ethnic—as well as national—identity, then, is something that Viscusi is struggling to hold on to. "Columbus is central to the very history and myth of America," explained Peter Carravetta in *Differentia,* "and his is . . . a major point of reference in the cultural unconscious of the Italian Americans." Although Viscusi acknowledges that there is much mythology surrounding Columbus that disguises a dark side to American history, "the *Oration* is singing the disintegration of America with bitter and melancholy tones, and though it does not conflate the myth of Columbus with that of America, it does expound how one has been the analogon, at times, or the metaphor, of the other, how both have been shorn of their former grandeur and recklessness, and how the way Columbus Day is sinking in the popular estimation, so may soon America become a ghost of its more demonic self." Viscusi's poem, Carravetta concluded, "is a major addition to the growing body of Italian American literary culture . . . [that] will stand out as a rich, problematic, indeed troubling and yet unavoidable critical ganglion in the current literary history network."

Viscusi followed up *Oration* two years later with his critically acclaimed autobiographical novel, *Astoria.* Like his poem, the novel's central theme concerns the migration of Italians to America and their sense of ethnic identity. The title comes from the name of an Italian neighborhood in Queens, where Viscusi's mother was raised. But the term "Astoria" also has a dual meaning of both "history" and "fiction." Thus, the name "Astoria" represents Italy for Viscusi. Written at a time when he was mourning his mother's recent death, the narrative drowns in nostalgia while the author attempts to describe the past in terms of the future so as to explain how he has been shaped by his environment. In the story, the narrator travels to Paris in 1986 to teach at the university. The journey, however, also inspires much personal reflection on his Italian-American background, as well as on his role as an educator with a more than passing interest in the philosophies of Jacques Derrida and Jacques Lacan.

In Paris, the narrator is stunned to find his mother buried in Napoleon's tomb. After this, he finds that everywhere he goes, from Rome to New York City, he finds his mother memorialized in one way or another, and that this always leads him back to Astoria. Endeavoring to rid himself of his mother's hold on him, he writes books and theorizes about what he is experiencing, but he cannot escape her as she symbolizes the Great Migration of his Italian ancestors. Describing Viscusi's complicated work variously as a "metanovel," "autobiography," "epiphany," "postcolonial allegory," and "a revisionist historical fiction," Peter Carravetta said in his *Melus* assessment that *Astoria* "is a memoir, a tortured recounting of the irreparable loss, a testament of filial love. . . . The author becomes narrator, and as narrating voice can finally let go, uttering the portentous question: Who was my mother? and therefore: Who were my forebears. Who, what, am I as a result of being the descendant of these and only these special people?" A *Kirkus Reviews* contributor called the novel a "difficult and sometimes rewarding debut" that "buries some genuine wit and moments of real insight in a relentlessly self-conscious fiction." *Library Journal* critic Ellen R. Cohen concluded that *Astoria* "will appeal to readers who relish extensive philosophical ruminations."

BIOGRAPHICAL AND CRITICAL SOURCES:

BOOKS

Boelhower, William, and Rocco Pallone, editors, *Adjusting Sites: New Essays in Italian American Studies*, Forum Italicum, 1999, pp. 57-71.

PERIODICALS

Chelsea, Volume 60, 1996, Adele La Barre Starensier, review of *Astoria*, pp. 135-137.
Choice, June, 1986, R. T. Van Arsdel, review of *Max Beerbohm; or, The Dandy Dante*, p. 1545.

Differentia, spring-autumn, 1994, Peter Carravetta, "An Other Columbiad," pp. 311-320.
Kirkus Reviews, June 15, 1995, review of *Astoria*, p. 810.
Library Journal, August, 1995, Ellen R. Cohen, review of *Astoria*, p. 121.
Melus, fall, 1999, Peter Carravetta, "*Figuras* of Cultural Recognition: A Reading of Robert Viscusi's *Astoria*," pp. 141-154.
New York Times, October 11, 1997, David Gonzalez, "A Poet Finds a New Muse in Christopher Columbus"; April 22, 2001, Felicia R. Lee, "Italian Stories, without Bullets."
Queen's Quarterly, autumn, 1986, Paul Boytinck, review of *Max Beerbohm; or, The Dandy Dante*, pp. 688-690.
Rethinking History: The Journal of Theory and Practice, spring, 2000, Santa Casciani, "[Re]creating Italian American Historiography: *Astoria* and the Truth of Narrative," pp. 7-19.
Victorian Studies, summer, 1987, Kerry Powell, review of *Max Beerbohm; or, The Dandy Dante*, pp. 558-560.
Virginia Quarterly Review, autumn, 1986, review of *Max Beerbohm; or, The Dandy Dante*, p. 123.

ONLINE

Italian Academy, http://www.italianacademy.columbia.edu/ (March 24, 2001).
Italian American Writers' Association, http://www.iawa.net/ (March 24, 2001).*

*   *   *

VRIENS, Jacques 1946-

PERSONAL: Born 1946, in Den Bosch, Netherlands; married; wife's name, Thérèse; children: Boris, Caspar. *Hobbies and other interests:* Acting, reading, walking, photography.

ADDRESSES: Agent—c/o Author Mail, Van Holkema & Warendorf, Bussum, Netherlands.

CAREER: Primary school teacher, then principal, first of De Manse primary school and then of De kle kapitein primary school; full-time writer, 1993—.

AWARDS, HONORS: Zilveren Griffel, 1979, for *Zaterdagmorgen/Zondagmorgen,* and 1991, for *Tinus-in-de-war;* named Knight of the Orde van de Nederlandse Leeuw, 2001; Pluim van de maand maart, 2002, for *Oh mijn lieve Augustijn;* winner, Nederlandse Kinderjury, 2003, for *Meester Jaap maakt er een puinhoop van.*

WRITINGS:

Zaterdagmorgen/Zondagmorgen, illustrated by Ivo de Weerd, Van Holkema & Warendorf (Bussem, Netherlands), 1978.

De vader-en-moeder-wedstrijd, Van Holkema & Warendorf (Weesp, Netherlands), 1985.

Een bende in de bovenbouw, illustrated by Joep Bertrams, Van Holkema & Warendorf (Houten, Netherlands), 1988.

Ik ben ook op jou, Van Goor (Amsterdam, Netherlands), 1992.

En de groeten van groep acht, illustrated by Mance Post, Van Holkema & Warendorf (Houten, Netherlands), 1995.

Meester Jaap, illustrated by Annet Schaap, Van Holkema & Warendorf (Houten, Netherlands), 1997.

Weg uit de Peel, illustrated by Henk Kneepkens, Van Holkema & Warendorf (Houten, Netherlands), 1997.

De verdwijning van de mislukte barbie, illustrated by Annet Schaap, Van Holkema & Warendorf (Houten, Netherlands), 2001.

Also author of numerous other titles, including *Bonje in het bonshotel,* 1991; *Tinus-in-de-war,* 1991; *Ha/Bah naar school,* 1992; *Het raadsel van de regenboog,* 1992; *Grootmoeder, wat heb je grote oren,* 1997; *Meester Jaap doet het weer,* 1998; *Meester Jaap gaat nooit verloren,* 1999; *De gekste avonturen van Tommie en Lotje,* 2000; *Achtste-groepers huilen niet,* 2000; *Het geheim van de verliefde hulpkok,* 2001; *Oh, mijn lieve Augustijn,* 2002; *De school is weg,* 2003; *Meester Jaap maakt er een puinhoop van,* 2003; *Eindelijk actie; De redding van de zwevende oma; De vondst van het stiekeme circus; De jacht op de afgepakte sterren; Die rotschool met die fijne klas; Ik doe niet meer me; Vaders, moeders? Hardgekookte eieren; Ga jij maar op de gang; Het achtste groepie tegen het soepie; Eeen stelltje mooie vrienden; De dikke Meester Jaap; Jelle en de maan; Jelle en de trein; Jelle en de baby; Jelle en de klok; Allemaal Poppenkast; Lieve dikke juffrouw; Willem en dikke Teun; Nog één nachtje slapen; Drie ei is een paasei; O, denneboom; Dag, Sinterklassje; Jij bent een kip!; Ik wil als vriend . . .; Poes is weg; Geen schoenen voor Bram; Alex krijgt een baby; Ik ben ook op jou; Tommie en Lotje; De spannendste avonturen van Tommie en Lotje; De stoutste avonturen van Tommie en Lotje; De liefste avonturen van Tommie en Lotje; Tommie en Lotje gaan op vakantie; De vrolijkste avonturen van Tommie en Lotje; Oh min lieve Augustijn;* and *Napolean, de stoerste kater (van de buurt).*

BIOGRAPHICAL AND CRITICAL SOURCES:

ONLINE

Jacques Vriens Home Page, http://www.jacquesvriens.nl/ (March 1, 2004).*

W

WADE, (Henry) William (Rawson) 1918-2004

OBITUARY NOTICE—See index for *CA* sketch: Born January 16, 1918, in London, England; died March 12, 2004, in Fulbourne, Cambridgeshire, England. Educator, attorney, and author. Wade was considered a giant among scholars of British academic law, specializing in constitutional, real property, and administrative law. Attending Cambridge University, he received his B.A. from Gonville and Caius College in 1939, and his M.A. from Trinity College in 1946; he was called to the Bar of Lincoln's Inn that year. A fellow at Trinity from 1946 until 1961, he was also a lecturer at Cambridge from 1947 to 1959, a reader there from 1959 to 1961, and Rouse Ball Professor of English Law from 1978 to 1982. In the 1960s and early 1970s, furthermore, Wade was Professor of English Law and fellow at St. John's College at Oxford. From 1976 to 1988, he served as Master of Gonville and Caius College. This distinguished career was supplemented by his extensive research and publishing endeavors, releasing such textbooks and other scholarly works as *Administrative Law* (1961; eighth edition, 2000), *Towards Administrative Justice* (1962), *The Law of Real Property* (1959; seventh edition, 2000), and *Constitutional Fundamentals* (1980); he also edited the *Annual Survey of Commonwealth Law* from 1965 to 1976. In his books, published articles, and his teaching, Wade supported a more open government, complained about the English constitution and the disparities between public and private law, and offered insightful interpretations on legislation such as the European Communities Act of 1972 and the Human Rights Act of 1998. A fellow of the British Academy from 1969, for which he served as vice president from 1981 to 1983, Wade received several honors for his contributions to the study of law, including being named a Knight of the British Empire in 1985 and receiving an honorary doctorate from Cambridge in 1998.

OBITUARIES AND OTHER SOURCES:

PERIODICALS

Daily Telegraph, March 18, 2004.
Guardian (Manchester, England), March 24, 2004, p. 23.
Independent (London, England), March 19, 2004, p. 35.
Times (London, England), March 26, 2004, p. 33.

*   *   *

WADE, Mary Dodson 1930-

PERSONAL: Born July 30, 1930, in Morrilton, AR; daughter of Graydon A. (an educator and businessman) and Bonnie (an educator; maiden name, Bearden) Dodson; married Harold L. Wade (an engineer), 1953; children: Bruce Dodson, Dana Leigh. *Education:* Attended Arkansas State Teachers College (now University of Central Arkansas), 1947-49; Baylor University, B.A. (cum laude), 1951; Texas Woman's University, M.A., 1961. *Politics:* Independent. *Religion:* Baptist. *Hobbies and other interests:* Travel (has visited Egypt, Greece, China, Japan, Peru, the Philippines, Jamaica, England, Ireland, and Germany).

ADDRESSES: Agent—c/o Author Mail, Colophon House, 17522 Brushy River Ct., Houston, TX 77095. *E-mail*—marydwade@aol.com.

CAREER: Pine Bluff, AR, and Richardson, TX, teacher, 1951-56; Cleveland, OH, school librarian, 1963-68; Sharon, MA, school librarian, 1968-77; Sugar Land, TX, school librarian, 1980-90. Colophon House, Houston, TX, founder. Speaker at schools, workshops, and conferences.

MEMBER: Society of Children's Book Writers and Illustrators (regional advisor, Houston chapter), Texas State Historical Association, Ladies Reading Club of Houston.

WRITINGS:

Easter Fires, illustrated by Patty Rucker, Eakin Press (Austin, TX), 1984.

Milk, Meat Biscuits, and the Terraqueous Machine: The Story of Gail Borden, Eakin Press (Austin, TX), 1987.

David Crockett: Sure He Was Right, Eakin Press (Austin, TX), 1992.

Amelia Earhart: Flying for Adventure, Millbrook Press (Brookfield, CT), 1992.

I Am Houston, illustrated by Pat Finney, Colophon House (Houston, TX), 1993.

Austin: The Son Becomes Father, Colophon House (Houston, TX), 1993.

Little Fish and Big Question, Island Heritage, 1994.

Ada Byron Lovelace: The Lady and the Computer, Dillon Press (New York, NY), 1994.

Cabeza de Vaca: Conquistador Who Cared, Colophon House (Houston, TX), 1994.

Estevan, Walking across America, Colophon House (Houston, TX), 1994.

Benedict Arnold, F. Watts (New York, NY), 1994.

Guadalupe Quintanilla: Leader of the Hispanic Community, Enslow Publishers (Springfield, NJ), 1995.

I'm Going to Texas = Yo voy a Tejas, illustrated by Virginia Marsh Roeder, translated by Guadalupe C. Quintanilla, Colophon House (Houston, TX), 1995.

The Alamo: Flash Point between Texas and Mexico, Discovery Enterprises (Carlisle, MA), 1996.

Opa's Stories, illustrated by Pat Finney, Colophon House (Houston, TX), 1996.

Homesteading on the Plains: Daily Life in the Land of Laura Ingalls Wilder, illustrated by Harvey Dunn, Millbrook Press (Brookfield, CT), 1997.

The Road to San Jacinto, Discovery Enterprises (Carlisle, MA), 1997.

I'm Going to California = Yo voy a California, illustrated by Virginia Marsh, translated by Juan M. Aguayo, Colophon House (Houston, TX), 1997.

Jane Long's Journey, illustrated by Virginia Marsh Roeder, Colophon House (Houston, TX), 1998.

George W. Bush: Governor of Texas, W. S. Benson (Austin, TX), 1999.

T Is for Texas, illustrated by Virginia Roeder, GHB Publishers (St. Charles, MO), 2000.

Walter's Worries, illustrated by Philip Webb, Learning Media (Wellington, New Zealand), 2001.

ALS—Lou Gehrig's Disease, Enslow Publishers (Berkeley Heights, NJ), 2001.

(With Nanci R. Vargus and Katharine A. Kane) *El Dia de los Muertos,* Children's Press (New York, NY), 2002.

George W. Bush, Forty-third President of the United States, W. S. Benson (Austin, TX), 2002.

Tsunami: Monster Waves, Enslow Publishers (Berkeley Heights, NJ), 2002.

Types of Maps, Children's Press (New York, NY), 2003.

Map Scale, Children's Press (New York, NY), 2003.

Condoleeza Rice: Being the Best, Millbrook Press (Brookfield, CT), 2003.

People of Texas, Heinemann Library (Chicago, IL), 2003.

Texas Plants and Animals, Heinemann Library (Chicago, IL), 2003.

Christopher Columbus, Children's Press (New York, NY), 2003.

Cinco de Mayo, Children's Press (New York, NY), 2003.

Uniquely Texas, Heinemann Library (Chicago, IL), 2004.

Texas History, Heinemann Library (Chicago, IL), 2004.

All around Texas: Regions and Resources, Heinemann Library (Chicago, IL), 2004.

Texas Native Peoples, Heinemann Library (Chicago, IL), 2004.

Presidents' Day: Honoring the Birthdays of Washington and Lincoln, Enslow Publishers (Berkeley Heights, NJ), 2004.

Joan Lowery Nixon: Mystery Writer, Enslow Publishers (Berkeley Heights, NJ), 2004.

Also contributor to children's magazines. Wade produced a ten-minute iconographic video of *Easter Fires* in 1990.

SIDELIGHTS: Mary Dodson Wade is the author of a multitude of historical and biographical books for students of many ages, from kindergarten through high school. Her books have often been praised by critics as solid, well-researched, student-friendly introductions to their subjects, which range from the people and culture of Wade's home state of Texas to scientific topics such as tsunamis.

Written for high school students, *ALS—Lou Gehrig's Disease* contains both scientific information about the disease and the human stories of some of the men and women afflicted with the disease, including Nobel-prize-winning scientist Stephen Hawking, star baseball player Lou Gehrig, and gymnast Marcie Gibson. The book "will leave readers moved yet heartened by the heroism demonstrated by so many of those affected," Mary R. Hofmann commented in *School Library Journal.* To *Booklist* reviewer Roger Leslie, a strong point of the book was its clear definitions of terms and explanations of scientific concepts, which "are generously supported with simple diagrams."

Condoleeza Rice: Being the Best is a biography of President George W. Bush's National Security Advisor written for late-elementary to early-middle-school students. The book has several features that make it accessible to its target audience, claim reviewers. *School Library Journal* contributor Marlene Gawron noted that "the facts are presented in short sentences in large print," making it easy to read, and the book was praised by both Gawron and *Booklist*'s Ilene Cooper for its many photographs, including some of Rice's childhood. "This is an attractive addition to the Gateway Biography series," Cooper concluded.

"The sound of words has always fascinated me," Wade once commented. "I love to roll them around in my head, and I love to create moods by moving them around on paper.

"My first efforts at writing were some poems when I was ten or twelve. As poetry, they were awful! But my mother kept them because she knew they were important to me. They serve to remind me that writing is like any skill—if you practice, you get better at it.

"Most of my writing is based on history. I love to know how things used to be and to make connections with what is today. What I have discovered is that people react much the same way to circumstances, regardless of the physical surroundings of the time. When writing biographies, I try to understand that this was a living, breathing individual, who reacted to something that was going on. In trying to capture that real person, I use autobiographies, if they are available. And I try to find what someone who knew the individual wrote. A biographical subject with a strong personality can provoke intense like or dislike, however, and that forces me to seek the motivation behind what was said.

"Even my fiction has some basis in reality. I find writing pure fiction is hard work. As an author, I must come up with a believable character who has a real problem, to which the character finds a reasonable solution. Research, especially eyewitness accounts, can provide wonderful details that bring a story to life."

BIOGRAPHICAL AND CRITICAL SOURCES:

PERIODICALS

Booklist, April 15, 1993, Kay Weisman, review of *I Am Houston,* pp. 1510-1511; March 1, 1995, Kay Weisman, review of *Benedict Arnold,* p. 1242; May 1, 1995, Kay Weisman, review of *Ada Byron Lovelace: The Lady and the Computer,* p. 1571; March 1, 1996, Susan Dove Lempke, review of *Guadalupe Quintanilla: Leader of the Hispanic Community,* pp. 1176-1177; January 1, 2002, Roger Leslie, review of *ALS—Lou Gehrig's Disease,* p. 840; March 1, 2003, Ilene Cooper, review of *Condoleeza Rice: Being the Best,* pp. 1207-1208; May 1, 2003, review of *Cinco de Mayo,* pp. 1602-1603.

Book Report, May-June, 1995, Phyllis Press, review of *Ada Byron Lovelace,* p. 46.

Review of Texas Books, fall, 1992, p. 3; winter, 1993, p. 6.

School Library Journal, November, 1992, Rita Soltan, review of *Amelia Earhart: Flying for Adventure,* p. 106; May, 1995, Margaret B. Rafferty, review of *Benedict Arnold,* p. 117; February, 1996, Linda Greengrass, review of *Guadalupe Quintanilla,* p. 106; July, 1997, Denise E. Agosto, review of *I'm Going to California = Yo voy a California,* pp. 77-78; February, 2002, Mary R. Hofmann, review of *ALS—Lou Gehrig's Disease,* pp. 150-

151; October, 2002, Eva Elizabeth, review of *Tsunami: Monster Waves,* p. 195; December, 2002, Ann Welton, review of *El Dia de los Muertos,* pp. 127-128; April, 2003, Marlene Gawron, review of *Condoleeza Rice,* p. 194; January, 2004, Christine E. Carr, review of *Christopher Columbus,* p. 123.

Texas Books in Review, spring, 1993, p. 18.*

*   *   *

WALFORD, Roy L(ee, Jr.) 1924-2004

OBITUARY NOTICE—See index for *CA* sketch: Born June 29, 1924, in San Diego, CA; died of respiratory failure and complications from amyotrophic lateral sclerosis, April 27, 2004, in Santa Monica, CA. Physician, adventurer, and author. A gerontologist and researcher at the University of California—Los Angeles (UCLA) who drew national attention as one of the scientists who inhabited Biosphere 2, Walford was concerned with finding ways to extend life, which he believed he had accomplished through a strictly controlled diet. Throughout his life, he was known to his friends, family, and colleagues as a quirky personality. For example, after completing his medical degree at the University of Chicago in 1948, he and a friend earned over forty thousand dollars gambling in Las Vegas, taking the money to buy a yacht to sail the Caribbean for a year and a half. He also wrote a spoof of Christopher Marlowe's *Dr. Faustus,* loved riding motorcycles, and was considered to be a "cultural provocateur" by his friends. After completing his residency at the Veterans Administration Hospital in Los Angeles, Walford was chief of laboratory service at Chanute Air Force Base before joining the UCLA faculty in 1954. Rising to the position of professor of pathology and hemopathology in 1966, he also worked as an attending pathologist at area hospitals while conducting research in the lab. Walford felt, however, that science was more than just lab work and would break up his studies on lab rodents with field research in such places as India and Africa. His most famous exploit, however, came in 1991 when he was the oldest scientist to participate in Biosphere 2, a three-acre enclosure located near Tucson, Arizona, that was designed to see whether a small human colony could survive in a self-sustaining structure on another planet such as Mars. Unfortunately, the experiment went awry when nitrous oxide began to build up in the atmosphere. The scientists all became ill and had to

abandon the structure. However, during their stay Walford was able to demonstrate that a low-calorie, controlled diet among the Biosphere 2 staff greatly improved their overall health. It was just another example of what Walford had been researching for many years by that point. He had already demonstrated in mice that low-calorie diets greatly extended the animals' life spans and vigor, an experiment that was shown to work in other species of animals, as well, including primates. Walford himself followed a 1,600-calorie-per-day diet that he felt improved his life greatly. However, he attributed his stay in Biosphere 2 and his prolonged exposure to high levels of nitrous oxide to his onset of ALS. Despite this, he asserted that his dietary practices greatly extended his survival after contracting the disease. Walford's theories are published in his books, which include *Maximum Life Span* (1983), *The One-Hundred-Twenty-Year Diet* (1986), *Anti-Aging Diet* (1994), and *The Anti-Aging Plan: Strategies and Recipes for Extending Your Healthy Years* (1994), the last written with Lisa Waldrop. He was also the author of several medical books and contributed to many other publications.

OBITUARIES AND OTHER SOURCES:

PERIODICALS

Chicago Tribune, May 3, 2004, Section 2, p. 13.
Los Angeles Times, May 1, 2004, p. B18.
New York Times, May 4, 2004, p. C15.

*   *   *

WALKER, Edward Joseph 1934-2004
(Ted Walker)

OBITUARY NOTICE—See index for *CA* sketch: Born November 28, 1934, in Lancing, West Sussex, England; died March 19, 2004, in Valencia, Spain. Educator and author. Walker was an award-winning author of plays, fiction, and children's books, but drew the most praise for his poetry. After an idyllic life spent near Lancing beach in England before World War II, he explored poetry as a young student at Steyning Grammar School, where he cofounded a poetry magazine called *Priapus.* His career began in 1953 as a schoolmaster and French and Spanish teacher at High

School for Boys in Chichester; three years later, he earned his B.A. at St. John's College, Cambridge; he would remain in Chichester until 1967, when the success of his writing led him to become a freelance writer and broadcaster. His early poems, published under the pen name Ted Walker, include *Those Other Growths* (1964), *The Solitaries* (1967), and *Gloves to the Hangman: Poems, 1969-1972* (1973), among others. Adept at formal verse, Walker wrote very personal poems that are notable for their fresh imagery; many of his pieces appeared in the pages of the *New Yorker*. Despite his success with poetry, however, his verse output slowed as he turned to writing fiction as a way of earning a better income. His short stories sold well, and some of these are collected in *You've Never Heard Me Sing* (1985). His prose work, indeed, allowed him to become a freelance writer, though he accepted an appointment as poet-in-residence and professor of creative writing at New England College in Arundel, Sussex, where he would remain from 1971 until 1992. He also turned to writing autobiography in the books *The High Path* (1982) and *The Last of England* (1992), travel writing with *In Spain* (1989), and children's poems in *Granddad's Seagulls* (1994), as well as penning a screenplay version of *Wind in the Willows* (1995). Walker returned to his first love, poetry, with one of his last books, *Mangoes on the Moon: Poems, 1992-1998* (1999), but his last publication, *He Danced with a Chair: Fictions and Factions* (2001), was a collection of prose works. Suffering increasingly from ill health later in life, he moved from England to Spain for the warmer weather, making Alcalali his permanent home in 1997. Named a Fellow of the Royal Society of Literature in 1975, Walker's contributions to literature were diverse; however, he will likely best be remembered for his poetry, for which he received such honors as the Cholmondeley Poetry Award and the Alice Hunt Bartlett Prize.

OBITUARIES AND OTHER SOURCES:

BOOKS

Contemporary Poets, seventh edition, St. James Press (Detroit, MI), 2001.

PERIODICALS

Guardian (Manchester, England), April 2, 2004, p. 29.
Independent (London, England), March 30, 2004, p. 35.
Times (London, England), March 26, 2004, p. 33.

WALKER, Ted
See WALKER, Edward Joseph

*   *   *

WALL, Kathryn R. 1945-

PERSONAL: Born June 14, 1945; married; husband's name, Norman; children: two stepsons. *Education:* Attended Indiana State College, 1963-64; Lorain County Community College, associate's degree (applied business), 1982.

ADDRESSES: Home—Hilton Head, SC. *Agent*—c/o Author Mail, St. Martin's Press, 175 Fifth Ave., New York, NY 10010. *E-mail*—kathy@pennynovels.com.

CAREER: Novelist. Formerly worked as an accountant; co-owner, with husband, of manufacturing tooling distributorship, 1990-94.

MEMBER: Mystery Writers of America, Sisters in Crime, Island Writers Network (founding member).

WRITINGS:

In for a Penny, iUniverse.com, 2001, Coastal Villages Press (Beaufort, SC), 2002.
And Not a Penny More, Coastal Villages Press (Beaufort, SC), 2002.
Perdition House, St. Martin's Press (New York, NY), 2003.
Judas Island, St. Martin's Press (New York, NY), 2004.

SIDELIGHTS: Kathryn R. Wall has written several mystery novels featuring Lydia Baynard "Bay" Tanner, a former financial consultant who now lives in Hilton Head, South Carolina, as does Wall herself. The "Bay Tanner" mysteries are set in the coastal region of South Carolina where plush beach resorts and old plantations are commonplace. This blending of the old and new South is also found in Wall's plots, which combine elements of the traditional and the modern.

The initial "Bay Tanner" mystery, *In for a Penny,* was self-published by Wall through iUniverse.com. Sales of the novel in South Carolina soon caught the attention of regional publisher Coastal Villages Press, which released a new edition of the book, as well as her second mystery, *And Not a Penny More.* New York-based St. Martin's Press has since picked up the popular series.

In for a Penny finds Tanner grieving after the murder of her husband Rob in a car bombing. After a year of mourning and living as a recluse, she is called upon to help an old family friend who has gotten herself involved with a shady real estate scheme and now stands to lose all her money in the fraudulent deal. As Tanner looks into the matter, with the help of her retired judge father, Talbot Simpson, she meets a handsome man with whom she becomes infatuated; unfortunately, he may be a land swindler and murderer. "The chemistry between them seems real," as Joyce Dixon noted in *Southern Scribe,* "but how much is he involved in the threats on her life?"

Tanner is contacted by old classmate Jordan Herrington in *And Not a Penny More.* Herrington has a strange story to tell. His mother was found murdered in a hotel room while on a cruise to South America. As Tanner looks into the incident, she finds that other women have also been killed on similar cruises. Her investigation becomes an international effort when she books a cruise herself and her father contacts an old friend in Interpol for assistance. Tanner and the Interpol agent work together to find the serial killer. "What follows is an intense race in a hurricane through the islands," Dixon explained in *Southern Scribe.*

Bay is visited by a distant relative in *Perdition House.* Fifth cousin Mercer Mary Prescott phones after being arrested for vagrancy and asks for Tanner's assistance in getting out of jail. After springing Mercer, the trouble really begins as strange characters show up in town looking for Mercer. Tanner discovers that Mercer had earlier trouble with the federal authorities for trespassing in a nuclear plant. When Tanner's housekeeper is attacked, she decides to look into the situation herself, unearthing a secret from her family's past in the process. A critic for *Publishers Weekly* noted that "Wall nicely blends the manners and mores of the aristocratic Southern tradition with more modern sensibilities, creating in Bay Tanner a woman who's equally at home in the tea room or out jogging." "This

terrific tense thriller takes readers on quite a ride," according to Harriet Klausner in *Books 'n' Bytes,* while a *Kirkus Reviews* found *Perdition House* to be "a taut, tasty chiller."

Speaking to Dixon, Wall described what it has been like for her to go from self-published author to a contract with a major national publishing house: "All in all, I'd have to say it's been a positive experience. While each level I've been a part of—self-publishing, small press, and major New York publisher—has its pluses and minuses, each has taught me a great deal about this strange business, and each step was necessary to get me to the place I'm in right now. I wouldn't trade any of it."

BIOGRAPHICAL AND CRITICAL SOURCES:

PERIODICALS

Kirkus Reviews, April 15, 2003, review of *Perdition House,* p. 577.
Publishers Weekly, May 5, 2003, review of *Perdition House,* p. 202.

ONLINE

Books 'n' Bytes, http://www.booksbytes.com/ (October 13, 2003), Harriet Klausner, review of *Perdition House.*
Kathryn R. Wall's Home Page, http://www.kathrynwall.com (May 15, 2004).
Southern Scribe, http://www.southernscribe.com/ (October 13, 2003), Joyce Dixon, "Lowcountry Mysteries: An Interview with Kathryn R. Wall," and reviews of *In for a Penny, And Not a Penny More,* and *Perdition House.**

*   *   *

WALLIN, Pamela 1943-

PERSONAL: Born 1943, in Wadena, Saskatchewan, Canada; daughter of William (a businessman and X-ray technician) and Leone (an English teacher) Wallin; married Malcolm Fox (a cameraman), 1987 (divorced, c. 1992). *Education:* College of Bandol (France), certificat d'etudes françaises; University of Regina, graduated (with honors), 1973.

ADDRESSES: Office—Canadian Consulate General, 1251 Avenue of the Americas, New York, NY 10020-1175.

CAREER: Newscaster and television personality. Owner of production companies, including Current Affairs Group Limited and Prime Media Group. Canadian consul-general to New York, NY, 2002—. Appeared on television series, including (as Ottawa contributor, then chief of Ottawa bureau, then cohost) *Canada A.M.,* Canadian Television (CTV), 1980-1992; *Question Period,* CTV, c. 1991; (as cohost) *Prime Time News,* Canadian Broadcasting Corporation (CBC), 1992-1995; (as host) "Pamela Wallin Live," *CBC Newsworld,* 1997-1998; (as host) *Pamela Wallin's Talk TV,* began 2001; also appeared on *Maclean's TV,* CTV; and *The National,* CBC. Also coproducer of *Maclean's TV.* Appeared as herself in the television movie *A Colder Kind of Death,* Lifetime, 2001; and in the television special *Who Wants to Be a Millionaire,* CTV, 2000. Guest star as herself on several episodes of *Royal Canadian Air Farce,* 1995-2000. Journalist with the *Toronto Star* newspaper, first Toronto, Ontario, Canada, then Ottawa, Ontario, Canada bureau, began 1979. Journalist for radio programs, including *Saskatchewan Today,* CBC Radio, 1974-75; (story producer) *As It Happens,* CBC Radio, 1977-79; and *Sunday Morning,* CBC Radio. Social worker at the Prince Albert Penitentiary, Canada, 1973-74. University of Regina, Regina, Saskatchewan, James Minifie Memorial Lecturer, 1992.

MEMBER: Canadian Journalism Foundation (chair, 2002—), Canadian Women in Communications (past chair), Academy of Canadian Cinema and Television (past vice chair), News Theatre (member of board of directors), University of Waterloo Board of Governors, University Health Network Board of Trustees, Pheromone Sciences Corp. Board of Directors, Ontario Cancer Research Network Board of Directors, Historica (council member), Genesis Foundation (patron), Career Edge 2000 (past national chair).

AWARDS, HONORS: Named Outstanding Canadian Achiever, Queen Elizabeth II, 1982; Skelton-Clark fellow, Queen's University, 1990; Gordon Sinclair Award for best broadcast overall journalist, Gemini Awards, 1992; President's Medal, 1993; named Broadcaster of the Year, Radio and Television News Directors' Association, 1994; Women of Influence Award for broadcasting, *Toronto Life,* 1994; Galaxi Award for best on-camera performance on a pay or specialty channel, Canadian Cable Television Association, 1997; Outstanding Achievement Award, Women in Film and Television, 1997; UNIFEM Canada Award, United Nations, 1999, for "outstanding contributions towards the advancement of women"; Saskatchewan Order of Merit, 1999; Lifetime Achievement Award, Canadian Association of Broadcasters; named Woman of the Year, Canadian Women in Communications, 2002; Her Majesty Queen Elizabeth's Golden Jubilee Medal, 2002; Variety Diamond Award, 2002. Honorary doctorates from Loyalist College, 1996; Wilfrid Laurier University, 1999; Ryerson University; 2000, University of Western Ontario, 2000; St. Thomas University, 2002; and University of Regina, 2002.

WRITINGS:

Since You Asked (memoir; also published as *Pamela Wallin: A Memoir*), Random House (New York, NY), 1998.
Speaking of Success: Collected Wisdom, Insights and Reflections, 2001.
The Comfort of Cats, photographs by Anne Bayin, Prometheus Books (Amherst, NY), 2003.

SIDELIGHTS: Pamela Wallin is one of the most recognizable faces in Canadian journalism. With the exception of her former boss Barbara Frum, Wallin may have done the most of any reporter to pave the way for Canadian women to take on serious roles in the traditionally male-dominated world of journalism. In just one example, in 1982 Wallin found herself in the unusual position of female war correspondent when Canadian Television (CTV) sent her off, with less than three hours' notice, to the Falkland Islands to cover the war there between Argentina and Great Britain. Her supervisor said to her as she left, "Screw this up and you'll ruin it for all women who want to be war correspondents." Wallin performed well in the difficult situation. In fact, her journalism so impressed her superiors that a few years after returning to Canada she became the first woman in the history of Canadian television journalism to hold the job of Ottawa bureau chief.

Shortly after Barbara Frum passed away in 1992, Wallin was given the job of co-anchor of the Canadian Broadcasting Corporation's (CBC's) nightly news program *Prime Time News.* In a well-publicized move, Wallin was let go from this job in 1995, reputedly because of personality conflicts between Wallin and others on the show's staff. When Wallin published her memoirs in 1998, readers hoped that Wallin would give her side of the dismissal story. Her settlement with the CBC forbade her to give most details of her departure, but still, "Wallin's is as frank a disclosure of the internal workings of the CBC as I've seen in print," a reviewer wrote in *Quill and Quire.* In addition, Wallin discusses her childhood in the small prairie town of Wadena, Saskatchewan, her rebellious teenage life, and her early years in journalism, including her first big break, when a friend asked her to fill in for the ill host of a call-in radio show for a month because he did not know anyone other than Wallin who could talk for an hour at a stretch. *Since You Asked* is a book "that should be mandatory reading for any young woman even thinking of a career in journalism," Barbara Wickens wrote in *Maclean's.*

BIOGRAPHICAL AND CRITICAL SOURCES:

PERIODICALS

Chatelaine, March, 1993, Philip Marchand, "Pamela Power!," pp. 58-61; June, 1996, Don Gillmor, interview with Wallin, pp. 49-52; January, 2003, Hilary Davidson, review of *The Comfort of Cats,* p. 14.

Contemporary Canadian Biographies, August, 1997, "Pamela Wallin."

Globe & Mail (Toronto, Ontario, Canada), May 14, 1997, "Journalist Wallin Wins Cable Award," p. C4; November 27, 1997, John Allemang, "Television: Footing the Bill for Pamela Wallin," p. C2; November 7, 1998, review of *Pamela Wallin: A Memoir;* August 3, 2000, Theresa Ebden, "Why Pamela Wallin's No Regis in a Skirt—Yet"; August 28, 2001, Michael Posner, "Pamela Wallin to Undergo Surgery for Colorectal Cancer"; October 27, 2001, John Allemang, interview with Wallin; June 26, 2002, Campbell Clark and Heather Scoffield, "Chretien Names TV's Wallin New York Consul-General," p. 1; June 27, 2002, "Wallin on Broadway," p. 1; July 9, 2002, John MacLachlan Gray, "Gray's Anatomy: Why Wallin Gets to Eat Fiddleheads in the Big Apple," p. 1; December 4, 2002, Gloria Galloway, interview with Wallin.

Maclean's, October 26, 1992, Diane Turbide, interview with Wallin, pp. 95-96; April 17, 1995, Brian D. Johnson and E. Kaye Fulton, "Inside Stories," pp. 20-23; November 16, 1998, Barbara Wickens, review of *Since You Asked,* p. 87; November 23, 1998, Allan Fotheringham, review of *Since You Asked,* p. 156; December 7, 1998, review of *Since You Asked,* p. 70; February 8, 1999, Peter C. Newman, "Pamela Wallin Could Be the Next CBC Boss," p. 58; October 21, 2002, Sharon Doyle Driedger, review of *The Comfort of Cats,* p. 76.

Quill and Quire, November, 1998, review of *Pamela Wallin: A Memoir,* p. 33.

Saturday Night, June, 1997, Anne Kingston, "Pamela Wallin's Wild Kingdom," pp. 38-46.

Toronto Life (Toronto, Ontario, Canada), April, 2003, Nathalie Atkinson, "Babe in the Woods," p. 10.

ONLINE

Consulate of Canada, New York Web site, http://www.dfait-maeci.gc.ca/ (August 6, 2003), "Biography: Pamela Wallin."

January Magazine, http://www.januarymagazine.com/ (November, 2001), Linda Richards, interview with Wallin.

Pamela Wallin Home Page, http://www.pamelawallin.com (July 10, 2003).*

*   *   *

WANG, (John) Wayne 1949-

PERSONAL: Born January 12, 1949, in Hong Kong, China; father, a businessperson and engineer; mother, a painter; married Cora Miao (an actress). *Education:* Attended Foothill College; California College of Arts and Crafts, M.F.A.

ADDRESSES: Agent—Bart Walker, International Creative Management, 40 West 57th St., New York, NY 10019.

CAREER: Director, producer, and screenwriter. Director of films, including *A Man, a Woman, and a Killer,* 1975; (and producer, editor, and narrator) *Chan Is Missing,* 1982; (and producer) *Dim Sum: A Little Bit of Heart,* 1985; *Slamdance,* 1987; (and producer) *Dim*

Sum Take-Outs, 1988; *Eat a Bowl of Tea,* Columbia, 1990; (with Spencer Nakasako) *Life Is Cheap . . . but Toilet Paper Is Expensive,* Silver Light, 1990; *The Stranger,* 1992; (and producer, with others) *The Joy Luck Club,* Buena Vista, 1993; (with Paul Auster) *Blue in the Face,* Miramax, 1995; (with Paul Auster) *Smoke,* Miramax, 1995; (and producer) *Chinese Box,* Trimark, 1998; *Anywhere but Here,* Twentieth Century-Fox, 1999; *The Beautiful Country,* 2001; (and producer) *The Center of the World,* Artisan Entertainment, 2001; *Maid in Manhattan* (also known as *The Chambermaid* and *Made in New York*), 2002; *Because of Winn-Dixie,* 2005 (in production), *Good Cook, Likes Music,* 2005 (in production); and *Last Holiday,* 2005 (in production). Also director of the short film *1944;* assistant director of the Chinese sequences, *Golden Needles.* Producer of the film *Lanai-Loa* (also known as *Lani Loa: The Passage*), Chrome Dragon Films, 1998. Director of the television special "Small Sounds and Tilting Shadows," *Strangers,* Home Box Office (HBO), 1992. Appeared as himself in the television specials *Slaying the Dragon,* 1988; *I Love New York,* 2002; and *Intimate Portrait: Jennifer Lopez,* 2002.

WRITINGS:

SCREENPLAYS

Life Is Cheap . . . but Toilet Paper Is Expensive, Silver Light, 1990.
(With Paul Auster) *Blue in the Face,* Miramax, 1995.
(With Jean-Claude Carrière, Larry Gross, and Paul Theroux) *Chinese Box,* Trimark, 1998.
(With Paul Auster, Miranda July, and Siri Hustvedt) *The Center of the World,* Artisan Entertainment, 2001.

Also author of (with Richard A. Richardson and Richard R. Schmidt) *A Man, a Woman, and a Killer,* 1975, and (with Isaac Cronin) *Chan Is Missing,* 1982.

SIDELIGHTS: Wayne Wang may be best known for directing such wide-audience Hollywood films as *The Joy Luck Club* and *Maid in Manhattan,* but he has also made some smaller-budget films from his own screenplays that have been critical if not always commercial successes. Born in Hong Kong to Chinese parents who were refugees from the Communist regime in mainland China, Wang was named after

American Western movie star John Wayne. Wang went to a Jesuit high school in Hong Kong, and after he graduated he came to California to attend college. Wang has remained there, in the San Francisco Bay area, ever since.

Wang's first successful film, *Chan Is Missing,* was made on a budget of a mere 22,000 dollars in grants from the American Film Institute and the National Endowment for the Arts. Shot in black and white, *Chan Is Missing* documents life and prejudice in San Francisco's Chinatown through the eyes of two cab drivers in search of a mysterious man Chan, who owes them 4,000 dollars. The movie became a surprise box office hit, and, as many reviewers later noted, its visual style presaged that of many of Chan's later works, including *Chinese Box.* In both films, Wena Poon explained in *Film Quarterly,* Wang's camera frequently pauses on such minutia as an elderly person peering out of a doorway or a cigarette dangling from a bystander's mouth, in what "amounts to a type of time-capsuling, an archeological preservation of poignant fragments that will perhaps vanish in the near future."

Filmed in Wang's native Hong Kong on the eve of that colony's return to China from the British, *Chinese Box* follows a dying British journalist, played by Jeremy Irons, as he films the streets of Hong Kong and becomes involved in the lives of two Chinese women, a bar owner (played by famed Chinese actress Gong Li, in her first English-speaking role) and a hustler (played by Hong Kong star Maggie Cheung). Each character's struggles parallel those of one of the geopolitical players in the Hong Kong handover: Irons is dying, just as the British presence in Hong Kong is; Li is trying to live down her checkered past and to figure out where to go in the future, as is mainland China; and Cheung, like Hong Kong, has been abused by those who control her but is determined to keep going no matter what. Despite its political overtones, on a personal level *Chinese Box* is still a "poetic and well-told story," a reviewer commented in the *News and Record.* Likewise, Richard Huntington noted in the *Buffalo News* that Wang "saturates this sorrowful movie with lovely and intricate shades of feeling."

"A lot of people asked me, why don't you use the mindscape of a Chinese in approaching [*Chinese Box*]," Wang told Bergen County, New Jersey *Record* interviewer Laurence Chollet, instead of using an Englishman as the main character. "Well, I'm not really a Chinese. I was brought up a colonial subject. . . . I was very influenced by the English." Wang has also rebelled against the idea that as a Chinese-American filmmaker he should stick to "ethnic" subjects, instead of making films like *Blue in the Face* and *The Center of the World* that lack an Asian angle. As Wang told *New York Times* interviewer Bernard Weinraub in 1993, "I'll eventually get back to [making films with Chinese themes]—I'm sure I will—but at the same time, I feel I'm just as American as anyone else. There are stories and characters about America that I want to tell."

The Center of the World was released amid a swirl of controversy in 2001. A gritty film about the difficulties of making romantic connections in hyper-commercial modern America, *The Center of the World* was released unrated because it was too explicit for an R, and several newspapers refused to run an advertisement for the film that they considered to be too suggestive. The film stars Peter Sarsgaard as a young dot-com millionaire who hires a stripper, played by Molly Parker, to entertain him during a weekend getaway in Las Vegas. Parker is adamant about the fact that she is not a prostitute and lays down several ground rules for the weekend, which include no intercourse, no kissing, no talking about feelings, and separate rooms. Despite Parker's insistence on maintaining a businesslike relationship, an attraction begins to develop between the two, but they still find themselves unable to connect on a meaningful level. "*The Center of the World* is sober and serious and downright glum, ultimately an all-too-familiar portrait of lonely souls unable to break through their own isolation," Sean Axmaker concluded in the *Seattle Post-Intelligencer.*

BIOGRAPHICAL AND CRITICAL SOURCES:

BOOKS

Notable Asian Americans, Gale (Detroit, MI), 1995.

PERIODICALS

America's Intelligence Wire, March 5, 2003, interview with Wang.

Arizona Daily Star (Tucson, AZ), May 25, 2001, Phil Villarreal, review of *The Center of the World,* p. F26.

Asia Africa Intelligence Wire, March 13, 2003, Shogo Hagiwara, review of *The Center of the World.*

Atlanta Journal-Constitution, May 1, 1998, Eleanor Ringel, review of *Chinese Box,* p. P10; May 4, 2001, Bob Longino, review of *The Center of the World,* p. P9.

Boston Herald, May 15, 1998, James Verniere, review of *Chinese Box,* p. 5; May 1, 2001, Stephen Schaefer, interview with Wang, p. 34; May 4, 2001, James Verniere, review of *The Center of the World,* p. 18.

Buffalo News (Buffalo, NY), May 22, 1998, Richard Huntington, review of *Chinese Box,* p. G27; May 25, 2001, Jeff Simon, review of *The Center of the World,* p. G5; May 26, 2001, Jeff Simon, interview with Wang, p. D1.

Cincinnati Enquirer (Cincinnati, OH), May 25, 2001, review of *The Center of the World,* p. W6, Robert Denerstein, review of *Center of the World,* p. 6B; June 7, 2001, Margaret A. McGurk, "Edited Movie Yanked at Esquire," p. B1.

Daily Herald (Arlington Heights, IL), May 1, 1998, Lisa Friedman Miner, review of *Chinese Box,* p. 38; May 4, 2001, Dann Gire, review of *The Center of the World,* p. 41.

Daily News (Los Angeles, CA), April 22, 2001, Rob Lowman, review of *The Center of the World,* p. L11.

Daily Telegraph (Surry Hills, New South Wales, Australia), November 4, 1999, John Spence, review of *Chinese Box,* p. T6.

Daily Variety, December 2, 2002, Robert Koehler, review of *Maid in Manhattan,* p. 6.

Dayton Daily News (Dayton, OH), June 15, 2001, Dusty Smith, review of *The Center of the World,* p. 11.

Detroit News, May 4, 2001, Susan Stark, review of *The Center of the World,* p. 3.

Entertainment Weekly, April 24, 1998, Lisa Schwarzbaum, review of *Chinese Box,* p. 56; April 27, 2001, Owen Gleiberman, review of *The Center of the World,* p. 88.

Evening Standard (London, England), September 20, 2001, Andrew Alexander, review of *The Center of the World,* p. 30.

Film Journal International, January, 2003, David Noh, review of *Maid in Manhattan,* p. 43.

Film Quarterly, fall, 1998, Wena Poon, review of *Chinese Box,* p. 31.

Guardian (Manchester, England), September 21, 2001, Peter Bradshaw, review of *The Center of the World,* p. 13.

Herald Sun (Melbourne, Victoria, Australia), February 13, 1999, Leigh Paatsch, review of *Chinese Box,* p. 108.

Houston Chronicle, May 1, 1998, Louis B. Parks, review of *Chinese Box* and interview with Wang, p. 4; April 29, 2001, Eric Harrison, interview with Wang, p. 11.

Independent (London, England), April 18, 1996, Robert Hanks, review of *Smoke,* p. 15; May 16, 1996, review of *Blue in the Face,* p. 10; September 21, 2001, review of *The Center of the World,* p. 10.

Independent Sunday (London, England), March 30, 1997, Jo-Jo Moyes, review of *Chinese Box,* p. 14; September 16, 2001, Matthew Sweet, review of *The Center of the World,* p. 8.

Knight Ridder/Tribune News Service, April 30, 2001, Glenn Lovell, review of *The Center of the World,* p. K4633; May 24, 2001, Jay Boyar, review of *The Center of the World,* p. K6120.

Los Angeles Magazine, May, 2001, Steve Erickson, review of *The Center of the World,* p. 126.

Los Angeles Times, April 17, 1998, Kevin Thomas, review of *Chinese Box,* p. 6; April 30, 1998, Mark Chalon Smith, review of *Chinese Box,* p. 6; April 20, 2001, Kevin Thomas, review of *The Center of the World,* p. F15.

Maclean's, May 14, 2001, Brian D. Johnson, review of *The Center of the World,* p. 64.

Nation, May 28, 2001, Amy Sohn, review of *The Center of the World,* p. 34.

New Republic, May 4, 1998, Stanley Kauffmann, review of *Chinese Box,* p. 27.

News and Record (Piedmont Triad, NC), October 8, 1998, review of *Chinese Box,* p. D1.

New York Post, April 18, 2001, review of *The Center of the World,* p. 56.

New York Times, May 30, 1982, Tony Chiu, interview with Wang, pp. 17, 35; September 5, 1993, Bernard Weinraub, interview with Wang, section 2, pp. 7, 15.

Plain Dealer (Cleveland, OH), April 19, 2001, "Newspapers Refuse to Run Suggestive Ad for Movie," p. 5E.

Record (Bergen County, NJ), April 17, 1998, Laurence Chollet, interview with Wang, p. Y1.

Rochester Democrat and Chronicle (Rochester, NY), November 12, 1999, Jack Garner, interview with Wang, p. 3C.

Rocky Mountain News (Denver, CO), May 8, 1998, Robert Denerstein, review of *Chinese Box,* p. 8D.

St. Louis Post-Dispatch, May 22, 1998, Joe Holleman, review of *Chinese Box,* p. E5.

San Francisco Chronicle, April 12, 1996, Edward Guthmann, review of *Smoke,* p. D12; April 22, 1998, Ruthe Stein, review of *Chinese Box,* p. C1; May 8, 1998, Edward Guthmann, review of *Chinese Box,* p. C3; February 2, 2001, Ruthe Stein, "Theaters Balk at Incendiary Trailer for Wang Film," p. C4; April 8, 2001, Bob Graham, review of *The Center of the World,* p. 40.

Sarasota Herald Tribune (Sarasota, FL), October 16, 1995, Terry Lawson, review of *Blue in the Face;* May 29, 1998, George Meyer, review of *Chinese Box,* p. 12; June 1, 2001, Philip Booth, review of *The Center of the World,* p. 19.

Seattle Post-Intelligencer, May 1, 1998, William Arnold, review of *Chinese Box,* p. 28; May 4, 2001, Sean Axmaker, review of *The Center of the World,* p. 36.

Seattle Times, April 26, 1998, review of *Chinese Box,* p. M1; May 1, 1998, review of *Chinese Box,* p. F7; May 4, 2001, John Zebrowski, review of *The Center of the World,* p. G37.

Star-Ledger (Newark, NJ), April 21, 1998, Allen Barra, review of *Chinese Box,* p. 31.

Star Tribune (Minneapolis, MN), May 22, 1998, Jeff Strickler, review of *Chinese Box,* p. 5E.

Tampa Tribune (Tampa, FL), May 25, 2001, review of *The Center of the World,* p. 4.

Tennessean (Nashville, TN), June 8, 2001, Gene Wyatt, review of *The Center of the World,* p. F20.

Variety, April 23, 2001, Dennis Harvey, review of *The Center of the World,* p. 17; June 11, 2001, Dana Harris, "Artisan Yanks Edited *World* in Cincinnati," p. 4.

Washington Times, May 15, 1998, Gary Arnold, review of *Chinese Box,* p. 17; May 11, 2001, Gary Arnold, review of *The Center of the World,* p. 9.

ONLINE

Internet Movie Database, http://www.imdb.com/ (May 21, 2004), "Wayne Wang."

Onion A.V. Club, http://www.theavclub.com/ (April 30, 1998), Keith Phipps, interview with Wang.*

* * *

WARD, Amanda Eyre 1972-

PERSONAL: Born 1972, in New York, NY; daughter of Gary B. Ward (an investment banker and manager) and Mary-Anne Westley (a communications manager); married Timothy Ashworth "Tip" Meckel (a geologist); children: one son. *Education:* Williams College, B.A.; University of Montana, M.F.A.

ADDRESSES: Home—Waterville, ME. *Agent*—c/o Author Mail, MacAdam/Cage Publishing, 155 Sansome St., Suite 550, San Francisco, CA 94104-3615; MacAdam/Cage Publishing, 1900 Wazee St., Suite 210, Denver, CO 80202. *E-mail*—aeyreward@yahoo.com.

CAREER: Has taught creative writing at the University of Texas.

AWARDS, HONORS: Violet Crown Book Award, for *Sleep toward Heaven.*

WRITINGS:

Sleep toward Heaven (novel), MacAdam/Cage Publishing (San Francisco, CA), 2003.
How to Be Lost, MacAdam/Cage Publishing (San Francisco, CA), 2004.

Contributor to books, including *Politically Inspired,* edited by Stephen Elliott and Gabriel Kram, MacAdam/Cage Publishing (San Francisco, CA), 2003. Short fiction has appeared in periodicals, including *Mississippi Review, Story Quarterly, New Delta Review,* and the *Austin Chronicle,* and on the Web site *Salon.com.*

ADAPTATIONS: Film rights for *Sleep toward Heaven* were acquired by Sandra Bullock and Fortis Films, a division of Warner Brothers.

SIDELIGHTS: When New York native Amanda Eyre Ward moved to Austin, Texas, to teach at the University of Texas, she could not ignore the frequent news reports of murders and executions in the state. "Just when I moved to Texas, there were executions on the news every day," Ward said in an interview for the *Portland Press Herald* in Maine. "The aspect that seemed most interesting to me was the seven women on death row. I was told they watched Oprah together and made afghans together," Ward continued. Although she was never able to interview any of the women, she thoroughly researched them and their pasts. "I sort of got obsessed," Ward admitted.

The result of her work, whether dedication or obsession, is her first novel, *Sleep toward Heaven.* The three women in this tale, each touched by violence and murder in some way, provide three distinct narratives that weave together into the novel. Karen Lowens, known as the Highway Honey because she robbed and killed her victims at rest stops, sits on death row, ravaged by AIDS and condemned to die for the murders of men she says she killed in self-defense. Karen seeks peace with herself, her victims, and her traumatic childhood before facing the deadly injection. Celia Mills mourns for her husband, Henry, Karen's final victim, who was shot during a botched convenience store robbery; she drifts through life in a near stupor, wondering if she can ever forgive the women who took her beloved Henry from her. Franny, meanwhile, deals with her flight from her fiancé and New York home after a young cancer patient dies in agony following a procedure she recommended. These three lives grow ever closer together until they finally intersect during an oppressively hot Texas summer. Into all their lives enters Dr. Franny Wren, the prison doctor, who struggles to reconcile her profession as a healer with the fact that she treats women who know to the minute when they are scheduled to die.

"Ward's impressive debut novel is a powerhouse of melancholic emotions channeled through the jagged lives of her intricate cast of female characters," remarked Elsa Gaztambide in *Booklist.* The author's "spare but psychologically rich portraits are utterly convincing," observed a *Publishers Weekly* reviewer further. "Ward's no-nonsense, unflinching prose and her complex but never confounding structure make this novel very tough to put down," commented Pam Houston in *O, the Oprah Magazine.* "But her greater triumph is her ability to humanize all of these characters" in the novel and make them recognizably individual and distinctly human.

BIOGRAPHICAL AND CRITICAL SOURCES:

PERIODICALS

Austin Chronicle, May 9, 2003, Marc Savlov, "Ward Wows Warners Dept."
Booklist, March 15, 2003, Elsa Gaztambide, review of *Sleep toward Heaven,* p. 1277; September 1, 2004, review of *How to Be Lost,* p. 66.
Kirkus Reviews, February 15, 2003, review of *Sleep toward Heaven,* p. 268; August 15, 2004, review of *How to Be Lost,* p. 776.

O, the Oprah Magazine, April, 2003, Pam Houston, "Her Final Days: A First Novel Imagines Life on Death Row," pp. 149-152.
Portland Press Herald (Portland, Maine), March 14, 2004, Ray Routhier, "Auspicious Debut; The Waterville Author's Revelatory First Novel Binds the Lives of Three Very Different Women, Including a Convicted Murderer on Death Row," p. 10E.
Publishers Weekly, March 3, 2003, review of *Sleep toward Heaven,* pp. 54-55; August 9, 2004, review of *How to Be Lost,* p. 228.
Texas Monthly, August, 2003, Mike Shea, "Killing Time: Two Young Novelists Offer Compelling Portraits of Serial Murderers—One Skin-Crawlingly Odd, the Other Surprisingly Sympathetic," pp. 62-64.

ONLINE

Amanda Eyre Ward Home Page, http://www.amandaward.com (April 6, 2004), biography of Amanda Eyre Ward.*

* * *

WATFORD, Christopher M. 1978-

PERSONAL: Born October 2, 1978, in Thomasville, NC; son of Jeffery (a sanitation worker) and Lisa (Gibson) Watford. *Ethnicity:* "White." *Education:* Appalachian State University, B.A., 2000; attended University of North Carolina—Greensboro, 2003. *Politics:* Democrat. *Religion:* Methodist.

ADDRESSES: Home—4495 Denton Rd., Thomasville, NC 27360. *Office*—Davidson County Community College, P.O. Box 1287, Lexington, NC 27293-1287. *E-mail*—cmwatford@hotmail.com.

CAREER: Davidson County Schools, Lexington NC, teacher of at-risk students, 2000—. Also affiliated with Davidson County Community College.

MEMBER: North Carolina Society of Archivists, Civil War Roundtable of North Carolina, Davidson County Writers Guild.

AWARDS, HONORS: Commendation, Davidson County Civil War Roundtable, 2001, for *The Civil War Roster of Davidson County, NC: Biographies of 1996 Men before, during, and after the Conflict.*

WRITINGS:

The Civil War Roster of Davidson County, NC: Biographies of 1996 Men before, during, and after the Conflict, McFarland and Co. (Jefferson, NC), 2001.
(Editor) *The Civil War in North Carolina: Soldiers' and Civilians' Letters and Diaries, 1861-1865: The Piedmont,* McFarland and Co. (Jefferson, NC), 2003.
(Editor) *The Civil War in North Carolina: Soldiers' and Civilians' Letters and Diaries, 1861-1965: The Mountains,* McFarland and Co. (Jefferson, NC), 2003.

WORK IN PROGRESS: Editing *The Life and Letters of William G. Morris,* the biography of a North Carolina carpenter, Confederate colonel, and state legislator, including more than one hundred letters from the Civil War period; editing *The Charles C. Blacknall Papers,* a collection of letters and diaries related to the Twenty-third North Carolina Regiment of the North Carolina Infantry; research on the life of Wilbur J. Cash, author of *Mind of the South;* research on the role of Scales's North Carolina Brigade at the Civil War battles of Chancellorsville and Gettysburg; research on the military band members of World War I.

* * *

WEBER, William 1950-

PERSONAL: Born 1950; married Amy Vedder (a wildlife conservationist and writer); children: Noah, Ethan. *Education:* University of Wisconsin at Madison, Ph.D.

ADDRESSES: Home—Yorktown Heights, NY. *Office*—Wildlife Conservation Society, 2300 Southern Blvd., Bronx, NY 10460.

CAREER: Wildlife observer and conservationist in Africa and America, 1978—; Wildlife Conservation Society, Bronx, NY, director of North American Programs.

WRITINGS:

African Rain Forest Ecology and Conservatism: An Interdisciplinary Perspective, Yale University Press (New Haven, CT), 2001.

(With wife, Amy Vedder) *In the Kingdom of Gorillas: Fragile Species in a Dangerous Land,* Simon & Schuster (New York, NY), 2001, published in England as *In the Kingdom of Gorillas: The Quest to Save Rwanda's Mountain Gorillas,* Aurum, 2002.

SIDELIGHTS: William Weber and his wife Amy Vedder began observing mountain gorillas in Rwanda in the late 1970s as part of a team headed by Dian Fossey. While Fossey brought the plight of the dwindling gorilla population to the attention of the world, it was Weber and Vedder who proposed and helped to implement viable programs to conserve the gorilla's habitat. Weber has been at the forefront of the eco-tourism movement, encouraging African governments to see their unique wildlife as a means to generate revenue from tourism dollars. Additionally, as director of North American programs for the Wildlife Conservation Society, Weber has spearheaded projects to improve conditions for wildlife in America, from introducing wolves back into Yellowstone Park to studying less invasive ways to harvest timber.

In the Kingdom of Gorillas: Fragile Species in a Dangerous Land recounts Weber and Vedder's experiences in the field watching gorillas as well as the subsequent vicissitudes the nation of Rwanda faced in the 1990s. The book sounds notes of optimism amidst a tale of spectacular brutality. Although a virulent civil war in Rwanda led to almost a million deaths in the time period the book covers, remarkably the gorilla population actually increased. Weber believes that this is due to the fact that both sides in the civil war realized that gorillas help the Rwandan economy by attracting tourists. In her *New York Times* review of *In the Kingdom of Gorillas,* Natalie Angier wrote: "Folksy, inspiring, amusing, didactic, depressing, sheerly horrifying, and, finally, quietly optimistic, the book highlights the tremendous difficulty of working on behalf of gorillas in a country that is among the poorest and most densely populated regions of Africa."

Although Weber and Vedder express hope that the mountain gorilla population will stabilize in Rwanda, they still warn that more needs to be done to support the species—and that the gorillas' needs conflict with subsistence pressures on the human population. In the *Times Literary Supplement,* David W. Macdonald observed: "Conservation is not a simple matter of good people pursuing unambiguously worthy goals—it is

about human affairs and as such is bedeviled by rivalries, anxieties and complexities of politics of every scale. As a primer for the often uncomfortable, sometimes unbecoming (but perhaps improvable) reality that lies ahead, every starry-eyed would-be conservationist should read this book."

Other reviewers found *In the Kingdom of Gorillas* successful on a variety of levels. According to Jonathan Shipley on *Bookreporter.com,* "The story of the gorilla is sparking with emotional force, and the chronicling of their plight and their growing success . . . makes for an informative and ennobling story." *Geographical* correspondent Miranda Haines wrote: "As a testament of suffering, survival and ultimately hope, this book is a fascinating read." Steven N. Austad maintained in *Natural History* that the authors "provide a vivid portrait of a land desperately trying to put itself back together," and *Library Journal* contributor Clewis Crim felt that the book "is a case study in how conservation must be grounded in the realities of people."

BIOGRAPHICAL AND CRITICAL SOURCES:

PERIODICALS

Geographical, September, 2002, Miranda Haines, "Gorilla Warfare," p. 57.
Kirkus Reviews, August 15, 2001, review of *In the Kingdom of Gorillas: Fragile Species in a Dangerous Land,* p. 1202.
Library Journal, October 1, 2001, Clewis Crim, review of *In the Kingdom of Gorillas,* p. 138.
Natural History, November, 2001, Steven N. Austad, review of *In the Kingdom of Gorillas,* p. 82.
New York Times, January 15, 2002, Natalie Angier, "Joy in Rwanda: Signing On with the Gorillas," p. F1.
Publishers Weekly, September 24, 2001, review of *In the Kingdom of Gorillas,* p. 82.
Times Literary Supplement, October 18, 2002, David W. Macdonald, "Gregorians in the Mist," p. 32.

ONLINE

Bookreporter.com, http://www.bookreporter.com/ (May 8, 2003), Jonathan Shipley, review of *In the Kingdom of Gorillas.*

Environmental News Network, http://enn.com/news/ (September 26, 2001), Stacy Fowler, interview with Amy Vedder.

Northcounty News, http://www.northcountynews.com/ (November 6, 2002), Margaret and Bill Primavera, "Bill Weber and Amy Vedder: Conservation, Gorillas and Lacrosse."*

*   *   *

WEBSTER, Jason 1970-

PERSONAL: Born 1970, in San Francisco, CA; married Salud (a flamenco dancer). *Education:* Attended Oxford University.

ADDRESSES: Home—Valencia, Spain. *Agent*—c/o Author Mail, Doubleday Broadway, Random House, 1745 Broadway, New York, NY 10019.

CAREER: Author, Arabic scholar, and flamenco guitarist.

WRITINGS:

Duende: A Journey into the Heart of Flamenco, Broadway Books (New York, NY), 2003.
Andalus: Unlocking the Secret of Moorish Spain, Doubleday (New York, NY), 2004.

Contributor to periodicals such as *Independent Sunday* (London, England).

SIDELIGHTS: Educated in Arabic at Oxford, accustomed to international living after years in England, Egypt, and Germany, and recently dumped by his longtime girlfriend, Jason Webster did what many would not have the nerve to do: he turned away from an assured but sedate life as a scholar to pursue, almost on a whim, the growing passion he felt within himself for flamenco guitar and the flamenco lifestyle. Webster writes about his resolute pursuit of *duende,* the emotional experience triggered by flamenco, in his book, *Duende: A Journey into the Heart of Flamenco.* The *duende* of the title is difficult to define, even for those who have experienced its ecstatic effects. Michael Emery, writing in *Birmingham Post* (Eng-

land), described it as "the transcendental moment when singer, dancer, and guitarist become as one, and transmit their conjoined emotion to the audience."

Starting out with his guitar and few playing skills, Webster lands in Alicante, Spain, where he polishes his playing with lessons from Juan. To make a living, he teaches English in a local college headed by Vincente and his wife, Lola. Though Lola is the boss's wife and is old enough to have children who are Webster's age, she is also an accomplished flamenco dancer. She and Webster are soon involved in a deeply passionate affair.

When Webster discovers that Vincente deserves his nickname of "El Killer," he seeks safer lodging in Madrid. There, he works to gain the acceptance of a gypsy flamenco troupe. Eventually, he is accepted into the group, but as little more than a curiosity—"El [Niño] Rubio," the blond boy—and at the very bottom of their social pecking order. Soon, he realizes that the flamenco lifestyle he traveled so far to find, that he worked so hard to immerse himself into, is little more than continual drinking, drug-taking, fighting, and stealing. He develops a cocaine habit and goes along on car-stealing trips. When his friend Jesus is killed during a car theft, Webster begins to realize that the lengths he has gone to in pursuit of flamenco and *duende* may not be worth the risk. "By the end of the book, Webster has found love with a woman called Salud," observed Miranda France in the Manchester *Guardian.* "The name means 'health.'"

"I don't believe that everything in *Duende* is true," France remarked. "It doesn't matter—Jason Webster is an exceptional writer, and this is a great book." *Duende* "sweeps along from one harmonious chord to the next and builds into a crescendo that is as rich in atmosphere and emotion as the world it seeks to portray," wrote Anthony Sattin in the London *Sunday Times.* "*Duende* is a fascinating book, the most gripping I have read for years," France stated. "Although the story occasionally hits a flat note, Webster makes up for it by fluidly interlacing his foreigner's perspective with edgy and often perilous cravings to live the life of a genuine flamenco guitarist," commented a reviewer in *Publishers Weekly.* Elsa Gaztambide, writing in *Booklist,* called *Duende* a "daring account of the lengths one man will go to in order to be accepted in a world that revolves around tormented passions."

Webster delves deeper into the history of his newly adopted Spanish homeland in *Andalus: Unlocking the*

Secrets of Moorish Spain. After saving illegal Moroccan immigrant Zine from a murderous band of farmers, Webster travels through Spain with Zine, seeking evidence of Moorish culture and influence on Spanish life and history. While Zine sneaks away for romantic liaisons with local women, Webster finds Moorish influences in architecture, language, and culture. "Webster imparts, with much verve, a lot of tumultuous Andalusian history" in the book, commented Tom Rosenthal in London's *Daily Mail,* who added that Webster illuminates "the richness of Moorish culture from cuisine to philosophy, from music to language, from medicine to architecture and how, without these vital ingredients, Spanish culture would be seriously impoverished."

BIOGRAPHICAL AND CRITICAL SOURCES:

PERIODICALS

Albuquerque Journal, April 25, 2004, David Steinberg, "Spanish Strings," p. F8.

Birmingham Post (Birmingham, England), February 1, 2003, Michael Emery, "Flourish of Flamenco in Real Spain," p. 49.

Booklist, February 1, 2003, Elsa Gaztambide, review of *Duende: A Journey into the Heart of Flamenco,* p. 963.

Chicago Tribune, May 4, 2003, June Sawyers, "The Resourceful Traveler," section 8, p. 18.

Daily Mail (London, England), April 30, 2004, Tom Rosenthal, review of *Andalus: Unlocking the Secrets of Moorish Spain,* p. 57.

Daily Telegraph (London, England), January 24, 2004, Patrick Ness, review of *Duende;* April 10, 2004, Nicholas Shakespeare, "Peel Back a Layer or Two to See Spain's Arab Past," p. 8.

Express (London, England), January 4, 2003, Jane Warren, "Jason Webster Gets to Grips First with His Guitar, and Then Himself," p. 40.

Guardian (Manchester, England), December 28, 2002, Miranda France, "Let the Spirit Move You: Travel Books Can Be Tedious, Says Miranda France. But a Picaresque Account of Joining a Gypsy Flamenco Community Is So Engrossing She Ignored Her Children's Screams to Finish a Chapter," review of *Duende,* p. 7; April 24, 2004, Mark Cocker, "Moor the Merrier: Mark Cocker Follows a Cheery Quest for Spain's Arabic Roots," p. 13.

Herald Sun (Melbourne, Australia), March 1, 2003, Alison Barclay, "Dream Run for Author," p. W30.

Independent (London, England), January 18, 2003, Liz Thomson, "The Gypsy King," p. 26; April 2, 2004, Robert Irwin, review of *Andalus,* p. 26.

Independent Sunday (London, England), December 28, 2003, Laurence Phelan, review of *Duende,* p. 14; June 6, 2004, Anthony Barnes, "Acclaimed Travel Book Is Paella in the Sky, Claims Flamenco Tutor," p. 16.

Irish Times (Dublin, Ireland), February 1, 2003, Shane Hegarty, "Searching for the Heart of the Rhythm," p. 60; February 7, 2004, Shane Hegarty, review of *Duende,* p. 62; May 29, 2004, Paddy Woodworth, "Moor Culture, Less Substance," p. 60.

Kirkus Reviews, January 15, 2003, review of *Duende,* pp. 134-135.

Library Journal, February 1, 2003, Joan Stahl, review of *Duende,* p. 94.

New York Times Book Review, June 1, 2003, Michael Pye, review of *Duende,* pp. 8, 30-31.

Observer (London, England), January 5, 2003, Stephanie Merritt, "A Dance to the Music of Time: Jason Webster Vividly Captures the Spirit of Spain's Most Celebrated Artform," p. 15; April 4, 2004, review of *Andalus,* p. 17.

Publishers Weekly, January 27, 2003, review of *Duende,* p. 246.

Scotland on Sunday (Edinburgh, Scotland), January 12, 2003, David Archibald, "Duende: Fruitless Search for the Musical Soul of Spain," p. 7.

Scotsman (Edinburgh, Scotland), January 11, 2003, John Burnside, "Mediterranean Mix of Flamenco, Fact, and Fiction," p. 5.

Sunday Telegraph (London, England), January 12, 2003, John Preston, "Castanets and Car-Jacking; John Preston Enjoys an Account of the Tribulations Which Faced a Would-be Flamenco Guitarist."

Sunday Times (London, England), January 19, 2003, Anthony Sattin, "The Gypsy Heart of Spain," p. 35; February 9, 2003, Paul Donovan, review of *Duende,* p. 65.

Times (London, England), December 21, 2002, Margaret Reynolds, "The Flamenco Kid," p. 15.

Times Literary Supplement, February 7, 2003, Robert Carver, "On the Trail of Flamenco," review of *Duende,* p. 33.

Washington Post Book World, March 30, 2003, Lily Sheehan, "Fiery Spirits," p. 15.

ONLINE

BookPage Web site, http://www.bookpage.com/ (June 30, 2004), Alison Hood, review of *Duende.*

Books at Transworld Web site, http://www. booksattransworld.co.uk/ (January 4, 2004), interview with Jason Webster.

Culture Court Web site, http://www.culturecourt.com/ (June 30, 2004), Lawrence Russell, review of *Duende.*

New Zealand Listener Web site, http://www.listener.co. nz/ (February 21-27, 2004), Natasha Hay, "Dance Me to the End of Love"; (June 19-25, 2004), Natasha Hay, "A Visit to the Alhambra."

Observer (London, England) Web site, http://www. observer.guardian.co.uk/ (January 11, 2004), Gemma Bowes, review of *Andalus.*

Rain Taxi Web site, http://www.raintaxi.com/ (July 15, 2004), John Toren, review of *Duende.**

*   *   *

WEEKS, James Powell 1950-
(Jim Weeks)

PERSONAL: Born 1950. *Education:* Pennsylvania State University, B.S., M.A., Ph.D. (American history), 2001; University of Pittsburgh, M.L.S.

ADDRESSES: Agent—c/o Author Mail, Princeton University Press, 41 William St., Princeton, NJ 08540-5237. *E-mail*—jpw5@psu.edu.

CAREER: Pennsylvania State University, University Park, PA, instructor in American history; scholar in residence at Pennsylvania Historical and Museum Commission. Research and editing fellow, Papers of Abraham Lincoln, 2003.

WRITINGS:

(Under name Jim Weeks) *Gettysburg: Memory, Market, and an American Shrine,* Princeton University Press (Princeton, NJ), 2003.

SIDELIGHTS: An American history instructor at Pennsylvania State University and scholar in residence at the Pennsylvania Historical and Museum Commission, James Powell Weeks has written a study of his state's—and the nation's—most famous battlefield: Gettysburg. While hundreds of books focus on the dramatic days of the battle itself, Weeks has chosen to explore the battlefield's history since then in *Gettysburg: Memory, Market, and an American Shrine.*

Ever since Abraham Lincoln used the battlefield as the backdrop for his immortal "Gettysburg Address," Americans have seen it as "hallowed ground," and Weeks' book explores the ways that attitude has played itself out. *History Today* contributor Adam Smith found that "Weeks demonstrates in this engrossing book that adding and detracting in the name of making the hallowed ground more purely hallowed has been the obsession of successive generations." The critic added, "The story told here is a multifaceted one. Most obviously it offers a fresh perspective on the contested memory of the Civil War. It is no less important as a window on the social history of leisure and tourism." The first visitors to the battlefield were genteel Victorian families who came in a spirit of contemplation and appreciation of the soldiers' noble sacrifice. Later, trainloads of tourists would come, seeking entertainment as much as edification. Today, "heritage tourists," such as Civil War reenactors, come seeking authenticity. "In a book of rare intelligence and eloquence, Weeks sifts through the tangled mass of memorabilia, images, remembrances . . . and more to show how this 'hallowed ground' was created and exploited for myriad interests," wrote *Library Journal* contributor Randall Miller.

BIOGRAPHICAL AND CRITICAL SOURCES:

PERIODICALS

History Today, December, 2003, Adam Smith, review of *Gettysburg: Memory, Market, and an American Shrine,* p. 56.
Library Journal, May 1, 2003, Randall Miller, review of *Gettysburg,* p. 136.

ONLINE

Civil War News, http://www.civilwarnews.com/ (April 29, 2004), review of *Gettysburg.**

WEEKS, Jim
See WEEKS, James Powell

* * *

WEXELBLATT, Robert

PERSONAL: Male. Education: University of Pennsylvania, B.A. (cum laude), 1966; University of Michigan, M.A., 1967; Brandeis University, Ph.D., 1973.

ADDRESSES: Home—12 Mague Ave., West Newton, MA 02165-1538. Office—Department of Humanities, 871 Commonwealth Ave., Boston University, Boston, MA 02215. E-mail—wex@bu.edu.

CAREER: Boston University, Boston, MA, professor of humanities, 1970—.

MEMBER: Phi Beta Kappa.

AWARDS, HONORS: Woodrow Wilson fellowship, 1966-67; award for best essay from Arizona Quarterly, 1980; Theodore Christian Hoepfner Prize for best story from Southern Humanities Review, 1983 and 1984; Metcalf Cup and Prize for excellence in teaching, both from Boston University, both 1983; honorable mention from Cape Rock poetry competition, 1986; award for best story from San Jose Studies, 1987; first prize for fiction from Kansas Quarterly and Kansas Arts Commission, 1987-88; award for best essay from San Jose Studies, 1990; Richter Award for Interdisciplinary Teaching from Boston University, 1993.

WRITINGS:

(Author of introduction) Lynne Alvarez, Ceremonies of Earth, (New York, NY), 1976.
Life in the Temperate Zone and Other Stories, Rutgers University Press (New Brunswick, NJ), 1990.
Professors at Play: Essays, Rutgers University Press (New Brunswick, NJ), 1991.
The Decline of Our Neighborhood: Stories, Rutgers University Press (New Brunswick, NJ), 1993.

Contributor to The Fathers' Book, G. K. Hall (Boston, MA), 1986. Contributor to periodicals, including American Literature, Arizona Quarterly, Bostonia, Cache Review, Cake, Carolina Quarterly, College Literature, College Teaching, Crab Creek Review, Denver Quarterly, Descant, English Language Notes, Essays in Literature, Four Quarters, Gestus, Hawaii Review, Hiram Poetry Review, Iowa Review, Kansas Quarterly, Lamar Journal of the Humanities, Literary Review, Massachusetts Review, Midwest Quarterly, Monocacy Valley Review, Notes on Modern American Literature, Orphic Lute, Piedmont Literary Review, Poem, Poetry Northwest, San Jose Studies, Small Pond, Southern Humanities Review, and Sou'wester.

SIDELIGHTS: Robert Wexelblatt is an accomplished fiction writer, essayist, and poet. Among his books is Life in the Temperate Zone, and Other Stories, which Fred Marchant, writing in the Harvard Book Review, described as a volume of "fine and gentle stories." Wexelblatt's style in this 1990 publication is rather demanding, for he employs a rich vocabulary and shows a penchant for the more intellectual, and somewhat absurd, aspects of life. The fourteen-story volume includes a tale in which a professor notes ties between Edgar Allan Poe and baseball; one featuring a musicology student who studies under a professional wrestler; and another about an aging professor determined to dissuade a former student from suicide. Marchant praised the book, "[The book] is laden with wit, wry observation, gentle sarcasm, and wicked ironies." A reviewer for Publishers Weekly suggested the volume is "best read with a dictionary in hand, this dense gallimaufry of intellectual games may prove rewarding to those intelligent and patient enough to penetrate it."

The Decline of Our Neighborhood, Wexelblatt's 1993 volume of eleven short stories, is comprised of similarly rich and inventive tales. In one particularly memorable narrative, "The Savior, Ishl Teitelbaum," Jewish prisoners in a concentration camp ponder their own persecution. Other tales, while less unnerving, are equally compelling. In "Benton's Top Banana," for example, a dashing widower brings his new love, a Jewish comedienne, back to his Midwest home to meet his aging parents. And in "The Alpha Company Artists' Collective," seven art students become inextricably united during World War I, after which their art—and their lives—are consequently altered. These stories are dense with devises, such as stories appearing within stories and comments on a story within a story. For example, "Baby in the Air" is interrupted by a conversation between "the author" and "the inquisitor" about the story and the creative process.

Critics were mostly impressed with *The Decline of Our Neighborhood.* Zofia Smardz, from the *New York Times Book Review,* noted that Wexelblatt's stories "seem trenchant while you're reading them, but the ideas don't stick for very long." However, Smardz did find his writing, "Loaded with wit, bristling with irony, draped in erudition and studded with metaphysics." It is irony that stands out in the short stories of Wexelblatt; in fact, a number of critics find his use of irony to be a superior characteristic of his writing. Jay L. Halio from *Studies in Short Fiction* wrote that Wexelblatt has a "gift for irony in all of its arresting forms" and found that irony weaves its way throughout the eleven stories in order to echo "contemporary political and/or social situations." In an interview with the Boston University newspaper, *Boston University Today,* Wexelblatt addressed his use of irony, "Irony is in one sense a function of education, of having learned contradictory truths and believing them both. When writing I look for ironies, but I don't really know where they come from and have no control over them." A *Publishers Weekly* reviewer commended Wexelblatt's writing, noting that "Wexelblatt constructs rich stories that make heavy subjects dance weightlessly before the reader's eyes." Kathleen De Grave, from the *Midwest Quarterly,* also enjoyed *The Decline of Our Neighborhood,* "Characters are drawn sharply; the language is at once erudite, witty, and graceful." She continued, "Wexelblatt's collection is funny, engaging, and an intellectual tour-de-force." *Booklist*'s David Cline praised the book as an "extraordinarily inventive and magnetic work."

Wexelblatt also is the author of *Professor at Play,* a collection of essays. In this wide-ranging volume Wexelblatt writes about Platonism and Franz Kafka's fiction; artists—in this case Heinrich von Kleist, Soren Kierkegaard, and Kafka—who forsake marriage for solitude; and the moral implications of a ringing telephone. *Midwest Quarterly* reviewer Donald Wayne Viney observed that the essays are "entertaining and insightful," yet they "lack a central focus." However, Viney concluded that "readers will be both amused and edified by Wexelblatt's meanderings."

In addition to the aforementioned writings, Wexelblatt has published poems in various periodicals; supplied the introduction to Lynne Alvarez's *Ceremonies of Earth,* which appeared in 1976; and contributed to the 1986 publication *The Fathers' Book.*

BIOGRAPHICAL AND CRITICAL SOURCES:

PERIODICALS

Booklist, March 1, 1994, David Cline, review of *The Decline of Our Neighborhood: Stories,* p. 1182.

Boston University Today, January 17-23, 1994, Jim Graves, story on Robert Wexelblatt and *The Decline of Our Neighborhood.*

Harvard Book Review, spring, 1991, Fred Marchant, review of *Life in the Temperate Zone and Other Stories,* p. 36.

LINK, October, 1990, review of *Life in the Temperate Zone and Other Stories.*

Massachusetts Facility Development Consortium Exchange, spring, 1994, Susan A. Holton, review of *Professors at Play,* p. 6.

Midwest Quarterly, fall, 1992, Donald Wayne Viney, review of *Professors at Play,* pp. 139-141; summer, 1994, Kathleen De Grave, review of *The Decline of Our Neighborhood,* pp. 470-472.

New York Times Book Review, March 6, 1994, Zofia Smardz, review of *The Decline of Our Neighborhood.*

Publishers Weekly, March 23, 1990, review of *Life in the Temperate Zone and Other Stories,* p. 67; December 13, 1993, review of *The Decline of Our Neighborhood,* p. 66.

Studies in Short Fiction, winter, 1996, Jay L. Halio, review of *The Decline of Our Neighborhood,* pp. 136-138.*

*   *   *

WHEELER, Shannon L. 1966-

PERSONAL: Born August 13, 1966, in San Francisco, CA. *Education:* University of California—Berkeley, B.A., 1989.

ADDRESSES: Office—Adhesive Comics, P.O. Box 14549, Portland, OR 97293. *E-mail*—wheeler@tmcm. com.

CAREER: Graphic artist, writer, comic creator. *Austin American-Statesman,* cartoonist, 1991—; Adhesive Comics and Press, Portland, OR, publisher and editor-in-chief.

AWARDS, HONORS: Eisner Award, 1993, for "Too Much Coffee Man."

WRITINGS:

Too Much Coffee Man: Guide for the Perplexed, Dark Horse Comics (Milwaukie, OR), 1998.
Too Much Coffee Man's Parade of Tirade, Dark Horse Comics (Milwaukie, OR), 1999.
Too Much Coffee Man's Amusing Musings, Dark Horse Comics (Milwaukie, OR), 2001.

Creator of *Too Much Coffee Man,* the comic book, the magazine and the strip, beginning c. 1995; coproducer of *Jab* (comic anthology).

SIDELIGHTS: Shannon L. Wheeler is the creator of the strip and comic book that after ten years became a magazine titled *Too Much Coffee Man* (TMCM). The strip appears primarily in alternative newspapers, and Wheeler's work has also been collected in several volumes. Wheeler maintains a Web site dedicated to his postmodern superhero.

Texas Monthly contributor Andrew Goldman noted that when the comic anthology *Jab,* that first featured Wheeler's character, failed to achieve popularity, Wheeler arranged to have every issue shot with a bullet as a marketing ploy, and sales tripled. When he featured his character in his own black-and-white comic, the cup-headed, espresso-loving, caffeine-jittered character who spends much of his time in front of a television took off. Wheeler first gave away a mini version of the comic in the Seattle area, but it soon blossomed into an indie comic. Goldman wrote that the TMCM character is "not even much of a crime-fighter. When he encounters evil deeds, he flees—cautiously, of course, so as not to spill his coffee."

In the *Washington Post Book World,* Mike Musgrove reviewed *Too Much Coffee Man's Guide for the Perplexed,* noting that other characters include Too Much Espresso Guy and Too Much German White Chocolate Woman with Almonds. Musgrove said that "there is an occasional burst of action in TMCM's life . . . but for the most part, this superhero leads an average life of quiet desperation." In one of the episodes, TMCM has a run-in with the law when he is mistaken for Too Much Crack Man.

Tom Waters wrote about the comic's transition from comic to magazine for *Acid Logic* online, saying that "a few issues later and the cult has grown and the magazine is the buzz of the Starbucks jet set. All the mom and pop chains that entertain people who mooch free refills and spend the majority of their evening swilling mud and breaking down the latest Woody Allen film. The magazine is really brilliant for a newcomer. It takes chances, and it's not . . . homogenized."

Waters interviewed Wheeler and asked him if he sees his character "as a vehicle to tackle political, religious, and philosophical topics now, or has he taken on a life of his own?" Wheeler replied, "Yes and yes. Early on I figured out that I would get bored if what I was going to do was coffee jokes, that it would end very quickly. What I was thinking about was personal responsibility and our obligation to the planet and the quandary of our lives."

Waters asked Wheeler if he found Seattle supportive, and Wheeler said, "I have a hard time in Seattle, because I think they hate their own reputation. They see me as part of the problem, so outside Seattle I might become a symbol for Seattle, but the town needs to look past the obvious aspect of TMCM."

The magazine, each issue of which has a special focus, contains interviews, articles, comics, including work by others, and complete coverage of the coffee industry. TMCM t-shirts and coffee cups are popular with fans of Wheeler's character and magazine.

Yankthechain.com interviewer Eric R. related that Wheeler "once did a whole strip that was just a Balzac speech about coffee. In it, Balzac concludes that coffee makes you 'brusque,' 'ill-tempered,' makes you 'argue about everything,' and 'harangue with monumental bad faith.' He also states that coffee makes ideas 'march through your head' and makes you extremely 'lucid.' Do you share this conclusion? Do you often work while or after drinking coffee? Do you avoid drinking coffee in social situations?"

Wheeler replied, "sort of," and said he likes the part of the speech in which Balzac says that coffee "makes the boring more boring. But it's a great little drug that does many different things to different people. Also, I think he was talking about drinking coffee in a great excess."

BIOGRAPHICAL AND CRITICAL SOURCES:

PERIODICALS

Texas Monthly, July, 1995, Andrew Goldman, review of *Too Much Coffee Man,* p. 80.
Washington Post Book World, July 26, 1998, Mike Musgrove, review of *Too Much Coffee Man: Guide for the Perplexed,* p. 10.

ONLINE

Acid Logic, http://www.acidlogic.com/ (August 1, 2003), Tom Waters, interview with Wheeler.
Shannon Wheeler Home Page, http://www.toomuchcoffeeman.com (December 4, 2003).
Twoheadedcat.com, http://www.twoheadedcat.com/ (September 30, 2002), James Cosby, interview with Wheeler.
Yankthechain.com, http://www.yankthechain.com/ (September 22, 2003), Eric R., interview with Wheeler.*

* * *

WHITE, Karen 1964-

PERSONAL: Born May 30, 1964, in Tulsa, OK; married Tim White (a bank officer), September 5, 1987; children: Meghan, Connor. *Ethnicity:* "Caucasian." *Education:* Tulane University, B.S., 1986. *Hobbies and other interests:* Singing in a church choir, playing piano, reading.

ADDRESSES: Office—P.O. Box 450181, Atlanta, GA 31145-9998. *Agent*—Karen Solem, Spencerhill Associates, P.O. Box 374, Chatham, NY 12037.

CAREER: Writer.

MEMBER: Romance Writers of America, Georgia Romance Writers (president, 2001-03).

AWARDS, HONORS: Holt Medallion, Virginia Romance Writers, 2002, for *Whispers of Goodbye.*

WRITINGS:

ROMANCE NOVELS

In the Shadow of the Moon, Dorchester Publishing (Wayne, PA), 2000.
Whispers of Goodbye, Dorchester Publishing (Wayne, PA), 2001.
Falling Home, Kensington Publishing (New York, NY), 2002.
After the Rain, Kensington Publishing (New York, NY), 2003.
(Coauthor) *Blessings in Mossy Creek,* Belle Books (Atlanta, GA), in press.

WORK IN PROGRESS: The Color of Light.

SIDELIGHTS: Karen White told *CA:* "Whenever anybody asks me why I decided to become a writer, I simply tell them that the career chose me. And then when they tell me they've always wanted to write a book, I tell them that, first, they need to read, read, read—especially in the genre in which they wish to write, and second, they need to sit down in a chair and just do it!"

BIOGRAPHICAL AND CRITICAL SOURCES:

PERIODICALS

Booklist, May 15, 2002, Alexandra Shrake, review of *Falling Home,* p. 1582.

* * *

WHITTINGTON, Brad 1956-

PERSONAL: Born March 12, 1956, in Fort Worth, TX; married; wife's name, Milly; children: Daniel, Sarah. *Education:* Attended East Texas Baptist College; Baylor University, B.S. (secondary education), 1979; graduated from Texas State Technical College, 1985. *Religion:* Christian. *Hobbies and other interests:* Reading, playing guitar.

ADDRESSES: Home—Kai, HI. *Agent*—Broadman & Holman Publishers, 127 Ninth Ave. N., Nashville, TN 37234. *E-mail*—author@fred.texas.com.

CAREER: Telecommunications worker. Has worked variously as a janitor, math teacher, computer programmer, Web page developer, and editor.

WRITINGS:

Welcome to Fred, Broadman & Holman (Nashville, TN), 2003.

Contributor of articles to magazines and newspapers.

WORK IN PROGRESS: Two sequels to *Welcome to Fred.*

SIDELIGHTS: In 2003 Brad Whittington published his debut novel *Welcome to Fred,* "a simple coming-of-age tale about a young man seeking to find out who he is and where he belongs," wrote *Library Journal* contributor Wilda Williams. Set in the late 1960s, the novel concerns Mark Cloud, a worldly adolescent who experiences growing pains after his family moves to the small, isolated town of Fred, Texas. The son of a Baptist preacher, Mark wrestles with issues of faith and identity, and his beliefs are tested during a family trip to California. In an interview with Daniel Whitfield published on the *Welcome to Fred* Web site, Whittington stated that his work addresses universal concerns: "I think most people experience some sense of alienation while they are growing up and strive to fit in. Everybody yearns for romantic love. Everybody struggles with the questions of God and religion."

"What elevates this book above others of its kind—if in fact there are others of its kind in the Christian market—is Whittington's ability not only to create believable, well-rounded characters but also to give them believable, well-rounded dialogue to work with," wrote Marcia Ford on the *Faithful Reader* Web site. A *Publishers Weekly* critic offered a mixed view of the novel, stating that "the reader sometimes feels more like an observer than a participant. However, there are lovely details, generous portions of humor and plenty of nostalgia." Reviewing *Welcome to Fred* in the *Honolulu Advertiser,* Wanda Adams observed that

Whittington "evokes adolescence with humor and more than a nod to the rueful embarrassment that comes of remembrances of one's early and unformed self."

BIOGRAPHICAL AND CRITICAL SOURCES:

PERIODICALS

Bookpage, April, 2003, review of *Welcome to Fred.*
CBA Marketplace, May, 2003, John Bernstein, review of *Welcome to Fred.*
Honolulu Advertiser, August 17, 2003, Wanda Adams, "*Fred* Reaches at Times but Is Thoroughly Enjoyable."
Honolulu Star-Bulletin, April 6, 2003, review of *Welcome to Fred.*
Library Journal, April 1, 2003, Wilda Williams, review of *Welcome to Fred,* p. 86.
Publishers Weekly, March 17, 2003, review of *Welcome to Fred,* p. 54.

ONLINE

Christian Book Preview Web site, http://www.christianbookpreviews.com/ (May 2, 2004), review of *Welcome to Fred.*
Faithful Reader Web site, http://www.faithfulreader.com/ (May 2, 2004), Marcia Ford, review of *Welcome to Fred.*
Welcome to Fred Web site, http://www.fredtexas.com/ (April 26, 2004), Daniel Whitfield, interview with Whittington.*

*   *   *

WILDER, Buck
See SMITH, Tim(othy R.)

*   *   *

WILKINSON, David Marion 1957-

PERSONAL: Born 1957, in Malvern, AR; son of Martin (a Presbyterian minister and petroleum engineer) and Alice (self-employed; maiden name: Johnson) Wilkinson; married Bonnie D. Bratton (an attorney); children: Dean, Tate. *Ethnicity:* "Scotch-Irish; French." *Education:* University of Texas—Austin, B.A., 1980.

ADDRESSES: Agent—Anna Cottle and Mary Alice Kier, c/o Cine/Lit Representation Literary Enterprises, P.O. Box 802918, Santa Clara, CA 91380-2918; fax: 661-513-0278. *E-mail*—remylogan@austin.rr.com.

CAREER: Writer. Has worked variously as a carpenter, legal investigator, mortgage loan officer, and oil field worker domestically and abroad.

MEMBER: Western Writers of America, Ozark Creative Writers (vice president), Writers League of Texas.

AWARDS, HONORS: Violet Crown Award, Writers League of Texas, 1997, for *Not between Brothers: An Epic Novel of Texas;* Spur Award for short fiction, Western Writers of America, 2000, for "Opening Day"; Oklahoma Book Award finalist, Oklahoma Center for the Book, and Spur Award, Western Writers of America, both 2003, both for *Oblivion's Altar.*

WRITINGS:

Not between Brothers: An Epic Novel of Texas, Boaz Publishing Company (Albany, CA), 1996.
The Empty Quarter, Boaz Publishing Company (Albany, CA), 1998.
Oblivion's Altar: A Novel of Courage, New American Library (New York, NY), 2002.
Only One Ranger, University of Texas Press (Austin, TX), 2004.

Contributor of short fiction to publications such as *ReadWest Online Magazine.*

SIDELIGHTS: David Marion Wilkinson draws upon his personal experiences and historical facts of life in the American West to fuel his novels and short stories. An award-winning Western novelist, Wilkinson's first book, *Not between Brothers: An Epic Novel of Texas,* was the recipient of the Violet Crown Award from the Writers League of Texas. The book covers four decades of early Texas history during a time when immigrants were trying to stake out a piece of Texas land while coming into conflict with the Indian tribes who already lived there. In the story, Remy Fuqua arrives in Texas, practically penniless, and proceeds to make his fortune by sheer force of will. He marries into a prominent Mexican family, becomes a father, and establishes a wealthy ranch. But he knows the dangers in the area and is prepared to do what he must to protect his family and property.

In contrast, Penateka warrior Kills White Bear has experienced first-hand the downfall of his people and his way of life. Disease, the destruction of once-rich hunting areas, and the continuing expansion of settlers have deprived his tribe of what once was theirs without question. Angry and resentful, Kills White Bear finds no room in his life for the Anglos or Mexicanos, and realizes there will be no peace between them. War is inevitable, as is the meeting between Kills White Bear and Remy Fuqua.

"For me, the story is a look back at a young America before her bloody boundaries were drawn," Wilkinson said in a statement on his Web site. His deep research required him to "read sixty non-fiction, historical, and primary source works in order to write my own," Wilkinson said. "I strove for historical accuracy first and foremost."

Though the book had the potential for controversy in its portrayals, Wilkinson did not seek to glamorize or apologize for any of his characters. "The intent was for the reader to see how things were, and then judge for him or herself," Wilkinson commented on his Web site. He wanted readers to see the world in which their ancestors lived, to find the dignity and courage the early Texas residents possessed, and to "forgive them for their faults," Wilkinson remarked. In the end, Wilkinson described *Not between Brothers* as "an American story of determination, healing, and hope against all obstacles and all odds." The book has also been optioned by actor Kevin Costner's Tig Productions for a potential television miniseries.

Wilkinson's second novel, *The Empty Quarter,* is based on his experiences working in the oilfields of Saudi Arabia and the North Sea. "It's not often that a writer has the opportunity to draw upon a life-changing experience to mold years later into a work of fiction," Wilkinson wrote on his Web site. The book's main character, Logan Wilson, clings tenaciously to the lifestyle of an oilfield worker in the Rub Al Khali desert, a life that he has long known, until events in the novel jolt him powerfully from his entrenched life. A similar experience propelled Wilkinson himself from the oil-rich desert sands. "It took a disastrous upheaval to drive me from that dark and empty place, the story of which forms the core of the novel I now offer you," Wilkinson commented.

Wilkinson returned to the Western genre with his third novel, *Oblivion's Altar.* During the sixty-year timespan of the novel, covering 1776 to 1839, Wilkinson presents an "entertaining, imaginative, and historically informed story" that examines the U.S. government's "ruthless displacement of the Cherokee Nation from its Georgia homeland," wrote James S. McWilliams in the *Austin Chronicle.* Ridge, a Cherokee chieftain born Ka-nung-da-tla-geh, or The Man Who Walks the Mountaintops, is a prominent farmer who believes the treaties and words of conciliation offered by then-president Andrew Jackson. But Jackson, named Sharp Knife by the Cherokee, has no intention of honoring the treaties or helping the tribe in a bitter, vicious land battle against the U.S. government. Ridge attempts to resist the land-grab through peaceful means and strategic resistance rather than through bloodshed, a stance that jeopardizes his reputation within the Cherokee community. Education becomes Ridge's weapon; he sends his son John off to an East Coast missionary school, where the boy becomes a lawyer. John takes the fight for Cherokee lands to the government's own favorite battlefield and wins cases for the Cherokee in the courts. However, the victories are blatantly ignored by the government; the tribe is forced from its lands in a violent displacement that initiates the Trail of Tears and the difficult migration of Indians westward.

"Ridge is a tragic hero, a good man who did everything he could to protect his people," wrote a *Publishers Weekly* reviewer, but a hero who is ultimately doomed by betrayal by both the white men he trusted and the Cherokee people he championed. "Wilkinson's tale packs a strong emotional punch" in its depiction of Ridge's defeat and the historically accurate portrayal of the Cherokee displacement and the origin of the Trail of Tears, the *Publishers Weekly* critic continued. "Wilkinson effectively, and at times brilliantly, illuminates the blood and guts of a Cherokee history seen from West to East," McWilliams observed.

Wilkinson's short story, "Opening Day," appeared in *ReadWest Online Magazine* and was the winner of the 2000 Spur Award for short fiction from the Western Writers of America.

BIOGRAPHICAL AND CRITICAL SOURCES:

PERIODICALS

Austin Chronicle, November 15, 2002, James S. McWilliams, review of *Oblivion's Altar.*
Publishers Weekly, October 21, 2002, review of *Oblivion's Altar,* p. 56.

ONLINE

David Marion Wilkinson Home Page, http://www. dmarionwilkinson.com (July 14, 2003).
Nashville Public Radio WPLN, http://www.wpln.org/ (July 14, 2003), biography of David Marion Wilkinson.
ReadWest Online Magazine, http://www.readwest.com/ (July 14, 2003), profile of David Marion Wilkinson.*

*   *   *

WILLIAMS, Carla 1965-

PERSONAL: Born 1965, in Los Angeles, CA; daughter of Wendell and Evelyn Williams. *Ethnicity:* "African American." *Education:* Princeton University, B.A., 1986; University of New Mexico, Albuquerque, M.A., 1988; M.F.A., 1996. *Politics:* Green Party. *Hobbies and other interests:* Committed to political activism.

ADDRESSES: Agent—c/o Author Mail, Temple University Press, 1601 N. Broad St., 306 USB, Philadelphia, PA 19122. *E-mail*—carlagirl@earthlink.net

CAREER: J. Paul Getty Museum, Los Angeles, CA, Department of Photographs, intern, 1991-92; Schomburg Center for Research in Black Culture, New York Public Library, New York, NY, Prints and Photographs Division, curator, 1992-93; Topanga, CA, private collection, curator, 1993-97; Pomona College, Claremont, CA, instructor in photography, 1994; freelance writer and editor, 1995—; J. Paul Getty Museum, Los Angeles, CA, Collections Information Planning Department, writer, art access, 1997-99; Thaw Art History Center, College of Santa Fe, Visual Resource curator, 1999-2002; College of Santa Fe, Santa Fe,

NM, Marion Center for Photographic Arts, adjunct professor of history of photography and photography, spring, 2001 and spring, 2002; Stanford University, Drama Department, lecturer, 2003. Lecturer and panelist at universities. *Exhibitions:* Group exhibitions include *Reflections in Black: A History Deconstructed,* various venues and dates; *Disclosures,* Calvin College, Grand Rapids, MI, 2001; *Precedence: Emmet Gowin and His Students,* Fosdick-Nelson Gallery, New York State College of Ceramics at Alfred University, 2000; *Past, Present, Future,* College of Santa Fe Fine Arts Gallery, 2000; *Treatment: Women's Bodies in Medical Science and Art,* Dinnerware Gallery, Tucson, AZ, 1999; *The Human Figure in Photography,* Graff Fine Arts Center Gallery, Dixie College, St. George, UT, 1998; National Juried and Invitational Exhibition, National Black Arts Festival, Georgia State University Art Gallery, Atlanta, GA, 1998; *Alternatives '98,* Ohio University, Athens, OH, 1998; *25 and Under,* traveling exhibition, Center for Documentary Studies and *Doubletake* magazine, 1996-98; *Searching for Memories: Black Women and the 1895 Atlanta Exposition,* collaboration in *Messages from the Everyday World: The Bathhouse Exhibition,* Arts Festival of Atlanta, Atlanta, GA, 1995; *African American Women Photographers,* Salena Gallery, Long Island University, Brooklyn, NY, 1993; *Of Pride and Pain: Photographs by Christian Walker, Deborah Willis, and Carla Williams,* The Light Factory, Charlotte, NC, 1992-93; *LACPS Annual Exhibition,* University of Southern California Lindhurst Gallery, Los Angeles, CA, 1992; *Contemporary Women Photographers,* University Art Museum, University of New Mexico, Albuquerque, NM, 1991; *How to Read Character,* The Teaching Gallery, University of New Mexico, Albuquerque, NM, 1991; *National Exposures 90,* Sawtooth Building Galleries, Winston-Salem, NC, 1990; *National Aperture 3,* Sawtooth Building Galleries, Winston-Salem, NC, 1988. Collections on exhibit at University Art Museum, University of New Mexico—Albuquerque; The Art Museum, Princeton University; Light Work, Syracuse, NY.

MEMBER: Society for Photographic Education National Conference (proposal review panel member), Arts Advisory Committee, Museum of the African Diaspora (San Francisco, CA), Publications Committee for Society for Photographic Education, Center for the Arts of the African Diaspora (advisory board member, 1998—), Los Angeles Center for Photographic Studies (member, board of directors, 1993-95); Los Angeles Department of Cultural Affairs (peer review panelist, 1993, 1996, 1997).

AWARDS, HONORS: Canon Excellence Award, April 1988, for *National Aperture 3* exhibition (contributor of photographs); Infinity Award, International Center for Photography, New York, 1994, for *Picturing Us: African American Identity in Photography* (contributor of essay); Golden Light Award Book of Merit, Maine Photographic Workshops, 1996, for *25 and Under* (contributor of photographs); Bronze Award from the National Gold Ink Awards, 2002, for *The Black Female Body: A Photographic History;* Rockefeller Fellow in the Black Performing Arts, Humanities Center, Stanford University, 2002-03.

WRITINGS:

Thurgood Marshall: 1908-1993, Child's World (Chanhassen, MN), 2002.
The Underground Railroad, Child's World (Chanhassen, MN), 2002.
(With Deborah Willis) *The Black Female Body: A Photographic History,* Temple University Press (Philadelphia, PA), 2002.

Contributor to journals, including *Fotophile: The Journal for Creative Photographers, Black & White Magazine,* and *Image;* contributor to encyclopedias, including *Black Women in America: An Historical Encyclopedia,* Oxford University Press (New York, NY), and *Encyclopedia of African American Art and Architecture,* Grolier Academic Reference; contributor to anthologies, including *Skin Deep, Spirit Strong: The Black Female Body in American Culture,* University of Michigan Press (Ann Arbor, MI), 2002, *Our Grandmothers,* Stewart, Tabori & Chang (New York, NY), 1998, and *Picturing Us: African American Identity in Photography,* New Press (New York, NY), 1994; contributor to online magazines and Web sites, including *PhotoPoint Magazine.* Contributor to exhibition catalogs, including *Picturing the Modern Amazon,* New Museum of Contemporary Art (New York, NY), 2000, and *Portraits at Imperial Courts,* Los Angeles Center for Photographic Studies (Los Angeles, CA), May 15-June 15, 1999; writer and editor for newsletter *Subtext: The Group at Strasberg,* 2002—.

WORK IN PROGRESS: Biography of Maudelle Bass; anthology on the Hottentot Venus.

SIDELIGHTS: Photographer and writer Carla Williams is a contributor to numerous publications, through both her writing and her photographs. In 2002 she published two historical-interest books for children, *The Underground Railroad* and *Thurgood Marshall: 1908-1993. The Underground Railroad* covers a significant period in African-American history, the clandestine freeing of slaves through the help of a network of both black and white supporters paving their safe passage from the South to northern U.S. cities. A reviewer for the *Horn Book Guide* found the prose simple enough to appeal to all readers and thought the anecdotal material was "intriguing." *Thurgood Marshall,* about the great African-American jurist, is also written for young readers. Marlene Gawron, in a review for the *School Library Journal,* said the books in this series "humanize these super-achievers." Both books feature plenty of photographs, which add to their interest, according to a *Horn Book Guide* critic.

Also in 2002, Williams' lengthy collaboration with photographer and writer Deborah Willis resulted in publication of *The Black Female Body: A Photographic History,* a collection of approximately 185 photographs of black women from the nineteenth through the twenty-first centuries, with accompanying text. The authors found photographs in old books, art museums, private collections, and archives in Europe and the United States. Combining their education and experience as photographers, they put together a book that Meredith Broussard, of *Citypaper.net,* called "a gorgeous, remarkable work, full of empowering perspectives about the artistic representation of African-American women."

In an interview with Annette John-Hall of the *Philadelphia Inquirer,* Williams and Willis said they met when a professor told Willis that a graduate student at the University of New Mexico (Williams) had been photographing her own behind. Williams said she made the photos for her photographic series *How to Read Character* because she had not seen any photos in her studies that looked like her. One of these photos is reproduced in *The Black Female Body* as a tribute to the African-American woman Saartjie Baartman, known as the Hottentot Venus. The nude Baartman was presented as an attraction at freak shows in the early nineteenth century because of her large and protuberant buttocks.

The Black Female Body is divided into four parts: "Colonial Conquest," "The Cultural Body," "The Body Beautiful," and "Reclaiming Bodies and Images." The photographs represent work by such well-known photographers as Gordon Parks, James Van Der Zee, Carrie Mae Weems, Adrian Piper, Chester Higgins, Renee Cox, Catherine Opie, Walker Evans, and Dorothea Lange, as well as anonymous photographs taken in the 1800s and 1900s to document the black female body for anthropological and less-noble purposes, such as pornographic interest. These include photos of the Hottentot Venus, the "Jezebels," and the "noble savages."

As described by Regina Woods, in the *Black Issues Book Review,* the book "moves back and forth between images of female bodies as specimens, metaphors for colonized territories, signifiers of hypersexuality, neutered mammies, and self-defined subjects." A reviewer for Temple University Press acknowledged that the authors "offer counterpoints to these exploitative images, as well as testaments to a vibrant culture." Many of the subjects are nude, but others are dressed in finery. Still others are photos of black women athletes and bodybuilders. Others are famous personalities, or simply mothers, daughters, grandmothers. Esther Iverem, writing for *SeeingBlack.com,* stated, "Williams and Willis . . . have compiled a tour de force of images and text that will make you think differently not only about African and African American history but also about the unique struggles that Black women have within that larger history."

In a review for *Library Journal,* Shauna Frischkorn commented that the book "provides a fascinating view into a long-neglected and even taboo subject." Williams' accompanying text, according to Stephanie Dinkins, of *Afterimage,* "seeks to deconstruct and (re)contextualize the images presented to reveal the ways in which perceptions of black women have been informed and constructed by Western photographic practice." Themes of negation, sexualization, and objectification recur throughout the book, and the authors succeed in allowing readers to confront these images as the professional photographers have done in hopes of forging, as Dinkins said, "a broader, self-determined vision of the black female physique."

Another function of the book is to show how representation, as in photographs, influences self-image and creates culture. A contributor to *Ebony* wrote that the book not only provides a photographic history but also chronicles "the long struggle for civil rights and the socio-political impact of artistic expression." A contributor to *Publishers Weekly* observed that the "point here is more the unmasking of stereotypes, which the book does very well." A contributor to *Choice* called the book "an important contribution" to the history of women, photography, and popular culture. John-Hall commended Williams and Willis on their "evenhanded, meticulously researched text."

Williams spoke about her self-portraits in a 2001 essay for *FemmeNoir.net*. She said they were "initially informed by the history of portraits made by male photographers of their wives, lovers, and muses" and that she wanted to make the photos of herself rather than "wait for someone else to want to make them of me." Nor did she want to photograph others in the same way. "With the self-portrait I could photograph exactly what I was feeling and decide later whether or not to display them," she said. When in graduate school a professor described her photographs as those of "a young black woman," she realized that "most viewers would always see a black body regardless of my intent." She then began to research historical photos of black women for her "Character" exhibit. Her later photographic work has centered around the changing body, with age, weight gain, and other factors. Although Williams has, over the years, periodically stopped making images and focused more on her writing, photography is still an important part of her life. She said in the 2001 essay that she sees her self-portraits as "highly personal, almost diaristic visual note-taking that functions in an ongoing continuum."

Williams told *CA:* "In 1999 I developed and launched http://www.carlagirl.net. The site functions as an archive of my photographic images, as well as past and current writings. The site also includes an extensive research library related to black artists and images of black women with more than 300 annotated entries, plus hundreds of regularly updated links to other sites related to black artists, especially women artists, gay and lesbian artists, and related photography and art sites. It includes a comprehensive calendar of arts events worldwide.

"The biggest influence on my work is black women. Black women inspire me, and I want to honor them with my work. Looking around at contemporary culture, I am determined that we not be overlooked and we not be misunderstood. Popular culture is really important to me, too. I hope that my work engages with popular culture in a way that makes it accessible to a larger audience.

"I hope that my books will make people look more carefully at images and make them think about what they see, and trust what they think they see rather than believe what they've been told. These images are now compiled in a single volume for people to reference for years to come. If that happens, we've more than achieved success."

BIOGRAPHICAL AND CRITICAL SOURCES:

PERIODICALS

Afterimage, May, 2002, Stephanie Dinkins, *The Black Female Body: A Photographic History,* p. 19.
Black Issues Book Review, March-April, 2002, Regina Woods, review of *The Black Female Body.*
Choice, October, 2002, review of *The Black Female Body,* p. 272.
Ebony, April, 2002, "Book Shelf: Picture Perfect: *The Black Female Body,*" p. 22.
Horn Book Guide, spring, 2002, review of *Thurgood Marshall: 1908-1993,* p. 180; spring, 2002, review of *The Underground Railroad,* p. 204.
Library Journal, October 1, 2002, Shauna Frischkorn, review of *The Black Female Body,* p. 93.
Philadelphia Inquirer, February 21, 2002, Annette John-Hall, "For Love of the Body,"
Publishers Weekly, February 4, 2002, review of *The Black Female Body,* p. 71.
School Library Journal, January, 2002, Marlene Gawron, review of *Thurgood Marshall,* p. 152; January, 2002, Margaret C. Howell, review of *The Underground Railroad,* p. 162.

ONLINE

Carla Williams Home Page, http://www.carlagirl.net (September 15, 2003).
CityPaper.net, http://www.citypaper.net/articles/ (February 21-28, 2002), Meredith Broussard, review of *The Black Female Body.*
FemmeNoir.net, http://www.femmenoir.net/ (May 8, 2003), Carla Williams, "Carlagirl Photo."
SeeingBlack.com, http://www.seeingblack.com/ (May 24, 2002), Esther Iverem, "Body Images, Then and Now."
Temple University Press Web site, http://www.temple.edu/tempress/ (May 8, 2003), review of *The Black Female Body.*

WILSON, Emma

PERSONAL: Female.

ADDRESSES: Office—Department of French, Faculty of Modern and Medieval Languages, University of Cambridge, Sidgwick Avenue, Cambridge CB3 9DA, England. *Agent*—c/o Author Mail, Columbia University Press, 61 West 62nd St., New York, NY 10023. *E-mail*—efw1000@hermes.cam.ac.uk.

CAREER: Author and educator. Cambridge University, Cambridge, England, senior lecturer in the Department of French.

WRITINGS:

Sexuality and the Reading Encounter: Identity and Desire in Proust, Duras, Tournier, and Cixous, Oxford University Press (New York, NY), 1996.

French Cinema since 1950: Personal Histories, Duckworth (London, England), 1999.

Memory and Survival: The French Cinema of Krzysztof, Legenda (Oxford, England), 2000.

Cinema's Missing Children, Columbia University Press (New York, NY), 2003.

WORK IN PROGRESS: A study of the films of Alain Resnais.

SIDELIGHTS: A faculty member of the University of Cambridge's Corpus Christi College, Emma Wilson specializes in French literature and contemporary film. In her first book, *Sexuality and the Reading Encounter: Identity and Desire in Proust, Duras, Tournier, and Cixous,* Wilson focuses on these four notable French writers, discussing the works of several theorists and incorporating the "queer theory" of reading into her analyses of scenes and presentations of pleasure, pain, eroticism, and loss presented in the authors' works. In the process, Wilson examines the complex relationship among the reader, the author, and the text with a focus on how a reader's sexual desire and orientation can be affected and possibly even changed by the reading of a literary novel.

In a review of *Sexuality and the Reading Encounter* in the *Times Literary Supplement,* Nicole Ward Jouve said she doubted "that reading is as formative" as the author argues. However, the reviewer called the book "a highly intelligent, up-to-date, well-informed study." *Modern Philology* contributor Martha Noel Evans noted that the book was "badly served by its copyeditors," especially in terms of using the either/or pronoun forms (such as s/he and him/herself). Evans also commented, however, that the book "never ceases to stimulate, provoke, and enlighten." Kate Ince, writing in *Modern Language Review,* said that the chapters on Proust and Duras were the book's high points. Ince also noted, "The book is impeccably researched and written with evidently painstaking care."

Wilson takes a critical look at some of the most widely watched and studied works of French cinema in her book *French Cinema since 1950: Personal Histories.* She focuses both on classic, widely known films such as François Truffaut's *The 400 Blows* and Jean Luc Godard's *Breathless,* as well as works little known outside of France such as *Irma Vep,* by director Jean-Pierre Leaud. Wilson begins by examining the young directors of the 1950s, such as Truffaut and Godard, who wanted to raise filmmaking to the level of classic literature. Wilson analyzes the biographical and autobiographical elements of several films, especially in terms of their creators' responses to various public events. *Times Literary Supplement* contributor Robin Buss called Wilson's critical approach "promising" but added that it was hindered by "poor argument and a certain lack of consideration for the reader." Writing in *Choice,* reviewer M. Yacowar said that *French Cinema since 1950* contained too much unnecessary information that took away from a more comprehensive analysis but was a valuable introduction to many lesser-known French films. Yacowar also noted, "The conclusion provides a touching fusion of the scholarly and personal."

In her 2003 book *Cinema's Missing Children,* Wilson discusses how numerous contemporary films approach the issue of the loss of a child, a long-time archetype in stories and fables, such as *Little Red Riding Hood.* Wilson contends in her introduction that "one of the central fears and compulsions explored in recent independent and art cinema is the death or loss of a child." In looking at the motif of the dead, missing, or murdered child, Wilson discusses how filmmakers use cinema to express and transform both their own and the viewer's response to the intense pain and horror at the loss of a child. To illustrate her themes and theories, Wilson draws on modern psychological and sociological research as she discusses such films as *Three Colours: Blue, All about My Mother,* and *Portrait of a Lady,* all of which discuss how a surviving mother deals with all-consuming grief and changes as the result of a child's death.

In a review on *Kamera.co.uk,* contributor Antonio Pasolini wrote that Wilson's contention that the missing child was central to modern art films is an exaggeration. Pasolini also commented that the book used too much academic language and was a "monotonous read." Nevertheless, the reviewer concluded, "Despite the style difficulties *Cinema's Missing Children* is faced with, it is certainly an original book that may pave the way for more in the field." Writing for *PopMatters Book Review,* James Oliphant also found the book's language to be too academic but noted, "That never detracts from the weight of [Wilson's] intellect or scholarship." Oliphant also commented that Wilson's book "makes for compelling reading for anyone interested in thoughtful and compelling film analysis."

BIOGRAPHICAL AND CRITICAL SOURCES:

PERIODICALS

Choice, January, 1997, F. C. St. Aubyn, review of *Sexuality and the Reading Encounter: Identity and Desire in Proust, Duras, Tournier, and Cixous,* p. 802; March, 2000, M. Yacowar, review of *French Cinema since 1950: Personal Histories,* p. 1309.
Modern Language Review, July, 1997, Kate Ince, review of *Sexuality and the Reading Encounter,* pp. 741-742.
Modern Philology, November, 1998, Martha Noel Evans, review of *Sexuality and the Reading Encounter,* p. 284.
Times Literary Supplement, June 6, 1997, Nicole Ward Jouve, review of *Sexuality and the Reading Encounter,* p. 33; September 3, 1999, Robin Buss, review of *French Cinema since 1950,* p. 32.

ONLINE

Kamera.co.uk, http://kamera.co.uk/ (November 7, 2003), Antonio Pasolini, review of *Cinema's Missing Children.*
PopMatters Book Review, http://www.popmatters.com/ (July 24, 2003), James Oliphant, review of *Cinema's Missing Children.**

WINNER, Thomas G(ustav) 1917-2004

OBITUARY NOTICE—See index for *CA* sketch: Born May 4, 1917, in Prague, Czechoslovakia (now Czech Republic); died of complications from pneumonia, April 20, 2004, in Cambridge, MA. Educator and author. Winner was a professor of comparative literature who was considered an authority on Russian literature, especially the works of Anton Chekhov. Winner, who was Jewish, was a fortunate recipient of a Harvard University scholarship that allowed him to escape Europe just as Nazi Germany was invading Poland at the start of World War II. At Harvard, he was a vocal protestor against the Nazis, while working to earn his master's degree in 1942. During the war, he served as a translator of the Office of War Information; with the war over, he returned to his studies, earning a Ph.D. in 1950 from Columbia University. Fluent in twenty languages, Winner accepted a teaching position at Duke University, where he taught until 1958. This was followed by eight years at the University of Michigan, and in 1966 he joined the Brown University faculty as professor of Slavic languages. In 1977 he became a professor of comparative literature, retiring as professor emeritus in 1982. From 1977 to 1983, he also worked as director of the Center for Research in Semiotics, and beginning in 1984 was director of the Program in Semiotic Studies at Boston University. The author of *The Oral Art and Literature of the Kazakhs of Russian Central Asia* (1958) and *Chekhov and His Prose* (1966), Winner was editor of several scholarly texts in Russian and English, including the coedited *The Peasant and the City in Eastern Europe: Interpenetrating Structures* (1982) and *Sign System and Function* (1984).

OBITUARIES AND OTHER SOURCES:

PERIODICALS

New York Times, April 29, 2004, p. A25.

*   *   *

WOODRING, Jim 1952-

PERSONAL: Born 1952, in Los Angeles, CA; married; children: one son.

ADDRESSES: Agent—c/o Author Mail, Fantagraphics Books, 7563 Lake City Way NE, Seattle, WA 98115. *E-mail*—jim@jimwoodring.com.

CAREER: Cartoonist, writer, illustrator, animator. Creator of the comic book series *Jim* and *Frank;* commercial illustrator for clients that include *The Whole Earth Catalog* and Microsoft.

AWARDS, HONORS: Harvey Award for best colorist, 1993, for *Tantalizing Stories Presents Frank in the River; Booklist*'s Top Ten Graphic Novels, 2004.

WRITINGS:

Tantalizing Stories Presents Frank in the River, Tundra (Northampton, MA), 1992.
The Book of Jim, Fantagraphics Books (Seattle, WA), 1993.
(With others) *Star Wars: Jabba the Hutt,* Pan Macmillan, 1995.
(With Kilian Plunkett) *Aliens: Labrinth,* Dark Horse Comics (Milwaukie, OR), 1997.
Frank (two volumes), Fantagraphics Books (Seattle, WA), 1997.
(With others) *Aliens: Kidnapped,* Dark Horse Comics (Milwaukie, OR), 1999.
Trosper, Fantagraphics Books (Seattle, WA), 2002.
The Frank Book, introduction by Francis Ford Coppola, Fantagraphics Books (Seattle, WA), 2003.
Jim Woodring Dream Journal, Dark Horse Comics (Milwaukie, OR), 2003.

Also author of *Trosper.* Work represented in anthologies, including *Flock of Dreamers: An Anthology of Dream-Inspired Comics,* Kitchen Sink Press, 1998; contributor to periodicals, including *Wired, World Art, Weirdo, Kenyon Review,* and *Zoetrope.*

SIDELIGHTS: Although Jim Woodring is best known for his wordless comic *Frank,* in his autobiographical *Jim,* he is generous in using dialogue to express his emotions and put his dreams down on paper. James Donnelly reviewed the four issues published as *The Book of Jim* in *Whole Earth Review,* saying that the stories "are composed with the pacing, tension and eloquence of a wholly mature, if overtly peculiar, artist."

Woodring grew up in Southern California and, according to his Web site, "enjoyed a childhood made interesting by frequent hallucinations, apparitions, disembodied voices, and other psychological malfunctions. Despite the generally frightening nature of his delusions, he learned to accept them as part of life and was accordingly a reasonably cheerful and good-natured lad."

Woodring moved up and down the West Coast and worked at a variety of jobs while he submitted his work to underground publications, a number of which used it. He found work as an animator in Los Angeles, where he says he "worked on some of the worst cartoons this degraded planet has ever seen." The self-taught artist self-published *Jim* and then met Gary Groth, founder of Fantagraphics, in 1984, and Groth published it as a thirty-two page magazine. When Fantagraphics moved to Seattle in 1986, Woodring relocated, and from that point, he became a full-time comix artist.

Richard Seven wrote in an article for the *Seattle Times: Pacific Northwest Online* that Frank "is a buck-toothed, wide-eyed, balloon-cheeked character who looks like a skinny cat that walks on two legs. There's no telling how old Frank is and he never talks. He lives in an unidentifiable place that can be pastoral one frame and hellish the next. Frank mutely moves through adventures full of strange offers, morphing objects, and creepy nooks just on the other side of some portal. A lot happens to Frank, but he comes out unscathed and none the wiser." Seven commented that "the work is steeped in symbolism and messages that Woodring himself doesn't always understand immediately."

The other creatures in *Frank* are bizarre and include the repulsive Manhog, a thin devil-like creature named Whim, Frank's satchel-shaped pet Pushpaw, and the Jerry Chickens, geometrically shaped fowl who play cards. Andrew D. Arnold wrote for *Time.com* that Woodring "keeps the stories wordless, both as a challenge to himself—'like writing a novel without the letter "e,"' he has said—but, more importantly, as a way to avoid cultural currency. Not using words keeps the 'Frank' stories timeless and universal. . . . Wordless, sequential drawings have been the purest form of communication since prehistory."

Robotfist reviewer Joseph Caouette called Frank's world "an empty world, and the pretty landscapes take on a deathly stillness because of the unsettling desolation that haunts them. In fact, one of the most fascinating aspects of these stories is that creeping sense of isolation. Even with a recurring cast of characters, the world seems so vast that our little dramatis personae cannot hope to fill the emptiness."

On her Web site, Kathleen E. Bennett wrote in a review of the series that Woodring "uses both stained glass/acid trip colors and rich, woodcut-like ink drawings to evoke different moods, two facets of the same world, which is both transparent and inscrutable. . . . If Frank is a hero, he's a Taoist or Zen one rather than a conqueror seeking personal victory or gain. While the world is trickster, Frank is the fool of tarot, with all of his human foibles and innocence." Bennett noted that while the stories illustrate basic concepts like death, spirituality, evil, pleasure, solitude, and friendship, "the strange landscapes, bizarre creatures, otherworldly colors and shapes, and often inexplicable actions that make up the stories are alien, at least to our conscious minds."

In an interview with Groth for *Comics Journal* online, Woodring said, "I wanted to be beyond any kind of place or time or culture. I do put in occasional cultural artifacts like hammers or party horns and things like that just for a little shock now and then. Besides, I'm sure every civilization has had something to pound with and something to make noise with at celebration times. But there would never be anything in there as modern as a television, or anything having to do with electricity. Everything is very primitive."

Woodring has branched out over the years and added commercial clients from Microsoft to the Experience Music Project. He designs CD covers and freelances for Japanese companies who push him to create ever-weirder art. He has also been involved with children's books, including his own creation, *Trosper,* which stars an elephant-like creature with a human face. The book comes with a CD of music by Bill Frisell.

The two have performed together, with Frisell playing guitar to Woodring's surreal stills and films. Ben Ratliff reviewed a seventy-minute performance in the *New York Times,* writing that Woodring and Frisell, "a superb draftsman and a superb technician, for those who had come to gawk at sheer skill, are on to a good idea."

The Frank Book collects all of the series since its 1991 debut, including the covers. A *Publishers Weekly* contributor wrote that "Woodring's talent is finally captured in a definitive collection that lives up to his genius."

BIOGRAPHICAL AND CRITICAL SOURCES:

PERIODICALS

Booklist, August, 2003, Gordon Flagg, review of *The Frank Book,* p. 1942.
New York Times, June 11, 2002, Ben Ratliff, "Music Review: A Visual Collaborator and His Accompanists," p. E5.
Publishers Weekly, September 15, 2003, review of *The Frank Book,* p. 46.
Whole Earth Review, winter, 1993, James Donnelly, review of *The Book of Jim,* p. 112.

ONLINE

Comics Journal, http://www.tcj.com/ (summer, 2002), Gary Groth, interview with Woodring.
Jim Woodring Home Page, http://www.jimwoodring.com (January 13, 2004).
Kathleen E. Bennett Home Page, http://www.drizzle.com/~kathleen/Comix/frank.html (January 13, 2004), review of *Frank.*
Robotfist, http://www.robotfist.com/ (July 16, 2003), Joseph Caouette, review of *The Frank Book.*
Seattle Times: Pacific Northwest Online, http://www.seattletimes.com/ (March 18, 2001), Richard Seven, "The Misunderstood Art."
Time.com, http://www.time.com/ (February 9, 2001), Andrew D. Arnold, review of *Frank.**

* * *

WOOLLEY, Peter J. 1960-

PERSONAL: Born February 23, 1960; son of Arthur (an Episcopal priest) and Alma (a nursing educator) Woolley; married; wife's name, Mary. *Education:* University of Pittsburgh, Ph.D. *Politics:* Independent. *Religion:* Episcopalian. *Hobbies and other interests:* Croquet, chess, piano.

ADDRESSES: Home—30 Ferndale Rd., Madison, NJ 07940. *Office*—Department of Social Sciences, Fairleigh Dickinson University, Madison, NJ 07940; fax: 973-443-8799. *E-mail*—woolley@fdu.edu.

CAREER: Fairleigh Dickinson University, Madison, NJ, professor of comparative politics, 1987—. Public Mind, executive director.

WRITINGS:

American Politics: Core Argument/Current Controversy (anthology), Prentice-Hall (Tappan, NJ), 1998.
Japan's Navy: Politics and Paradox, 1971-2000, Lynne Rienner Publishers (Boulder, CO), 2000.

WORK IN PROGRESS: Geography and Japan's Foreign Relations.

*   *   *

WU, Chin-Tao

PERSONAL: Female. *Education:* City University, M.A.; University College London, Ph.D..

ADDRESSES: Agent—c/o Author Mail, Verso Books, 180 Varick St., 10th Fl., New York, NY 10014-4606. *E-mail*—chintao2@ms52.hinet.net.

CAREER: Bethnal Green Museum of Childhood, London, England, part-time art worker, 1991-2000; University of East Anglia, School of World Art Studies and Museology, J. Paul Getty post-doctoral research fellow, 1998-99; University College London, Department of History of Art, honorary research fellow, 1999—; Nanhua University, Taiwan, assistant professor, 2001—.

WRITINGS:

Privatising Culture: Corporate Art Intervention since the 1980s, Verso (New York, NY), 2002.

Contributor to *New Left Review* and *Kunst und Politik Jahrbach der Guernica-Gesellschaft.*

SIDELIGHTS: Chin-Tao Wu earned a Master of Arts degree in arts administration and also a Ph.D. in the history of art. Her degrees, along with her work and research, have earned for her the status of an internationally recognized specialist on corporate art patronage and cultural politics.

In *Privatising Culture: Corporate Art Intervention since the 1980s,* Wu examines the increasing amount of corporate involvement in the visual arts since the 1980s in the United States and in Great Britain. Corporations in both countries now fund visual art programs, sponsor art awards, include art exhibits and galleries in their places of business, and their executives are also board members of various art institutions. Wu explains the benefits and losses to the art world as a result of this increasing corporate involvement. She also discusses the benefits that corporations receive because of their involvement in the arts. A *Publishers Weekly* contributor concluded, "Wu convincingly tells an ugly story of seduction and betrayal . . . one that anyone who cares about the future of art needs to hear." *Library Journal* contributor Carol J. Binkowski called *Privatising Culture* "A superbly researched and invigorating study," and later stated, "Wu offers a well-documented and intelligent analysis of these complex partnerships and their mutual impact." *Journal of Cultural Economics* editor J. Mark Schuster noted that this study "goes well beyond prior studies of corporate cultural influence."

BIOGRAPHICAL AND CRITICAL SOURCES:

PERIODICALS

Afterimage, September-October, 2002, Jennifer Pearson Yamashiro, "Privatizing Culture," p. 17.
Art in America, October, 2002, Robert Atkins, "Co-opting the Arts," pp. 53-54.
Art Review, July 1, 2001, John Henshall, "In bed with big business," p. 70.
Journal of Cultural Economics, May, 2003, J. Mark Schuster, review of *Privatising Culture: Corporate Art Intervention since the 1980s,* pp. 143-146.
Library Journal, October 15, 2001, Carol J. Binkowski, *Privatising Culture,* p. 74.
New Left Review, November-December, 2002, Sarah James, review of *Privatising Culture,* pp. 154-160.
Publishers Weekly, July 2, 2001, review of *Privatising Culture,* p. 64.
Socialist Review, June, 2002, Chris Nineham, "An artful business," pp. 31-32.
Sociological Review, February, 2003, Victoria D. Alexander, review of *Privatising Culture,* pp. 161-163.
Times Higher Education Supplement, June 28, 2002, Rudi Bogni, "Art, money, and modern Medici," p. 30.
Times Literary Supplement, November 23, 2001, David Hawkes, "Avant-Garde plc," p. 26.
Washington Post, June 4, 2002, Chris Lehmann, "Culture's Corporate Lords," p. C3.

Y-Z

YORK, Robert
See ESTRIDGE, Robin

*   *   *

YOUNG, Terence 1953-

PERSONAL: Born 1953; married Patricia Young (a poet); children: two. *Education:* University of British Columbia, M.F.A., 1996.

ADDRESSES: Home—Victoria, British Columbia, Canada. *Agent*—c/o Author Mail, Raincoast Books, 9050 Shaughnessy St., Vancouver, British Columbia V6P 6E5, Canada; fax: 604-323-2600.

CAREER: Writer and educator. High school creative writing teacher. Founder and editor, *Claremont Review.*

AWARDS, HONORS: British Columbia Governor General's Literary Award nominee in poetry, 1999, for *The Island in Winter;* Fiddlehead fiction contest winner; *This Magazine* fiction contest winner; PRISM International fiction contest winner; Journey Prize nominee.

WRITINGS:

Fooling Ourselves (poems), Reference West (Victoria, British Columbia, Canada), 1996.
The Island in Winter (poems), Signal Editions (Montreal, Quebec, Canada), 1999.
Rhymes with Useless (short stories), Raincoast Books (Vancouver, British Columbia, Canada), 2000.

Contributor of fiction and poetry to publications such as *Event, Grain, Arc,* and *Malahat Review.*

SIDELIGHTS: Poet and short-story writer Terence Young teaches his craft to high school students in Victoria, British Columbia, Canada. He has given readings at various schools and universities, including Trent University, and conducted writing workshops at the Victoria School of Writing and elsewhere.

A sense of family, and of what emotional havoc family members can inflict on themselves and each other, infuses Young's short story collection, *Rhymes with Useless.* "In sharp, colloquial prose, Young traces the cracks just beneath the surface of familial life in his haunting, sometimes heartbreaking tales," commented a *Publishers Weekly* reviewer. In one story in the collection, "Yellow with Black Horns," Evelina finds evidence of her parents' deteriorating relationship and escalating arguments in her drinking cup, smashed on the floor and left where it lay. A young husband considers a marriage-breaking dalliance with his temporary worker at the same time his wife visits an investment counselor, seeking ways to secure their future in "Fast." In the book's title story, a wife's conversion to vegetarianism has an unexpected result for her husband: no meat also means, inexplicably, no sex. And the mother in "The Berlin Wall" is cut off from her children after her husband is caught selling marijuana out of their house. Other stories include "Dead" and "Maintenance." In the first, seventeen-year-old Anna agrees to have sex with her boyfriend, but she discovers that her search for all the pleasures and distractions that life has to offer does not always live up to her expectations. And in "Maintenance" a mourning widower realizes that "the real cataclysm was not that the world would end all at once but that it was ending one person at a time."

"These are fine, sensitive stories, chronicling loss and disaffection without resorting to bland generalities," the *Publishers Weekly* critic remarked. Young's "stories work to elicit sympathy in his readers, as his characters go about their jobs and try to understand their beloveds; as they try to act dutifully to others, to themselves, in their attempt to ward off what one of his poem's speakers calls 'whatever hunts us down,'" observed Harold Hoefle on the *Danforth Review* Web site. The repetitively downbeat tone of Young's stories "starts to leave the reader numb," commented Aaron Hamburger in *Village Voice*. "Still, his sharp renderings of oddballs in distress remind us that stories can do more than amuse with clever conceits—they have the power to disturb us, to bump us out of our comfortable grooves." Hoefle concluded, "In Young's stories, much of humanity breathes; because of his art, we want these characters to breathe easier."

BIOGRAPHICAL AND CRITICAL SOURCES:

PERIODICALS

Publishes Weekly, February 5, 2001, review of *Rhymes with Useless,* p. 67.
Village Voice, January 23, 2001, Aaron Hamburger, "Oddballs with Problems," p. 62.

ONLINE

Canada Council for the Arts, http://www.canada council.ca/ (October 19, 1999), "The Canada Council for the Arts Announces Nominees for the 1999 Governor General's Literary Awards."
Danforth Review, http://www.danforthreview.com/ (April 4, 2004), Harold Hoefle, review of *Rhymes with Useless.*
Trent University, http://www.trentu.edu/ (April 4, 2004), biography of Terence Young.
University of British Columbia, http://www.public affairs.ubc.ca/ (April 4, 2004), biography of Terence Young.
Victoria School of Writing, http://www.victoria schoolofwriting.org/ (April 4, 2004), biography of Terence Young.*

ZACKS, Mitch(ell)

PERSONAL: Male. Education: Yale University, B.S. (economics; cum laude); University of Chicago, M.B.A. (analytic finance; with high honors).

ADDRESSES: Office—Zacks Investment Research, Inc., 155 North Wacker Dr., Suite 300, Chicago, IL 60606. *Agent*—c/o Author Mail, HarperBusiness, 10 East 53rd St., New York, NY 10022.

CAREER: Lazard Freres, New York, NY, former investment-banking analyst; Zacks Investment Research, Chicago, IL, vice president; Zacks Investment Management, Chicago, portfolio manager.

WRITINGS:

Ahead of the Market: The Zacks Method for Spotting Stocks Early—in Any Economy, HarperBusiness (New York, NY), 2003.

Columnist for *Chicago Sun-Times.*

SIDELIGHTS: In *Ahead of the Market: The Zacks Method for Spotting Stocks Early—in Any Economy,* investment analyst and *Chicago Sun Times* columnist Mitch Zacks presents a method of evaluating the research of Wall Street analysts in order to find stocks on the verge of strong appreciation in price. The basis of Zacks' method is to locate companies whose projected earnings estimates are being revised higher. This method often reveals companies that are growing fast. Zacks recommends averaging the earnings estimates of a number of analysts to find those stocks most likely to increase in value. Patrick J. Brunet, reviewing the book for *Library Journal,* found that "the system is logical and convincingly presented." Robert Barker, in *Business Week,* called Zacks "a veteran tracker of analysts' earnings estimates."

BIOGRAPHICAL AND CRITICAL SOURCES:

PERIODICALS

Business Week, March 31, 2003, Robert Barker, review of *Ahead of the Market: The Zacks Method for Spotting Stocks Early—in Any Economy,* p. 99.
Library Journal, April 1, 2003, Patrick J. Brunet, review of *Ahead of the Market,* p. 111.

ONLINE

Zacks Web site, http://www.zacks.com/ (May 19, 2004), "Mitch Zacks on Investing."*

*   *   *

ZUCKOFF, Mitchell 1962-

PERSONAL: Born 1962, in Brooklyn, NY; son of Sid (a history teacher) and Gerry (a bookkeeper) Zuckoff; married Suzanne Kreiter (a newspaper photographer); children: two daughters. *Education:* University of Rhode Island, B.A. (summa cum laude), 1983; University of Missouri, M.A. (journalism), 1987.

ADDRESSES: Home—14 Ridge Rd., Newton, MA 02468. *Office*—Boston University School of Communications, Commonwealth Ave., Boston, MA. *Agent*—Richard Abate, ICM, 40 West 57th St., New York, NY 10019. *E-mail*—zuckoff@yahoo.com.

CAREER: Journalist and author. *Bridgeport Post,* Bridgeport, CT, bureau chief, 1983-84; Associated Press, New York, NY, wire service reporter, 1984-87; States News Service, Washington, DC, Washington reporter, 1987-88; *Boston Globe,* Boston, MA, business reporter, then national and investigative reporter, 1989—. Batten fellow, University of Virginia—Darden, 2003-04; member of journalism faculty, Boston University, 2003—.

AWARDS, HONORS: Benjamin Fine Award, 1992; Heywood Broun Award, 1994; Livingston Award for International Reporting, 1995; Pulitzer Prize finalist, 1997; Associated Press Managing Editors' Award for Public Service, 1998; National Media Award, American Association on Mental Retardation, Media Award, National Down Syndrome Congress, Distinguished Writing Award, American Society of Newspaper Editors, Christopher Award, and Tash Image Award, all 2000, all for "Choosing Naia: A Family's Journey" (newspaper series).

WRITINGS:

Choosing Naia: A Family's Journey, Beacon Press (Boston, MA), 2002.
(With Dick Lehr) *Judgment Ridge: The True Story Behind the Dartmouth Murders,* HarperCollins (New York, NY), 2003.

WORK IN PROGRESS: A book on Charles Ponzi, tentatively titled *Ponzi: The Greatest American Schemer,* for Random House, expected publication in 2005.

SIDELIGHTS: Mitchell Zuckoff is a journalist whose multi-award-winning newspaper series about a couple's decision not to abort a child with Down syndrome inspired his 2002 book, *Choosing Naia: A Family's Journey.* Chronicling interracial couple Greg and Tierney Fairchilds' five-year journey after discovering that their child would be born with a heart defect, Zuckoff examines the complex emotional, moral, and medical issues raised as a result of the technological advances in prenatal testing, while also painting a sensitive portrait of two people who must make difficult moral judgments and ultimately chose a difficult, heartbreaking path in deciding to raise a disabled child. The Fairchilds are unusual; faced with a similar prognosis for their unborn fetus, ninety percent of American couples chose to abort.

In *Booklist* contributor Vanessa Bush praised Zuckoff's "searing" account of the Fairchilds' predicament as "an inspiring look at one family that offers profound lessons for us all." Noting that Zuckoff's subject remained centered due to the fact that the Fairchilds are pro-choice with regard to the abortion issue, *Library Journal* contributor KellyJo Houtz Griffin found *Choosing Naia* to be valuable in particular for detailing the ironic "heartbreak that arises when modern medicine's astounding ability to identify problems" clashes with "its inability to do anything about them." Taking a different slant, a *Publishers Weekly* contributor cited Zuckoff's book as "At once a powerful argument against abortion and an eye-opening look at how a functional couple handles an extremely vexing decision." Noting that "Zuckoff doesn't shrink from pointing out the hardships and sadness of raising a disabled child," *New York Times Book Review* contributor Maggie Jones dubbed *Choosing Naia* "a refreshing tale in an age in which medical technology encourages us to strive for perfection in ourselves and in our children."

BIOGRAPHICAL AND CRITICAL SOURCES:

PERIODICALS

Booklist, October 15, 2002, Vanessa Bush, review of *Choosing Naia: A Family's Journey,* p. 369.
Kirkus Reviews, July 15, 2002, review of *Choosing Naia,* p. 1022.
Library Journal, August, 2002, KellyJo Houtz Griffin, review of *Choosing Naia,* p. 132.

New York Times Book Review, December 15, 2002, Maggie Jones, "A Diagnosis Is Not a Name," p. 26.

Publishers Weekly, June 3, 2002, review of *Choosing Naia,* p. 73.

ONLINE

Batten Institute Web site, http://www.darden.edu/batten/ (January 21, 2003), "Mitchell Zuckoff."